OXFORD HISTORY OF
THE CHRISTIAN CHURCH

Edited by

HENRY AND OWEN CHADWICK

THE
PAPAL MONARCHY

The Western Church from 1050 to 1250

━━

COLIN MORRIS

CLARENDON PRESS · OXFORD

*This book has been printed digitally and produced in a standard design
in order to ensure its continuing availability*

OXFORD
UNIVERSITY PRESS

Great Clarendon Street, Oxford OX2 6DP

Oxford University Press is a department of the University of Oxford.
It furthers the University's objective of excellence in research, scholarship,
and education by publishing worldwide in

Oxford New York

Athens Auckland Bangkok Bogotá Buenos Aires Cape Town
Chennai Dar es Salaam Delhi Florence Hong Kong Istanbul Karachi
Kolkata Kuala Lumpur Madrid Melbourne Mexico City Mumbai Nairobi
Paris São Paulo Shanghai Singapore Taipei Tokyo Toronto Warsaw

with associated companies in Berlin Ibadan

Oxford is a registered trade mark of Oxford University Press
in the UK and in certain other countries

Published in the United States
by Oxford University Press Inc., New York

© Colin Morris 1989

ISBN 0-19-826925-0

To Brenda with love

Christ left to Peter, not only the whole church but also the whole world, to govern (Pope Innocent III).

> Once, kings and emperors,
> Dukes, counts and officers,
> Valiant knights of theirs,
> Governed the land.
> I see the clergy stand
> In the lords' places,
> Traitors and thieves
> Who have hypocrites' faces.

(Peire Cardenal, troubadour)

FOREWORD

The twelfth-century scholar saw himself as a dwarf sitting on the back of a giant, and this volume rests uneasily on the shoulders of a vast mass of previous scholarship. There is no way of adequately expressing my debt to the writings and conversation of others, except through the inadequate medium of the bibliography, which provides some introduction to the wealth of discussion made available by modern research.

I owe debts of gratitude to the Leverhulme Trustees and the British Academy for generous research grants, to Pembroke and Wolfson Colleges at Oxford for their very kind hospitality during periods of research. It is impossible to detail the archivists and librarians from whom I have received help, but I must mention in particular the Bodleian Library, which has provided a pleasant setting for work and access to magnificent collections of material. I am grateful, too, to the Society for Promoting Christian Knowledge for permission to quote from my previous book, *The Discovery of the Individual*.

From my own University of Southampton I have received much help, including a grant for research which enabled me to have for a time the valuable help of two research assistants, Alison Bideleux and Joan Wardrop. The Library staff have dealt with innumerable obscure bibliographical inquiries with great efficiency and good humour, and Mark Farley, of the Department of Education gave indispensable help in putting the material into machine-readable form suitable for transmission to the Press. My thanks are also due to Jean Colson, and to my pupil Claire Burch, for assistance in preparing the index. I am very specially indebted to two colleagues, Dr Ernest Blake and Dr Brian Golding, who have been an unfailing source of ideas and comments and whose reading of the manuscript has saved me from many errors and misinterpretations. Finally, my thanks are due to the History Department at Southampton for providing such a congenial and stimulating academic setting during the years in which this book was under preparation.

CONTENTS

ABBREVIATIONS

AASS	*Acta Sanctorum*, ed. J. Bollandus (Antwerp, 1643–)
AFH	*Archivum Franciscanum Historicum* (Florence)
AFP	*Archivum Fratrum Praedicatorum* (Rome)
AHC	*Annuarium Historiae Conciliorum* (Paderborn)
AHP	*Archivum Historiae Pontificiae* (Rome)
AKg	*Archiv für Kulturgeschichte* (Cologne)
Alberigo	J. Alberigo *et al.*, *Conciliorum Oecumenicorum Decreta* (Basle, 1962). (There is also a third, enlarged edition at Bologna, 1973.)
Annales	*Annales. Économies, sociétés, civilisations* (Paris)
Bernard, *Opera*	J. Leclercq *et al.* (eds.), *S. Bernardi Opera*, 8 vols. (Rome, 1957–77)
BMCL	*Bulletin of Medieval Canon Law* (Berkeley, Calif.)
C&S	*Councils and Synods, with other Documents relating to the English Church*, 2 vols (4 parts) (Oxford 1964–81)
CCM	*Cahiers de civilisation médiévale* (Poitiers)
CC(CM)	Corpus Christianorum, continuatio mediaevalis
CF	*Cahiers de Fanjeaux* (Toulouse)
CISAM	Centro italiano di studi sull'alto medioevo (Spoleto)
CMH	*Cambridge Medieval History*
CNSS	*Actes du congrès national des Sociétés Savantes* (Paris)
CSSSM	Centro di studi sulla spiritualità medievale (Todi)
DAEM	*Deutsches Archiv für Erforschung des Mittelalters* (Cologne)
Dic. DC	*Dictionnaire de Droit Canonique*, ed. R. Naz (Paris, 1935–)
Dic. TC	*Dictionnaire de Théologie Catholique* (Paris, 1899–1972)
EHR	*English Historical Review*
FM	A. Fliche and V. Martin (eds.), *Histoire de l'église*, 21 vols. (Paris, 1939–)
Foreville	R. Foreville, *Latran I, II, III et Latran IV*, Histoire des conciles oecuméniques 6 (Paris, 1965)
Gall. Christ.	*Gallia Christiana*, 16 vols. (Paris, 1715–1865, repr. 1970)
Greg. VII. Extrav.	H. E. J. Cowdrey, The Epistolae Vagantes of Pope Gregory VII (Oxford, 1972)

Greg. VII. *Reg.*	E. Caspar (ed.), *Das Register Gregors VII.*, MGH Ep. 2
HJb	*Historisches Jahrbuch* (Munich)
HZ	*Historische Zeitschrift* (Munich)
ICMCL	*International Congress of Medieval Canon Law* (Vatican)
JEH	*Journal of Ecclesiastical History*
JMH	*Journal of Medieval History*
LdM	*Lexikon des Mittelalters* (Munich)
Le Bras	*Études d'histoire du droit canonique dédiées à G. Le Bras*, 2 vols. (Paris, 1965)
MA	*Le Moyen-Âge* (Brussels)
Mansi	J. D. Mansi (ed.), *Sanctorum Conciliorum collectio nova* (Venice 1748–)
MCSM	Miscellanea del Centro di Studi Medievali (La Mendola)
MGH	Monumenta Germaniae Historica
LdL	Libelli de Lite
Leges	
Schriften	
SS	Scriptores
SSRG	Scriptores rerum Germanicarum in usum scholarum
MIC	*Monumenta Iuris Canonici*
MIOG	*Mitteilungen des Instituts für Österreichische Geschichtsforschung*
Misc. Med.	Miscellanea Medievalia (Rome)
MS	*Mediaeval Studies*
n.d.	no date
Ordericus Vitalis	Marjorie Chibnall, *The Ecclesiastical History of Ordericus Vitalis*, 6 vols. (Oxford, 1969–80)
PBA	*Proceedings of the British Academy*
PL	Patrologiae Latinae cursus completus, series Latina, ed. J.-P. Migne (1844–)
QFIAB	*Quellen und Forschungen aus italienischen Archiven und Bibliotheken* (Tübingen)
RHC	Recueil des Historiens des Croisades
Occ	Historiens occidentaux
RHDFE	*Revue historique de droit français et étranger* (Paris)
RHE	*Revue d'histoire ecclésiastique* (Louvain)
RHEF	*Revue d'histoire de l'église de France* (Paris)
RR	*Renaissance and Renewal in the Twelfth Century*, ed. R. L. Benson and G. Constable (Oxford, 1982)
RS	Rolls Series
RSCI	*Rivista di Storia della Chiesa in Italia* (Rome)

Sb	Sitzungsberichte
SC	Sources chrétiennes
SCH	*Studies in Church History*
SGrat	*Studia Gratiana* (Rome)
S Greg	*Studi Gregoriani* (Rome)
SSCISAM	Settimane di Studi del Centro italiano di Studi sull'alto medioevo (Spoleto)
TRHS	*Transactions of the Royal Historical Society*
VuF	Vorträge und Forschungen (Sigmaringen)
ZKg	*Zeitschrift für Kirchengeschichte* (Stuttgart)
ZSSRGkA	*Zeitschrift der Savigny-Stiftung für Rechtsgeschichte, kanonistische Abteilung* (volume numbers are those of the main series)

REFERENCES TO CANON LAW

The standard edition is E. Friedberg, *Corpus Iuris Canonici*, 2nd edn. 2 vols. (Leipzig, 1922). Gratian, *Decr.*C. XII, q. 2, c. 3 (1223) means Causa XII, questio 2, capitulum 3 of the *Decretum* in column 1223 of Friedberg vol. i. Greg. IX, *Decretals*, IV. 2.5 (673) means book IV, questio 2, capitulum 5 of the Gregorian Collection in column 673 of Friedberg vol. ii.

INTRODUCTION

The title of this book expresses a paradox, not a fact. A papal monarchy was in principle and in practice inconceivable in medieval Europe. One of the distinctive features of Christianity has been a clear separation between church and state. The awareness of two powers, each with its own area of authority, was founded upon the ministry of Christ and embodied in his command, 'Render to Caesar the things that are Caesar's, and to God the things that are God's' (Mark 12: 17). The distinction between sacred and secular, between kingdom (*regnum*) and priesthood (*sacerdotium*) is a commonplace of Christian thinking, and it was not forgotten between 1050 and 1250. On the contrary the sense of opposition between clergy and laity grew stronger, as clergy were discouraged from secular employment and debarred from those activities of government which involved the use of force and imposition of death sentences. In the proper sense of the words, papal monarchy was impossible. A pope could no more rule a kingdom than a king could say mass. Yet the language of papal monarchy is inescapable in our sources, and the popes adopted imperial dress and ceremonial. Rhetoric and symbolism expressed a complex reality. In part they described the supremacy of papal authority within the church, a supremacy which was widely recognized although it was rarely defined as absolutism. But papal claims went further. The ineffectiveness of state power at the beginning of our period meant that the clergy supervised activities which in the ancient or the modern world alike have been the business of the state or of voluntary societies. These included the provision of hospitals and schools, jurisdiction over marriage and probate, the defence of Christendom against the infidel, and the preservation of peace within its borders. As the supreme authority within the church popes had final responsibility for all these matters, and it is striking to find how many major initiatives were undertaken directly by the Roman Church: the history of the crusades, of the friars, and of the inquisition, for example, was shaped by papal decisions. Moreover since the clergy were answerable for the souls of laity, the *sacerdotium* appeared superior to the *regnum* and popes to kings. There was much argument about how such supremacy should be defined in practice, but many writers were prepared to see in the papacy an authority above earthly kings, and such language was not always rejected by the lay powers, however carefully they defended their customary rights. The impression of dominance was strengthened by the fact that bishops and abbots controlled great estates, and even duchies and counties, so that German bishops in the thirteenth century could be described as 'kings and priests'. Over the centuries the Roman Church accumulated a great mass of claims to secular power, including the Papal State in central Italy and suzerainty over Sicily, England, and other kingdoms. The forged Donation of Constantine included a formal grant of imperial style to the pope. All this put the two-power theory under grave strain, and makes it appropriate to speak of papal monarchy as a special feature of the centuries after 1050.

The beginning of the period is easy to define. Although much use was made of earlier precedents the elaboration of the rhetoric of papal monarchy scarcely began before the middle of the eleventh century, and was then rapidly developed in the circle of Gregory VII (1073–85). There is no similarly clear terminal date. The language of sovereignty stamped itself upon the Roman Church, and its echoes remained clear in Boniface VIII, in the popes of Avignon, in Sixtus V, and in Pius IX. In spite of the Second Vatican Council, it is still alive in some recent utterances by authority. The year 1250, however, offers a natural break. By then, all the great initiatives of the medieval papacy had been put into effect. The two centuries covered by this book were the supreme age of papal monarchy. Christendom was ruled by kings and princes under the supervision of the clergy, and especially of the Roman Church, which alone possessed the fullness of power.

The ideal of Christendom, whatever its splendour, is an embarrassment to the historian of the church, for it provides no limit to his subject-matter. In an age when every man was a Christian, and when the patronage and responsibility of the church extended throughout society, its history comprises architecture and literature, philosophy and music, estate administration, law, crusades, the empire, national states and their churches. Of the making of such a book, there would be no end. There is fortunately one central theme which provides a natural line of investigation: the creation of an international culture which increasingly bound together the diverse, and often hostile, peoples into one Christian people or *populus Christianus*. The expanding authority of the papacy was only one of the new forces which moulded this international culture. Other influences include the appearance of religious orders which extended into every part of Europe, a common learning stimulated by the universities, a common discipline enjoined by councils, and a common defence provided by the crusades. Such a study offers a number of points of interest. What we are seeing is the making of Christendom in its later form, for there are innumerable institutions and attitudes which did not exist in 1050 but which by 1250 were firmly established, and which remained characteristic of modern history. Among them were the birth of theology as an academic discipline, the inquisition, central direction of the affairs of the regional churches, the growth of the friars, prince-bishops, diocesan records, chivalry, the crusades, regular confession, and the elevation of the host. This is the Europe of tradition, 'the world we have lost', whereas to go back before 1050 is to enter a region which is by comparison alien to our own. To historians who worked in a culture where the ideal of Christendom was still vital, these developments came to appear inescapable, and to Catholic scholars they appeared also right. These convictions shaped the approach of many of the ablest scholars of medieval church history, such as Augustin Fliche, and have contributed to the vocabulary of historical study: the ideals of the papal reformers have come to seem the central and creative force in subsequent ecclesiastical history, and the single word 'Gregorian' has been applied to almost everything that was new and enlightened in our period.

For those who live in post-Christian Europe the aura of inevitability has been removed. The dominant impression is not of evolution determined by earlier traditions, but of an abundance of new energies which were refashioning society in unprophesiable ways: the transformation of the economy and social structure and the rise of the cities and universities brought with them appeals to public opinion, demands for new teaching and devotional patterns, and an agonizing tension between privilege and poverty which is difficult to parallel from the preceding generations. The effect was to leave scope for individual policies which had a long-lasting impact upon the history of the church. It would have been hard to foresee

Gregory VII's disconcerting sympathy for social revolution, Urban II's decision to rescue the church of Jerusalem, Alexander III's practice of legislating by letter, and Innocent III's remorseless determination to destroy the German hegemony in Italy, let alone the impact of charismatic personalities such as Bernard of Clairvaux and Francis of Assisi. If these men and their policies were in some sense an expression of existing ideas, they developed them in quite unexpected directions. Jean Leclercq has rightly warned us that 'Christian experience is never to be reduced to or explained by social, economic, political or ideological pressures.' The uncertainty principle is fundamental to both history and religion. It is always tempting for the historian to focus on those movements which had the greatest influence on the future, and the immense creativity of our period makes it easy to fall into such a trap. But it is vital to remember that the forces which were shaping a new international culture were destroying older values inherited from the Carolingian past. Karl Leyser has suggested that they actually aborted the growth of a common culture which can be discerned in the first half of the eleventh century. The new international culture had a fragmenting as well as a unifying impact, for it stamped new divisions upon society, between clergy and laity, Latins and Greeks, and papacy and empire. Already within our period we can see those divisions being deepened by a pattern of protest and reaction. Heresy was at least in part a protest against clerical authority, and crusade and inquisition followed in an attempt to preserve doctrinal unity from the corrosion of heresy.

The speed of change was so great that I have found it necessary to subdivide the book at 1122 and 1200. This arrangement has inconveniences. The divisions are unsuitable for some topics, in which they disrupt a story of continuous development. What is more, identical processes took place at different times in different regions: the founding of local churches was almost complete in south-eastern England in 1100, and was barely beginning in some parts of eastern Europe in 1250. The use of these chronological divisions also panders to the historian's besetting temptation to be a follower of fashion. The assumption that what is newest is also most significant is difficult to resist. But an original book sometimes was little read whereas traditional writings continued to have a vast influence disseminated through the inclusion of extracts in collections or *florilegia*. The work of modern editors, invaluable as it is to historians, may entangle them more deeply in the embrace of new fashions, for understandably there are far more definitive editions of works surviving in one manuscript than of those which exist in hundreds. Yet it was this latter group, spreading through countries and centuries, which maintained older ideas and values across the boundaries between periods. It will therefore be essential to move fairly easily across our chronological divisions, but it is important to have them. Medieval history is misrepresented if we study it in units of several centuries, for, while Innocent III was obviously in some sense the successor of Gregory VII, he was confronted by different problems and disposed of different resources with which to solve them. At times, too, our period falls into three ages with an accuracy which would have delighted the heart of Abbot Joachim of Fiore, for we have in turn the ages of the Cluniacs, the Cistercians, and the friars; or the times of little heresy, of growing heresy, and of the inquisition. Similarly the Concordat of Worms in 1122 and the death of Henry VI in 1197 mark points of real change in the relations of church and empire. In a dynamic age, more is gained than lost by marking the differences between the generations. One further difference will inevitably shape this book: the extremely rapid increase in record evidence. Even very basic information is denied us in the middle of the eleventh century, whereas 200 years later we know a great deal about the operation of many institutions. As a result there is a good deal more detail included, even in a volume of this general kind, as the period advances. This has the effect of keeping Gregory VII in his proper place. Great man that he was, his ideas were not the only, or even the most decisive, influence in the restructuring of the medieval church.

The common features in the new Europe (both of unification and fragmentation) will be the central theme, but they must not lead us to undervalue the continuing regional characteristics of medieval Europe. There are plenty of local features, such as the Gilbertine order in England or the houses of Fiore in southern Italy, and the appearance of a widely diffused phenomenon may conceal vast local divergences: the Franciscans were very different in the Apennines and the Rhineland. The question of continuity and change is at its most teasing in the area about which one would most like to have full information: the religious awareness of the ordinary member of the church. Here the basic problem is the obvious one that little people leave no records. We have virtually no first-hand statement of the ideas of peasants or townsmen in this period. There are reports by inquisitors, preachers, and recorders of miracles, and some of them were careful observers. But they are not sufficient to enable us to form a coherent picture of popular opinion and they are subject to caution, because a clerk was always liable to make an unfamiliar belief conform to something he knew from his textbooks. It is almost certainly wrong to suppose that there was a pattern of unchanging superstition at the roots of society. Recent work has made us aware of the concern of the hierarchy, especially in the thirteenth century, for the teaching of the populace as a whole, and it would be perverse to suppose that these endeavours were totally without effect. We are also beginning to recognize, thanks to the work of Jacques le Goff, Jean-Claude Schmitt, and others, that Christianity itself provided a great deal of material to popular fable and ritual, and it has been suggested that the twelfth and thirteenth centuries saw a profound transformation of the folklore which circulated in the west. Popular culture was being transformed at the same time as the learned world around it. In a general volume of this kind I have had to eschew a full exploration of this fascinating field, where the achievement of broad conclusions is still a distant prospect. The reader will find a good deal about pastoral and teaching techniques and the response of the authorities to dissent and heresy; and I have attempted to give some overview of the 'religion of the illiterate'. Perhaps the secret history of the people of God cannot be written for any generation. We are not yet ready to do so, in any event, for the Middle Ages.

In accordance with the policy of the series the footnotes do not include detailed discussions but are limited to references to quotations in the text. There are separate volumes allocated to the Iberian peninsula and to the eastern churches; the latter volume, by Dr Joan Hussey, has already covered the development of relations between Rome and Constantinople. With these exceptions, this book attempts to give an account of the religious history of the Latin west between 1050 and 1250.

PART I

THE PAPAL REFORM MOVEMENT AND THE CONFLICT WITH THE EMPIRE (*c.* 1046–1122)

INTRODUCTORY

The second half of the eleventh century was a particularly decisive time in the history of the church. To mention only three of the more important developments, the popes emerged as the leaders of an international reform movement in western Europe; they became involved in a dispute with the empire whose effects were to be long-lasting; and they directed the military efforts of Christendom against Islam, most notably in the First Crusade. The papal reform movement, the investiture contest, and the crusades went far beyond any previous precedents for papal activity, and were to have a profound impact upon the future history of the church. Behind them lay one of the most remarkable features of this period: the influence of monasticism. In general it has been rare for a monk to become pope, but from 1073 to 1118 the chair of St Peter was continuously occupied by men with monastic training, and monastic advisers were prominent in the formulation of papal policy. Monasticism was itself in turmoil, for while existing abbeys were expanding rapidly many new ones were being founded and challenges to traditional ideals were being vigorously expressed. Yet monasticism was only one (although a very important) element in an international movement for the reform of the church and redefinition of the place of the laity within it. Behind these developments were major changes in society. A new structure of lordship was emerging, along with a money economy and urban communities. Closely related with these social changes was a great expansion of learning, the first stages in the movement which was to produce the distinctive medieval contribution to European scholarship.

There were thus five great forces transforming the history of the church: papal revival, monastic renewal, international reform, social change, and the growth of learning. It is not easy to define their mutual influence, or even to determine their chronological priority, since change necessarily took place over a long period, and at very different speeds in different parts of Europe. Nevertheless, the first part of this book must be concerned with an attempt to understand the way in which these new forces became dominant within the life of the church.

I

CHRISTIAN SOCIETY IN THE MIDDLE OF THE ELEVENTH CENTURY

i. *Introduction*

It is hard to give a fair account of the church of the mid-eleventh century. The severe criticisms of the reformers of the next generation came to be accepted by subsequent catholic thinkers, and left their mark on the work of historians until recent times. What is more, men of the earlier eleventh century did not leave an abundant record of their point of view, for they lived in a largely pre-literate age. This does not mean simply that many people were unable to read or write, but that it was not natural to resort to writing as a means of record or communication. The usual mode of formal expression was a symbolic action. A man was known to be king because he had been publicly anointed and crowned; another was known to have been appointed bishop because he had received the gift of ring and staff. Land was transferred through a material token such as a knife or a clod of earth. Some written record might be made of a donation, but even then it would not often define the privileges and duties which were being conferred. While bishops and abbots valued the documents which validated their rights of possession, lay nobles felt a healthy contempt for writing, and were not prepared to give weight to a mere scrap of parchment. The advocate (or lay protector) of the abbey of Prüm in the Rhineland expressed his feeling clearly in a dispute in 1063: 'he laughed at the record, and said that a pen can write more or less anything. He was not going to lose his rights because of that.'[1] This was not simply the attitude of a backwoods nobleman without sense or education; it was a fact that the available documents were unreliable, and that it was almost impossible to detect a competent, or even an incompetent, forgery. The memory of sworn witnesses seemed more worthy of trust than title-deeds of

[1] Cited H. Bresslau, *Handbuch der Urkundenlehre für Deutschland und Italien*, 2nd edn. (Leipzig, 1912), i.651 n.

doubtful authenticity, and for a long time after 1050 it continued to be accepted that witnesses were the best evidence in a legal tribunal. This reluctance to use writing was also reflected in the relatively small amount of controversy on contemporary issues. A well-read man in 1050, and that with rare exceptions meant a monk or member of the upper clergy, would be familiar with works from the distant past: the Scriptures, monastic writings such as the *Collations* of Cassian and the Rule of St Benedict, patristic and Carolingian commentaries and saints' lives, and doctrinal and pastoral works by a small number of the Fathers. To an extent which we would find unimaginable there was a lack of contemporary written work, and not much demand for it: the great letter-collections of the succeeding age, for example, were anticipated in the early eleventh century only by that of Fulbert of Chartres. A limited number of chronicles, such as those of Thietmar of Merseburg in eastern Germany and Adhemar of Chabannes in Aquitaine show that intelligent contemporaries were reflecting on the issues facing their society and that creative thinking did not begin in 1050, but they offer a relatively small amount of material in which we can overhear the anxieties of the age.

In governing and educated circles, the Carolingian inheritance was still strong. It is true that the world of Charlemagne and his descendants had been transformed: its political unity had been shattered, kingdoms had passed to other families, and bishoprics and monasteries had been ravaged by barbarian invaders. Nevertheless, readers of the volume in this series by Michael Wallace-Hadrill on *The Frankish Church* will recognize how attitudes and institutions which went back to the Carolingians still provided the framework for thinking in the eleventh century. From that source had come the idea of a western empire with a special relationship with the Roman Church, and so had the idea of the God-given ruler, who like a new David championed the Christian people in war against the unbeliever. The respect of the Frankish church for Rome, reflected in the cult of St Peter and in liturgical borrowing, offered a basis for claims to Roman primacy in a new age. Germany in particular had preserved much from the Carolingians. The title of emperor, the royal direction of great monasteries and bishoprics, and a variety of other practices of government maintained that continuity, as did institutions such as the court chapel, or *Hofkapelle*, of the German kings. The Rhineland and Lotharingia displayed a particularly strong continuity with the past in architecture and scholarship. The immense majority of Carolingian manuscripts had been devoted to the text of the Bible, the liturgy, or the four major Latin Fathers, Ambrose, Jerome, Augustine, and Gregory; and this remained the dominant pattern for book production until well into the twelfth century. Ideas and styles created by Carolingian scholars were taken up by their successors. Thus the interpretation of the liturgy by Amalarius of Metz, which his contemporaries had found unduly daring, became the basis for expositions of the mass, while the dispute over the presence of Christ in the eucharist between Ratramnus of Corbie and Paschasius Radbertus was to be revived by Berengar of Tours in the middle of the eleventh century on a much more public platform. Collections of canon law (most notably the pseudo-Isidorian decretals forged about 850) provided the basis for church discipline in the new age. Even the reformers' originalities testify to the pervasive late Carolingian atmosphere. Gregory VII's policy was directed not only against recent corruptions, but also against the Carolingian polity itself, rejecting liturgy and laws which were not truly Roman and the Rule of Aix which permitted canons to own individual property, which Gregory saw as the result of improper imperial interference in church affairs.

By 1050 the conversion of Europe was almost complete, at least in terms of formal allegiance. The older Christian lands were now ringed by nations in the process of accepting the faith: Norway, Denmark, Poland, and Hungary. To the north there remained untouched the more remote areas of the Baltic, and the Slavonic tribes on the frontier of Saxony. In southern Europe much less progress had been made, and Sicily and most of Spain were still under Moslem rule. The chronicler Raoul Glaber explained that on the cross Christ had his face to the west and his right hand to the north, to symbolize the fact that conversions would be more abundant there.[2] Within these wide boundaries, people were acquainted with unbelief only as represented by the Jews, who were increasingly moving from the countryside to form communities in the cities, or by pagan cults brought from outside by settlers. By 1050, moreover, there were few remains of non-Christian worship in former Viking areas, although the church in eastern England and in parts of Normandy was still suffering from the damage done by the Viking invasions through the seizure of property and suppression

---

[2] Raoul Glaber, *Historiae*, i. 5 (PL 142.626C).

of bishoprics and monasteries. With few exceptions, western Europeans worshipped in Latin liturgies, reverenced Rome as the mother of churches, and drew on a common stock of ceremony and symbolism. Among the learned at least, there was a clear awareness of the Latin world as a cultural unity which had grown apart from Greek tradition embodied in the great Christian empire of Byzantium. Lanfranc of Bec could call 'almost all the Latin world' as witness to the truth of his doctrines.[3]

Yet there was no sense of living in a stable age of secure faith. Contemporaries were aware of the threat posed by the heathen outside and of their duty to proclaim the Gospel 'in every place and to every people without exception'.[4] They were also troubled by the power of demons within their own homeland, for, as Raoul Glaber warned his readers, they were 'abundant all over the world, and especially in springs and trees'.[5] The world was seen not only as the abode of demons, but also as a centre of corruption and depravity. A favourite text was 1 John 5: 19, 'the whole world is in the power of the evil one'. The learned German monk, Hermann the Lame, gave on his death-bed in 1054 the message *tedet quidem me vivere* (it is a bore to be alive): 'This present world, with all that belongs to it, and this mortal life itself is despicable and wearisome to me, and in contrast that future and intransitory world and that eternal and immortal life fill me with such ineffable desire and love . . . that I count all transitory things as vain nothings.'[6] This world-rejection, so characteristic of the eleventh century, was to continue as a dark background to spiritual life throughout our whole period, and contributed one of the important elements within the growth of a new monasticism. Yet paradoxically the monks who had abandoned the world were also concerned for the general well-being of the church. While some thinkers were filled with despair about the secular order, another strand of Christian belief was confident in the divine power to govern the affairs of men.

ii. *The Pattern of Divine Government.*

The passion and resurrection of Christ had established him as king:

---

[3] Lanfranc, *De Corpore et Sanguine*, 2 (PL 150.410A): 'huius rei testis est tota fere Latinitas.'
[4] Glaber, *Historiae* i. 5 (PL 142.626C).
[5] Glaber, *Historiae* iv. 3 (675A).
[6] Berthold, *Annales, sub anno* 1054 (MGH SS V.268).

Triumphat ille splendide	He triumphs gloriously on high,
et dignus amplitudine,	Is over all accounted great.
soli polique patriam	The fatherland of earth and sky
unam fecit rempublicam.[7]	He now has made a single state.

In spiritual matters as in political ones the contemporary idea of authority was different from ours. The king was a hero-figure or a bearer of sanctity, and men looked to him not for a uniform administration but for interventions to promote justice and right-eousness. Similarly Christ's government of the world consisted in particular manifestations of power. Miracles were specially impor-tant in imparting a sense of God's presence. As Lawrence of Amalfi wrote, 'he waters the dryness of our minds by the joyful manifes-tation of his miracles'.[8] The learned Bishop Gerard of Cambrai told a synod of clergy at Arras in 1025 about the frequent presence of heavenly beings: 'Often when these holy mysteries are celebrated choirs of angels are seen by many going about the table of the altar . . . like knights in attendance on the service of their king.'[9] What Herbert Marcuse has called the one-dimensional character of modern awareness is wholly alien to the experience of medieval man.

Even the ordinary affairs of men depended upon the intervention of celestial powers. There was no confidence in an autonomous human capacity to conduct business without intervention from above. The saints in particular inspired the minds of men by their examples, and they performed many valuable social functions. Men turned to them when they needed healing, or victory in judicial combat, or the birth of an heir. Saints acted as intercessors for God's forgiveness, and sinners who were not ready to enter a monastery could hope for mercy by performing a pilgrimage to one of the great shrines. Above all, the saint was the patron of his church, its protector and in a real sense its owner. His (or, much more rarely, her) power resided specially in his relics, contained in a magnificent casket of gold and silver preserved in the crypt or, increasingly, beside the high altar. In southern France it became customary to house the relics in a golden image of the saint, such as the statue of Ste Foy which still survives at Conques. The lives of the saints,

---

[7] F. J. E. Raby (ed.) *The Oxford Book of Medieval Latin Verse* (Oxford, 1959), no. 128, ascribed to Bishop Fulbert of Chartres.

[8] Lawrence of Amalfi, *Vita S. Zenobii Episcopi*, prol., F. Newton (ed.), *Opera* (MGH Quellen 7, 51).

[9] Mansi, xix.435C.

which were written in abundance, told of invaders of church lands who had been brought to repentance or punishment by their power; monks might take the relics with them when they went to plead in a law court, as the community of Stavelot did before the Emperor Henry IV at Liège in 1071; and relics were regularly carried into battle to harness the victory-bringing power of the saint. The veneration of the saints was not a primitive practice which survived from the barbarian past and was destined to fade away with higher standards of education. On the contrary, their shrines were increasingly important centres in the eleventh-century world, and pilgrimage to them, which in the Carolingian period had been mainly the prerogative of clergy and nobles, was becoming widespread and popular. This was true of the greatest international centres: pilgrimage to Jerusalem was on a larger scale than ever before, and from about 1050 the shrine of St James at Compostella in northern Spain began to attract visitors from abroad in ever growing numbers. In many parts of Europe the century saw the establishment of major pilgrimage centres. The popularity of the shrine of Ste Foy at Conques increased markedly from about the year 1000; Vézelay under Abbot Geoffrey (1037–52) acquired the body of St Mary Magdalen; Bavaria received its first major centre of pilgrimage in 1049 when Pope Leo IX consecrated the church of Heiligkreuz, Donauwörth, specially built to house a fragment of the cross brought from Constantinople; the body of St Matthew was discovered at Salerno in 1080; and the international fame of the image of Christ, the *Santo Volto*, at Lucca seems to date from the late eleventh century. Raoul Glaber was justified in entitling one of his chapters 'the relics of the saints discovered on all sides'.[10] The new importance of pilgrimage was such that the word *peregrinus*, which had previously meant a foreigner or exile, now came to be used to mean a visitor to a shrine, a pilgrim in the later sense. This confidence in the power of the saints will be more comprehensible to us if we remember that it was, as a matter of hard fact, effective. The standing of a church really did depend on the greatness of its patron saint. The authority of Rome was derived from St Peter and St Paul, and Compostella would have been nothing without St James. Lands were restored out of love or fear of the saints, the poor and the sick could hope for relief at their shrines, and the donations of

---

[10] Glaber, *Historiae*, iii.6 (PL 142.655B).

pilgrims helped to finance new and splendid buildings. It is understandable that these wonders were ascribed to the mysterious powers which resided in the bodies of holy men. Sin and sorrow could not be overcome by human arrangement, but by sacred power.

The shrines of the saints were by no means the only places where men might have recourse to the help of the sacred. The judicial system depended in difficult cases on recourse to divine judgement through the practices which we know as ordeals, but which were at the time described by the simple term judgement, *iudicium*. When human testimony was lacking, the accused might appeal to divine witness in the ceremonies of hot iron, or hot or cold water, ceremonies for which a liturgy was provided and which frequently took place in the cathedral itself. Once again we encounter the same distrust of human possibilities and the conviction that the innocent can only be vindicated by sacred power.

God's care for his people was shown not only in the shrines of the saints and the ritual of the ordeal, but in the provision of authorities to govern Christian society: 'The greatest gifts of God to mankind, bestowed by the divine clemency, are indeed the priesthood and the empire, the one ministering in divine things, the other presiding and taking care over human affairs: both proceed from the same origin and adorn human life.'[11] This declaration of Roman Law embodied what is generally known as the Gelasian principle: the affirmation that God had provided two powers for the government of men, the royal and the priestly, *regnum* and *sacerdotium*. Gelasius I (492–6), the pope from whom it received its name, had been clear in his declaration of the duality but had implied the greater dignity of the *sacerdotium*, which dealt with spiritual and eternal things. To medieval men, this duality was a matter of common sense, and so was the duty of the two powers to co-operate for the well-being of the Christian world. It was also necessary that each power should respect the boundary between them, and its definition was to become one of the most important issues of the succeeding centuries. In practice in the middle of the eleventh century the two powers were not equal, for in most parts of Europe the organization of the church depended heavily upon the rule of the anointed king.

A glance at the historical atlas reveals a pattern of kingdoms which

[11] *Corpus Iuris Civilis*, iii, Nov. VI pr. ed. R. Schoell and W. Kroll (Berlin, 1954), 35–6.

are recognizably the ancestors of the states of modern Europe, even if their frontiers are different in detail, and their names still undefined. Spain was not a political term at all, and Germany and Italy were only slowly being distinguished within the general concept of the empire. Gregory VII was adopting an unusual style in 1076 when he spoke of the 'kingdom of the Teutons and of Italy'.[12] The rulers of these kingdoms had little by way of administrative machinery at their disposal. The classical term for a state, *respublica*, was relatively rare in eleventh-century writing; *patria* referred more commonly to the heavenly country than the earthly; and the king was ruler of a people, *rex Anglorum* rather than *rex Anglie*. He was their father and protector, whose task it was to save them from oppression and injustice, and he was their leader in war. The nature of the royal office at the beginning of our period is declared in materials which, although highly evocative, are hard to interpret with precision: coronation liturgies, panegyrics, and the symbolism of royal insignia. It is a fact of prime importance that there was not, at the beginning of our period, a clear area of separate governmental responsibilities which could be firmly labelled as secular. Although the lay ruler's military role was peculiar to his office, in other respects (as guardian of peace and justice and protector of the church) his functions interlocked with those of bishops and of patron saints. Carolingian bishops had certainly seen the preservation of the peace as part of the emperor's function, but had themselves co-operated actively with him. Monastic writers of the tenth and eleventh centuries had sometimes stressed the king's standing as a sacred person, and esteemed such rulers as Robert the Pious of France (996–1031) and the Emperor Henry II (1002–24) because of their asceticism, whether real or imagined: the virtues of the king overlapped with those of the monk. The definition of responsibilities, which could be made so confidently in the time of Justinian, was no longer clear.

Of the rulers of the west, the greatest was the emperor, whose dominions included Germany, northern and central Italy, and the old middle kingdom of Burgundy. It was accepted by this time that the imperial dignity was vested in one of the leading families of Germany, and in 1050 the emperor was the brilliant Henry III (1039–

---

[12] Greg. VII, *Reg.* iii.6 (253). Gregory also regularly used the word 'Teutonic' in his letters. It seems to have expressed a new perception of national relations, and conceivably reflected the pope's awareness of his Roman origins.

56), the second of the Salian house. The existence of the imperial title has sometimes misled historians into supposing that it expressed a strong ambition for political unity: 'as Christendom is subject to the pope, so all peoples must obey the emperor'.[13] It is true that language was used which appears to imply this. The emperors regarded themselves as the legitimate heirs of Rome, and already in the tenth century they used the title *Imperator Augustus Romanorum*. When the style of Roman imperialism was combined with the belief that the emperor was God's anointed, propaganda inevitably took on a universalist ring. Thus Wipo, chaplain of Henry III, wrote

> Henry the Third, the friend of virtue, reigns.
> Next after Christ he rules across the earth.[14]

The practical significance of such phrases was slight. The Salian emperors did not claim fealty or tribute from other monarchs except where they had special grounds for doing so, and the universal empire scarcely existed as an ideal, let alone as a reality. Even in the early eleventh century the assertion was being made in France that 'each king devoutly exercises Christian empire within the bounds of his realm'.[15] The distinctive thing about the empire was not that it was universal, but that it was Roman. The emperor claimed lordship over the city of Rome, where alone he could receive his crown, and he was protector of the see of Rome, the greatest of all the western churches.

All kings, the emperor included, were God's agents, set apart for government by the anointing which they had received: 'Kings and priests . . . are found to be called God and Christ on account of the mystery of the ministry which they have received.'[16] In the great prayer *Deus inenarrabilis*, which was used in coronation orders throughout the whole of our period, the king was seen as the means by which peace and virtue were bestowed upon his people: 'and so may this people thrive under his government and be blessed with eternal life'.[17] The anointing of a king could take place only once, but he could show himself many times at a crown-wearing or coronation. So similar were the functions of a king and of a patron saint

---

[13] For these words of Ludwig Hahn and similar views, see R. Schlierer, *Weltherrschafts-gedanke und altdeutsches Kaisertum* (Tübingen, 1934), 20–4.

[14] Wipo, *Tetralogus*, vv. 18–19, ed. H. Bresslau, *Die Werke Wipos* (Hanover, 1915), 76.

[15] Abbo of Fleury, *Collectio Canonum*, 9 (PL 139.482B).

[16] Peter Damian, *Liber Gratissimus*, 10 (MGH LdL. i.31).

[17] R. Elze, *Die Ordines für die Weihe und Krönung des Kaisers* (Hanover, 1960), no. iv. A.2 (p. 10).

that the ceremonial proper to the one was transferred to the other. The regalia often contained relics or even were relics—the German kings were invested with the lance of St Maurice, into which had been set a nail from the cross of Christ. The king was displayed to his people as the Lord's anointed and as a walking relic-collection. It is not surprising that at one of William the Conqueror's crown-wearings a spectator fell down, crying out, 'Behold, I see God!' Marc Bloch has seen this period as the time when the custom of 'royal healing' or touching for scrofula arose, although its regular use may belong rather to the thirteenth-century cult of kingship.[18] The sacred office of kingship gave its holder a special responsibility for the church. He was acknowledged as vicar of Christ, and even, in a title which belonged to Christ himself, as head of the church.[19] The Old Testament provided many texts and examples to support the idea of the godly king ruling over a faithful people. The New Testament is considerably less enthusiastic about the secular power, but contemporaries did the best they could with its few helpful texts, such as Romans 13: 1: 'Let every person be subject to the governing authorities. For there is no authority except from God, and those that exist have been instituted by God.' The responsibility of a conscientious ruler towards the church is expressed in a charter of Edward the Confessor:

It will be right and proper for us, who are said to have been appointed by God as ruler over men, prudently to endeavour by the inspiration of divine mercy and after the measure of our judgement . . . especially to take in hand and in kindly measure investigate the affairs of the church.[20]

While the lay power therefore accepted responsibilities for the welfare of the church, the collapse of royal power, most notably in France, had led the bishops to assume what had primarily been royal functions, and to take the initiative in defending the peace. The beginning of the Peace of God movement is usually identified as the council of Le Puy in 975, where Bishop Guy demanded from an assembly of laymen an oath to preserve the peace and to respect the property of the church and of the 'poor', that is the ordinary population. There followed a sequence of councils, mainly in

---

[18] Milo, *Vita Lanfranci* xiii.33 (PL 150.53CD). On 'royal healing' see works cited in the bibliography.

[19] Wipo, *Vita Chuonradi* 3, ed. H. Bresslau, 23; K. Strecker, *Die Tegernseer Briefsammlung* no. 125 (MGH Epistolae Selectae III p. 142). The title 'head of the church' is from Eph. 5: 23, and had already been used of the royal office in a work falsely ascribed to St John Chrysostom.

[20] Cited and discussed by F. Barlow, *The English Church 1000–66* (London, 1963), 35.

southern France but spreading into the north and other regions, in which peace was enjoined upon the military classes under the threat of ecclesiastical censures. Associated with this were measures, first evident at the council of Toulouges in 1027, prohibiting violence at certain seasons, initially on Sundays but extending to include Fridays, Lent, and other days of special significance. By the time of the council of Narbonne in 1054 an impressive body of legislation had been assembled, which had reached the point of prohibiting any Christian from killing another. John Cowdrey has suggested that this was the culmination of the movement, which afterwards did not show the same vitality in its original form.[21] By this time it had moved far from its Carolingian roots and had developed features which were to be of great significance in the development of medieval society. The bishops were no longer the assistants of the lay power in keeping the peace, but had accepted that responsibility themselves, seeking the support of princes where possible, taking oaths from knights, and even on occasions organizing peace-keeping militias. The calling of special peace councils, where the presence of relics contributed by local monasteries added to the force of the injunctions, similarly went far beyond ninth-century precedents. The theological foundation of this enterprise was also significant, for it was seen as a realization of the peace which the apostles received from their Lord: 'How fair is the name of peace, and how beautiful is the reputation of unity, which Christ left to the disciples when he ascended into heaven.'[22] These themes (the church's duty to defend and provide for the welfare of Christian society, employing militias and oaths when necessary for the purpose; and the restoration of the apostolic age) will be appearing again in this history. The peace movement was a seed-bed in which many of the growths of the following century were germinated.

iii. The Church and the Lay Powers

Although the extent to which lay powers intervened in ecclesiastical affairs differed from one part of Europe to another, the general pattern was of heavy involvement. Apart from their moral responsibility, they were compelled to take a close interest because of the large landholdings of monasteries and bishoprics, and the clergy's

---

[21] H. E. J. Cowdrey, 'The Peace of God and the Truce of God in the Eleventh century', *Past and Present* 46 (1970) 53.

[22] Council of Poitiers (*c.* 1011–14), prol. (Mansi, xix. 267).

influential position in local society. When William I became king of England in 1066 he found thirty-five monasteries in existence with an aggregate income of £11,000, almost a sixth of the annual revenue of the whole country, while their links with the nobility tended to make them centres of opposition to the Norman conquerors. It was even more vital to control the great churches of Germany and Italy, for from the late tenth century the emperors had endowed them with secular privileges on an even greater scale than elsewhere: counties, immunities, tolls, markets, the minting of money, and other rights were transferred into the hands of favoured bishops, so that, for example, the diocese of Utrecht received no less than eight counties in the course of the eleventh century. It was assumed that the resources of the churches were available for the assistance of the ruler: in particular, bishops were expected to provide hospitality in their cities for the royal court on its incessant journeys, to bring troops to the support of royal expeditions, and to attend the court to give counsel. Royal grants of protection or *tuitio* were seen as creating a formal relationship between the Crown and the church which received them. The emperors were quite open about the service which the churches were expected to provide, and Henry II granted the abbey of Helmershausen to Bishop Meinwerk of Paderborn 'because it could be of no use to the kingdom in providing facilities or servants'.[23] The government of the German and Italian churches has often been described as the 'imperial church system'. This was not a clearly structured institution, for personal relations were pre-eminent in the functioning of the emperor's government. Even the most important services, such as participation in the military expeditions to Italy, were performed mainly by bishops closely associated with the king, who visited most frequently a relatively small number of favourite cities. The services thus rendered were in practice repaid by the grant of generous privileges. Especially under Henry III, bishops were appointed from the clerks who had acquired personal links with the court through their membership of the royal chapel and of a small group of chapters such as Bamberg, Magdeburg, and Henry's own beloved foundation of St Simon and St Jude at Goslar. Although most German bishops and abbots were of noble birth, lineage was not the only consideration in episcopal appointments. The choice was influenced by

---

[23] *Vita Meinwerci* 144 (MGH SS XI. 137).

bishops at court who appear as sponsors for candidates by officially 'intervening' in elections, and the evidence is that they used their position to secure the advancement of pupils whom they had taught, canons of their cathedrals, or other clergy whom they had encountered during their careers. It was a solid structure founded not on constitutional powers but on an old-boy network on an impressive scale. The central position of the Crown was made clear by the king's custom of giving to each new bishop a ring and staff, signs of the episcopal office which had originally been placed on the altar for his consecration, but were now bestowed by the emperor as the sign of nomination. The gift of the pastoral staff was by this time a long-standing tradition, and it is probable that the ring was added by Henry III himself. It is not certain whether Henry supposed that he was giving the spiritual office of bishop on God's behalf, or whether he intended only to bestow the land and rights which emperors had so abundantly given. In the empire, there are no texts from his reign which distinguish between the gift of temporal possessions and of the cure of souls, whereas this distinction was recognized in some parts of France before the middle of the century.

The position of the ruler in the German church was an extreme example of a general situation. In England the right of the king to participate in episcopal elections was clear, and although it is not certain whether the Anglo-Saxon kings invested with the pastoral staff, their Norman successors undoubtedly did so after 1066. In France royal authority was only effective in the north, in the area of the Île de France, and elsewhere the appointment of bishops had fallen into local hands. The great princes were not necessarily bad rulers of their regional churches: the dukes of Aquitaine helped to sponsor the Peace of God movement, and during the middle years of the century the monasteries of Normandy saw a brilliant revival under ducal patronage. In many cases, however, the bishopric was controlled at a still more local level. There are a few examples of bishoprics which had actually become hereditary. At Quimper in Brittany, a certain Benedict or Budic was describing himself as 'count and bishop' in the early eleventh century, and the two offices then descended in different branches of his family until 1123. Similar succession from father to son can be found at Rennes and Nantes, and seems to have been characteristic of the Breton church. Outside Brittany there was a long family tenure at Poitiers, held by the Isembart family from 986 to 1087. French bishops were usually drawn from the local nobility of the diocese; the replacement of an uncle by a nephew was quite common, but it was rare for the same family to retain the see for more than two generations. The new bishop was in many cases expected to provide a gift or *donum* to the count. At its best, such a system could secure an easy co-operation between clergy and lay nobility; it provided bishops whose connections and social status enabled them to act effectively in a society dominated by the lay aristocracy; and the payment of the *donum* confirmed, according to prevailing custom, their security of tenure. It is quite wrong to suppose that only bad bishops could be appointed under these customs. In most cases, we do not know enough about them to decide one way or the other, but it is not difficult to find bishops whose appointment was by later standards gravely improper, but who were effective administrators of their sees. The system, however, had obvious dangers. The exaction of gifts might be on such a scale as to ruin the endowments of the church, and the lay nobles, being the relatives and allies of the upper clergy, were in a good position to establish themselves as tenants of church lands. They could also acquire spiritual revenues: tithes had often passed into lay hands, and we even hear of a layman holding an archdeaconry as a fief by hereditary right.[24]

The influence of lay owners was even more marked at the level of local churches. The character of these varied from one region to another, according to the density of settlements and the length of time for which Christianity had been established, but there were some important common features. In each district there was a mother-church, often originally founded at a royal estate. Such a church (the old minster of England, or the *plebs* or *pieve* of Italy) was a meeting-place for worship and centre for baptisms and burials. A range of revenues had been attached to it for its upkeep, the most important being tithes, a tenth of the income of all inhabitants. At some of these churches there was a resident community of clergy, although this could only be found at a minority in the eleventh century, and probably such team ministries had never been general. In addition to the mother-churches, many other chapels and oratories had been founded. These had been designed to serve the private estates of bishops, abbeys, or lay lords or to meet the needs of villagers distant from their local church. The impact of private ownership upon this structure was complex. It was inevitable that

---

[24] Ordericus Vitalis, iii (ii. 152).

the rights of the founder would be dominant in the churches which he had provided and which were on his estates, where the priest was in a sense the chaplain of the lord to whom the church belonged. In some parts of Europe, most notably in France, these churches rapidly acquired the rights originally belonging to the baptismal churches. They secured their own tithes, font, and cemetery and thus emerged as parish churches in the later sense, although there was not in this period a clear distinction in usage between the words 'parish' and 'diocese', *parochia* and *diocesis*. In Italy, the older pattern of ministry survived much longer. The characteristic system there, throughout the twelfth century, was one of mother-churches and outlying chapels, *plebes cum capellis*. The advance of private ownership here took the form of the alienation of the rights of the *plebes* to laymen, which can be observed from at least the tenth century. When Alexander II (1062–73) drew up a list of the rights of the bishopric of Lucca, only five of the fifty *plebes* there remained in the possession of the bishop. The mightiest holder of *plebes* was probably Marquis Boniface of Tuscany, who is listed in a document of about 1052 as owning, in the diocese of Reggio alone, eleven and a half *plebes* with a number of chapels, while fourteen more were listed under 'castles and *plebes* which the bishop holds with all his knights'.[25] Boniface repented of his acquisition of church property, and his family was to be a pillar of the reforming papacy. At the other end of Europe we can observe a similar development, when in the middle years of the eleventh century the estates of the great church of Bosham (Sussex) were being alienated to oblige an earl and provide for the royal clerks of Edward the Confessor.[26] The lord of a church might expect to enjoy revenue from tithes and lands and to control the appointment of the priest, and to a remarkable extent churches were treated as legal property like the mill or oven. They could be inherited and given as fiefs, so that the church of Huntingdon changed its lord five times in a generation, being sold twice and once given as security for a loan. In France it was common for charters to refer to churches which were possessed by hereditary right.[27] It was quite normal for a lay owner to grant a church with all its appendages, including tithes,

[25] For detailed evidence, see C. Violante, 'Pievi e parocchie nell'Italia centrosettentrionale', MCSM 8 (1977) 658 f., 669–70.

[26] Barlow, *The English Church 1000–66*, 190–1.

[27] Ibid., 192–3; *Cartulaire noir de la cathédrale d'Angers*, ed. C. Urseau (Angers, 1908), no. 66, p. 132, granting 'ecclesias de Mellomartis . . . sicut eas hereditario jure huc usque possedi'.

burial rights, first-fruits, offerings, and other revenues which clearly
derived from the spiritual functions of the priest. It seems that in the
early eleventh century thè idea of the church as a local community,
or even as a body capable of possessing rights, had been largely lost.
Ecclesia meant a building, and charters were phrased so that land was
given *to* God and the saints *at* the church. 'The idea of corporate
personality was too abstract to lay hold of men's minds.'[28] The lay
control of local churches was matched by the intrusion of lay
interests into monasteries and collegiate churches. With the decay of
royal government in France during the century before 1050, the lay
advocate of each monastery, whose task had been to represent it in
the law-courts, had to become its defender against neighbouring
nobles, and from a protector he rapidly became an exploiter. It was a
matter of status for a landowner to have a family monastery, and if
an abbey was too expensive, then a small collegiate church could be
founded. This was particularly a feature of northern France, where
the petty nobles, enjoying wide independence, created many such
churches during the eleventh century, several of them being
endowed with lands which had been taken from nearby abbeys.
There is clearly much to support the description of this period as 'the
church in the power of the laity'.[29]

Yet that description contains a revealing assumption, that the
church should normally be controlled by the clergy. This was to be
the thrust of the argument of the reformers, with their strong sense
of a distinction between the two orders; but it fails to cover
important aspects of the situation. By no means all proprietors were
laymen. Monasteries were large owners of churches, and their
holdings were steadily increasing as lay lords transferred their
ecclesiastical rights to them—a movement which antedates the
middle of the century. Clergy were no less eager than laymen to
exploit the cash value of their spiritual functions. The bishops' duties
of oversight were transmuted into collections of profitable rights,
which in Normandy were known as 'episcopal customs'. Charges
were made at synod and visitation, and it is by no means certain that
the occasions actually took place, or whether they had merely
become the name of a tax; fines were levied for moral offences; and
churches were sometimes quite openly offered for sale, although this

---

[28] A. Dumas, 'La notion de la propriété ecclésiastique', *RHEF* 26 (1940) 17.
[29] Especially by E. Amann and A. Dumas, *L'Église au pouvoir des laïques (888–1057)*, FM 7
(Paris, 1942).

perhaps was unusual. As far as we can judge from surviving documents, the prevailing concept of the bishop's office was that of a spiritual lord, who performed important liturgical functions and was the proprietor of a large body of particular rights. The distinctive thing, in fact, was not lay lordship but private ownership. In the church as in the kingdoms the idea of corporate institutions with public functions had collapsed into bundles of rights owned by individual proprietors. It was a seigneurial church which had adopted the practices of the world in which it lived.

The whole system has been described by German historians as *Eigenkirchentum*. This may be translated, to adapt a modern term to an ancient practice, as the privatization of churches. The concept has the merit of emphasizing that we are dealing with a genuine type of customary law, which had its own cogency, even though it was in conflict with both ancient and modern canon law. Ulrich Stutz traced the idea of *Eigenkirchentum* back to the early Germanic assumptions about possession, and he is undoubtedly right in believing that it had ancient foundations and that it had for centuries posed problems for the church. More important from our point of view, however, are indications that the process of privatization had advanced very rapidly between 950 and 1050. It is not surprising that this should be so, for it coincided with precisely the same process in the state, where royal rights and public functions were being taken into private hands: the seigneurial revolution proceeded in parallel in the secular and spiritual spheres. Increasingly it presented the church with a critical situation and posed four problems. One of these, the huge lay intrusion into ecclesiastical revenues, has already been mentioned. The advance of privatization also brought with it a collapse of clerical communities. Monasteries had suffered from the Viking invasions, which had obliterated some ancient abbeys and led elsewhere to the replacement of the monks by lay canons. The changes of the later tenth century had in their turn a grave impact upon certain abbeys, but even more upon colleges of canons in cathedrals and other great churches. The Rule of Aix (816), while insisting on a corporate life, had allowed the ownership of individual property, and under the impact of privatization many communities dissolved. We hear, for example, that the canons of Arezzo in Tuscany had wives and families and divided the common property among themselves, and that St Romuald about 1005 'assigned canons and clerks who were living in the world like laymen to

provosts and taught them to live in a common congregation'. [30] A
third problem was posed by the married clergy. Not many people in
the year 1000 thought there was much wrong with clerical marriage,
but it had certainly become more prominent than before, with the
appearance of married canons in major churches, the growing
number of local churches served by married priests, and the tendency
for son to succeed father in them.

The fourth effect of the growth of *Eigenkirchentum* is the most
prominent of all in the thought of the period: simony, or the
procurement of spiritual privileges by payment of money. It is most
unlikely that the widespread purchase of ecclesiastical appointments
and revenues was a new thing. In Germanic society, the exchange of
gifts was a normal custom, and convention would require a counter-
gift from a clerk who had received the grant of a living; to render
some appropriate return would have been good manners, as well as
confirming his entitlement to hold the office. If that is so, the
question presents itself why the issue now began to cause so much
excitement. To this there are perhaps two answers. One is that the
use of money for commercial purposes was becoming very much
more common in the eleventh century. The present given to a bishop
or a lay lord therefore appeared much more like a cash payment than
a conventional gift, and the intensity of the reaction was increased by
the fact that some leading reformers, such as Peter Damian, showed
fierce hostility to the whole development of a money economy. It is
unlikely to be a coincidence that Italy, which was foremost in
commercial development, was also a forerunner in radical protests
against simony. The other cause for growing anxiety about simony
may have been the progress of privatization itself, which gave rise to
a large number of business transactions in church rights. It is
probable, therefore, that we are not simply the victims of an optical
illusion: even allowing for the greater volume of evidence, the
church of 1050 really was much more dominated by simony than
that of 850. The growth of a money economy and of seigneurial
jurisdiction had increased the grip of simony, and the chink of
money round the altar had become impossible to ignore or to accept.

iv. *The Beginnings of a Reform Ideology.*

The roots of the great reforming movement, whose manifestations

---

[30] *Historia Custodum Aretinorum* (MGH SS XXX.2.1473); Peter Damian, *Vita Romualdi* 35
(PL 144.986–7). This life was written about 1042.

will occupy a great part of this volume, were already in existence before 1050, and we can discern three spheres which were particularly significant.

We noticed earlier that the idea of the church as a community had almost disappeared, and that churches were being treated as buildings which were as susceptible to ownership as a mill or an oven. At best, they were seen as property owned by God or the patron saint. Yet in some influential circles the old concept of the church as a community was being actively revived. It was kept in memory in part by the fact that Isidore of Seville had defined the church as an assembly of people.[31] At the abbey of St Victor, Marseille, a major centre of monastic growth, it was realized that the use of the word *ecclesia* to mean a building is strictly incorrect: 'preaching freely that Jesus Christ is the son of the living God, (the apostles) ordered the building of material houses both in wood and stone, in which they could readily instruct the assembled faithful in the Lord's teaching. These houses from that time onwards the faithful incorrectly called "churches" '.[32] This sense of community was particularly expressed in a growing devotion to the apostles. In France and Germany, there was an increasing observance of the feast of *Divisio apostolorum*, kept normally on 15 July to commemorate the separation of the apostles to preach the Gospel. At the same time, it was becoming fashionable for churches to adopt patron saints from among the apostles, who sometimes replaced the less familiar martyr or missionary of the traditional dedication; or, as in the case of St Martial at Limoges, there was a move to obtain recognition of the patron as having apostolic rank. This devotion to the apostolic past was not a mere formality, but was accompanied by an attempt to understand and appropriate the spirituality of the first generation of Christians. It has already been mentioned that the Peace of God movement saw itself as inspired by the peace which Christ had given to the twelve, and there was growing excitement about the description of the apostolic church in the New Testament: 'Now the company of those who believed were of one heart and soul, and no one said that any of the things which he possessed was his own, but they had everything in common' (Acts 4: 32).

The proud duty of living the apostolic life belonged in the first place to monks, and the passages from the *Acts of the Apostles*

---

[31] Isidore, *De Ecclesiasticis Officiis* I.i.2 (PL 83.739–40): 'ecclesia autem vocatur proprie, propter quod omnes ad se vocet et in unum congreget', echoing a definition by St Augustine.

[32] M. Guérard, (ed.), *Cartulaire . . . de S. Victor de Marseille* (Paris, 1857), I, no. 33, p. 52.

provided them with a vision of community which they could set against the sombre background of a world of which they had despaired. The monasteries were seen as the historical continuation of the apostolic church at Jerusalem. This idea was expounded by Bishop Pons of Marseille in his *carta liberalis* for St Victor, Marseille, in 1005. Having quoted Acts 4: 32, he continued

At Jerusalem the whole multitude of believers was of a kind which it is now difficult to find among the few who are in monasteries. But when by the preaching of the apostles the necks of all the peoples were subjugated to the yoke of the Lord, and the number of believers was infinite, and when the holy apostles had departed from the world in the glory of martyrdom, that holy fellowship and institution of the apostles began little by little to grow lukewarm. Seeing this, those whose minds were fervent in the doctrine which they had received from the apostles separated themselves and began to live together. They were called in Greek cenobites, that is 'living communally'. From that monasteries took their origin.[33]

These ideals were shared by many monastic leaders, and provided a programme for such great houses as Cluny and St Bénigne, Dijon, and were also, as we shall see later, beginning to impinge on the secular clergy, among whom houses of canons were already, before the middle of the century, returning to a common life and common ownership of property.

A further source of reforming ideas was canon law. This was thought to have absolute authority, so that Abbot Siegfried of Gorze wrote in 1043 that 'it is sure and undoubtedly true that the authority of the canons is the law of God'.[34] It was, however, hard to study and apply the canons, for existing collections were arranged chronologically and were difficult to consult on any particular matter. The two most widely circulated were the Dionysia-Hadriana, which was the nearest thing to an official compilation that existed, and the pseudo-Isidorian decretals. In the years before 1050 the situation was being changed by the dissemination of a new collection, the *Decretum* of Bishop Burchard of Worms, completed before 1020, and admirably designed to meet the needs of bishops who had to hear ecclesiastical disputes, for the compilation was arranged by themes and so was much easier to consult. It spread throughout western Europe, appeared in Rome and central Italy by

---

[33] *Cartulaire . . . de S. Victor* I, no. 15, p. 18.
[34] Letter to Abbot Poppo of Stavelot, cited W. von Giesebrecht, *Geschichte der deutschen Kaiserzeit*, ii (Brunswick, 1860), doc. 10, p. 663.

about 1050, and remained influential until the end of the century. For some fifty years or more it was the most generally authoritative of canonical collections, and the character of the reforming ideology was influenced by the fact that many extracts from papal letters, which were believed to represent the teaching of the early church, were in fact drawn from the forged decretals of pseudo-Isidore. Thinking was therefore being shaped, not so much by catholic tradition in its historical form, as by the image of tradition in the minds of the ninth-century forgers.

The apostolic ideal, the monastic and clerical revivals, and the application of canon law all had features in common, and their objectives were actively supported by some of the German emperors, notably by Henry II (1002–24) and Henry III (1039–56). The most important feature of all was the attack on simony, which was condemned in the synods of Ravenna and Rome: 'if any one shall consecrate a bishop or priest or deacon or any form of holy orders for money, he shall be anathema and the ordainer shall be deposed'. The attack on simony was pursued on an international scale: in France it was condemned at the synod of Bourges 1031 and in the chronicle of the Cluniac Raoul Glaber; in England lay domination and the sale of churches were attacked in the sermons of Ælfric; in Germany the *Decretum* of Burchard of Worms preserved the ancient legislation against simony; and in Tuscany monastic founders included provisions that an abbot who obtained office by simony should be expelled.[35] The attack on clerical marriage was not as persistent, but it was a central theme of the synod of Pavia in 1022, while Burchard of Worms preserved from earlier collections legislation which limited the intervention of lay powers in pastoral affairs.

The Roman Church was not a major source of reforming enterprises. Until the crisis of 1045–6 the papal office was held by members of the great family of Tusculum. They have often been regarded as an expression of its degradation, and certainly contemporary criticism of Benedict IX (1032–45) was severe. Recent study has however shown that the Tusculan popes were more concerned for the upholding of canon law, and more active on the international scene, than has usually been supposed. Even under Benedict IX there

---

[35] See e.g. M. Fornasari, ed., *Collectio Canonum in V Libris*, i.72, CC(CM) 6 (1970), 63. See also W. Goez, 'Reformpapsttum, Adel und monastische Erneuerung in der Toscana', VuF 17 (1973), 222 n.

was a group at Rome based on the household of John Gratian, who was to become pope briefly as Gregory VI in 1045. This party probably had connections with reformers such as the hermit Peter Damian, Abbot Odilo of Cluny and the exiled Archbishop Lawrence of Amalfi. It also included the youthful clerk Hildebrand, who may have been a relative of John Gratian and certainly began his fiery career under his auspices.

The dignity of the church of Rome rested, in the eyes of contemporaries, on its standing as the shrine of the apostles. There were many people, great and small, who like Count Haimo of Corbeil 'went to Rome to the tombs of the apostles Peter and Paul for the sake of prayer'.[36] The foundation-texts of the Roman Church were the promises given by Christ to Peter, with power to bind and loose, but these were not generally regarded as giving jurisdiction over all other churches. Isidore had taught that the powers of Peter had been conferred on all the apostles, and his teaching was quoted at the synod of Arras in 1025.[37] In line with this, Burchard of Worms declared that the order of bishops had begun with Peter, so that Rome was to be reverenced as the first see and enjoyed a primacy among bishops; but its bishop could not properly be termed chief of the bishops or their prince (*princeps sacerdotum* or *summus sacerdos*).[38] Papal influence north of the Alps was limited to a narrow range of specific issues. In the first half of the century it was very rare for a pope to travel outside Italy, and many bishops had never visited Rome. There was no regular channel of communication, and it is probable that many dioceses never received a papal letter of any kind. Nevertheless there were still signs of a view which had been expressed by Leo I and Gregory I and had been sharpened in the Carolingian period, that the see of Rome was the special recipient of the Petrine commission and enjoyed a general authority of binding and loosing in the church as a whole. The materials for such an interpretation were contained in papal letters and in canon law, and had been increased by the fertile imagination of the pseudo-Isidorian forger, whose work was already known at Rome. There was only one area of activity in which this primacy had received significant application before 1050: the emergent practice of exempting great

[36] C. Borel (ed.), *Vie de Bouchard le Vénérable par Eudes de S.-Maur* (Paris, 1892), 5–6. The life was written in 1058 although it tells of earlier events.

[37] Isidore, *De Officiis Ecclesiasticis*, II.v.5 (PL 83.782A); Mansi xix.444A.

[38] Burchard, *Decretum* i.1–3 (PL 140.549–50).

monasteries from the control of the bishops. John XIX linked the exemption which he granted to Cluny with the claim that the apostolic see 'has the right of judging over every church, and no one is permitted to quibble about its decree nor to judge its judgement.'[39] This was saying a great deal, but before 1050 it was very rare for the claim to be put into effect.

Between about 1020 and 1050, then, there were important groups who were looking for a revival of apostolic standards in opposition to the practices which generally prevailed. The work of monastic renewal, the reform of collegiate churches, and the more effective application of canon law and legislation by councils and synods did not begin in the middle of the century, however much they may have been accelerated thereafter. The rediscovery of the church of Christ and the apostles—in its own way, a quest for the historical Jesus—had already emerged as an ideal, and is a striking illustration of the renewal of the church by the recovery of the past, or of what was conceived to be the past. As Hans Küng has said, 'Christianity means the activation of memory', and the process was already happening before 1050.[40] Scholars have been unable to agree how close the reform movement of those years had come to the ideals which became dominant in the second half of the century. Many of the principles were certainly being stated already: there was not much later legislation about simony, for example, which was not already in essence contained in the collection of Burchard of Worms. One difference we can notice at once: there was before 1050 no very clear statement of a programme, and no co-ordination of the reforming endeavours by an authority which could champion them throughout western Europe. These were provided only by the dramatic change within the Roman Church after the intervention of Henry III in 1046. The implementation of the programme, more-over, could take place only in the context of developments in society as a whole, which were only beginning in the middle of the eleventh century, and to which we must turn in the next chapter.

[39] See H. E. J. Cowdrey, *The Cluniacs and the Gregorian Reform* (Oxford, 1970), 41–2 n.
[40] H. Küng, *On being a Christian* (London, 1974), 121.

2

THE PATTERN OF SOCIAL CHANGE

It is not possible in studying the medieval world to distinguish clearly between the history of the church and that of secular society. The chronicler Otto of Freising, remembering St Augustine's distinction between the city of God and the earthly city, thought it could hardly be applied to his own times: 'because not only the whole people, but also the princes, with a few exceptions, were catholics, it seems to me that I have written the history, not of two cities, but only of one, which I call the church'.[1] The great changes which we shall have to study in the organization and spirituality of the church were responses to the transformation of society, and at the same time they helped to bring the transformation about. What is more, the actual concepts which we must use in understanding the period were themselves moulded by ecclesiastical writers. Such groups as the knights (*milites*) or the poor (*pauperes*) may seem to us to be sociological phenomena, but to twelfth-century writers they were theological and moral conceptions, significant for the function which they fulfilled in the divine purpose for the world. Social changes cannot be examined separately from the religious thought which helped to bring them about and shaped the information we receive about them. The purpose of this chapter is to consider these wider changes before turning to those developments which are more specifically ecclesiastical.

i. *The Extension of Economic Activity: the Countryside*

In the eleventh century a great part of the countryside in western Europe was still unpeopled. River valleys were unprofitable marsh-lands, and low-lying coasts, notably those of Flanders, Holland, and northern Germany, were covered with sand-dunes and salt-marsh. Still more characteristic of the landscape were the great forests. Even in the more thickly settled areas such as England or northern France,

[1] Otto of Freising, *Chronica*, v. prol., ed. A. Hofmeister (Hanover, 1912), 229.

there were extensive woods, each of which had its own name, like
rivers and mountains on the modern map: Wychwood, Sherwood,
Weald, Yveline, La Bière. Perhaps the most fully developed
countryside was that of Lombardy, but even there estates had been
allowed to lapse from cultivation, the marshes at the mouth of the Po
valley were unrecovered, and at the heart of the most fertile area a
village near Mantua had still in 1114 the legal obligation to assist the
lord when he pursued wild beasts in the woods.[2] While even the
more populated lands had a good deal of undeveloped space,
Germany still had huge areas of primeval forest untouched by man,
and its internal colonization was going to produce one of the major
shifts in political power in our period.

The years after 1050 have been christened the Age of Clearance.
All over Europe, there were in progress the settlement of wastes, the
clearance of forests, and the draining of marshes. The timing of this
great enterprise varied from one region to another. In France the
activity was most intense between 1050 and 1150, although in some
areas, such as the county of Mâcon on the Rhône in the neighbourhood of the great abbey of Cluny, it had begun in the late tenth
century. In Flanders, Count Baldwin V was congratulated around
1060 because 'you have made fertile by your care and industry land
which was uncultivated until recently'.[3] In the Île de France new
settlement, or resettlement of land which had become waste during
the past century of disorder, was specially evident when Louis VI
(1108–37) was creating new villages beside the crucial road from
Paris to Orléans through the heart of the royal territory, and when
Abbot Suger of Saint-Denis (1122–51) was restoring the abbey lands
and settling colonists, *coloni* or *hospites*. Germany provided specially
abundant opportunities for clearance. In this land of great forests, it
had perhaps never wholly stopped, but evidence suggests that it had
slowed around 900 and that progress had become rapid by the late
eleventh century. Peasant settlers were moving into Austria, while in
the north Archbishop Frederick of Hamburg-Bremen made an
agreement with a group of Hollanders in 1106 to drain land which
was 'until now uncultivated and marshy and useless to the
inhabitants of the country.'[4] Princely houses were able to build up
territories under their own control, as the Zähringen did in the Black

---

[2] See the evidence in J. K. Hyde, *Society and Politics in Medieval Italy* (London, 1973), 25–6.
[3] Letter from archbishop of Reims (MGH SS XV.ii.855).
[4] Cited G. Duby, *Rural Economy and Country Life in the Medieval West* (London, 1968), 391–3.

Forest and the Hohenstaufen in Alsace and Suabia. The same possibility was open to the ecclesiastical princes, and the question of *territorialpolitik*, the clashes over the control of territories, became increasingly significant in the relations between the German monarchy and bishops. Land for settlement was particularly abundant on the eastern frontier. In 1108 the bishops and lay nobles of Saxony drafted a manifesto inviting peoples from the German lands to join in an expedition against the pagan Wends and to settle in the east: 'here you can save your souls and, if you wish, acquire the best of land to dwell in'.[5] The process of settlement made it easy to find the land needed for founding or extending monasteries. Thus (to take one of many possible examples) in 1101 Abbot Windolf of Pegau on the river Elster undertook the settlement of a place which was called after him Abbatisdorf, 'to root out the trees and bushes everywhere and, having destroyed the dense woods, to lay out new lands. A church was built there and a manor (*curia*) properly provided for the use of the inhabitants.'[6]

The process of clearance was associated with a growth in population in many parts of western Europe. Some of the new lands were brought into cultivation by immigrants, like the Hollanders at Bremen, who had probably been driven away by the growing population and consequent land shortage in their home districts. It is likely that several different causes were combining to produce a great demographic increase. It must in part have been due to the cessation of invasions from outside which had made the ninth and tenth centuries such a troubled time all over the west. Improvements in technology helped: an upsurge in iron production made available more iron tools (the woodman's axe, the heavy plough for rich soils), while better systems of harnessing improved the performance of draught animals. Nutrition played its part, with the extension of fields devoted to leguminous crops; as Lynn White has suggested, medieval people were literally full of beans. It is difficult to give a firm chronological framework to these changes, but they were certainly having a significant impact in the course of the twelfth century. It may well be, too, that the continent was experiencing one of the cyclical changes in the world's weather, and that the longer

[5] The expedition did not set off, and there is some doubt whether the manifesto was circulated. See P. Knoch, 'Kreuzzug und Siedlung: Studien zum Aufruf der Magdeburger Kirche von 1108', *Für die Geschichte Mittel-und Ostdeutschlands* 23 (1974), 1–33.

[6] *Annales Pegavienses* for 1101 (MGH SS XVI.247). For the background see M. Meiner, *Wiprecht von Groitzsch und Abt Windolf von Pegau* (Grossdeuben bei Leipzig, 1927).

and drier summers, which had grave consequences for the economy of hot and arid regions such as Iraq at precisely this time, made the processes of draining and clearance much easier in the wetter conditions of the west. The emergence of cities interacted with the countryside by producing a demand for its products; the new prosperity of the Île de France was founded on the supply of corn and wine to the industrial towns of Flanders. The reasons are speculative, but the increase in the population, and of the settled area, is an important fact in most of western Europe.

Contemporaries were aware of the problem of over-population. One account of the speech of pope Urban II, when he proclaimed the First Crusade at Clermont in 1095, strikingly ascribes to him a recognition of the need for *Lebensraum* in the east:

The land which you inhabit is closed in on all sides by the sea and the chains of mountains and is crowded by your large numbers, so that it does not suffice for the supply of riches and scarcely provides food for its cultivators. That is why you quarrel among yourselves, wage war and often wound and kill each other.[7]

The pressure of population upon the land, that most fundamental of resources, shaped social customs and ethical ideas. It lay behind the growth of practices designed to prevent the disintegration of estates through subdivision among many heirs. The most obvious of these was primogeniture, the rule that the eldest son inherited the whole of the estate. It made the propertied classes interested in new strategies of marriage which might enable them to safeguard or acquire land, and this interacted with the thinking of theologians and canon lawyers to produce a quite new marriage law. Another strategy for a hard-pressed nobility was chastity. It is evident to us that one reason for monastic growth was the need to remove some of the sons and daughters from competition for the family lands, and it is interesting to discover that this was recognized at the time. Bishop Otto of Bamberg (1102–39) explained his many monastic foundations by the fact that 'now, at the end of the ages, when men are multiplied beyond number, is the time of continence'.[8]

The expansion of settlement into hitherto uninhabited areas had large implications for the organization of religious communities and the emergence of new ways of thinking. It was now possible to

[7] Robert the Monk, *Historia Iherosolimitana*, i. 1 (RHC Occ. iii.728).
[8] Herbord, *Dialogus de vita Ottonis*, i.18 (MGH SS XX.710).

create stable monastic foundations in what had previously been wilderness. The growth of new orders in the hills and forests would not have been possible a century earlier, and the economic success of the Cistercians would have then been unthinkable. The expansion was also creating a climate of greater confidence. The wastes which had once been the abode of beasts and demons were falling to the axe and becoming the home of men, and the wolf was literally being driven from the door. The land was being clad in a white robe of churches. This provided the physical background to the sense of dominance over nature and belief in human capacity which was to become a feature of the new age. At the same time the movement of considerable elements of the population from their ancestral villages tended to disrupt the system of kin or clan which had provided belonging and security. Many men were 'compelled by the constraints of hunger to leave their land and their kindred'.[9] Their move took them into a variety of different environments. They might enter a newly founded settlement or *villeneuve*, enjoying land of their own regulated by the lord's charter, or settle within the walls of a fortified village (*castello*) of the sort which was numerous in central Italy. The inhabitants of these entered a structured community, even if the move uprooted them from their old kindred and neighbourhood. Others might be driven from their land by warfare, famine, acquisitive landlords, or population pressure without a secure place of refuge.[10] Migrants came to live in the growing cities, where they remained in poverty at the mercy of the changing demand for unskilled labour, and others moved into the forest to settle in small clearings. To some of them the pilgrim routes offered a source of escape, and we find that they sometimes ended as beggars who travelled from one shrine to another, existing on charity as perpetual pilgrims. Economic activity, therefore, produced the new social problem of the 'poor'.

Poverty in the modern sense of the word had long been endemic in a world troubled by outside invasion, internal war, poor technology, and natural disasters. In Carolingian usage, however, *pauper* did not primarily refer to those who lacked financial resources. The classic opposition had been between *potens* and *pauper*, between the great proprietors and the subject population which required protection to

---

[9] *Annales Cameracenses* for 1144 (MGH SS XVI. 516).

[10] The causes of poverty are well illustrated in J. M. Bienvenu, 'Pauvreté, misères et charité en Anjou', *MA* 72 (1966), 389–424; 73 (1967), 5–34, 189–216.

safeguard its land. We even find a contrast between the *pauper*, a small holder, and the *egenus*, the needy man whom we would more naturally call the poor. The Carolingian thinking was exactly in line with the words of the psalmist: 'May he judge thy people with righteousness, and thy poor with justice! . . . May he defend the cause of the poor of the people, give deliverance to the needy, and crush the oppressor!' (Ps. 72: 2–4). In the eleventh century, the meaning of the word became diversified. It could be used for unarmed peasants, incapable of defending themselves against nobles and knights who were oppressing them—an adaptation of the old distinction to a new social reality. The 'poor' were also very frequently the voluntary poor, monks or hermits who had renounced their worldly inheritance for the sake of Christ. Finally, and most significantly from our point of view, the 'poor' were seen as a distinct group of the dispossessed. They were those who had lost their lord, their land and kindred; whose provisions would not suffice until the next harvest; who had fallen into the hands of rural money-lenders. The word *pauperes* was thus already being used in the eleventh century to identify a new problem of poverty: the existence of groups who had fallen through the net of protection which, inadequate as it was, had formerly been provided by the family and the village community. This problem of poverty was to have a profound effect upon the spiritual ideals and functions of the church in our period.[11]

ii. *The Extension of Economic Activity: the Cities.*

At the beginning of the eleventh century the culture and economy of the west were almost wholly rural. It is true that many of the old Roman cities still existed, and moreover that they were important. Not only were they walled towns and centres of defence, but they contained the cathedrals and therefore the remains of diocesan administration. Nevertheless their population was small and there were relatively few Roman cities in northern France and England and none at all beyond the Rhine and Danube. Only in Italy was something like an urban culture preserved. Even there the economy, outside a few ports such as Venice and Amalfi, was agricultural, and

[11] I have here adopted amendments to the views of M. Mollat proposed in an important article by C. Violante, 'Riflessioni sulla povertà nel secolo XI', *Studi sul medioevo cristiano offerti a R. Morghen* (Rome, 1974), ii. 1061–81.

the possibility of an industrial and commercial society seemed scarcely imaginable. About 1025 a writer at Pavia, one of the largest inland cities, noted with amazement that the people of Venice did not cultivate crops or vineyards.[12] Nevertheless, the larger Italian cities contained not only a cathedral, but a palace and court administration, the residences of the nobility, and a group of lay judges and notaries. These varied a good deal in their legal learning, but they were the nearest thing to a professional class anywhere in the west, and their leading members might become men of outstanding importance, like the family of Leo at Lucca, who were large landowners and held administrative authority in more than one city.

The demographic expansion which gave rise to the clearances in the countryside was also reflected in the growth of the cities. Indeed, they were part of the same process. Most cities grew because of the increasing vitality of the economic life of the region which they served, for a larger population and greater production required better centres of exchange. To that must be added the growth of transcontinental trade. By 1150 the outlines of the later medieval commercial pattern had been firmly sketched. The Italian ports controlled the carrying trade to Constantinople, Syria, and Egypt, while they themselves obtained cloth from the industrial towns of Flanders. For its raw materials, Flanders in turn drew from a wide area: wool from England, corn and wine from the Île de France. The cities therefore ranged in importance from small regional markets to trading centres with connections in every part of the world. Almost no numerical evidence remains of their population, but an indication of their growth is given by the walls. At Cologne, the Roman walls enclosed ninety-seven hectares, and these already had received a minor extension in the tenth century. In 1106, there was a further small extension, and then a major new wall in 1180, which enclosed 401 hectares, one of the largest city areas in Europe. At Paris the Roman settlement south of the river Seine on the Mont Sainte-Geneviève had not survived the Germanic invasions, and urban life continued mainly on the tiny Île de la Cité, with an area measuring only eight hectares. Rapid expansion apparently began late in the eleventh century, and the walls built by Philip Augustus early in the thirteenth century encompassed almost 273 hectares. The growth of Paris was produced by a combination of the features which were encouraging urban development. On the right bank of the Seine was

[12] *Honorancie Civitatis Papie*, 4 (MGH SS XXX.ii.1453).

a commercial centre, from which the merchants controlled trade on the river from Rouen eastwards. From the reign of Louis VI (1108–37) Paris became increasingly the centre of royal government, and at the same time the famous schools began to attract students from all over Europe. Under Abbot Suger the abbey of Saint-Denis, just to the north, developed into a national shrine and centre of pilgrimage.

The century from 1050 to 1150 also saw the growth of Flanders as a populous industrial area, and extensive developments in the civic life of Italy. The fleets of Venice, Genoa, and Pisa were handling large-scale trade with Asia and Africa, while the collapse of the old political order had led to the emergence in Lombardy of a society whose authority was in the hands of the cities. The disintegration of imperial control, which can already be discerned in some cities in the tenth century, developed apace during the minority of the emperor Henry IV after 1056 and continued throughout the bitter papal-imperial conflict. The destruction of the palaces of the emperor or the margrave in cities such as Pavia, Lucca, and Bologna symbolized the end of an order. The ruling classes of the cities, nobles, judges, and knights of the bishops' households, increasingly exercised authority in the name of the community, displacing the bishop who had once acted on its behalf. By 1150 virtually every city in northern Italy was governed by elected consuls and organized as a commune. Rome itself, the head of the world, *caput mundi*, was also touched by the new vigour of urban life, but in a way occasioned by its unique history. The vast Antonine walls had, even in the classical period, enclosed a good deal of countryside, and by 1100 they bore no sort of relationship to the size of the city, whose population had shrunk during the intervening ages. The great basilicas situated near the walls, including the cathedral church of St John Lateran itself, formed villages separated by open country from the main city. The new growth of population was centred in the Tiber valley and in Trastevere on the west bank, which provided a power-base for new families such as the Pierleoni, whose possessions on Tiber Island controlled one of the main bridges. Also on the west bank, the basilica of St Peter at the Vatican had been given its own protective wall as early as the ninth century. Most Italian cities were influenced by their memories of the classical past, and this was supremely so at Rome. Extensive church-building there was stimulated by the need to make provision for the densely settled areas by the Tiber and also to repair damage done, along the edges of the main inhabited area, by the Normans in 1084. Splendid buildings such as San Clemente and Santa Maria in Trastevere were in neo-classical style, designed in basilican form and decorated by mosaics inspired by those of the early centuries. The citizens' desire for liberty was subsequently expressed in classical forms with a Senate meeting at the Capitol. Rome was not, for most of our period, a satisfactory basis for the exercise of papal authority. It did not, until centuries later, possess the commercial or banking resources of the cities further north, nor did its schools share in the brilliant developments of those of France or Lombardy; most of its cultural history was written from outside. There were powerful groups always ready to go into opposition or to ally with the emperors, and for long periods the popes were unable to settle in their own city or conduct their administration from it. Their seat of power was a travelling household, not the Vatican or the Lateran basilicas.

The rising cities expressed themselves in the social and religious forms which came most naturally to the age. Almost invariably they were governed by a small group of leading families, a patriciate descended from the local aristocracy or from officers of the bishop's household. Like any monastery, the cities sought for charters of privilege and exemption, and they protected their security by that most standard of contemporary devices, a mutual oath – for that was the meaning of the 'commune' which so many cities wished to establish. It was an oath of peace with strong similarities to the oaths exacted from participants in the Peace of God movement. The cities often found in their patron saint their sense of identity and guarantee of protection. The body of St Mark was Venice's proudest possession, while at Lucca the generation which saw the appearance of the first consuls was also responsible for the recarving of the city's most splendid relic, the *Santo Volto* or statue of Christ, believed to record his exact appearance. The new greatness of the city of Bari was celebrated by the theft in 1087 of the body of St Nicholas from the shrine in Asia Minor in which it was housed, and at Verona the tympanum of the church of San Zeno, carved by the mason Nicholas in the 1130s, showed the saint bestowing a banner on the forces of the commune. Some bishops, especially in smaller cities, identified themselves closely with the aspirations of the citizens against castellans who were also trying to gain control. Bishop Bruno of Segni's last words were a promise 'that no tyrant shall in future construct a tower or any fortification in the city of Segni to dominate or oppress them, and they shall enjoy for ever the joys of liberty, which the divine munificence has given them'.[13] The impact of the saints upon the new cities was such that it brought about a major reconstruction of traditional ceremonies and superstitions. 'Folklore' seems to have been told anew in many cities in the twelfth century. For example, the relics of St Martha of Bethany were discovered at Tarascon on the Rhône in 1187, when the town was beginning to enjoy a new prosperity. Within the next few years a life of St Martha told of her capture of a local monster, *la Tarasque*. The Tarasque procession on Whit Monday, and the celebration of the capture on the saint's day, 29 July, continued at least sporadically into the twentieth century. It is striking that in the medieval materials the description of the saint and details of the capture are of common form, easy to parallel from other legends, whereas *la Tarasque* is a beast with distinctive features and strong local connections. The conclusion lies ready to hand that the original ceremonial and story-telling of the region were being altered to accommodate the rising power of the new saint. *La Tarasque* was tamed by urbanism and the power of the church, but without wholly losing her original features, which survived long enough to give us some indication of the transformation which had taken place in folk belief.

Before the middle of the twelfth century the expanding towns were showing signs of a new cultural and political importance. The cathedral schools were emerging as a major intellectual force, and the cathedrals themselves were increasingly the finest architectural monuments of the time. The outbreak of the conflict between Henry IV and Gregory VII turned on the struggle for Milan, and the support which most of the German cities gave Henry was crucial in excluding his opponents from the major bishoprics. On the First Crusade the navies of the Italian ports played an essential part in the capture of Antioch and Jerusalem. Increasingly, an urban style of life emerged, for the towns, small as they seem by twentieth-century standards, were posing unprecedented problems of scale. Their inhabitants needed hospitals, almshouses, leper-houses, schools, brothels, taverns, and churches, and the provision of all these things was rapidly extended. The cities also offered new opportunities for propagandists to sow the seeds of discontent, as Ariald did so effectively at Milan in the 1050s. Some of them acquired a nasty reputation for riot: 'the people is fickle and disorderly, and therefore

[13] *Vita* (*AASS* July IV 484DE).

is sometimes disturbed with seditious movements'.[14] One of the most famous insurrections was that at Laon in 1112, when the townsmen found their disreputable Bishop Gaudri hiding in a wine barrel and murdered him there. It is not surprising that these episodes of tumult led some clergy to declare themselves hostile to the whole urban movement; Abbot Guibert of Nogent, a close observer of the troubles at Laon, regarded 'commune' as a 'new and most evil name'.[15] Some historians have therefore regarded the cities as forming an intrusive element in society, 'hostile to the aristocracy and the feudal system', but at best this is a half-truth.[16] According to local circumstances citizens might rise against their bishop, or act as his ally against the local nobility; while some listened to anticlerical preachers, others were cathedral builders and devotees of their patron saint.

Some thinkers rejected the city entirely, not because of any clash of interests, but because they abhorred the whole ethos of commerce and careerist education. 'I will not dwell in cities', declared Norbert of Xanten, the founder of the Premonstratensians, 'but rather in deserted and uncultivated places,' while Bernard of Clairvaux urged Henry Murdac, master of the school at York, to seek God in the heart of nature: 'You will find something more in forests than in books. Woods and rocks will teach you what you cannot learn from masters.'[17] Their abhorrence of city life was increased by the part which money was coming to play in it. It is hard to trace in detail this growth in the availability of money, which indeed by later standards was still limited: throughout the period covered by this book there was no successful minting of a gold currency by a western government, and credit techniques were very primitive before the thirteenth century. Nevertheless, by about 1050 an increased level of financial activity was becoming quite widely evident. One of its effects was to act as a solvent on older forms of social organization. We have already observed an apparent link between the growing concern about simony and the rise of a money economy, and the demand for cash and credit also had a disastrous impact upon the

[14] At Tournai, *Vita S. Macharii altera*, 22 (MGH SS XV.ii.617).

[15] Guibert, *De Vita Sua*, iii.7: E.R. Labande (ed.), *Guibert de Nogent: Autobiographie* (Paris, 1981), 320.

[16] F. Heer, *The Medieval World* (London, 1962), 75. A more balanced statement of the same view is in E. Werner, 'Heresie und Gesellschaft im 11 Jh.', Sb der sächsischen Akademie, phil.-hist. Kl., 117.5 (1975), 11 ff.

[17] Hermann, *De Miraculis S. Mariae Laudunensis*, iii.3 (PL 156.991C); Bernard, ep.106 (*Opera* vii.266–7).

position of the Jews. They had previously formed a minority which, if little loved, had been tolerated, but they were now pressed into acting as the money-lenders which Christian society required, and became hated for the efficiency with which they performed their new role. The radical enthusiasts for poverty found the impact of money wholly objectionable, but the emergence of a cash economy also opened a great range of new possibilities. Alexander Murray is right in his judgement that 'money, rather than being a solvent of medieval society as it might first appear, was a prerequisite for its most characteristic achievements—such as cathedrals, pilgrimages and crusades.'[18] The flexibility provided by the wider use of money was essential for the range of international undertakings which, as we shall see shortly, was one of the most characteristic features of the new age.

iii. *The Expansion of Education.*

The medieval church in its years of fullest development depended heavily upon learning. Its theology was sophisticated and its administration shaped by skilled canon lawyers. This is particularly striking in view of the fact that in 1050 the level of learning was low and good education available to very few. Large monasteries needed a school for the training of their monks, and might open it to favoured pupils from outside or supplement it with an external school designed for students outside the community. Other major churches were required by Carolingian legislation to provide instruction, and in practice they had at least a song school designed to train boys to sing the service. Before the twelfth century, the word *schola* meant a choir rather than a school in our sense, and the training was often in the hands of the precentor, who was in charge of the music. The requirement of the Council of Rome in 1078 that bishops should provide for the teaching of letters in their churches and supervise the care of their ornaments emphasized the link between education and liturgy.[19] In Germany the emperors had encouraged the development of cathedral schools, and by 1050 such schools as Liège, Bamberg, and Magdeburg were the recruiting-grounds of the next generation of canons, and therefore of bishops. Henry III was a noted champion of these centres; indeed, he drew all his bishops

---

[18] A. Murray, *Reason and Society in the Middle Ages* (Oxford, 1978), 55.
[19] Greg. VII, *Reg.* VI.5b (402).

from this source. The Augsburg annalist noted succinctly that in Henry's time there was 'most famous study everywhere'.[20] In smaller towns it is unlikely that teaching was available other than from the parish priest, whose efforts would be directed (if he possessed the modest skill required) to training boys to help in church. It was a system which made natural the hereditary benefice, in which the son was trained up to follow his father's business.

There were indeed monasteries and cathedrals with fine libraries. Fleury on the river Loire and Reichenau and Saint-Gall in southern Germany were literary and artistic centres, and the activity of learned abbeys and their external schools kept the Meuse valley in the forefront of European culture. Even at its best, however, monastic writing in the eleventh century showed the marks of a non-speculative education. There were hymns, lives of saints, and annals in abundance, but not much serious theology or philosophy, whose absence from a Christian culture may be unexpected to the modern reader. Outside the monasteries, it was even more difficult to secure an advanced education. At times an outstanding master would emerge, such as Gerbert of Reims in the late tenth century or Fulbert of Chartres in the next generation, and Fulbert had a large group of pupils who later became heads of schools or *scholastici*. It has been suggested that Italian cities still possessed schools under lay masters, and it is at least true that cathedrals such as Milan and Pavia provided teaching to quite a high level. The core of their training was rhetoric, the art of public speaking, but it included a considerable amount of law and a good knowledge of the classics.

As against these rather frail beginnings, rapid progress took place from the second half of the eleventh century. There was a general improvement in the level of literacy among the clergy. Abbot Guibert of Nogent, writing about 1115, reflected on the change which he had seen:

A little before that time, and still partly in my own time, there was a great shortage of teachers of grammar. Almost none could be found in towns, and scarcely any in cities; and those who could be found were slender in knowledge, and were not even comparable with the wandering scholars of our own day.[21]

Some local schools at least had teaching of high quality: Bernard of Clairvaux acquired excellent Latin without attending any of the great

<hr />

[20] *Annal. Aug.* for 1041 (MGH SS III 125).
[21] Guibert, *De Vita Sua*, i.4, ed. E.-R. Labande, 26.

centres, and in England Gilbert of Sempringham, the founder of a major religious order, began his career as a local schoolmaster. The facts support the impression of a great expansion of education. Not merely were vastly more books being written in the early twelfth century, but many were composed in elegant Latin. The years from 1080 to 1130 saw the work of Anselm of Canterbury, Hildebert of Lavardin, Marbod of Rennes, Baudri of Bourgueil, Peter Abelard, and the young Bernard of Clairvaux, to mention only a few names. These were literary artists of high quality, with whom scarcely any writer of the previous century could be compared, and they had clearly enjoyed a good foundation in the mastery of Latin.

The general rise in the level of instruction was accompanied by the rapid expansion of higher education, especially in the schools of northern France. This was not at first the result of new institutions, but of new masters. Some of the earliest were monks: the teaching of Lanfranc and Anselm at Bec in Normandy was particularly famous. Much more typically, these teachers were secular masters attached to a cathedral. Assemblies of students began to be added to the traditional cathedral community. We are fortunate in having an account of a cathedral school in this early phase of expansion from the time of Master Odo of Tournai (1087–92). Odo personally supervised the attendance and conduct of his pupils at services, while at the same time providing a wide-ranging syllabus, including dialectic and astronomy, which attracted about 200 students 'not only from France, Flanders or Normandy, but also from far-distant Italy, Saxony and Burgundy'.[22] After 1100 the number of famous masters increased. At Laon there was Anselm (c.1080–1117), an innovator in theological method with a wide reputation. In the same generation there was William of Champeaux at Paris and Bernard of Chartres. The masters were not on the staff of established institutions, but were liable to move from one school to another or, not infrequently, to join a radical group of monastic reformers. Bruno of Reims became the founder of La Grande Chartreuse in 1084, and Odo established a small community at Tournai. When the master moved, the stream of pupils flowed to other centres, but before 1150 Paris had become an outstanding centre with a substantial group of masters permanently teaching there.[23]

---

[22] Hermann, *De Restauratione Abbatiae S. Martini Tornacensis*, i.1–4 (PL 180.41–5).

[23] It used to be thought that Chartres was another centre with a tradition of learned teachers and its own distinctive theological outlook, but an argument is in progress whether this group of masters was really based there or whether they primarily taught at Paris.

The masters were now becoming an important element in the life of the church. They began to attain high office, among the earliest being Lanfranc and Anselm (successively archbishops of Canterbury), William of Champeaux (bishop of Châlons 1113–22), and Gilbert the Universal (bishop of London 1128–34). By 1150 a large proportion of bishops had studied in the schools, and masters had many influential pupils. At Reims Bruno had taught the future Pope Urban II, who in 1090 invited him to Rome; Anselm of Laon's former students included cardinals, bishops, and abbots; and Bernard of Clairvaux, campaigning against Peter Abelard, was worried about the influence of his pupils who were now in the papal curia. The masters were playing an exciting and troubling part on the European stage. Disciples adored their masters, and they flocked after Abelard asking him to lecture. The sober Hugh of St Victor made fun of the dewy-eyed admiration which some students expressed: ' "We have seen them", they will tell you. "We studied under them. They often used to speak to us. Those great and famous men were our acquaintances." '[24]

While this spectacular growth was taking place in the city schools, monastic schools were declining. The monasteries could now recruit literate members, and did not have to train them themselves. The new monastic orders set their face against accepting boys for training, and this approach began to prevail within traditional abbeys also. External schools were either abandoned or placed under the direction of lay masters. This failure to expand the monastic schools did not mean that the orders had lost the spiritual leadership of the western church. The years from 1050 to 1150 were among the most creative ones in monastic history, and monasticism had a marked ability to attract outstanding masters into its ranks. Peter Damian, Bruno of Reims, Robert of Arbrissel, Peter Abelard, and Henry Murdac, to mention only a few, began as masters and ended as monks, and the number of masters who joined the regular canons was even greater. For a time the religious were able to find leaders among men who had been trained in the world and had deliberately rejected secular values and who were consequently champions of a revivalistic and radical spirit. It was only later, and with the coming of the friars, that the monasteries wholly lost the leadership of learning which had been theirs since the sixth century, but which now passed to the universities.

[24] Hugh of St Victor, *Didascalicon*, iii. 14 (PL 176.773D).

The basic syllabus was still, formally speaking, that of the Carolingian period: the three subjects of the *trivium* (grammar, rhetoric, and logic or dialectic) and the four of the *quadrivium* (arithmetic, geometry, astronomy, and music). This was by this time a threadbare and conventional classification, but it was a neat formula which survived several far-reaching attempts to revise it, such as those in the *Eptateucon* of Thierry of Chartres and the *Didascalicon* of Hugh of S. Victor. It was in any case being reformed by changes within it. Gerbert had introduced into the syllabus the logical works of Aristotle in the sixth-century versions of Boethius. They opened to students techniques of argument and of categorization which, when developed, made possible the ordering of major new fields of study. Outstandingly in the schools of northern France, and to an extent in those of Germany and Lombardy, dialectic became the central and most exciting part of the *trivium*. Grammar itself was changing in its methods and matter. Since the Carolingian period a wider range of classics had been brought into the syllabus to replace or supplement the early Christian poets as literary models. Rhetoric was adapted to form the basis of a higher secretarial theory, the *ars dictaminis* or art of correspondence, whose first clear manifestation was in Italy in the *Precepta dictaminum* of Adalbertus Samaritanus (1111–15), which was specifically designed, the author said, for 'the wise and powerful of this world'.

Further modifications in the syllabus arose from the fact that the greater schools were attended by older students intent upon advanced work. One field of advanced study which was well established by 1150 was divinity, the *sacra pagina*. Two great masters of the eleventh century, Lanfranc and Bruno, had written commentaries on the Biblical text, and Master Anselm had made Laon a major centre for theology in the years before his death in 1117. In about 1113 Peter Abelard began his controversial career as a teacher of theology, without ever having had a master in the subject. The character of Christian thinking was to be deeply influenced by the fact that theology was increasingly studied in a non-monastic environment and was shaped intellectually by techniques learned from the study of dialectic. Similar forces were at work in the schools of northern Italy, but the dominant discipline was Roman Law. It had long been a staple subject there, and early in the eleventh century Peter Damian had acquired a substantial legal knowledge in the course of his schooling. From about 1070 there are signs that at

Bologna law was becoming specially important within the framework of the arts course, and professional advocates (*causidici*) were appearing in the courts of Tuscany, many of them from Bologna or Ferrara. By 1100 Irnerius, the first of the great legal masters, was becoming famous for his exposition at Bologna of the texts of the civil law.

The world of learning in the early twelfth century had become a diversified scene, within which it was possible to study a range of different subjects to an advanced level. They had just one feature in common: the purpose of study was the elucidation of the texts of the past. The authority might be the Bible, or the Fathers, or Roman law, or the canons, or the pagan philosophers or poets (or, in the case of monastic reformers, Cassian and the Rule of St Benedict); in all these cases, the object was the exploration and application of inherited wisdom. The recovery of the past was the crucial feature of twelfth-century learning.

iv. *The Aristocracy*

Medieval Europe was a seigneurial society, a world dominated by its lords. This was never more completely true than during the eleventh and twelfth centuries. The breakdown of Carolingian government had, especially in parts of France, been accompanied by the collapse of public jurisdiction, and its replacement by the dominance of local noble families to create the seigneurial society which was the secular equivalent of the privatization of rights within the church. The old county courts had been succeeded by honorial courts in which the lord exercised jurisdiction only over his own men, and the ties of land tenure or personal dependence replaced public obligations and duties. The visible symbol of the new order was the castle, which had already become significant in France early in the eleventh century, and which spread to England after the Norman Conquest in 1066 and, in subsequent years, to Germany. Each neighbourhood was dominated by the castellan and his strong-armed men, who imposed levies on the peasantry and tried to establish his claim to be advocate or protector of local monastic lands. It was around 1100 that families began to acquire surnames (Montfort, Clare, Hohenstaufen) based on their most important castle. The twelfth-century noble had literally a local habitation and a name in a way which had not been true of his predecessors. In France, where the fragmentation had gone furthest, the Capetian kings themselves had begun to act as a private household, abandoning the old official diploma and issuing grants modelled on the private charter. In many French regions the castellans in 1050 were virtually independent powers uncontrolled by any superior authority, although the extent of the disintegration varied. The dukes of Normandy and counts of Flanders, for example, retained large powers of control within their territories. In England and the empire the position of the royal house was strong enough to prevent a total fragmentation and to preserve an awareness of the authority of the king over the whole of society. The private ownership of rights and jurisdiction had made large strides there without having obliterated the old order.

The situation was, however, not stable. At a date which varies according to the district, it became possible once again to build up the administration of a large territory. Louis VI on the Capetian royal domain campaigned strenuously to subdue the independence of the local nobles, and the same tendency is visible elsewhere. The colonization movement, the availability of revenues from tolls and markets, as well as such technical developments as the stone castle, weighted things in favour of the greater nobles, and led to the creation of larger units of government. What in France produced greater national integration had the opposite effect in Germany, where the princely *territorium* grew to the detriment of royal power. All over Europe the power of the aristocracy was enormous. It was said of Robert of Meulan, the friend and adviser of Henry I of England, that the kings of England and France made war and peace at his will.[25] The two northern French families of Anjou and Blois illustrate to perfection the international nobility at its highest point of power. The counts of Blois combined with their large county of Blois-Chartres the even richer territory of Champagne, married into the house of William the Conqueror, and produced a king of England in Stephen (1135–54). Anjou secured the throne of England in the person of Henry II (1154–89), and his grandfather Fulk had earlier become king of Jerusalem (1131–43). These families of the highest rank were obviously not typical, but at a lower level the international connections of the nobility might be widespread. Norman families might have relatives in England, Wales, Sicily, and Syria, and French nobles commonly had members of their families who had visited Spain or the Holy Land.

[25] Henry of Huntingdon, *De Contemptu Mundi*, 7 (RS 74, 306).

The centre of a noble's activity was his household (*familia*) or court (*curia*). Here in a domestic setting his tenants, officers, and counsellors would gather round him, and here he could impose the stamp of his patronage upon their activities. The courts of the greater nobles might be major cultural centres, and could vary greatly in kind. Under the counts of Poitiers their courts became a centre of troubadour poetry from 1100 onwards, while at the same time Countess Adela of Blois was a patron of new monasticism and in touch with many of the leading scholars in northern France. Even more remarkable was the patronage of Countess Matilda of Tuscany, who from the 1070s turned her court into a centre for the dissemination of Gregorian ideas. The development of the city schools did not destroy the importance of this lay patronage of learning, because it was in the courts of princes that the masters sought careers and influence. Until recently, it has been the fashion to write European history from a national viewpoint, and the story of the growth of the monarchy has been told in preference to the cultural importance of the nobility; but the wide scope of private lordship, which had almost superseded public authority in France and played an important part in every country, also requires recognition. True, the Carolingian model remained alive in Germany and England, and by the middle of the twelfth century the kingdoms of England and Sicily had taken the first steps towards renewed centralization. The exchange of ideas was furthered by royal councils, attended alike by bishops and lay lords. Yet we are still a long way from effective royal government. The king as a rule had only the same limited machinery of administration as was available to nobles, and like them he governed through his household. The most distinctive feature of the king was the sacred gift of anointing, which no noble ever received, but even so dukes and counts were regarded as the rightful defenders of churches, and they all bore the proud title *dominus*, lord, which belonged to God from whom all dominion came. In 1043 the synod of Narbonne excommunicated those who had invaded the abbey lands of Saint-Michel, Cuxa, but exempted Count Guilhem and his brothers, 'because we think it unworthy to subject to excommunication those whom we would wish to be patrons or defenders of the said monastery'.[26] Jacques le Goff has remarked that kings were always in a sense strangers in the medieval world, and this paradox is

---

[26] Mansi xix.602.

particularly applicable to the century between 1050 and 1150, when the nobility had a wide range of action and the ability to drive society along new paths.

v. *The Dissemination of Ideas.*

Medieval society lacked those technical means for the rapid dissemination of ideas and exchange of information which the modern world so abundantly possesses, but the interchange of cultural influences was of great importance. Movements of international scope were characteristic of the emerging society: the preaching of the crusades, ideals of chivalry, reverence for the see of Rome, and the influence of new monastic orders, all spread throughout the west, in some cases with remarkable speed. This could not have happened without an effective network for the interchange of ideas. The peculiarity of this pattern, as judged from our own standpoint, was the relative insignificance of the national level. The state as an organism was weak, and even where the bishops were royal nominees, this did not engender in them a primarily national consciousness. In one sense their loyalties were narrowly local, for their devotion was directed to the patron saint of their church, and to the preservation of its rights and privileges. It was St Augustine or St Cuthbert, St Denis or St Benedict, who provided the impetus and motivation for their policies. At another level Christendom was their natural unit. The world of scholarship was peculiarly international, and it was common to settle in foreign lands to study and teach, as did Lanfranc and Anselm in Normandy and John of Salisbury and William of Tyre at the schools of northern France. A similar pattern prevailed in economic affairs. There was much activity at a local level, and an international trade in high-value commodities carried mainly in Italian shipping, but there was no national economic policy, nor even the idea of one. Such an international civilization required a system of information elaborate enough to give unity to the culture of Christendom.

There were, moreover, features of contemporary society which rendered publicity not less necessary than in our own day, but more so. The inadequacy of the system of record meant that transactions had to be brought to public notice. Charters and grants were designed to inform the community as a whole of what had been done, and commonly began with such a formula as 'let it be known to all our faithful who shall see this present charter'. A new bishop had to be received by the people of his city, a parish priest to be installed in the presence of the deanery chapter; otherwise there would be no public knowledge, and therefore no secure tenure. Administrative processes were the property of everybody in a way which modern champions of open government might envy. The extent to which the 'public' included the whole population would vary from one issue to another. Frequently it was enough to address oneself to a small and privileged group, but there were occasions (and they were more frequent than has sometimes been supposed) when a very wide circulation was needed. The appeal to join the crusades was addressed very generally; so were demands for support in the conflicts between empire and papacy; and the requirement of annual confession was designed to be heard and obeyed by every adult in the west. The growth of the cities was crucial in the effectiveness of this mass propaganda, for it was relatively easy to reach the whole population of a town, which in addition served as a meeting-point for the surrounding countryside. The fact that there was no single absolute authority, as existed in the empires of Rome or China, and that there was not even an effective national unit which controlled opinion, made the techniques of conviction and persuasion quite remarkably important.

There was, of course, a physical problem of communication, and there were attempts to improve the difficult conditions of travel. This was one aspect of the Peace of God movement. The hierarchy strove to protect travellers; pilgrims and crusaders were guarded by manifold privileges; and at first attempts were made to defend merchants from interference, although in the twelfth century the distaste for commercial gain became so strong among the extremists who influenced papal policy that this course of action was not sustained. Bridge-building was seen as a charitable work, and in the course of the twelfth century brotherhoods were established at important river crossings to establish and maintain a bridge there. In the past, travel had been made possible not only by the availability of accommodation in monastic guest-houses, limited as this was in the early Middle Ages, but also by customs of hospitality which required a visitor to be maintained for the night by the host who encountered him; but the rapid increase in numbers on the roads made this impossible to operate. The last legislation requiring the old convention comes from a German Landpeace of the late eleventh century. It was already being replaced by two alternative provisions: the rise of taverns, where supplies could be readily obtained, and the creation of hostels or hospitals where travellers might stay, of which one important early group was the guest-houses established by the Hospitallers before 1113 in the main ports on the pilgrim route to the Holy Land.

At the same time, the media of exchange were being employed to publicize ideas, policies, programmes, and doctrines. The circulation of ideas was greatly assisted by the existence of Latin as the medium for the universal expression of scholarship, liturgy, and controversy. Some vernaculars also functioned as a *lingua franca* beyond the boundaries of any one nation. French was spoken in the twelfth century by the aristocracy not only in northern France, but also in England and Syria, and to some extent in southern Italy. The monasteries had originally been representatives of strong local or regional cultures, with each house independent of others and attached to its own diocese. In the eleventh century they began to be attached far more to international structures. The growth of exemption led abbeys such as Cluny and St Victor, Marseille, to look for protection to Rome, and the Cluniac houses were in theory all part of the mother abbey of Cluny. In the twelfth century the process went further, with the Cistercians, Carthusians, and others observing a standardized way of life in houses in many different countries. Pilgrimage was yet another influence which made for a common culture. The shrines proclaimed their message in the decoration of the buildings, in hymns and sermons, in songs and stories, and some of the cults (James of Compostella, Nicholas, Alexis, Mary Magdalen) were adopted in many European countries.

The Roman Church was particularly active in creating links to enable its reforming programme, and its controversies with the empire, to reach all the provinces of the west. As Gerhoh of Reichersberg said, the Romans 'paint, speak and write, indoors and out', to communicate their message.[27] Above all, they sought to establish close connections between Rome and the provincial churches. Metropolitans were required to collect their *pallium* or scarf of office in person from the pope, and were subsequently invited or ordered to pay regular visits. Legates were sent to every part of Europe, often men who were close to the pope personally, to

[27] Gerhoh, *De Investigatione Antichristi*, i. 72 (MGH LdL iii.393), referring to claims of supremacy over the emperors.

represent his policy. Councils and synods were held under the presidency of a legate or of an archbishop acting on papal instructions. A major synod would bring together numbers of clergy and laity to hear the settlement of a wide range of disputes, as well as the enactment of decrees, and thus spread information and instructions widely. Assemblies which had a primarily spiritual purpose rather than a legal one could also serve an important purpose in the distribution of information. Leo IX (1049–54) and Urban II (1088–99) on their long tours north of the Alps were active in visiting great churches and consecrating them, and one must suppose that the meetings, no doubt with a sermon by the pope, helped to create the sympathy between the pope and upper clergy which is a feature of both pontificates. Leo IX is indeed the prime example of a pope whose activity was less legal and administrative (although he did not neglect these spheres) than charismatic: the power of his preaching, the dramatic repentance of simoniacs, and their even more dramatic deaths gave an impetus to the cause of reform which no legislation could have achieved. In the pattern of changing social structures the improvement of the means for disseminating ideas was of major importance, for it involved the localities of Europe, still in many ways remote from each other, in the great issues which were central to the new age. No church could regard itself as exempt from these imperatives: as Ulrich of Cluny sharply pointed out, what God can do in France, he can also do in the neighbourhood of Speyer.[28]

[28] Ulrich of Cluny, preface to customs in PL 149.638CD.

3

MONASTIC GROWTH AND CHANGE

At a time therefore when there were no establishments for monks except in the oldest monasteries, new structures were begun everywhere . . . In villages and towns, cities and castles, and even in the very woods and fields, there suddenly appeared swarms of monks spreading in every direction and busily engaged, and places in which there had been lairs of wild beasts and caves of robbers resounded with the name of God and the veneration of the saints.[1]

The truth of this contemporary description is confirmed by a great abundance of evidence. At no other period in the history of the church has there been so rapid a growth in the number of monks, the variety of forms of monastic life, and the scale of monastic possessions. In this whole process of rapid change there were three different but connected developments. There was, first, the growth of existing monasteries. One of these, the abbey of Cluny, enjoyed an expansion so enormous, and of so special a kind, that it has to be discussed as a second element in the monastic scene. Thirdly, there were varied groups which may be loosely described as 'hermits', which were seeking a different type of monastic obedience from the one which had become traditional.

i. *The Expansion of the Monasteries.*

There were already many great monasteries in the eleventh century, with a long history behind them and large landed endowments. One of the most famous of all was Monte Cassino, to the south of Rome, where St Benedict himself had lived, and which was described as the 'head and beginning of all monasteries'.[2] The disorders attendant on the collapse of Carolingian government had been a time of trouble for many of these houses; the number of monks had fallen, and the

---

[1] Guibert of Nogent, *De Vita Sua*, i.11 E.-R. Labande (ed.), *Autobiographie* (Paris, 1981), 72.
[2] L. Duchesne (ed.), *Liber Pontificalis* (Paris, 1886–1957), ii.311.

estates suffered from the aggression of nearby laymen. The eleventh century saw an increase in the size of most communities, sometimes a very large one. We know, for example, that Monte Cassino had about 100 monks at the beginning of the century and 200 in 1071. St Aubin at Angers showed a sustained increase over a period of a century from 11 monks in 970 to 57 in 1038 and 105 in 1082, while at Gloucester there was dramatic growth from 10 monks to 100 under Abbot Serlo (1072–1104).[3] Greater numbers required larger churches and buildings for the accommodation of the monks, and the new architecture often expressed the power and wealth of the abbeys. One of the greatest of these projects was Abbot Desiderius's new basilica at Monte Cassino, whose consecration by Alexander II on 1 October 1071 was a magnificent affair with a huge attendance. At Cluny the third church, built between 1088 and about 1130, was the largest building ever designed for Christian worship apart from the later St Peter's at Rome. These were the two most celebrated churches of all, but many other abbots were building big. A specially impressive building campaign was undertaken in England after the Conquest by the Norman abbots, the size of whose new churches may still be seen at such places as St Albans and Durham. Almost all the really outstanding ecclesiastical buildings were monastic until the time of Abbot Suger's reconstruction of Saint-Denis in the middle years of the twelfth century. Thereafter, although there were still fine abbey churches being built, the leadership in architectural innovation passed mainly to the cathedrals and city churches.

This expansion had to be supported by increased resources, and the second half of the eleventh century was in general a time of development of monastic lands. Admittedly there were setbacks: we hear complaints from monastic chroniclers about the intrusion of knights onto monastic land in England by the new Norman rulers. But by and large the nobility was disposed to be generous to monasteries, and in almost all parts of Europe the number of recorded donations increased. The restoration of church lands was an important part of the policy of the reforming popes, and great families valued their association with the devotions of the monks, apart from more secular advantages of prestige or profit: the authentication of their status by the recognition of a great abbey, the

---

[3] For references see H. Hoffmann in H. Dormeier, *Montecassino und die Laien im 11. und 12.Jh.*, MGH Schriften 27 (1979) 1; J. Dubois, 'Les moines dans la société du Moyen Âge', *RHEF* 60 (1974) 5–37; and D. Knowles, *The Monastic Order in England* (Cambridge, 1950), 126.

benefits of hospitality and the ability of the monks to bring into profitable cultivation land which was outside the control of the dominant family. All these motives gave an opportunity to abbots to extend their holdings. At Monte Cassino the extension and strengthening of the land of St Benedict, the *terra Sancti Benedicti*, began before the middle of the eleventh century. Under Abbot Desiderius (1058–87) the abbey made a close alliance with the Norman princes who were then in the process of establishing their power throughout the south of the Italian peninsula, and the monk Amatus wrote a history in praise and justification of their triumph. The abbey lands benefited from their patronage on a vast scale. The land of St Benedict was further extended, an access to the sea secured in 1066 at Torre a Mare beside the mouth of the river Garigliano, and large grants received in southern Italy as a whole. The importance attached to this expansion of land and revenue is evident from the magnificent bronze doors which a member of the Amalfi ruling class, Maurus Pantaleone, gave for the old basilica in 1066, on which was inscribed a list of the abbey's possessions, including 47 *castella* and 560 churches. The Norman conquerors of England were similarly generous to their family monasteries at home in Normandy. In some regions, the process of rebuilding and extending the estates was more delayed: the restoration of those of Saint-Denis was primarily the work of Louis VI and Abbot Suger in the second quarter of the twelfth century. The study of the muniments became an essential part of the strategy of the abbeys: Leo, chronicler of Monte Cassino and cardinal-bishop of Ostia (*c.* 1102–15), and Suger of Saint-Denis both founded their future reputations on their work as young monks in the abbey's archives. When documents were missing it was necessary to supply them: Leo's successor as chronicler at Monte Cassino was a talented and imaginative forger, Peter the Deacon. The growth of the abbey lands was not just a matter of donation or recovery. Some monasteries were able to take advantage of the rapid growth of the cities by selling or leasing land for building; this process has been studied at Arras, where a great part of the town belonged to the abbey of St Vaast, and at Genoa.[4] There was also the opportunity to make loans in cash or treasure on the security of a piece of land. This was certainly being done on a considerable scale by the monasteries, and Cinzio Violante has

---

[4] See C. Violante, 'Monasteri e canoniche nello sviluppo dell' economia monetaria', MCSM 9 (1980) esp. 375–6.

emphasized that the major purpose of most of these loans was the extension of the estates. In northern Europe land given as security for a loan was usually held in mortgage, which gave both possession and revenue to the monastery, and the terms of the loan were designed to discourage its repayment, with the object of securing a permanent increase in the abbey lands. With the partial exception of Italy, there was no attempt to secure repayment within a limited term in order to facilitate further investments in new commercial projects. This insertion of the monasteries into the money economy has to be understood, however, not as a commercial undertaking, but as part of the domanial policy of the rich monasteries and collegiate churches.

The increase in monastic resources did not come only from lordship over land. The development in the private ownership of ecclesiastical rights had already placed in the hands of the monks tithes and churches which canon law assigned to the supervision of the bishop. More significantly still, very many churches and tithes were in the hands of laymen, who during the eleventh century granted them to abbeys in a movement which was called 'restitution', inaccurately because the revenues were not properly monastic ones. During the period 1038–1126 Monte Cassino received 193 donations of churches, 186 of them from laymen.[5] In northern France the process went so far that lay ownership had been almost extinguished by 1200. In the diocese of Angers, for example, 44 churches were transferred between 1050 and 1100, and a further 102 between 1050 and 1100. In northern Italy the rights of the baptismal churches, the *pievi* or *plebes*, were extensively recovered from lay proprietors between 1050 and 1125 and put into the control of communities of canons. The resulting balance of lordship over local churches between laymen, monks, and bishops varied a great deal. In England and Normandy many lay patrons remained, although with reduced rights. In a few places, churches were largely taken into the bishop's hand, usually for a special reason: in Italy the small dioceses of Latium made the bishop a dominant force, and in Brittany 'restitution' took place late, at a time when the authority of the diocese had been revived, so that it was able to benefit directly from the transfers. More typically the beneficiaries were the monks. Houses such as Déols (Berry) or Farfa (central Italy) acquired huge numbers of dependent churches. In the diocese of Bourges, the

---

[5] See the table in H. Dormeier, *Montecassino und die Laien*, 56.

archbishop ended with the patronage of only 7 per cent of the churches; none remained in lay patronage; all the rest belonged to the great churches, usually monastic ones. At Lyon and Besançon the pattern was similar. In the same way, monasteries were acquiring grants of tithe from the lay lords who had misappropriated it.

The most obvious reason for the large-scale restitutions was the prohibition of lay ownership of churches and tithes which became a firm part of the policy of the reforming popes. At Reims in 1049 Leo IX forbade the possession of ecclesiastical revenues by laymen, and at Rome in 1050 he ordered that all revenues of churches were to be returned, and tithes paid to the clergy.[6] From this time, it was consistently held by the Roman Church that it was simony for laymen to hold such rights. There was no question of simony if they were transferred to monasteries, but there was still a problem, because in canon law the division of tithes, and the government of local churches, was a matter for the bishop. Papal policy on this point was not wholly consistent, but as a rule it followed the principle which can already be found in a major decision by the Roman Church in 1060: monasteries were permitted to retain 'tithes or any ecclesiastical property' which had been theirs for thirty or forty years, but more recent acquisitions required the consent of the bishop.[7] This probably did not present much of an obstacle, for reforming bishops were in favour of the extension of the power of clerical communities over local churches, and in any case the bishop presumably had little real option: if he refused permission, the revenue would remain in the hands of the lay lord, to the danger of his soul, and the monastery would be deprived of a gift to no good purpose. The process of restitution was a success for papal policy, but it is more difficult to say how far commitment to reform was the real motivation for the lay lords. In a few cases it is possible to associate grants with a local reforming council or similar event, and sometimes the lord records his awareness of the sin which he is committing by detaining ecclesiastical revenues: 'struck by the fear of God, and coming to archbishop Richard lest they die accursed, they voluntarily relinquished into his hands the church which they wrongfully possessed'.[8] But such mentions are few among a huge

[6] For the evidence see G. Constable, *Monastic Tithes from their Origins to the Twelfth Century* (Cambridge, 1964), 85–7.

[7] Ibid. 87–8.

[8] Grant made under Archbishop Richard of Bourges (1071–90); see G. Devailly, 'Le clergé régulier et le ministère pastoral', *Cahiers d'Histoire* 20 (1975), 262 n.

mass of surviving charters (only two, for example, among the
donations to Monte Cassino), and it is striking that the process had
begun at least a generation before the development of the strenuous
papal reform movement about 1050.[9] Many of these grants must
have been straight financial transactions in return for a payment or a
loan. The reformers' programme encouraged both donors and
recipients to feel that churches and tithes were particularly appropriate ways to endow a monastery, and also introduced a prohibition on
ecclesiastical owners from granting them to laymen, thus ensuring
that it became a one-way process which resulted in a vast reduction
in lay holdings to the advantage, above all, of the monasteries.

In addition to the landed endowments and ecclesiastical revenues
which they were accumulating, many abbeys had a privileged legal
status, which they derived from grants of three kinds. From kings
and princes they had received charters of immunity, excluding royal
officers wholly or partly from their estates and freeing them from
services which were normally due from their tenures. In England,
for example, several abbeys had a specially privileged zone or
banleuca which often extended for a mile or more around the house.
An abbey might also have received one of the grants of papal
protection or 'liberty' which were being issued from the late ninth
century. They were designed mainly to protect the estates by
spiritual sanctions to supplement the royal power which was
becoming steadily less effective as a defence. A third type of privilege
prevented the bishop from exercising his usual rights over the house,
for example by forbidding the holding of diocesan synods there or
allowing the abbot to invite any bishop he chose to consecrate altars
or ordain members of the house. It came to be known as 'exemption'
in the twelfth century, when the legal position was defined with
much more precision.[10] With the progressive increase in papal
activity the number of grants of protection and exemption increased
considerably, but for most monasteries the main source of privilege
was still their ancient charters, extended by forgery and custom. The
bishops of the century before 1050 had been in no position to
supervise their dioceses effectively, and abbeys tended to exercise
autonomous control both over their own affairs within the house and
over the churches which they owned. The revival of the bishops'

---

[9] H. Dormeier, *Montecassino und die Laien*, 58–62.

[10] The term first occurs in a diploma of Nicholas II to St Martin, Autun in 1059: 'et ab omni
alia jurisdictione et subiectione liberum sit et exemptum' (PL 143. 1327C).

authority provoked a series of disputes, like that between Arch-bishop Hildebrand of Capua and Monte Cassino from 1065 onwards, in which even the greatest abbeys had to defend their traditional position in face of the attempt to subject them to the powers of the diocese under canon law.

One further feature in the monastic scene has to be noted here. Almost all monasteries reverenced the Rule of St Benedict, but their routine was governed by customs which differed from one abbey to another. The Rule was a revered authority rather than a piece of legislation which had to be followed in every detail. The daily order of most abbeys went back to the reforms of Benedict of Aniane in the early ninth century, and this meant that all spent longer in singing services than St Benedict had envisaged, for new offices had been added together with hymns and sequences, and provisions had been made for the saying of private masses by the increasing number of monks in priests' orders. The monastery had become above all a liturgical body dedicated to the performance of God's work, the *Opus Dei*. The Carolingian pattern was most directly continued in eleventh-century Germany. There monastic renewal was very closely connected with the royal family, for the emperor was the protector of major abbeys. A series of houses (first St Maximin at Trier, later St Emmeram at Regensburg) had acted as centres of inspiration, sending out their monks and customs to reform or found new monasteries, which however remained autonomous under imperial patronage.

Outside Germany the eleventh century saw the emergence of what can best be called monastic empires, in which one abbey governed a whole series of smaller houses. The reasons for the creation of structures of this type were various. One was the subjection of several monasteries to an outstanding monastic leader, such as William of Volpiano, for the purpose of reform. During the leader's lifetime at least the group of houses tended to remain under his supervision. In other cases an abbey which, like St Victor, Marseille, had been specially fertile in founding others would continue to exercise responsibility, to safeguard its distinctive customs in the daughter-houses., Another reason was the granting of estates at a great distance from the original abbey, which could only be administered by installing nearby a small cell or priory with two or three monks in residence. It was a form of monastic colonialism, increasingly characteristic of French monasticism, and very specially of the Normans in England. In the first generation, they founded few new abbeys (the Conqueror's thanksgiving monastery of Battle is an important exception) but gave generously to their monasteries at home. The exploitation of south Wales was even cruder, for there was not a single new abbey created there until 1130, whereas there were nineteen dependent priories, of which only a few ever became independent.[11] From these causes there arose groups of houses run, with varying degrees of efficiency and centralization, from a mother-abbey; and the greatest of these was Cluny.

ii. *The Golden Age of Cluny*

In Germany and in England there was an effective royal authority to which the monasteries could look for protection. In France, where there was not, monasticism began to develop in a different direction. Cluny, which was to become the most influential of all French houses, looked not to the power of the king but to an understanding with the aristocracy and papal protection. At its foundation in 909 Cluny was given immunity from all secular jurisdiction and was made the property of the Roman Church, being dedicated appropriately to St Peter and St Paul. The popes not only involved themselves directly in the preservation of Cluny's rights, but in 1024 granted it, with its dependencies, extensive independence from the diocesan bishop. Cluny came to symbolize the liberty or exemption of the church in a way unknown in Germany. In spite of fundamental similarities in the way of life of Cluniac and German monasticism derived from their Carolingian inheritance, there were important distinctions in their organization and attitudes.

The privileges which had been conceded to Cluny were the more significant in that the abbey became the centre of a system of subordinate monasteries. The foundations of this had been laid before the middle of the eleventh century, but the great expansion was the work of Abbot Hugh of Sémur (1049–1109). The mother-house itself grew progressively larger. It probably had 100 monks at Hugh's accession, 200 in 1080, and 300 by the time of his death. The massive extension of both the church and the monastic buildings was produced by this influx of numbers, and Abbot Hugh, who was not at first enthusiastic about new building, was eventually convinced of its necessity. The enormous abbey church, 531 feet in length, was

[11] F. G. Cowley, *The Monastic Order in South Wales* (Cardiff, 1977), 9 ff.

begun in 1088, and by 1095 the east end was sufficiently complete to be consecrated by Pope Urban II, although the whole building was not finished until well into the following century. The growth of the mother-house was parallelled by the expansion of its influence. In 1052 or shortly afterwards, for example, estates were given for the endowment of a priory on the river Loire near Nevers, which became known as La Charité-sur-Loire because of the abundant provision made there for the poor. Hugh's brother, Geoffrey of Sémur, founded the first nunnery in the order at Marcigny in 1056, with their sister Ermengarde as prioress. This, too, was a large house planned for ninety-nine nuns, the Virgin Mary being the hundredth and the titular abbess. In other instances, existing monasteries, including some ancient and famous ones like St Pierre, Moissac, were taken over, the customs of Cluny introduced and the authority of its abbot enforced. These transactions were sometimes bitterly opposed by the monks involved, and it is far from clear (although it was often said) that in every case a decayed house was being reformed. St Martial Limoges was subordinated to Cluny in 1062 only as a result of relentless pressure by vicomte Adhemar II, who seems to have had a financial interest in the deal.[12] Southern France was the centre of the Cluniac empire, but houses were also founded in Spain, where the personal devotion of Alfonso VI of Castile and Leon led him to grant a handsome annual tribute. Abbot Hugh was opposed to the creation of dependent priories far distant from the mother-house, but so vigorous was the impetus behind the expansion that it could not be stopped. St Pancras, Lewes, and other priories were founded in England, and foundations made in Lombardy.

This spectacular success was due in part to a series of talented abbots, and especially to the combination of authority and moderation characteristic of Hugh, whom Gregory VII described as a gentle tyrant, *blandus tyrannus.* Cluny also expressed in its life much of the spirituality of the age. It was above all a cultic centre and a power-house of prayer. It has often been supposed that at Cluny the contemporary fashion for magnificent and lengthy services reached its extreme. It was not necessarily radical in welcoming liturgical innovation, but sheer size meant that it became the symbol of rich and elaborate ceremonial. Cluny's special ministry, however, and

[12] N. Hunt, *Cluny under S. Hugh* (London, 1967), 137 and 153–4; H. E. J. Cowdrey, *The Cluniacs and the Gregorian Reform* (Oxford, 1970), 90–4.

the one which made it so influential, was its function as a refuge for penitents. Cluny developed to its widest extent the system of associating noble families in the brotherhood of the monks. The word 'association' is a crucial one in understanding this relationship. Certainly these aristocratic patrons were anxious to benefit from the intercessions of the monks, but they did not see themselves as 'buying' prayers and masses as actions of value in themselves. It was rather that they became spiritually members of the community, enjoying an inclusion which might be expressed in burial within the monastery precinct. In a period when Christian burial had become accessible, indeed obligatory, to everyone, and when the poor were required to be buried in the cemetery of their local churches, the aristocracy sought association with the far more splendid liturgy of the great abbeys. The Cluniac extension of prayers for the departed, including the widespread adoption of All Souls' Day within the order, must be understood in the sense of prayer for the community and its lay associates; the observance of All Souls' was rare outside the order until the end of the twelfth century. Cluny was also particularly ready to admit members of the aristocracy as monks. Many of the recruits which were increasing its numbers were, it is true, secular clergy or monks from other houses, since Cluny had the remarkable privilege of receiving any monk it chose to admit; but others were laymen. These 'converts' or *conversi* must often have been without the Latin necessary to participate in the offices, but they were regarded as full monks. The house was divided into the choir, the boys, and the *conversi*. The latter were given minor tasks in the liturgy, and sometimes (but by no means invariably) were trained as choir-monks. Hugh treated the susceptibilities of lay nobles kindly. Those who had committed grave offences in the world were readily admitted, including the murderer of Hugh's own brother. In these ways Cluny exercised a genuine ministry of forgiveness toward the nobility, and it was associated with some important initiatives among them. Older historical views went too far in discovering the influence of Cluny almost everywhere, but it probably assisted in some degree in the growth of the Peace of God movement, the recruitment of French knights to fight the Moors in Spain, and even in the preparation of the First Crusade.

In its relations with its dependent monasteries Cluny introduced some remarkable innovations. Notionally the whole fellowship constituted one single abbey, with Hugh himself as the sole abbot.

Each monk was supposed to journey to the mother-house to make his profession, and the subordinate houses had priors, not abbots, at their head, with the exception of a few great monasteries which had been brought under Cluny. This divergence from Benedictine principles was the deliberate policy of Hugh, who sought to downgrade abbeys into priories, and was denounced on one occasion as an 'arch-abbot'.[13] It may reasonably be described as the first monastic order, as long as we remember that to contemporaries the word 'order' still meant the way of life followed by a monastery. It would, however, be a great mistake to see Cluny as a centralized and inflexible body. It was at once its strength and weakness that it possessed no machinery for co-ordinating policy and discipline. There was, for that matter, no clear distinction between Cluniac priories proper and houses which had adopted its customs, whose representatives attended the great council summoned by Peter the Venerable to discuss the customs of Cluny in 1132. A lot of freedom, too, was allowed to individual monks. Around Cluny itself there were hermitages where monks could go on retreat, and Anastasius, who was brought to the abbey by Hugh himself in 1067, lived in a markedly individual style in the community. Cluny had a broad bottom. There was plenty of room for people of divergent temperaments.

During the abbacy of Hugh, Cluny's prestige was enormous. He was one of the small group of people addressed by Gregory VII in terms of close friendship, and Gregory at the synod of Rome in Lent 1080 delivered a remarkable tribute to the abbey, 'which belongs to St Peter and to this church by special right as its own particular property'.[14] Cluny's esteem was also great in the imperial family, and Hugh was invited by Henry III to act as the godfather of his son, the future Henry IV. Cluniac customs were, however, only slowly adopted within imperial territories, as princes and bishops began to found monasteries without tight imperial control. Bishop Adalbero of Würzburg in 1046 encouraged monks from Gorze to settle at Schwarzach am Main, whence a large group of abbeys was founded in the south-east and Saxony. In the 1070s Archbishop Anno of Cologne, influenced by the ideals of Fruttuaria in northern Italy, summoned monks from there to Siegburg near Cologne.

---

[13] *Vita Bernardi Tironensis*, vii. 58 (PL 172. 1401D). Thus at Sauxillange 'reducta est abbatia in prioratum per S. Hugonem magnum': cited J. Evans, *Monastic Life at Cluny* (London, 1931), 26.

[14] Printed H. E. J. Cowdrey, *The Cluniacs and the Gregorian Reform* (Oxford, 1970), 271–3.

Fruttuaria had early historical connections with Cluny, and contained little of the traditional German respect for imperial authority. Soon afterwards, Abbot William of Hirsau deliberately adopted the customs of Cluny. He had visited Rome in 1076, and come back as a fervent partisan of Gregory VII and an admirer of Cluny, which he saw as the model of monastic perfection, 'so that if any traces of sanctity may still be seen in other monasteries, there is no doubt that the particular streams flowed from thence, as from a living and unfailing spring'.[15] The customs of Cluny were recorded by Ulric of Zell for use in southern Germany, and Hirsau's influence rapidly carried them to other houses. This group of disciples of Cluny was passionately hostile to imperial policy in the dispute with Gregory VII, and fiercely critical of traditional German monasteries, with whom they engaged in bitter controversy. Paradoxically, these enthusiasts never became constitutionally part of the Cluniac family: they retained a link with lay patrons (much valued by the south German nobles who were their protectors) and owed no formal obedience to Cluny while they were following its customs. They were, in fact, a polemical group distinct from the more mellow outlook of the French Cluniacs, but representing the passionate admiration felt for Cluny within the papal reforming party. That, however, is another matter, to which we must return later.

iii. *Hermits*

There had always been a place for hermits in Benedictine tradition. The Rule itself had listed among the various types of monks the hermits who 'go out well armed from the battle-line of their brothers to the solitary combat of the desert', and it was a common practice for monasteries to make provision for their members to retire to the wilderness.[16] Hermitages were built close to abbeys, and some have left remains which can be seen today, like the chapel of St Saturnin on the hill above the abbey of St Wandrille in Normandy, or the hermitage at Scex, perched on a cliff high above St Maurice at Agaune in Switzerland. Monks might go on retreat into the isolation of the forests surrounding the abbey, as at Cluny, and for some monks residence in a cell distant from the mother-house was an opportunity to live a life of isolation and contemplation. Retirement

---

[15] Constitutions of Hirsau, prol. (PL 150.929AB).
[16] A. de Vogüé and J. Neufville, *Le règle de S. Benoît* (SC 181 (1972) c.1, i.436–8).

into a hermitage was an option chosen by former abbots or officers, like Hugh of Selby in 1122 and Gerald le Vert, who is described by Peter the Venerable of Cluny as residing on a remote mountain until his death in 1133.[17]

One of the most striking features of the religious life of the eleventh century was the growth of enthusiasm for the eremitical life. In estimating the dimensions of this movement, we are faced with a problem of sources. Hermits do not require records, as a monastery does, and often we only know about a hermit because he came to be venerated locally as a saint and therefore was recorded in a *Life*. To piece together these lives is to form a picture of holy men whose witness formed the basis of local cults in many parts of Europe. Such hermits can be traced in almost every region of Italy throughout the eleventh and twelfth centuries until they came to be associated with the Franciscans or (after the end of our period) linked in loosely organized societies. The majority of those who were called hermits at this time, however, were not solitaries. The emphasis in their writings is not so much upon privacy as upon a retreat to the wilderness, sometimes with one or two companions, sometimes with a group of disciples; and such retreats seem often to have alternated with preaching campaigns or an active ministry in the world. They were men who could not find a calling within the traditional pattern of received monasticism, and who withdrew to found new communities outside it. It has been said that 'much confusion could have been avoided if these new hermits . . . had presumed to call themselves "holy men" '.[18] They remembered that the word 'hermit' properly means a wilderness-dweller, and were essentially men seeking an alternative way of life, which was severe but not necessarily solitary. They also present us with a paradox, because in many cases groups which began by rejecting monastic discipline ended by being incorporated into a monastic order, sometimes a highly organized one. There is often a large gap between the first foundation of a hermitage and the recording of customs and, in the case of successful houses, the creation of a family of monasteries, so that it is often far from clear whether the fully developed order accurately reflects the intentions of the founding fathers. There is no simple chronology to this process, for we can see

---

[17] For references and other examples see G. Constable, 'Eremitical Forms of Monastic Life', MCSM 9 (1977), 256–7.

[18] H. Leyser, *Hermits and the new Monasticism* (London, 1984), 1.

the hermit urge at work throughout our whole period, but the time of rule-writing is to be found primarily in the twelfth century. It belongs to a general tendency to codify, which is also apparent in canon law and theology and which brought to an end the great age of hermit experiments.

Enthusiasm for the eremitical life became apparent in Italy at the turn of the tenth and eleventh centuries when Nilus, who had been trained in Calabria in the Greek tradition of austerity and eremitism, founded a house at Grottaferrata near Rome. Soon afterwards, Romuald, a monk from the abbey of St Apollinare at Ravenna, left the house, and after travelling widely settled at Camaldoli just after 1010. He was followed by Peter Damian, the most outstanding hermit-leader of the century, who disseminated the way of life originally created by Romuald.[19] Another movement in the Appenines, of a different kind, was initiated by John Gualbert, a monk of San Miniato, Florence, who about 1036 settled at Vallombrosa. Gualbert was a champion of the cenobitic way of life, and the nine monasteries which were following his teaching by the time of his death in 1073 were organized on Benedictine lines. But they diverged from traditional monasticism in stressing the need to observe the Rule in conditions of poverty and severity, and even more distinctively in the intensity of their campaign against simony. The emergence of similar hermits in France was not long delayed. They can be found in the first companions of the knight Herluin at Bec in Normandy in the 1030s and in Robert of Turlande, a canon who settled in 1043 in a remote part of the Auvergne and founded what was to become the great abbey of La Chaise-Dieu (*Casa Dei*). The last twenty years of the century saw enormous eremitical activity. In the Limousin, Stephen settled at Muret about 1076, having lived with hermits in Calabria, and established the beginnings of the later order of Grandmont. In 1080 Gerard of Corbie founded the community of Sauve-Majeur in the diocese of Bordeaux. There was also an important group of hermits in Burgundy in the forest of Colan. Outstanding among them was Robert, who had left the abbey of Tonnerre where he was abbot, became a hermit, founded Molesme in 1075, abandoned it in 1098 to found Cîteaux ('with his usual levity', a papal legate impatiently observed), and finally returned to Molesme. One of his companions for a time was Bruno

---

[19] For the argument that Peter was codifying rather than creating a way of life, see Leyser, *Hermits*, 29.

of Cologne, a master of the school of Reims, then founder of La Grande Chartreuse in 1084, adviser to Urban II, and finally founder of the austere house of Squillace in Calabria. In north-western France an active movement was also beginning, with Robert of Arbrissel, son of a priest and himself a Paris scholar, settling in the 'desert' of Craon, preaching, founding a house of canons, and finally in 1101 establishing the house of Fontevraud. A preaching ministry seems to have been a particular feature of this region, where Bernard of Tiron and Vitalis of Savigny were also prominent. Hermit activity is a little more difficult to find in the eleventh century outside Italy and France, but we must note that the re-establishment of monasticism in northern England (Durham, Jarrow, St Mary's York, for example) was initiated by monks from Evesham and other southern abbeys who were inspired by eremitical ideals; and that the Hirsau movement in southern Germany, although from the beginning it accepted the customs of Cluny, had a strong share of the hermit spirit.

These varied examples of a widespread dissatisfaction with traditional monasticism constituted what historians have come to call 'the monastic crisis'. The term is a misleading one, at least if it is understood as describing a failure of traditional monasticism: the total picture is, on the contrary, one of the extension of the religious life both within and outside its accustomed forms. Many enthusiasts were abandoning the old structured life. Some were influenced by the eremitic element which, as we have seen, still existed within Benedictine communities, and by older pre-Benedictine practices which were to be found in some areas. Celtic hermits were still to be found in the far west: we know, for example, of Caradog, a hermit who lived in a number of places in south Wales until his death in 1124. The Greek hermit-tradition in Calabria had been strengthened by the migration of monks from Moslem-controlled Sicily. We can trace connections between the new hermits and these areas; some of them lived with Celtic hermits for a time, Stephen of Muret apparently obtained his training in southern Italy and Bruno settled in Calabria. But neither the links nor the similarities are very strong, and we have to seek another source for the new spirit. One major feature was the desire for participation in the religious life by groups who felt excluded from the old monasteries. The classic figure in Benedictine monasticism was the monk who had been brought up since boyhood within the house and trained in its traditions. The leaders of the new movements came on the whole from elsewhere. Some were monks, but had entered as converts (Romuald, John Gualbert), and quite rapidly had found their way of life unsatisfying. Some were from the city schools (Peter Damian, Bruno of Cologne, Robert of Arbrissel). Yet others were canons (Robert of Turlande and Bruno of Cologne). Laymen were prominent: Bec was founded by the converted knight Herluin, Afflighem in Flanders in 1083 by knights who gave up their life of brigandage and settled around a wandering preacher, and many of the small hermit groups, like that at Muret, included laymen who were treated on equal terms with the clergy. A feature of some of the leaders was their concern to make provision for women: Robert of Arbrissel in particular included them among his followers, to the alarm of some of those who were otherwise in sympathy with him. The older monasteries had not wholly failed to make provision for the interests of these groups— canons could certainly be admitted as monks, and Cluny had its active ministry to laymen. But the provision for laymen, and still more for women, was in general insufficient, and scholars or canons would not necessarily wish to accept traditions of worship which were foreign to them, and in which they had not been trained. The new hermits represented the ambitions of groups which were being brought into prominence by the social changes discussed in the last chapter; such 'new men' were the knights and the growing urban aristocracy, and a more learned secular clergy, educated by their work in the schools to criticize accepted practice and to look to earlier and different models of organization.

These forces acted as a solvent upon the accepted monastic values of stability and association in the liturgy of a traditional community. In the new movements total withdrawal from the world was uneasily linked with concern about growing social problems. The most obvious of these was simony. Almost all the hermit leaders felt passionately about it, and in particular refusal to tolerate simony within the abbey of San Miniato had been the starting-point of John Gualbert's withdrawal thence and his foundation of Vallombrosa. There were other questions, too. One was the concern to open the Gospel to the whole world, which we can see in Romuald and Robert of Arbrissel, and later in Francis of Assisi. The reason why this basic element of Christianity became so prominent at this time was perhaps that as large numbers of people broke away from their traditional structures, assembled in cities, moved on the pilgrim roads and made settlements in the forests, their needs became more obvious, and the inadequacy of the old order in meeting them became more apparent. This would explain the urgency of Romuald's desire 'to turn the whole world into a wilderness, and to associate the whole multitude of people to the monastic order'.[20] It is significant that there is a marked shift in the attitude to poverty at this time. Traditionally, monasteries had been aware of their duty to provide for the poor, but it was pre-eminently the rich who were blessed, for they had the means of earning God's pleasure; we hear, for example, of a pilgrim at Bourges who thought that God and the saint would not be willing to heal a poor man.[21] The eleventh century saw the beginning of a reversal of these values. The new movements insisted not simply on largesse, but on identification with the poor. Their settlements in the wilderness had at first only the bare necessities of life, and some of them were marked by a deliberate and conscious poverty. Stephen of Muret had a deep love for the poor, and Norbert of Xanten is said to have desired 'naked to follow the naked cross'.[22] The new attitude was summed up in the story of St Alexis, which told of a young Roman nobleman who had given up all his possessions and who spent long years in disguise in his parents' house living as a servant. This legend spread rapidly in the eleventh and twelfth centuries and expressed the ideal of poverty as an individual way of life embodying the values of the Gospel. The general concern for those in need also expressed itself in ministry to particular groups of people. Robert of Arbrissel, Peter the Hermit, and others were anxious to provide an escape for women of the cities from a life of prostitution; and Stephen of Muret, although in one sense he represented the ideal of withdrawal in an extreme form, was willing to instruct knights how to go on campaign without sin.

As they followed no traditional set of customs, the new societies were guided by their leader, who generally had the title 'master'; at Obazine, where the priest Stephen settled with followers in the course of the 1120s, 'since no law of any order had been accepted, the institutes of the master were taken as law; these demanded nothing other than humility, obedience, poverty and discipline and, on top of these, continual charity'. [23] The master's own teaching was based on the following of Christ after the example of the apostles. This did not

---

[20] Peter Damian, *Vita Romualdi*, 37 (PL 144.988AB).

[21] *Miracula S. Austregisili*, iii.4 (*AASS* May V. 237★C).

[22] 'nudam crucem nudus utique sequi deberet', *Vita* iv. 22(PL 170.1272AB). For Stephen of Muret, see C. Pellisstrandi, 'La pauvreté dans la règle de Grandmont': M. Mollat (ed.), *Études sur l'histoire de la pauvreté* (Paris, 1974), i.229–45.

[23] *Vita Stephani Obazinensis*, i.16 ed. M. Aubrun (Clermont-Ferrand, 1970), 70.

exclude the use of the Rule of Benedict, or the lives of the desert Fathers, as guides, because they were thought to embody this example. But some deliberately went behind these later texts to the simple word of Scripture; Stephen of Muret exclaimed, in a spirit worthy of Francis of Assisi later, 'there is no other Rule than the Gospel of Christ!'[24] For most of these reformers, the thing which captured their imagination was the common life of poverty which the apostles had lived at Jerusalem, as the *Acts of the Apostles* described it. For monks this way of life was embodied in their customary order, but increasingly there were people who saw a contrast between the complexity of monastic observance and the simplicity of the first fellowship, which they sought to revive in their own age. The life of perfection no longer had to be learned in long years in the monastery school, but was open to all men.

iv. *Canons*

It is both inconvenient and necessary to distinguish canons from hermits. It is inconvenient because there was a large overlap between the two movements. Some leading hermits were originally canons, and hermit foundations sometimes adopted customs designed for canons. The diversity of forms of religious life was puzzling to contemporaries, so that Stephen of Muret was later said to have been asked by two visiting cardinals whether he had been instructed by a monk, a canon, or a hermit.[25] In principle, however, canons were distinct from hermits, just as they were from monks. Under Carolingian legislation they were subject to the Rule of Aix of 816, which was very different from that of Benedict. Communities of canons were intended to officiate in public, and in contrast to the older monastic tradition their members were normally expected to be priests. They were required to live the common life in refectory and dormitory, but were permitted to retain private property. In the disorders of the tenth century, many houses of canons lost their distinctive discipline, and became colleges of married clergy who lived in their own houses and had no common dormitory or refectory.

The apostolic life movement had, even before the middle of the

---

[24] *Liber de Doctrina* prol.: J. Becquet (ed.), *Scriptores Ordinis Grandimontensis*, CC(CM) 8 (1978) 5.
[25] *Vita Stephani ampliata*, 32, Becquet 121.

eleventh century, made its impact upon communities of canons. The most obvious objective was the restoration of the common life according to the Rule of Aix, but some reformers had already gone beyond this to the ownership of common property. The chapters in German cathedrals were being reshaped in accordance with the new principles under the encouragement of such emperors as Henry II: Bamberg and other houses were used for the training of future bishops in the imperial churches. In some places complete common ownership seems to have been adopted, as at Hildesheim, where it was said that the chapter 'in their profession as canons observed the strictness of monks'. In Italy the old baptismal churches or *pievi* had often been run by teams of clergy, and the popularity of a full common life was growing among reformers at cathedrals, *pievi* and hermitages. When Romuald *c.*1005 'taught canons and clergy who lived in the world like laymen to be obedient to a provost and live the common life in a congregation' he may have been prescribing customs more demanding than those of Aix.[26] Through imperial influence the reform of canons spread into the province of Ravenna under Archbishop Gebhard (1027–44); there the theory of the movement was stated by Bishop John of Cesena in 1042 in a diploma for his cathedral chapter. In Tuscany bishops and lay nobles were active supporters of the movement, notably at Florence and Lucca (from which Popes Nicholas II and Alexander II were to come to Rome). Elsewhere in 1039 four canons of Avignon were authorized by the bishop to retire to the church of St Ruf 'to live the religious life there', and founded a house which was to become the centre of a great collection of communities of canons. The issue received precise definition at the Lateran Council of 1059, when Hildebrand spoke in praise of some clergy who had renounced their goods 'by the example of the primitive church', and launched an attack upon the Rule of Aix for its laxity. It was specifically the permission to enjoy private property which was Hildebrand's target. The Council of 1059 made it obligatory for clergy to live at the churches which they served and share a dormitory and refectory, and exhorted them to practise 'the apostolic, that is the common life'.[27] The same policy was strenuously advocated by Peter Damian in his pamphlet *Contra Clericos Regulares Proprietarios*.

The idea that canons, like monks, should take the apostolic church

[26] Peter Damian, *Vita Romualdi*, 35 (PL 144.986–7).
[27] Canon 4, MGH Leges Const.I, no. 384, p. 547.

of Jerusalem as their model was not entirely new, for Augustine himself had proposed this in sermons which were quoted in the Rule of Aix. It was strengthened by the use of two decretals from pseudo-Isidore, ascribed to Clement and Urban I. Clement was said to have written that 'the common life is necessary to all . . . and especially to those who desire to serve God blamelessly and wish to imitate the life of the apostles and their disciples'. These decretals were incorporated by Anselm of Lucca in his collection in the 1080s.[28] One necessity for the reformers was to find a Rule to express these more stringent ideals, and by the end of the century canons had been provided with one. The first reference to a community living according to the Rule of St Augustine seems to be at St Denis, Reims, in 1067. At first this was perhaps only an allusion to the statements by Augustine contained in the Rule of Aix, but by 1100 there were many foundations which had accepted as their rule a collection of writings known as the Third Rule or *Regula Tertia*. It was believed, perhaps correctly, to be authentically the work of Augustine. Before the end of the century, the canons had been provided, not only with a Rule, but also with a history of their descent from the apostles, parallel to that claimed by monks. The classic definition was formulated by Urban II in a bull to the house of canons at Rottenbuch in southern Germany in 1092:

From the beginning of the holy church two ways of life were instituted for its sons: one to strengthen the debility of the weak, the other to perfect the blessed life of the strong . . . Those who hold to the lower make use of earthly goods; those who hold to the higher despise and abandon earthly goods. The path which by God's favour is turned from earthly things is divided into two sections with almost the same purpose, that is canons and monks. The latter of these, by the mercy of God, now shines forth in great numbers in almost the whole world, but the first has almost become extinct because of the indifference of the people.[29]

Urban thus subdivided the clergy into classes which soon became generally recognized: secular clergy (including canons living under the Rule of Aix) who retain private property, and regulars who imitate the life of the apostles, and who are in turn divided into monks and canons. The statement in the Rottenbuch bull was

[28] Gratian, *Decr.* C. XII, q. 1, c. 2 (676). On these decretals see G. Le Bras, 'Note sur la vie commune des clercs dans les collections canoniques', MCSM 3 (1962) 16–19.

[29] PL 151.338CD. There is a similar statement of theory in the customary of Lethbert at St Ruf, Avignon, about 1100 (PL 157.718–9).

incorporated into privileges to several other major houses of canons and became a crucial element in determing their self-awareness. The term 'regular' canons was increasingly adopted for those living according to the Augustinian Rule in order to distinguish them from the 'secular' canons who observed the Rule of Aix or lived individually, without a common dormitory and refectory.

All over Europe there were vast numbers of churches served by canons, ranging from cathedrals and rich collegiate foundations to baptismal churches and castle chapels. The obvious priority was to 'regularize' these communities, and in southern Europe this took place on a very considerable scale. When the canons of a cathedral were unwilling to change their way of life, bishops sometimes encouraged seceders to form a separate community nearby. St Ruf at Avignon may be an early example of this process, as may St Denis, Reims; St Quentin, Beauvais, whose provost Ivo became bishop of Chartres from 1093 to 1111 and an important propagator of the regular canons; and St Victor at Paris, founded by William of Champeaux in 1108. In northern Europe, little progress had in fact been made by the end of the eleventh century in replacing secular canons by regulars, but the canonical life had shown itself very attractive to hermit communities. At Arrouaise, for example, a lay hermit Roger was joined by two clerks about 1090. One of these two, Cono, became head of the community, which was given the statutes of regular canons by Bishop Lambert of Arras, who had links with St Quentin, Beauvais, and Bishop Ivo. Some hermit groups applied to existing houses of canons to secure a Rule and customs, as did Walcher of Aureil in the Limousin and the community of Chamouzey in Lorraine; both houses obtained their customs from St Ruf, Avignon. It must appear paradoxical that men who had opted for withdrawal from the world decided to shape their communal life according to norms designed for clergy with pastoral responsibilities, but on reflection the attraction was a natural one. To accept a set of monastic customs was scarcely an option for many hermits, who had gone into the wilderness either because traditional monastic life was not available to them or because they found it too relaxed. The Rule of St Augustine, moreover, contained much less detail than that of Benedict, and left room for the community's own practices. It also allowed a ministry of preaching or charity to the poor, which many hermits combined with their withdrawal into contemplation. Thus when just after 1086 a priest named Geoffrey, who was teaching at Limoges, was considering retirement from the world, Abbot Hugh of Cluny recommended him to become a monk; but Geoffrey did not wish to accept 'the burden of monastic rule', and he first became a hermit at le Chalard near Limoges, and soon afterwards a regular canon. Already in the eleventh century the status of regular canon, and the Rule of St Augustine which was its mark, could be found throughout the whole gamut of religious life, from cathedral chapters to small, charitable communities in remote regions, and it was to become a significant element in the policy of the papal reformers and to make an important contribution to the building up of Christian society in the following century.

4

THE PAPAL REFORM 1046–1073

i. *Introduction*

In the middle of the eleventh century, there were many signs of dissatisfaction with the prevailing conditions within the church. The concern of Cluny for monastic dignity and purity, the beginnings of the eremitical revival and the desire to restore the apostolic life, the sympathy for reform in imperial circles, the circulation of the *Decretum* of Burchard of Worms and the 'restitution' of local churches from lay to monastic control were all pointing towards a change. At Rome itself there was in the household of John Gratian a group with contacts among reforming enthusiasts in the church outside. It was evident that there was going to be an attack on the evils of *Eigenkirchentum* and there were hopes that the Roman Church would be a participant in it. What could not have been foreseen was the scale of the offensive, its suddenness, the coherent ideology which was developed to support it, and the decisive impact which it was to have on the whole history of the western church. In the course of twenty-five years, the popes began to intervene vigorously in the affairs of other churches and became the leaders of an international reform movement. After many decades in which the Roman Church had been controlled by the local noble families, influential positions came to be held by men from outside Rome, and of the line of reforming popes only Gregory VII himself was Roman by birth or education. Monks came to play a role in the direction of papal policy for which no previous example can be found: significantly, the great apse mosaic at San Clemente, composed as a manifesto for the reforming papacy and completed perhaps about 1120, showed the Fathers of the church dressed in monastic habit. Most startling of all, the dominant thinking in the Roman Church took on a strongly anti-imperial tinge, in defiance of the traditional idea that *regnum* and *sacerdotium* should co-operate in the service of God. And the change was rapid. The appointment of the first German pope led almost at once to the promulgation of reform, and only a generation divided Henry III's intervention in 1046 from Henry IV's excommunication in 1076.

In an attempt to explain the rapid development of this remarkable course of events historians have sometimes looked for a single, or at least a principal, moving force. It has been suggested, for example, that the Cluniac reform was the source from which the reformers' thinking flowed. Augustin Fliche, while he painted the background on a broad canvas, stressed the importance of Lotharingia (Lorraine), the province which was now part of the empire, but which had originally been within the middle kingdom between France and Germany. There Fliche discerned a tradition of radical thinking about the state which entered the Roman Church under Leo IX. Other writers have pointed to the arrival at Rome of the pseudo-Isidorian decretals, with their emphasis on the autonomy of churches from royal power. There is no doubt that Cluny, reformers from Lotharingia, and pseudo-Isidore all had a part to play in the papal reform, but none of them can be regarded as the primary explanation of the course of events. The ideas of Cluny needed much adaptation before they could be applied to the government of the clergy as a whole, and while it is true that the influence of Cluny and Monte Cassino was great at Rome, it must not be forgotten that their fullest development did not precede the papal reform, but was most evident under Abbots Hugh and Desiderius, two contemporaries of Gregory VII. Lotharingia produced its quota of radical thinkers, but it is hard to say that they were specially characteristic of the province, whose finest scholar, the long-lived Sigebert of Gembloux, remained a stalwart imperialist until his death in 1112. The pseudo-Isidorian decretals certainly provided a good deal of the material needed to formulate the new ideology, and in that sense their importance can scarcely be exaggerated; but they were a resource (especially in the convenient form provided by Burchard of Worms) rather than a single precipitant of change.

In looking for an explanation of what was to happen, we need to keep in mind some much more general considerations. One is the coexistence of several currents of reform in the middle years of the eleventh century. Although no truly international programme had emerged to unite these scattered endeavours, there was a real coherence between them. The attack on simony, and less obviously on clerical marriage and on the lay invasion of ecclesiastical rights, rested on a determination to restore the clergy to the apostolic life which was described in *The Acts of the Apostles* and in canon law. It was not yet a programme, but it was capable of becoming one. It was sharpened, and disseminated throughout Europe, by the expansion of monasticism and the insistence on sanctity and poverty which accompanied it. The sudden leap forward within the generation after 1046 was the consequence of the take-over at Rome by a group of enthusiastic reformers; and that in turn was made possible by the existence of special political circumstances in Italy which allowed leaders from outside to be imposed by imperial authority, and then to sustain themselves in control against the power which had originally placed them there. Also significant was the broad pattern of social change which we considered in Chapter 2. The growth of learning made possible an exchange of ideas and formulation of programmes which would not have been conceivable a century before: the papal reform was to generate the first great pamphlet war since the fall of Rome. Equally important was 'the appearance of the crowd on the stage of public events'.[1] Connections between the Roman Church and radical groups in the cities, especially at Milan, were of crucial importance, and one of the weapons of the new papacy was an appeal to laymen to go on strike against corrupt priests by refusing to attend their masses. But these broad considerations will not suffice as explanations without bearing in mind the remarkable ability of some of the leaders, and particularly of the ministry of all the talents assembled in the Roman Church by Leo IX. Without Lenin, the Russian revolution would have been very different; without Leo IX and Gregory VII, the papal reform would not have acquired its distinctive characteristics.

The movement which we have now to study is often known as the Gregorian Reform. The term was made famous by Augustin Fliche, whose major study, *La réforme grégorienne*, was named after the leader who, as Subdeacon and Cardinal Hildebrand and then as Pope Gregory VII, was almost continuously associated with the reform for forty years. Its very wide use has obscured the fact that 'ecclesiastical reform in the eleventh century was more complex and less papally oriented than the title, Gregorian Reform Movement, has suggested'.[2] It was, indeed, rather a series of movements

---

[1] R. I. Moore, 'Family, Community and Cult on the Eve of the Gregorian Reform', *TRHS* V. 30 (1980), 49.

[2] J. Gilchrist, 'The *Epistola Widonis*', *Authority and Power: Studies presented to Walter Ullmann* (Cambridge, 1980), 49–58. Fliche did not originally intend the all-purpose use which has been made of his concept.

operating at a number of different levels. There was, first, a series of overlapping initiatives, in various parts of Europe and different sections of the church, which had become apparent before 1050 and thereafter made steady progress. Not all of these were papally inspired: some great archbishops were opponents of simony and of clerical marriage, but resented the activities of papal legates in their provinces. Among these movements, and steadily assuming the direction of them, was the reforming party in control of the Roman Church. This group was itself split by the policy of Gregory VII. Whether or not his ideas were a logical consequence of earlier policies, their application created a new situation, with an open breach with the emperor and a schism in the papal office. The indiscriminate application of the term 'Gregorian Reform' tends to obscure the special character of Gregory's policy, which alienated some of the most ardent reformers, as well as over-simplifying the complicated interrelationship of the reforming movements as a whole. I shall therefore reserve 'Gregorian' for the actions of Gregory himself and his successors in the papal schism, using the terms 'papal reform' or 'reforming papacy' for the directing group at Rome from 1046 onwards.

One final word of warning has to be given to the reader. It is often difficult in the eleventh century to reconstruct a course of events precisely, but this difficulty becomes quite extreme with the history of the papal reform. The early chronicles are slight and poorly informed, and the fuller accounts which were written later, like those of Benzo of Alba and Bonizo of Sutri, are distorted by controversy. Record evidence is thin and complicated by forgery and interpolation. In spite of an enormous volume of scholarly work, there is still no agreement on such basic questions as the intentions of Henry III in 1046, the purpose of the papal election decree of 1059, or the timing of the prohibition of lay investiture in relation to the breach with the empire in 1076. Some attempt will be made to indicate where there are major disputes still current; more than that, within reasonable limits of space, cannot be promised.

ii. *The Beginnings of Papal Reform (1046–1057)*

The tenure of the papal office by members of the great Roman family of Tusculum was interrupted in the middle of the 1040s. It is reasonable to assume that expression of reforming ideals in the groups around John Gratian and the unpopularity of Benedict IX were among the causes of the crisis, but we have little solid knowledge of the situation beyond the bare facts. In autumn 1044 Benedict was expelled from Rome by its citizens and replaced by Bishop John of Sabina as Sylvester III. Although Benedict was quickly restored his position seems to have become untenable, and on 1 May 1045 he resigned his office in favour of John Gratian, who took the title of Gregory VI and was eagerly greeted by the Italian hermit leader Peter Damian as the bringer of a new age. Gregory was thereafter recognized as pope, since Sylvester was an intruder and Benedict had resigned, and the suggestion that an appeal was made for Henry III to come to Rome to disentangle a threefold schism, although it is an understandable one, is not correct.

It is more probable that Henry's journey to Rome in 1046 was coincidental, caused not by events in the city but by his intention to reassert his rights in Italy and secure the imperial crown at the hands of the pope, as all his predecessors had done since Otto I. He was a remarkable man, who took very seriously his divinely given duties. It was his custom to make his confession before wearing the royal insignia, and his scrupulous rectitude won him the name of *Linea Iusticie*, the measure of righteousness. He was conscientious in the appointment of bishops and, by reputation, entirely free from simony. Even among the zealous reformers of the next generation, he was revered as 'a religious king, very ecclesiastical and devout in matters of worship'.[3] He was a particularly scrupulous champion of the royal authority over the church which had been characteristic of the government of Germany since the time of Otto I. He also embodied some of its more domineering features: he dealt with his bishops in a masterful way, and was not unduly troubled about the niceties of canon law—in particular, his marriage with the Empress Agnes was well within the prohibited relationship and provoked protests in stricter circles. Henry can be seen, moreover, as having deliberately extended this Ottonian supremacy to the Roman Church itself. He nominated a series of German bishops as pope, and chose men who were model products of the imperial church system: Germans of noble birth, several of them nearly related to the emperor, products of the royal chapel and cathedral schools. Henry was no enthusiast of monk-bishops, appointing only one in his seventeen years of rule in Germany, and to this extent he was out of tune with one important reforming element which was eventually to

[3] Chronicle of St Bénigne, Dijon (MGH SS VII.237); Peter Damian, *Liber Gratissimus*, 38 (MGH LdL.i.71–2); and, most striking of all, Humbert, *Adversus Simoniacos*, iii.7 (LdL.i.206)

dominate the movement at Rome. The signs are that he intended to change the character of the Roman Church in a new and lasting way. He was recognized by the citizens of Rome as *patricius,* a title which was regarded as giving a decisive voice in the appointment of future popes; and his first appointment significantly called himself Clement II, a revival of the name of the early pope who was usually taken as the direct successor of Peter. It was a dramatic announcement of the restoration of the Roman Church to apostolic purity.

To interpret Henry III's reign as the highest expression of royal ecclesiastical supremacy is, however, to disregard the ambiguities in his government—ambiguities which were to become critical in later decades. At one and the same time, he accepted the ideas of apostolic renewal which were beginning to circulate in reforming circles, and he disregarded the provisions of canon law in his dealings with the bishops. The assumption of the title *patricius* was itself a product of such ambiguity, since it based his claim to nominate the pope, not on the divine authority of the anointed emperor, but on a secular title recently exercised by the Roman aristocracy. In all probability Henry, a practical ruler in an age not noted for theoretical refinement, was unaware that such principles existed in uneasy tension below the surface of his policy. If we had more information about his detailed intentions, and the procedures which he followed in his dealings with the Roman Church, we might discover a clearer line of policy, but the evidence leaves these matters uncertain.

Henry entered Italy in the autumn of 1046. He met Gregory VI at Piacenza, amicably as far as we know. At some point, however, it was reported that the retirement of Benedict IX had been secured by the payment of money, and that Gregory VI's position as pope was thus stained by simony. At the synod of Sutri on 20 December, Gregory VI was removed, and any remaining claims of Sylvester and Benedict set aside. Henry's motives in taking action against Gregory were probably the obvious ones: he was an opponent of simony, and would have had no wish to be crowned by a pope whose accession could be questioned. The procedure adopted at Sutri is very variously reported: Gregory may have been deposed by Henry or by the bishops in synod, or resigned of his own free will, or deemed not to have been properly elected because of the charge of simony.[4]

[4] There is little doubt about the truth of the accusation of simony. For a possible explanation, see Herrmann, *Das Tuskulanerpapsttum* (Stuttgart, 1973), 155–6. The view that Gregory was not deposed by the synod has been reasserted by F.-J. Schmale, 'Die "Absetzung" Gregors VI', *Annuarium Historiae Conciliorum,* 11 (1979) 55–103. The possibility that Henry had

Gregory went into exile in Germany, accompanied by his young clerk, Hildebrand. For a replacement Henry turned to the ranks of the German bishops and appointed Suidger of Bamberg. On Christmas Day 1046 the new pope was enthroned, with the name Clement II, and he in turn crowned Henry and his wife Agnes as emperor and empress.

The reform of the Roman Church was widely welcomed, but it did not go unchallenged. Burchard of Worms had already incorporated in his *Decretum* some texts which limited royal authority in spiritual matters, and in the reign of Henry III a number of critical voices were raised against the exercise of his royal priesthood. When the Benedictine Halinard was appointed to the archbishopric of Lyon in 1046 he refused to swear an oath of fealty, alleging both the New Testament command not to swear, and the command of the Rule that a monk should separate himself from secular affairs. A much more jealous defender of the division between the two powers was Bishop Wazo of Liège, whose remarks, admittedly, were only recorded some years later. When Henry took action against Widger, the archbishop-elect of Ravenna, in 1046, Wazo protested against the procedure and declared in resounding fashion that bishops owed obedience to the king in secular affairs, but in spiritual ones to the pope. It was a distinction which in essence would have been familiar to Carolingian churchmen, and suggests that their tradition of thought was not dead. Wazo is also said to have compared Henry's royal unction with the greater dignity of the anointing of bishops, and to have denied the validity of the deposition of Gregory VI. A still sharper attack was contained in the tract *De Ordinando Pontifice*, probably of French origin, in which the whole issue of imperial authority in the church was raised in radical terms: 'where do we read that emperors have obtained the place of Christ?'[5] The new age was in any event dawning slowly. German popes proved vulnerable to the Italian climate. Clement II died on 9 October 1047 and his

been told of the simony charge in Germany and had intervened for that reason cannot be excluded, but is less likely than the version in the text. By the same token we do not know whether Henry's design for a long-term reform of the Roman Church, for which I have argued in the text, was originally conceived in co-operation with Gregory VI or was developed after the breach with him.

   [5] H. H. Anton, *Der sogenannte Traktat 'De Ordinando Pontifice'* (Bonn, 1982), 83. The question of authorship and intent is fully discussed there, with full references to earlier studies. The title of the tract is modern and does not properly describe the contents. For Wazo, see Anselm, *Gesta episcoporum Leodiensium*, 65 (MGH SS VII.228–9).

successor Damasus II survived for only three weeks after his enthronement on 17 July 1048.

The future character of the reforming papacy was determined by the next pope, that *papa mirabilis* Leo IX.[6] Perhaps few elements in his policy were completely new, but he implemented it with a force and vision which in a few short years changed the character of the Roman Church and its standing in western Christendom. At his appointment Bruno was 46 years old, the son of a count in Alsace, a relative of the Emperor Henry III, and bishop of Toul, where he was already noted for his activity in combatting simony. Having been welcomed by the clergy and people of Rome he was enthroned as pope on 12 February 1049. One of Leo's most important contributions was the recruiting of a group of outstanding reformers into the senior ranks of the Roman Church. Some were from his own diocese of Toul, including Humbert, a monk of Moyenmoutier (who became cardinal-bishop of Silva Candida), Hugh Candidus from Remiremont (cardinal-priest of San Clemente) and Udo (papal chancellor). From elsewhere came Frederick, archdeacon of Liège and brother of Duke Godfrey of Lorraine (also papal chancellor) and the Subdeacon Hildebrand, who now after the death of Gregory VI returned to the Lateran palace. Other prominent reformers in close touch with Leo were Archbishops Halinard of Lyon and Hugh of Besançon, and the hermit leader Peter Damian. These talented men, whose names include two future popes, were to sustain the reforming cause throughout the next generation.

The purpose of this recruitment was to provide Leo with the means for an ambitious attack on abuses within the western church. In his five years in office he held eleven or twelve synods which issued canons against simony and clerical marriage, and reasserted the validity of canon law and the necessity of the canonical election of bishops. Contemporaries were struck by his conviction of the international responsibility of the Roman Church, which was vividly expressed in his travels in 1049 in northern Italy, Germany, and France and in the synods of Reims and Mainz in the autumn of that year:

What pastor of the Roman Church, since that golden age in which Leo and Gregory shone clearer than crystal as lights of spiritual doctrine, has arisen as diligent and watchful as you, holiest of bishops . . .? You were not

[6] John of Fécamp, *Epistola ad S. Leonem IX* (PL 143.797C).

content in your own see of the city of Rome to care for one people . . . but also visited and examined with synodical scrutiny the churches north of the Alps.[7]

This sense of the revival of the glories of the early church was confirmed by Leo's charismatic gifts. He was not simply a legislator; rather, it was characteristic for him to preside at the consecration of great churches and other liturgical occasions, some of which, like the translation of St Remigius at Reims in 1049, he converted into reforming synods. He had a strong sense that through him God was speaking to the Christian people, and a remarkable ability to call down judgement upon evil-doers. At Leo's first synod at Rome the bishop of Sutri collapsed and died as he defended himself against a charge of simony; at Reims the spokesman for Bishop Hugh of Langres became tongue-tied as he tried to present his case, and years later one of the clergy present remembered how the assembly had been terrified by Leo's proclamation of God's wrath against simoniacs.[8] His ministry set the fashion for treating the reforming popes as saints, whose lives and miracles should be recorded. This charismatic power was precisely what was needed to give impetus to the campaign against simony and to force public opinion to take it seriously.

To modern eyes there is a sharp contrast between the two parts of Leo's short pontificate. From 1051 onwards, although his concern for reform did not cease, the main focus of his policy was the Norman menace in southern Italy. They had entered the country as mercenaries, but were now engaged in establishing themselves as its rulers under their formidable leaders Richard of Aversa and Robert Guiscard. The clash of interests began when Leo accepted the lordship over Benevento which its inhabitants offered him, and in 1052 the pope appealed to Henry III for support, which was not forthcoming. Leo, while carrying on negotiations with the Byzantine emperor, therefore decided to put himself at the head of an army and to suppress the Normans from his own resources. In Leo's eyes the expedition was not a mere political matter. The papal claims to authority in southern Italy were large; indeed, the Donation of Constantine, another ninth-century forgery, provided a basis for claiming dominion over the whole region. He was also shocked by

---

[7] John of Fécamp (PL 143.797C).
[8] Will of Udalric of Reims (PL 150.1547C).

the violence of the Normans and was pressing them to treat the inhabitants justly: 'he showed them how God is persecuted when the poor are persecuted, and God is satisfied when the poor are well treated. And he charged them that they should faithfully protect the priests and the goods of the church.'[9] The pope was therefore driven by the defence of the possessions of St Peter and the suffering of the people of Apulia, as well as by an attempted alliance with Byzantium, to give high priority to action against the invaders. The result was an anti-climax. The papal army was overwhelmed at Civitate on 18 June 1053 and Leo himself was captured. The Normans kept him in honourable captivity for almost a year, and he died at Rome on 19 April 1054 shortly after his release.

He had been pope for only a short time, and the end of his pontificate was occupied by the disastrous Norman campaign; but Leo's work had been great. He had manifested the authority of Rome north of the Alps, emphasized the binding power of canon law, given a new and dramatic life to the campaign against simony and clerical marriage, provided a startling precedent for papally conducted warfare, and set a stamp on future dealings with the Greek Church. There was so far little sign of the deteriorating relations with the empire which were to be a feature of the following decade, although it was significant that Henry III, finding himself under pressure in Germany, had been unable to provide the resources for which the pope had asked to fight the Normans. There were also some complaints that Henry had fallen away from his original high aims and was disappointing the expectations which he had aroused. As far as relations between pope and emperor were concerned, however, these were the distant whisperings of a storm whose coming no one foresaw.

Leo's successor was Bishop Gebhard of Eichstätt, who was enthroned at Rome as Victor II. Another relative of the emperor, his policy followed the general lines of Leo's, and he secured from Henry a promise that he would render to St Peter what was rightly his.[10] By this time Henry's hold over Italy was becoming increasingly insecure. Countess Beatrice of Tuscany, the greatest landowner of northern Italy, had married Duke Godfrey of Lorraine, a long-standing enemy of Henry III, and it was only with difficulty

---

[9] V. de Bartholomaeis (ed.), *Storia de' Normanni di Amato di Montecassino* (Rome, 1935), iii. 16 (130–1).

[10] *De episcopis Eichstetensibus*, 38 (MGH SS VII. 265).

that the pope was able to reconcile the emperor with them. Hardly had he done so when Henry died on 5 October 1056, in the presence of the pope, to whom he commended his small son Henry. In a sense Victor was the heir to the imperial policy, but he did not long survive, and died at Arezzo in Tuscany on 28 July 1057. The line of popes appointed from the ranks of German bishops had come to an end, and so had the close co-operation of papal reformers and the imperial court.

iii. *The Reformers Come of Age (1057–1073)*

The deaths of Henry III and Victor II completed the transformation of the Italian political situation. Until the early 1050s, conditions had been favourable for maintaining the imperial interest in the Roman Church in co-operation with the German popes. Now, imperial policy was in the weak hands of the Empress Agnes, regent for the boy Henry IV; the formidable power of Lorraine-Tuscany, in the hands of Duke Godfrey, dominated much of the north of the peninsula; and, to the south of Rome, Norman power had been consolidated by the victory at Civitate. The quiescence of the Roman nobility was also coming to an end. Their failure to challenge the position of the German popes had been notable in the preceding years. The reason may well be that the Tusculan family had depended heavily on the control of the papacy for its power and had been disabled by losing it. Moreover, until the death of the former Benedict IX in 1055 the Roman nobles were in practice unable to unite behind a convincing local candidate. Thereafter, they recovered their freedom of action, which they were to use in ways which threatened the reformers and jeopardized their good relations with the imperial court.

When news arrived at Rome of the death of Victor II an assembly of clergy and people immediately elected Frederick of Lorraine as Pope Stephen IX, and he was enthroned on 3 August 1057. The new pope had been brought to Rome by Leo, who had made him chancellor, and he had subsequently been elected abbot of Monte Cassino. For the first time since 1045 an election had been made without prior consultation with the German court, and the choice of Godfrey of Lorraine's brother probably indicates an appeal to him for his protection. Stephen was the first monk to be elected pope for many years, and he proceeded to strengthen the monastic position within the Roman Church by appointing Peter Damian as bishop of Ostia, the senior cardinal-bishop, and Humbert as papal chancellor. His term as pope was too short for more than these first measures, since he died at Florence on 29 March 1058.

His death gave rise to a schism. The clergy and laity at once proceeded to an election at Rome, choosing Bishop John of Velletri, who was installed as Benedict X on 5 April 1058. By this time, the new men had established themselves sufficiently firmly to be able to challenge the old nobility. They turned for support jointly to the Empress Agnes, with whom Hildebrand conducted the negotiations, and to Duke Godfrey. The new pope was another Tuscan connection, Bishop Gerard of Florence, who had been prominent in the reform movement there. He was escorted to Rome by the troops of Duke Godfrey and installed as Nicholas II on 24 January 1059.

Within the party which thus renewed its control of the papal office there were three outstanding men. The oldest of them was Peter Damian. He had been born at Ravenna about 1007, had studied at Faenza and Parma, and been a master, probably at Ravenna. In 1035 he entered the hermitage of Fonte Avellana in the Appenines and became prior in 1043. Peter was at once an advocate of withdrawal, given to ascetic practices of an exaggerated kind, and a propagandist for reform. The clash of loyalties within his mind produced a number of eccentricities and indiscretions: his fierce attack on homosexual practices in monasteries, the *Liber Gomorrhianus*, was regarded somewhat coolly by the popes. On the other hand on major issues of theology Peter's was the voice of moderation. He asserted firmly the tradition that it was the emperor's task to be the defender of the church, and that the pope should look to him for assistance in reform. His *Liber Gratissimus* (1052) was one of the finest theological works of the century and a classic criticism of the rigorist approach to the problem of simony.

The second of these three men, Hildebrand, may have been related to the Roman nobility, although there is little solid evidence that, as was formerly believed, he was a member of the rising Pierleone family. He was educated in the school in the Lateran palace and at the monastery of St Mary Aventine, where he was probably professed as a monk in boyhood.[11] After exile in northern Europe with Gregory

---

[11] Gregory was certainly a monk, but it is hard to be sure where he made his profession. In spite of a clear statement of Bonizo of Sutri that this took place at Cluny in 1047–8 an earlier profession seems more probable.

VI he returned to Rome under Leo IX, and his arrival at a position of prime importance was indicated by his part in negotiating the election of Nicholas II. By 1059 he had become archdeacon of the Roman Church. Peter Damian, who was far from being an uncritical admirer, nicknamed him 'holy Satan'.[12]

The third member of the group was Humbert. Originally a monk of Moyenmoutier, he had come to Rome with Leo IX and been nominated archbishop of Palermo, a nominal title as the town was in Moslem hands; he was then made cardinal-bishop of Silva Candida and subsequently papal chancellor. Humbert was a learned man, who apart from wide reading of the Latin Fathers also knew some Greek, and he enjoyed a great deal of influence with the popes from 1050 until his death in 1061. He had a large involvement in negotiations with Constantinople, and in the politics of reform he represented the rigorist party, which refused to recognize the orders conferred by simoniac bishops. There has been much discussion among historians about the body of writing which may be assigned to Humbert, who at one time was in danger of becoming the residuary legatee of every anonymous pamphlet written in his lifetime. The fact is that the only major work which can be securely assigned to him was the *Adversus Simoniacos*, 'Against the Simoniacs', which he composed about 1058 as a reply (although not expressly) to Peter Damian's *Liber Gratissimus*. It is striking for its statement of the rigorist view and its early attack on lay investiture, and we shall have to return to it shortly. It was, however, little circulated; it is important, not because it became well known, but because its author was influential in papal circles for a decade.

The pontificate of Nicholas II, which was deeply influenced by these three men, has sometimes been seen as embodying the first application of the ideas which were fully implemented by Gregory VII after 1075. The question is an important one, because if this view is correct it would mean that the policy had been both formulated and applied (presumably under Humbert's influence) at this early stage in the development of the papal reform. On this interpretation, Nicholas not only re-enacted the reforming legislation of Leo IX but added to it a prohibition of lay investiture, a decree on papal elections designed to free the papacy from imperial influence, a stringent

---

[12] Opuscula 20,1 (PL 145.444AB). Dr Blake has suggested to me that the reference is to Matt. 16: 23, and that Peter was complaining about the pressure put on him by Hildebrand to involve himself in the affairs of the world rather than withdraw to his hermitage.

attempt to oblige canons to adopt individual poverty, and a treaty which provided Norman protection for the reform party. It was not surprising, the argument runs, that by 1061 there was an open breach between the reform party at Rome and the imperial advisers in Germany. Does an examination of Nicholas' policy support this understanding of it?[13]

The new pope celebrated his victory in the schism by summoning a great synod at the Lateran, including 113 bishops, and its decrees were published to the western church in the letter *Vigilantia universalis*. This provided a summary of the reforming programme, including the measures against simony and clerical marriage which had become a standard part of it over the last ten years. The discussion of the common life of canons was marked by a sharp attack, led by Hildebrand, on the permission to own private property contained in the Rule of Aix, which had been adopted under Louis the Pious in 816; but the resulting decree was moderate in its wording, for canons were only exhorted (not compelled) to give up the use of private possessions. The papal election decree, which was the most striking piece of new legislation, appears to have been designed for three purposes: to justify the procedures which had in fact been followed in electing Nicholas II; to secure the hold upon the Roman Church which the reform party had almost lost and to ensure that future elections should be carried out according to the principles of canon law. The contorted provisions were the result of trying to achieve these different, and not completely consistent, aims. There was in fact no real guidance in canon law about the method of electing the Roman pontiff, and this decree was the first attempt to define procedure: 'First the cardinal bishops shall together discuss with most careful consideration, then they shall associate with themselves the cardinal clerks, and thus the remaining clergy and people shall join in consenting to the new election.'[14] The common electoral procedure at the time was for an inner group, which acted as a nominating committee in modern terminology, to hold a preliminary discussion or *tractatio* and produce a name for election by the wider body. The influential place of the cardinal-bishops, in whose ranks the reformers were strongly entrenched, is evident. Another drafting problem was presented by the rights of the emperor, for there was nothing in canon law to justify his influence upon elections. It was solved rather evasively by allowing to Henry

[13] The question of the alleged decree on investiture is considered later in this chapter.
[14] Papal election decree 3 (MGH Leges IV Const.I, p. 539).

IV the 'due honour and dignity' which had been granted by the apostolic see. The precise significance of this measure has been the subject of a great deal of controversy. It is unlikely that it was intended to exclude the emperor from any part in papal elections, but his role was reduced to a privilege granted by the Roman Church, a change which marked a sharp difference from the days of Henry III, when the all-important *tractatio* had been held at the imperial court.

In the same year there was a reversal of Leo IX's policy towards the Normans. It is uncertain whether this was mainly the work of Desiderius, abbot of Monte Cassino, or of Archdeacon Hildebrand. Whoever was the initiator, the new pope was persuaded to seek a rapprochement with Richard of Capua and Robert Guiscard. At Melfi in August 1059 he recognized their right to most of southern Italy. Robert received investiture of Apulia, Calabria, and Sicily, most of which were still in Greek and Moslem hands. In return the Norman princes swore obedience to the papacy, promising to pay an annual tribute and to defend the rights of St Peter. The arrangement achieved several things: it recognized the large papal claims to southern Italy, envisaged an effective extension of Latin Christendom against Moslems and Greeks, and promised financial and military assistance to the popes. Neither the papal election decree nor the Norman alliance was directly anti-imperial; they were rather attempts to fortify the position of the reformers in a world in which (at least during the minority of Henry IV) the imperial interest had become only one, and not the most powerful, of the forces to be taken into account.

In the meantime a new front in the campaign against simony and clerical marriage had opened with the beginning of the troubles at Milan. In this great and traditional church, both the payment of fees and the marriage of priests were customary. The move against the ecclesiastical establishment began with the preaching of the deacon Ariald against clerical marriage: on 10 May 1057 the clergy, assembled for the translation of the relics of St Nazzaro, were surprised by an uprising of the laity and compelled to swear that in future they would observe chastity. Before long, Ariald had widened his attack to include simony, and had come to feel that marriage was a secondary matter if clergy were involved in simoniacal heresy: 'it hardly matters whether heretics have wives or not.' Perhaps at this time his followers received the insulting name *Patarini*.[15] To settle

---

[15] Andrew of Strumi, *Vita sancti Arialdi* 10 (MGH SS XXX.ii.1055).

this crisis Nicholas II sent as legates Peter Damian and Bishop Anselm of Lucca, who imposed a solution along the lines advocated in Peter's *Liber Gratissimus*. The clergy were obliged to renounce simony and concubinage and to do penance, but they were permitted to keep their offices. It was an insecure settlement, which did not satisfy the radical demands of the *Patarini*, who had meanwhile established within the city a community devoted to living the apostolic life.

Nicholas II died on 27 July 1061, leaving behind him an awkward situation. In the months before his death, relations with the German church had deteriorated gravely, apparently as a result of a clash with Archbishops Anno of Cologne and Siegfried of Mainz.[16] The quarrel has often been explained as the result of imperial resentment at the papal election decree and the alliance with the Normans, but there is no clear evidence for this view. The dispute reached the point where a synod of German bishops met to condemn the pope and declare his acts invalid, and this was to have grave consequences for the new election. At Rome Bishop Anselm of Lucca was elected and enthroned as Alexander II on 30 September or 1 October 1061. He was a member of the Milanese family of da Baggio and had been associated with the reforming group at Rome.[17] He owed his elevation to the support of Archdeacon Hildebrand and the presence of a Norman force brought there in fulfilment of the oath of 1059. This time the German court was not even informed, and an embassy from the Roman nobility induced Henry IV at the council of Basle on 28 October 1061 to nominate Bishop Cadalus of Parma as Honorius II. Alexander's prospects at first appeared poor, but a *coup d'état* by Archbishop Anno of Cologne reversed the policy of the imperial court. Alexander was able to secure himself in Rome, and at Pentecost 1064 the synod of Mantua finally secured his general recognition as pope.

Alexander's policy stood firmly in the tradition of Nicholas II, whose legislation he repeated almost verbatim in his first synod after Easter 1063, attended by more than 100 bishops. There was

---

[16] Unfortunately the details of this important episode are obscure, and we depend on a short account by Peter Damian, *Disceptatio Synodalis* (MGH LdL i.87–8), supplemented by Deusdedit (LdL ii.309) and Benzo of Alba (MGH SS XI.672). There is no contemporary support for a connection between the quarrel of 1061 and the events of 1059.

[17] The weight of evidence is against the traditional views (although they rest on early statements) that Alexander was a former pupil of Lanfranc at Bec, and that he had been a founder of the *Patarini*.

nevertheless a shift of power among his advisers, with the death of
Cardinal Humbert in 1061 and the determination of Peter Damian to
return to his hermitage. Most contemporaries thought that the
direction of policy was now in the hands of archdeacon Hildebrand.
Peter Damian acidly remarked that, if you wanted to live at Rome,
you had to obey the pope's lord rather than the lord pope.[18] The
evidence does not enable us to measure precisely the correctness of
this impression, but it does seem clear that Hildebrand was in charge
of policy towards Milan, a city of crucial importance which was
moreover the birthplace of Alexander. The pontificate saw a steadily
increasing intervention in the regions of Europe in the cause of
reform, a policy implemented by the despatch of legates and by the
approval of military endeavours in support of the papacy. In France,
where papal legates had already been active, a further series visited
the country, including Peter Damian who was sent to hear a dispute
between the abbey of Cluny and the bishop of Mâcon in 1063. A
closer watch was also kept on appointments to bishoprics there. In
1065 the pope wrote that Hildegaire was believed to have seized the
bishopric of Chartres with the connivance of the advisers of the
young Philip I, and he threatened an interdict on the royal court
unless it withdrew its support for him. Alexander was not
challenging all lay interest in appointments, but was reacting with
vigour to any suggestion of purchase or the use of force. In England
the Norman Conquest provided an occasion for the reorganization
of the church. This was welcomed at Rome, for Archbishop Stigand
of Canterbury (1052–70) was an intruder and a scandalous pluralist,
and had obtained the pallium, the emblem of his authority, from the
'anti-pope' Benedict X. William I welcomed the visit in 1070 of
Bishop Ermenfrid of Sitten who came to remove some of the
English bishops, Stigand included. William was following a policy
of gallicizing the English church, and by the end of his reign in 1087
only one bishop, Wulfstan of Worcester, was English by birth. It
can, however, not be said that papal power had made a spectacular
breakthrough in England. King William regarded himself as responsible for the church in collaboration with his adviser and friend,
Archbishop Lanfranc of Canterbury (1070–89). Lanfranc was a north
Italian who had moved to Normandy and won recognition as one of
the outstanding scholars of his generation. The imperialist Pope
Clement III, admittedly when he was angling for his support,

[18] Peter Damian, *Carmen*, 149 (PL 145.961D).

described him as 'the most splendid star of Europe'. He had become
a monk in 1042 at the newly founded house of Bec, and then in 1063
been appointed by Duke William as abbot of his new foundation of
St Stephen's, Caen. Lanfranc was an active reformer, but he neither
expected nor welcomed direct intervention from Rome, and was
concerned to secure his own recognition as primate, with authority
over the archbishop of York and effective headship over the whole
British church.

In Germany the young King Henry IV was assuming control from
about 1066, after ten years of minority government. He was as
deeply religious as his father had been and took pleasure in discussion
with the learned clergy whom he appointed as his chaplains. Later in
his life his personal copy of the psalter became so worn with use that
one of his chaplains, the future Bishop Otto of Bamberg, had it
bound for him as a surprise. At first there was little disposition to
challenge the principles of church order which Henry III had
imposed, but in practice it was becoming more difficult for the king
to govern the imperial church. As regent, Archbishop Anno had
forced his relatives into vacant sees, including his brother Werner,
who became archbishop of Magdeburg in 1063, and he caused so
much annoyance in 1066 in trying to appoint his nephew Cuno as
archbishop of Trier that Cuno was murdered there. The increasing
independence of cathedral and other canons led to arguments about
episcopal appointments, and so did the growing collision of interest
between the Crown and some of the great princes, who were seeking
to build up their territories and, as part of the process, to found
monasteries under their patronage. Archbishop Anno of Cologne,
Duke Rudolf of Suabia, and others brought in monks from
Fruttuaria and other houses outside Germany, which did not share
the tradition of imperial headship. The growing alienation between
the court and the reformers was reflected in the position of Henry's
mother, the Empress Agnes, who had retired to Rome and who
intervened in Germany several times in order to reconcile Henry
with Alexander II, the southern princes, and Gregory VII in turn. It
may be that a more statesmanlike approach by Henry IV would have
won support, but he followed the natural line of trying to force his
nominees into bishoprics. Hermann of Bamberg was probably a
good appointment, although very much a royal favourite, while
Charles of Constance was a much less suitable nomination, and both
provoked fierce complaints from the canons of their cities. With the

growth of these divisions, papal authority was drawn into the affairs of German churches in a way unknown in the past. At Trier, following Cuno's murder. Alexander II approved the election of Udo, the first case of promotion in Germany without the approval of the royal court. Bishop Hermann of Bamberg was pursued with false charges of simony, and Charles of Constance resigned under pressure at the synod of Mainz in 1071. The campaign of the canons there had been led by the head of their school, Bernard, and inspired him to a study of canon law. It is our first mention of the Constance tradition of canonists, who were to be a major element in the development of papal theory under Gregory VII.

The Roman Church was even more directly involved in the local movements of protest in Italian cities. At Florence the Vallombrosan monks whipped up popular feeling against Bishop Peter and insisted on arranging an ordeal by fire in which one of their number proved the bishop guilty of simony. At the Rome synod of 1068 Alexander II bowed to the inevitable and deposed him. More influential for future events was the renewal of the troubles at Milan, where the settlement of 1059 had not endured. The *Patarini* had acquired a new leader in Erlembald, a layman who acted with violence against clergy charged with simony: his critics said that he was like a pope to judge the priests, and like a king to bruise the peoples. Rome showed a remarkable lack of reserve in giving its support to Erlembald. The conservative party remained strong at Milan, however, and in June 1066 Ariald, the founder of the *Patarini* was murdered; the movement now had its martyr. A few years later the struggle led to a schism which was to have international consequences. In 1072 the city was divided between two claimants to the archbishopric, Godfrey who had been invested by Henry IV, and Atto the *Patarini* candidate. The Roman Church promptly recognized Atto, and at the Easter synod of 1073 Alexander II excommunicated the advisers of Henry IV for their part in the investiture of Godfrey. When Alexander died on 21 April 1073 he left a crisis, with an almost open breach between the pope and the German king. The situation had been partly produced by the papal support for a party whose appeal to the people, and violent conduct, had created both a social upheaval and a schism in the Milanese church. Probably Hildebrand had been the champion of this policy of direct involvement; and his was to be the voice which determined the policy of the Roman Church during the next ten years.

iv. *The Principles of Papal Reform*

Between the synod of Sutri in 1046 and the accession of Gregory VII in 1073, a group of dedicated men had secured the senior positions in the Roman Church and established it as a co-ordinating force in international reform. They had begun to show a sturdy independence towards old-established powers and by 1073 they had come to the brink of a confrontation with the authority of Henry IV. Many of these leaders were monks, and a set of common principles underlay the monastic revival and the papal reform movement. Both were imbued with the spirit of *contemptus mundi* or rejection of worldly values. Abbot John of Fécamp explained what this meant:

We find that in the Scriptures those who love the world are called *the world*. So what can be more properly called *the world* than kings and dukes, marquises and counts, fleshly bishops and every one who is given up to fleshly desires? For we see abbots bound in friendship to such men, and monks diligently serving them.[19]

This dismissal of the political order expresses the spirit which also underlay the work of the papal reformers, and is embodied in its most extreme form in Humbert's work *Adversus Simoniacos*. Against this mass of evil, papal and monastic reformers agreed on the source of remedy: 'let us turn back, dearly beloved, to the innocence of the primitive church'.[20] In their imaginations these men lived again in the pages of the *Acts of the Apostles*, when Simon Peter strove with Simon Magus. While papal and monastic reformers shared these principles in common, their practical programmes were necessarily different. Leo IX, Humbert, and Hildebrand stood for the correction of abuses among the clergy as a whole, who had subjected themselves to the dominance of the worldly laity. Tellenbach said of Hildebrand as Gregory VII that he 'stands at the greatest—from the spiritual point of view the only—turning-point in the history of Catholic Christendom; in his time the policy of converting the world gained once and for all the upper hand over the policy of withdrawing from it'.[21] This large claim rests on the solid fact that the function of a pope is different from that of an abbot, and that the reforming popes, with their enlarged sense of authority, saw

---

[19] Letter *Tuae quidem*, 7, J. Leclercq and J.-P. Bonnes, *Jean de Fécamp* (Paris, 1946), 203. John was abbot of Fécamp from 1028 to 1078, but the letter contains no indication of date.

[20] *Sermo* 53 ascribed to Peter Damian (PL 144.806C).

[21] G. Tellenbach, *Church, State and Christian Society* (Oxford, 1940), 164.

themselves as responsible for the well-being of the western church and issued legislation and published it through legates and synods in a way which would not have been conceivable for Hugh of Cluny or Desiderius of Monte Cassino.

Yet the difference of roles does not necessarily imply a difference of attitudes, and it is arguable that the papal reform movement did not mark the abandonment of the monastic approach so much as its adoption as the policy of the Roman Church. One of the fundamental aims was to separate the clergy from the rest of society, preferably into communities living under rule with common property, but at least stripped of the ties such as simony and marriage which bound them to the world. The classic statement is that of Humbert:

Just as clergy are forbidden to interfere with secular business, so are laymen with ecclesiastical business . . . In the same way as clergy are distinct from laymen in their dress and profession, so they should also be in deeds and conversation, so that neither party should take upon itself the office or hereditary status of the other, but each respect the bounds appointed by the holy Fathers and orthodox princes. Just as the clergy are separated within the walls of basilicas from the offices and areas allotted to laymen, so they ought to be identifiably separate in business. Thus laymen should arrange and provide for their own business, which is secular, and clergy for theirs, which is ecclesiastical.[22]

The stress on separation was not new. It was implicit in the Gelasian principle, and the rules of canon law which forbade the clergy to become involved in secular affairs had already been cited in Burchard of Worms. But the separation of the clergy from worldly affairs was not a simple restoration of the past, because it was being applied to a society in which the churches had landed endowments and secular duties, and it was accompanied by the attempt to strip away from the priesthood all family ties and segregate it into communities. The first generation of reformers looked to abbeys such as Cluny and Monte Cassino, with the empires of local churches under their control, as natural allies in implementing their policy. At a later stage, as we shall see, the growth of the regular canons and the possibility of using the bishop as the effective power in the reform of the local churches led to an 'episcopal revival' and to an emphasis upon the withdrawal of monasteries from involvement in the secular church.

---

[22] Humbert, *Adversus Simoniacos*, iii.9 (MGH LdL i.208).

The priority in this reform was the need to purify the clergy for the performance of their liturgical functions, for it was through the means of grace dispensed in the sacraments, and above all in the mass, that salvation was made available to believers. It was for this reason that there were agonized discussions about the impact of simony upon the administration of the sacraments, and that Humbert and other leaders committed themselves passionately to a doctrine of Christ's physical presence in the bread and wine consecrated by the hands of a faithful priest. Johannes Laudage has emphasized that the concern for the purification of the clergy as the channel of sacramental salvation runs through the whole of the reforming movement. It represents a welding of a monastic demand for purity with a pastoral concern proper to secular clergy, and it is reflected not only in the legislation of reforming councils but in a new type of saint's life, in which miracles were given much less prominence than the demand that the clergy should follow Christ as his disciples. One early example of this style was the *Life of Ariald* by Andrew of Strumi, written about 1075 with its stress on Ariald's characteristic message: 'Behold, Christ says, "whoever is my minister must follow me".'[23] We must, however, be careful not to state this concept of reform in too modern a way. Historians have often stressed that, whatever the disagreements may have been over the proper discipline of the church, there were men of good will who were united in the desire for moral reform of the clergy; but this is a misconception, at least if we think of 'moral reform' in terms which would be natural today. There is little in the whole literature of the papal reform movement about the need to make clergy personally more devout, to build up their character, or to provide better instruction or pastoral care for the laity. Indeed, there is only a limited amount of discussion designed to define the priestly office in its inner character. These things do indeed become important in the thirteenth century, but in the age of Leo IX and Gregory VII we are still in a primitive society, in which it is more accurate to think in terms of cultic reform. The church and clergy must be freed from practices which made them ritually impure. Simony and clerical marriage were often discussed not as obstacles to pastoral service, but in terms of physical corruption. Simony was like disease; trafficking in money was described in anal language, as dirt and ordure. It was a terrible impurity for the priest to go from a woman's

---

[23] *Vita sancti Arialdi*, c. 10 (MGH SS XXX.ii. 1052), citing John 12: 26.

bed to handle the body of the Lord on the altar. Churches had to be rescued from defilement by lay possession through transfer to monastic ownership; the effect on the parishioners was almost never considered. The objective of the reformers was not pastoral efficiency in a modern sense, but purification of the clergy from secular service, money, and women, and in consequence simony (not ignorance or incompetence) was the enemy against which all reforming endeavours must be directed.

v. *The Reform of the Clergy*

There are fashions in sin, as in everything else. In our own age the prime offence is racial discrimination, but in the second half of the eleventh century simony came to hold the position of the thing abhorred above all others by scrupulous men. It was an ancient evil whose name was derived from Simon Magus, who had offered money for the power of the Holy Spirit and been condemned for it by St Peter (Acts 8: 9–24). The main outlines were already contained in the canons collected by Burchard of Worms; the novelty was the vehemence with which simony was condemned rather than the way it was defined. It had long been seen as a heresy, *simoniaca heresis*, and included the sin of giving money for holy orders, and indeed for any ecclesiastical office. What was more, it was simony to obtain ecclesiastical promotion by secular service or flattery, even if no money were paid—an extension of the concept which can already be found in Gregory I. The campaign against simony was an expression of the major objectives of the reformers: the purification of the clergy for divine service by their separation from the world and the pursuit of apostolic perfection. It was an unsubtle concept which offered a dramatic symbol presented to the faithful in preaching and art, through which they could see the danger of priests whose holy office had been polluted by money, and the hope that once more Peter would deliver the church from the machinations of Simon Magus. In the sculpted capital at Autun, for example, we see him hurled headlong to destruction by the apostle's prayers.

In spite of several condemnations of simony in synods, it was still said around 1050 to be almost universal 'throughout Germany and Gaul and the whole of Italy'.[24] The purchase of orders and benefices

---

[24] Humbert, *Adversus Simoniacos*, ii.36 and iii.7 (MGH LdL i.85, 206). See also Peter Damian, *Vita Romualdi*, 35 (PL 144. 896C) and Raoul Glaber, *Historiae*, ii.6 (PL 142.636AB).

was prohibited by Clement II at Rome in 1047 and Leo IX at Reims in 1049, and Leo began a determined effort to remove bishops guilty of simony. In 1059 Nicholas II's *Vigilantia universalis* contained a general condemnation of the securing of ecclesiastical office by simony, and Alexander II's version of it incorporated a lengthy definition of the practice. Gregory VII could fairly say in 1075 of the canons against simony and clerical marriage that 'our holy and apostolic mother church has ever since the time of the blessed pope Leo often, in councils and by legates and letters, admonished, asked and ordered, by the authority she has received from St Peter, the peoples committed to her care to restore and observe these, neglected as they have been in the past'.[25] There was, however, sharp disagreement about the discipline which should be imposed against simony. The radical view was set out by Humbert in his *Adversus Simoniacos* of 1058 and widely circulated in the so-called *Letter of Wido*. It denied the charge could be avoided by pleading that the cash had been paid not for the sacrament but for the income arising from the appointment: 'if someone objects that they are not selling consecration, but the goods which arise from consecration, he may sound as if he is saying something, but he is making no sense at all'. Orders and the possessions of churches are as inseparably united as body and soul.[26] Still more drastic was the argument that, since simony is heresy, a bishop who has been simoniacally consecrated has received no authority and is incapable of ordaining clergy. Peter Damian reported a conversation with a clerk who had been ordained by a simoniac bishop:

'Did you possess', I asked, 'anything within yourself of those grades you previously received from the bishop?' 'Nothing at all', he said, 'for what was there for me to receive?' And I added, 'so you were no different from a layman, in fact you *were* just a layman.' 'That's right', he said, 'just simply a layman, with nothing clerical about me at all.'[27]

The theory had spectacular implications. Given that simony was common, it followed that there were whole dioceses, even whole countries, in which priests had not been properly ordained, and at the end of the century it was still being asserted by some people that 'the priesthood has been extinguished in the church'.[28] It was

---

[25] Nicholas II, *Vigilantia universalis*, 9 and (for Alexander II) 1 (R. Schieffer, *Investiturverbot* 215–22); and Greg. VII. *Reg.* II. 15 (183–4).

[26] For the importance of the letter, see Gilchrist, 'The *Epistola Widonis*' and the text of the longer version in *DAEM* 37 (1981), esp. 595.

[27] Peter Damian, *Liber Gratissimus*, 35 (MGH LdL i.68).

[28] Bruno of Segni, *Libellus de Symoniacis*, 1 (MGH LdL ii.547).

possible to maintain that this radical view was in accord with catholic tradition, especially as the anti-Donatist writings of St Augustine, which were the classic statement of the validity of orders conferred outside the church, were little known. The main champion of a more moderate position was Peter Damian in his *Liber Gratissimus* (1052), a work widely circulated but by no means readily accepted in reforming circles. The controversy arrived at Rome with Leo IX, who probably (the matter is not completely clear) attempted to annul (*cassare*) the orders of clergy ordained by simonist bishops, and re ordained some of them. Fuel was added to the fire in 1059 when Peter Damian, as legate at Milan, allowed penitent simonists to remain in office, and Nicholas II arrived at a rather awkward compromise: considering the exigencies of the present time, innocent clergy ordained by simoniacs might remain in office, but the concession would not be applied to later ordinations.[29]

Second only in importance, in the eyes of the reformers, to the freeing of the church from simony was the attempt to enforce chastity. Canon law in the western church forbade the marriage of clergy in major orders (although not in the subordinate grades) but there was no bar to the ordination of married men provided they remained continent. Since the minimum age for ordination as priest was 30, many bishops and priests were already married and had a family. The position was complicated by the fact that the institution of concubinage or 'subsidiary marriage' was an accepted one in society generally, and was widespread among the clergy. The evidence suggests that a high proportion of priests lived with wives or concubines, had families, and hoped that they might succeed them in their benefices. It was the intention of Leo IX to enforce the canon law, above all because of the danger that the Lord's body would be touched by impure hands: 'if you commit incest with your spiritual daughter, with what conscience do you dare to handle the mystery of the Lord's body?'[30] There had already been attempts to enforce celibacy on those in major orders, and Leo IX issued canons to the same purpose. One of the aims of the synod of 1059 was legislation against the concubinage of clergy in holy orders, that is priests, deacons, and subdeacons. Peter Damian wrote his *De Celibatu Sacerdotum* and *Contra Intemperantes Clericos* in the same cause, and identified the heresy of the Nicolaitans, known since New Testament days, as consisting in the defence of the marriage of priests.

[29] MGH Leges IV Const.I, p. 550, dated 1059 or 1060.
[30] Peter Damian, *De Celibatu Sacerdotum*, 3 (PL 145.385A).

The term was an artificial invention, and never secured the same currency as *simoniaca heresis*. It was one of the innovations of the reformers. Another was the insistence that married men must leave their wives on receiving holy orders, whereas the older canons, while prescribing continence, stressed that the marriage should be maintained and the wife supported. It was also new to attempt to enforce these regulations by what was effectively a lay strike: in 1059 the faithful were instructed to absent themselves from the masses of married priests, a measure repeated by Alexander II and Gregory VII.[31]

The protests against this policy were loud. Pamphlets were produced against it, notably the *Rescriptum* of Bishop Ulric of Imola in 1060 (a popular work, widely copied and adapted) and the *Apologia* of Sigebert of Gembloux shortly after 1075, and there were riots in synods when bishops attempted to issue regulations separating priests from their wives. The reforming Archbishop John of Rouen was driven with stones out of his diocesan synod in 1072, exclaiming 'O God, the heathen are come into your inheritance!'; and in 1074 there were angry scenes in various parts of Europe, including Paris, where the clergy condemned the reforming decrees as 'intolerable and therefore unreasonable'. Opposition became stronger as a new and increasingly powerful element entered the situation: the conviction that a married priest was not really married in law. The idea rested on secular custom rather than on the canons. Before 1050 there was both in France and Germany a belief that sons of clergy were illegitimate and therefore incapable of inheriting, and a law of Justinian, which required the deposition of clergy who married after ordination, was applied to all married clergy in major orders.[32] It became standard in papal decrees to refer to the women of priests, whether married or not, as concubines, and eventually the Roman Church gave the force of law to the denial of the validity of the marriage of priests. The Second Lateran Council in 1139 declared a marriage entered into by a priest, deacon, or subdeacon not to be a marriage, *matrimonium non esse*. Although this covered only mar-

---

[31] *Vigilantia universalis* 3: R. Schieffer (ed.), *Investiturverbot*, 218–19.

[32] For the practice in France, see the synod of Bourges 1031 can. 8 (Mansi xix. 504); for Germany, A. Hauck, *Kirchengeschichte Deutschlands* iii (Leipzig, 1896), 567–8. The law of Justinian was probably the basis for decrees at Pavia in 1022 and the oath imposed on the Milanese clergy in 1057.

riages after ordination, it was an important step towards the norm of a wholly celibate priesthood.[33]

The ideal way of securing the liberation of the clergy from secular dependence and family ties was to bring them into communities living under rule, and we saw in the previous chapter how the reforming popes were enthusiastic advocates of the regular canons. Nicholas II, Alexander II, Gregory VII, and Urban II all had close links with the movement, and the council of 1059 made the promotion of the common life part of the official programme, at least in the moderate form that canons were commanded to live in community, but simply urged to accept the apostolic ideal of poverty as to their own possessions.[34] The implementation of this programme took some decades, and even then it did little for the large numbers of country churches, where it would scarcely have been possible to form a clerical community. It is hard to find any indication that much thought was given to this problem, perhaps because in Italy the baptismal churches or *pievi* still exercised supervision over the rural chapels, and the Roman Church tended to take this pattern as a model. The attack on clerical marriage and promotion of houses of canons could never have been a viable reform for the large dioceses of northern Europe, where the common life movement created many communities of regular canons but had little impact on the village clergy as a whole.

Another important element of reform was the control of the appointment of bishops. The principle governing this was defined in a text of Leo I: 'Reason does not allow them to be counted among bishops who are not elected by the clergy nor requested by the people nor consecrated by the bishops with the approval of the metropolitan.'[35] The exact meaning of these broadly defined requirements was unclear. The normal procedure in the eleventh century involved a discussion or *tractatio* in the presence of the lay ruler followed by the giving of the pastoral staff, reception by the

---

[33] There is a canon ascribed to the First Lateran Council (1123) ordering that the partners of such a marriage should be disjoined, *disiungi*, but the text is of doubtful authenticity, and in any case may only be a repetition of the demand for separation. The more stringent rule was first formulated at the council of Pisa in 1135.

[34] *Vigilantia universalis* 4 ed. Schieffer, 220.

[35] *Epistola ad Rusticum* (PL 67.288B). Other texts commonly quoted in the eleventh century were Celestine I, 'Nullus invitis datur episcopus' (PL 67.276D) and Leo I, 'qui praefuturus est omnibus, ab omnibus eligatur' (PL 54.634A).

clergy and people of the diocese, and consecration by the archbishop. Dangers began when one of these constituent parts, usually the ruler, ignored the rest and sought to impose its own candidate by force. It was not easy to devise a system which would prevent this, and when Leo IX at Reims decreed that 'no one shall be promoted to ecclesiastical office without the election of clergy and people', he probably intended simply to exclude the cruder sort of intrusion, such as that which had caused a long schism in the archbishopric of Besançon.[36] In 1058 Humbert's *Adversus Simoniacos* for the first time interpreted the canon law as prohibiting lay investiture. Earlier popes, he wrote, had commanded that

by the judgement of the metropolitan the election of the clergy shall be confirmed, and by the consent of the prince the petition of the laity shall be likewise. Nevertheless the sacred canons are being rejected and the whole Christian religion confounded because these things are done backwards . . . For the secular power comes first in electing and confirming, and then whether they like it or not there follows the consent of the clergy and people and finally the judgement of the metropolitan.[37]

We do not know of any other expression of reservations about lay investiture in papal circles in the 1060s. The decree of Nicholas II that 'no clerk or priest should in any way accept a church from laymen, whether freely or for payment' has been interpreted as a prohibition of lay investiture, but it was certainly not applied in that sense.[38] Alexander II, as we saw in a previous section, resisted the cruder forms of lay dictation in the appointment of bishops, and there are signs in a privilege to the archbishop of Salzburg in 1070 and in his support for Atto at Milan in 1072 that he was moving towards the promotion of free election, but he never to our knowledge expressed any opposition to lay investiture. When, early in his pontificate, Gregory VII consulted the cardinals he received the reply that royal

[36] Mansi xix.741. A variant reading of this text is 'episcopal election shall lie in the common consent of the clergy and people of the vacant diocese': U.-R. Blumenthal, 'Ein neuer Text für das Reimser Konzil Leos IX (1049)', *DAEM* 32 (1976) 36. It is quite likely that Leo, legislating at a synod in France, had in mind the situation there, and not in the empire.

[37] Humbert, *Adversus Simoniacos*, iii.6 (MGH LdL i.205).

[38] *Vigilantia universalis*, 6, ed. Schieffer, 222. Unhappily we have only the title, and it is conceivable the text referred to local churches and not bishoprics. See G. Borino, 'L'investitura laica dal decreto di Nicolo al decreto di Gregorio VII', *S. Greg.* 5 (1956), 349–59. The papal election decree, which placed the conduct of the proceedings in the hands of the cardinal-bishops and left the German king with a vague traditional honour, showed an attitude unfavourable to lay influence in elections but is not directly relevant to the customary investiture of bishops.

investiture 'was the usage of the church and considered as legal, although it rested on no authority'.[39]

The basis of action of the reformers was the authority of the Roman Church. Their thought rested on papal teaching in past centuries, and the Tusculan popes before them had at times made claims to general authority. But important elements were new, and above all the primacy of Rome was taught with more warmth and vehemence than ever before. Peter Damian formulated the doctrine that all other churches have founders, but Christ alone founded the Roman Church.[40] It may already have meant to him what it certainly did a generation later, namely that St Peter had appointed the patriarchs of the east and the bishops of the west. In Rome, according to Leo IX and his contemporaries, all churches could find their mother, their head, and their hinge (*cardo*). The title 'universal', which Gregory I had explicitly refused to use, was now advanced officially.[41] Rome was the judge of the catholicity of all other churches.[42] The new status of the apostolic see was reflected in the emergence of a new term, apparently first used by Clement II in 1047: papacy, *papatus*. Constructed on the analogy of bishopric, *episcopatus*, it expressed the idea that there existed a rank or order higher than that of bishop.

The hope was that in a reformed papacy the prince of the apostles, St Peter, himself could manifest his power. Peter Damian, who expressed so much of the new ideology, was keenly aware of this potential source of energy for the renewal of the church: 'How great is the privilege of the Roman Church to preserve the rule of canonical equity and justice, and how great is its force in enforcing the discipline of the ecclesiastical order, can only be clearly understood by those engaged in ecclesiastical business.'[43] To define the apostolic authority of Rome, it was necessary to go back to the canon law and the documents of the early centuries. Leo IX drew at length on the Donation of Constantine when he expounded the

---

[39] Hugh of Flavigny, *Chronicon*, ii (MGH SS VIII 411–12).

[40] Peter Damian, *Disceptatio Synodalis* (MGH LdL i.78). The idea was based on the Isidorian decretals, esp. pseudo-Anacletus: 'This holy Roman Church received the primacy, not from the apostles, but from the Lord our Saviour himself' (Gratian, *Decr.* D. XXII, c. 2(73)).

[41] Synod of Reims 1049 (Mansi xix.738) and papal election decree 1059 (MGH Leges IV Const I. no. 382 p. 539).

[42] See Peter Damian in PL 144.241A and the bull of 1054 to the patriarch of Constantinople (PL 143.1004C). The origins of this idea are discussed in J. J. Ryan, *Saint Peter Damiani and his canonical Sources* (Toronto, 1956), no. 145.

[43] Peter Damian, PL 145.89B.

nature of Roman authority to Michael Cerularius, patriarch of Constantinople; and Hildebrand asked Peter Damian before 1059 to compile a collection of texts on the prerogatives of the apostolic see. The irony was that most of the material which was being used, although of this they had no conception, was the product of ninth-century forgery, and they were thus reconstructing, not the apostolic age, but a church order designed for polemical purposes by the imagination of a Carolingian author. At this early stage, however, there was no close definition of the legal rights which the pope might exercise over other churches, and in fact much of the exposition of papal theory is to be found in Leo IX's correspondence with Constantinople and other eastern churches. In practice the authority of the Roman Church was beginning to impinge intermittently upon the other western churches in such matters as the disputed appointment of bishops, and papal legates were visiting France and Spain in particular. Even by 1061 there had been serious tension with the archbishops of Germany. Nevertheless, such episodes were rare. The time when popes would seek to exercise any sort of general administrative supervision over Latin Christendom was still remote, but some important steps in that direction were to be taken in the pontificate of Gregory VII.

5

THE DISCORD OF EMPIRE AND
PAPACY 1073–1099

i. *Gregory VII*

Immediately after the death of Alexander II a tumultuous election took place at Rome on 22 April 1073. The new pope was Archdeacon Hildebrand, who had long been a powerful influence at the Lateran palace and who now took the title Gregory VII. The proceedings were irregular, for the 1059 decree was totally disregarded: there was no preliminary discussion among the cardinal-bishops, and no consultation of the German court, nor indeed any other acknowledgement of the due honour which the decree had vaguely reserved to the emperor. The questionable character of the election was to figure among the many charges which Gregory's enemies would direct against him.

He was recognized by contemporaries as one of those rare personalities who can make or mar a world: 'the Christian people is divided into two, with some saying that he is good and others calling him an imposter and a false monk and an anti-Christian'.[1] He had been called, he believed, to care for the cause of righteousness, *iusticia*, and there were almost no limits to the extent of his responsibility. He was deeply impressed by the mass of evil which confronted him in the world, and one of his favourite quotations was Philippians 2: 21: 'they all look after their own interests, not those of Jesus Christ'. He saw those who afflicted the church as 'members of Antichrist' and therefore signs of the approaching end of the world, although it is hard to be sure how literally he intended this language to be understood.[2] Against the ranks of iniquity he devoted himself to fighting God's war, a war which was not only a metaphor, for he showed no hesitation in using force against the unrighteous. His

---

[1] Wido of Ferrara, *De Scismate Hildebrandi*, i.2 (MGH LdL i.535).
[2] For the evidence see K. J. Benz, 'Eschatologisches Gedankengut bei Gregor VII', *ZKg* 97 (1986), 1–35.

enemies were threatened with punishment in this life as well as in the life to come, and in the crisis of 1080 Gregory prophesied that if Henry IV 'has not repented before the feast of St Peter he will be dead or deposed. If this does not happen you ought not to believe me any more'.[3]

Gregory's vision of the world as a place where great forces of good and evil were contending underlies his whole conduct of the papal office. He believed that all men were committed to the struggle, and repeatedly quoted a text of Jeremiah: '*Cursed is he who keeps back his sword from bloodshed*, that is the word of preaching from the rebuke of fleshly men.'[4] This sense of urgent involvement led Gregory to support unreservedly those whom he saw as friends of God and the Roman Church, and moderates were alienated by his association with men of violence such as Erlembald and by his choice of intransigent legates. His urgency was connected with his conviction, unique in its intensity among all the popes of the period, of his identification with St Peter. He believed that Peter and Paul had summoned him to headship in the Roman Church: 'I have not chosen you, but you have chosen me, and imposed upon me the most heavy weight of your church.' He was empowered to address others on their behalf: 'blessed Peter answers by me'.[5] Obedience to the commands of the apostolic see became, for him, increasingly the test of righteousness and even of catholic belief.

Gregory shared the conviction of the reformers as a whole that it was their duty to restore the perfection of the apostolic church. Like them, he looked for models in the New Testament, canon law, and monastic tradition. He was prepared on occasions to compromise, but was at heart a man who wanted to sweep away accepted practices which obstructed the path of righteousness. It was perhaps Gregory who introduced the famous remark: 'if by chance you are in opposition to a custom, it must be observed that the Lord said, "I am the truth and the life". He did not say, "I am the custom", but "the truth".'[6] Accordingly, there was a new urgency in his reference to

---

[3] Bonizo, *Liber ad amicum*, ix (MGH LdL i.616). The correct date is almost certainly 1080 rather than 1076.

[4] Reg. I. 15 (23). The text is from Jer. 48: 10, the interpretation from the *Regula Pastoralis* of Gregory the Great, and the text occurs more than ten times in the register.

[5] See Reg. VII. 14a (483); IV.2 (293); I. 10, 13, 42 (17, 22, 65); and VIII.21 (561).

[6] The words probably originated with Tertullian and were cited by other Fathers. They were quoted by Urban II to Count Robert of Flanders in 1092 (ep. 70. PL 151.356C) but also occur in another letter perhaps by Gregory himself. See Greg. VII *Extrav.* 67 (151) and G. B. Ladner, 'Two Gregorian Letters', *S. Greg.* 5 (1956), esp. 225–35.

canon law, and he actively encouraged the production of collections. Inevitably, Gregory shared the same distorted idea of the early church as did his associates. Many of the texts to which he attached most importance were forgeries from the Carolingian period, and his idea of the apostolic age was an amalgam of history, legend, and misunderstanding. There was also a further distorting element in Gregory's vision of the ancient traditions. His concern to enforce the laws of the church was so pressing that when he encountered resistance he responded by taking the matter under his immediate supervision. He listened to a small group of favourite advisers, which included his faithful supporters Countesses Beatrice and Matilda of the house of Tuscany. Even within the Roman Church, the cardinals found that policy was decided without consultation, and their discontent turned to open rebellion in 1084. In his dealings with the provinces Gregory worked through the ranks of his own confidants, who were appointed to an office of a new kind, as resident legates for long periods. The sole precedent for this arrangement was the legateship in Spain of Cardinal Hugh Candidus under Alexander II. Notable among these appointments were Bishop Hugh of Die, subsequently archbishop of Lyon, in Gaul from about 1075; Bishop Amatus of Oléron in southern Gaul and Spain in 1077; Bishop Altmann of Passau in Germany in 1080; Bishop Anselm II of Lucca in Lombardy in 1081; and Abbot Richard of St Victor, Marseille, in Spain in 1079. The powers entrusted to such legates were great, and they had an almost vice-regal status, exercising a wide range of papal powers of intervention, in some cases for a period of years.

Contemporaries and modern historians have disagreed about the long-term intention of this policy. Of the increasing initiative displayed by the Roman Church there is no doubt, but it is questionable whether Gregory was seeking a permanent change in the constitution of the western church. The difficulty in assessing his design is expressed in the summary of the powers of the apostolic see inserted in his register. This document, the so-called *Dictatus Pape*, made some very large claims, to which it will be necessary to return in detail later. It is a crucial text in the interpretation of Gregory's policy, and something must therefore be said about the technical problems involved in its interpretation. *Dictatus Pape* is not strictly a title but a rubric, occasionally used elsewhere in the register and apparently meaning that the pope dictated the particular item himself. It is found among the letters for the spring of 1075, but the text is undated and there are reasons for thinking that the earlier years of the register were written up as a block.[7] We cannot therefore say with confidence whether the document was designed as a papal response to the conflict with the German archbishops or monarchy, or whether it was a broad policy statement to clarify Gregory's future actions. The majority view of historians has been that it consists of headings for a small collection of canons defining the authority of the papacy. Some scholars, however, have taken precisely the opposite view: this arbitrary collection of claims was composed precisely because it was not possible for Gregory to find a basis for his actions in traditional canon law. It was thus an expression of his 'contempt for antiquity' of which some historians have written. There is no ready solution to this dispute. The case for seeing the *Dictatus Pape* as an interpretation of canon law rests on the similarity between its claims and those made by later 'Gregorian' canonical collections, notably that of Cardinal Deusdedit, and these resemblances seem to me convincing. Undoubtedly, its emphases were very different from those of the older collections, but it was probably intended to reinterpret the canonical tradition, not to supersede it. The actual character of the claims suggests that its main purpose was not to provide a blueprint for papal absolutism, but to define the emergency powers inherent in the Roman see to enable it to take action for the reform of the church.

In all probability, Gregory himself would not have admitted to a wish to deprive bishops and metropolitans of their authority. On the contrary, he hoped to liberate them from subservience to lay rulers; he aimed at giving back to metropolitans a real power of supervising episcopal elections; and from time to time he cited many of the standard canonical texts about the dignity of bishops. He had no machinery for centralizing their powers in his own hands, and the permanent legates, who had very varied commissions, could not have functioned as a replacement for the normal constitution. The threat to the traditional position of the bishops did not arise from a conscious project for centralization but from Gregory's sense of urgency in pressing the reform of the clergy, which led him to

---

[7] There is a further question whether Reg. Vat. 2 is the original working register from the papal writing-office, or whether it is a collection made subsequently. The nature of the *Dictatus Pape* is however not affected by this uncertainty. Perhaps spring 1076 is the more likely date. We do not know that Gregory composed the sentences; the existence of very similar texts in other manuscripts suggest that he did not.

intervene repeatedly in the ordinary course of ecclesiastical discipline. This drew him into conflict with some of the great regional powers in the western church, and consequently into alliance with dissatisfied groups. He supported the extreme policies of Erlembald at Milan, and at Bamberg, Constance, and elsewhere welcomed the charges made by dissidents against their bishops. The metropolitans with whom he came into conflict were often not corrupt, but were champions of an older order. At Reims the removal of Archbishop Manasses was more the result of his defence of his rights than of a record of simony. In England Gregory succeeded in alienating the devout and influential Archbishop Lanfranc of Canterbury, who grew impatient at the demands made on him to visit Rome, and who eventually lapsed into neutrality in the papal schism. Even given the assumption that Gregory's interventions were essentially emergency measures, conservatives were right to be worried: subsequent events were to show that it was easier for the papacy to assume authority than to restore it once regional powers had lost the directing initiative. It was a series of interventions of this type which provoked collisions with archbishops and princes in many parts of Europe, and above all with the German government under Henry IV.

ii. *The Breach with the Empire*

The confrontation between Gregory VII and Henry IV is one of the episodes of medieval history which has entered into popular awareness, and in Germany 'Canossa' has more than once become a political slogan. In recent years, some historians have suggested that the drama of these events has led to their receiving too exclusive a treatment, and that it would be preferable to displace our attention towards the spiritual aspects of Gregory's work. The fact remains, however, that Gregory was 'less a man of far-reaching ideas than of decisive action'.[8] The collision with the empire is the most important example of his determination to implement the policy of the papal reformers, even at a cost which would have seemed unthinkable a few years before, and it was to have a profound effect on the papacy and on the structure of the church.

The first stage was one of conflict with the archbishops. Between

---

[8] R. Schieffer, 'Gregor VII. Ein Versuch über die historische Grösse', *HJb* 97 (1978), 106. A different approach is represented by G. Fornasari, 'Dal nuovo su Gregorio VII?', *Studi Medieval* iii.24 (1983), 315–53.

1073 and 1075 the decrees of Roman synods against simony and clerical concubinage were circulated with instructions to have them published locally, and as a result there were uproars of clergy in centres such as Passau and Erfurt, as there were also at Paris. Gregory was bitterly disappointed by the attitude of some bishops. In face of clerical opposition, Archbishop Siegfried of Mainz moderated the decrees (as did Lanfranc in England), and when Gregory sent his legates to publish them Liemar of Bremen, who was no friend of simony, objected angrily to their activity. He described Gregory as a dangerous man, who ordered bishops about as if they were his bailiffs.[9] Gregory showed no inclination to compromise in face of this opposition. He summoned several bishops to Rome to answer accusations, and in July 1075, after many delays, he pronounced the final deposition of Hermann of Bamberg for simony. It was an innovation to intervene to such an extent in the provinces of metropolitans, and still more so to hear complaints of subordinates against their bishop.[10] In a letter of 11 January 1075 Gregory made plain his intention to counter the disobedience of bishops by resorting to innovations, 'for it seems to us far better to re-establish divine justice by means of new counsels than to allow the souls of men to perish along with the laws which they have neglected'.[11] What to the pope was the declaration of a state of emergency appeared to the German bishops as the subversion of traditional order. By 1076 the German prelates had reached the verge of withdrawing their obedience, because Gregory had surrendered 'the control of ecclesiastical affairs to the ravening fury of the mob'— a reference to his appeal to laymen not to attend the masses of married or simoniac priests.

At this point the relation of pope and bishops became entangled with a quarrel between pope and king. The estrangement which had taken place at the end of Alexander's pontificate over Milan was suddenly healed when, in the summer of 1073, Henry IV was faced with a major rebellion in Saxony. Unwilling to fight on two fronts, Henry wrote an abject apology for his simony in a letter the like of

[9] It is not in fact clear that Lanfranc's relatively conservative legislation was in any way influenced by Gregory. See M. Brett, 'The Canons of the First Lateran Council in English Manuscripts', *ICMCL* 6, 13–28.

[10] Peter Damian had already defended this procedure in ep. I.12 (PL 144.215–6). The power was stated in *Dictatus Pape* 24 (Reg. II. 55a (207)): 'Quod illius precepto et licentia subiectis liceat accusare.'

[11] Letter to south German princes, Reg. II.45 (184). It is uncertain whether the reforming decrees which provoked the archbishops' hostility were issued in 1074 or 1075.

which, wrote the gratified pope, 'we do not recall that he or his predecessors ever sent to Roman pontiffs'. [12] The letter inaugurated a period of two years of relative friendship. When in 1075 the relations between the two powers reached crisis point the background was a new papal policy towards the election and investiture of bishops (to which we shall return shortly); but the occasion was Milan. A renewed outbreak of violence by the *Patarini* in March led to the burning down of the cathedral, and then to a conservative reaction in which Erlembald was killed and the *Patarini* greatly weakened. The now dominant conservatives asked Henry to end the troubles by setting aside both claimants and investing a new archbishop. Henry at first hesitated; but when, in alliance with the south German princes, he heavily defeated the Saxons in June 1075, he resolved to take the initiative in Italy. He therefore nominated the young Milanese deacon Tedald as archbishop. Gregory reacted sharply in a letter of 8 December 1075, which ended with a full-blooded assertion of Henry's duty to God and St Peter, but what did the damage was probably a verbal message accompanying the letter, threatening that if Henry did not behave as a faithful son of the church he would be excommunicated and deposed. [13] Henry's exaggerated response has to be explained by his concern for his royal dignity: given his assumptions about his God-given power, Gregory's message must have sounded blasphemous, and the idea of withdrawing his allegiance from Gregory, and thus annulling in advance any sentence of excommunication, would have been attractive. There were also other parties pressing him to take action, including the aggrieved German bishops and Gregory's opponents at Rome, whence Cardinal Hugh Candidus had travelled north to co-ordinate action against the pope. A synod of German bishops assembled at Worms on 24 January 1076, and there they issued a letter to complain about the discord which 'brother Hildebrand' had caused and of his disorderly election. The bishops therefore withdrew their recognition of him, and Henry as *patricius* invited the Romans to depose him. It was a drastic action, widely publicized by the issue of

[12] Reg. I.25 (42) to Erlembald, 27 Sept. 1073. Henry's letter is Reg. I.29a. We do not know whether it was Henry's own iniative—a sort of preview of Canossa—or whether he was coerced into writing it by Rudolf of Suabia and the southern princes, who were mediating between the Saxons and the king, and whose support was crucial to Henry.

[13] Reg. III.10 (263–7) (the date in the register, 8 Jan. 1076, must be a copyist's error); Bernold, *Chronicon* (MGH SS V.432). Was the threat of excommunication, if indeed it existed, the sanction expressed in the investiture decree of spring 1075? In that case investiture, while not in itself the main issue, played a crucial part in the outbreak of hostility.

propaganda versions of the letters. Brother Hildebrand was in no way overawed, and at the Lent synod of 1076 he withdrew from Henry the government of Germany and Italy and excommunicated him.[14] In this unparalleled exchange of outrages Henry appeared to public opinion as the aggressor. Some of the bishops had been coerced into joining in the sentence at Worms, and these quickly made their peace with the pope. Still worse, Duke Rudolf of Suabia and the southern princes were alienated, and the Saxons given an opportunity to resume their opposition. The situation was perilous for Henry, but his enemies were far from united. We are not quite clear about Gregory's objectives in the summer of 1076, but he may have been looking for Henry's submission followed by a council at which the pope could judge the affairs of the German church and kingdom. Within the German opposition, there were differing policies: one group, led by the Saxons, had given up all hope of a settlement with Henry and was pressing for his removal. Others (including several bishops) were primarily concerned to secure a reconciliation between king and pope. When the princes met at Tribur on 16 October 1076, the conflicting demands rapidly became obvious. The result was a compromise. Henry was required to swear obedience to Gregory and to revoke the sentence of Worms. The princes also swore no longer to recognize Henry if he did not obtain absolution within a year of his excommunication, and to meet at Augsburg in Gregory's presence early in 1077. It was a notable humiliation for the king, but the plan was a ramshackle one which involved a number of uncertainties, and which in the event was to enable Henry to bring off his coup at Canossa, which transformed the situation.

Gregory set out for the meeting, but the deadline was not realistic and the princes had no means of escorting the pope across Lombardy, where the strongly imperialist bishops were powerful. Late in January the pope reached Countess Matilda's castle at Canossa, and there Henry arrived to ask for absolution. His pleas were supported by Matilda and by his godfather, Abbot Hugh of Cluny, and after being obliged to wait for three days in the garb of a penitent he was absolved on 28 January 1077. The one condition of absolution was that Henry promised to meet the pope and the princes and to do justice according to Gregory's decision. The arguments about the significance of Canossa began immediately and

[14] Reg. III.6* (253–4).

have continued ever since. From Henry's point of view the three-day penance may have been perceived as a further humiliation, following the one he had suffered at Tribur, and it certainly seemed so to some contemporaries; and he had been obliged to promise to accept the decision of the forthcoming council. On the other hand, it was not unprecedented for kings to do public penance; his policy at Worms had already been abandoned under the pressure of the princes, and so he lost nothing further by his reconciliation with Gregory; he had obtained absolution in the time demanded of him, and had opened the way to winning back the moderates whom he had alienated the previous year. Gregory's policy was still fixed upon the goal of a council. He had secured no specific assurances, not even about Milan, and had failed to make clear whether Henry could now be regarded as legitimately king or not. Without the assembly of pope and princes to judge Henry the pope's policy made no sense.

It may well be that both sides hoped to find in Canossa a genuine reconciliation, for a complete breach between empire and papacy was a new and disquieting possibility. If that was their aim, they had reckoned without their supporters. The Lombard bishops refused to withdraw their hostility against Gregory and insisted on negotiations being abandoned, thus making the journey to Germany effectively impossible. There, the opposition met at Forchheim on 13 March 1077, refused to delay until the pope's arrival, and elected Rudolf of Suabia as king in Henry's place. The country was now in civil war, and Gregory acknowledged with distress that the dispute 'has grown to a most severe conflict and almost to the division of the whole country'.[15] Rudolf's ecclesiastical policy was ostentatiously Gregorian in character and he was supported by the papal legates, Cardinal-deacon Bernard and Abbot Bernard of St Victor, Marseille, as well as by many leading prelates, including Archbishops Siegfried of Mainz and Gebhard of Salzburg, and Bishops Adalbero of Würzburg and Altmann of Passau. The new ecclesiastical policy had a good deal to offer the southern princes. Their impact on the appointment of bishops had hitherto been fairly slight, for royal control and the power of the bishops at court had prevented the local nobility from acquiring the sort of influence which was relatively common in France. The Gregorian party broke away from the old system: none of its nominees had served in the royal chapel and many were monks, some of them belonging to the families of the southern

[15] Reg. IV.25 (339) and V.7 (356), 9 June and 30 Sept. 1077.

nobility. The pope continued to strive to establish a tribunal to judge
the dispute, but in the disorder this was impossible. Rudolf's
authority was rapidly reduced to Saxony and a small part of Suabia,
and several Gregorian bishops had to take refuge in Saxony. As
Henry's military position improved he became more intransigent,
and by the beginning of 1080 Gregory had abandoned all hope of a
council or of any other form of settlement with Henry.

At Easter, 7 March 1080, Gregory pronounced his sentence at
Rome. Henry was condemned for impeding the assembly and
ruining the churches of Germany. He was deprived of his royal
power and SS Peter and Paul were asked to implement the
sentence.[16] Gregory prophesied that the king would be deposed
within a short time. But in 1080 the position was not as favourable as
in 1076. Even the moderates were growing impatient with Gregory.
Egilbert, archbishop-elect of Trier, refused him the name of
Christian, 'because he does not have the sign of Christ, which is
peace and charity'.[17] Even so, they were still hesitant, and the
decisive act of schism was carried out by an assembly consisting
mainly of the intransigent Lombard bishops. At Brixen on 25 June
1080 it was declared that Gregory had been wrongly elected, and in
his place Archbishop Wibert of Ravenna was elected as Clement III.
Clement was no mere creature of Henry IV. He was a capable man, a
sincere opponent of simony, and a defender of papal rights. He was
cast in a more conservative mould than the radical Gregory: his
propaganda was received sympathetically by the episcopate, by a
number of kingdoms, and even by part of the governing group
within the Roman Church, but he made no attempt to appeal to
broad strata of the population or to the armed force of the laity other
than to the traditional protection of the emperor. The western
church was in a state of formal schism between the representatives of
conflicting ideals.

The critical year 1075 was also the point at which Gregory
abandoned the tolerance of lay interference in episcopal appointments. In his first year or two he had accepted investiture with ring
and staff and the participation of rulers in the nomination of bishops.
From 1075, his correspondence shows a clear determination to
restrict their intervention and to have the election supervised by the
pope or metropolitan. At the Lent synod of 1080 the new procedure,
which the pope was already following, was clearly spelled out:

[16] Reg. VII. 14a (486–7).
[17] P. Jaffé, *Bibliotheca rerum Germanicarum*, 5 (Berlin, 1869), no. 61, p. 128.

When on the death of the pastor of any church another has to be canonically substituted, at the instance of a bishop who shall be sent as visitor by the apostolic or the metropolitan see, the clergy and people without any secular desire, fear or favour shall, with the consent of the apostolic see or their metropolitan, elect for themselves a pastor according to God.[18]

The prohibition of lay investiture is clearly associated with this new policy. It was reported that in 1075 the pope 'openly forbade the king henceforth to have any right in giving bishoprics and removed all lay persons from the investiture of churches'. It is probable that the issue of this decree arose from his conviction that the existing situation was intolerable, for he said himself that it was 'a truth necessary for salvation'.[19] If this decree of 1075 was intended to be generally applicable, it seems that Gregory regarded it as negotiable, for in the crucial letter of December 1075 he offered to discuss outstanding problems with Henry, and no attempt was made to implement the policy in England until after 1100. Whatever modifications Gregory might have contemplated, his decree in the Roman synod of autumn 1078 gave the subject maximum publicity, commenting that such investitures 'are, as we know, being made in many regions by lay persons against the statutes of the holy Fathers and as a result many disorders are arising in the church from which the Christian religion is afflicted'.[20] Since episcopal churches had no defined electorate and no experience in using this new liberty, the withdrawal of royal influence tended to place appointments in the hands of the pope or metropolitan. It is unfortunately impossible to be sure what connection there was between the adoption of this new policy and the breach with Henry IV. Certainly the traditional name for the whole dispute, 'the investiture contest', is wrong in implying that investitures were the primary issue. In the minds of the controversialists there was a much wider range of questions, and it was only after 1100 that the royal right of investiture became the central, and intractable, issue.

After the final breach in 1080 the position of the Gregorians

---

[18] Reg. VII.14a (482). Letters to Montefeltre and Gubbio, 2 Jan. 1075 (Reg. II.41 (178)); Chartres. 4 Mar. 1077 (Reg. IV.14 (318) and V.11 (364)); Aquileia 17 Sept. 1077 (Reg. V.5–5 (352–5)). See also the letter to Philip I on 27 Dec. 1080 (Reg. VIII.20 (543)).

[19] Reg. III.10 (266). The decree of 1075 is mentioned only in Arnulf, *Gesta Archiep. Mediolan.* iv.7 (MGH SS VIII.27). It has been doubted whether the decree was issued at all in spring 1075, but the early synods of Gregory are poorly recorded and references in Dec. 1075 and in May 1077 confirm its existence. The evidence is excellently presented by R. Schieffer, *Die Entstehung des päpstlichen Investiturverbots für den deutschen König* (Stuttgart, 1981), 114–52, although the conclusions are controversial.

[20] Reg. VI 5b (403).

continued to decline. Their party soon suffered a severe setback with the death of King Rudolf of his wounds in the battle of the river Elster on 15 October 1080. He was buried under an inscription which proclaimed him as a martyr: 'Where his men triumphed, he fell, war's sacred victim. For him, death was life. He died for the church.'[21] His successor as anti-king was a feeble figure, and Henry was left free to bring pressure upon Gregory in Italy. The pope tried to buttress his power with a new alliance. Almost since his accession he had been on terms of bitter hostility with Robert Guiscard, who was now the most powerful Norman leader, but in June 1080 they were reconciled and Guiscard did homage to the pope at Ceprano. The new policy brought little immediate benefit to the pope, for the Norman leader's ambition was set on a campaign against the Byzantine empire. The resistance of the citizens of Rome and of Gregory's other supporters was sufficient to oblige Henry to spend three years in building up his position in northern and central Italy, but his pressure opened a gap between Gregory and a large, discontented group within the Roman Church. The tension was already visible in May 1082, when the Roman clergy refused to allow the treasures of their churches to be employed for the defence of the city, and early in 1084 thirteen cardinals, much of the staff of the Lateran palace, and even the papal chancellor changed their allegiance to Clement III. On Easter Day 1084 Henry, along with his empress Bertha, received the imperial crown at the hands of Clement III. In practice neither of the contending popes could hold Rome. In May a Norman army under Robert Guiscard arrived, forced Clement to retreat, and ravaged the city from the Lateran to the Colosseum. Gregory in turn was obliged to withdraw with the Normans, and spent the last year of his life under their protection.

His determination to continue the battle was expressed in an encyclical letter late in 1084: 'Ever since by God's providence mother church set me upon the apostolic throne . . . my greatest concern has been that holy church, the bride of Christ, our lady and mother, should return to her true glory and stand free, chaste and catholic.'[22] Odo, cardinal-bishop of Ostia, was sent to rally the Gregorians in Germany early in 1085. They were still established in parts of Saxony and the south, but the imperialist cause was in the ascendant. Most of the cathedral cities were controlled by bishops who recognized

---

[21] Inscription on tomb slab of Rudolf of Suabia in Merseburg cathedral.
[22] Greg. VII, *Extrav.* 54 (133).

Clement III, and Henry was able to hold a magnificent council at Mainz in May. When Gregory died at Salerno on 25 May 1085 he was an apparent failure. He had alienated from his cause many who shared his desire for a renewal of the church, had failed to defeat Henry and had stirred up a civil war which did grave harm to the German churches. He left Rome, the city he loved, in disorder, damaged at the hands of his Norman allies. The western church was in schism and the once fruitful co-operation between papacy and empire replaced by suspicion and hostility. It was an inheritance which in the long term deeply marked the character of the papacy.

iii. *The Revival of the Gregorian Papacy 1085–1099*

The years 1085–99 were the high point in the fortunes of the imperialist pope, Clement III. He was at least precariously in control of Rome, where seventeen of the twenty-eight cardinal-priests are known to have been firmly on his side, although only one of the cardinal-bishops was; and he commanded the allegiance of much of the empire, Denmark, Poland, and Hungary, while England had taken up a position of neutrality. Throughout this region he appears to have been a responsible pope, conscious of papal rights, with a policy of moderate reform, and not obviously inferior to his main rival Urban II. Meanwhile the Gregorians were unable to produce an agreed successor. The Normans pressed for Abbot Desiderius of Monte Cassino, but he was fiercely opposed by some of Gregory's closest associates as being dangerously soft towards the emperor. Eventually Odo, cardinal-bishop of Ostia, gave way and consecrated Desiderius as Victor III on 9 May 1087. His pontificate was short, for he died on 16 September, expressing a wish for Odo to succeed him. The election took place at Terracina on 12 March 1088, and Odo took the title Urban II. He was a Frenchman, educated at Reims, where St Bruno had been one of his masters. By about 1074 Odo had become grand prior of Cluny, and probably in 1080 he was appointed cardinal-bishop of Ostia. In that capacity he was closely associated with Gregory VII, and was unkindly described as Gregory's personal slave, *pedisequus*. Urban himself issued a resounding declaration of his loyalty to the principles of Gregory.[23] He was, nevertheless, far from being an unimaginative imitator. He was more prepared than his predecessor to permit exceptions when

---

[23] Ep. 1 (PL 151.284A) to the bishops of Germany.

they seemed advantageous, as when he allowed former supporters of Clement III to continue in their orders and benefices. Concessions of this kind were criticized by hard-line Gregorians, but they were facilitated by the growing clarity of the theory of dispensation. It was not a new idea that the pope could dispense from the requirements of the canons, but Urban set out more precisely the right to suspend the rules of law.[24] Urban also relied far more than Gregory on consultation. There is little in his letters about a personal relationship with St Peter, and he spoke not as a man with a private illumination, but as head of the Roman Church after discussion with its clergy. He had learned the lesson of 1084 and associated the cardinals in the conduct of business. As the unquestioned choice of his party, who had inherited and not caused the schism, he was in a position of moral authority.

These advantages had to be set against his initial political weakness. The Normans in southern Italy were convulsed by civil war, and although they offered the valuable facility of a territory in which Urban could reside and hold synods, they were in no position to give support in central Italy. Within the empire Urban depended on two main circles of supporters, both of them held together no doubt in part by political interest, but more obviously by spiritual and ideological aims and by the more subtle ties of friendship and proximity. They have been called 'friendship circles', and in the broader medieval sense of *amicitia*, participation in a common cause which extended beyond simple personal affection, this is a good name for them. One of them had its centre in the court of Countess Matilda of Tuscany. Her enormous estates, including both fiefs and allods under her direct ownership, extended from Verona as far as Lucca, and therefore dominated a large area of northern Italy and controlled several of the most important roads between Germany and Rome. For much of our period the Matildine lands were to play an important part in papal-imperial relations. She was not only one of the most powerful landowners in Europe, but a cultivated woman with a considerable library, who corresponded with influential church leaders and was an important patron of learning and of her family monasteries of Santa Apollonia, Canossa, and San Benedetto,

---

[24] On the earlier history of the idea, see S. Kuttner, 'Urban II and the Doctrine of Interpretation', *S. Grat*, 15 (1972), 53–85. Urban's theory of dispensation is stated in a fragment of a letter to Bishop Peter of Terracina 1088 (S. Loewenfeld, *Epistolae Pontificum Romanorum ineditae* (Leipzig, 1885), no. 121, p. 59), and it was discussed by Bernold of Constance in his *De Excommunicatis Vitandis*.

Polirone. She may have encouraged the work of Irnerius on Roman law at Bologna, and she certainly asked John of Mantua to write his commentary on the *Song of Songs* in 1081–3—an early example of a theme which was to be very fashionable in the following century. The great canonist Anselm II of Lucca was a friend. There were times when Matilda almost appeared as the conscience of the Gregorian party. It was to Matilda that the dissidents appealed in the crisis over Desiderius' election, and she was resolute in her loyalty to Urban.

The nexus of his supporters in southern Germany was more complex. At its heart was the school at Constance. The collection of canonistic material there had apparently been begun by the master, Bernard, before his move to Hildesheim in 1072, and was continued by his talented successor Bernold. As a result of the presence of an unusually fine collection of texts, Bernold was able to make an important contribution to the polemic which began in the late 1070s. Another element was supplied by the work of the enthusiastic Gregorian Abbot William of Hirsau, the monks of whose foundations became notable for their propaganda. Archbishop Gebhard of Salzburg (1060–88) and Bishop Altmann of Passau (1065–91) were associated with the group, and through them the houses of canons centred on Rottenbuch (founded *c.*1070). The protection of the lay nobility greatly increased the importance of this ecclesiastical circle. After the death of Rudolf of Suabia the south German princes, now under the leadership of Berthold of Zähringen and Welf of Bavaria, had continued to be opponents of Henry IV, founders of monasteries and champions of the new ideals of church reform. They also had a personal connection with Urban, who as Cardinal-bishop Odo of Ostia had been sent as legate to rally the German opposition in 1085. The personal links which held together these south German Gregorians may be seen in the able Bishop Gebhard of Constance, who effectively became the leader of the south German Gregorians. Gebhard was a former monk of Hirsau and brother of Berthold of Zähringen and had been consecrated by Odo of Ostia. The loyalty of this connection was the more important because the Gregorian position had wholly crumbled in Saxony, where the nobility had been reconciled with Henry IV in 1088.

For Urban the central religious problem in his dealings with the empire was the schism with Clement III. Gregorian extremists argued that all who had dealings with excommunicates were themselves excommunicate, a rigorist view which unchurched most of Germany, since all the subjects of a schismatic bishop would fall under the ban. Urban did not question their position and saw himself faced by 'a contagion of general evil', but he prescribed light penances for those who had sinned out of ignorance or fear.[25] Although in principle he adopted the rigorist view about clergy ordained by simoniacs, he was willing to dispense them completely on occasions, as at Milan in 1088 where clergy ordained by Archbishop Tedald were allowed to remain in office unless they were personally guilty of simony. Urban has sometimes been seen as a moderate, a Cluniac rather than a Gregorian pope, but his attitude to the schism suggests that he was a rigorist who was prepared to use his discretion freely for the general good of the church. In a society which lived, not by general laws but by franchises and privileges, this appeared a legitimate attitude to a complex situation.

One of Urban's persistent aims was to strengthen his party in Lombardy. In 1088 he secured the submission of Archbishop Anselm of Milan, thus ending the long alliance between the church there and the emperor. From 1090 onwards the presence of Henry IV in Lombardy strengthened the imperialists, but early in 1093 his son Conrad deserted him and was crowned king of the Lombards by Archbishop Anselm at Milan. During the next three years, while Germany remained faithful to Henry, he was himself isolated in Lombardy by his enemies' control of the Alpine passes. Urban took advantage of this turn of fortune by moving from southern Italy, and met Conrad at Cremona, where the young king ceremonially performed the service of a groom to the pope and swore fidelity to the Roman Church.[26] In March 1095 Urban was able to hold the first general assembly of his supporters in the synod of Piacenza. A variety of matters was considered: the relations of Philip I of France with Bertrada of Montfort, the complaints of Praxedis, second wife of Henry IV, against his alleged maltreatment, and the appeal for help of an embassy from the Byzantine Emperor Alexius I. The main business however was the re-enactment of Gregory VII's legislation. Simony was condemned, and it was decreed that anything by way of holy orders or ecclesiastical rights obtained by money was 'unlawful

---

[25] Ep. 15 to Bishop Gebhard of Constance (PL 151.297–8), Apr. 1089.

[26] MGH Leges IV Const. I, no. 394 (p. 564) and Bernold, *Chronicon* s.a. 1095 (MGH SS V.463). Urban was following the proposal by Gregory VII in 1081 that the successor of Rudolf of Suabia should take an oath of obedience to him (Reg. IX.3 (575–6)). Probably in both cases an oath of spiritual fidelity, not of vassalage, was intended.

(*irritum*) . . . and never possessing any force'.[27] A final ruling was given that the orders of Clementist clergy were only to be recognized in special circumstances. Urban followed his triumph in Lombardy by making the first papal visit to France since Leo IX's brief appearance at Reims in 1049. The high point of the French tour was the great assembly at Clermont in November 1095, in the presence of about thirteen archbishops, eighty-two bishops and innumerable abbots. The most famous episode was the proclamation of the First Crusade, which must be considered later, and in addition Philip I was excommunicated because of the Bertrada affair. The bulk of the assembly's business however was the provision of a comprehensive body of reforming regulations. They included a broad condemnation of the lay ownership of churches and the prohibition not merely of investiture, but also of the performance of homage by bishops and priests to lay rulers. This was a natural extension of the investiture decree, and was probably directed against the solemn hand-oath rather than all forms of sworn allegiance. The canons of Clermont were an impressive expression of the policy which Urban had inherited, and which he summarized in words taken from Gregory's last encyclical: 'the church shall be catholic, chaste and free: catholic in the faith and fellowship of the saints, chaste from all contagion of evil, and free from all secular power.'[28]

Meanwhile other churches were being persuaded by judicious concessions to support Urban. About 1095 King Eric III of Denmark quarrelled with Liemar, the strongly Clementist archbishop of Hamburg, and undertook a dramatic journey to Italy to meet Urban. He secured a promise of independence from Hamburg, which led to the foundation of the archbishopric of Lund in 1103. England under William Rufus acknowledged Urban in 1095 in return for a promise to send no legates there without the king's permission. In 1098 Urban's loyal supporter Count Roger of Sicily received an even larger grant, the position of perpetual legate within his territories. In the course of ten years Urban had immensely strengthened the position of the Gregorian line of popes. At the time of his death on 29 July 1099 he was still not secure in Rome, but he had succeeded in laying the foundations of the triumph of Gregorian ideas of church government over those of Clement III, the representative of the older

---

[27] C. of Piacenza c.2 (MGH Leges IV Const. I no. 393, p. 561). There is no evidence that the investiture decrees were renewed at Piacenza, but Urban assumed in his negotiations with Conrad that they were still in force.

[28] R. Somerville, *The Councils of Urban II: Decreta Claromontensia* (Amsterdam, 1972), 90.

pattern of imperial protection of the church. The programme enunciated by Gregory had been brought to much wider acceptance. This, however, was not the whole of his achievement. He began to build the papal administration on new foundations, and he turned papal policy away from its concentration on the empire. Certainly there were precedents for this, for the involvement with southern Italy and Spain dated back to the time before Gregory VII. Urban developed these relationships and added to them a much closer link with the French church, which reflected his own French origins, and he originated the great enterprise of the First Crusade. By 1099, although Clement III survived him, Urban had visibly made himself the head of the greater part of Christendom.[29]

iv. *The War of Ideas (1076–1099)*

We are told that when Gregory VII proclaimed the excommunication of Henry IV the chair of St Peter was miraculously split in two, thus showing how the church was divided against itself. To Manegold of Lautembach it seemed that St Augustine's two cities, the earthly and the heavenly, had separated themselves 'so that there is scarcely a city in the whole Latin world which does not have defenders of both sides in this affair'. There was schism, too, in the minds of men:

Often I reflect how many people there are in support of each party, and how they are as well advanced in learning as men can be, and most serious-minded, and how it would therefore be wrong to believe that one side or the other is deliberately acting in defiance of justice or of the peace of the church. So I find that my own small judgement begins to waver, and I am covered with a dark cloud of doubt.[30]

Some important European churchmen, in face of this unprecedented hostility between pope and emperor, withdrew into neutrality. Lanfranc of Canterbury seems to have done so, and Abbot Hugh of Cluny was less than whole-hearted in his advocacy of Gregory's cause. Cluny commemorated the emperors in its prayers, and Hugh made attempts to reconcile the two parties; indeed, his biographer regarded it as one of the most striking instances of his notable work

---

[29] The First Crusade and the development of the papal administration are discussed in subsequent chapters.

[30] Manegold, *Contra Wolfelmum*, 23, ed. W. Hartmann, MGH Quellen 8, 102; Wido of Osnabrück (MGH LdL i.462).

as a mediator. One aspect of Gregory's actions which was widely resented was the involvement of the laity and even of the lower classes in the controversy. Henry's supporters complained angrily of seditious preaching:

> But the lord pope says, 'He is perverse, to whom you gave your oath. He is wicked, and a perjuror, and a criminal; you do not owe fidelity to him.' This indeed, my lord pope, we read in your writings, this indeed we have heard carried throughout the world by your evangelists.[31]

The material for this appeal to public opinion, in the market place and the pulpit, was provided by a pamphlet war for which there had been no real parallel since the ancient world.

The controversy is recorded in the register of Gregory VII, in collections of canons, and in polemical treatises. The register of Gregory's letters is a unique survival before Innocent III. They were major vehicles of propaganda, and the most crucial of them, such as the second letter to Bishop Hermann of Metz in 1081, were widely known in Germany. 'The first decade of the history of the polemical literature of the Investiture Contest is dominated by the circulation of the letters of Gregory VII.'[32] At first the papal reformers had not found it necessary to produce lawbooks of their own, but used traditional collections supplemented by the more recent work of Burchard. When the controversy raised questions which these collections were not designed to answer, thematically arranged extracts began to be produced in the Roman Church itself, in the circle of Countess Matilda and by the canonists of the Constance group. They all bore the marks of the crisis but by no means all reflected Gregory's own position in detail. The one most closely associated with him was the *Dictatus Pape* entered in his register in 1075 or 1076. At about the same time a collection called *Diversorum Patrum Sententie* (or alternatively the Collection in 74 Titles) was beginning to circulate in Italy and Germany, although its origin is not clear.[33] The great period of new collections was the 1080s, when there came from within the Roman Church the *Capitulare* of Cardinal Atto and (in 1087) the work of Cardinal Deusdedit, each reflecting the ideas of different groups among the cardinals. The

---

[31] Wenrich of Trier 6 (LdL i.294).

[32] I. S. Robinson, 'The Dissemination of the Letters of Pope Gregory VII', *JEH* 34 (1983), 193.

[33] Once regarded as the earliest of the reformers' collections, it is no longer clear that it reflects Gregorian thinking, and there is no firm evidence for its existence before 1070.

collection of Bishop Anselm of Lucca, prepared in Lombardy about
1083, was specially important in disseminating Gregorian thinking
since it supplied much material to the subsequent authoritative books
of Ivo of Chartres and Gratian. This canonistic activity was viewed
with distaste by imperialists, who continued to use the traditional
books in place of the systematic excerpts preferred by the Gregorians
and complained about the 'fraudulent compilations' produced by
Hildebrand, Urban, Anselm of Lucca, and Deusdedit.[34] There were,
finally, many occasional works of controversy. These include
histories written in a strongly partisan spirit, such as the *Ad
Heinricum IV Imperatorem* by the imperialist Benzo of Alba and the
Liber ad Amicum by the papalist Bonizo of Sutri. Pamphlets were
written to answer other pamphlets, as when Wenrich of Trier's
criticism of papalist arguments was in turn answered by Manegold of
Lautembach's *Liber ad Gebhardum*.

Gregory and his followers based their case on the responsibility of
the Roman Church, and it is somewhat surprising that they did not
offer much theological reflection about the source of its authority.
Gregory's longest statement of this is therefore worth quoting:

You all know in your charity . . . that care and *anxiety for all the churches* (II
Cor.xi.28) have been committed to us, little as we are, by God. For the lord
Jesus Christ appointed St Peter the chief of the apostles, giving him *the keys
of the kingdom of heaven* and the power of binding and loosing in heaven and
on earth. Upon him he also *built his church* (Mt.xvi.18–9), commending to
him his sheep to be fed (Jn.xxi.17). From that time onwards that supremacy
and power passed down through St Peter to all those who receive his see, or
who shall receive it until the end of the world, by divine privilege and
hereditary right. As a successor to that see it is incumbent on us, as a
necessity which we cannot avoid, to bring help to all the oppressed and to
fight even to the death if necessary with *the sword of the* holy *spirit, which is
the word of God* (Eph.vi.17), in defence of righteousness against the enemies
of God until they be converted.[35]

In this passage Gregory was drawing from both Paul and Peter, the
founders of the Roman Church, while defining its relations with
Peter in decidedly contemporary terms as 'privilege and hereditary
right'. Since the pope shared the supreme apostolate of Peter he had a
right to intervene in other dioceses. At this point the papal theorists

---

[34] Cardinal Beno in MGH LdL ii.416. On the approach of the two sides to collections of
canons, see the interesting article by H. Fuhrmann, 'Pseudoisidor, Otto von Ostia und der
Zitatenkampf von Gerstungen', *ZSSRGkA* 99 (1982) 52–69.
[35] Greg. VII, *Reg.* IX.35 (622–3).

were precise. The *Dictatus Pape*, which has sometimes (wrongly) been regarded as a definition of Gregory's reforming programme, was primarily a list of the special prerogatives of the Roman Church. The pope has power, even without a synod, to depose and restore bishops (clauses iii, xxv). He may translate them, unite bishoprics and ordain clergy of any church (vii, xiii–xv). All 'greater causes' ought to be referred to the apostolic see (xxi). The pope has power to depose the guilty even in their absence (v). Legates, even of inferior rank, take precedence over bishops (iv). Accusations can be heard from subjects against their superiors (xxiv). All of these rights are supported by material in the collections of Deusdedit and Anselm and most of them had some precedent in earlier canon law. Yet the claims of the *Dictatus Pape* represent a slanted version of canonical tradition. They contravened many of the normal legal principles: that judgement should be given in synod, that inferiors might not accuse superiors, and that the accused should not be condemned in his absence. These principles protected established rights, and the claiming of power to overrule them was a declaration of a state of emergency.

Gregory was bringing into question all the accepted principles of obedience to traditional authority, and it was only one stage further to the assumption that Rome has absolute supremacy over all churches: 'the Roman Church has obtained the primacy from Christ'. [36] Rome alone was guaranteed from error: 'the Roman Church has never erred nor, by Scripture's authority, will ever err'. [37] It was even held that the Roman Church could decide which canons were authentic: 'Peter is the goldsmith's stone, which tests the gold, whether it be true or false.' [38] This was a large shift of emphasis, but it was limited by the expectation that the pope would be guided by canon law, into which, in fact, not much material was incorporated from the eleventh-century popes. Gregory provided a balanced statement of the position: 'it is customary for the holy and apostolic see to tolerate many things on mature consideration, but never in its decrees and constitutions to depart from the concord of canonical tradition'. [39] These claims nevertheless gave the pope a

[36] W. von Glanvell, *Die Kanonessammlung des Kardinals Deusdedit* (Paderborn, 1905), prol. p. 6.

[37] *Dictatus Pape* 22 (Reg. II 55a (207)). The reference is to Luke 22: 31–2.

[38] Atto, *Capitulare*, prol. (A. Mai, *Scriptorum Veterum Nova Collectio* VI (Rome, 1832): *Trium Attonum Scripta*, 61.) See also J. J. Ryan, *S. Peter Damiani and his Canonical Sources* (Toronto, 1956), nos. 18–20, pp. 29–30.

[39] Greg. VII, *Reg.* II. 50 (191), 24 Jan. 1075.

quasi-royal position within the church, and Bernold of Constance made the analogy precise: 'Each bishop does not have so great a power over the flock committed to him as does the apostolic prelate, for although the latter has divided his cure into particular bishoprics he has in no way deprived himself of his universal and principal power; just as the king has not diminished his royal power although he has divided his kingdom among different dukes, counts and judges.'[40] This authority was expressed in the language of imperial splendour. Alphanus of Salerno addressed Peter,

> Caesar and consul both, command the Roman senate.
> Behold, the world beneath the sky obeys your word.[41]

The pope now acquired, along with his bishop's mitre, a crown or *regnum*. We first hear of a papal coronation in 1059 and from 1075 we hear of ceremonies in which, as at a royal crown-wearing, the pope appeared with crown and imperial robe. Gregory claimed that only the pope could use imperial insignia and boasted that the law of the Roman pontiffs has prevailed in more lands than the law of the Roman emperors.[42]

This is a claim to papal monarchy, but it is hard to determine its exact meaning. One significance was the eschatological one. The New Testament had taught that the Roman empire was the force which restrained the coming of Antichrist, but since 1076 the empire had fallen away and this function devolved upon the pope.[43] The imperial claim also expressed the duty of the pope as described in the commission to Jeremiah: 'see, I have set you this day over nations and over kingdoms, to pluck up and to break down, to destroy and to overthrow, to build and to plant' (Jer. 1: 10). Gregory's duty to strive for righteousness, *iusticia*, is expressed frequently in his works, and he believed that the papal office had been established for this very purpose. Primarily, this meant the liberty and purity of the church; it was only rarely that he intervened in a case of secular oppression where the interests of the church were not involved. To Gregory's

---

[40] Bernold, *Apologeticus*, 23 (MGH LdL ii.88).

[41] J. Szövérffy, 'Der Investiturstreit und die Petrus-Hymnen des Mittelalters', *DAEM* 13 (1957), 230.

[42] *Dictatus Pape* 8 (Reg. II.55a (204) and Reg. II.75 (237)). There were even charters issued in Burgundy in 1082–3 *domino nostro papa Gregorio Romanum imperium tenente* (C. U. J. Chevalier, *Cartulaire de l'abbaye de S. Bernard de Romans* (Romans, 1898), nos. 186, 188), but this is very unusual.

[43] 2 Thess. 2: 6–7 was usually understood as referring to the restraint of Antichrist by the Roman Empire, as by John of Mantua just after 1080: B. Bischoff and B. Taeger, *In Cantica canticorum . . . ad comitissam Matildam*, Spicilegium Friburgense 19 (1973), 64–5.

eyes the sphere of religion was incomparably more important than secular affairs. They differed as do sun and moon, gold and lead, and even a simple exorcist, since he can command demons, is mightier than a king.[44] Gregory continued to see *regnum* and *sacerdotium* as both founded by God, and by the monarchical symbols he was claiming not a right to worldly authority, but a power better than that of the world.

It was his conviction that in a critical situation it was his duty to recall secular rulers to the way of righteousness, which caused the final breach. The *Dictatus Pape* asserted that the pope can depose emperors and absolve subjects from their allegiance, and these powers were actually exercised against Henry IV.[45] The precedents were argued in the second letter to Hermann of Metz, and were on the whole poor. Gregory also sought to involve the whole Christian people in his apostolic struggle against evil. Just as he appealed for lay support against simoniac clergy, so he enlisted sympathetic princes, such as those of southern Germany, into a *militia* of St Peter, as he described it, bound to serve the Roman Church even against 'non-catholic' monarchs, including their own lord Henry IV. Gregory even proposed in 1081 that the next German king should take such an oath of obedience.[46] To conservatives the attack upon the position of Henry IV was an outrage:

It is a new thing, and unheard of in all previous ages, that popes should wish so easily to divide up the kingdoms of the peoples; to wipe out in a sudden conspiracy the name of kings, which was found from the beginning of the world and afterwards established by God; to change the anointed of the Lord like common villeins whenever they please; to order them to come down from the throne of their fathers and, if they do not do so at once, curse them with an anathema.[47]

Conversely Bonizo held that 'the dispute between the pope and the king arose from nowhere else but this, that . . . without judgement he attempted to drive from his see the lord pope of the elder Rome.'[48] The controversialists, while aware of other causes, saw the heart of the matter in the deposition of pope by king and king by pope.

---

[44] Reg. IV.2 (296); IX.37 (631); VIII.21 (555–6). In each instance Gregory specifically based his claim on patristic authority.

[45] *Dictatus Pape*, 12, 27 (Reg. II.55a (204, 208)).

[46] Reg. IX.3 (575–6).

[47] Wenrich of Trier 4 (MGH LdL i.289).

[48] Bonizo, *Liber ad Amicum*, ix (LdL i.617–8).

It has even been argued, notably by Karl Jordan, that Gregory extended his programme of enlisting the princes in the service of St Peter into an ambitious project to reduce the lay rulers generally to feudal obedience. The Normans in southern Italy and the kingdom of Aragon were already bound by an oath and a commitment to pay tribute; Gregory also asserted a similar supremacy in England, and proposed an oath to the Roman Church for future German kings; and there are indications that he regarded the crowns of Denmark and Poland also as bound to the suzerainty of Rome. The existence of this element in his policy is undeniable, but we should not interpret it as a grand design to secure the recognition of papal overlordship throughout the west. For Gregory, obedience to the see of Rome was the supreme test of righteousness, and in the ethos of the period it was natural to express this obligation in terms which we would regard as feudal. It certainly did not imply that he had any intention to direct the political affairs of the country in question, and as a matter of fact, he was not even very active in advancing these 'feudal' claims: in southern Italy and Aragon they had been inherited from the past, and in England he was asserting what he believed to be an established right of the Roman Church, based either on Alexander II's supposed grant of the kingdom to William the Conqueror or on the payment of Peter's Pence. Ties of this sort indicated Gregory's concern to enlist the princes on the side of the angels against the simoniac Henry and expressed their obligation to assist the Roman Church.

The outburst of pamphlet controversy has been seen as the foundation of the western tradition of political thought. There is truth in this, but the argument about political theory was confined within some specific issues: was Gregory properly elected? Was Henry a just king, and if he was not had his subjects a right to rebel? Had the pope a right to dispense them from their allegiance? Had the lay power a right to invest bishops and receive their homage? The answer to these questions had to be found in canon law, and canonists were prominent in the controversy. When canon law did not provide a clear solution, appeal was made to historical precedent. The Gregorians believed themselves to be restorers of a right order which had existed in the past, and zealously assembled instances of popes who had excommunicated rulers and been parties to their deposition. Between the two sides there remained a large agreeement about political principles. Almost all the imperialists rested their arguments on the traditional two-power theory:

Whoever carefully considers this disposition of God according to the divine ordinance of the two powers must certainly conclude that in this a great iniquity has been worked by Hildebrand and his bishops, who, although they ought not on account of the episcopal dignity to interfere in any secular affairs, usurped the institution of royal dignity against the ordinance of God and against the custom and discipline of the church.[49]

The Gregorians similarly defended themselves in the name of the separation of powers: 'Let kings have what belongs to kings, and priests have what belongs to priests. So shall they keep peace towards each other and respect one another in the one body of Christ.'[50] These words of Paschal II in 1105 were faithful to the tradition of Gregory VII, who in 1074 wrote to William the Conqueror that it was the king's duty 'to take counsel for the churches committed to you to defend'; and who even contemplated the possibility of leaving the Roman Church in the care of Henry IV 'that you may preserve it as your holy mother and defend its honour'.[51] The controversy over particular issues took place on the common ground of the two-power theory.

There were some exceptions. Benzo of Alba made unlimited claims for the royal office, reminding the bishops that they were appointed 'by the hands of the king, not by the hands of Foldebrand'.[52] Among the Gregorians the two-power theory was under strain. In the second letter to Hermann of Metz Gregory ascribed the creation of kingship to the sins of men. Even if he was referring to non-catholic or pagan kings, the argument represented a debasement of the monarchical dignity which cannot easily be paralleled. Good Christians were seen as having more right to a royal title than bad kings.[53] The old idea of Christian order had not been formally rejected, but on occasions the Gregorian party was eroding it by the way the Petrine primacy was now affirmed.

[49] *Liber de Unitate*, ii.15 (MGH LdL ii.226).
[50] Paschal II, ep. 164 (PL 163.175B).
[51] Reg. II.31 (167) and I.70 (101).
[52] Benzo, *Ad Heinricum Imperatorem*, iv prol. (MGH SS XI.634).
[53] Reg. VIII.21 (557), with reference to the royal priesthood of 1 Pet. 2: 9.

6

GREEKS AND SARACENS

i. *The Situation in the Mediterranean World*

The Cluniac monk Raoul Glaber had already before the middle of the eleventh century commented that the preaching of the Gospel in the north of Europe had enjoyed much greater success than in the south.[1] The Roman Church recognized the need to assist in the organization of the new churches in Scandinavia and to send missions to the remoter regions, but its attention was more occupied by the Mediterranean. There the frontier between the Latin, Greek, and Moslem worlds lay close to Rome itself, and the popes were conscious of the Christian churches which were subject to Moslem rule in Sicily, Spain, and north Africa. The arrival at Rome of the reforming party, with its policy based on a new ideology and implemented by northerners who were unfamiliar with the attitudes of the south, would in any event have led to changes. The desire for a new policy is illustrated by Leo IX's appointment of Humbert as archbishop of Sicily in 1050. Perhaps he was chosen because he knew some Greek, but it was a paper appointment, significant only as a declaration of intent. As it happened, the new approach by Rome coincided with a new chapter in the centuries-old conflict of Islam and Christianity.

The most obvious feature in the new political situation was the expansion of the Byzantine empire under the Macedonian dynasty, a process which continued until the death of Basil II in 1025. Its frontiers were extended far into Syria, to the Danube, and into southern Italy, so that in 1050 they were wider than at any time since the rise of Islam. False modesty was never a Byzantine defect, and the consequence of this brilliant story of success was to confirm the impression that Constantinople was the centre of the civilized world. The contrast between the great eastern Christian empire and the Roman Church of the early part of the century, with its limited

[1] Raoul Glaber, *Historiae*, ii. 5 (PL 142.626C).

power and local interests, was vivid. By 1050, it was becoming blurred as Byzantium faced growing problems and the Roman Church reasserted its role of leadership, and the distance between image and reality was one of the reasons for the crisis of 1054. The Byzantine control of the eastern Mediterranean facilitated communications with the other patriarchates, Antioch, Jerusalem, and Alexandria, with which contact had been poor, and in particular made possible an enormous growth in western pilgrimage to Jerusalem, both through the Balkans and by sea. The Greek advance into southern Italy had included within the empire areas of Latin speech and practice and brought the frontier quite close to Rome itself. The changes in the eastern Mediterranean had been echoed, much more feebly, in the west also. There, the joint expedition of Pisa and Genoa to remove the Moslem bases from Sardinia in 1015–16 marked the end of the period of Saracen naval dominance, although it was a long time before the Christian fleets were strong enough to go seriously onto the offensive. In Spain a sustained Christian advance was beginning in the middle years of the century, and its first major chapter culminated in the fall of Toledo to Alfonso VI of Castile in 1085; but that is another story, reserved for a separate volume in this series. The growth of easier communications throughout the Mediterranean as a whole is illustrated by the correspondence of Patriarch Peter of Antioch with Leo IX, in which he lamented the long isolation of Rome from the eastern churches, and with Dominic of Grado, the head of the Venetian church, in 1052–3. Leo was also in touch with the remains of the once great church in north Africa, where he noted in 1053 that scarcely five bishoprics remained in a province in which once 205 bishops had met in council at Carthage.[2]

The source of later developments is primarily to be found in southern Italy. It was a meeting-place of three cultures, with Sicily dominated by the Moslems, a traditional Byzantine presence in the coastal regions on the mainland, and a Lombard population inland. This unstable region had been further disturbed by the extension of Byzantine power, and even more by the arrival of the Normans. By 1050, they were already regarded by Byzantium as a dangerous threat. Some areas of southern Italy were heavily Greek in culture, notably Calabria and the southern peninsula of Apulia, while elsewhere Greek officials and Greek bishops were governing a

[2] Letter of 17 Dec. 1053, PL 143.728A.

largely Latin population. The extent to which the church still existed in the island of Sicily is a matter of controversy. Norman chroniclers tell us of Christians who welcomed the arrival of the conquerors, but the signs are that the faith survived in restricted areas and primarily among a subject rural population. There is an indication that the direction of the Sicilian church had been transferred to Reggio on the mainland, although when the Normans captured Palermo they discovered a bishop there, 'timid and of Greek nationality'. We hear of only one other Greek bishop in Sicily, a certain James of no known see in 1103, and the supposition is that the Normans had arrived just in time to encounter the last ruins of the former hierarchy. Although some historians have been optimistic about the survival of Sicilian monasticism of an eremitical type, we hear much more of hermits migrating onto the mainland, and it is doubtful whether many survived on the island.

The Normans were to become the appointed agents of the Roman Church for the restoration of Latin Christianity, but the policy of the popes was for a long time delicately balanced between their need for Norman support and their apprehensions of Norman expansion into the neighbourhood of Rome. The definitive alliance of 1059 established the main lines of future policy, but there were many withdrawals from it, particularly under Gregory VII, who was in bitter conflict with the Norman leader, Robert Guiscard, from 1073 to 1080. But the Norman alliance had not yet been formed when the complex politics of southern Italy provided the occasion for the breach between Rome and Constantinople in 1054.

Over the centuries the Greek and Latin churches had been growing apart in customs and attitudes. The closer contact which was resumed in the mid-eleventh century did indeed include some attempts at active co-operation, but its effect was much more to reveal the distance between Rome and Constantinople. There were three issues. The first was the question of usages: the Latins used unleavened bread in the eucharist and observed different practices in fasting and in the observance of Lent, and western canon law forbade priests to live as married men. Both sides were quite capable of being tolerant about these customs, but considerations of high policy made their amicable discussion difficult. The reforming party at Rome, with its belief that Roman practices were apostolic practices and its determined attack on clerical marriage, found it hard to regard Greek customs as permissible divergences. The Byzantines saw uniformity in the main points of the liturgy as important, and their sense of grandeur made it hard for them to be sympathetic to the comparative barbarians of the west, while they had a political problem of their own in the need to secure conformity from the Armenians, who had been incorporated in the empire by Basil II and whose customs were in some way similar to those of the Latins. The second issue which had developed over a long period was the *filioque*. The western church had added the word to the creed to describe the Holy Spirit as 'proceeding from the Father *and the Son*'. The point of trinitarian doctrine which this expressed was a relatively arcane one. Latin theology had always stressed the equality of the three persons of Father, Son, and Holy Spirit and the closeness of their common bond of unity, while the Greeks sought the same unity in the Father as its source. The issue was made much more acute by the addition of the word to the Creed, for Byzantium regarded this as an ecumenical document which could only be changed, if at all, by a council of the whole church. The change had originated in western Europe outside Rome, which had been resistant to it for a long time. It was probably the inclusion of the *filioque* in the letter which Sergius IV had sent to Constantinople in 1009 which led the patriarch to withhold formal recognition of him; thereafter, no pope's name was included in the diptychs or formal prayer lists there. If this was a schism, it was a very technical one, but at least it recorded the existence of an unresolved issue.

In the light of the later history of Græco-Latin relations, the most significant issue was the claim to supremacy which the Roman Church was increasingly making in terms unacceptable to Constantinople. It can be discerned in the background of the particular disputes in the eleventh century, but surprisingly it rarely became overt. The concern of Greek theologians about the 'scandal' of papal claims was a future development.[3] The theology of Roman supremacy over other patriarchates was still undeveloped. Cardinal Deusdedit, good Gregorian as he was, insisted towards the end of the century on the concord which should exist between the ancient patriarchates in essential matters of faith and order, and when Leo IX wished to expound the privileges of the Roman Church he had to resort to huge quotations from the Donation of Constantine, which in effect gave them a secular and not a theological origin.

The quarrel with Constantinople began paradoxically with an

[3] See D. M. Nicol, 'The Papal Scandal', *SCH* 13 (1976), 141–68.

attempt at an alliance. Leo IX's interest in joint action against the Normans was eagerly echoed by the Byzantine Emperor Constantine IX and by the Lombard governor, Argyrus, whom he had just appointed to control southern Italy. Unhappily the patriarch, Michael Cerularius (1043–58), was a flamboyant politician, fiercely hostile to the Latins and to imperial policy and popular in the capital. The trouble started when the patriarch closed the churches observing the Latin rite in Constantinople, and when there arrived in the west a tract written by Archbishop Leo of Ochrida attacking the Latin use of unleavened bread and other practices. Westerners believed that Cerularius inspired, or even wrote, Leo's tract, and was engaged in a piece of unprovoked aggression against the Latins. The exact progress of the correspondence is difficult to chart, but it was fatally complicated by the defeat of Argyrus in February 1053 and the capture of Leo IX by the Normans at Civitate in June. Thereafter Cerularius was convinced that the pope was not in control of affairs, and that the western reaction was being manipulated by his own bitter enemy Argyrus and by a group of cardinals. On the western side, Humbert was certainly involved, perhaps both translating Greek letters and writing Latin ones, and he was little disposed towards compromise with Constantinople. The pope responded to the tract of Leo of Ochrida with the first letter to Michael Cerularius, asserting the authority of Rome (and therefore of its customs) in extremely firm terms, drawn largely from the supposed Donation of Constantine, a western forgery not known in the east. It is not clear that this hard-line letter was ever sent; it may have been held back because of the arrival of more amicable messages from the patriarch and the emperor. An embassy set off from Rome, consisting of Humbert, Frederick of Lorraine, and Archbishop Peter of Amalfi. We do not know its purpose, other than to carry the papal reply to these two letters. It may have been designed to restore good relations, or more specifically to renew the alliance against the Normans. Whatever the intention, the result was disastrous. The ambassadors were welcomed by the emperor and ignored by the patriarch, while an atmosphere of controversy and vituperation grew in the city. Finally on 16 July 1054 the legates entered St Sophia and laid on the altar a bull excommunicating Michael Cerularius, Leo of Ochrida, and all their followers. The document was full of wild charges against the Greeks, who were declared to be prozymite (leaven-using) heretics. At a synod at Constantinople on 24 July the events were rehearsed and the responsibility fixed upon the three irresponsible westerners and Argyrus, who was blamed for the contents of the letters which they brought with them.

The bizarre proceedings of 1054 came to be regarded as the starting-point of the definitive schism between the two great branches of the Christian church, and were symbolically revoked as a gesture of reconciliation by both pope and patriarch in 1965. To regard them in this light is a great oversimplification. The estrangement of Greeks and Latins was a process which began before the eleventh century and continued long after it. Soon after 1054 popes were again in touch with Constantinople, and it is clear that on the Greek side the condemnations were directed against four specific people, who were not treated as representing the Roman Church. It is less certain that Humbert regarded the excommunication as a personal one. The inclusion not only of Cerularius, but of all his followers, and the denunciation of the Greeks as prozymite heretics, does look like a condemnation of the whole Byzantine church until it should change its practices. The most important fact was that future popes did not assume that they were dealing with heretics or schismatics at Constantinople, and this prevents us from regarding it as the genuine date of the schism; but the action of a high-powered legation from the west in treating the Greeks as a whole as heretics, even if under great stress and in a highly complex situation, had to be regarded as a bad omen for future relations.

ii. *The Conquest of Sicily and Apulia*

The oath which Robert Guiscard took to Pope Nicholas II in 1059 to inaugurate the alliance between Normans and papacy was a remarkable one. Some of its terms were naturally addressed to meeting the immediate needs of the Roman Church, such as the protection of papal elections, but it was formed by a wider vision. The new vassal described himself as 'by the grace of God and St Peter duke of Apulia and Calabria and by their help future duke of Sicily'. He thus announced a programme of conquest of the Greek provinces and of Moslem Sicily. He also swore to the pope that 'I will put into your power all the churches which are in my dominion with their possessions and I will be their defender'.[4] It is unlikely that this was a promise to Latinize the churches there, since it does not apply

---

[4] J. Déer, *Das Papsttum und die süditalienischen Normanannenstaaten* (Göttingen, 1969), 17–18.

specifically to Greek churches. The policy of Latinization which he subsequently followed was inspired by Norman as well as papal interests, although there is no reason to suppose that the pope was uneasy about it, and in 1067 Alexander II commented on the task of Guiscard 'to build Latin monasteries in place of those of the Greeks'.[5]

The process of conquest proceeded rapidly on the mainland, assisted by the fact that the attention of Byzantium was distracted elsewhere, and a serious defence could only be provided at a few important places. By 1071, with the fall of Bari, the whole of the mainland was in Norman hands. In spite of deep divisions among the Moslems of Sicily, their resistance was more protracted. Count Roger, Guiscard's younger brother, secured Messina in 1061, but had great difficulty in maintaining himself in the island, and only did so by a victory over great odds at Cerami in 1063, with divine aid it was believed.[6] It was only when Guiscard was free to come to his assistance that a joint operation secured the conquest of Palermo in 1072 after a long siege, and the final surrender of the last Moslem strongholds took place as late as 1091. Historians have given very different accounts of the policy of the Norman conquerors. They have been seen in particular as creating, especially in Sicily itself, a multi-cultural society highly unusual in the intolerant medieval world. On the island Count Roger had relative freedom in shaping the new Christian settlement, for he was confronted by a Moslem establishment and a ruined Greek church. The mainland presented a different issue, for there Robert Guiscard, scourge of Byzantine emperors, ruled a land of mixed, but predominantly Greek, religious tradition. Here again, historians have varied in their views between a policy of imposing Latin men and manners as far as the situation permitted, and (alternatively) the creation of an amalgam, of 'Norman Byzantinism'. What were the attitudes of the first generation of conquerors, with whom we are now concerned?

The overall impact of Guiscard's policy on the mainland is one of strong Latinization. This is not necessarily a by-product of his anti-Byzantine foreign policy, but may well be a simple reflection of his belief in the superiority of Latin over Greek customs. It was his policy to found Latin monasteries. He completed the development of

---

[5] A. Pratesi, *Carte Latine di abbazie calabresi* (Vatican, 1958), no. 3, p. 5.

[6] Our account of the battle of Cerami depends almost wholly on the later description by William of Malaterra. He gave it great prominence, but may have exaggerated its importance.

Holy Trinity, Venosa, near Melfi (dedicated 1059). The second abbot, Berengar, built it up to a community of a hundred monks, and it received enormous endowments, many of them assets stripped from Greek monasteries. It was designed as the ducal foundation of the Hauteville family, and Guiscard himself was to be buried there. In the strongly Greek province of Calabria, he founded Sant'Eufemia (1062) and, in conjunction with his brother count Roger, Holy Trinity Mileto (1080). Great donations were bestowed on Monte Cassino and La Cava, often including Greek priories and even some major Greek monasteries such as St Peter, Taranto, given to Monte Cassino in 1080. The building up of these monastic empires was not solely a matter of enforcing Latin religious supremacy, but was a process of improving monastic organization by submitting small houses to the discipline of great abbeys. It is not surprising that most indications of serious decline were to be found among the Greek houses, including some large ones such as Santa Maria Roccella near Catanzaro, built soon after the Norman conquest but in disuse shortly after 1100. This picture of decline is not universal, but the few stories of persistence or growth in Basilian (Greek) monasticism were confined to strongly Greek regions. Except where there were large Greek populations, it was also the practice to appoint Latin bishops. The important archbishopric of Reggio was, after some resistance, firmly in the hands of a Latin bishop from 1086 at the latest. In the totally Greek town of Rossano in 1093 an attempt to intrude a Latin had to be abandoned in face of the opposition of the inhabitants. In solidly Greek areas, the Greek rite and Greek bishops survived for many centuries, but they are the exception, a compromise with reality on the part of a Latinizing government. On the island, the total collapse of the hierarchy left Count Roger a free hand to create a Latin episcopate. The first bishop at Palermo was Nicodemus, presumably the 'timid Greek' found by the Normans on their entry, but within the following twenty years a Latin hierarchy had been created at centres such as Troina (1080–1), Syracuse, Mazaro, Catania, and Agrigento (1086–8), almost entirely with bishops from France. Roger has often been credited with a revival of Greek monasticism in Sicily, and it is clear that he did found a number of Basilian houses in the last twenty years of the century. Ménager has argued strongly, however, that it is a mistake to see this as deliberate encouragement of Greek culture. What was happening was a move away from the mainland houses under the pressure of

Latinization there, a counter-migration from areas colonized originally by Sicilian hermits escaping from Moslem pressure. Count
Roger was doing no more than providing facilities for this
migration: the apparent 'Basilian renaissance' was always artificial,
and within a generation the new houses were on the verge of
collapse. It is certainly true that Roger was importing skilled Greek
administrators from Apulia to help in running Sicily, but that is a
different matter. In ecclesiastical policy, the evidence justifies us only
in finding vigorous Latinization on the mainland, combined with a
readiness in Sicily itself to accept the dissatisfied Basilians who were
impelled to move there.[7]

The Norman conquest of Apulia and Sicily was an important
precedent for the future, for it was much the most dramatic example
of the extension of the frontiers of Latin Christianity under papal
encouragement, and it was accompanied by propaganda about the
operations as being wars fought on God's behalf. The message is
strongly put in both the major chronicles of the Norman conquests,
by Amatus of Monte Cassino and William of Malaterra.[8] It is present
in the speech of Robert Guiscard: 'I wish to deliver the Christians and
Catholics, who are subjected to the servitude of the Saracens. My
great desire is to free them from their servitude and avenge the injury
done to God.'[9] The armies make their communion and receive
absolution before battle; at Cerami, we are told that St George
appeared on the field to fight for the Christians, who subsequently
received the gift of the banner of St Peter from Alexander II. Urban
II saw Roger as 'champion of the Christian faith'.[10] This did not, on
the other hand, mean that the Normans were active in the conversion
of the Sicilian Moslems, or were intended to be; when some of them
in the army at the siege of Capua in 1098 were moved by the sanctity
of Anselm of Canterbury to think of conversion, they dared not take
the step because of the hostility of Count Roger. In a real sense,
Roger was the refounder of the Sicilian church. Gregory VII and

---

[7] See especially L.-R. Ménager, 'La "byzantinisation" religieuse de l'Italie méridionale et la
politique monastique des Normands d'Italie', *RHE* 53 (1958), 747–74 and 54 (1959), 1–40.

[8] It must be noticed that William of Malaterra wrote after the First Crusade, and may have
been reading back its ideas into the conquest of Sicily. Amatus of Monte Cassino had finished
his chronicle by about 1085, although it only survives in a much later French translation.

[9] V. de Bartholomaeis (ed.), *Storia de' Normanni di Amato di Montecassino* (Rome, 1935),
v. 12 (234).

[10] Urban II, ep. 59, Mar. 1092 (PL 151.340C). For the expression of some reservations
about the 'crusading' character of the Norman conquests, see C. Erdmann, *The Origin of the
Idea of Crusade*, tr. and notes by M. W. Baldwin (Princeton, 1977), 134 n. 64.

Urban showed great confidence in him, and Urban (after attempting the appointment of a bishop as resident legate) recognized Roger himself as possessing legatine authority. The concession was a striking one, and reflects the position of Roger as a warrior who had restored to the church one of its lost provinces. With the exception of this special treatment of the office of legate, the ethos of the Norman conquests anticipates that of the First Crusade more closely than any other wars of the period.

iii. *The Rise of Christian Militarism*

One of the most striking features of our period is that it is the age of the crusades. To those who know the New Testament, they must be a surprising development. They are the more remarkable because the scholars of the time were well aware of the injunctions of Christ to seek peace and to forgive wrongs without seeking vengeance, and of the teaching of St Augustine which permitted Christian princes to use force to defend their rights and to protect the church, but only in strictly limited circumstances. In particular the principle that unbelievers may not be coerced into baptism was traditionally accepted and was widely known in this period. Collections of canon law did not give a great deal of space to the ethics of warfare, but such material as they included was heavily drawn from the Augustinian tradition. It is difficult to find in the collection of Anselm of Lucca any hint of a justification for the First Crusade which was to take place in the following decade. The impression that the church was committed on the side of peace is confirmed by the activity of bishops in promoting the Peace and Truce of God and by the prohibition of the carrying of arms by clergy, a canonical rule repeatedly stressed by reforming councils in the eleventh century. The assumption that participation in warfare was in itself an evil was widespread in ecclesiastical circles. Norman warriors were obliged to do penance after the battle of Hastings for those they had killed or injured there and Guibert of Nogent, commenting on the change produced by the preaching of the First Crusade, pointed out that in the past knights could only attain salvation by giving up their appointed way of life, that is by becoming monks. [11]

There was, however, a contrary tradition. The defence of Christendom against unbelievers had increasingly been seen as

[11] Guibert, *Gesta Dei per Francos*, i, RHC Occ. iv.124.

blessed by God. In the ninth century Popes Leo IV and John VIII gave assurances of forgiveness and eternal life to those who were killed in battle against the heathen, and such warriors were sometimes seen as martyrs for the faith. Epics or *chansons de geste* designed to entertain nobles and their knights centred largely on war against the Saracens, a theme as persistent as cowboys and Indians in early 'westerns'. Surviving versions of these *chansons* date from the twelfth century, but they were unquestionably in circulation before then, and it is reasonable to assume that from at least 1050 stories of the heroic deeds of Roland and William of Orange against Islam were widely known. Even within Europe, the clergy had been obliged to accept warfare as a fact. Blessings of arms can be found from the tenth century onwards, and it is probable that at the time of the conversion the priests of the new religion had taken over from the old the function of protecting weapons from evil magic by appropriate rituals. A further element had been added by the growth of the Peace of God movement itself. It may seem odd to use this as a benchmark in the rise of militarism, since its whole purpose was the restraint of violence, but it did contain features which pointed in another direction. The failure of the central authority to maintain order in large parts of Europe, and most notably in France, left bishops with no real alternative but to defend themselves, and the movement towards the militarization of bishops' households was very general in the eleventh century. It was said of Bishop Wulfstan of Worcester (1062–95), the last surviving Old English bishop, that he was obliged to fill his court with knights as the Norman king and bishops required.[12] The Peace of God movement was the point at which the bishops took the responsibility for public order which kings could no longer discharge, and at times they assembled peace militias from their own resources and those of their allies and directed them to the repression of evil-doers. True, most warriors were still seen as agents of evil, and the pun *militia—malitia* survived for a long time; but it had been recognized that they might also be engaged in the task of fighting for peace.

The arrival of the reforming party in control of the Roman Church was, in this as in so many respects, an important turning-point because 'the church reformers were the very men who stood for the idea of holy war and sought to put it into practice'.[13] Their

---

[12] R. R. Darlington (ed.), *The* Vita Wulfstani *of William of Malmesbury*, Camden Series iii.40 (1928), 55–6.
[13] Erdmann, *Idea of Crusade*, 143.

willingness to use force to maintain control in central Italy and to combat the enemies of the Roman Church is striking, and goes beyond a simple response to the exigencies of the situation. One contributory reason was probably the experience of the early reform popes in commanding their own armed forces as German bishops. The ecclesiastical contingents were a particularly important element in German armies, and Leo IX, who had already been engaged in expeditions in the service of Henry III as bishop of Toul, would not have found his Norman campaign as strange as some contemporaries did. There were also more fundamental reasons of ideology. The reformers assumed that they had a duty of leadership within Christendom. Far more than in the previous Peace of God movement, they were prepared to do what the lay power had left undone, and if necessary to challenge rulers who obstructed their reforms. Leadership of this type necessarily involved decisions about the use of force, which was so fundamental a part of the duties of government. A further reason was the profound conviction of the papal reformers that God was calling them to restore right order in Christian society. For clergy, this meant the ending of simony and a celibate life in community; for the aristocracy, it meant to put their swords at the disposal of God and the Roman Church. The devout warrior now stood beside the holy priest in the attainment of a church which would be free, catholic, and chaste: the first clear statement of the duties of the Christian knight is to be found in the extreme Gregorian Bonizo of Sutri.[14]

The first striking manifestation of the new papal militarism was the expedition of Leo IX against the Normans in 1053. Its aim was to defend the territories of the Roman Church and to protect the population against Norman savagery, and it was undertaken after an appeal to Henry III had failed to persuade the emperor to repress the Norman menace. The personal participation of the pope shocked some contemporaries, including Peter Damian, and Leo himself was worried about what he had done, especially after the disastrous defeat at Civitate. He was reassured, his biographer tells us, by a vision of the fallen in heaven, where they were placed in the ranks of the martyrs. Subsequent popes used force to secure their control of the Roman countryside, and the growing spirit of militarism may be seen in the practice of Alexander II in sending the banner of St Peter

---

[14] Bonizo, *Liber de Vita Christiana*, ed. E. Perels (Berlin, 1930), 248–9.

as a sign of approval of a campaign. It is true that there are some questions about the despatch of these banners, but it is likely that they were sent to Erlembald, the Patarine leader at Milan, in 1063, to Roger of Sicily in the same year, to the leaders of the Barbastro campaign in Spain in 1064, and to William of Normandy for his invasion of England in 1066. There are reasons for thinking that Hildebrand was the inspirer of this policy, which he continued as Gregory VII in orchestrating the opposition to Henry IV, encouraging armed resistance by the princes, and associating his sympathizers in the ranks of the 'militia of St Peter'. The phrase is very rare before Gregory, and the concept, a military fellowship of those who are sworn to implement papal policy, was totally new. Gregory was militarizing the traditional idea of the 'faithful', and seeing the *fideles*, not indeed as vassals, but as warriors in St Peter's service. Historians of the crusades have often noticed the way in which in the thirteenth century the idea was deflected for use in western Europe against the enemies of the Roman Church. This did indeed happen, as we shall see later, but in a sense it was a return to the origins of the movement, for the eleventh-century popes employed armed force against their European enemies before they directed it against the infidels elsewhere.

At the same time the idea that warfare should be undertaken in the service of God against the unbeliever was becoming more generally accepted. The Christian frontiers were under attack at various points throughout the century, and moreover almost all the territories of Islam had once been Christian, so that the western expeditions in Spain, Sicily, Syria, and even north Africa could be seen as lawful attempts to recover territory of which Christendom had been deprived by force. There had already been a period of vigorous activity in the early years of the century. The Venetian defence of Bari against Moslem attack in 1003 was said by the chronicler John the Deacon to have been undertaken 'not out of worldly fear but out of the fear of God'.[15] Much more remarkable was the response to the news that the Egyptian Caliph Hakim had ordered the destruction of the church of the Holy Sepulchre in 1009. A letter of Pope Sergius IV urged the coastal cities to assemble a fleet which might go to the rescue of the city, and offered a promise of forgiveness to all those who took part. If this letter is authentic, it is the first suggestion of an

[15] G. Monticolo (ed.), *Cronache veneziane*, Fonti per la Stona d' Italia 9 (1887), 166.

expedition to the east under papal direction.[16] Nearer to home, Benedict VIII supported the Pisan and Genoan attack on Saracen bases in Sardinia in 1015–16.

The continuous history of warfare against Islam in the Mediterranean began just after 1059. The Norman expansion in Sicily was an important part of it, and Alexander II's sponsorship of the expedition to Spain in 1064 spread the policy there; although the papal involvement in this campaign is in doubt, and in general Spanish historians have moved away from the older idea that 'holy war' was a tradition in the Spanish kingdoms, which provided a forcing-ground for the growth of crusading in the eleventh century. The Pisan raid on Palermo in 1063 was consciously undertaken in the service of Christendom, and the spoils were used to begin the magnificent new cathedral there. In 1087, Pisa attacked the great north African city of Mahdia, and a poem celebrated the triumph there as God's work. It is interesting to notice that the French were prominent in many of these expeditions and that almost all had a pilgrimage element somewhere in the background. Frenchmen were attracted to Spain by the shrine of St James at Compostella, and Normans to southern Italy by that of St Michael on Monte Gargano: while in 1087 the Pisans combined their voyage with a pilgrimage to Rome. In spite of the theoretical incompatibility of war and pilgrimage, since the pilgrim could not carry arms, the two things went closely together. By this time, moreover, events in the eastern Mediterranean had created a new area of concern for both warriors and pilgrims.

iv. *The First Crusade*

The transformation in the Middle East was the result of the Seljuk invasion. In the middle years of the eleventh century the defences which protected Persia from the nomadic peoples of Central Asia had collapsed, thus allowing the creation of a great Seljuk empire and also a large influx of nomads into the settled lands. At the battle of Manzikert in 1071 the Byzantine army was overwhelmed, and this defeat had two consequences for the Christian world. The most

---

[16] See text in H. Zimmermann, *Papsturkunden 869–1046* ii (Vienna, 1985), no. 445, pp. 845–8. The authenticity of the letter has been denied by A. Gieysztor, 'The Genesis of the Crusades: the Encyclical of Sergius IV', *Medievalia et Humanistica* 5 (1949), 3–23 and 6 (1950), 3–34. He regards it as a piece of propaganda designed for the First Crusade. It is certainly an odd letter, but I do not myself think that its peculiarities are removed by transporting them to 1095.

obvious was the loss of the Greek province of Anatolia (modern Turkey), where Turkish nomads took over the plateau, and a Seljuk prince established the sultanate of Rum, with its capital at Nicaea. The threat to the Byzantine empire was acute: Turkish forces were close to Constantinople, while armies of Pecheneg nomads from the Russian steppes were raiding the Balkans, and Bari, the last possession in southern Italy, had been lost to the Normans. There was also a less direct consequence. The Seljuk invasion led to the establishment in Syria of a series of Turkish principalities, with Jerusalem itself in dispute between the Turks and the Fatimite government of Egypt. We know little about the route for western pilgrims to Jerusalem, but the signs are that with the collapse of Byzantium and the disorders in Syria, it had become much more dangerous. Even by 1064–5 a large German pilgrimage had been attacked and had to defend itself with improvised arms. Apart from the persecution by Caliph Hakim in 1009, the Fatimite rulers had been tolerant towards Christians. The nomads from the steppes were less so, and the breakdown of order would by itself have been enough to make the journey more hazardous.

Manzikert brought a quick attempt at a response from the west. The Byzantine Emperor Michael VII appealed to both Gregory VII and Robert Guiscard for assistance. The negotiation was delicate because the two were in bitter discord, and what emerged from Gregory's side was a proposal in 1074 to lead an expedition himself which would first defeat Guiscard and then go to the assistance of the Byzantines. We know of the project only from a few letters, for it barely seems to have existed except on paper. It is interesting that Gregory briefly mentioned his intention that the expedition should continue to Jerusalem, perhaps (although this is not quite clear) as a pilgrimage after the relief of Byzantium.[17] Michael's negotiations with Robert Guiscard were more successful and led to a marriage alliance; but the consequences were tragic, because Michael was deposed in 1078 by Nicephorus Boteniates. By 1081 Nicephorus also had fallen, and the new emperor, Alexius I Comnenus, was confronted by a large-scale Norman invasion of Greece with the blessing of Gregory VII. The first western attempts to intervene had originated with the crisis of 1071, but had misfired disastrously.

It is more difficult to discern why the First Crusade was

<hr>

[17] Greg. VII, *Reg.* II.31 (166).

proclaimed in 1095. Modern historians have been inclined to see it as designed for the relief of Byzantium, and there are some arguments for this view. Alexius I (1081–1118) certainly made several attempts to secure western help; he had been reconciled with Urban II in a friendly correspondence between 1089 and 1090; and there were Greek ambassadors at Piacenza in the spring of 1095 asking for assistance, although we have few details of their appeal. On the other hand, Alexius had considerably improved the Byzantine position by 1095, and the despatch of a large expedition to Jerusalem in that year seems a strange response to the situation. There was a story told, probably during the crusade itself, that Peter the Hermit had brought back an appeal for help from the patriarch of Jerusalem because of the oppression of the church there; an appeal confirmed, it was said, by a vision of Christ in the church of the Holy Sepulchre. This account has for a long time been dismissed as a legend, but on insufficient grounds, and if true it would help to explain the timing of the expedition and the choice of Jerusalem as objective better than the theory that the action was designed exclusively for the assistance of Byzantium. It would also mean that the hermit movement, which made an impact on western culture in so many different ways, was influential in the genesis of the First Crusade as well.[18] Whatever the correct explanation of the date, it was, unknown to the westerners, a happy accident, for in 1092 the Seljuk empire had lost both its sultan, Malik Shah, and its vizir, Nizam al-Mulk, and its enormous forces were convulsed in civil war and could not be efficiently deployed against the Latin invaders.

The council of Clermont met in November 1095, and it was probably on 27 November that Urban II announced the project for an expedition to the east: 'whoever for devotion alone, not to obtain honour or money, shall set out to free the church of God at Jerusalem, that shall be counted to him for all penance'.[19] Urban probably had in mind the sufferings of the eastern churches in general, for his subsequent letters mention Constantinople, Antioch, and Jerusalem. The spiritual inducement was a handsome one, offered in terms of the contemporary penitential system. Participants

---

[18] See E. O. Blake and C. Morris, 'A Hermit Goes to War: Peter and the Origins of the First Crusade', *SCH* 22 (1985), 79–107, in contradiction to the view of H. Hagenmeyer, *Peter der Heremite* (Leipzig, 1879).

[19] R. Somerville, *The Councils of Urban II: 1. Decreta Claromontensia* (Amsterdam, 1972), 74. For a view of the origins of the Crusade which differs from the one in the text, see H. E. Mayer, *The Crusades* (Oxford, 1972), 10–11.

would be freed from any requirement to perform penance; or, to put it another way, they would receive immediate forgiveness of sins. The effect, for a knight, was to allow him to go on the expedition as a warrior, bearing arms, and yet with the full promise of salvation.[20] It has sometimes been suggested that Urban's motives must be seen in strictly western terms: he was anxious, at a time of schism, to be seen to be directing the forces of Christendom, while Henry IV cut a feeble figure of inactivity. Certainly, there is a western dimension to what was happening. The development of a heavy western cavalry and the growth of the Italian fleets were sufficient (but only just sufficient, as events showed) to make the expedition feasible. Moreover, Urban may have been attracted by prophecies that Jerusalem would be delivered by a godly emperor; in the absence, as he saw it, of any legitimate emperor, the task had fallen to the papacy. Yet the decision to send large forces from his supporters to the east could not have risen from political calculation, but from a conviction that it was God's will to deliver Jerusalem. Urban had been in close contact with all the forces which were active in the holy war in the western Mediterranean: a Frenchman himself, he had spent a number of years with the Normans in southern Italy, had actively encouraged the Spanish reconquest, and had visited Pisa on his way north to Piacenza and Clermont. The principles of action learned in the apprenticeship in the west were now to be applied on an even larger stage in the east. The motto 'God's will! *Deus lo volt!*' was chosen by the pope to be the warcry of the armies, and the sign of the cross to be their badge. The preaching of Peter the Hermit enlisted a large force consisting of a number of knights and many poor, but the cutting edge of the expedition consisted of contingents of great Lords: Raymond of St Giles, Count of Toulouse, Duke Robert of Normandy, Counts Stephen of Blois and Robert of Flanders, Duke Godfrey of Lorraine with his brother Baldwin, and the able Bohemond of Taranto, son of Robert Guiscard, who joined the crusade uninvited as it crossed Italy. Bishop Adhemar of Le Puy was appointed as the pope's vicar on the expedition.

The intention was that the leaders would co-operate closely with the Emperor Alexius, but this was a precarious hope from the

---

[20] Again, contrast Mayer, *The Crusades*, 26–9. Earlier popes had offered a general assurance of salvation; Alexander II, probably in 1064, had ordered penance to be imposed and then remitted. Urban's cancellation of all penance for all sins was both more precise and more radical than any previous grant.

beginning. Tension began with the problems of supplies for the crusaders, made more acute by the fact that the first contingent to arrive in Constantinople was the relatively undisciplined force assembled by Peter the Hermit. Feelings were roused when Alexius demanded that each leader should take an oath of homage to him. The crucial breach, however, came over Antioch, which the crusaders captured in June 1098. Some of the leaders argued that Alexius had failed to keep his promise to assist them. They had been left in a grave situation from which they had only been extracted by the military talents of Bohemond and the inspiration given to them by the discovery of the Holy Lance, whose presence in the cathedral at Antioch was revealed to a poor crusader, Peter Bartholomew, in a vision. The problems in the army were made much more acute by the death of Bishop Adhemar shortly after the fall of the city, and after fierce disputes among the leaders it was agreed not to return Antioch to the emperor as they had promised, but to give the city to Bohemond, who had master-minded its capture. This marked one of the stages in the alienation of eastern and western Christians, for the fate of Antioch, the second Greek city in the world, was something which Alexius could not ignore. The leaders were lukewarm in their desire to continue to Jerusalem, and it was only after a long delay, under pressure from the mass of poor crusaders, that the march was resumed. Even then, the army moved forward without the help of Bohemond and Baldwin, who were occupied in establishing themselves in their new possessions at Antioch and Edessa. Jerusalem fell on 15 July 1099, and victory was marked by a massacre of the Moslem population. Duke Godfrey was established as ruler, and confirmed his tenure of the city by a victory at Ascalon over the Egyptians on 12 August.

The remarkable success of this extraordinary expedition was partly due to the moral cohesion of an army which, in spite of divisions and rivalries, had a conviction of a divine call. The western forces arrived at a time when the Seljuk empire was paralysed by civil war, while Syria, their main objective, was politically fragmented and religiously divided between Sunnites and Shiites. Moslem rulers felt no obligation to unite to oppose the crusaders, and it was only some forty years later that an effective propaganda campaign was opened to proclaim a *jihad* or holy war against the Frankish intruders. The westerners' heavy cavalry proved highly effective against opponents who were not familiar with its methods of fighting, and assistance from the fleets of Italian cities was crucial in the sieges of both Antioch and Jerusalem. The naval power of Venice, Genoa, and Pisa was even more vital in the following phase, when a relatively small number of Frankish settlers, assisted by large forces of pilgrims who came each summer to fight and pray, not only succeeded in defending Jerusalem but was able to complete the conquest of the whole Syrian coastal strip. By 1125 the Franks had created the four Christian states of Jerusalem, Tripoli, Antioch, and Edessa and controlled the coast from Antioch to the outskirts of Ascalon.

The triumph of the First Crusade had a rapid impact upon the awareness of western Europeans. Not only was it described at length in major chronicles, such as those of William of Malmesbury and Ordericus Vitalis; it also formed the sole subject of many works, in a way which had rarely happened to any historical event in the past. There were histories by eyewitnesses, such as that of Raymond of Aguilers and the anonymous *Gesta Francorum*. These were then worked into longer studies such as those of Robert of Reims and Baudri of Bourgueil. The spirit of much of this writing is reflected in the proud title of Guibert of Nogent's book, *Gesta Dei per Francos*, 'God's Deeds through the Franks'. There was an immediate desire to support the Franks in the east, including an ambitious but unsuccessful attempt to reinforce them in 1101. The dissemination of relics carried crusading ideology with them; although the Holy Lance rapidly disappeared, there was the Cross, fragments of which were widely distributed, and many new finds, such as the bodies of the patriarchs at Hebron (or, as the Franks called it, St Abraham) about 1118. Once the way was opened to pilgrims, this time by sea, very large numbers began to come to the Holy Land. The spreading of devotion to the Passion and the historical life of Jesus, which we shall have to consider in a later chapter, was undoubtedly accelerated by these means. The crusade also produced its own vocabulary. This was not, perhaps, quite what we would expect, for the term 'crusade' never really emerged: the nearest equivalent (*crucesignati* or cross-signed) almost never occurs before the Third Crusade, and older terms such as pilgrimage or expedition remained current. More significant was the common use in crusading chronicles of such words as 'Christians' and 'Christendom', which had been rare in the past and expressed a sense of polarization against the outside world which had come with the crusade. Even more common was the phrase *milites Christi*, knights of Christ, which became a standard way of referring to the crusaders. In the past it had normally been used for monks, and its adoption reflected the conviction that the military calling could be pleasing to God; knighthood was becoming a vocation.

Finally, westerners discovered a new interest in the world of Islam. Before 1095, they had known very little indeed about it. Now there was a series of attempts by Hugh of Fleury, Sigebert of Gembloux, Guibert of Nogent, and Embricho of Mainz to produce a life of Mahomet. Derived ultimately from Byzantine anti-Moslem propaganda, their contents were decidedly strange, but they form the first attempt at understanding the enemy.[21] A very different picture of Saracens appeared in the *chansons de geste*, where they were presented as idolaters and polytheists, in absurd contrast with the theological reality of Islam. Interestingly this picture only appears in rather pale colours in the chronicles written at the time of the First Crusade, and it is tempting to think that the new interest in the Moslems provoked by the Crusade explains the appearance of a highly satirical and savage description of them in the *Song of Roland* and thence in later poems. We do not know, however, at what date this element appeared in the *Roland* materials. Whatever the reality of this last speculation, there is no doubt that in general the First Crusade opened a range of new ideas and interests which was to help shape the distinctive character of the twelfth century.

[21] Three of these lives of Mahomet, included within longer histories, were written within a year or two of 1110. The fourth, a separate work by Embricho of Mainz, unfortunately cannot be dated accurately, but was probably written at about the same time.

7

THE CONFLICT RENEWED: THE QUESTION
OF INVESTITURE (1099–1122)

i. *Paschal II (1099–1118)*

At the turn of the century a series of deaths marked the end of the long-continued schism in the Roman Church. Urban II died at Rome on 29 July 1099, with his hold on the city still insecure. On 13 August the cardinals of his party elected Rainier, cardinal-priest of San Clemente, who took the title of Paschal II. Like his predecessor he was a monk who had come to Rome in the time of Gregory VII, entered papal service, and acted as a legate. His situation was simplified by the death in September 1100 of Clement III. Thereafter, there was no serious anti-pope. Several elections were attempted, but in most cases with little support from the imperial court. With the death in 1101 of the young anti-king Conrad, a further obstacle to mutual recognition by pope and emperor was removed, and neither side was inclined to continue the state of schism within the papacy or empire. In the long series of negotiations which followed, the popes showed a willingness to compromise on some vital issues. In the course of the settlement with Henry V in 1105–6, they did not insist on the removal of all bishops and clergy ordained in obedience to Clement. Nor was there any proposal to renew the onslaught upon simony and concubinage which had marked the early stages of papal reform, and occasioned the clash with the German bishops in the early days of Gregory VII. Simony was regarded with as much abhorrence as ever, but as far as we know the possibility was never even considered of requiring, as part of a settlement, the removal of clergy in Henry's obedience who had obtained their offices for money. We can only guess why such a course of action was ignored: the consciousness may have dawned by now that a charge of simony was difficult to prove and the prosecutions would have been ruinous for better relations between papacy and empire. Perhaps also the Gregorians were aware of the painful fact that simony was much more common in the loyal province of southern France than in the schismatic empire, and concubinage of clergy still almost universal. Whatever the reason, simony (while remaining formally the gravest of sins) had become something of a ghost issue, hiding behind the concrete and demonstrable question of lay investiture.

It was the decision of Paschal II to maintain this prohibition which determined the character of the second phase of the struggle between the popes and the Salian emperors. He made his decision early: in 1102 at the Lateran synod both lay investiture and the performance of homage to laymen were prohibited. In one respect he went further than his predecessors, who had tolerated it silently in many parts of the west. While lay investiture continued in the decent obscurity of eastern Europe, Paschal clearly regarded the prohibition as one for universal enforcement. He may not have sought the conflict in England, where Archbishop Anselm raised the question in 1100, but his response there, as in the empire and in France, was decisive. We have no clear evidence why the pope and his advisers decided to maintain the struggle over a ceremony, when so many pastoral and political considerations pointed to peace. It is quite true that logically it was a difficult practice to defend; whatever the king's role in the appointment of a bishop, it was hard to see that he should exercise it by bestowing the spiritual insignia of ring and staff. It was, however, difficult for the lay power to concede because this was the traditional way of giving to a new bishop the endowments, estates, and jurisdictions of his church, and the increasingly technical discussion of the subject uncovered profound differences about the nature of the church's endowments and of the secular services which were due for them. Almost certainly, Paschal's policy was based on the very clear opinion of his Gregorian supporters, for when circumstances led him in 1111–12 on the paths of compromise or surrender, their rejection was immediate. The Gregorians maintained a deep loyalty to the good old cause for which many of them had suffered, and some had personal, emotional, and political reasons for continued hostility to the empire; and there was no doubt that the prohibition of investiture was firmly in the tradition. It had been fully and formally condemned in 1078; at Clermont in 1095 Urban renewed the prohibition and in addition forbade bishops and priests to do homage to laymen. The investiture question had been one of the many issues involved in the controversy between *regnum* and *sacerdotium* but it now became the primary obstacle to agreement between the two powers. If ring and staff were given by laymen it nullified the possibility of a free election, and opened the way to simony. The doctrine that investiture was 'the seedbed of the heresy of simony' had already been stated by Cardinal Deusdedit, and it was affirmed by Paschal II in a letter of 1102 and in the first phase of the negotiations in 1111.[1] At the opposite extreme a few writers held that it was within the power of the king to create bishops by investiture: this was the position of the so-called Anglo-Norman Anonymous about 1100, and of the *Orthodoxa Defensio* which was written at the great imperialist abbey of Farfa to justify the actions of Henry V in 1111. This argument was fortified by documents of Popes Hadrian I and Leo VIII granting to Charlemagne and Otto I the right to exercise investiture. These were certainly imperialist forgeries, written almost certainly in Ravenna circles in the 1080s.

Yet even the most resolutely royalist writers were progressively showing the influence of a middle position which was far more characteristic of imperialist polemic than was the absolute claim to nominate bishops. This view held that investiture was the grant, not of a church, but of the lands and jurisdictions (*regalia*) which the king had given to it. Such thinking had been adumbrated by Wenrich of Trier, and more clearly by Wido of Ferrara, and in France the distinction between the grant of possessions and of spiritual authority went back for some decades. Its most famous expression was in a letter of Bishop Ivo of Chartres to Hugh of Lyon, the papal legate, in 1097, arguing that Urban's legislation at Clermont was not intended to forbid lay rulers to grant temporal possessions to a new bishop:

What does it matter how this grant is made—by hand, or nod, or word, or staff—provided that kings do not intend to give anything spiritual, but only to assent to the request of petitioners or to concede to the bishops-elect the churches' vills and other external properties which they receive from the generosity of kings?

This was a forced interpretation of the Clermont decree, but the letter became widely known and made familiar the distinction

---

[1] Deusdedit, *Contra Invasores et Simoniacos*, i.15 (MGH LdL ii.314); Paschal, ep. 93 to Archbishop Anselm of Canterbury (PL 163.91B); and MGH Leges Const.I, no. 90, p. 141. For the text of the decree of 1102, see U.-R. Blumenthal, *The early Councils of Pope Paschal II 1100–10* (Toronto, 1978), 17–20; and for the supposed grant of Leo VIII, and references to it, see H. Zimmermann, *Papsturkunden 896–1046* (Vienna, 1985), i, no. 165, pp. 314–17.

between the bishopric itself and the *regalia* attached to it. Hugh of Fleury shortly afterwards made a similar distinction with an important variant: the bishop-elect should receive 'the investiture of secular things' from the king, but not by ring or staff, and the cure of souls was given by the archbishop at consecration.[2]

The first clash arising from Paschal's firm position occurred in England. Archbishop Anselm of Canterbury had been in exile on the Continent and had attended the councils of Bari in 1098 and Rome in 1099. At the latter he heard, apparently for the first time, the papal prohibition of lay investiture and homage. When in 1100 Anselm was invited to return to England by the new king Henry I (1100–35) he accordingly refused to consecrate any bishop who had received royal investiture, and also declined to do homage himself. Since Paschal would not modify the decrees Anselm was once more obliged to leave the country. The controversy waged fiercely for some years, but a settlement was reached at a meeting of king and archbishop at Laigle in Normandy in July 1105 and confirmed at London in August 1107. The pope showed considerable dexterity in avoiding an open concession, for, while lifting the sentence of excommunication from all who had offended against the decree, he simply authorized Anselm, until the king should come to a better mind, to consecrate bishops who had done homage for their temporal possessions. In return Henry I agreed to surrender the right to invest bishops. Nothing seems to have been said about the conduct of elections, but a York writer, Hugh the Chantor, commented that the concession cost the king 'little or nothing—a little, indeed, of his royal dignity, but nothing at all from his power to enthrone whomever he chose'.[3] The English settlement is sometimes regarded as a triumph for Ivo's principles, but its terms do not really fit his teaching and it looks more like a compromise in which homage was tolerated in exchange for the surrender of

---

[2] Ivo of Chartres, ep.60 (PL 162.73BC); Hugh of Fleury, *De Regia Potestate et Sacerdotali Dignitate*, i.5 (MGH LdL ii.472).

[3] C. Johnson (ed.), *Hugh the Chantor, History of the Church of York* (Edinburgh, 1961), 14. On the other hand, Anselm's biographer Eadmer claimed that the king 'nec personas quae in regimen ecclesiarum sumebantur per se elegit, nec eas per dationem virgae pastoralis ecclesiis quibus preficiebantur investivit': R. W. Southern (ed.), *The Life of S. Anselm* (Edinburgh, 1962), c. 63, p. 140. Anselm's attitude is puzzling: it is hard to believe that he had not previously heard of the decrees, especially as he had sent a representative, Boso, to Clermont in 1095 where they were enacted. There are signs that in the eleventh century the decrees of a council were binding on the clergy present, and this may be the explanation of Anselm's rigid adherence to legislation which he had previously ignored.

investiture. In France an agreement was reached relatively easily. The king renounced both investiture and homage but retained the right to grant temporalities to new bishops and to receive an oath of fealty. The settlement was probably negotiated under the influence of the young Louis VI, who was emerging into prominence in the last years of his father's reign, and must have been reached at least by the time of the meeting in 1107 between Paschal, Philip I, and Louis VI.

The intractable problem arose in the empire. Although Henry IV wanted a settlement with Paschal, it proved difficult to initiate serious negotiations until in December 1104 the young Henry, now heir to the throne, rebelled either in frustration at his exclusion from power or from conviction that it was essential to resolve the interminable struggle against the papacy. He at once won the support of the remaining German Gregorians and of Paschal himself, although his victory was only complete with the death of his father at Liège on 7 August 1106. Many bishops were reconciled with the pope and others were replaced, but beneath the general pacification there lurked the problem of investiture. Paschal had no intention of making concessions on this issue. In November 1105 he wrote a firm letter to Archbishop Ruthard of Mainz saying that investiture was the cause of all the conflict between *regnum* and *sacerdotium*. At the synod of Guastella in October 1106 the gap between the pope and Henry's delegation proved to be so great that Paschal abandoned his intention to visit Germany and went to France instead.

Henry V had succeeded in uniting behind him a wide range of German opinion, and in the second half of 1110 he entered Italy to receive imperial coronation, to restore his political position there, and to settle the investiture issue. The great Liège scholar Sigebert of Gembloux had previously prepared a paper on investiture, the *De Investitura Episcoporum*, which argued the case for lay investiture on the ground that it was essential to maintain royal rights over *regalia* in churches as handsomely endowed as those in the empire.[4] Henry had entered Italy with perhaps the biggest army that had so far been raised by a German ruler, and the presence of this force goes far

---

[4] On authorship and purpose, see J. Beumann, 'Sigebert von Gembloux und der Traktat *De Investitura Episcoporum*', VuF Sonderband 20 (1976) and *DAEM* 33 (1977) 37–83; and, for a different view, A. J. Stoclet, 'Une nouvelle pièce au dossier du *Tractatus de investitura episcoporum*', *Latomus* 43 (1984), 454–9. The theory of Augustin Fliche that this tract ascribed to the emperor the right to invest with both spiritual and temporal powers has not been generally accepted by scholars.

towards explaining the events of 1111. He was met by a radical proposal from the pope: that the emperor should give up investiture, and in return the churches would surrender the regalian rights which they held. It seems that the pope intended these to comprise 'cities, duchies, marches, counties, mints, toll, market rights, royal advocacies, hundred rights and vills which are manifestly royal, with their attachments, military service and royal castles'.[5] The proposal looks like a response to the idea of the *De Investitura Episcoporum* that investiture was made necessary by the church's large landed endowments. In the past, historians have seen it as a striking attempt to draw the church onto the road of voluntary poverty by forcing the bishops to live only on tithes and offerings, a policy which 'if it had been applied would have opened genuinely revolutionary prospects for the church of the time'.[6] This idealistic interpretation led to a picture of Paschal as a saintly extremist with few political skills. It is clear, however, that there was no intention of giving up all the possessions of the church. The draft agreement expressly freed them from imperial control: 'we decree that churches with their offerings and hereditary possessions, which did not manifestly belong to the kingdom, shall remain free'.[7] The 'manifest' *regalia* must have been those lands for which an imperial grant was extant, or perhaps those which owed a definite service; all others would, at least in the eyes of the pope, have been part of the 'hereditary' lands of the church. In return the pope would receive, not only the abandonment of lay investiture, but a promise by Henry V to restore the papal lands in Italy to their fullest extent—a promise to which Paschal attached great importance. The proposal was designed to free the clergy from secular duties disliked by Gregorian theorists, not to reduce them to apostolic poverty. Henry's advisers seem at first to have been suspicious about the proposals, but the terms were finally agreed at Sutri on 9 February 1111. The treaty was concealed from the imperial bishops in an ill-advised attempt to deny them a chance to discuss it.

On 12 February a great assembly met at St Peter's for Henry's coronation, and the reading of the agreement produced an uproar. Unsurprisingly each side blamed the other: the details are impossible

---

[5] MGH Leges Const. I, no. 90, p. 141. The imperial version shows the pope as surrendering all land and castles without qualification, but this is a polemical distortion.

[6] G. Miccoli, *Storia d'Italia: la storia religiosa, 3: la riforma gregoriana* (Turin, 1974), 511.

[7] MGH Leges Const. I, no. 90, p. 141.

to discern clearly, except that the protests of the German bishops were loud and clear. It was impossible to continue with the ceremony, and the day ended with Henry arresting the pope and many of the cardinals. The course of events strongly suggests that he had not planned this breakdown, and he had great difficulty in getting his captives out of the city. Paschal did not easily give way to Henry's demands, but he was in a desperate position. Not only was he a captive, but virtually the whole of the papal territory was occupied by a large German army. Henry was hinting at schism, and with many of the senior Roman clergy in his hands he might have been able to impose an anti-pope at Rome. At the negotiations of Ponte Mammolo Paschal surrendered, promising to grant Henry the free right of investiture, to crown him emperor, and never to excommunicate him. In return Henry would release his captives and restore the papal patrimony in full, an important undertaking which he made no real effort to fulfil. The coronation took place on 13 April. Henry had secured more than he had originally even thought of asking.

The privilege of 1111 created bitter divisions among the Gregorians. Paschal was reluctant to take the easy way of revoking the concessions on the grounds that they were forced, and may have thought of resigning in order to allow his successor to nullify the agreement. Meanwhile he was subjected to extremely hostile criticism from the old Gregorian Bishop Bruno of Segni and a group of French churchmen led by Abbot Geoffrey of Vendôme and Archbishop Josserand of Lyon, who argued that lay investiture was a heresy, and the pope was a heretic if he permitted it. The theory behind this unyielding position was expressed by Placidus of Nonantula in his *Liber de Honore Ecclesie*, which held that the material possessions of the church formed part of the spiritual dignity of the bishop and therefore that no compromise with the lay power was possible on the issue. Even the settlement permitted in France would have been excluded by this argument, since the lay power had nothing to give the bishop-elect and there was no place for any sort of ceremony. The Lateran synod of 18 March 1112 ended in a rather confused compromise between the pope and his critics. The privilege (now neatly christened the *pravilegium*) was cancelled, apparently by the synod in Paschal's presence, but investiture was not formally denounced as a heresy and the emperor was not excommunicated. For some of the opposition, this was too little and too late. In

September 1112 the synod of Vienne, assembled by Archbishop Guy, excommunicated Henry V and threatened to withdraw obedience from Paschal if he did not do the same. It is a salutary reminder of the complexity of the politics of the period to notice that Guy of Vienne was by no means a sea-green incorruptible Gregorian, and that his powerful family had a long history of opposition to Henry V in Burgundy. Paschal's own legate, the influential Cardinal-bishop Cono of Praeneste, also pressed him to confirm the sentence of excommunication, and at the Lateran Synod of 1116 the pope was still being accused of heresy. This time he had far more support than in 1112, but the episode had stamped the developing theory of Roman primacy with the awareness that a pope had arguably become a heretic, and that it was the energy of the cardinals and the authority of a synod which had led the Roman Church out of peril.

Meanwhile the unity of German opinion in support of the emperor had broken. The cause was not initially the investiture problem but the clash of territorial interests, which produced bitter quarrels in 1112 with Duke Lothar of Saxony and with Adalbert, the one-time friend and chancellor of Henry but now an assertive archbishop of Mainz. For the moment their opposition was suppressed and they were personally humiliated, and Henry was able to celebrate his marriage with Matilda of England on 7 January 1114 with unparalleled splendour. 1115 was the year of decision. In February Henry's forces were defeated by the Saxons at Welfesholze, and later the townsmen of Mainz forced the king to release their captive archbishop. Henry's power, which had been impressive for almost a decade, never recovered from the double blow. 'From then on the unhappy empire, which had only experienced a few years of rest, was once again torn asunder and divided on both sides of the Alps.'[8]

The opposition demanded a settlement with Rome. Even the lay princes, who had some sympathy with the emperor over the preservation of his rights of investiture, were impatient to see an end to the interminable quarrel, while Adalbert of Mainz, now a bitter enemy of Henry, had adopted a strongly papalist line in which he was supported by Frederick of Cologne and the bishops of the province of Salzburg, for long a bulwark of Gregorian ideas. While the position of Henry V was crumbling in Germany, Italian affairs

---

[8] Otto of Freising, *Chronicon*, vii.15, ed. A. Hofmeister (Hanover, 1912), 329–30.

were turning to his advantage. Henry had established good relations
with Countess Matilda, who at her death in 1115 bequeathed to him
her vast estates. She had already in 1102 conceded to the pope a
nominal overlordship (at least, that is the most probable interpretation of her intention) and the consequence of the double bequest
was to create a curious situation in the former Matildine lands. For
the time being, Henry took possession of them, apparently without
objection from Paschal. The pope, in any case, had reason to be
worried about the situation at Rome. The Pierleoni, stalwart
upholders of papal reform, had received great privileges within the
city, and other families were increasingly resentful. By the time of
the death of Paschal on 21 January 1118 the tension there was acute.
The cardinals chose John of Gaeta as the new Pope Gelasius II,
presumably as a safe man who would follow the traditional paths,
since he had been papal chancellor since the days of Urban II. His
brief pontificate was a troubled one. He was immediately kidnapped
by Cencius Frangipani, the leader of one of the noble factions, and
was then chased from Rome by Henry V, who refused to recognize
him and appointed an unconvincing anti-pope, Archbishop Maurice
of the Spanish see of Braga, as Gregory VIII. Gelasius followed the
path of his predecessors to France and died at Cluny on 29 January
1119. Paschal had been stubborn in defending the prohibition of lay
investiture, and skilful in extricating himself from the consequences
of his forced concession in the *pravilegium*, but by 1119 the long
dispute had reached no conclusion. The one real prospect of a
solution came from the determination of the opposition in Germany
to force Henry to the conference table.

ii. *The Concordat of Worms*

The cardinals who were in France, in choosing Gelasius' successor,
were almost certainly not thinking of a compromise with the
emperor, for their choice fell on Archbishop Guy of Vienne, one of
the 'ultras' of 1112, a man who, although he was a relative of the
Salian house, belonged to a family with a tradition of political
resistance to it. For the first time for over half a century, a pope was
chosen from outside the monastic orders. The new pope took the
name Calixtus II. His immediate objective was to secure the
unconditional surrender of investiture by Henry V, and his hope of
doing so was founded on the strong demand within Germany for a

settlement. He very nearly succeeded. In negotiations at Strasburg, where the arrangements in France were explained to him, Henry expressed himself satisfied, and in further preliminary negotiations he was persuaded to agree to a blanket renunciation: 'I surrender all investiture of all churches.' Encouraged by this, Calixtus arranged to meet the emperor in person at Mouzon on the Franco-German frontier and summoned a large council at Reims for 20 October 1119 to confirm the terms of the triumph. The result was a serious discomfiture for the pope. The arrival of a large German army at Mouzon revived uncomfortable memories of 1111, and the papal advisers had begun to have reservations about the surrender formula, which contained nothing about the possessions of churches: 'if the king is really acting sincerely, these words are satisfactory, but if he is inclined to quibble about the terms, it seems to us that we need a clarification. Otherwise, he could try to claim the ancient possessions of the churches for himself, or else start investing bishops with them again.'[9] Whatever the intentions of Henry V, he was not willing to alter the already agreed formula. Calixtus had to return, exhausted, to Reims to report failure, and his annoyance was increased when he found that he could not even prevail on the council to issue a general condemnation of investiture. The draft decree condemning 'the investiture of all churches and ecclesiastical possessions by lay hands in any form' had to be softened to 'the investiture by lay hands of bishoprics and abbeys'.[10]

This setback at the brink of apparent victory was very disappointing, and probably convinced the new pope that he must look, not for a blanket condemnation, but for a detailed agreement. His underlying situation remained favourable. He was recognized everywhere outside the empire, and no one was taking the anti-pope seriously. Even the emperor had in practice abandoned him, and Calixtus was able to travel to Rome and take control of the city. In Germany a renewal of hostilities between Henry and the Saxons led to a meeting between the princes on both sides at Würzburg on 29 September 1121, where they concluded a 'firm peace' among themselves and advised the emperor to seek a final settlement with the pope, and to secure his absolution from the excommunication which had been

---

[9] Hesso, *Relatio* (MGH LdL iii.25).
[10] Hesso (iii.27). The opposition was probably occasioned by reluctance to cancel the rights of lay patrons in local churches, but the wording makes no mention of ecclesiastical possessions and is less comprehensive than the renunciation offered by Henry.

imposed when he recognized the anti-pope Gregory VIII. The way was opened for what, in the event, proved to be the decisive negotiations.

The representatives of the Roman Church were Lambert, cardinal-bishop of Ostia, and Cardinals Saxo and Gregory, a distinguished group which included two future popes. It became clear that they would have to make large concessions in order to obtain the end of lay investiture, for even the princes did not wish to see its abandonment and attacked Archbishop Adalbert as a 'destroyer of the empire' when he argued against it. The agreement took the form of two documents setting out the renunciations made by each side. The emperor surrendered 'all investiture by ring and staff' and granted canonical election and free consecration in all churches of the empire. The pope allowed that in Germany the election of bishops might take place in Henry's presence, that he might settle disputed elections with the advice of the bishops of the province, and that the elect would receive the *regalia* from him by a sceptre and would do what was by law required (an evasive phrase intended to avoid saying bluntly that the pope was permitting homage before consecration). On these terms, the surrender of imperial investiture in Germany could only be regarded as a technical change, which did not even greatly alter the traditional ceremonies. Elsewhere in the empire far more of the imperial rights were signed away, and the only concession to the emperor was that a new bishop should do homage within six months of consecration.[11] The agreement was announced outside the walls of Worms on 23 September 1122, and met with considerable opposition from the advisers of the pope. Adalbert of Mainz tried to persuade him to disown it, and there was trouble at the First Lateran Council (as it is usually named) which met to ratify it on 18 March 1123. When the papal concession was read, there were loud shouts of *non placet!* The resistance was overcome only by the plea that the arrangements should be tolerated for the sake of peace, and radicals such as Gerhoh of Reichersberg continued afterwards to be troubled by the concessions made by the church. None the less, the agreement was approved. After almost fifty years of hostility, papacy and empire were at last at peace.

iii. *Papal Administration.*

The new responsibilities of the popes were by this time bringing

[11] MGH Leges Const. I, no. 108, p. 161.

with them a change in the government of the church. The Roman
Church in the eleventh century had been designed for worship. The
liturgy at the cathedral, St John Lateran, was maintained by the seven
bishops of the suburban sees of Ostia, Porto, Albano, Palestrina,
Silva Candida, Tusculum, and Sabina. The four other great basilicas
of St Peter, San Paolo *fuori le mura*, San Lorenzo *fuori le mura* and
Santa Maria Maggiore were eached served by seven priests who held
parishes or 'titles' in the city. The seven bishops and twenty-eight
priests were known as cardinals, because they were 'incardinated'
(hinged, dovetailed) into the liturgical arrangements of the great
churches. Rome was unique only in the scale of the provision made
for worship, for other churches had cardinals and Roman cardinals
had no special standing in the western church as a whole. Apart from
their liturgical duties, they were not clearly distinguished from the
other clergy of the Roman province, and they had no function within
the papal administration. The structure of the Roman Church was
not designed to sustain any policy of intervention in the affairs of
other churches. The main officers were the judges or *iudices palatini*,
who were responsible for finance, almsgiving, and the supervision of
the writing-office, but they were far from being mere agents of papal
policy and were closely connected with the nobility of the city. The
notaries or scriniaries who prepared papal documents were still at the
beginning of the century using papyrus, which was almost unknown
elsewhere in Europe, and their distinctive script, the *littera Romana*,
could not even be read north of the Alps. The papal household itself
was located in the Lateran palace and was accordingly termed the
sacrum palatium Lateranense. The title reflected the tendency, from the
time of the Ottonian interventions at Rome, to adopt a more
dignified or even imperial style, but the Lateran palace cannot be seen
as a government. The judges were only members of it in a rather
limited sense, and the clerical staff were concerned with daily
running rather than with major decisions. The papal household was
rooted in the Roman earth and had to be transformed before it could
assume a directive role on an international scale.

The policy changes of the period up to the end of Gregory VII's
pontificate had less impact upon the structure of papal administration
than might be expected. The one major change was the increasing
weight of administration discharged by the clergy of the Roman
church, a tendency which had already been apparent under the
Tusculan popes. The Roman synod became a regular occasion at
which canons were issued and notified to the western church

generally. More striking still was the transformation of the cardinal-bishops, whose ranks were filled with able men often drawn from outside Rome. The city parishes were similarly used to advance leading advisers of the reforming popes. The cardinal-bishops and priests provided legates to represent the Roman Church in other regions and formed a body of advisers who began, especially under Alexander II, to act as witnesses to papal documents. These changes seem to have been both conscious and deliberate: at an early stage Peter Damian saw the Roman Church as an imitation of the curia of ancient Rome, with the cardinals acting as the 'spiritual senators of the universal church'.[12] There were also signs of increasing activity by deacons and subdeacons attached to the Lateran palace and of a body of chaplains there. There are other instances, too, of the growing administrative importance of senior clergy. The office of papal chancellor had emerged well before the middle of the century, and in the 1050s it was occupied by important advisers such as Frederick of Lorraine and Humbert of Silva Candida. It may also be that Hildebrand, as archdeacon of Rome from 1059 onwards, took over some of the financial duties of the older officers, but the matter remains obscure. All of this represents a significant development of Roman clergy to meet enlarged responsibilities for policy-making in the church as a whole, and some of the changes were to be of great importance for the future. Nevertheless, we must regard 1084 rather than 1046 as the starting-point of the new structure through which the Roman Church was to exercise control in the later Middle Ages. The innovations of the forty years after 1046 had not led to an overhaul of the method of government. The writing-office was not systematically reorganized by the chancellors, who introduced notaries from the north alongside the old officials who continued to produce documents in the traditional forms. The *iudices palatini* lost some of their status within the papal household, but retained their functions. Moreover, the progress towards a new organization was not a smooth one. Gregory VII actually moved away from some of the new features introduced by his predecessors, partly because of his autocratic style and partly, perhaps, because he had himself been trained in the old Roman Church. His tendency to take decisions by his own authority or with a small group of confidential advisers, his neglect of the views of the cardinal-priests, many of whom were

---

[12] *Contra Philargyriam*, 7 (PL 145.540B).

uneasy about the breach with Henry IV, his use of his personal confidants as legates, and the financial problems caused by his policies led to the wholesale abandonment of Gregory in the crisis of 1084. The *iudices*, the chancellor, the archdeacon, and many of the priests in the Roman titles went over to Clement III.

Urban II and Paschal II were faced with the need to reconstitute the papal administration, and they had to do so largely in isolation from Rome, where between 1084 and 1122 they were never really secure. The circumstances inevitably removed some of the features of the old order. The *iudices* lost their administrative functions within the household and became primarily ceremonial or civic officials. The Roman synods, which had been so important in formulating policy until the last years of Gregory VII, were never revived in their old form. The central feature of the new structure was the authority given to the cardinals as a whole. The theory was stated by Deusdedit, who was himself a cardinal-priest: 'the name cardinals is derived from the hinges (*cardinibus*) of a door, because they so rule and act that they move the people of God . . . to the love of God by holy doctrines'.[13] Consciously or not, this marked the abandonment of the original derivation of the term from their duties in the basilicas. With the weakening of this liturgical aspect, it became possible to enlist the deacons of the Roman Church in the ranks of the cardinals. The emergence of the cardinal-deacons, a title virtually unknown before 1090, completed the membership of the college in its later form. The use of the cardinals to attest papal bulls, which had occurred under Alexander, was resumed and extended by Urban, and by the time of Paschal they were being consulted about all questions of importance. In 1087 Victor III had already involved them in the election of Oderisius, his successor as abbot of Monte Cassino, and their advice was taken about the renewal of the emperor's excommunication in 1089 and about disputed elections to bishoprics, such as those at Halberstadt and Arras in 1094.[14] The general activity of the cardinals in the government of the western church has a continuous history from the pontificate of Urban II. It was very

[13] W. von den Glanvell (ed.), *Die Kanonessammlung des Kardinals Deusdedit* (Paderborn, 1905), ii. 160. The same derivation was given by Leo IX to the patriarch of Constantinople (ep. 100 c. 32, PL 143.765B), but with an important difference: for Leo, it meant only that the cardinals were close to the hinge, which was the apostolic see.

[14] Peter the Deacon, *Chronica Monasterii Casinensis*, iv.1 (MGH SS VII.760); J. Sydow, *Studien und Mitteilungen zur Geschichte des Benediktiner-Ordens* 63 (1951) 49; Urban II, ep. 100 (PL 151.375C); Lambert, *De Primatu Sedis Atrebatensis* (PL 162.638A).

much a reality under Paschal II: the cardinals were closely involved in the crisis in relations with Henry V in 1111–12, both as guarantors of the surrender at Ponte Mammolo, and then paradoxically as agents in its repudiation; and the college included some of Paschal's most bitter critics. The role of the cardinals as papal electors was also recognized at much the same time. The decree of 1059 had given special authority in elections to the cardinal-bishops, but it had never been properly applied. At least from the time of Urban II's election in 1088 there was participation by all ranks of cardinals, and other groups were increasingly excluded. The use of cardinals as legates became normal practice under Paschal, and their role as legal advisers was beginning to develop. Shortly after 1100 the bishop of Barbastro in Catalonia raised some questions of canon law with cardinal Albert of St Sabina, who explained that he had consulted the cardinals as a body before replying, and by 1120 Baudri of Bourgueil, archbishop of Dol, was calling them 'those senators who obtained the primacy of the whole apostolate'.[15]

In the meantime the papal household was being reorganized into a pattern much closer to that of the courts of northern Europe. The chamber emerged as the principal financial office. Urban probably took the idea from his old abbey of Cluny. The first known papal chamberlain was a Cluniac monk, Peter, who was in office for some years from 1099 onwards, and at first the chamber actually seems to have been located there. The tie with Cluny lasted until 1123, when Calixtus appointed a Roman clerk, Alfanus. The chancery was reshaped under John of Gaeta, cardinal-deacon of St Maria in Cosmedin, who became chancellor in September 1089 and held the office for almost thirty years until he became pope as Gelasius II. During this time a standard diploma and formal prose or *cursus* was adopted for use and replaced the old formulary, the *Liber Diurnus*, which had long provided the examplar for papal documents, but which ceased to be used soon after 1087. The papal chaplains were becoming a more structured body, and Paschal II is said to have promoted to the cardinalate nine of his 'chaplains and writers', while the papal household was acquiring a distinctive rite of its own, separate from that in the basilica of St John Lateran. The terms 'chapel' and 'chaplains' were still not standard under Paschal, but the

---

[15] H.-W. Klewitz, 'Die Entstehung des Kardinalskollegium', *Reformpapsttum und Kardinalkolleg* (Darmstadt, 1957), 110; Baudri, *Vita S. Hugonis*, 6 (PL 162.637A), reflecting his contemporary situation back into the past.

reality was beginning to appear. With its chamber, newly organized writing-office, and chapel the papal household was taking on a different appearance. It was also acquiring a new name, curia, which first appears in a papal document in 1089. We must not exaggerate the abruptness of the change. The word *curia*, in the sense of assembly, had occasionally been used in the eleventh century, and it was in any case becoming fashionable as the standard word for royal or princely courts. Moreover, it was not frequent under Urban and Paschal. The reason why it was to become the standard description for the papal household was its widespread use for 'lawcourt', which is precisely what the curia was going to become. But that, in 1122, lay mainly in the future.

iv. *The Achievement of the Papal Reform Movement*

Calixtus II celebrated the Concordat of Worms and the return of the papacy to the Lateran by inaugurating a major rebuilding of the palace there. In particular he undertook the construction of the chapel of St Nicholas, which a few years later was decorated with a triumphal fresco. The chapel was demolished in 1747 but several sketches remain of the painting, which depicted the victory of the true popes over Clement III and the other anti-popes. It was a dramatic depiction of the papal belief that a long chapter of struggle had reached its end.

For all that the Roman Church had done to promulgate a new vision of ecclesiastical order, the impact of popes upon many regional churches was still slight. In writing a history of (for example) the English church during the first quarter of the twelfth century, the chapter on the influence of Rome would be a relatively short one. The importance which the papal reformers have assumed so far in this book is the result of concentration upon the church as an international body. That is not to say that their significance is an optical illusion, rather that it is a matter of perspective: they bulk large from the viewpoint where we are standing. It must also be remembered that the group of reformers who established themselves within the Roman Church was only one of many movements, which had strong ties of sympathy but which cannot by any device be consolidated into one great international Gregorian party. Cluniacs and canonical reformers, Hirsau and hermits, *Patarini* and Vallombrosans, Countess Matilda and the school of Constance, Deusdedit

and Anselm of Lucca, form a whole within which constituent parts
had close associations, but also differing priorities. The objective of
the papal reformers was to create a church which, to use the formula
of Gregory and Urban, was catholic, chaste, and free; that is,
delivered from the pollutions of simony, concubinage, and lay
control. The programme went back to the days of Leo IX, but from
the beginning it seemed to its advocates that it could only be applied
if Christendom would honour the words and authority of the see of
Peter. As time went on, their policy became more specific still as
attention was focused upon lay investiture as the central issue. Some
of these objectives were shared by men of good will generally. It was
possible to be an enemy of simony without wishing to see the
authority of the bishops suspended or the rights of the anointed king
subverted. Modern historiography has made us aware that the
Gregorians were not necessarily right in their analysis of what was
needed for the church. We do not have to agree with Gregory in his
belief that the victory of Clement III would have been the triumph of
Simon Magus over Simon Peter. Even the title 'papal reformers' is a
term of art, if a useful one. Clement, too, was a papal reformer, but
one who desired to reform corruptions in the traditional way, by
securing the co-operation of the emperor.

One of the most outstanding successes of the reformers was the
formulation of a coherent programme and the persuasion of hearers
who were not at first eager to receive it. While Burchard of Worms
and others had laid a basis for this already, the ability of Leo IX and
his successors to secure the adoption of a clear set of priorities
remains impressive. There were not many precedents for the means
by which the programme was disseminated: the importing of
outstanding men into the leadership of the Roman Church, the
promulgation of decrees and their circulation by legates (sometimes
even with the aid of miracles); the creation of an effective system of
polemics supported by theme-centred collections of canon law; and
an appeal to lay support which deployed strikes against decadent
clergy and rebellion against obstructive kings. Equally successful
was the defence of their dominant position within the Roman
Church, which was essential for the continuance of the movement.
In 1059, 1084, and 1111 the position of the papal reform seemed
desperate, but in each case it was rescued by tough and clear-minded
action. It was a model of how an initially small group can make,
disseminate, and defend a revolution. There were other striking

successes by the papal reformers or their allies. The expansion of monasticism was impressive. So was the progress made in the spread of the common life among canons, which they regarded as particularly important in the establishment of clerical discipline on a sound basis. The leadership which the popes gave to the expansion of Christendom in the Mediterranean also had some dramatic results, and in particular produced the remarkable achievement of the First Crusade. Whatever we may think about the sending of military expeditions to distant places, the establishment of Christian rule in Jerusalem was seen at the time as a God-given triumph.

These achievements, however, are in the last resort peripheral to the problems which had brought the reform movement into existence. Had the hold of simony and concubinage on the church been weakened by the campaign which had been waged against them? One thing certainly had been achieved. There is little doubt that they had become more repugnant to public opinion. But if the reformers had won the argument, had they reduced the evils? Something may have been achieved at those points on which the reformers concentrated. Money probably passed less frequently at episcopal elections, and there was certainly a lower proportion of married canons in 1120 than there had been in 1050. But it remained common for country priests to have a family life and to pass their church to a son; the reformers had not been in a position to do much about the ordinary clergy. It is also clear that customary payments continued which to the modern eye look decidedly like simony: it was still accepted, in the 1120s and later, that bishops received a fee for the consecration of chrism each year, and that applicants for admission to monasteries had to bring an endowment with them. Moreover, the reformers allowed themselves to be sidetracked in the war against simony. Their hostility was deflected from the routine task of eliminating cash payments to the struggle with the adherents of the schismatic pope and the attempt to end the practice of lay investiture. To the Gregorians it seemed that victory in these causes was essential before simony could be overcome and that Clementists and investers were by definition simonists. Even if we accept this analysis without challenge, it postponed the removal of simony from ordinary transactions to a distant future. The reformers had formulated an ideology as a basis for spiritual reform, and ended by fighting for the ideology rather than the reform. This was implicit in their whole approach, which was designed to ensure the ritual purity of the clergy rather than to improve their pastoral efficiency. From this point of view they attached importance to the process of 'restitution', which had immensely reduced the number of benefices to which laymen were appointing. The change did little or nothing for the pastoral care of the parishioners, for almost all the grants were made to monasteries who probably exploited the revenues more thoroughly than the lay lords had done. But that is a different viewpoint: the papal reformers were not seeking revenues for an effective pastorate, but purity from lay contamination.

The price paid for these limited and ambiguous successes was the creation of a series of rifts within the common culture of Christian Europe. It is a curious paradox that the very period which saw the adoption of 'Christendom' as a standard expression also saw the disruption of its post-Carolingian inheritance. The separation of clergy from laity was a major feature of the reforming programme, and its effects will be studied in more detail in the next section. If the traditional dating of the schism between the Latin and Greek churches to 1054 is an over-simplification, the events of that year crucially worsened relations just when Christian unity was going to be required in face of the revived threat of Islam in the east; and the First Crusade, whatever Urban II's intentions, further jeopardized the mutual understanding of the two great traditions. Germany was divided internally and was divided from the western kingdoms with which it had been closely linked in earlier centuries. It would be foolish to make the papal reformers solely responsible for all these changes. The movement towards a society of 'estates' or separate professional groups was in any case pointing towards a clear distinction of clergy and laity, and the different historical experiences of Germans and French after the end of common Carolingian government and of Latins and Greeks from a much earlier date, were separating them into distinct, and mutually antagonistic, cultures. The effect of the papal reform movement was to exaggerate these schismatic trends and to formalize them as the basis of the new church order.

The most obvious of all the divisions was the hostility between empire and papacy. Here, the Concordat of Worms was a compromise which on paper was dearly bought by the reformers. They had to concede to Henry V a range of privileges which offended Gregorian principles: the election of bishops in the presence of the king, royal control over disputed elections, and the performance of homage before consecration. If Calixtus II proclaimed it as a triumph, that was partly a necessity of propaganda, for there were influential critics of the Concordat and he could not afford to concede that it was no more than half a victory. Yet there was substance in his argument. The central issue in contention, lay investiture with ring and staff, had been resolved in favour of the papal viewpoint, and in the Italian churches the papal demands had been conceded to an extent which gravely eroded the prospects of imperial control there. In addition, the death of Henry V in 1125 removed the danger that the German Crown would use its privileges under the Concordat to secure the predominance of the royalist bishops, and instead inaugurated a period of co-operation between empire and papacy. It was only after 1152 that the popes were faced with the determination of the German court to enforce all, and more than all, its rights under the agreement, and by then this was only one of a range of issues which led to the renewal of conflict after a generation of peace between the two powers.

PART II

THE GROWTH OF
CHRISTENDOM (1122–98)

INTRODUCTORY

Hans-Walter Klewitz saw the 1120s as 'the end of the reform papacy'. The signing of the Concordat of Worms, shortly followed in 1125 by the death of the Emperor Henry V, marked a profound change in the relationship of empire and papacy. It coincided, moreover, with the emergence of new forces which were increasingly to shape the history of the church in western Europe. That is not to say that the next generation of leaders renounced the inheritance which they had received from Gregory VII and his followers; but their concerns were significantly different, and the extension of the word 'Gregorian' to cover their policy is unhelpful.

The hostility which had for so long marked the policy of the Roman Church towards the German emperors was transformed, for thirty years, into an alliance. Some historians have seen these years as a successful expression of papal overlordship over secular kingdoms, and others have called them after one of the outstanding churchmen of the time, 'the age of St Bernard'. We shall have to consider the appropriateness of these descriptions; certainly one cannot disregard a new warmth in the relations of *regnum* and *sacerdotium* or the prominence of a number of great churchmen (Bernard himself, Suger of Saint-Denis, Wibald of Stavelot among them) who combined respect for papal authority with influence upon the policy of kings. With the middle of the century, we have a sharp change in atmosphere: the succession of two powerful and strong-minded rulers, the Emperor Frederick Barbarossa and King Henry II of England, brought a renewal of conflict between church and state, although the issues were largely different from those of the years before 1122.

The second characteristic of the period was the creation of a new monasticism. The groups of hermits who had been experimenting with forms of communal living outside the established houses were brought together not only into monasteries, but into huge families or orders, some of them including hundreds of houses. The Cistercians,

Premonstratensians, Carthusians, Gilbertines, Fontevrault, Grandmont, and the families of regular canons transformed the monastic scene with remarkable speed.

The third feature was the expansion of Christendom. Literally, the frontier was being pushed forward: there was missionary and military expansion in the Baltic and in Spain and structures of support were provided, if in the end unsuccessfully, for the Latin states in Syria. This was accompanied by the building of a Christian culture within western Europe. Cathedrals and pilgrimage churches were provided on a previously unparalleled scale, local churches increased in number or rebuilt in stone, and patterns of living proposed for the laity through the formulation of ethics of marriage, chivalry, charity, and even (reluctantly and slowly) of commercial conduct. This remarkable drive towards Christianization can be seen in part as a 'post-Gregorian' feature. The definition of the special character of the clergy as an order distinct from the rest of the Christian people, which had been so prominent in the reformers' policy, led to a concern for the proper definition of the role of the laity within the divine economy. This became more urgent as the ranks of the laity became more diverse, more skilled, and also more inclined to demand religious provision, if necessary by joining heretical groups. There was also a colonization of inner space. Before 1120 not much had been written about personal experience in prayer. The works of Peter Damian and some devotions of John of Fécamp and Anselm of Canterbury had been forerunners of the new age, but they are small in volume when set beside the output of spiritual theology which was specially the achievement of the Cistercian writers. The working of the human spirit became a subject of central interest. William of St Thierry's books opened a new approach to psychology, and in ethics the intention of the individual was given much more importance in the assessment of conduct. These ideas were directed in the first place to an audience of monks and scholars, but they show a kinship with developments in wider strata of society: pilgrimage and the cults of the cross, the Blessed Virgin, and Mary Magdalen echo Cistercian meditations on the heavenly Jerusalem, the passion, the incarnation, and penitence. Twelfth-century thinkers were well aware of the progress which was going on around them and used a variety of concepts to explain it. Some saw themselves in direct continuity with the culture of former generations, but others were conscious of a gap between the 'ancients' and 'moderns'; yet others were aware of the power of innovation which was the special quality of Nature, *parens Natura*; and a few like Otto of Freising and Anselm of Havelberg saw their own age as occupying a special place in the historical process and began to strain the limits of a model of Christian history which had remained largely unchanged since the time of St Augustine. New developments in the concepts of nature, history, and eschatology were thus implicit in what was happening in the history of the church. It is with this range of developments in mind that I have given this section of the book the subtitle (metaphorical, admittedly) 'the Growth of Christendom'.

The description which has won most favour among modern historians to represent this outburst of creativity is that of the twelfth-century Renaissance. When C. H. Haskins introduced the concept in 1927 he had in mind primarily the revival of classical learning in the city schools. It was not a term used at the time, for men of letters did not feel the need to deny their immediate predecessors and revive the values and style of the classical world; they were attempting to recover and apply the wisdom of all past ages, Cicero and Seneca, civil law and canon law, Augustine and Ambrose, Gregory and Benedict, without categorizing any one group of authorities as being pre-eminently 'classics'. The title is justified in that the growth of understanding was based on the recovery of past wisdom; like a dwarf on the back of a giant, to use a favourite image, the scholar was lifted up by ancient learning so that he could see the horizon. This appropriation of the treasures of the past can be seen not only in the schools, but in the new monasteries and the lay courts. It was a threefold renaissance which rested (among many other things) on Latin learning, early monastic writing, and Roman law. For our purposes it had quite specific relevance to the history of the church in the development of theology as a structured subject of study, in the growth of a new legal system controlled by the papal curia, and in the development of better administrative control, through the availability of a class of well-educated clerks, both in church and state.

This remarkable creativity had another side to it: codification. While experiments in monastic community continued, the really distinctive feature of the twelfth century was the acceptance of constitutions and rules which regulated the life of the new monastic orders. The drive to Christianize society was embodied in the creation of increasingly elaborate lawcodes. In attempting to chart its progress, we shall often have occasion to cite the *Decretum* of Gratian, the collection of canons (with comments) of about 1140 which summed up the existing state of the law of the church; and, at a later stage, the papal decretals, especially those issued by Alexander III (1159–81), which attempted to shape legal norms for all the churches subject to the decisions of Rome. The achievement of an elaborate system of law for enforcement through the ecclesiastical courts was an illustration of an element in the culture of the twelfth-century church which contrasts markedly with the more open elements: the defence of ecclesiastical privilege. Fear of the laity as the invaders of the just rights of the clergy was part of the Gregorian heritage. It is impossible to know whether it might have been assuaged if church lands had been freed from all lay obligations, as the reformers intended. In fact, the Concordat of Worms and similar compromises left the bishops with continuing commitments in the political order, and canon law set itself to define the limits of these and to extend the exemptions of the clergy from the government of the lay princes.

One final introductory remark needs to be made. The period from 1122 to 1198 offers us a paradox. Papal control over the provincial churches grew steadily, but there is no clear equivalent for the firm reforming policy stated by Leo IX and revised by Gregory VII nor for the much more elaborate programme championed by Innocent III. The popes of the twelfth century, even Alexander III, failed to provide the same leadership. In part the explanation was personal: a Gregory VII does not achieve authority in every generation. It was also the case that the apparatus of government in both church and state essentially functioned by response to appeals or complaints from subjects, and was not adapted to the formulation of high policy. The popes did not have the means of defining governmental objectives and securing their acceptance by the bishops as a whole. Their legal activity was impressive, but it was designed mainly to ensure that the Roman Church was able to respond consistently to the many pleas which parties were bringing before it. The most obvious place at which a policy could be formulated and accepted was a council, and there were indeed some important ones. Yet at first they were directed to the solution of immediate problems (it is not an accident that the Lateran Councils of 1123, 1139, and 1179 were held to celebrate the end of a schism), and the concept of a programme of legislation proved difficult to achieve. This was partly because of technical problems: popes were lax about even providing proper records of conciliar decrees, diocesan records were totally inadequate for the exercise of control, and the use of local synods to promulgate central decisions was rare. It was only in the last quarter of the century that steps began to be taken towards a solution of these problems, and the way was thus being opened to the impressive formulation of policy by Innocent III and the Fourth Lateran Council. It is no doubt true that all government (twentieth-century included) is a matter of response, usually belated, to a rising storm of protest, but medieval rulers did not have at their disposal the means of devising general programmes which could be universally applied. Innocent III was rare in the extent to which he succeeded in finding these means; in the meantime, it must be noted that, for all the growth in papal administration, central initiative was not a large feature in the life of the twelfth-century church.

8

THE ROMAN CHURCH AND THE EMPIRE
IN THE TWELFTH CENTURY

i. *After the Concordat of Worms (1122–1153)*

The end of the controversy over investiture marked a change in the relationship between Rome and the rest of Christendom. The popes had to respond to the growing power of a new spirituality; to the crisis of a schism, this time generated within the Roman Church and not imposed from outside; and to the new opportunities provided by a period of co-operation with the empire and other secular powers. The changing character of the papacy was illustrated by the type of men who were elected. In the forty-six years from 1073 to 1119 the four popes all came from a Benedictine or Cluniac background. From 1124 to 1159 this predominance disappeared. Of the seven popes, four had been regular canons and one a Cistercian; men from the new orders were pope for twenty-one of the thirty-five years.[1] From 1130 onwards, Bernard of Clairvaux, the passionate advocate of the Cistercian order, was influential at Rome, especially under the Cistercian Pope Eugenius III (1145–53).

The smooth development of the Roman Church in the period after Worms was disrupted by the election of 1130. Division among the cardinals was no new thing. A large party had abandoned Gregory VII in 1084, and there had been bitter conflicts over the *Pravilegium* after 1112. In the 1120s, after Calixtus II had returned to Rome, one of the dominant personalities in the curia was Peter Pierleone. It was said of him about 1125 that 'he stands so high at Rome that all Rome speaks or is silent at his nod'.[2] He was a member of a Roman family which had grown great in the service of the Gregorian popes.

---

[1] The number of popes who were regular canons has been overestimated by historians. There is no solid reason for thinking that Innocent II, Anastasius II, or chancellor Haimeric were regular canons, but the extent of the change remains impressive. The calculations omit the Cluniac Anacletus II.

[2] For this and other references, see H. Bloch, 'The schism of Anacletus and the Glanfeuil forgeries', *Traditio* 8 (1952), 163–4n.

Already under Calixtus we can discern the rising influence of other groups, among them the noble family of the Frangipani. Above all, in 1123 the influential office of papal chancellor was given to the dynamic Cardinal Haimeric, a Frenchman imported by a French pope. The tension came to the surface at the death of Calixtus II on 13 December 1124, when in disorderly proceedings Bishop Lambert of Ostia, the candidate of Haimeric and the Frangipani, was recognized as Honorius II. Pandulf, the author of the *Lives of the Popes* for this period, regarded the coup of 1124 as the root of the later schism. By 1130 it was clear that the conflict of factions was threatening the orderly election of a new pope, and the cardinals agreed to appoint an electoral college of eight. In the prevailing atmosphere it would have been difficult to reach agreement, but any hope of peace was extinguished by the conduct of Haimeric's supporters, who on the death of Honorius II unilaterally elected Cardinal Gregory of St Angelo as Innocent II. The rival party then assembled its adherents and elected Peter Pierleone as Anacletus II. The Frangipani soon abandoned Innocent, leaving Rome solid for Anacletus; but Haimeric and his supporters appealed to their contacts in northern Europe, and the schism was to last for eight years. It shocked public opinion to see how 'in many monasteries two abbots appeared, and in bishoprics two prelates struggled for office, one of them supporting Peter Anacletus and the other favouring Gregory Innocent'.[3] The Anacletians were in a slight majority, but against that Innocent had the support of five of the six cardinal-bishops. Anacletus was the candidate of the older men. Half his supporters had been appointed by Paschal II before 1118, whereas among the nineteen Innocentians only two, one of them Innocent himself, went back to Paschal's time. Cardinal Peter of Porto described them as 'a handful of new boys', *novitii*.

A recent tradition of historical writing has argued that the schism in the college of cardinals was the product of the changed spirituality in the curia. Beginning with an article by H.-W. Klewitz significantly entitled 'The End of the Reform Papacy', this school has identified the supporters of Anacletus with the old Gregorian party, hostile to the empire, unhappy about the Concordat of Worms, and closely linked with the older Benedictine monasticism; while Innocent is seen as the candidate of the party of Haimeric, marked by

---

[3] Ordericus Vitalis, xiii.1 (vi.418–19).

strong links with France and the new monastic orders and well-disposed to co-operation with the rulers of France and Germany. The analysis of the parties does not confirm the more exaggerated claims which have sometimes been made about them: the Innocentians included only one regular canon and two Frenchmen, and among the cardinals created by Innocent II there were several Benedictine abbots. We should not think in terms of coherent parties, but of interest groups forced into conflict by Haimeric's determination to secure the papacy for his own candidate in 1130.

The fate of the two claimants was determined by the contacts of their supporters. Anacletus II rapidly made an alliance with Roger of Sicily, recognizing his control on the mainland and granting him the royal title. Meanwhile Haimeric had carried the papal chancery and an extensive network of correspondents into Innocent's service, and the kings of France and Germany were rapidly informed of his election. They were brought onto his side largely by the pressure of sympathetic churchmen: Suger of Saint-Denis, Peter of Cluny, Norbert of Magdeburg, and Walter of Ravenna. Bernard of Clairvaux rose to international prominence as a skilful and ruthless propagandist. The allegiance of France was declared for Innocent at the council of Étampes, and that of Germany at Würzburg, and Innocent travelled north to meet Henry I of England, Louis VI of France, and (in a splendid gathering at Liège in March 1131) Lothar of Germany. An expedition in 1133 secured for Lothar the imperial Crown, but Innocent was forced again to retreat to the north. Even a much larger army in 1137 had to withdraw without inflicting a decisive defeat on Roger. The resolution of the schism was finally made possible by the death of Anacletus on 25 January 1138, and in the following year Innocent, having failed again to overcome Roger, recognized him as king. The victory of the Innocentians was a mark of the growing power of international opinion and of its limitations. It had sustained his cause effectively, but the resolution of the schism had to await its natural end through his rival's death.

The Concordat of Worms, which had initiated this new period, had been a compromise, but the events of the next thirty years confirmed the claim of Calixtus II to have won a victory for the church. The two most powerful kingdoms of the north, England and Germany, had been cautious about the Gregorian papacy or hostile to it, but in both the situation was transformed. The incidence of a disputed succession between Stephen and Matilda in 1135 left the contending parties in England anxious for the support of pope and bishops. In Germany the Salian monarchy was succeeded by two kings, Lothar of Saxony (1125–37) and Conrad of Hohenstaufen (1138–52), specifically committed to a close relationship with the papacy. The exact character of this relationship has been much disputed by historians. Some have seen the popes as aspiring successfully to general control in the west; Eugenius III is said in 1147–8, during the Second Crusade, to have been 'on the direct road to universal rule'.[4] An alternative view, while not denying the existence of this triumphalist element in the curia, stresses that it did not intend to overthrow the independence of the secular power in its own sphere: co-operation, not complete supremacy, was the ideal for church-state relations.

The changed character of the German monarchy was illustrated by the elections of 1125 and 1138. Under the influence of Archbishop Adalbert of Mainz, an extremist who had serious reservations about the Concordat, the electors in 1125 turned their backs on Salian policy, passing over the nephew of Henry V and choosing instead Lothar, a long-standing enemy of Henry whose whole political alignment had been with the Gregorian party. The choice of Conrad III in 1138 was primarily the work of Archbishop Adalbero of Trier, who arranged the election in the presence of the papal legate, Cardinal Theodwin. In both cases the result was the election of a king whose policy was alignment with papal interests, and whose independence of action was impeded by civil war. The division of Welf and Waibling (Hohenstaufen), or Guelph and Ghibelline, which was to underlie party warfare in the Italian cities, now appeared for the first time in imperial history. So did the 'ecclesiastical principality', a territory within which the bishop possessed most important rights of government. The effect of the Investiture Contest had been to bring to power men who had not been trained in the imperial chapel and who did not think in the ways instilled by the Salian emperors. Lothar III, in sharp contrast with his predecessors, found very few of his bishops from the clerks of his chapel. The prelates of the early twelfth century such as Ruthard of Mainz (1089–1109), Frederick I of Cologne (1100–31) and Bruno of Trier (1101–24) steered their way between the conflicting claims of pope and emperor and concentrated on building up their local territorial

---

[4] H. Gleber, *Papst Eugen III* (Jena, 1936), 176.

power. This policy reflected the increasing difficulty of relying on the effective protection of the emperor: like the French bishops a century before, the Germans now had to make their own plans for the security of their churches. The old traditions of the imperial church had not been so severely disrupted that it was beyond the possibility of renewal by Frederick I after 1152, but the bishops whom he found in office had been trained in a very different school from those of Henry III's reign.

One direct consequence of the change of government was the effective limitation of the rights of the Crown by the Concordat. The report that Lothar had renounced his remaining rights at his coronation is almost certainly incorrect, but in his first years there were cases of elections out of the royal presence and occasionally bishops were consecrated before investiture. At Liège in 1131 and Rome in 1133 Lothar raised the issue of investiture, and he eventually secured a confirmation of the right to give investiture before consecration. After 1133 one can trace a significantly greater royal influence in elections. It remained true that papal representatives were judging questions which Henry V would have treated as part of the royal prerogative: at Magdeburg the disputed election of 1126 led to the nomination of Norbert by Archbishop Adalbert and the papal legates, and in 1131 Adalbero of Trier owed his see to the support of Innocent II. The partial weakening of control over appointments did not mean that the special relationship between the emperor and the German churches had been destroyed. Lothar insisted on the performance of military service and other duties by bishops and abbots, and increased the number of abbeys under direct imperial protection.

In Italy the imperial position had been much weakened by the Concordat. The pope was able to control abbatial elections at imperial abbeys such as Farfa and Monte Cassino, and Ravenna, which for a long time had been the centre of opposition to Roman influence, came into the hands of Archbishop Walter (1119–44), a regular canon and enthusiastic supporter of the papal cause. The question of the Matildine lands was resolved by compromise: Innocent II granted them to Lothar and his son-in-law Henry the Proud to hold from him. The whole approach of the curia towards secular powers radiated a new confidence. Conrad III was anointed by a papal legate; Stephen of England boasted in 1136 that he had been 'confirmed' by the pope, and Eugenius III 'approved' the election of Frederick Barbarossa in 1152. At Liège in 1131 Lothar had acted as the pope's marshal, assisting him to dismount. Innocent II decorated the Lateran palace with a painting which showed Lothar's oath to preserve the privileges of the city of Rome, his investiture (perhaps) with the Matildine lands, and his imperial coronation. An inscription claimed that 'he becomes the pope's man', *homo fit papae*.[5] The fresco later aroused the angry protest of Frederick Barbarossa, but before 1152 propaganda of this kind does not seem to have provoked annoyance in government circles in Germany; under Conrad his principal adviser on foreign policy, Abbot Wibald of Stavelot, was a strong supporter of friendly relations between the two powers.

The supremacy of the Roman Church was expressed by the splendid Second Lateran Council, celebrated by Innocent II in 1139 to mark the end of the schism. In his opening discourse he is reported as asserting 'that Rome is the head of the world, that promotion to ecclesiastical dignity is requested from the Roman pontiff as if by the custom of feudal law and is not legally held without his permission'.[6] The legislation enacted there was largely drawn from the canons of Innocent's earlier councils such as Clermont 1130, Reims 1131, and Pisa 1135, and diverged in only a few details from that of earlier popes, thus providing its final formulation on the eve of the publication of Gratian's *Decretum*. The pontificate of Eugenius III, with the pope sponsoring the Second Crusade and advising regents about the conduct of government during the absence of rulers in the east, seemed to confirm the reality of the papal triumph, but one must notice its limitations. Innocent and Eugenius were bringing under the control of the Roman Church rights which were essentially ecclesiastical: to summon a crusade or anoint a ruler. They did not normally claim to direct rulers in the exercise of their governmental powers. What is more, their policy generated a reaction. Radicals such as Bernard of Clairvaux and Gerhoh of Reichersberg were critical of the growing judicial and political commitments of churchmen, and there was increasing lay resentment. In 1143 the Romans rose in rebellion against Innocent II and

---

[5] The exact nature of the painting, and even the number of scenes illustrated, are disputed. See A. Frugoni, 'A pictura cepit', *Bulletino dell' Istituto Storico Italiano* 78 (1967), 123–36, whose view of the evidence is followed in the text here. W. Heinemeyer in *Archiv für Diplomatik* 15 (1969), especially 183–97, argues that the inscription, with its claim to supremacy, was a later escalation of the painting, which was itself a more general assertion of papal dignity.

[6] *Chronicon Mauriacense*, III (PL 180.168A).

set up a city government based on Roman models and anti-clerical in tone. In spite of the alliance between the popes and the German kings, there were a few significant moments of tension between them. When in 1137 Lothar had overrrun much of southern Italy, they had a sharp exchange about the control of Monte Cassino and the right to invest the new duke of Apulia. The German princes too were becoming increasingly concerned about clerical privilege. A growing series of complaints was sharpened by awareness of the unhappy condition of a Germany in the throes of civil wars. When Frederick Barbarossa in 1152 and Henry II in 1154 took over in Germany and England and resolved to restore the dignity of the Crown, they were to find plenty of support.

ii. *Frederick I and the Renewal of the Empire*

'By our careful application the catholic church should be adorned by the privileges of its dignity, and the majesty of the Roman Empire should be reformed, by God's help, to the original strength of its excellence.' In these words from the letter of March 1152, announcing his election to Pope Eugenius III, Frederick I already struck the keynote of his reign.[7] He named himself *pater patriae*, father of the fatherland, ruling a 'kingdom conferred on him by God', and saw himself as obliged to defend the 'venerable decrees and sacred laws' of his predecessors. The relationship between church and state was to be determined by the principle laid down by Gelasius I: 'there are two things by which this world is chiefly ruled, that is the sacred authority of the pontiffs and the royal power'. The major part of Frederick's programme had thus been stated at the beginning of his reign. He interpreted these claims in their widest sense. The statement that the empire was conferred by God (which the popes in one sense did not deny) meant to the new emperor that the pope did not bestow it. The development of the cult of the Three Kings at Cologne and the canonization of Charlemagne also expressed the holiness of the royal office. Frederick's desire for co-operation with the pope and bishops was genuine, as was his piety; at Bamberg he left the reputation of having been a 'lover of the churches'. But he took a large view of the directing power of the Crown. While he accepted the validity of the Concordat of Worms he differed from his

[7] R. L. Benson in *RR*, 361. The letter is printed in MGH Leges IV Const. I, no. 137, pp. 191–2.

predecessors in that he exercised all, and more than all, the rights which it guaranteed to the monarchy, including the adjudication of disputed elections. In the same way in Italy Frederick was to press to the maximum his rights to govern and to tax lands which the Roman Church believed to be its own patrimony.

The change in tone in 1152 was dramatic, but the elements of the new rhetoric can be found in the preceding period. There is a direct continuation between the letters written by Wibald of Stavelot on behalf of Conrad III and his draft for the announcement of Frederick's election. It was the arrival of a new and glamorous monarch in Germany which made it possible for Abbot Wibald to gather together the claims which had been made piecemeal in recent years into a coherent position. Frederick, the nephew of Conrad III, was in his late twenties and already duke of Suabia, a commanding personality whose striking appearance is recorded in a description by the chronicler Rahewin and in a silver-gilt bust which he presented to his godfather, Otto of Cappenburg. His red-gold hair led Italians to give him the nickname Barbarossa, by which he is still known. He was well placed by descent to bring unity to Germany, for his father was a Hohenstaufen and his mother a Welf. The position formulated by Frederick and his advisers was in some important ways an innovation. The self-conscious proclamation of the majesty of the empire was new, as was the abundant use of Roman law. In order to restore to obedience the great cities of Lombardy, which had grown in prosperity and independence since the days of Henry V, Frederick harnessed new techniques of administration and legal doctrines. But the heart of his ideology was a return to the past glory of the empire, tarnished by recent events. There was a conservatism about his approach which rendered him, for all the tactical skill which he often showed in diplomacy, unable to make use of new forces. He rejected the approaches of the Roman commune as emphatically as he demanded the submission of the greater cities of the north, and (unlike his grandson, Frederick II) he made no use, even for propaganda, of radical critics of the curia. He was clumsy in relations with the rising kingdoms of the west and under the influence of Rainald of Dassel allowed their rulers to be described as kings of provinces or as *reguli*, petty kings. The heart of the matter was a return to the past, and although the concessions of recent kings were not cancelled, they were interpreted in such a minimalist style that a conflict was almost inevitable with the Italian cities and with the Roman Church.

Eugenius III and Frederick were not looking for a quarrel. Both believed in the collaboration of the two powers, and Eugenius had strong reasons for seeking imperial support. The papal territories in central Italy were threatened by the pressure of the Norman kingdom of Sicily, which now stretched to within a few miles of Rome. Even more serious was the Roman commune, which claimed to exercise sole jurisdiction within the city through its senate on the Capitol and which had welcomed Arnold of Brescia and his message that the hierarchy should give up its privileges and return to the simplicity of the apostles. The grandiloquent language which the leaders had drawn from the imperial past now sounds absurd but the threat to the papal position was real. Eugenius therefore urged the emperor to carry out the expedition to Rome which had already been promised by Conrad III, and the conditions for the enterprise were ratified on 23 March 1153 at the Treaty of Constance. As 'special advocate of the holy Roman Church' Frederick was to defend and recover its territories. The pope promised to crown him, to 'enlarge the honour of the empire' and to excommunicate its enemies.[8]

The first signs were reasonably hopeful. While the expedition was in preparation, papal legates co-operated with the emperor in the affairs of the German church except in the case of Magdeburg, where Frederick had used his supposed right to adjudicate in a disputed election to appoint Wichmann as archbishop, and now impeded the legates' attempts to hear the dispute. Even there, Eugenius's short-lived successor Anastasius IV (1153–4) backed down, to the anger of some members of the curia. When Frederick began his first Italian campaign with a small army, it was as an ally of the Roman Church. He was met in Italy by a new pope. On 4 December 1154 Nicholas Breakspear, cardinal-bishop of Albano, had been elected, the only Englishman ever to be pope. He had been abbot of the great house of regular canons, St Ruf at Avignon, and had become a cardinal probably in 1149. Thereafter much of his time had been spent on a very successful legation in Scandinavia. His character has been variously assessed. Some historians have seen him as tough and inflexible, but others as a relatively mild man whose policy was fashioned by some authoritative advisers, notably Roland, who was already papal chancellor at the time of Hadrian's accession, and Boso, the papal chamberlain. Hadrian's main priority was the

[8] MGH Leges IV Const. I, no. 144–5, pp. 201–3.

security of Rome itself. By imposing an interdict on the city he was able to force the commune to expel Arnold of Brescia, and then to secure his arrest by Frederick and execution by papal officers. Papal lands and fortresses were energetically built up within the Patrimony under Boso's effective guidance. In a short pontificate, Hadrian did more than any of his predecessors to secure the papal position in central Italy, but he was much less successful in his conduct of relations with the empire.

The first meeting of Frederick and Hadrian was unfortunate. It took place at Sutri on 8 June 1155 as the emperor was on his way to Rome for the coronation. Frederick at first refused to honour the pope by performing the service of marshal as Lothar had done. This may merely have been a mistake in protocol, but it is more likely that he was aware of the Lateran picture showing Lothar as the pope's man. After this mishap both parties tried to observe their obligations under the Concordat. The emperor refused to listen to representatives of the Roman citizens, and the pope crowned him on 18 June 1155. At this point, with the commune still in control of Rome and without any action against the Normans, the German princes urged that the army should return home, and Frederick reluctantly agreed. Hadrian was left to face the Normans alone and in June 1156 he was obliged to sign the Treaty of Benevento. William I was recognized as king subject to homage and a large tribute, and his special powers as legate in the island of Sicily were confirmed with a few amendments. However reluctantly, Hadrian had departed from the policy of co-operation with the empire. Meanwhile the German court had moved an important step in the opposite direction with the appointment of the talented Rainald of Dassel as chancellor. Rainald, a fervent imperialist, was chosen from outside the chancery and his arrival gave a new edge to the ideology expressed in royal letters and diplomas.

The extent of the breach was shown in 1157. Hadrian sent two legates to the imperial court, the chancellor Roland and Bernard of San Clemente, who met the emperor at Besançon in October. In his letter the pope reminded Frederick that he had conferred on him the imperial Crown, and said that he would gladly give him greater *beneficia* if it were possible. *Beneficium* is the normal Latin for a benefit or gift; it was also in Germany the standard term for a fief, and Rainald, who was translating, chose this meaning and rendered it as *Lehen*. The emperor had to intervene to prevent his princes from lynching the legates. A letter of the German bishops to the pope and a manifesto from the emperor to his subjects for the first time stated the imperialist ideology in a clearly anti-papal form. The emperor asserted that the imperial Crown was a divine *beneficium* and was initially bestowed by the election of the princes. Hadrian was obliged, in a letter to the court at Augsburg, to explain away his original language: *beneficium* meant a benefit and by 'conferring' the crown he meant placing it on the emperor's head. On any showing it was a signal diplomatic defeat, but historians are not agreed whether the pope's choice of feudal language was inadvertent or deliberate. The truth is probably that he was using triumphalist language to emphasize his supremacy without troubling about its precise legal implications. His inflated rhetoric enabled Rainald to manœuvre him into an embarrassing position.

By this time Italian affairs were causing further difficulties between pope and emperor. The decrees of Roncaglia in 1158 had claimed for the emperor a large range of political and financial rights within the Lombard cities, and led to a final breach with the great city of Milan, which was put to the ban of empire in April 1159. The curia was becoming concerned at the invasion of the privileges of the Roman Church by the imperial legates, Counts Guy of Biandrate and Otto of Wittelsbach, and a letter from Hadrian complained about the emperor's failure to observe the Treaty of Constance, the exaction of homage from Italian bishops, the excessive levy of hospitality from bishops, the taxation of the lands of St Peter, and interference by imperial representatives in papal territories, including Rome itself.[9] Relations were at breaking-point and reports were circulating that Milan and its allies had reached an agreement with the curia which would involve the excommunication of the emperor. The coalition of papacy, Lombards, and Normans, which was eventually to wreck Frederick's ambitions, had thus probably come into being under Hadrian IV, but the final breakdown of the long peace was not to be the result of a direct declaration of war. It was occasioned by the growing division within the college of cardinals between the 'Sicilian' party and the imperialist sympathizers, which came to a head at the death of Hadrian IV on 1 September 1159.

iii. *The Alexandrine Schism (1159–1177)*

During three days of tense negotiations after the funeral of Hadrian

[9] MGH Leges IV Const. I, no. 179–80, pp. 250–1.

IV on 4 September 1159 rival groups of cardinals elected two candidates, Roland the papal chancellor as Alexander III and Octavian, cardinal-priest of St Cecilia, as Victor IV. It was the third major schism in less than a century, following those of 1080–1100 and 1130–8. The propaganda from each side gave different accounts of events. The Victorines alleged that the 'Sicilian' party had committed the papal curia to hostility to the empire by allying with the Norman kingdom and with Milan, had taken an illicit oath only to elect from their own number, and finally had broken an agreement to proceed to an election with the cardinals as a whole. The Alexandrines complained of the interference of the imperial representative in Rome, Otto of Wittelsbach, in advancing the cause of Victor. It is no longer possible to discover the truth behind these two sets of allegations, but they agree in finding the cause of the schism in political circumstances. The scene was set by Frederick Barbarossa's enforcement of imperial authority in Italy. No previous emperor had enjoyed such control for at least a century, and the cardinals were divided in their reactions. One group welcomed the prospect of imperial protection against the Norman kingdom and intended to continue the alliance which had prevailed before 1156, but the other saw the emperor as a growing menace. It was this group which elected Alexander, and it was fairly rapidly joined by the uncommitted cardinals. Out of a total college of thirty-one, Victor's supporters originally may have numbered nine or more, but they soon dropped to only five. The rules governing papal elections were vague, since the decree of 1059 had never been effectively applied and was now in complete abeyance. The large Alexandrine majority was an obvious weakness in the imperialists' case, but it must be remembered that if the accusations of sectional oaths and breach of procedure were true, Alexander's election would have been very questionable.

Both candidates had already had distinguished careers in curial service. Victor was a native of the Roman Campagna, a member of a family of the highest nobility which had a tradition of loyalty to the empire. Roland was one of the new men who had risen through the schools and papal service. Descended from one of the major families of Siena (later tradition said it was the Bandinelli), he had taught theology at Bologna and then become a canon of Pisa. From there he was summoned to papal service by Eugenius III, probably in 1148, and then had been appointed papal chancellor. He has for a long time been identified with M. Roland, a Bologna canonist, but there are no grounds for this. M. Roland had studied at Paris; but with the abandonment of the identification we lose any firm evidence that Cardinal Roland had done so, although the support which he received from the French schoolmen suggests they found him a natural champion. Circumstances forced him to formulate the papal position in face of imperial power, but he did so cautiously, using little of the exaggerated rhetoric of Gregory VII. His letters are full of traditional claims: the pope can be judged by no one, the emperor is invading the rights of the church and fomenting schism. Only rarely do we find political actions justified by large statements of papal supremacy. It was a marked retreat from the style of Hadrian, whether or not this had been inspired by the new pope as Cardinal Roland.

The first period of the schism was dominated by the strength of Frederick I's position in Italy, which was confirmed by the unconditional surrender of Milan after a long siege in 1162. The emperor claimed that, as advocate of the Roman Church, it was his duty to summon a council to adjudicate in the disputed election, although he ostentatiously left the decision to the bishops. Alexander refused to attend on the grounds that the pope could not be judged, and when the council of Pavia, consisting of about fifty bishops from imperial territories, met on 5 February 1160 it found in favour of Victor, whom the emperor formally recognized. A great part of the German church accepted him, with the Alexandrine sympathies of the province of Salzburg being tolerated by the emperor; at first, indeed, even radical reformers such as Gerhoh of Reichersberg were predisposed to Victor because Alexander was blamed for the treacherous creation of the papal alliance with Sicily. Alexander responded to the council of Pavia by excommunicating Frederick and releasing his subjects from their allegiance, but unlike Gregory VII he did not pronounce a sentence of deposition. His political support came initially from the kingdom of Sicily and the Lombards, but soon a series of negotiations in England and France led to his recognition by both kingdoms at a joint meeting at Beauvais in July 1160. Alexander decided to follow the trail blazed by several predecessors and to move to France, where he arrived in April 1162. On 19 May 1163 he opened an impressive council at Tours with some 118 bishops, at which the excommunication of the emperor was renewed.[10] Frederick was putting heavy pressure upon Louis

---

[10] On the date of the opening of the council, see R. Somerville, *Pope Alexander III and the Council of Tours* (Los Angeles, 1977), 11.

VII of France to withdraw recognition from Alexander, but without success.

The support for Victor IV was now largely confined to lands under the direct control of the emperor, and the death of Victor on 20 April 1164 was a serious blow to the imperial cause. Rainald of Dassel, apparently without instructions from the emperor, arranged for the election of Cardinal Guy of Crema as Pope Paschal III, but the deliberate continuation of the schism lost a good deal of support, and several leaders of the German church, including Archbishops Conrad of Mainz and Hillin of Trier, recognized Alexander as pope. By determined action, Frederick removed any prospect of an early peace. His motives were explained in a conversation with Gerhoh of Reichersberg, to whom he said that he would never obey a pope who strove to diminish the rights of the empire, or who 'under the name of pope wishes to rule not only over the clergy but also over the kingdom'.[11] His determination was strengthened by the hope, which proved vain, that the split between Henry II of England and Archbishop Thomas Becket might lead to the abandonment of Alexander there. At a major assembly of German bishops at Würzburg at Pentecost 1165 an oath was imposed never to acknowledge Alexander as pope, and a few bishops who proved intractable were replaced. In particular, Conrad at Mainz was succeeded by the emperor's military-minded chancellor Christian. The western church was now closer to a state of permanent schism than at any time before the Great Schism of the fourteenth century. Frederick also took steps to deal with a deterioration of the situation in Italy. There the foundation of the League of Verona had marked the emergence of a new resistance to Frederick's dominance, and in 1165 Alexander returned to Rome. The emperor attempted to resolve the situation by mounting a major expedition to Rome and was successful in occupying the Vatican basilica and in having Paschal enthroned as pope on 22 July 1167. At this point, disaster visited the German cause. A devastating infection, probably malaria, decimated the army and killed many of its leaders, including Rainald of Dassel. The Lombards took the opportunity offered by German weakness to renew the League on 1 December 1167, and to rebuild Milan and found a new city, called Alessandria in honour of the pope. The discomfiture to the imperial cause was completed by the death of Paschal on 20 September 1168.

[11] P. Classen, *Gerhoch von Reichersberg* (Wiesbaden, 1960), 276 with references.

In the remaining years of the schism the conflict between the Lombard League and the emperor was in the foreground. Alexander III now committed himself firmly to alliance with the renascent League, and in his letter *Nullum est dubium* to the Lombard consuls in March 1170 the pope prohibited the making of any new association under pain of excommunication, commanded that all should obey the rectors of Lombardy, and threatened to deprive any city which seceded from the league of its status as a diocese. Moreover the new imperialist pope, Calixtus III, was in a weak position, having been elected by only a tiny rump of cardinals. The apparently dominant position of Alexander was, however, weakened by continuing problems with the city of Rome. He was scarcely able to enter the city for ten years after 1167, and the Roman clergy and commune showed alarming signs of neutrality in the schism. Some deeds were dated simply by the year of the schism, and a tract in 1171 argued that unjust excommunications were invalid and that 'a man can be saved without the Roman pontiff'.[12] Frederick's return to Italy with a considerable army in 1174 led to an attempt at a negotiated settlement with the Lombard League, but the League's refusal to abandon Alexander provoked a renewal of hostilities. The defeat of the German army at the Battle of Legnano in May 1176 finally convinced the emperor that he had to come to terms with the pope.

These were agreed at Anagni in November 1176 and finalized in a personal meeting at Venice on 24 July 1177. Frederick was obliged to renounce Calixtus III and to acknowledge Alexander, to whom he did the marshal-service which had provoked controversy in the past. A truce for six years was made with the Lombards, leaving them in practice in possession of most of the disputed rights of self-government, and another for fifteen years with Sicily. But the agreement was very far from being an unconditional defeat for the emperor, and there is a striking contrast between the preliminary conditions at Anagni and the final settlement at Venice. There it was agreed that the emperor was to retain the revenues from the former Matildine lands for fifteen years, pending a full discussion of the title to them, and the undertaking to restore the papal possessions in central Italy was made in distinctly vague terms. The settlement of the affairs of the German church left Frederick in complete possession of the extensive rights which he had claimed to direct its

<hr/>

[12] J. Petersohn, 'Papstschisma und Kirchenfrieden', *QFIAB* 59 (1979), 163.

affairs, and he secured special terms for the leading imperialist churchmen. In particular, Mainz was kept by the ultra-imperialist Christian in preference to the Alexander's supporter Conrad, who was to have the next vacant archbishopric in Germany.

Considering the stress which had been placed in Alexander's propaganda upon the struggle for the liberty of the church, this was a remarkable end to the affair. It can be explained in part by the pope's need for the support of imperial arms to secure access to Rome, from which he had virtually been excluded by the commune. A still stronger reason may be found in the general desire for peace, which burst out in great rejoicing when the settlement was announced. The policy of never recognizing Alexander adopted at Würzburg in 1165 had threatened an almost indefinite schism, to avoid which it was worth making many silent concessions. In company with Archbishop Christian, Alexander returned to Rome. The commune was to keep the liberties it had possessed since 1143, but the senators took an oath to the pope and restored papal *regalia*. Alexander followed the examples of 1123 and 1139 in marking the end of the schism by the assembly of the Third Lateran Council of 1179. The council was apparently envisaged as early as the negotiations at Anagni, and opened in the presence of over 300 bishops on 5 March 1179. Part of its business was to wind up the schism, notably by the issue of a decree which required the consent of two-thirds of the cardinals for the election of a new pope. A series of decisions regulated the question of ordinations and appointments made under the schismatic popes—a difficult issue because of the exemptions which Frederick had already secured. Apart from this immediate business, the council issued canons regulating the affairs of the western churches as a whole, which mark an important step between the ideals of the Gregorian reformers and the legislation of Innocent III. The schism was finally over, and Frederick and Alexander were seemingly determined on co-operation. It was true, however, that the peace had been bought at the price of silence over many issues which were to give rise to trouble in the future.

iv. *The Papacy under Pressure (1177–1198)*

During the twenty-five years following the end of the schism the Roman Church was under intense political pressure. At no other time was imperial government in Italy so close to being a reality. The relations of emperors and popes were not uniformly hostile, for both sides had an interest in reaching an agreement. Frederick I and Henry VI needed the settlement of Italian affairs to be confirmed by concordat with the papacy, and the popes required support for their campaign against heresy and for the defence of the Holy Land, a question which became very urgent with the fall of Jerusalem to Saladin in 1187. There were three issues, left unsettled at the Treaty of Venice, which shaped papal-imperial relations during these years.

The first was the control of the German church. The emperor's claims had scarcely been affected by the agreement with Alexander III. He continued to exercise a strong influence on the election of bishops and to settle disputed elections. Apart from Urban III in 1186 the popes did not seriously attempt to interfere with the ordinary course of royal control over the church in Germany, but two major *causes célèbres* at Trier and Liège caused severe problems. A shift in the pattern of political control also affected the position of the church with the overthrow in 1180 of Henry the Lion, head of the house of Welf and former ally of Frederick I. The power of the great dukes was now finally transferred to a larger number of princely families, who aimed at the promotion of their own members to local bishoprics: we are told that on 8 September 1191 Liège was crowded with nobles who had come for the election. At a political level, it also proved impossible to eradicate the power of the Welfs, and the ability of Henry the Lion to exploit dissatisfaction against his Hohenstaufen rivals was a major problem for the emperors. The second issue between emperors and popes was the question of territorial rights within Italy. From the Peace of Venice onwards, Barbarossa's new policy was to base his power solidly on the Matildine lands and on imperial claims in central Italy, where in 1177 he appointed two of his most trusted agents to govern the duchy of Spoleto and the march of Ancona. On 25 June 1183 he signed the Peace of Constance with the representatives of the Lombard League, and in addition he made an alliance with Milan, formerly his bitter enemy. On the papal side, as a natural reaction, there was a more active interest in the title deeds of the territorial claims of the Roman Church contained in the forged Donation of Constantine, the grants of former emperors, and other documents. These were embodied in the *Liber Censuum* compiled by the papal chamberlain Cencius in 1192 and formed the basis for the policy of recuperation which was to be directed against the empire immediately after the death of Henry VI. The third issue was the radical realignment of diplomatic relations created by the alliance of Germany and Sicily. These two powers, whose hostility had been persistent throughout our whole period, were linked by the betrothal in 1184 of Henry and Constance, the heirs to the imperial and Sicilian thrones, and were united when Henry VI enforced his claim to Sicily in 1194. The change implied long-lasting domination of central Italy by Hohenstaufen power. The union of kingdom and empire also prompted a series of attempts to make succession to the empire hereditary as a means of ensuring the continued unity of the two powers, and this directly involved the papal right to crown the emperor.

After the death of Alexander III in 1181 Frederick Barbarossa was confronted by a series of short-lived popes. The first of them, Lucius III (1181–5), was an elderly Cistercian who was seriously interested in an amicable settlement. In 1183 Frederick suggested that the Roman Church surrender its territorial claims in return for a large annual pension from the imperial revenues in Italy; alternatively a commission could be appointed to determine boundaries and possibly arrange exchanges.[13] He also proposed a summit conference with the pope, which in fact took place in November 1184 at Verona. There a discussion which began well ended in frustration. Some issues were readily agreed: co-operation against heresy, the planning of a new crusade, and (at the request of the pope) the return to Germany of the banished Henry the Lion. There was a discussion of the appeal of Folmar, one of the candidates in the disputed election at Trier in May 1183, against Rudolf of Wied, whom the emperor had invested. The cause of the subsequent breakdown of the conference is obscure: some sources ascribe it to the arrival of news that Henry VI had resorted to violence against Folmar's adherents in Germany. The announcement at Augsburg on 29 October of the betrothal of Henry and Constance must also have come as a bombshell if the plans were not already known to the curia, but the timing suggests that the pope had already been informed, even if there is no reason to accept Johannes Haller's view that Lucius himself forwarded the Sicilian marriage project. Whatever the precise breaking-point, anti-imperial cardinals pressed Lucius to resist, and Frederick left Verona without a settlement of the Trier

[13] MGH Leges Const. I, no. 296, pp. 420–1.

dispute or of the question of the Matildine lands and in face of a papal refusal to crown Henry VI as emperor during his father's life-time.

After the death of Lucius III the state of opinion among the cardinals was reflected in the unanimous election on 25 November 1185 of the archbishop of Milan, a fierce opponent of the emperor, as Urban III. Urban embarked on a systematic campaign against Barbarossa's policy. Not only did he maintain the refusal to crown Henry, but he decided the Trier election in favour of Folmar in May 1186 and attacked the royal exercise of rights over the German bishoprics. The Hohenstaufen counter-attack was formidable: Henry occupied the Patrimony of St Peter, while the German bishops at Gelnhausen on 28 November 1186 supported Frederick and protested at the pope's conduct. Urban, threatening to excommunicate the emperor, died at Ferrara on 20 October 1187, after a brief pontificate which had demonstrated the weakness of the political position of the curia. Another swing of opinion among the cardinals led to the election of the papal chancellor Albert of Morra, who was reputedly an imperialist sympathizer. The pontificate of Gregory VIII (21 October–17 December 1187) was one of the shortest in papal history, but it began the response of western Christendom to the loss of Jerusalem with the issue of *Audita tremendi*, the encyclical which launched the Third Crusade.

The next pope, Clement III (1187–91), has often been regarded as another imperialist, but it is more accurate to see him as essentially a Roman. He was Paolo Scolari, a member of a noble family who had been educated at the basilica of Santa Maria Maggiore and become cardinal-bishop of Palestrina. His agreement with the commune of Rome made it possible for the popes to reside there again; his numerous nominations of cardinals, which virtually recreated the sacred college in the space of four years, filled it with men of Roman birth and training; and he was the first of a line of Roman popes who were to occupy the papal throne for over fifty years. All of this was a very marked break with the past, for Rome had only intermittently been a base for the popes since 1084 and popes of Roman birth had been rare since Gregory VII. Clement was no Innocent III, but he created the preconditions for Innocent's policy. He was by disposition a compromiser. The settlement with the Roman senate on 31 May 1188 involved the return to the pope of the *regalia* and several major Roman churches, but also compensated the Romans for the resulting loss of income. Tusculum, the city which had long resisted the senate, was to be surrendered to its vengeance—a provision which in practice the pope was unable to fulfil. A further compromise with the emperor followed in spring 1189. It included the deposition of Folmar as archbishop of Trier and a promise by the pope to crown Henry as emperor. The territorial terms were embodied in a rescript from Henry VI on 3 April restoring a list of places in the Patrimony of St Peter to the pope 'in possession, saving the right of the empire as to both property and possession'. In effect this reconstituted the region surrounding Rome as a papal domain, but no mention was made of the rest of central Italy or of the Matildine lands, which remained in the emperor's control.[14] It was a blueprint for an Italy under Hohenstaufen influence, and it has been rightly said to 'mark the final triumph of imperial policy' at the end of Barbarossa's reign.[15]

A new situation was created by two deaths. The first was that of William II of Sicily on 18 November 1189. Up to that point the prospect of a Hohenstaufen succession in Sicily was fairly remote, for although William was childless he was still only in early middle age. With his death, the danger that the Hohenstaufen would dominate the peninsula became real. Clement III, who had worked in co-operation with the empire, now supported the opposition party in Sicily in the election of Tancred of Lecce, an illegitimate member of the royal family. A few months later the report arrived of the death of Frederick I during the Third Crusade on 10 June 1190 in an accident at a river crossing in Anatolia. His heir Henry VI thus became emperor in his own right. He was of a very different temperament from his father. A man of considerable learning, whom Godfrey of Viterbo greeted as a philosopher-king, he possessed neither Barbarossa's striking physique nor his ability to win affection and loyalty, and in Henry the Hohenstaufen drive for power was not balanced by other qualities.[16] His political aims, however, were close to those which Barbarossa had followed in his later years. They included secure control in Italy and an active interest in the eastern Mediterranean. Historians have sometimes attributed to Henry a desire for world dominion which would necessarily have been a challenge to the papacy, and it is true that in addition to Sicily he received the homage of Richard of England and of the kings of Armenia and Cyprus in the east, and he was also

---

[14] Const. I. no. 322–4, pp. 460–3.   [15] A. L. Poole, *CMH* v.459.
[16] Godfrey of Viterbo, *Memoria seculorum* (MGH SS XXII 103).

thought to be striving for the submission of Philip Augustus of France. Henry was undoubtedly convinced of the superiority of the imperial office over that of kings, and exacted their deference to his higher status, but that is not the same thing as seeking the power to govern other kingdoms or even to intervene politically there. The issues dividing Henry from the papacy were much more concrete.

Clement III, in spite of disagreement over the Sicilian question, did not attempt to avoid his commitment to crown Henry, who was in the neighbourhood of Rome for the ceremony when Clement died. His successor Celestine III was the oldest man ever to be elected pope. He was a Roman of noble birth, Hyacinth Bobone, and had been educated in France where he had been a pupil of Peter Abelard. He was about 85 at the time of his election, much the most senior man among a body of new cardinals. His opposition to Henry VI has often been described as passive resistance, but that is a great understatement: he was a determined and resolute opponent. If he did not excommunicate Henry, it must be remembered that the precedents for this action, by Gregory VII and Alexander III, were both in circumstances where the emperor was attempting to depose the pope. After some delay and bargaining Celestine proceeded with the coronation on 15 April 1191. Henry's first attempt to enforce his claims in Sicily rapidly failed, and in June 1192 the pope signed the Concordat of Gravina with Tancred, who in return for his investiture with the kingdom surrendered many of the rights which his predecessors had held over the Sicilian church.

The opposition in Germany was exacerbated by two scandals at the end of 1192. Albert of Brabant had been elected bishop of Liège by a majority of the voters but rejected by the emperor. His claim was upheld by Celestine III and he was consecrated at Reims, where he was murdered by a party of German knights on 24 November 1192. The similarity to the case of Thomas Becket of Canterbury was underlined by Albert's biographer, who quoted Dean Ralph of Reims's remark, 'Behold a greater than Thomas is here!'[17] A month later, Richard I of England, on his way home through Germany at the end of the Third Crusade, was captured by his personal enemy Leopold of Austria and surrendered to the emperor. In the eyes of his enemies Henry had now been responsible for the killing of a bishop and imprisonment of a crusader. The powerful relatives of Bishop

Albert made common cause with the Welf allies of Richard of England, with the support of Tancred and the pope. Henry extricated himself from this dangerous situation by adroit negotiations with Richard. The terms for release included not only a huge ransom and homage for England, but a close alliance against Philip Augustus of France and an undertaking to make peace with the Welfs. The transformation of the situation was completed by the death of Tancred on 20 February 1194. With peace in Germany, central Italy in the control of his officers, and funding from the English ransom, Henry rapidly overran Sicily and was crowned at Palermo on Christmas Day 1194. The next day his triumph was completed by the birth of a son, baptized Frederick Roger, who was to be his heir in both kingdoms.

To make this succession a reality Henry needed the agreement of the German princes and the pope. To reopen negotiations with the pope he took a crusading vow, and there followed a long series of discussions culminating in November 1196. The emperor's aim, we are told by the Marbach annalist, was that the pope 'should baptize his son . . . and anoint him king', that is king of the Romans and therefore acknowledged heir to the empire.[18] Henry was in effect proposing a major change in the constitutional relations of empire and papacy, and to obtain it he relied in part upon the coercion of the papal territories by his officers. He also envisaged important concessions. In a letter of 17 November 1196 he reminded Celestine that he had offered 'such things . . . as had been offered . . . neither by our father . . . nor by any other of our predecessors'.[19] Unfortunately there is no record of the nature of these. It has been widely accepted that Henry undertook to put a canonry in every collegiate church of the empire at the disposal of pope and cardinals—a plausible suggestion in view of the development of papal provisions in precisely this period. Other scholars have suggested that Henry was willing to receive investiture of the empire as a fief from the pope by means of a golden orb, or again to make large territorial concessions in central Italy in return for the coronation of his son. These suggestions, however, rest on sources which are of dubious relevance to the negotiations of 1195–6, and the matter has to be left open.

[18] *Annales Marbacenses* s.a. 1196 (MGH SS XVII.167).
[19] MGH Leges Const. I, no. 376, p. 525. For the date, see G. Baaken, 'Die Verhandlungen zwischen Kaiser Heinrich VI und Papst Coelestin III', *DAEM* 27 (1971), 457–513.

The discussions led to no agreement, and must have been broken off at the latest in May 1197, when a major conspiracy in Sicily designed to murder Henry, to which Celestine may have been privy, was ferociously repressed by the emperor. Henry was meanwhile pressing ahead with his plans for a crusade, and the major part of the expedition had actually left for the east when the emperor fell ill and died at Messina on 28 September 1197. With a 2-year-old boy as his heir, his political system collapsed. Celestine, with the initiative thus unexpectedly restored to him, at once took effective action to recover the lands claimed by the papacy, and was rapidly able to organize a league of Tuscan cities directed against the German oppressors. He also, in a curious mirror-image of the 'hereditary empire' scheme, held a discussion among the cardinals at Christmas of the succession to the papacy and offered to resign if Cardinal John of St Paul, his closest adviser, were elected as the new pope. The cardinals wisely refused to establish such a startling precedent. The continuation of the papal counter-offensive against the Hohenstaufen after the death of Celestine on 8 January 1198 was to be continued by other, and very much younger, hands.

9

THE GOVERNMENT OF THE CHURCH IN THE TWELFTH CENTURY

i. *Concepts of Papal Authority*

The opening address at the Third Lateran Council in March 1179 was delivered by the canonist Bishop Rufinus of Assisi, and we may safely assume that the description of papal authority was one which Alexander III wished the bishops to take to their home churches:

There are many things to wonder at in the sight of an assembly of such noble fathers, and as I look I see this blessed gathering of prelates as presenting the image of a magnificent city, where there is the king, nobles, consuls and also a crowd of people. Is not the chief pontiff the king? The nobles or magnates are his brothers and flanks, the lord cardinals; the archbishops are the consuls; and we other bishops and abbots are not ashamed in so noble a city to take the place of the people.[1]

It is clear that we are presented here with an image of papal monarchy in the government of the church; the question is what sense the thinkers of the twelfth century gave to that idea. In a diverse culture, there were different assumptions. Theologians glorified the papal office by the rhetorical use of Biblical symbolism, led by the need to find in Rome protection for privileges or leadership in the struggle against abuses. Canonists came to see the pope as the supreme judge. At the same time the ancient texts on which both disciplines were founded expressed limitations which created a complex pattern within which papal supremacy was at once affirmed and restricted.

The twelfth century introduced some important innovations in the vocabulary of papal monarchy, which were to reach their full significance under Innocent III. For the first time, leaving aside a few precedents in the distant past, the pope came to be addressed as the

---

[1] G. Morin, 'Le discours d'ouverture du concile général du Latran (1179)', *Memorie della pontificia Accademia Romana di Archeologia*, III.2 (1928), 116-17.

vicar of Christ. Taken by itself it was not a remarkable title, for anybody who acted on behalf of Christ could be called his vicar, and the term had been used of both kings and bishops. The new development was to treat it as unique to the pope. The statement that the pope acts in place of Christ (*vice Christi*) appears in Peter Damian and in a few writers of the early twelfth century, but the first application to the pope of the precise title 'vicar of Christ' seems to be early in the twelfth century in Honorius's *Jewel of the Soul*, (*De gemma animae*), which makes its special character quite clear: 'the pope is the vicar of Christ and all the bishops are vicars of the apostles'. Its appearance about 1150 in the *De consideratione* of Bernard of Clairvaux was particularly significant because of the huge influence of the work. The first pope to use the title was Eugenius III in 1153, and thereafter its acceptance was widespread.[2]

Another term which was winning increasing significance was 'fullness of power', *plenitudo potestatis*. It had a long history beginning with a letter of Leo I, but up to the time of Gratian it had attracted little notice. Its use was confined to Leo's letter and two pseudo-Isidorian texts based on it, and it simply contrasted the authority of the apostolic see with those (such as legates or metropolitans) who had been authorized to perform a subordinate function. It was Bernard's *De consideratione* which introduced a new interpretation when he wrote to Eugenius III that 'according to your canons, others are called to a share in caring; you, to the fullness of power. The power of others is confined within fixed limits; yours extends also to those who have received power over others.'[3] In spite of the specific reference to canon law the meaning is new, because Bernard understood it as referring to the universal power of the Roman pontiff to intervene in all parts of the church. The term, which was to be a favourite of Innocent III's, was used several times by the curia in letters of his predecessor Celestine III. Other concepts were also to be found with increasing frequency: Rome was the mother and mistress, the head and hinge, of all the churches. Its bishop alone could rightly be called universal, a title which came into use in spite of Gratian's preservation of older texts which prohibited it. As Rufinus noted, 'this is not observed today, for we regularly in our letters call the chief pontiff universal'.[4]

---

[2] For the references see M. Maccarrone, *Vicarius Christi. Storia del titolo papale* (Rome, 1952), esp. 86–100.

[3] Bernard, *De consideratione*, II.viii.16, *Opera*, iii.424.

[4] Gratian, *Decr.* D. XCIX, c. 4–5 (351); H. Singer (ed.), *Die Summa Decretorum des Magister Rufinus* (Paderborn, 1902), 194.

This terminology expressed the headship of Rome over the church, but it had implications also for the political actions of the popes which are revealed in the development of the terminology of the two swords. It was at the beginning of our period that writers first applied to the church-state relationship the words in Luke 22: 38: 'And they said, "Look, Lord, here are two swords." And he said to them, "It is enough."' The image was seized on by imperialist writers to express their two-power theory and was used in this sense by writers on both sides, since both agreed that the secular power existed for the sake of righteousness. A significant change in vocabulary is found in Bernard of Clairvaux: 'Both therefore belong to the church, the spiritual and the material sword; but the one is to be used for the church, the other by the church; the former by the hand of the priest, the latter by that of the knight, but at the indication of the priest and the hand of the emperor.'[5] It was common ground that spiritual and material power was to be used in the service of the church, but Bernard refashioned this by assuming that 'the church' properly meant the bishops, and above all the pope, who therefore had authority to request the aid of the emperor to defend the interests of Christianity. The argument was not that royal authority was in principle derived from the pope; Bernard would have been the last man to make a constitutional point of that sort, and he had in mind practical situations such as the crusades. The same point could, however, be expressed in a way which sounded like a claim to universal authority, as in Eugenius III's statement that God founded the Roman Church and committed to it 'the laws of both heavenly and earthly empire'.[6]

The core of the argument lay in the supremacy of Rome over other churches. To canonists this signified its position as head in matters of justice, administration, and discipline. This had some foundations in tradition, for it had always been recognized that Rome had cognizance of certain 'major causes', and the False Decretals had extended these to cover a range of rights to intervene in other churches. Mostly, however, the rights claimed for the Roman Church were new, as was the framework of law within which they were exercised. Some writers saw the pope as the source of canon law, from which he could dispense and exempt. Gratian expressed the claim in an extreme form: 'The holy Roman Church imparts right and authority to the sacred canons, but is not bound by them.

---

[5] Bernard, *De consideratione*, IV.iii.7, *Opera*, iii.454.
[6] P. Jaffé, *Regesta Pontificum Romanorum*, 2 vols. (Leipzig, 1888), 9149.

For it has the right of establishing canons, since it is the head and hinge of all churches, from whose ruling no one may dissent. It therefore gives authority to the canons without subjecting itself to them.' The canonists took up the idea of the universal authority of the Roman Church, which Huguccio described as 'the common and general forum of all clergy and all churches'.[7] This function became even more important with the increasingly juridical way in which decisions, even in matters of faith, were reached. Since the curia was head of the judicial system, larger areas of the life of the church fell by this means under its control.

This concept sat rather uneasily within the framework of an older theology which saw the Roman Church as the guardian of the catholic faith, founded by God and preserved from error by divine promise. Any divergence of customs, as in the Mozarabic liturgy in Spain or the Ambrosian rite at Milan, was assumed to have arisen because the local church had departed from apostolic practice, which could be reliably observed in the Church of Rome. The clearest statement of this position is in the *Dialogues* of Anselm of Havelberg:

For this purpose the holy Roman Church was chosen before the others by the Lord, was given by him and blessed with a special privilege, and stands above all churches as if by prerogative, and by divine right excels them. For the others from time to time have been invaded by various heresies and wavered in the catholic faith; but she, founded and established upon a rock, has always remained unshaken.

The title-deeds of the Roman Church were the familiar Petrine texts, but these were not interpreted as applying solely to the pope. Thus the declaration of Matthew 16: 18, 'on this rock I will build my church', was usually regarded as a reference not to Peter, but to Christ or to the confession of faith, and it was held that the powers of binding and loosing belonged to all the apostles (Matt. 18: 18) while being given principally to Peter, as Matthew 16: 19 implies. The contemporary idea of Peter's ministry was expressed by Anselm in a fine passage:

Peter was the senior in age of the apostles, more sure in faith, more simple in hearing the words of eternal life . . . more ready in responding among Christ and the apostles, more effective in healing the sick even with the shadow of his body. After the Ascension of the Lord he took over in place

---

[7] Gratian, *Decr.* C. IX, q. 1, dictum post c.16 (1011); Huguccio, cited J. A. Watt, 'The Theory of Papal Monarchy in the Thirteenth Century', *Traditio* 20 (1964), 270.

of Christ that young and primitive church . . . Therefore it is not right that any of the faithful should in any way doubt or put in question, but they should hold most firmly that Peter was appointed by the Lord chief of the apostles. [8]

Such statements did not indicate precisely where authority lay, and for most purposes no distinction was made between the terms Roman Church, apostolic see, and pope (usually under the title 'supreme pontiff'), while the growth of the college of cardinals left it uncertain how much the pope could undertake without them. The phrase 'Roman Church' was quite often used even more widely, to include the whole body of the faithful, and if the prevailing tendency was to identify it with the pope, this did not rest on any basis of theory and was held in check by interpretations which imposed limits on papal authority. In particular, Gratian had preserved material which threw doubt on the absolute authority of the pope in matters of doctrine. The crucial text here was the statement that the pope 'is the judge of all men and is himself judged of no one, unless he is found to be erroneous in faith'. [9] This last phrase made it clear that a pope could be a heretic, and Gratian accepted this without much misgiving. He was not familiar with Pope Honorius, whose heresy was to bulk large in post-Reformation controversy, but Anastasius II (496–8) served as the type of the heretic pope. [10] In recognizing that a pope might fall into error Gratian was a man of his time. The extreme Gregorians had accused Paschal II of heresy when he surrendered to Henry V, and one canonist went so far as to comment that 'it would be dangerous for us to commit our faith to the decision of one man'. [11] Nor did the canonists assume that the pope had unrestricted rights even in matters which were not a question of faith, for they stressed his duty to uphold the *status ecclesie*, the constitution or welfare of the church. St Bernard saw this as involving the obligation to defend the traditional hierarchy against the threats posed by appeals and exemptions. Huguccio's statement is a fair summary of the balance of opinion in the twelfth century: 'In those things which pertain to salvation, as is contained in the Gospel, the Law and the prophets, he cannot amend. Also in those which

[8] Anselm, *Dialogi*, iii. 5 (PL 188. 1214C) and 10 (col. 1222–3).

[9] Gratian, *Decr.* D. XL, c. 6 (146). The passage first appeared in Deusdedit, where it was wrongly ascribed to St Boniface. It appears to be part of a treatise composed at Rome in the eleventh century.

[10] Gratian, *Decr.* D. XIX, c. 9 (64).

[11] *Glossa Palatina*, cited B. Tierney, *Origins of Papal Infallibility* (Leiden, 1972), 32 n.

concern the state of the church, as in the sacraments and articles of faith, he cannot dispense.'[12] Twelfth-century thinkers commonly accepted that the Roman Church had a God-given primacy and that it was preserved from heresy by the promise of Christ. The Roman Church could not in practice reach a decision without the pope, but the prevailing view did not accept that the supreme pontiff alone could define in matters of faith, alter the structure of the church, or exploit for his own purposes the property of other churches.

ii. *The Exercise of Papal Power*

The pope's principal agents in the exercise of his authority came from the college of cardinals. We have seen in an earlier chapter the origins of their change from liturgical duties to governmental functions: by the time of the Concordat of Worms they were being consulted about the wide range of decisions which came to the apostolic see. The early ascendancy of the cardinal-bishops had vanished except as a matter of ceremony, and for practical purposes no distinction was made between the various orders. The total possible number of cardinals was in theory over fifty, but some titles were left vacant for long periods and others amalgamated, so that there were only thirty at the time of the schism of 1159, and as few as nineteen when Clement III became pope in 1187. The popes had the power to nominate, and in two cases used it to flood the college with supporters. In 1123 in face of the protests against the Concordat, Calixtus II appointed fifteen cardinals, and Clement III created twenty-five to fill the college with men of Roman birth and education. The later practice of nominating leaders of other national churches as cardinals outside the curia was still rare, and most cardinals were Italians, together with some Frenchmen and a handful from other nationalities. Bernard of Clairvaux's plea to Eugenius III to recruit them widely ('should they not be chosen from the whole world, who are to judge the world?') remained without permanent effect.[13]

The changing role of the cardinals can be illustrated by their part in the election of a new pope. Traditionally this had belonged to the clergy and laity of the Roman Church, dominated by the local nobility, and the first step away from such practice was the grant in

---

[12] Cited by G. Post, *SGrat* ix. 372.
[13] Bernard, *De consideratione*, IV.iv.4, *Opera*, iii.456.

1059 of power to the cardinal-bishops to process the election in a *tractatio*. By 1100 the cardinals as a whole seem to have been participating in papal elections, although not yet to the exclusion of other Roman clergy and laity. Werner Maleczek considers that the first pope to be elected by cardinals alone was Innocent II in the disputed election of 1130.[14] This system was formalized by the election decree of 1179, *Licet de vitanda*, which thereafter gave the decision to the cardinals as a whole, voting by a two-thirds majority: a striking statement of the equality of all the members irrespective of their standing as bishops, priests, or deacons, and of the monopoly which they had established over papal business.[15] Their theoretical position as joint rulers of the Roman Church was now acknowledged. The decretist Huguccio held that new laws should be discussed in consistory with the cardinals, and saw them as guaranteeing the inerrancy of the Roman Church even if the pope should stumble.[16] New popes were elected almost entirely from the ranks of the cardinals. From them most papal legates were appointed, and the rapidly growing number of appeals was handled largely by the cardinals as auditors. This involvement in legal business at the highest level naturally made the cardinals unpopular with satirists, whose attacks on the Roman curia regularly assumed that the pope was surrounded by cardinals even more involved in extortion than the pope himself.

The period between the schism of 1084 and the Concordat of Worms had seen the creation of a papal curia with its own chamber and chancery, separate from the traditional officers of the city of Rome. The next phase in its history was shaped by the need to provide for the flood of appeals which effectively began in the 1130s. Early in the twelfth century Paschal II reminded Henry I of England of the two types of causes which should be heard by the apostolic see: *causae maiores* (greater causes) and appeals from all who believed themselves to be oppressed.[17] The former were a group of special issues long recognized in canon law and greatly extended in the course of the twelfth century. The latter category was based mainly on canons from the pseudo-Isidorian decretals, which did not define the groups who might appeal; but the matter was one of secondary

---

[14] W. Maleczek, *Papst und Kardinalskolleg 1191–1216* (Vienna, 1984), 218.
[15] III Lateran can. 1 (Alberigo 187) = Greg. IX, *Decretals*, I.6.6(51).
[16] See B. Tierney, *Foundations of the Conciliar Theory* (Cambridge, 1955), 71, 81.
[17] Eadmer, *Historia novorum in Anglia*, ed. M. Rule (RS, 1884), 233.

importance, because the possibility of a volume of appeals which would swamp the existing machinery still seemed remote.

The growth of appeals was to some extent the result of the increased initiative in the life of the western church under the Gregorian papacy, for when an instruction or a privilege had come from Rome disputes about it would naturally involve papal authority. In practice appeals extended far beyond these special cases and included litigation about matters of routine. By 1160 it was already regarded as usual for a dispute over the possession of a parish church to be appealed to the curia. Technically this had become possible because the revival of Roman law had provided procedures which could be linked into a system for the handling of appeals, but beneath this lay a more fundamental change. Papal activity was the outstanding example of what has been called 'rescript' government. This means that letters or rescripts were issued in response to petitions from outside the curia, and that they often simply echoed the wording of the request. It was the task of the papal officials to ensure that the answer was in accordance with the law, but there was no investigation of facts or even a proper check to make sure whether an incompatible instruction had been issued. Clement III noted the difficulty of making sure that the same case was not delegated to different sets of judges, and commented that 'when one commission frustrates another it makes the Roman curia look frivolous'.[18] This administration by response left most of the initiative in the hands of petitioners and meant that a vast amount of paperwork might imply only a minimum of true policy-making. It was not unique to the papacy: on the contrary, it was a style of government which was emerging rapidly and can be traced in the rise of common law in England. Central governments did not have the resources to enforce their authority evenly in the manner of a modern state, but instead were providing a jurisdiction to which parties could turn in the settlement of local disputes. At the heart of what may seem a very active administration the pope or king was passive, responding to applications without, in many cases, any real capacity to assess the situation. A picture of this kind helps us to understand the popes' remarkable failure (as it has seemed to historians) to carry through a systematic reform of the western church. This was not mainly because the Roman curia was itself corrupt but because the structure

---

[18] Cited by Pitz, *Papstreskript und Kaiserreskript im Ma.* (Tübingen, 1971), 327.

was not designed for the exercise of major initiatives or the application of consistent policies. The papacy was not surprisingly a monarchy of its period, far removed from the absolutism which became possible in later centuries.

Inevitably there were protests. It was an unattractive idea to turn the household of St Peter into a set of tribunals for property rights, and some influential advisers were anxious to limit the juridical activity of the curia to matters of genuine spiritual significance. Bernard of Clairvaux warned his protégé Eugenius III that he was in danger of undermining the proper hierarchy of the church: 'Abbots are being withdrawn from their bishops, bishops from their archbishops . . . You have been appointed to preserve for each the grades and orders of honours and dignities, not to prejudice them', and similar complaints were made in indignant terms by the hierarchy of the provincial churches.[19] Appeals provided a highly convenient machinery by which abbeys could obtain Roman protection for their privileges, and could extend them into full exemption from episcopal authority. Several popes attempted to restrict the growth of appeals, but on the whole the weight of opinion was in favour of freedom of appeal. Gratian had assigned to appellants almost unrestricted rights: they could appeal at any time (not just after sentence); any person could appeal who felt himself oppressed (not simply against a faulty judgement); and the bishop had no power to restrict appeals.[20] So great was the liberty extended to complainants that many actions were brought straight to the curia without any hearing before the diocesan or other local authorities.

We only know a limited amount about the arrangements within the curia before Innocent III. Although the pope personally heard cases the numbers were too great for this to be the normal procedure, and many were referred to groups of cardinals for decision. The key to the growth of appeals lay in the delegation of cases to judges in the country of origin by papal mandate. It is not possible to give a precise starting-date for this, because the reference of individual cases to local judges went back far into papal history, and the legal possibility of delegation was recognized in the collections of Anselm of Lucca and Deusdedit. The new features were the increasingly large number of cases and the development of standardized letters initially based on the mandates known to Roman civil law. The full

---

[19] Bernard, *De consideratione*, III.iv.14, *Opera*, iii.442.
[20] Gratian, *Decr.* C. II, q. 6, dictum post c. 14 (470).

development of such common-form mandates is mainly to be ascribed to the time of Alexander III, but the large-scale use of judges delegate goes back before the middle of the century. Most historians see the pontificate of Innocent II as the time when a steady flow of delegations began. In England Robert of Béthune, bishop of Hereford (1131–48), already had a reputation for hearing causes as a judge delegate, while Bishop Roger of Worcester (1164–79) can be found acting as a delegate in about a hundred cases. It is probable that there were many others of which we have no record, because a register of Archbishop Henry of Reims, who died in 1175, indicates that he received no less that 423 papal letters, of which the larger proportion concerned lawsuits. The use of judges delegate enabled a litigant to escape from the jurisdiction of the bishop, who might well have his own interests or sympathies, and to submit his plea to a tribunal of three experienced judges.

The system of appeals was financed by fees to curial advocates and notaries and by presents which were barely distinguishable from bribes. Nevertheless the papacy found itself in severe financial difficulties. For much of the century the popes were unable to obtain access to their revenues from the city of Rome, and their income from the Patrimony of St Peter outside it was threatened by local cities and nobles as well as by imperial pressure. The political and military costs of resistance to the Hohenstaufen must have been formidable: as Hadrian IV put it, 'no one can make war without pay'.[21] One effect of the isolation of the curia from the city of Rome was to diminish the financial significance of the traditional officers, and from the middle of the century the chamberlain was completely in charge of papal revenues. He was invariably a cardinal, and two holders of the office, Boso under Hadrian IV and Cencius (the later Honorius III) under Celestine III, were major political figures. The concern of the curia about its finances was reflected in a series of attempts to list its revenues. The process had already begun with Deusdedit's collection of canons, which focused particularly on the rights of the Roman Church, and it culminated in the *Liber Censuum* completed by Cencius in 1192. This was designed to continue in use under his successors, with gaps left for new entries. It was a reasonably thorough piece of work, but all these works were marked by an 'unsurpassed conservatism'.[22] They are lists of legal rights

[21] *nemo potest sine stipendiis militare*, cited V. Pfaff, 'Päpstliche Finanzverwaltung am Ende des 12 Jhs', *MIOG* 64 (1956), 21.
[22] V. Pfaff, 'Päpstliche Finanzverwaltung', 12.

combined with other liturgical and historical material: the collections are a major source of information about the *Ordo Romanus* which governed the ceremonial of the Roman Church. The image of a papacy bound up with the traditional life of the city is preserved here, although in view of the long absences from Rome it must have been on the way to being an anachronism. Unfortunately no list of receipts and outgoings survives from the chamber for this period; such a list might have given a more workmanlike impression of its operation.

The revenues recorded in the *Liber Censuum* would have been inadequate for the needs of the popes. Historically the principal income of the Roman Church came from its landed estates in central Italy and from the proceeds of lordship such as tolls and judicial revenues; but there had been large losses and many estates yielded only nominal rents. Cencius records only two types of income derived from the western church outside Italy: the *census* due from exempt abbeys and the tribute payable by certain kingdoms and principalities. Such tributes had emerged, mainly in the eleventh century, with the acknowledgement of papal overlordship by the Normans in Sicily and other states; they also included Peter's Pence from England, Scandinavia, and Poland, a customary gift of uncertain origin which was interpreted by the curia as a sign of subjection. Peter's Pence was notionally a levy of a penny on the house of every freeman, but it had been eroded by custom so that the annual sum actually produced by England was just under £200. The total revenue implied by the *Liber Censuum* is hard to estimate because the items are stated in many different currencies, but V. Pfaff has assessed it as 1,214 gold ounces. By international standards this was very small, amounting to less than 5 per cent of Richard I's annual income from England; and it must be added that some of the items, particularly the sums due from princes and exempt monasteries, were not always paid.[23] On the other hand, there were important resources not included in the *Liber Censuum*. The income in cash and kind received from central Italy by papal rectors and other officers is not there, nor is the papal share of offerings in the great Roman basilicas adequately represented. These omissions are understandable, because the purpose was to provide a working list of sums due directly at the chamber, but they mean that the local

---

[23] V. Pfaff, 'Die Einnahmen der römischen Kurie', *Vierteljahresschrift für Sozialwissenschaft und Wirtschaftsgeschichte* 40 (1953), 97–118.

revenue of the popes must have been greater than Cencius has indicated and that the popes' acute concern about imperial pressure on their territories becomes readily understandable. Another important financial resource was the right to finance the journeys of popes and legates by taking 'procurations' or subsistence expenses from the churches which they were visiting. Carlrichard Brühl has shown that the claim for procurations for legates originated with Gregory VII, and for popes with Urban II's visit to France, and he has stressed the importance of this right in giving the popes freedom of action.[24] Procurations were sometimes, perhaps usually, taken in money as well as in free hospitality, and some legates were reported to have taken a large sum in silver back to the curia with them. This custom meant that the pope was able to conduct diplomacy and organize inspections without cost to himself, and possibly at a considerable profit to his agents.

There were also attempts to increase the international revenue of the curia. Perhaps the most important was the appeal for subsidies from sympathetic churchmen. The earliest of which we know was a request by Urban II to the clergy of southern France in 1093 for gifts 'in restoration of the liberty of the apostolic see'. Alexander III repeatedly asked for gifts from groups of clergy, for example the English prelates in 1173; and in 1184 Lucius III, excluded from Rome by the commune, asked Henry II for a grant from the English clergy. The level of such subsidies was presumably determined by the donors, for the age of papally imposed income taxes was yet to come. Sometimes they were more complex than simple charitable donations. We hear of 'the common collections made for the lord pope or his nuncios' as a custom at Genoa in 1187, and this becomes comprehensible in the light of the close financial relations between the papacy and Genoa, which had led Alexander III in 1162 to describe the city as 'the special chamber of St Peter'.[25] Papal support for Genoese mercantile operations brought in a good deal of money to the curia. The papacy attempted also to maximize the contributions from other churches by having payments made to its own appointed collectors, and began to provide curial officers with incomes by securing for them canonries in collegiate churches, two practices which were to be systematized in the thirteenth century. The effective papal revenue was thus larger than the *Liber Censuum*

[24] C. Brühl, 'Zur Geschichte der *procuratio canonica*', MCSM VII (1974), 419–31.
[25] Cited V. Pfaff, 'Päpstliche Finanzverwaltung', 21.

indicates; but it did not match the responsibilities. One can well understand the offers by Frederick Barbarossa and Henry VI of a reliable revenue to the curia in return for a settlement of territorial questions in Italy. Although they were not accepted, they were undoubtedly directed towards a pressing need on the part of the papacy.

In the twelfth century, therefore, the agenda for papal business was written by interested parties in Christendom as a whole. The machinery of the curia was designed to respond to petitioners and appellants; its revenues were inadequate and the attempts to increase them relied on improvisations pursued with little system. The idea of the papacy as an absolute monarchy able to decide at will the affairs of the provincial churches is an illusion. Nevertheless the Roman Church had other channels of communication which gave it considerable powers of direction. The machinery to which the popes turned for the dissemination of their policy was primarily the council. The synods of Rome, which had been important to the papal reformers of the late eleventh century, had ceased to exist in their old form as the consistory of cardinals assumed their place as the assembly of the Roman Church. A different type of council now emerged, presided over by the popes on their travels. The new councils were designed to bring together the curia and the bishops, and their assembly was usually a response to a crisis. Reims 1119 was intended to arrive at a settlement of the dispute over investitures, while Clermont 1130, Reims 1131, Pisa 1135, and Tours 1163 were designed to rally support in times of schism. The most famous, the three Lateran Councils of 1123, 1139, and 1179, were all called to resolve the issues posed by the ending of a schism and the return to Rome of the papacy after a long absence. The purpose of these councils, however, was not only political, for almost all of them issued important decrees about church discipline. In contrast with this legislative activity by the pope in council, archbishops and bishops issued few canons between 1123 and 1198. Even in England and Normandy, where the archbishops of Canterbury and Rouen had presided over important national or provincial assemblies in earlier decades, there seems to be a reduction of synodal activity until its revival under Innocent III. The initiative in legislation was being left to the pope, who summoned councils, notified the bishops by his legates or letters, and chose the preachers to give the keynote addresses. The decrees, were probably drafted in the curia; at Third

Lateran some of them reflect policies already applied in Alexander III's decretal letters. It would be wrong, however, to suppose that there was no genuine exchange between the curia and the provincial bishops. At Third Lateran, for example, canon 9 mentioned a 'vehement complaint by our brothers and fellow bishops' about the abuse of privileges by the Templars and Hospitallers, and there is a report of a sharp criticism by John of Salisbury, then bishop of Chartres, of the excessively legalistic procedure of the council.[26] The conciliar procedure provided an opportunity to formulate papal policy in the light of comments from the bishops.

One of the major lines of communication between the curia and the provinces was the legate. A marked change took place with the disappearance of the long-standing 'viceroys' whom Gregory VII had appointed from among his confidants to supervise the regional churches. The last examples of this type of appointment were Bishops Gerald of Angoulême and Geoffrey of Chartres, legates of the rival popes in the schism of 1130. The curia operated instead through legates who, although they had wide powers, were sent for a limited term and for a specific purpose. They often, in the twelfth century, had a political objective: to raise support for the pope in a time of schism, to safeguard the position of his allies in the Lombard League, or to negotiate peace between rival Christian powers. They were members of the curia, and almost always cardinals. The other development of the office of legate was quite different in kind: the appointment as resident legate with limited powers of a member of the local hierarchy. This might be the result of a desire to honour an archbishop who enjoyed the approval of the curia, or it could be a simple way of solving a local difficulty. Thus a long-standing quarrel about Canterbury's claim to primacy over the English church as a whole was evaded by making the archbishop of Canterbury the resident legate. This system, which continued with breaks from 1126 onwards, gave him precedence over the archbishop of York. The two different types of legate, the later *legatus a latere* and *legatus natus*, were thus in practice differentiated during this century.

There were other ways, too, in which the popes could take the initiative in introducing policies to the church as a whole. Although, as we saw earlier, the system of judges delegate was a response to the demands of litigants, it also involved the issue of decretal letters to

[26] III Lateran can. 9 (Alberigo 192) = Greg. IX, *Decretals*, V.3.9(751).

rule on points of law, and these allowed popes to imprint their own ideas, or those of their curial advisers, upon the law of the western church. The custom that a crusade was originated by a papal bull was widely accepted in the century. It did not mean that the pope's policy always prevailed; Bernard of Clairvaux probably exceeded his instructions in recruiting Conrad III for the Second Crusade, and Henry VI's crusade may have been wished on Pope Celestine III (the matter is not clear). But it did give the pope the opportunity to originate and plan crusades and to publicize his theology of crusading, as Gregory VIII did in his bull *Audita tremendi*. The century also saw a shift in the accepted method of creating a new saint. In the past this had normally been a response to the pressure of public demand authenticated by the decision of the diocesan, but in the twelfth century the official procedure shifted decisively in favour of seeking the permission of the pope in synod. In 1163 at Tours Alexander found himself faced by requests for no less than six canonizations, including Anselm of Canterbury and three who had died recently: Bernard of Clairvaux (1153), the Irish Malachy of Armagh (1148), and the Tuscan hermit William of Malavalle (1157). Finally with the increasing threat of heresy the bishops turned to papal authority for leadership, and the first steps toward decisive action were taken at Third Lateran and at the meeting of Verona in 1184. In these areas it was possible for the popes not merely to respond to pressures from outside but to offer a formative leadership to the western churches.

iii. *The Pastorate of the Bishops*

The European church was divided into dioceses, each with a bishop at its head. Their size varied enormously between the Mediterranean region and the north. To take extreme examples, Ravello near Salerno was less than two miles long, whereas Constance in Germany and Lincoln in England were immense, so that the standing of a southern Italian bishop was more like that of the rector of a city church in the north. Even within particular regions the accidents of history had left bishoprics of uneven size: the three Alpine dioceses of Tarentaise, Aosta, and Sitten contained less than 100 parishes each, whereas their neighbour Geneva had over 400. This network of dioceses was being extended to cover the whole continent. Apart from bishoprics founded in the mission fields the

Celtic churches in Scotland and Ireland were being transformed from their monastic structure to a diocesan one. Territories were also being defined more clearly. Whereas a bishopric had usually been described in papal diplomas by listing its major estates, after 1100 the assumption prevailed that a bishop's authority was defined by geographical limits. The *Collection in 74 Titles* had required that 'every one be content with his own boundaries' and Gratian was concerned to prevent bishops from ordaining clergy from else-where.[27] The older proprietorial assumption nevertheless left some scars on the body of the church in the form of outlying fragments of dioceses where a bishop had maintained his former interest, and in a few dioceses, notably Dol in Brittany, these scattered portions were larger than the handful of parishes in the core around the cathedral city.

The bishop was the primary authority. In the language of the developing canon law he was the 'ordinary', who held all spiritual jurisdiction unless it had been specifically devolved elsewhere. Admittedly, with rare exceptions, dioceses did not stand directly under the pope but were combined into provinces led by an archbishop or metropolitan (the two words, in this period, meant the same). The archbishop was important in terms of prestige and leadership, but his office was never designed to give general managerial authority over other bishops, and with the growth of papal initiative during the twelfth century its administrative function tended to be marginalized. Moreover the provincial synod, over which the archbishop presided, was to a considerable extent in abeyance during the twelfth century. The organization of the church into provinces did not abolish the place of the diocese as the primary structure.

St Anselm had defined the traditional idea of the office when he spoke to the bishops of the province of Canterbury: 'Brethren, I have summoned you to come to me because on you especially devolves the duty of handling, dispensing and maintaining the word of God. You are bishops: you are set in authority in the church of God: you are sons of God.'[28] It was essentially the ideal which Gregory I had set out long before in his *Cura Pastoralis*. After a period in which the

---

[27] *Collection in 74 Titles*, xxvi, ed. J. Gilchrist (Vatican, 1973), 119–21; Gratian, *Decr.* C. IX q. 2, opening dictum (602).
[28] Translation from G. Bosanquet, *Eadmer's History of Recent Events in England* (London, 1964), 85.

monasteries had been the leading powers in the church, the twelfth century saw a concerted attempt to rediscover the power of the bishop in what Cinzio Violante has called a 'new episcopalism'.[29] Around the middle of the century a series of writings set out to present a model of the good bishop. Hugh of St Victor explored the theology of the episcopate in his *On the Sacraments*, and Bernard of Clairvaux dedicated to Archbishop Henry of Sens a treatise *On the conduct and office of bishops*, and wrote a *Life* of Archbishop Malachy of Armagh. Gratian included a section on the personal qualities required of a bishop, basing it on 1 Timothy 3 and Titus 1: 7–9 and on passages from Gregory the Great; an innovation in the canonical collections of the period.[30] A further indication of the new episcopalism was the papal legislation giving the bishop authority over local churches and tithes, and in particular requiring his consent to their transfer to monastic ownership. The programme was essentially complete in the canons of the First Lateran Council:

No archdeacon or archpriest or provost or dean shall in any way grant the cure of souls or prebends of the church to anyone except with the judgement and consent of the bishop. Indeed, as is decreed by the sacred canons, the cure of souls and stewardship of ecclesiastical property are to remain in the power and judgement of the bishop.

A further canon insisted on the subjection of monks to their bishops and on the need for the bishop to grant cure of souls to priests appointed by monks to parish churches.[31] The policy was maintained by the later Lateran Councils and its principles were applied in many settlements over monastic rights throughout Christendom. This episcopalian tendency may also be reflected in the ending of the sequence of monk-popes after 1118 in favour of popes drawn from the ranks of the regular canons and elsewhere, but we must not see it as a simple reaction against monks or against Gregorian policy. Gregory VII and Urban II had already legislated to restore disciplinary power to the bishops, and the new orders such as the Cistercians supported the withdrawal of monks from involvement in the world and from ownership of parish churches and tithes. This movement in thinking came too late, however, to give the bishops

[29] C. Violante, 'Pievi e parrocchie nell'Italia centrosettentrionale', MCSM VIII (1977), 699.
[30] Hugh of St Victor, *De Sacramentis*, iii.12 (PL 176.428–30); Bernard, ep. 42 *De Moribus et Officio Episcoporum*, (*Opera* vii. 100 ff.) and *Vita S. Malachiae* (iii.297 ff.); on Gratian, see J. Gaudemet, 'Patristique et pastorale: la contribution de Grégoire le Grand au *Miroir de l'Evêque* dans le Décret de Gratien', *Le Bras* i.129–39.
[31] I Lateran can. 4, 16 (Alberigo 166, 169).

the full benefit of the massive shift in the ownership of parish churches from laymen to ecclesiastics; as was noticed in Chapter 3.i above, the primary beneficiaries of this movement were the great abbeys.

The bishop's control over his diocese was exercised through a network of subsidiary jurisdictions. The office of archdeacon, long established in France, was extended to other regions and its powers were more accurately defined. England does not seem to have had an organized archidiaconal system until after the Norman Conquest, and its introduction may have been connected with the decree of William I about 1072 transferring ecclesiastical causes to the hearing of the bishops. Italy never acquired archdeacons: this was understandable in the small dioceses of the south and centre, but they did not appear either in the large dioceses of the north. Northern French dioceses already had several archdeacons at the beginning of our period, and the twelfth century saw the clearer definition of their territories and the introduction of the practice of subdivision elsewhere. Lincoln had eight archdeacons before the middle of the twelfth century, with circumscriptions largely coinciding with the shires. The term 'archdeaconry', *archidiaconatus*, was coming into use around 1100, and in the following years the scope of the office was defined in a series of local settlements as it was at Paris, with papal approval, in 1126–7. Below the archdeacon was the archpriest, rural dean, or dean of Christianity (the term used varied from one region to another), presiding over a small group of parishes. The arrangement had earlier origins but became generally established in the twelfth century. Sometimes, as in the region of Liège, the deanery represented the remains of the authority of the old baptismal church before its subdivision into parishes; in Italy, where the system survived more intact than elsewhere, the head of the *pieve* functioned as archpriest. Elsewhere deaneries appear to be later constructions defined in terms of existing secular units, such as the hundred in England. By about 1150 in many parts of Europe the village church had thus been incorporated into a deanery and an archdeaconry, under the overall direction of the bishop. The increase in episcopal authority is given some statistical definition by the growing number of *acta* emerging from the bishop's writing office. At Orléans the surviving documents total 21 for 971–1096 (0.17 per year), 26 for 1096–1145 (0.53) and 244 for 1146–1207 (4.0).[32] At Angers we have

---

[32] C. Vuillez, 'L'évêque au miroir de l'*ars dictaminis*', *RHEF* 70 (1984), 277–304, from calculations of Mauricette Simon.

records of 165 letters of Bishop Ulger (1125–48), a huge increase on the recorded activity of any of his predecessors.

Such developments may suggest that the ideal of the bishop was approximating to the form which it was to take for much of the future history of the church: a pastor whose task was to instruct his clergy in their duties and to supervise their efficiency through his officers. To describe the function of the bishop thus would be a serious misunderstanding of the situation before 1200. The administrative structure was still very inadequate for the task of detailed supervision. Archdeacons were cathedral dignitaries in their own right and imperfectly controlled by the bishop, and the activity of the episcopal writing office, even though it had increased, was mainly concerned with confirmations of rights and properties and did not extend to maintaining proper records. Bishop Roger of Worcester (1164–79) may have kept a roll of clerks instituted to benefices, but if so he was innovating in having such a basic document as that. The signs are that the active supervision of the country clergy had scarcely yet been formulated even as an ideal. Action could be taken against scandalous clergy on occasion, but the instances in the letters of bishop Arnulf of Lisieux (1139–72) indicate that this sort of activity was only spasmodic. It was not clear what legal powers the bishop possessed to discipline local clergy, and Roger of Worcester found it necessary shortly after his consecration in 1164 to request a papal letter, *Inter cetera sollicitudinis*, to define his rights. The treatises designed to provide a mirror for bishops concentrated on their personal qualities: Bernard of Clairvaux stressed repeatedly the 'example' offered by Malachy of Armagh. The series of lives of the bishops of Auxerre written during the century was centred on their sanctity (especially their humility) and their administration, but this term meant the defence of the rights of the church of Auxerre. Nor do the bishops in reality seem to have been setting the tone for the spirituality of the period. It is significant that in Germany, only two twelfth-century bishops came to be venerated as saints, in contrast with seventeen in the preceding century. The fashionable spiritual ideals were being presented by the new monastic orders and the regular canons, and although both of these were defenders of episcopal authority, at least in theory, they were shaped by their own dynamic. The twelfth-century bishop's task was to be the liturgical head of his church, exemplary in his conduct and effective in his protection of its rights; the day-to-day supervision and instruction of the clergy was not a central part of his duties. It was only in the closing decades of the century that a new efficiency in diocesan administration and new ideas of the pastorate gave indications of a change to come, and to these we shall turn later in this book.

The character of the episcopate was naturally determined by its method of appointment. The demand for canonical election had become one of the keynotes of the Gregorian programme, and was enshrined in canon 3 of the First Lateran Council: 'no one shall consecrate a bishop unless he has been canonically elected'.[33] This left the procedure unclear, and the decretist Rufinus about 1157 defined it as involving 'the wishes of the citizens, the testimony of the people, the will of the nobles and of religious men, the election of the clergy, the confirmation of the metropolitan and bishops'.[34] While several of those elements remained, the characteristic development of the twelfth century was to isolate the act of election proper and confine it to the canons of the cathedral. A precedent for this development had been set long before in grants by the emperors of a right of election to canons of German cathedrals, but the first sign of its wider adoption was in the decree of the Second Lateran Council that 'we prohibit the canons of the episcopal see from excluding religious men from the election of bishops, but by their counsel an honest and suitable person shall be elected as bishop'.[35] It was uncertain at the time who were these religious men whose participation were being protected: the monks in the diocese, or its senior clergy as a whole? Forty years later, a letter of Alexander III to the church of Bremen showed a marked shift of policy:

although for the election of a bishop the favour and assent of the prince should be requested, yet laymen should not be admitted to the election. But the election is to be held by the canons of the cathedral church and the religious men from the city and diocese. However we do not mean by this that the objection of the religious should override the canons.[36]

By the early thirteenth century it was simply accepted that the canons elected the bishop. As we shall see in the next section, the exclusion of laymen from the election did not prevent kings and princes from influencing the choice, whereas papal intervention was still rare. There are a few famous cases when a disputed election led to an international uproar (Langres 1138, York 1140, Trier 1183), but

[33] Alberigo, 166.
[34] H. Singer (ed.), *Die Summa Decretorum des Magister Rufinus* (Paderborn, 1902), 155.
[35] II Lateran can. 28 (Alberigo 179).
[36] Letter to Bremen, 1171/2, PL 200.1270D.

these are abnormal. Much more common was a request for papal confirmation of an election after it had been made. Electors in fact were liable to turn to a range of different authorities in the search for security, and the Roman Church was the most frequently invoked. Requests for confirmation are a clear indication of growing papal prestige, but they are not the same thing as the exercise of a voice in the choice of the bishops. In Germany Carlrichard Brühl has counted only seven cases of papal intervention in an election in the eleventh century and nineteen in the twelfth. In France when Eugenius III appointed the first bishop of Tournai in 1146 he explained that this was because the see had just been re-established, and it was only in the years after 1180 that the papal influence became significant, with ten interventions in twenty years. The basic pattern remained election by the canons under the influence of the lay power.

The control of elections by the canons had obvious effects upon the choice of bishops. A very large proportion came from their ranks, many of them former archdeacons. Monks provided about 10 per cent of the German episcopate between 1000 and 1200; the proportion in France was rather higher, but not in the area of royal influence in the north. It is significant that as far as we know not a single bishop in Germany, France, or England was elected because he had been a successful parish priest. (The situation in the small dioceses of Italy was different.) Overlapping with the tendency to appoint canons of cathedrals was the nomination of royal servants, who had often been rewarded with such positions already. The major families of Capetian officers, such as Garlande, are well represented in the sees of northern France, and a crude example of the exercise of royal influence can be found in 1173 after the murder of Thomas Becket, when Henry II filled three of the six vacant bishoprics with royal officials who had been opponents of the martyr. When left to themselves, chapters tended to elect local men: only one bishop of Auxerre in the twelfth century came from outside the region, and he was also the one example of a papally influenced appointment there. The system also produced episcopal families. Sometimes these continued in the same see: the bishops of Chartres came from the family of Lèves between 1116 and 1155; five archbishops of Cologne were from the family of the counts of Berg between 1132 and 1216; and relatives of the Belmeis family provided several bishops of London. Such local and family ties were at least as strong in the twelfth century as they had been earlier; in particular, the ability of the German rulers to make appointments with an imperial horizon from their court chapel, as they had done before 1100, was restricted by the growing power of the territorial nobility. It was usually royal influence which broke into the local circle: the Capetians had a marked tendency to appoint Paris men in other parts of France, and Henry II introduced Normans into other parts of the Angevin empire. A few rulers (among them Roger II of Sicily and the Polish dukes) actively recruited foreigners for vacant bishoprics. The intensely aristocratic character of the twelfth-century episcopate does not imply that it was hostile to reforming tendencies. Some of the families mentioned, such as the Lèves at Chartres, were loyal supporters of Gregorian ideas, while Henry of France, the brother of Louis VII, who became an outstanding archbishop of Reims, had in earlier life renounced all his preferments to join the Cistercians. Most bishops, like most saints, were still drawn from the noble families who were qualified to protect the lands of the see and provide an example to their subjects.

iv. *Churches and Kingdoms*

The church saw western Europe as a grouping of kingdoms. In spite of the fact that ecclesiastical divisions frequently did not correspond with political ones the official record in the *Liber Censuum* of 1192 listed kingdoms first and provinces or archbishoprics as their subdivisions, and the curia preferred to correspond with kings about ecclesiastical business rather than with nobles. Historians have often seen the relations of church and state in the twelfth century as shaped by the triumph of Gregorian ideas, and have suggested that because the religious authority of the king was no longer recognized, he had to look for other foundations for his power. On this interpretation, by 'desacralizing' the monarchy the papacy had opened the road to the secular state. It is certainly true that the new papalist thinking had implications for royal government. The description of the pope as the vicar of Christ and as the possessor of fulness of power implied the superior dignity of the spiritual power, for the secular ruler could not make such claims. High-church writers categorized the king as a layman and denied that his anointing had the same character as that of a bishop. Royal unction disappeared from lists of sacraments. The functions of clergy and laity were clearly distinguished by the exclusion of laymen from the investiture of bishops and (with important exceptions) from presence at their election. At the same time the kingdoms, led by England and Sicily, were being provided with a more effective machinery of government and Frederick Barbarossa was formulating the theory of imperial power. These changes, however, cannot accurately be described as the emergence of a secular state or the desacralization of the monarchy. As we saw in Chapter 1, the God-given power of the king had always been seen as exercised in tandem with that of the priesthood, and kings in the twelfth century continued to use the language of divine authority. The monarchy, so far from giving up its claims, laid even more emphasis upon its religious origin.

It remained the official doctrine, alike of royal chanceries and of clerical reformers, that the king ruled by the power of God; indeed, the words of St Paul in Romans 13: 1 ruled out any other view. The argument of Gregory VII in the second letter to Bishop Herman of Metz that kings came into existence because of sin stripped the royal office of much of its dignity, but was rarely echoed by later writers. The ideology propounded by Abbot Suger of Saint Denis for Louis VI of France (1108–37) struck a very different note. Suger described the king as the vicar of God, bearing his image, and told how on his death-bed Louis required his son to swear 'to guard the church of God and defend the poor and orphans and maintain every one in his right'.[37] The sign of divine commission was the ceremony of anointing which inaugurated a new reign, and in spite of the distinction of this from episcopal anointing it continued to be regarded with great respect. The papalist Bishop Grosseteste of Lincoln wrote in the middle of the thirteenth century that 'royal unction is a sign of the prerogative of the reception of the most sacred sevenfold gift of the spirit'.[38] Pictorial presentations of the relations of church and state, in sculptures on cathedrals or illuminations in manuscripts of Gratian's collection of canon law, presented them as parallel authorities, each with a sphere of influence bestowed on it by God. The bishop or spiritual authority usually is given more dignity than the king or secular authority (although even that it not true in Germany) but the underlying duality of two powers is clear.

Belief in the sacred power of the king was disseminated widely in society by new or developed ceremonial. The first mentions of the

[37] Suger, *Vita Ludovici Grossi*, ed. H. Waquet (Paris, 1929), 134, 274.
[38] H. R. Luard (ed.), *Roberti Grosseteste Epistolae*, RS, 1861, ep. 124, p. 350.

healing power of kings ascribe it to Robert the Pious in France (996–1031) and Edward the Confessor in England (1042–66), but in both cases possibly the power was a function of their personal sanctity. It is likely that from the early twelfth century their successors in France and England were touching for scrofula, which was later to be known as 'the king's evil', although we cannot be sure that it had become a regular practice until the thirteenth century. The gift by a chamberlain to two Norman abbeys of basins which he had received from the hands of Henry I may well suggest a belief in the sacred touch of royalty.[39] Liturgical ceremonies also enhanced the dignity of the king's office. In most parts of Europe the funerals of great men had been simple and even (in the cases of William the Conqueror in 1087 and William Rufus in 1100) squalid. Now kings began to make careful preparation for their burials, building great churches for them as Henry I did at Reading Abbey and Stephen at Faversham. From Henry II onwards kings of England were probably buried in their coronation robes, and splendid tombs were provided, such as those of the Angevin royal house at Fontevraud or the Sicilian kings as Palermo.

The most striking development was the creation of a strong link between the royal family and the saints, preferably (where possible) with a member of the royal house. The German kings secured the canonization of the Emperor Henry II (died 1024) and his wife Kunigunde, and subsequently—although by an anti-pope— of Charlemagne himself. Henry II of England persuaded Alexander III to canonize Edward the Confessor in 1161. Other rulers promoted saints with whom they had been associated, as did Louis VII (1137–80) with the Cistercian Peter of Tarantaise and Thomas Becket. Political authority was as sensitive as the rest of public opinion to miracles worked by the saints. There was a spectacular episode at the abbey of Déols in May 1187 during a campaign between Philip Augustus of France and Richard Coeur de Lion, when it was observed that a statue of the Virgin had torn her robe in grief at the violence done to the countryside. Richard, who himself came forward as a witness of the miracle, hastily agreed a truce with his opponent. The most striking association of a royal family with a saint in the course of the century was, however, the Capetian link with Saint-Denis, which already existed but was made much stronger by the co-operation of Abbot Suger with his friend Louis

---

[39] M. R. James *et al.* (eds.), *Walter Map: de Nugibus Curialium* (Oxford, 1983), v.6, p. 490.

VI. In 1124, faced by a threatened invasion by the Emperor Henry V, Louis went to the abbey and received the banner of St Denis from the altar, where the relics of the saint and his companions were exposed as a defence in time of national danger. The banner was soon identified with the *oriflamme*, the traditional name of the banner of Charlemagne, and was to be carried by the French kings as long as the monarchy lasted. At about this time (unfortunately we cannot date it securely) there was composed the forged Donation of Charlemagne, granting the kingdom to the abbey of Saint-Denis and commending it to his protection. The significance of this association of the monarchy with the national saint was increased by the spectacular rebuilding undertaken by Suger in the first experiment in the 'Gothic' style, inspired by the theories of vision in St Denis's own supposed writings. St Denis was to become to France what the lion of St Mark was to Venice, the symbol of national identity and religious protection, and to this the rising French monarchy had linked itself firmly in the imagination of its subjects.

Among all the monarchies of Christendom, the Capetians provided the model for royal protection of the church. Once the informal agreement over lay investiture had been made during the visit of Paschal II clashes were rare. Louis VI occasionally collided with ecclesiastical authority over the reform of churches in which he had a direct interest, and the *politique de grandeur* (as Marcel Pacaut has called it) during Louis VII's early years gave rise to several quarrels, and culminating in the disputed election at Bourges in 1141 and a war with Theobald of Champagne, in which the pope and St Bernard strongly supported the count. Thereafter Louis was a friend of reform and of the papacy. The university of Paris was a major centre of papalist theory, and France was a refuge for Alexander III from 1162 to 1165 and for Thomas Becket from 1164 to 1170. This did not mean that the Crown was sacrificing its interests, for its customary rights enabled it to control and even exploit bishoprics and abbeys. Kings could ensure the election of their chosen candidates by use of the royal licence for election, and the new bishop had to take an oath of fealty to the king and receive from him the temporalities of the see. Henry II and Frederick Barbarossa insisted that the election be held in the king's presence and that the bishop perform the more formal act of homage, but the example of France suggests that gentler methods were ample to safeguard the royal interest.

Apart from this influence over appointments, churches were attached to the royal interest by their hope of generosity and protection. Royal benevolence could be on a splendid scale. At times it was inspired by directly religious motives. William the Conqueror founded the great abbey of Battle to celebrate his victory in 1066, and Philip Augustus founded La Victoire after his triumph at Bouvines in 1214. There was also a steady flow of donations on more routine occasions. It was not always the kings whom we regard as most 'ecclesiastical' in their policy who gave most. Barbarossa was a generous donor, and Louis VII gave more during his early grandiose years, when he was frequently in collision with the papacy, than he did later. Louis's pattern of donation has been analysed by Marcel Pacaut, who has found 452 acts surviving from the 43 years of his reign, 177 being new gifts and 275 confirmations of existing rights. Twenty-five per cent of these acts applied to the large areas of France outside the royal demesne, and the number of confirmations reminds us that, from the point of view of the clergy, the king's role in defending the possessions of the churches from depredation was at least as important as the prospect of obtaining new income from his good pleasure. Royal protection did not rest only on political calculation. It was an essential part of the king's function, and it was inspired by his own need, in turn, for the protection of God and the saints. It also had more measurable value for the monarchy, since 'protection' in medieval style implied control as well as responsibility. The clergy were important servants of the Crown. In strict canon law they should not have been, but in practice it was accepted that clerks, usually in minor orders, should be involved in the royal bureaucracy. Bishops and abbots might act as royal advisers: high churchmen saw the role of Suger under Louis VI and VII and Wibald of Stavelot under Conrad III as models. The growth of royal administration posed a more difficult question, since kings wanted to use bishops as officers of their government. At first the convention was for royal servants to resign on appointment to bishoprics, but in the late twelfth century there are important examples to the contrary. Rainald of Dassel, Barbarossa's chancellor from May 1156, was elected archbishop of Cologne in spring 1159 and thus added to his powers the formerly conventional post of arch-chancellor for Italy, and in 1159 Hugh of Champfleury remained chancellor of Louis VII on his appointment as bishop of Soissons. In 1162 it was Henry II's intention that Thomas Becket should continue as chancellor while

archbishop of Canterbury, and subsequently several bishops functioned as royal justices, while in the reign of Richard I Hubert Walter
was at the head of administration in both church and state, being
archbishop of Canterbury, papal legate, and justiciar, an early
foretaste of Cardinal Wolsey. Numerically such civil servant bishops
were the exception; much more characteristic was the enjoyment of
political support from bishops who were linked to the Crown alike
by advancement, interest, and convention. The Hohenstaufen
emperors enjoyed much support from the German hierarchy, and
Henry II was sustained in his quarrel with Becket by several of the
English bishops. There were, of course, exceptions, and it is
noticeable that when bishops acted independently, as they did in
England under Stephen and in Germany in the aftermath of the
Investiture Contest, the reason was often the weakening of royal
authority, which forced them to consolidate their territorial power in
order to protect themselves. The Capetians were able to extend their
power by intervening in areas outside the demesne (as Louis VI and
VII both did in the Auvergne) in response to appeals from bishops
against the local nobility; and they were to do so even more
spectacularly later when they intervened in the south against the
growing threat of the Albigensian heresy. It was not only oppression
but also the absence of protection which caused problems between
king and bishops.

The control of the church also had direct cash value for the
Crown. In almost every part of Europe vacant bishoprics and abbeys
were in its custody, and the richer ones provided an important source
of income. The English kings proved particularly susceptible to the
temptation to defer appointments in order to enjoy the income: there
were enormous vacancies at Canterbury (1089–93 and 1109–13) and
York (1181–91). The duty to provide hospitality was also important
in a century when most kings were continuously travelling, and in
the empire especially it was a formal and burdensome obligation.
Revenue came from the churches either as presents or feudal aids,
according to local custom, although with a few exceptions the
development of regular royal taxation of the church, like that of
papal taxation, belongs to the thirteenth century.

The interweaving of the interests of church and state was so close
that lay governments were involved in questions of ecclesiastical
organization. The clearest examples come from the edges of Europe,
where the structure of the church was in the process of definition.

Poland and Hungary had already at the beginning of our period obtained their own archbishoprics, and during the twelfth century Denmark (Lund 1104), Norway (Trondheim 1152), and Sweden (Uppsala 1164) were formed into provinces. In England the attempts of the archbishops of Canterbury to exercise an effective primacy over York were usually supported by the Crown, which also welcomed the attempts of York to establish itself as the metropolitan see in Scotland. This was eventually frustrated with the granting by Celestine III in 1192 of an extraordinary status to the Scottish church, which was to have no archbishop but be directly under the papacy. In Ireland there were signs at first that Canterbury was extending its authority there, but the reorganization of the Irish church into dioceses, completed at the Council of Kells under the papal legate John Parparo in 1152, provided the island with four provinces of its own. The expansion of Angevin authority into Ireland took place within this framework, but with papal support. Hadrian IV's bull *Laudabiliter* (assuming that it is not a forgery) granted the country to Henry II, and Henry's establishment of his authority there some years later was actively assisted by Alexander III.

The common interests between church and state were disrupted by a number of important issues. The greatest of these, the collision between empire and papacy in Italy, has been discussed in the previous chapter, but there were others. Most governments in the later twelfth century were less considerate than the Capetians in their dealings with the church, and Frederick Barbarossa, Henry II, the Sicilian kings, and the Lombard cities asserted wider rights over it and enforced them more toughly. This attitude, especially as it followed the greater liberty which the churches enjoyed under Stephen in England and Lothar in Germany, led to indignant complaints about royal oppression; John of Salisbury, a member of the papal curia and then secretary to the archbishop of Canterbury, saw the Hohenstaufen, the Angevins, and the Norman kings of Sicily as tyrants. Even so, the issues only occasionally led to an explosion. Kings usually based their claims upon custom, but often these customs had been recognized, however reluctantly, by earlier popes. Barbarossa's power over episcopal appointments rested on the Concordat of Worms. The kings of England, Hungary, and Sicily claimed the right to exclude papal legates from their territories, and it seems that this had been conceded in all three cases by Urban II, verbally or (in the case of the island of Sicily) in the diploma of 1098. There was tension over this issue, but the kings were able to maintain their position until the late twelfth century.

The expansion of the activity of church courts, when placed alongside the improved efficiency of royal ones, also created points of conflict. Clerical privilege, matrimonial suits, disputes over lay patronage, and other matters might all involve the interests of the Crown and nobility, and the growth of appeals potentially transferred the final decision outside the kingdom altogether. In general these conflicts of jurisdiction were dealt with as technical matters. Royal lawyers devised methods for defending their jurisdiction, such as writs of prohibition, and a great deal depended on the preference of litigants, who often could choose between the two tribunals. Kings were liable to interfere with appeals in cases where they had a strong interest, and occasionally suspended them altogether as a means of coercing the papacy, as Barbarossa did after the quarrel at Besançon . In two instances, such conflicts of jurisdiction led to long-lasting disputes between the two powers. Late in the century the liberties of the church in Norway were challenged by the extraordinary King Sverre, a native of the Faeroe Islands who had been educated for the priesthood and was (so he claimed) an illegimate son of the royal house. A talented soldier, he established an uncertain control in Norway by 1184, and forced into exile two archbishops in succession, Eystein in 1180 and Erik Ivarssoen in 1190. Sverre was excommunicated in 1194, and in 1198 Innocent III imposed an interdict on the entire kingdom. Sverre retained his position, however, until his death in 1202, and meanwhile issued in the vernacular an incisive 'speech against the bishops'. Its assertion of the supremacy of the secular power looked back to Scandinavian traditions of royal control of the church, and at the same time forward to claims which were to be advanced by the rising national monarchies of the later thirteenth century. In the eyes of western Europe as a whole, however, a much more important clash between church and state arose under Henry II of England, who in the 1150s and 1160s enforced the traditional ducal customs in Normandy, attempted to introduce them elsewhere in his Continental lands, and set out to restrict ecclesiastical jurisdiction in England. Before the death of Archbishop Theobald in 1161 the clergy of Canterbury were already complaining about the king's oppression. Even so, most of the English bishops, even papalists like Gilbert Foliot of Hereford and London, saw the issues as negotiable. The exception who proved the rule was Thomas Becket.

Thomas was a Londoner, educated for service of both church and state, but much less of a scholar than many of his episcopal colleagues. From 1155 he was at once archdeacon of Canterbury and royal chancellor, and an inseparable companion of Henry II. In 1162 under royal pressure he was appointed archbishop of Canterbury. We do not know whether Henry was hoping that he would sell out the interests of the church or whether he was seen (being both a Canterbury man and a king's friend) as an agent of an acceptable compromise. Both expectations were misplaced. Thomas emerged as an ardent champion of the liberties of the church. He resigned the chancellorship and annoyed Henry by refusing to co-operate about a number of issues. In October 1163 at Westminster Henry demanded an oath from the bishops to observe the customs of the realm, and after some opposition Thomas agreed. When the bishops offered to take the oath at Clarendon on 13 January 1164, Henry produced a written record of the customs. It was probably a fair statement of practice in the reign of Henry I, but several of the clauses were contrary to canon law and to prevailing practice in more recent years. The issue which provoked most public discussion was the king's claim that a clerk accused of a crime should, after trial in the bishop's court, be deprived of his orders and handed to the lay power for punishment. To this Thomas responded that 'God Himself does not judge his enemies twice'. He had perhaps learned this reference to Nahum 1: 9 from the theologians on his staff, for local custom and the teaching of canonists both varied considerably and Henry's position was a defensible one in canon law. We do not know when Henry resolved on the written formulation of the customs; it may have been his purpose from the beginning, or he may have decided on it in view of the bishops' resistance at Westminster. In either case he was demanding too much from the bishops. In response to this error, Becket made one of his own. After leading the opposition of the bishops, he suddenly reversed his position and without consulting them offered to accept the document. Thomas soon repented of his concession, but by then the bishops had lost their solidarity. Clarendon determined the pattern of the next seven years.

The king was now completely alienated from his former friend, and proceeded against him so fiercely that Thomas escaped to the

Continent in autumn 1164, looking to the protection of the king of France and the pope. He no longer enjoyed the support of his fellow bishops, several of whom, while refusing to sign the Constitutions, supported the king in his complaints about the archbishop. Alexander had no difficulty in condemning many of the Constitutions, but was more hesitant about what to do next, faced as he was by an intransigent archbishop, appeals by bishops against him, an uncertain legal situation and a king who might be tempted to transfer his allegiance to the imperialist pope. In 1170 each side moved into a more extreme position. Henry secured the coronation as his heir of his son Henry, the ceremony being carried out by Archbishop Roger of York in the absence of the archbishop of Canterbury, whose right it was; and the pope threatened excommunication and interdict. Henry drew back from the brink and came to an agreement with Thomas at Fréteval, but even then there was no real settlement of the issues. Thomas returned to Canterbury, already anticipating his death at the hands of his enemies, and on 29 December he was cut down in his own cathedral by four knights who had misunderstood (or correctly understood?) a threat spoken against him by the king.

The discussions after the murder of the archbishop confirmed the view of Gilbert Foliot and other bishops that the questions at issue were negotiable. Apart from the conditions of Henry's penance, which included the promise of a crusade and substantial help for the Holy Land, the king gave a qualified undertaking to allow appeals to the curia. He did not have to renounce the Constitutions, and the customs which they described continued in the royal courts. Even the issue of criminous clerks was only settled in subsequent negotiations in 1176. The quarrel, if not precisely over a non-issue, was over issues which elsewhere had caused little trouble, and Henry's control over the English church was scarcely disturbed. The reasons why the controversy proved so intractable and so caught the attention of contemporaries were in part personal: Thomas's defiant attitude and his changes of front exasperated the king (and some of his own friends) and led Henry to seek his deposition, and possibly his death. The situation was also particularly favourable to publicity: since the pope was in northern France at the time, the curia was intimately involved, as were the kings of England and France. Moreover, Thomas was not a former chancellor for nothing: his household issued a huge stream of propaganda, swelled by his allies in the schools at Paris and the Cistercians, and matched by the highly vocal Anglo-Norman bishops. Whatever the king's intentions, it was certainly true that the church of Canterbury was being persecuted: its pastor exiled, its clergy threatened and its lands impounded. In this situation, a martyrdom had a highly dramatic effect, so that within a few years Thomas had been canonized and his cult spread from Iceland to Palermo. In these ways the episode had no close parallels in the twelfth century, but it revealed the potentially explosive power of a technical issue between church and state, if unwisely handled. It was also a dramatic vindication of the wisdom of the Capetian approach as against the tough methods which the Angevins used in controlling the church.

10

THE NEW MONASTIC ORDERS

i. *From Hermitage to Monastery*

One of the features of the monastic scene in the late eleventh century had been the appearance of groups of hermits who lived outside existing rules and customs. The dominant characteristic in the twelfth century was the opposite: the emergence of new orders with clearly defined constitutions. Paradoxically, these monks were the lineal descendants of the hermits: the Cistercians and Carthusians trace their ancestry back to hermits gathered in Burgundy, while Fontevraud, Savigny, and Tiron have their origin in the poverty-and-preaching movement in north-western France. Historians have disagreed about the dynamics of the change: was it transition or treason?[1] Ernst Werner saw the movement from the freer life of hermits into regulated communities primarily as the result of pressure by the hierarchy, whereas Giles Constable and Henrietta Leyser have rejected any suggestion of a sharp contrast between hermits on the one hand and monks on the other, emphasizing there was a multitude of forms of 'eremitical monasticism', within which movement could take place in one direction or the other.[2] In any case, we must not exaggerate the speed of the transformation. There were certainly plenty of communities whose founders chose to accept a Rule from an established house, but when a community developed its own customs into a new form of religious life the process usually took a considerable time. Remarkably, in almost every such case the original founder had moved elsewhere, and there are doubts about the continuity of ideals; a feature common to Bruno at Chartreuse, Robert at Cîteaux, Cono at Arrouaise, William of Champeaux at St Victor, and Norbert at Prémontré.

---

[1] L. Milis, 'L'évolution de l'érémitisme au canonicat régulier . . .: transition ou trahison?', MCSM 7 (1977), 223–38.

[2] E. Werner, *Pauperes Christi* (Leipzig, 1956); H. Leyser, *Hermits and the new Monasticism* (London, 1984); and G. Constable, 'The Study of Monastic History Today', in his *Religious Life and Thought* (London, 1979).

There was no one reason for the change. In many cases a simple increase in numbers meant that an unstructured life was no longer possible. Some houses were worried by their liberty, as at Obazine, where 'they wanted to belong to an order authorized by the church, so that in the absence of their masters there would remain to them the unfailing authority of a written law', and at Fountains where 'it did not seem to them to be right to trust their own whims and intuition, lest they should be tricked and deceived'.[3] Sometimes a local crisis led to the acceptance of a Rule, as at Tournai when Odo impoverished the house by his gifts in the famine of 1095. Some groups indulged in careful discussions before they decided which Rule to adopt, and made modifications before it was accepted. Oigny resolved 'to follow the Rule of St Augustine and the eremitical life', living the common life according to the former and observing the austerity that was proper to the latter.[4] Sometimes the adoption of a structured monastic life did not emerge from the community itself, but was the result of pressure or persuasion by the bishop. This might be an expression of sympathetic concern for the hermits' ideals. Bishop Bartholomew of Laon was a source of strength and guidance to Norbert in the early days of the Premonstratensian movement, and archbishop Hildebert of Tours was concerned to provide for the hermit groups of his diocese. There were also times when considerable pressure was applied. Robert of Molesme, who at various stages abandoned all three houses of which he was abbot, was ordered to leave Cîteaux; Robert of Arbrissel was criticized for going about with bands of women and for leaving the communities which he had gathered at La Roë and Fontevraud in order to continue his preaching ministry; Gilbert of Sempringham seemed unable or unwilling to provide any proper structure for his double order of canons and nuns.

The monastic orders which emerged from hermit foundations often bore the marks of their origin. The Carthusians provided for a solitary life within the community, and in Italy Camaldoli and Fonte Avellana and their dependencies remained strongly eremitical. In one sense the Cistercians turned their back firmly on the hermit ideal, to which they were less sympathetic than the Cluniacs, but they carried into the cenobitic life features of hermit inspiration such as the

---

[3] For references, see Leyser, *Hermits*, 87, 89. The second case may be Cistercian propaganda; their certainty was their strength.

[4] *Propositum* of Oigny, printed by C. Dereine, *RHE* 43 (1948), 440.

severity with which they kept the Rule, manual labour, the reduction in the weight of monastic liturgy and the stress on withdrawal to the wilderness. Within the order of canons, a much more severe version of the Rule of St Augustine appeared. In these ways monastic and canonical tradition was changed by the eremitical movement. At the same time, the attractions of the more severe monasticism made themselves felt upon the remaining hermits, whose houses were inclined to affiliate rapidly with the new orders or to borrow their customs on a large scale. Inevitably some of the hermits' ideals were abandoned in the process. This is dramatically illustrated by the censorship to which some of the early founders' lives were subjected in order to bring them into conformity with the discipline which had developed, as when Petronilla of Fontevraud was first dissatisfied with the *Life* of Robert of Arbrissel which she had commissioned from Baudri of Dol, and then circulated its replacement by his chaplain André in a very truncated form. The movement towards formal monasticism lowered the status of lay members, who frequently began on equal terms with the clergy but ended as a subsidiary group of *conversi*. The relative freedom of the treatment of women by Robert of Arbrissel, Gilbert of Sempringham, and Norbert of Xanten was subsequently replaced by seclusion. In some places the hermit inspiration appears to have been wholly lost. Afflighem, founded by laymen in 1083, had within twenty years become a house following Cluniac customs, accepting the whole range of property which these allowed; and the highly aristocratic nunneries of the order of Fontevraud were far removed from the ideals of Robert of Arbrissel's earlier career.

In spite of the enormous scale on which transfers had taken place from hermitage to monastery, the old pattern of eremitical life still survived. One example among many was Galgano, a layman in southern Tuscany, who was called like Romuald almost two centuries before him to abandon his arms and take up the peaceful life of a solitary. He lived among a small group of followers for a short period and died about 1181. His foundation illustrates the pattern of mutual attraction and repulsion between monks and hermits, for the Cistercians shortly after 1191 sought to take over his cult and founded their largest abbey in Tuscany; but many of his original followers retired from the site, where the oratory and the abbey may still be seen side by side. Eremitism did not merely continue: by developing new forms it adjusted to the new society. Recluses, men or women living in cells beside a church, had existed in the past, but now became much more common and functioned as advisers for the neighbourhood and sometimes as visionaries whose comments manifested God's word in the midst of local problems. Such holy men and women as Mabel of Parma, who lived as a recluse at the church of St Eusebio, Vercelli, from 1189 to 1237, or as the Englishmen Wulfric of Haselbury and Godric of Finchale, brought the eremitical spirit to the people living in towns and cities. There was also an overlap between the ideals of the groups of hermits with whom we have so far been concerned, and movements in which the desire to follow Christ in preaching and in poverty was taking a still more radical form. In a few survivors of the old hermit ideas, such as Henry of Lausanne, the poverty and preaching movement fed the growing currents of heresy and dissent, and it escaped into the city streets and found recruits such as the Waldensians and Humiliati. St Francis of Assisi was to emerge from the background of Italian eremitism. But by that time, having moved far outside monasticism in any form then recognized, it was another story which must concern us later.

ii. *The New Orders*

Incomparably the most successful of all the new orders was that of Cîteaux. The speed of its expansion exceeded any similar movement in the whole history of monasticism, while it exerted a strong and direct influence on other new orders and had a major impact upon the spirituality of the twelfth century as a whole. It originated in a secession from the abbey of Molesme, which had been founded as recently as 1075. Abbot Robert and Prior Alberic led a party of monks, said to have been twenty-one in number, to found a 'new monastery' (the title by which it was at first known) at Cîteaux in a valley among the hills of Burgundy in the spring of 1098. Its early history was troubled. The monks of Molesme protested and, under the pressure of the papal legate, Robert agreed to return there, taking back with him those monks 'who did not love the wilderness'.[5] According to William of Malmesbury, only eight remained. The new abbot was Alberic, who governed the young community until his death early in 1109. He was succeeded by Stephen Harding, an

---

[5] *Exordium parvum*, vii.13. There are several good editions: see, most recently, J.-B. Auberger, *L'unanimité cistercienne* (Achel, 1986), doc. I/5, pp. 355–75.

Englishman who had been at Molesme, and who presided over the first expansion of the order, beginning with La Ferté (1113), Pontigny (1114), and Morimond and Clairvaux (1115). By the time of the first major confirmation of the constitution by Calixtus II in *Ad hoc in apostolicae* on 23 December 1119 rapid growth was in progress. Harding had been joined in 1112 or 1113 by Bernard of Clairvaux, one of the outstanding men of the century, whose contribution to the growth of the Cistercians was to be enormous; but it is unlikely, as Bernard's biographer later suggested, that Cîteaux was still in a perilous condition when he entered. The first important arrival of recruits and acquisition of property had probably taken place by then.

The distinctive features of the fully developed Cistercian Order were derived from an underlying principle: the commitment to observe the Rule of St Benedict literally. Unfortunately the stages by which this programme developed are uncertain because the dates of the early sources are a matter of controversy. The most significant of all is the *Exordium parvum*, a history of the origins which incorporates important documentary material. All the main outlines of the order's policy are included in it, and Chapter xv assigns the basic legislation to the time of Alberic. If this account is reliable, it suggests that the seceders had left Molesme, not simply because it had grown prosperous and lax, but because they objected to the modifications to the Rule introduced in all Benedictine houses. The argument, however, continues whether the *Exordium* was written before 1119, or was a polemical work produced about 1150 as a response to Cluniac criticism. The later dating would remove any evidence for regarding the special characteristics of the Cistercians as part of the programme brought from Molesme, and make it more natural to see them as produced by the influence of Stephen Harding or St Bernard. The foundation of Cîteaux would then be one of many hermit experiments, and in itself a non-event.[6]

Already in Molesme the desire had been expressed to observe the Rule more faithfully. Archbishop Hugh of Lyon, when dealing with the crisis produced by the secession, addressed the founders of the new monastery as wishing 'henceforth more strictly and perfectly to keep the Rule of St Benedict, which so far you have kept in a

---

[6] 'pratiquement banale', M. Pacaut, 'Cîteaux: recherche banale, expérience originale', *Cahiers d'Histoire* 19 (1974), 109–20, esp. 110.

lukewarm and negligent fashion.'[7] In the *Exordium parvum* the motto 'Back to the Rule' is asserted firmly: the Cistercian life is to walk 'in the straight and narrow way which the Rule points out'.[8] If this account is early, we have here the logical basis of the more detailed Cistercian usages. William of Malmesbury was impressed by the *ratio* which underlay the planning of Stephen Harding, whose policy rested on reasoned argument from the text of the Rule.[9] This involved the rejection of all alleviations which had been introduced by later Benedictine custom and the adoption of extreme simplicity in clothing, extra meals, and bedding and 'all those things which are contrary to the purity of the Rule'.[10] On the assumption that the Rule excluded whatever it did not specifically authorize, a much more severe monastic regime was required, and one which satisfied the contemporary aspiration to follow Christ in poverty. Another of the simplifications was the adoption of a habit of undyed wool in place of the traditional Benedictine black, so that the 'white' or 'grey' monks were visibly different from all others. On the same principle, the original provision for labour to be part of the monastic day was restored, and the Cistercians stressed it as an important element. Associated with this was the rejection of sources of income not mentioned by the Rule, 'churches and altars, or offerings or burial-dues or the tithes of other men, or ovens and mills, or vills or peasants'.[11] The refusal to accept such wealth was characteristic of several of the new orders, and in the Cistercians it was rooted in their programme for the literal observance of the Rule.

Yet there were difficulties in the literal observance of an ancient text, and in practice the Cistercians made innovations. One was the decision not to accept boys offered by their parents but to recruit only men old enough to decide for themselves. Most of the new orders opted for adult recruiting, and even in the older houses there was a tendency to close the internal schools designed to train boys. Ulrich of Cluny had already stressed to Abbot William of Hirsau that the best monks were those who joined the monastery 'not before years of discretion, nor by their parents' command, but of their own

[7] *Exordium parvum*, ii.2. Archbishop Hugh's phrases are more moderate than those of the narrative, and it is improbable that (as has been suggested) they were written into the letter later.

[8] Ibid., prologue.

[9] W. Stubbs (ed.), *Willelmi Malmesbiriensis monachi De Gestis Regum Anglorum*, 2 vols. (RS, 1889), 381–3.

[10] *Exordium parvum*, xv. 2.

[11] Ibid. xv. 5.

will, of mature years at the command of Christ alone'.[12] This move was typical of a society which offered an increasing range of choice and placed more emphasis on individual decisions. Another way in which the Cistercians departed from the Rule was the creation of a second order of monks, the *conversi* or lay or 'bearded' brothers. Cluny had already had a large number of *conversi*, and they existed in several of the new orders. According to the *Exordium parvum* Alberic had introduced them at Cîteaux 'because without their assistance they were unable to obey the precepts of the Rule fully day and night', but their existence in the order is not confirmed by other references until later, and they would more naturally belong to the period of growing property endowment under Stephen Harding.[13] The Cistercian practice differed from that of Cluny in that there was far more separation between choir monks and lay brothers; 'we now have within the enclosure of the monastery two monasteries, that is one of lay brothers and the other of clergy'.[14] The lay brothers were usually unlearned, said much simplified prayers, and were physically separated from the choir monks, residing in the west range outside the main cloister. The third advance beyond the Rule of Benedict was the creation of an effective system of common government. It was embodied in the *Carta Caritatis,* which probably originated in its initial form in 1113. The idea was that all the monasteries should observe the same customs, but respect for the Rule prevented the adoption of the Cluniac arrangement of one single abbot with power over the whole order. The scheme of central control can be seen in evolution through the various editions of the Charter of Charity. At first, a great deal depended on the abbot of Cîteaux, but increasingly control was exercised by the general chapter of all abbots, together with the abbots of the four senior daughters of Cîteaux. In addition, abbots throughout the order had the task of visiting daughter-houses to inspect discipline. By the 1120s at the latest the Cistercians had a programme which expressed many of the monastic aspirations of the period, together with an effective system of government.

The success of Cîteaux in embodying contemporary aspirations into a clear programme lay behind its enormous attraction for the next two or three generations. There was also a personal reason:

---

[12] Ulrich of Cluny, *Antiquiores consuetudines,* Epistola nuncupatoria (PL 149.636–7).

[13] *Exordium parvum,* xv. 10.

[14] *Dialogus inter Cluniacensem monachum et Cisterciensem,* iii, E. Martène and U. Durand, *Thesaurus novus anecdotorum* (Paris, 1717), v.1648A.

Bernard of Clairvaux. Bernard was a brilliantly successful persuader, and was also the most outstanding spiritual theologian in an age which had begun eagerly to reflect upon the religious life. We do not know what sort of spiritual teaching was being given at Cîteaux before his time, but recent historians such as J.-B. Auberger have seen Clairvaux as the source of a new spirituality, with more stress on the literal observance of the Rule, on asceticism, and on interior piety, whereas the Cîteaux of Stephen Harding stood closer to traditional Benedictine values. Whatever the truth of this, Bernard's thinking was extremely influential, and attracted still more recruits. Almost half of the abbeys in existence at his death in 1153 were daughters of Clairvaux, and this gives some measure of his contribution to the spread of the order. Another reason for the Cistercians' expansion was their withdrawal from the complexities of manorial life. In refusing mills, ovens, serfs, and tithes, they had opted for the running of their own estates 'in the wilderness'. They aimed for a solid block of land which they developed and exploited from a centre or 'grange'. which was run by the lay brothers. These *conversi* are sometimes seen as a peasant work-force, but it is clear that (except perhaps at one or two houses at the beginning) they were not numerous enough for that. They were the bailiffs who supervised granges and hired labourers, and were also the smiths and tradesmen whom the abbey needed and, increasingly, the merchants who resided at a hall in a nearby city and handled the abbey's commercial connections. We do not have enough information to be sure from what social groups the *conversi* were recruited, and undoubtedly this must have differed from one region to another. They included men of high birth and townsmen, attracted perhaps both by devotion and by the opportunity for using their skills on a larger stage. This method of estate administration was, as it turned out, the formula for economic success; a success which was increased by the fact that Cistercian regulations forbade expenditure on treasures or ostentatious building, so that surplus cash tended to be used in purchasing new land. They were soon making the wilderness blossom, and joining in the great clearance of forests and wastes. Houses were established in the Yorkshire Pennines, where Rievaulx was founded in 1132 and Fountains affiliated 1135, and on the Flemish seacoast, where Les Dunes, which joined them in 1138, eventually absorbed much of the coastline of modern Belgium. They became frontiersmen *par excellence*, and many of their richest houses were those established on the edge of the Christian territories, like those of Alcobaça (1148) or Poblet (1150) in the Iberian peninsula, or their foundations in eastern Germany.

They had the gift of drawing influential people from both the aristocracy and the schools, 'many noble warriors and profound philosophers' into the order.[15] These included recruits of royal status: Henry of France from the Capetian royal house, Conrad the Welf and Otto of Freising from the great families of Germany. Assisted by such influential members, they spread rapidly. By 1120, monks from La Ferté had crossed the Alps into Italy and founded the first house there at Tiglieto in Liguria. A series of acquisitions followed, including the ancient abbey of SS Vincent and Anastasius at Rome (the later Tre Fontane) offered by Innocent II to Bernard. Its first Cistercian abbot in 1140 was Bernard of Pisa, the later Eugenius III. In 1123 the order secured its first foundation in Germany, Camp or Altenkamp near Cologne, and between 1131 and 1135 monks from Clairvaux took over the important house of Eberbach. Meanwhile the Cistercians were entering England with a series of foundations, beginning at Waverley in Surrey. As a whole the order grew from one abbey in 1112 to 10 in 1119 and to 344 in 1153, by which time there were houses in every country from Norway and Poland to Portugal. By then, Louis Lekai has calculated, there must have been over 11,000 Cistercians in all, taking monks and lay brothers together, and his calculation perhaps errs, if at all, on the side of caution. The general chapter decreed in 1152 that no further houses should be founded, but even in an order subject to uniform regulations the decision affected different regions differently. In England and France foundations almost stopped, and this perhaps opened the way to sustained expansion by the Premonstratensians and other regular canons. In Germany and the east, where houses descended from Morimond were less isolated from society and were in growing demand for assisting settlement, the decree was little observed. By 1200 there were 530 abbeys in the order.

No other monastic confederation approached the international success of the Cistercians, but there were several which, in any age less expansionist than the twelfth century, would strike us as remarkable stories of development. Characteristically, their work was focused on their own large region, and not spread over western

---

[15] Ordericus Vitalis viii.26 (iv, p. 327).

Europe as a whole. La Chaise-Dieu (founded 1043) eventually became the mother-house of an order with 11 abbeys and 330 priories, the great majority of them in southern and central France. After Stephen's hermitage of Muret was moved to Grandmont in 1125, it received customs and an organization under Prior Stephen of Liciac (1139–63) and expanded to about 150 dependent houses in France and England. Fontevraud operated in the same area, with 129 foundations in the course of the twelfth century. The mother-house had been founded about 1101 by Robert of Arbrissel to provide separate refuges for the various groups among his mixed following, including aristocratic ladies, prostitutes, lepers, and clergy. Robert insisted on giving a woman head for the whole order, and appointed Petronilla of Chemillé as grand abbess shortly before his death in 1116. Petronilla's policy was to shape the order into something close to the traditional upper-class nunneries, and its expansion was the result of the shortage of aristocratic facilities of this kind in north-western Europe. In southern Germany the observances of Hirsau, closely based on Cluny, were followed by up to 100 monasteries, although there was no structure of centralized government in the group. Other monastic families, after a period of expansion, sought membership of a still larger federation, as when Savigny and Obazine with all their dependencies were affiliated with the Cistercians in 1147. Among these orders, the Carthusians were distinctive. It is clear that Bruno of Cologne did not intend to establish an order. After founding La Grande Chartreuse in 1084, he left it for papal service and eventually founded another house in Calabria, where the district of Serra San Bruno is still full of memories of him. Although the house eventually became Carthusian, it does not seem originally to have had the same customs or any direct governmental tie with Bruno's earlier foundation. The manner of life at La Grande Chartreuse is uncertain in the earlier years, but we know from the description by Guibert of Nogent that it had assumed its later form at least by 1115, that is thirty years after its creation. Under the fifth prior, Guigo (1109–36), the first dependent monasteries were acquired, and he wrote the first set of customs between 1121 and 1127. Expansion was slow, but by 1200 there were just under forty houses, with a concentration in Burgundy but some scattered as far away as western England. Some features were reminiscent of the Cistercians: the estates formed a 'waste' or wilderness directly exploited by the order, and there was a sharp separation between monks and lay brothers, which went even further than that at Cîteaux. The two groups occupied quite separate buildings, an 'upper' and a 'lower' house. The monks lived an eremitical life, each having a cell with a garden within the monastery; the community met only at worship in the church. Like the Cistercians, the Carthusians had a highly organized and disciplined programme of life; unlike them, they did not have the experience of unrestricted expansion which was to create many problems for Cîteaux.

Side by side with the new monastic orders, the regular canons were also expanding. Something has already been said in Chapter 3 about the development of the canonical movement; it continued apace in the twelfth century, with so many variations that its proliferation cannot be described in a short space. The underlying motivation is clear enough in a desire to live the apostolic life. This could be differently defined: some houses laid their emphasis on the service of the Christian community or the 'cure of souls'; others stressed poverty and withdrawal from the world. The latter group, among whom the Premonstratensians were prominent, are liable to strike us as monks by nature; but men who were already canons were liable to seek to purify their own order rather than to submit themselves to an unfamiliar monastic discipline. Although the name 'canon' should (from its Greek derivation) mean a clerk who was submitted to a rule, by the middle of the twelfth century it was being applied to four different groups: canons of ancient cathedrals and colleges who had individual incomes and houses in the manner of modern Anglican canons; communities living under the ancient Rule of Aix, in community but with personal property; those living under the milder Augustinian *Third Rule*; and those under a much stricter and more recent version of the Augustinian rule. From about 1130 the convention was to describe the Augustinians as 'regular canons' (tautologically, because both words meant the same thing) and the others as 'secular canons'. Even this description hugely understates the complexities, because the Rule of St Augustine was much less specific than that of Benedict, and allowed enormous variations in the customs which a house might follow, from a small group of brethren serving a hospital to a cathedral with immense endowments.

One of the interesting parts of the spectrum was formed by the regular canons who were the chosen agents of bishops for the reform of their dioceses. In southern Europe they controlled many of the cathedrals, including St John Lateran at Rome, Florence, and Lucca; Cefalù in Sicily; and in southern France Toulouse, Nîmes, and Carcassonne. The high point in the use of regular canons in the government of the church was in eastern Germany, where they occupied a key place in the policy of such men as Bishop Reinhard of Halberstadt (1107–23) and Archbishop Conrad I of Salzburg (1106–47) for restoring their churches after the ravages of the dispute between papacy and emperors. Bishop Reinhard found on his accession a 'wretched church', and when Conrad returned from exile in Saxony in 1121 or 1122 he found his diocese 'very poor and greatly devastated'. Before the end of his pontificate Conrad had regularized fourteen houses, including the cathedral, and the whole group was supervised by an assembly which met under his presidency. The houses of canons were centres of liturgical worship and of administration, since archdeaconries were sometimes located there, and they assisted the bishop in the supervision of his possessions. Eastern Germany showed the potential of the canons as an alternative system of government, where exceptional circumstances allowed them to be fully developed. It opened fascinating possibilities, for it represented a wholly different way of administering the church from the one which eventually triumphed; but it had only a limited spread in place and time, and even before the end of the century the common life was beginning to break down in many of the German dioceses.

In France and England, the secular cathedral chapters remained almost completely impervious to the efforts of the bishops to introduce the regular life. North of the Loire, only the chapter of Sées, a small cathedral in southern Normandy, reformed from St Victor at Paris, acquired a regular chapter, and in England only Carlisle, although many of the richest English cathedrals already had Benedictine chapters whose existence went back before the Norman conquest. It was, however, possible for bishops to establish regular canons in many of the smaller collegiate churches, and they did so by encouraging the growth of the great federations of Augustinians. St Ruf, Avignon, continued its growth until in 1158, when the community moved to Valence, it had about 100 houses following its customs, although the constitutional attachments were slight. St Victor at Paris was a specialist in the reform of other houses: its expansion came almost totally from the aggregation of existing communities. The Augustinians in England were highly favoured by the king's men who had made their fortunes under Henry I (1100–35): some of them, such as Waldef of Kirkham, had close links with the Cistercians and were essentially monastic in character, while others were in cities or small towns (St Bartholomew's, London, and Cirencester) and drew a great deal of their income from city rents and the ownership of parish churches, a source which was forbidden to Cistercians.

A new feature among the canons was the appearance of a more severe version of the Augustinian Rule, the *Ordo monasterii*, whose provisions included silence, fasting, and manual labour. This set of customs brought canons much closer to the new orders of monks, and naturally it appealed most strongly to those groups which had a hermit background. Springiersbach adopted it soon after 1100 and transmitted it to a group of houses in the Rhineland and Germany; Arrouaise accepted the new customs under Abbot Gervase, probably in 1126. Such groups formed the 'new order' of regular canons in contrast to the 'old order' which continued to follow the *Regula Tertia*. The most remarkable federation following the new order, however, were the Premonstratensians. Prémontré had its roots in the world of hermits and itinerant preachers. Its founder, Norbert, was a member of a noble German family and a canon of Xanten in the Rhineland. As a royal chaplain, he accompanied Henry V on his dramatic visit to Rome in 1111. Norbert experienced a deep personal conversion about 1115. He at first attempted to persuade the canons of Xanten to live as regulars, and having failed he set out to preach. Eventually, under the protection of Bishop Bartholomew of Laon, he founded a community in the forests at Prémontré in 1121. There, Norbert considered the customs of his new house. He decided not to apply for affiliation to the Cistercians, but to accept the Augustinian Rule, apparently on the ground of his original calling as a canon, 'for he wished now to live the apostolic life which he had undertaken in words'. [16] This was accepted in its stringent form of the 'new order', and at once had to contend with complaints from nearby 'old order' canons about the innovation. Norbert left the community in 1126 when he was appointed archbishop of Magdeburg. By then, it had begun to spread with great speed, with new houses already in 1122 at Floreffe and Cappenburg. It was indeed distinctive, among all the new federations of canons or monks, in that its expansion followed

[16] *Vita A*, MGH SS XII.683.

immediately upon the foundation of the mother-house, without a substantial period of development such as took place within Cîteaux or La Grande Chartreuse. The adoption of a set of customs, a modification of the *Ordo monasterii* in a moderate direction, and the organization of an order, whose system of government was heavily influenced by the Cistercian model, was the work of Norbert's successor, Hugh of Fosses. By 1200 there were about 100 abbeys, and their way of life spanned the monastic and the canonical. It was a severe order, with a great deal of sympathy with the Cistercians, but at the same time its houses, almost from the beginning, had acquired parishes to govern, and some of the Premonstratensians were leading apologists of the canons in the controversies with the monks which developed in the course of the century.

iii. *Controversy and Criticism*

Giles Constable has drawn attention to the change in the subject-matter of controversy between the eleventh and twelfth centuries. During the last quarter of the eleventh century the main interest lay in the relationship between the church and the secular power, and this was continued under Paschal II, although with a focus on more technical problems and especially on investiture. After 1125, public controversy was centred on the proper form of the religious life.[17] There were three major debates: between Cistercians and black monks, between monks and regular canons, and a third more general current of criticism by seculars directed in particular against the reformed orders.

The sharp exchanges between Cistercians and traditional monks should not be allowed to obscure a large degree of sympathy between them. They read the same literature and shared many of the same ideals. On the black-monk side, Guibert of Nogent about 1115 wrote warmly about the new monasticism, William of Malmesbury about 1125 wrote a very sympathetic account of Cistercian origins, and about 1131 Abbot William of St Thierry presided at Reims over a council of Benedictine abbots who resolved to introduce Cistercian-type usages into their own houses. Although Suger of Saint-Denis was in many ways a champion of traditional Benedictinism, Bernard of Clairvaux wrote him a warm letter of congratulation about his

[17] G. Constable, 'Papal, Imperial and Monastic Propaganda', *Preaching and Propaganda in the Middle Ages* (Paris, 1983), 179–99

reforms at the abbey and remained on good terms with him throughout their lives. The common ground was, in a sense, what produced the problem, because the Cistercian reform proved very attractive to ardent monks, and many wished to become Cistercians (as William of St Thierry did, eventually going to Signy in 1135 as a simple monk) or to import into their own lives the emphasis on silence and manual labour which was characteristic of the new orders. Many of the sharpest exchanges were generated by the migration of monks from one order to another or by a threat to traditional usages.

The outbreak of controversy between Cistercians and Cluniacs coincided with a scandal at Cluny. Pons of Melgueil, who had become abbot in 1109, was descended from a family notable for its support of the Gregorian papacy, and indeed was the godson of Paschal II. He governed the abbey and its dependencies in much the same spirit as his great predecessor, Hugh. The growth of dissatisfaction with him was probably the result of financial difficulties at the abbey. The vast building programme, which Hugh had adopted reluctantly, and the large provision for the relief of the poor were too much even for Cluny's considerable revenues, especially when events in Spain led to an interruption of the subsidy from Castile. The pressure was increased by the attempts of neighbouring bishops to restrict the exemptions of the abbey. Pons had to face complaints from both inside and outside, and when he met Calixtus II he found the pope unsympathetic. Calixtus had been a great metropolitan himself and was disinclined to continue the old Gregorian championship of monastic privileges, against which the tide was turning. Pons apparently resigned in anger and went on perpetual pilgrimage to the Holy Land. Peter the Venerable was elected in his place in 1122. Pons, however, returned to the west and settled as a hermit near Vicenza. In 1126, persuaded by his former supporters, he returned to Cluny and attempted to resume control, provoking disorders in the course of which the abbey was sacked. Summoned to Rome, he refused to answer for his conduct, and died there after a few months in a papal prison. This startling episode obviously reveals the tensions which existed within the community, but one must not conclude too hastily that Cluny was in decline. The abbey retained influence at Rome, and Cluniacs were in demand for bishoprics and as abbots for houses outside the order. Henry I of England helped with the finance needed for the completion of the new abbey church in 1133, and his own royal foundation at Reading in 1121 adopted the customs of Cluny. So did Faversham, the foundation of his successor Stephen in 1148. Stephen's brother Henry of Blois was a Cluniac who became bishop of Winchester (1129–71) and combined this office with that of abbot to wealthy Glastonbury and, for a time, with that of papal legate in England. The new abbot of Cluny, Peter of Montboissier or Peter the Venerable, was one of the most remarkable men in his generation. Although Peter staunchly defended Cluniac customs against Bernard of Clairvaux, when he wrote to his own monks he was a good deal more critical of the state of affairs and was anxious to correct the relaxed features of Cluniac life. He held a large reforming assembly at Cluny in 1132 and in 1146 published a consolidated edition of his new statutes. Both these steps reflected a concern to improve co-ordination within the Cluniac family, which had depended on the sole authority of the abbot. It must be admitted that some of the problems arising from the poor structure of government remained unsolved. At about the time of Peter's death the German monk Idung of Prüfening, a Cluniac turned Cistercian, contrasted the efficient system of Cîteaux with the chaos of Cluny: 'Since your abbots are without a head, like *acephali* with no master over themselves, everyone in his own monastery does what he wants and leaves out what he wants. This is the reason why religious life in your monasteries is not durable.'[18]

Idung's *Dialogue between a Cistercian and a Cluniac* belonged to a tradition of Cistercian criticism which apparently began about 1124 with an open letter addressed by Bernard of Clairvaux to his cousin Robert, who had left the Cistercians to become a Cluniac. It has been suggested that this was a device to intervene in the dispute raging inside Cluny between reformers and conservatives, of which the Pons affair was an expression, but it need not be more than a response to a case of 'migration' which had touched Bernard nearly. It was followed a few months later at the request of William of St Thierry by a more systematic attack in the *Apologia ad Guillelmum*, one of the masterpieces of monastic polemic. These works began a pamphlet war which continued for more than a generation. There were dignified replies from Peter the Venerable, and the adoption of

---

[18] *Dialogus*, iii, *Thesaurus*, v. 1641 E. The fall of Pons is difficult to interpret because of the large discrepancies between the account later given by Peter the Venerable and that of other contemporaries. See discussions listed in bibliography.

some of the changes advocated by Bernard by the abbots of the province of Reims produced an indignant reply by the Cluniac Matthew of Albano. The issues were still keenly felt in the 1150s, when Idung of Prüfening wrote, and about 1160 when they formed a central interest in the *Life of Amadeus of Bonnevaux*. The terms of the debate did not alter greatly during this period. The black-monk position was in part a sheer defence of the authority of accepted custom. As Matthew of Albano demanded to know, 'What is this new law? What is this new teaching?'[19] They found particularly offensive the Cistercian claim to a monopoly of the Rule of Benedict, which they alone observed literally: 'a new race of pharisees comes back to the world, who set themselves apart and prefer themselves to others'.[20] The Cistercians, on the contrary, argued that the black monks did not keep the Rule to which they had sworn, and they made much of the ease and display typical of the Cluniac life, of which the classic criticism is Bernard's *Apologia*. The buildings are vast, ornate, and decorated with unsuitable monsters and grotesques. The cooking is worthy of the *Good Food Guide*: 'Who could describe, for example, the different ways of preparing eggs alone, not to mention anything else? With great expertise they are beaten and mixed, or cooked in water or hard boiled or chopped small. They are served fried, roasted, stuffed, by themselves or with other things.'[21] The liturgy is inordinately long and splendid, and what silence remains is swallowed up in idle chatter. This comfortable life rests upon the exploitation of property rights and revenues not permitted by the Rule. Bernard's picture is that of the opposition between primitive simplicity and a decadent way of life which had moved away from the one to which monks were sworn.

While this argument was in progress, another was developing. Monks and canons were by now much more similar to one another than they had been in the Carolingian period. The tendency for monks to become priests, which had already been apparent then, had made steady progress, to an extent which was criticized in some quarters, as Abbot Rupert of Deutz noted: 'Why so many priests in

---

[19] U. Berlière, *Documents inédits pour servir à l'histoire ecclésiastique de la Belgique* I (1894), 101. Cf Ordericus Vitalis viii.27, (iv, p. 333): 'present-day teachers who prefer new traditions to the customs of the fathers of old, calling other monks seculars and presumptuously condemning them as violators of the Rule'.

[20] G. Constable (ed.), *The Letters of Peter the Venerable* (Cambridge, Mass., 1967), ep. 28, i. p. 57.

[21] Bernard, *Apologia ad Guillelmum*, ix.20 (*Opera* iii.98).

the monasteries?'[22] The process of 'restitution' had also put into the hands of monasteries great numbers of local churches and a large revenue from tithe, whose possession was defended on the ground that monks are entitled to exercise the cure of souls. While monks were thus in the process of becoming clergy, some clergy were on the way to becoming monks. The regular canons lived in community under a Rule, and those who had adopted the more severe 'new order' had accepted with it important aspects of monastic custom. Houses of regular canons did not necessarily exercise cure of souls, and they did not automatically serve the parishes which belonged to their monastery; indeed, the signs are that they had to obtain a special privilege to be allowed to do so. The similarity between monks and canons made the issues in dispute all the more significant.

One was the question of migration between the orders. The accepted doctrine was that an applicant could move only from a less to a more severe one. To Rupert of Deutz this meant flatly that 'it is lawful and always will be for a clerk to become a monk'.[23] The issue was technical, but it had large implications because the canons argued that their calling was superior, being more firmly rooted in the Gospel. The Premonstratensian Anselm of Havelberg, writing about 1150 to Abbot Egbert of Huysberg, referred to the types of ministry listed by St Paul in 1 Corinthians 12: 4–10 and asked: 'are these not sufficient . . . for the building up of the body of Christ, which is the church? Although this can exist in good shape without monks, still it is better and more attractively constructed and decorated with the variety given by different orders of the elect.'[24] The argument was to spill over into some important areas, including (as we shall see later) the interpretation of Christian history and its fulfilment.

The second subject of controversy was close to the first: the claim of the canons that they had a monopoly of pastoral care. This term was not a common one at the time, but the range of functions is described in a canon of the First Lateran Council of 1123 which established a solid basis for the canons' claim: 'We also forbid abbots and monks to give public penance, to visit the sick and to anoint them, and to sing mass publicly.' [25] The problem was posed by

[22] Rupert, *In Regulam S. Benedicti*, iii. 12 (PL 170.520A).
[23] Ibid., iv. 13 (PL 170.536D).
[24] Anselm, *Epistola apologetica pro ordine canonicorum regularium*, PL 188.1136C.
[25] I Lateran c. 16, Alberigo 169 n. See also the discussion in ch. 9. iii above.

Gratian, who devoted a whole section or *Causa* of his canonical collection to the question, in the form, 'is it permissible for monks to perform offices for the people, give penance and baptize?' His answer was that a monk, if a priest, could perform such functions, but only if appropriately appointed and authorized; in other words, he was in the same position as any other priest.[26] We do not know how frequently monks acted as clergy in churches owned by the monasteries, but the weight of evidence is that it was rare. The canons were firm in asserting their position: the Premonstratensian Philip of Harvengt held that not even a good monk should be promoted to clerical orders and that 'Christ gave to the apostles and to apostolic men, that is to clergy, the office of preaching'.[27] For the first time for many centuries the pastoral office was claiming to stand at the centre of the church's life, and to relegate the monks to a secondary position.

The Cistercians were not only under fire from the black monks for their innovations; they were also being increasingly criticized for abandoning their principles, and above all for greed. The management of Cistercian estates was designed to be quite different from that of the older monasteries. The *Exordium parvum* makes it clear that their houses were intended to be situated in the wilderness, far from cities, and to be supported, not by the revenue from peasant cultivations, mills, tithes, or churches, but by the direct exploitation of land by lay brothers and hired labour. In many abbeys the early days were difficult. The problems were such that the site of the monastery might have to be changed—this happened at twenty-one abbeys in England and Wales, and the abbey of Øm in Jutland established a record by moving four times between 1165 and 1172. Not all Cistercian houses supervised great clearances in the woodlands or marshes. Local circumstances might lead to an economy based mainly on animal husbandry, as at several Burgundian abbeys, but the clearance pattern was the more usual one. By the second half of the twelfth century, each Cistercian abbey was surrounded by a ring of granges, varying normally between five and fifteen in number, from which the needs of the monks were supplied. Eventually some abbeys were to develop this system into massive production for the market, as in the Yorkshire abbeys with their great sheep-runs, but on a large scale this was a thirteenth-century development. Why, then, was there criticism of the Cistercians as

---

[26] Gratian, *Decr.* C. XVI (761 ff.).
[27] Philip of Harvengt, *De Institutione Clericorum*, iv.72 (PL 203.762A).

landlords by writers who held no particular brief for the attitudes of earlier monasticism?

It is quite easy, even in the first half of the century, to find breaches of the rules set out in the *Exordium parvum*. Perhaps the 'wilderness' in which the early monks settled was always a theological concept rather than a topographical one. Not all the sites were savage, nor were they always remote from human settlement. More seriously, they were sometimes already occupied: there was even a chapel and several serfs on the site of Cîteaux. The technique on such occasions was to remove the inhabitants in order to have the land available for Cistercian exploitation. Only a thorough study of the twelfth-century foundations as a whole would reveal how common these clearances were, but the signs are that there were many. A study by G. Despy of three Lotharingian abbeys (Orval 1131, Villers 1146, Aulne 1147) reveals the destruction of existing settlements on all of them; even an intervention by ecclesiastical authority failed to save the peasants from expulsion.[28] We do know that on some occasions compensation was provided in the form of a new site, but of its adequacy we have no means of judging. These removals certainly left a bad taste in the mouths of contemporaries such as Walter Map, who commented that 'they make a wilderness so that they can be alone'.[29] In a sense, this policy indicates excessive enthusiasm to follow the principles of the order, by removing any inhabitants whose presence would be contrary to them. It also happened, however, that abbeys held property of the kinds renounced in *Exordium parvum*, particularly when an existing monastery joined the order. Thus Tre Fontane at Rome was permitted by Pope Eugenius III to have 'a certain castle and some other possessions'. When the monastic families of Savigny and Obazine were affiliated *en bloc* in 1147, they were allowed to keep the tithes which, under their own regulations, they lawfully owned, and their example proved infectious so that by 1200 most Cistercian abbeys had some revenue from tithe. From the 1160s onwards some abbeys were acquiring town houses, presumably for purposes of trade, in a way which was clearly contrary to the spirit of the early regulations. These instances probably reflect the inability of the general chapter to keep control of an order which was growing too quickly. Yet in 1200 the estates of a

[28] G. Despy, 'Les richesses de la terre: Cîteaux et Prémontré devant l'économie de profit', *Problèmes d'histoire du Christianisme*, ed. J. Préaux, 5 (Brussels, 1974–5), 58–80.

[29] M. R. James *et al.* (eds.), *Walter Map, De Nugis Curialium* (Oxford, 1983), i.25, p. 92.

Cistercian abbey were still very different in organization from those of a black-monk house, and their characteristics reflected the distinctive rules which had been established at the beginning. Income from tithes and other property was relatively small, and so was involvement in commercial affairs.

The basis for criticism, apart from distaste at the expulsions, was probably twofold. For one thing, the Cistercians had been too successful for their own good. Their formula of direct exploitation of the land had made them wealthy once the granges were in full production, and in the later part of the century they had all the irritating power of *nouveaux riches* who had come from nowhere to great prosperity. The same criticisms were directed against the new wealth of the military orders. The other major source of annoyance was the scale of their privileges. About 1150 Bernard of Clairvaux wrote strongly in his *De Consideratione* against such grants, but his order was already accumulating them. Essentially the privileges which they obtained emerged directly from the character of the order. When a bishop accepted the foundation of a house, he thereby recognized the Carta Caritatis and thus signed away most of his powers of discipline and jurisdiction there. By the time that Lucius III brought their privileges together into a general grant, *Monastice sinceritas*, in 1184, the order had escaped from almost all the normal obligations to bishops under canon law. A similar pattern may be observed with tithes. Monks had traditionally (although not always successfully) claimed that they need not pay tithes on new land (*novalia*), nor on estates which they directly cultivated themselves. An order which received no tithe, and which claimed to cultivate all its estates itself and moreover, in some parts of Europe, was a major colonizer of new land, was in a convincing position to advance such claims. The struggle to secure papal recognition of them continued until Innocent III provided a compromise, favourable to the order, which excused it from paying tithes on *novalia* already held, but prohibited any further expansion of the privilege. Even the friends of the Cistercians were growing uneasy about its prosperity: Alexander III's letter *Inter innumeras* of 1169, while thanking them for their support in the schism, gently reminded them of the need to follow the steps of their fathers; and Geoffrey of Auxerre, devoted as he was to his own order, feared that it was slipping back into the relaxation of traditional monasticism which it existed to remedy.[30]

---

[30] F. Gastaldelli, 'Tre sermoni di Goffredo di Auxerre', *Cîteaux* 31 (1980), 193–225.

iv. *The New Orders in Twelfth-century Society*

For a long time it was fashionable to describe the second quarter of the twelfth century as the age of St Bernard. He was the son of a minor Burgundian noble, born in 1090, who in 1112 or 1113, instead of continuing his studies in the schools, decided to withdraw to the nearby abbey of Cîteaux with a group of relations and companions. In 1115 he was sent to establish a new community at Clairvaux, and he remained abbot there until his death in 1153. He refused several offers of preferment, and his simple curriculum vitae suggests a man who spent his life in the retirement to which the Cistercians were dedicated. In reality, he was one of the most influential men of his lifetime, even when we have discounted the exaggerated importance assigned to him by his biographers. Bernard was a prolific correspondent and persuasive speaker, who visited Germany, Italy, and southern France in person and wrote letters to places as far apart as England and the eastern Mediterranean. He was essentially a propagandist, who used the available media with immense effect to transmit his message; he possessed no power except the ability to influence those who did. His major interventions in international affairs began with the schism of 1130, when he was a prominent supporter of Innocent II and spent a long time travelling with the pope and curia. He intervened in disputed episcopal elections, usually successfully and in the interest of the Cistercian candidate, and emerged as a champion of orthodoxy against those who seemed to threaten it, including schoolmen (Abelard 1140, Gilbert of Poitiers 1148), radical reformers (Arnold of Brescia) and the rising tide of popular heretics (in Cologne and southern France in the 1140s). It was at that time that he reached his highest level of influence with the election of his pupil Bernard as the first Cistercian pope, Eugenius III, in 1146. Eugenius continued to regard him as his mentor, asking for the book of spiritual advice, the *De Consideratione*, an incisive discussion of the papal office and a vade-mecum for many later popes. Bernard's own reading of the situation was disconcertingly revealed by his remark that 'people say that I am pope rather than you'; other accounts of the curia do not confirm this exaggerated notion.[31] Nevertheless, he took the lead in the preaching of the Second Crusade, perhaps going well beyond the commission which the pope had given him, and suffered from the criticism which was generated by its dismal failure.

---

[31] Ep. 239 to Eugenius III (*Opera* viii. 120).

Along with William of St Thierry and Ælred of Rievaulx,
Bernard was the leader of the most influential school of spirituality
which had existed since the patristic period. Bernard was also
instrumental in encouraging effective Cistercian participation in the
life of the church as a whole: up to the time of his death Clairvaux
provided over half the Cistercians who became bishops. The order's
presence in the cardinals' college and on the bishops' bench was
never spectacular, however, since it was rare to appoint monks as
bishops. The largest number of Cistercian bishops at any one time
was twenty-nine. A more significant contribution was perhaps the
use of Cistercians as 'shock troops' in critical situations: they were
sent to preach against heretics in southern France, and their abbeys
were important in assisting Christian settlement on the frontiers, in
Spain and eastern Germany. More than any other pope, it was
Innocent III who saw the Cistercians as his special agents—a warning
that we must not lay too much emphasis on the symptoms of decline
which some have discerned as already present in the twelfth century.
There is no escaping the element of paradox in this situation. An
order which stood for withdrawal from the world was intervening in
it more forcefully than Cluny. There are some considerations which
mitigate this tension. The Rule charged the abbot with representing
the monastery in the outside world, and this type of activity was
almost always undertaken by abbots. Moreover, Cistercians rarely
supplied regular advice about routine political affairs in the style of
Suger of Saint-Denis or Wibald of Stavelot. This element in the life
of the order was probably a special contribution of Bernard's, for he
began the tradition and was its most extreme representative. One
must accept that there was an element of contradiction in his whole
personality, for he was an enthusiast of contemplation who
happened to be outstandingly good at persuasion. He seems to have
been somewhat puzzled by his own predicament, and referred to
himself sadly as the chimera of his age, 'neither clerk nor layman;
I have long since abandoned the way of life, but not the habit, of
the monk'.[32]

The spectacular interventions of Bernard must not lead us to
overestimate his influence, and that of his order, upon the culture of
his time. Another very powerful influence was that of the regular
canons. Karl Bosl has even suggested that 1124–1159 should be
envisaged as the 'canonical period of papal history', and it is true

---

[32] Ep. 250 to Carthusian Prior Bernard of Porto (*Opera* viii. 147).

that, even if the number of regular-canon popes has been exaggerated, they were influential in the curia. Their members can be found in almost every important area of the church's life: they were scholars (Hugh of St Victor), radical reformers (Gerhoh of Reichersberg) or revolutionaries (Arnold of Brescia), and canonists (Ivo of Chartres, Gratian). Their total impact has to be assessed as greater than that of the Cistercians. We must also remember that the eye always tends to see what is moving rather than the stationary landscape, and acknowledge the continuing influence exercised by traditional Benedictine abbeys. Relatively few new ones were founded in the twelfth century, but a great number of priories were being created by existing monasteries. Individual abbots were still among the most important men on the European scene; in France, in the second quarter of the century, the most influential churchmen were Abbots Bernard of Clairvaux, Peter the Venerable of Cluny and Suger of Saint-Denis. This fact is certainly a tribute to the genius of Bernard, whose standing had been achieved solely by his own talent, while the others were the heads of very great abbeys, but it is wrong to see him as dominant among the three. This was perhaps the last generation in which traditional Benedictines were making a major contribution in the fields of artistic creation, as Suger was, or of scholarship, like Rupert of Deutz; after 1150, it is difficult to think of successors of the same calibre. Perhaps the greatest restraint on the influence of the new orders was the existence of other creative forces which had now appeared, notably the city schools. It is not altogether exaggerated to speak of Bernard and Abelard as contending for the youth of Europe.[33] The development of law and administration, too, was a new element which proved impossible to restrain; for all the influence exercised by Bernard's *De Consideratione* his attack on the growing legal responsibilities of the curia was wholly ineffective.

Apart from the influence of the new orders on European politics and culture, the sheer weight of new foundations had a great impact upon the countryside. The combination of monasteries of the new orders with additional Benedictine priories meant that almost every village lay within a short distance of a monastic community. The large diocese of Soissons in northern France will serve as an example. About 1070, it had four Benedictine abbeys with perhaps eight priories. There were two large houses of secular canons, the

[33] F. Heer, *The Medieval World* (New York, 1963), 115.

cathedral and St Corneille, Compiègne, and many small ones in castles or attached to nunneries or other churches, perhaps nineteen in all. By 1200 the situation had been transformed and the monastic presence was much greater. The four Benedictine abbeys remained, and so did the cathedral, probably the only surviving community of secular canons amid a tide which had swept the rest away, including Compiègne, which in 1150 had been taken over by a group of monks from Saint Denis amid fierce resistance. There were by that time over thirty Benedictine priories. There were also four Premonstratensian abbeys newly created, and although there was only one Cistercian, Longpont, it was a rich house with eleven granges. In addition there were several other houses of regular canons, which had very largely taken over the functions of the former secular communities, among them two further Premonstratensian houses.[34] The same picture of monastic impact emerges from the nearby Beauvais region, where the Cistercian and Premonstratensian granges were in the process of creating a new landscape and where their foundations were so numerous that it was necessary to agree that neither order would establish an abbey within four miles of a house of the other, nor a grange within one mile.[35] In the old kingdom of Burgundy, to take another example, there were 1,800 monasteries by 1200, and in the most settled region this amounted to as many as two in every parish.

Various views have been taken of the significance of this monastic landownership for twelfth-century society. Bernard Bligny has offered us a pessimistic reading. The houses of new orders were deliberately situated away from major centres, and were therefore of much less use than the old Benedictine abbeys for hospitality for travellers and succour for the poor. The Carthusians, in fact, did not regard poor relief as a major concern of theirs, since it would interfere with their isolation. Yet by the second half of the century, these were rich houses, even if the monks in them did not have individual property. Their wealth had been created ultimately at the expense of the peasantry, by withdrawing land from lay cultivation and sometimes by removing existing villages. This analysis is certainly true of some regions, but there is a balance on the other side. The Cistercians opened large areas for settlement, and the

[34] L. Duval-Arnould, 'Moines et chanoines dans le diocèse de Soissons', MCSM 9 (1980), 679–91.

[35] D. Lohrmann, *Kirchengut im nördlichen Frankreich* (Bonn, 1983).

consequent demand for wage-labour, which they required for working the estates, offered opportunities for employment which did not previously exist. At least during the twelfth century, their reputation as the pioneers opening new lands within Europe and on the frontier has a good deal of reality, and their wealth was a thing of new creation. [36] Not enough is known to be sure whether on balance the peasants gained or lost, but it must be agreed that the effect of their activities on peasant communities was, to the monks, a matter of very little interest.

[36] B. Bligny, 'Monachisme et pauvreté au XIIème siècle', *Atti del II Convegno internazionale . . . di Studi francescani* (Assisi, 1975), 105–47, with comments by P. Tomea, *Aevum* 51 (1977), 389–95.

I I

THE CHRISTIAN FRONTIER

i. *The Theory of Mission*

On the west front of the abbey church at Vézelay there is a carving of the glorified Christ sending his power upon the apostles. In the outer bands of the composition are representations of the peoples of the world, including the distant dog-headed races of whom geographers had told. This carving was a confident statement of the universal mission of the church, inspired perhaps by Abbot Peter of Cluny, and it stood at one of the centres of Christendom, where the Second Crusade was preached and the Third Crusade assembled. The missionary task was conceived in a very different way from the approach in more recent ages, which have seen religion as a matter of personal conviction. The medieval assumption, on the contrary, was that the Christian faith provided the framework of a healthy society. As they saw it, they were confronted outside Christendom with an evil society founded upon idolatry, and their task was to replace it by an order which rested upon the sure ground of reverence for the one true God. Thus in 1007 the synod of Frankfurt saw the purpose of the new bishopric of Bamberg as being 'both that the paganism of the Slavs may be destroyed and also that the memory of the Christian name may be forever celebrated there'.[1] To destroy pagan worship and to substitute for it the cult of the true God remained the double objective throughout our period; as the leaders of the First Crusade put it, their aim was 'that . . . when the strength of the Saracens and of the devil is broken, the kingdom of Christ and of the church may extend everywhere from sea to sea'.[2] As these words imply, the awareness was growing strong of a territorial division between the lands where Christ ruled, and the dominions of the false gods. The term *Christianitas* was not new, but its use greatly increased around 1100 as an expression for the geographical concept

---

[1] MGH Diplomata, III no. 143, p. 170.
[2] H. Hagenmeyer, *Epistulae et chartae ad historiam primi belli sacri spectantes* (Innsbruck, 1901; repr. Hildesheim, 1973), ep. XVIII, p. 171.

which we would call Christendom. The use of the word (even of the word 'Christian') was however rare until the First Crusade; it was in the chroniclers of the Crusade that the word first became a standard part of western vocabulary. To extend the boundaries of Christendom was a structural task and no more a matter of individual persuasion than, in the eyes of the Pentagon today, resistance to communism is a question of convincing individual Russians that they are wrong.

The northern and southern frontiers required different approaches. The beginning of expansion in the Mediterranean world was examined in Chapter 6. It was characterized by the aim of delivering Christian communities from Moslem oppression and hence by the resort to force under papal auspices, and it was complicated by the need to deal with Christians whose traditions were sometimes very different from those of Rome. In the north, the task was one of preaching the Gospel and building up the church in those pagan lands whose rulers were sympathetic to the new religion. It was much more obviously a missionary situation.

It is probable that the first Christian presence in Scandinavia and the Slavonic east had arisen from accidental contacts: trading, raiding, exile of royal families in England or Germany, and links with relatives who had colonized western provinces and become Christians there—processes which can be traced well before the year 1000. These contacts formed the basis on which native kings instituted a policy of deliberate Christianization. The correlation between the rise of new monarchies and the establishment of the church was close. The strength of pre-Christian cults rested on the kin or clan, and the church offered an attractive prospect to a ruler engaged in creating a new style of power. The missionaries were imbued with a traditional spirit of reverence for monarchy and were ready to recognize the king as enjoying a divinely-given authority. The introduction of clergy provided an impressive ceremonial, a network of connections in Europe, and secretarial and administrative support. The assumption that it was for the king, or for the body of chiefs as a whole, to decide on the people's religion was an accepted one, and the princes of Pomerania in 1128 expressed their dislike of the democratic methods of the early church:

In the primitive church, as we have heard, the religion of Christian faith began with the people and with common persons and spread to the middle classes and at length influenced the great princes of this world. Let us change the order of the primitive church and let it begin with us princes and, passing on from us to the middle classes by an easy progress, let the sanctifying influence of the divine religion enlighten the whole people and nation.[3]

The task of the kings in introducing Christianity was not a straightforward one. The clans were sometimes persistent in upholding the old deities, and there was a danger of a combination of rebellion and pagan reaction. Christianity might also mean the danger of foreign dominance, against which different strategies were adopted. In Poland and Hungary a hierarchy controlled by national archbishops was rapidly created. In Scandinavia there was no independent metropolitan until the twelfth century, but the kings retained a strong link of personal dependence with their bishops. One region alone, that of the Wends on the Elbe, reacted to the threat by attachment to the old religion. It was a pattern repeated in Prussia and Lithuania in the thirteenth century, but before 1200 the Wendish tribes were the one group among whom Christianity was not the chosen faith and preferred instrument of the local dynasties.

One of the basic methods in spreading the faith was by preaching. We have a detailed account of the work of Bishop Otto of Bamberg, who went to Pomerania under the auspices of Boleslaw III of Poland in the 1120s. The need for preachers did not at first lead to the creation of special missionary societies or orders. Stability was the mark of monastic life, and, although individual monks made major contributions, there were no organizations with a mobile membership which could be transferred at need. These only arose with the creation of the Templars (for military purposes) and later of the friars. In the same way, there were no central pressure groups for missions in the western church and no co-ordinated ways of financing them. Serious thinking about the subject was largely confined to the north of Germany, where already in the early eleventh century Thietmar of Merseburg had, in his chronicle, shown a concern with the assimilation of neighbouring peoples into Christian society. This tradition was continued in Adam of Bremen's work *The Deeds of the Archbishops of the Church of Hamburg* in the 1170s, and a century later in *The Chronicle of the Slavs* by Helmold of Bosau. The strategy was to baptize first, and then to instruct. Duke

---

[3] Herbord, *Vita Ottonis episcopi Bambergensis*, iii (MGH SS XII. 802–3).

Richard I of Normandy had said in an earlier age to his pagan allies, 'I will first have you baptized . . . and then further instructed in the full and perfect faith through preaching by the bishops.'[4] This remained the approach in the eleventh and twelfth centuries. It meant that, with rare exceptions, preaching was an official enterprise sponsored by authority, and in the early period of the conversion it is unlikely, given the small number of clergy and the unsuitability of their training, that much was achieved beyond the widespread baptism of the population. That is not to say that rulers were all content with a merely nominal acceptance of the Gospel. Gottschalk, the devout believer who was prince of the Wendish Obodrites until 1066, used to preach personally in the Slavic tongue, interpreting to the people the more difficult teaching of the clergy.[5]

Another major element in the expansion of Latin Christianity was settlement. The rising population led to migration outside the former frontiers, and the settlers took with them their religion and way of life. Villages of western character were established in Palestine, in the frontier zones in Spain and in the Slavonic east. Acre, an old Arab city, was thoroughly westernized, and a Moslem visitor was dismayed to find it full of pigs and crosses, those signs of Christian conviction. On the coast of the Baltic German cities were created, such as Lübeck and Rostock. The long-term fate of these Latin settlements varied: in Palestine they were doomed to perish in face of Moslem reconquest, but in Sicily the Lombards, and in eastern Europe the Germans, came to have cultural predominance. This does not indicate, as has sometimes been suggested, that the advance of Christianity beyond the Elbe was achieved by the annihilation of the original inhabitants. Wendish princes encouraged settlers from Saxony and Franconia in the hope of increasing the prosperity of their lands, and eventually adopted German language and culture. In almost all the frontier regions, the great ecclesiastical establishments were important agents in settlement. In Palestine the canons of the Holy Sepulchre introduced western peasants onto their great estates centred on Magna Mahumeria north of Jerusalem, and in the land of the Obodrites Bishop Bern of Schwerin had built up a network of prosperous estates by the time of his death in 1191.

    [4] Dudo of S. Quentin, *De Gestis Normanniae Ducum*, iii (PL 141. 745B).
    [5] B. Schmeidler (ed.), *Adam von Bremen, Hamburgische Kirchengeschichte* (Hanover, 1917), iii.20, p. 163.

Cistercian and Premonstratensian abbeys were also important. There is not much sign that they undertook direct missionary work, but their example was probably significant: Duke Bogislav of Pomerania expressed the hope that 'if we support good provosts and men of holy life we shall succeed in making our unbelieving people recognize the true faith'. More obviously important was their function as centres of settlement, bringing new land into cultivation under Christian auspices: the monks of Dargun received 'full power and perfect freedom in calling to themselves and settling . . . Germans, Danes, Slavs or people of any nation whatsoever and in setting up parishes and priests'.[6]

Where the faith could not be spread by preaching or settlement under the patronage of native rulers, western Europeans resorted to warfare, which was the primary instrument of expansion in Spain, Sicily, and Syria, and a significant one in eastern Germany. Christian tradition held that people should not be coerced into baptism. Pomeranian Christians protested in 1147 against the whole philosophy of warfare in the service of the Christ: 'if they have come to strengthen the Christian faith, they should have done so not by arms but by the preaching of bishops'.[7] These principles did not prevent the launching of crusades. This was partly because the military aristocracy was ready to use force when its interests were involved, as they were along the Elbe frontier. But the door to Christian militarism was opened more widely by the fact that the traditional theory of the just war permitted the use of force in self-defence or in the recovery of legitimate rights. In the Mediterranean it could always be argued that oppressed Christians needed defending or lost territories were being recovered in Spain, Sicily, and Syria, and even in the north Helmold remarked that in Holstein the masonry and landmarks of old Christian settlements, abandoned in face of pagan reaction, could still be seen. Strictly this did not justify compulsory baptism, but even the missionary-minded Otto of Bamberg in Pomerania threatened that recalcitrants would be punished, and it is not surprising that on the First Crusade there were clear examples of a choice between death and baptism, or that the *Song of Roland* approved the use of direct action:

---

[6] Cited E. Christiansen, *The Northern Crusades* (London, 1980), 68.
[7] Vincent of Prague (MGH SS XVII.663). It should be noted that the Pomeranian Christians were themselves being attacked by the crusaders.

Then to the font the pagans are compelled.
If any dare defy Charlemagne's command,
Then he is hanged or killed or burned with fire.
A hundred thousand men are thus baptized
And are made Christians . . .[8]

On the whole canonists and papal encyclicals never adopted
compulsory conversion as official policy, but there is one significant
exception in the so-called Wendish crusade of 1147, sponsored by
Bernard of Clairvaux and authorized by Eugenius III as a diversion
from the Second Crusade. Although there is disagreement about the
precise intention of Bernard's words, they do seem to demand the
conversion or annihilation of the pagans, and in that sense mark an
important invasion of official doctrine by more popular ideas. H.-D.
Kahl has made the interesting suggestion that Bernard was influenced by Sibylline prophecies of the end of the world, which spoke
of the conquest and conversion of the peoples of the north by a king
of the Romans and which Bernard applied to his contemporary
situation.[9] Just as the north provided a more purely missionary
framework, so it also offered a particularly clear example of holy
wars fought to extend the frontiers of faith.

ii. *Scandinavia*

By the middle of the eleventh century Christianity was the official
religion in both Denmark and Norway. Denmark had had Christian
kings for most of the preceding century and possessed several well-
established bishoprics. Under Swein II Estrithson (1047–74) it was
entering fully into the comity of Christian nations. Norwegian
Christianity was less securely based, but Olaf Tryggvason (995–
1000) had enforced its public acceptance in Norway and Iceland, and
his policy had been continued by Olaf Haraldson (1015–30), who
was to become the patron saint of the country. In Sweden, progress
was slower. Several missionaries were at work there under King
Stenkil (1057–66) and in some provinces the old temples were being
destroyed, but Stenkil did not dare to proceed against the great
shrine of Uppsala. His wisdom was shown when the attempt by his
successor Inge to destroy it set in motion a pagan reaction in which

---

[8] *Chanson de Roland*, laisse 266.
[9] H.-D. Kahl, 'Die Ableitung des Missionkreuzzugs aus sybillinischer Eschatologie', H.
Nowak (ed.), *Die Rolle der Ritterorden* (Torun, 1983), 129–39.

the king was forced to flee and the English missionary Eskil martyred. In the event this proved to be the last determined act of resistance, and about 1138 King Sverker celebrated the public triumph of the new faith by a great church at Uppsala, using material from the temple. Even so, the old practices lingered, and in 1181 Pope Lucius III, appointing Bishop Giles of Västeras, required him 'to root out paganism, to wipe out harmful practices, to implant Christianity and other salutary teaching'.[10] The last Scandinavian country to be evangelized was Finland. There is no evidence of a Christian presence there before the expedition of King Erik of Sweden in 1157 and the early years of the church are obscure. The first bishop, Henry, was martyred, and his successors met with severe difficulties. Pope Alexander III was gloomy about the Finns and remarked that they would only profess Christianity when threatened by an enemy army.

One of the striking features was the late date at which the new churches secured autonomy through the grant of a separate archbishopric. There were several reasons for this. It was difficult, especially in Norway and Sweden, to endow bishoprics because of the limited area of cultivated land and the nature of the property customs. Kings therefore preferred to treat bishops as court officials, and in the early years chose primarily clergy of English birth and education. The archbishopric of Hamburg-Bremen also had an entrenched position. Since the time of Ansgar in the ninth century it had been regarded as the missionary centre for the north and east and it enjoyed support from the German emperors. Its importance was also enhanced by the ambitious policy of Archbishop Adalbert (1043–72). He was, Adam of Bremen tells us, 'so affable and generous and hospitable, so desirous of both divine and human glory, that little Bremen was made famous like Rome by his power, and was visited in devotion by all parts of the earth, especially by all the northern peoples'.[11] Adalbert was committed to the missionary enterprise, and considered going north himself as a preacher until he was dissuaded by his friend King Swein of Denmark, who stressed the importance of knowing the language and customs of the people at first hand. Adalbert even devised a grandiose plan for a northern patriarchate with twelve subordinate bishops. He was unable to implement this project, but at least he managed to extend the

[10] Lucius III, ep. 12 of 30 Dec. 1181 (PL 201.1086A).
[11] B. Schmeidler (ed.), *Adam von Bremen*, iii.24, p. 167.

organization of his church. Denmark received additional bishoprics, but still no archbishop; and the first native bishop, Isleifr at the see of Skalholt, was provided for Iceland.

The first important step in the direction of an autonomous ecclesiastical structure was the creation of the archbishopric of Lund in 1104 by Paschal II, and the basis for the final organization was laid in a legatine mission in 1152 by Nicholas Breakspear, cardinal-bishop of Albano, later Hadrian IV. Norway received its own archbishop at Nidaros (Trondheim), shortly followed in 1164 by one for Sweden at Uppsala. By this time the whole immense region from Greenland in the west to Finland in the east had been provided with bishoprics, and few changes in the pattern of dioceses took place between then and the Reformation. Even so, Scandinavian Christianity continued to display some eccentric features. The memory of the old pagan legends was still alive in the early thirteenth century and was being used in the writing of sagas, although it is difficult to know how far it retained any religious import. The process of conversion had replaced temples by churches, which often occupied the same niche in society. Except in Iceland, the main centre of worship tended to be a 'folk-church', and it was difficult, for reasons already stated, to find endowments for a parish system on the same basis as in France or Germany. The monastic constitution was also different. In the tenth century several of the English missionaries had been monks, but in spite of this there were few Benedictine monasteries in Scandinavia. This was partly because the system of land tenure made it difficult to provide the landed endowments required for the support of the black monks, and partly a simple matter of chronology: the monastic foundations in the north took place during the great age of Cistercian expansion. In Sweden, for example, the first successful monastic foundation about 1143 was the Cistercian Alvastra, whose daughter-house Varnhem was to become the most important abbey in the country. In Denmark, two successive archbishops of Lund, Eskil (1138–77) and Absalom (1177–1201), both outstanding ecclesiastical statesmen, sponsored the arrival of the Cistercians. Although Eskil was a personal friend of Bernard of Clairvaux, the houses in Denmark did not preserve the original simplicity of the order and, for example, seem to have owned tithes from the beginning. In Ireland, another country outside the main body of continental Europe, monastic colonization was similarly carried out by the Cistercians, but there they overlaid a long-established tradition of native monasticism. The pattern of parochial and monastic organization in Scandinavia remained different from that in the west as a whole.

iii. *Eastern Europe*[12]

On the eastern boundary of the Latin world lay two countries, Poland and Hungary, which (like Denmark and Norway to the north) had formally accepted Christianity before the beginning of our period. Their churches had already obtained independence under their own archbishops, long before this happened in Scandinavia, but the position of the Crown, and of the church which it supported, was still insecure in the middle of the eleventh century. In Poland, where the Piast family had created a powerful monarchy, a combination of pagan reaction and Bohemian invasion in the years after 1034 swept away the archbishopric and several other sees. Since they had been supported mainly by levies on the royal estates it was difficult for the weakened ruling house to restore them. The problem was complicated by the fact that the archbishopric of Gniezno had in a sense been founded in the wrong place, for the true religious and cultural centre was Kraków, with its longer tradition of Christianity and its contacts with Bohemia and Hungary. When papal legates visited the country in 1075, there was no archbishop and probably only two bishops, at Kraków and Wrocław. With the support of Boleslaw II the legates restored Gniezno as the metropolitan see and created two further bishoprics, and in 1076 Boleslaw celebrated the restoration of the Polish church by receiving royal coronation—the last ruler to do so for many years. Under Duke Boleslaw III (1102–38) the structure of the hierarchy was completed with the creation of three more bishoprics, including one for newly conquered Pomerania. The claims of the archbishop of Magdeburg to authority over Gniezno were never effectively pursued, and were finally extinguished by a bull of Innocent II to Archbishop James of Gniezno in 1136.

The Polish church was dominated by the duke or king. It had been founded in the heyday of the Ottonian system and continued to live by its values. The earliest Polish chronicler, the 'Anonymous', who wrote early in the twelfth century and was probably a foreign monk,

---

[12] Relations of the Greek and Latin churches in the twelfth century are discussed in another volume in this series by J. M. Hussey, *The Orthodox Church in the Byzantine Empire* (Oxford, 1986), 167–83.

derived the special powers of the Polish rulers from a grant by the Emperor Otto III to King Boleslaw the Great, which was then confirmed by the pope. The Anonymous described Boleslaw as the 'patron and advocate of bishops' and said that he had the power of creating new bishoprics in pagan territories.[13] The position in Poland would thus have an origin like that in Sicily, where Roger I received legatine powers because of his service of the church in expanding the Christian frontier. The co-operation between Boleslaw II and Gregory VII in restoring the Polish hierarchy did not lead to any reduction in the dominant position of the lay power, which lasted in the old form longer than in the west. This was in part because of the intensely conservative senior Piast, Mesco the Old, who throughout much of the twelfth century strove to maintain the old polity. By that time, joint action between provincial nobles and bishops was already bringing about changes: at the conference of Leczyca in 1180 important concessions were made to the church by Casimir the Just, who had replaced Mesco as duke of Kraków. Even so, until the end of the twelfth century bishops were still invested in the old style by the lay ruler, and the first canonical election was at Kraków in 1207. One arbitrary use of royal power became important in Polish history or legend: in 1079 Boleslaw II executed Bishop Stanislas of Kraków for involvement in a conspiracy against him. Much later the canons of Kraków surrounded the episode with a halo of sanctity, but the earliest evidence suggests that Stanislas was neither a patriot nor a martyr, but a political bishop who fell foul of the ruler's tight control over the church.

The Piasts welcomed relationships with distant parts of Europe. In about 990 a loose tributary relationship had been established with Rome, and soon afterwards Poland was paying Peter's pence to the pope. The Lotharingian marriage connections of the royal house led to the import of clerks from the province, and the Benedictine abbeys of Tyniec, Lubin and Mogilno were founded by monks from there. Kraków soon had an excellent school, which had French masters and sent scholars to the west for further study, and ambitious westerners travelled to Poland to look for advancement, as did the young Otto, later bishop of Bamberg and apostle of Pomerania. Like him, many of the imports were imperialists by sympathy. Bishop Werner of Plock (1157–c.72) came from the region of Bamberg, was a strong supporter of Barbarossa and attended the

---

[13] C. Maleczynski (ed.), *Galli Anonymi Chronica* (Kraków 1952), 20.

ceremony for the canonization of Charlemagne. His predecessor, the Lotharingian Alexander of Malonne (1129–56), was a strenuous frontiersman, who was described later as 'both lamb and lion . . . bishop and knight, at once well-armed and devout'.[14] The extension of the faith within Poland was mostly achieved by the proliferation of houses of secular canons, of which seventy-six are known to have existed by 1200. Most were in Silesia or Little Poland (the province of Kraków), and in the rest of the country local provision was slight. Considerable areas remained untouched by the new faith; even in the thirteenth century there was pagan worship in remote districts and adult baptism was quite common. It was the ruling class and the more populated provinces which, under the patronage of the ducal dynasty, had been incorporated into the cultural framework of the west.

The history of the establishment of Christianity in Hungary displays some broad parallels with Poland. Stephen (997–1038) had created an imposing organization of two archbishoprics and eight bishoprics together with a number of monasteries, but as in Poland there was a long period of disruption in the middle years of the century. Ladislas I (1077–95) had taken refuge as a child at the Polish court, and his mother was Lotharingian. There are signs of the influence of personnel, liturgical books, and saints from that area. The reigns of Ladislas and his successor Koloman (1095–1114) confirmed beyond further question the Christian imprint on Hungarian culture. Stephen was canonized to become the model of Christian monarchy, the hierarchy was extended and its privileges defined in new legislation. The synod of Szabolcs in 1092 was concerned with the restoration of ecclesiastical discipline after the ravages of the civil wars, including the rebuilding of damaged churches and the payment of tithe.

While there are similarities between the two countries, there are also important differences. The impact of the Greek Orthodox church upon Poland was slight, whereas Hungary was one of the most important meeting-places of eastern and western influences. The Magyars had settled in an area where Greek missions had previously been active; some southern Magyar princes were early converted to the Greek use, and the population of frontier districts such as Sirmium were solidly attached to the Greek rite; and there were still Basilian monasteries in Hungary in the late twelfth

[14] For references see J. Kloczowski in MCSM 7 (1974), 442.

century. With the revival of Byzantine ambitions under the Emperor Manuel (1143–80) Hungary found itself under the political influence of Constantinople, and Bela III (1172–96) was brought up there. It is far from clear what determined the choice of the Latin rite, but once that was made the Hungarian church seems to have remained solidly Latin; when there was rivalry between 'eastern' and 'western' parties, it was a question of politics and does not seem to have involved any doubt about ecclesiastical allegiance. There was another important difference between the two churches. Poland was on the road to nowhere, but Hungary was a centre of international communications. The pilgrimages of the eleventh century and crusades of the twelfth crossed the Hungarian plains, and expansion into Croatia brought involvement with Venice. The kings of Hungary, like the dukes of Poland, valued their influence over the church, and their permission was necessary for a legate to enter the country or for an appeal to go to Rome, but far sooner than in Poland it was recognized that the old forms could not continue, and the right of investiture was surrendered at the synod of Guastalla in 1106. Clerical privileges in legal matters were acknowledged by about 1070 and were clearly asserted in the legislation of Ladislas and Koloman. In the twelfth century, Hungary was in many ways an up-to-date and influential western country, with a rich and effective monarchy which had accepted many of the principles of ecclesiastical government which were shaping the church in the west.

Scandinavia, Poland, and Hungary were all success stories, in which the church, championed by the ruling families, had established its dominance without too many protests or reactions. It was different on the Baltic coast among the peoples to the east of the Elbe. Here a rebellion in 983 had overthrown the Saxon lordship and fixed the eastern border of Germany along the Elbe and then northward on a well-delineated frontier through modern Holstein. The territory was occupied by a series of peoples largely independent of each other. Immediately east of the Elbe were tribes under the control of the prince of the Obodrites; then, moving eastward, the Wilzi or Liutizi close to the river Oder; beyond them, the Pomeranians; and finally the Prussians, far to the east of the Oder, who were largely untouched by Christianity until the thirteenth century. In the long run, the Obodrites and Pomeranians were converted by the same mechanism as the Poles and Hungarians, that is by the adoption of Christianity by a native dynasty; but this process was much slower than in other parts of the east.

Even in 1050 the Obodrites and the Wilzi, between them occupying what is now the northern part of the German Democratic Republic, were almost surrounded by Christian Saxony, Denmark, and Poland, and their remarkable powers of resistance therefore need explanation. One element was certainly the special character of paganism among the Wends (as we may conveniently call this group of peoples). It was remarkable for its great centres such as Szczecin in Pomerania or the temple of the god Sventovit on the island of Rügen or that of the god Redigast. These were more than local deities, and their cult was supervised by colleges of priests with extensive landed endowments. Both in Pomerania and among the Liutizi the pagan priesthood formed the hard core of opposition to conversion. In spite of recent archaeological work, our information about Polish paganism, which disappeared so much earlier, is insufficient to be sure whether it originally possessed the same structure and organization. It is however very possible that the structure was not indigenous, but was built up because of the political circumstances in which the Wends found themselves. Among the Wends, as among the Poles, the ruling house was relatively quick to accept Christianity, but the resistance of the provincial nobles was far more formidable in the Wendish territories. The explanation was almost certainly a political one. Although there were some problems in Poland about intervention from the empire, these were slight when compared with the heavy pressure of the Saxons (and to some extent of the Danes and Poles as well) upon the Wends, who were threatened by direct political dominance and economic exploitation. The result was that while in Poland and Hungary Christianity became the means of asserting national identity, that function among the Wendish peoples was performed largely by a pagan priesthood. During the twelfth century, there were Christian advocates of military conquest as the best way of establishing the church in the Wendish territories, and some historians have seen the eventual success as the result of the establishment of German political dominance there. This appears at best to be a gross over-simplification. Adam of Bremen and Helmold, both perceptive observers, thought that the Saxon demand for tribute did harm to the progress of the Gospel. Helmold acidly remarked that during the expedition of Duke Henry the Lion into

Slavia 'no mention has been made of Christianity, but only of money'.[15] As a result, the new religion seemed to offer the Slavs 'a German god'.[16]

Prospects for the rapid Christianization of the Baltic Slavs appeared good in the middle of the eleventh century. The prince of the Obodrites, Gottschalk, had established a stable authority and good relations with the Saxon princes. He was energetically building up the church under his rule, providing colleges of canons in the main towns and no less than three bishoprics (Oldenburg, Ratzeburg, and Mecklenburg). These hopes were overthrown by the rebellion of 1066, led by the Liutizi, in which Gottschalk was slain, several clergy executed, and the churches completely destroyed. The pagan victory began a period of more than half a century in which virtually no effort was made to convert the Slavs. Prince Henry of the Obodrites 1083–1127) was personally a Christian but did not attempt to extend the faith outside his own chapel.

A more fluid situation arose in the 1120s, partly because of the arrival of regular canons in eastern Germany. Vicelin, the apostle to the Obodrites, took charge of the frontier church of Faldera (later Neumünster) about 1127; Norbert became archbishop of Magdeburg in 1126; and Bishop Otto of Bamberg, the missionary to Pomerania, also had strong links with the new orders. The first major success was in Pomerania, and the way was opened by the conquest by Boleslaw III of Poland. He invited Bishop Otto, who had once lived at the Polish court, to carry out preaching missions in Pomerania in 1124–5 and 1128. Although this looks like Christianity by conquest, the situation was more complex, for Duke Wartislaw of Pomerania had been baptized in his youth at Merseburg, and he now encouraged the establishment of the church as a way of building up the coherence of the duchy. By 1140 it had acquired its own separate bishopric. The conversion of Pomerania left the Obodrites and Liutizi completely surrounded by Christian societies, but there was still no church in the territory, and the prince from 1131 to 1160, Niclot, was a firm adherent of the old religion. Pressure was increasing from the extension of settlement, Lübeck being founded as a German city in 1143. The long-vacant bishoprics of Oldenburg and Mecklenburg were filled in 1149, the former by the elderly Vicelin. Military action became more forceful: the Wendish Crusade

---

[15] B. Schmeidler (ed.), *Helmolds Slavenchronik* (Hanover, 1937), i.68, p. 129.
[16] Ebbo, *Vita Ottonis episcopi Bambergensis*, iii.1 (MGH SS XII.859).

of 1147, the first occasion on which the pope unambiguously sponsored a policy of 'conversion by conquest', proved futile, but in 1160 Duke Henry the Lion of Saxony completely overcame Niclot and he was able to treat the region as a conquered province. In the end, however, the prospect of introducing Christianity under Saxon military occupation proved illusory. In 1164 a rebellion restored power to a Christian son of Niclot, Pribislaw, and it was a Danish expedition which in 1168–9 achieved the destruction of the last major pagan temple, at Arkona on the island of Rügen. Peace in 1171 between Saxons, Danes, and Wends created the precondition for the secure establishment of the church. Pribislaw became a close ally of Henry the Lion. Their families were joined in marriage, and they went together on pilgrimage to Jerusalem in 1172–3. Bishop Bern of Schwerin (1158–91) supervised the process of building up the church. A Cistercian himself, he encouraged landowners to endow Cistercian abbeys. Doberan was founded by monks from Bern's own home community of Amelungsborn in 1171, and Dargun from Esrom in Denmark in 1172. The first, wooden, cathedral of Schwerin was consecrated on 9 September 1171, and at Lübeck a stone cathedral was begun in 1173 or 1174. Cathedral chapters were in existence by that time, and there were clergy working in the countryside. Both among Obodrites and Pomeranians, settlers from the west were welcomed. Westernization, after long decades of resistance, was now more rapid than in Poland, but the underlying process of the adoption of Christianity under the auspices of a native dynasty was the same. The Wends were never really conquered, let alone obliterated, by the Germans.[17]

iv. *The Defence of the Holy Sepulchre*

One of the disconcerting things about twelfth century thought is that it found no evident place for crusading. The very words 'crusade' and 'crusader' had no exact equivalent in contemporary vocabulary, at least until the appearance of *crucesignati* late in the century, and Gratian's compilation of canons contains no discussion of warfare with unbelievers. The explanation of this irritating unawareness of living in an age of crusading is primarily that from 1099 to 1187

---

[17] See the constrasting account in J. T. Addison, *The Medieval Missionary* (repr. Philadelphia, 1976), 56: 'the land was at last Christian, but the great bulk of its inhabitants were no longer Wends.'

Jerusalem was a Christian possession, and the theory of just war applied to its defence in the same way as to any other lawful right. There was no plan for an unrestricted offensive against the heathen, and no need to discuss its justification. Moreover between 1101 and 1187 there was only one general European expedition ('crusade') to the east. The link of the west with the Holy Sepulchre was not kept alive by crusades, but by institutions of a quite different sort: pilgrimages and military orders.

The twelfth century saw the development of pilgrimage to Jerusalem on a very large scale. The land route across Asia Minor was no longer practicable, and the pilgrims came by sea, usually to Acre but sometimes to Jaffa, a much poorer harbour but nearer Jerusalem. Contemporaries were deeply convinced of the value of praying in the place where Christ lived and died, and for those who could not travel Christ's presence was mediated by the fragments of the Cross and other relics of the Passion, and by the building of representations of the Holy Sepulchre, of which a fine example survives at Bologna. The spirit of the pilgrims is expressed in an early thirteenth-century song:

Allerêrst lebe ich mir werde,	Now my life has found a purpose,
sît mîn sündic ouge siht	For my sinful eyes behold
daz reine lant und ouch die erde	That fair land and holy country
der man sô vil êren giht.	Of which wondrous things are told.
mirst geschehen des ich ie bat,	My desire is granted now:
ich bin komen an die stat	I have seen the place which God
dâ got mennischlîchen trat.[18]	In a human body trod.

For the Franks in Palestine the pilgrims were a financial, military, and emotional lifeline to the west. Ansellus, the cantor of the church of the Holy Sepulchre, wrote to his old colleagues at Paris a letter which vividly captures the attitude of some settlers in the east:

Although I have now for twenty-four years been absent in body from your church and you, in which and with whom I was brought up and educated, yet in my mind I am still fervent in your love, and live in my mind with you in your church. I always talked with those who over the years have come from you to us, who knew you and were known to you, and inquired eagerly about the condition of your church, and what you are doing, and how you are, especially those of you whom I saw and knew . . . Often in dreams I seem to be taking part in your ceremonies and processions, and at your daily mattins and offices, and to be saying the psalms with you.[19]

[18] Walter von der Vogelweide, *Palästinalied*, ed. P. Stapf (Wiesbaden, n.d.), no. 171, p. 464.
[19] *Gall. Christ.* VII, Instr. no. 53, p. 44.

The churches and chapels at the sacred sites in Jerusalem were rebuilt—it is likely that most of them were still in ruins after their devastation by al-Hakim almost a century before. A splendid reconstruction was undertaken at the church of the Holy Sepulchre itself, bringing into one building for the first time the Sepulchre, the site of Calvary, and St Helena's chapel. It was consecrated in 1149 in time to celebrate the fiftieth anniversary of the fall of the city, and the new church was later depicted on the coinage of the kingdom under Amalric (1162–74). Meanwhile research, made fertile by imagination, was revealing new sacred sites. One of the major responsibilities of the authorities was the protection of pilgrims, especially on the southern route from Jaffa to Jerusalem which was exposed to raids from the Egyptian city of Ascalon. In the 1130s King Fulk established a series of castles and settlements to mask Ascalon and make such attacks more difficult. The pilgrims themselves also made a significant contribution to the safety of the kingdom, for many, perhaps most, came expecting to fight during the campaigning season. In the early years, when the Franks were very short of manpower, the influx of pilgrims each summer brought vital reinforcements, and is always carefully recorded by Fulcher of Chartres in his chronicle. From this mixed background of pilgrimage and warfare emerged one of the most remarkable innovations of the period: the military orders.

The appearance of the military orders was the final stage in the sacralization of knighthood, its conversion into an 'order' in the service of Christ. The basic thinking can be found already in the accounts of Urban II's speech at Clermont some ten years after the First Crusade. Baudri of Bourgueil presented him as saying, 'Holy church reserved for her defence a *militia*, but you have depraved it into *malitia* . . . If you want to save your souls, either throw away at once the belt of this sort of *militia* or proceed boldly as soldiers of Christ and go speedily to the defence of the eastern church.'[20] In 1118 a group of knights in the Holy Land, led by Hugh of Payns, devoted themselves to the protection of pilgrims on the way to Jerusalem, promising to live in obedience to the Rule of St Augustine at the Holy Sepulchre. They provided a nucleus for noble pilgrims who joined them temporarily on visits, but according to William of Tyre there were only nine with a full commitment as 'fellow-soldiers of Christ', *commilitones Christi*, to use their original title. In 1128 Hugh

---

[20] Baudri, *Historia Jerosolimitana*, i.3 (RHC Occ. IV.14).

came to western Europe to seek approval for the Rule and to recruit. The Rule, with some amendments, was approved at the council of Troyes, and endowments began to flow in with remarkable speed. In 1139, the bull *Omne datum optimum* granted almost complete freedom from episcopal authority, and by this time the knights had become known as the Templars from their principal headquarters at Jerusalem. Meanwhile, a different course was being followed by another order, the Hospitallers. Before the arrival of the First Crusade there was already a Hospital of St John at Jerusalem for the reception of western pilgrims. Its warden Gerard won the confidence of the new rulers and received handsome donations, including a gift from Baldwin I of a tenth of his possessions—a striking indication of his estimate of the importance of the pilgrim traffic. By 1113 the Hospital had hostels in the major ports in southern Europe used by pilgrims, and in that year Paschal II defined its status in *Pie postulatio voluntatis*, which effectively made it the first self-governing international order, a considerable time before either the Cistercians or the Templars achieved a similar position. It was still a wholly charitable organization, and the first clear sign of military responsibility only appeared in 1136, when King Fulk granted the castle of Bethgibelin, significantly designed for the protection of pilgrims on the Jerusalem road. In 1144 the donation of large territories on the frontier of the county of Tripoli indicates the existence of a real military potential.

The two orders acted as channels by which funds and manpower were sent to support the eastern Franks. They contributed materially to the defence of Jerusalem through the fortresses which they maintained and their well-disciplined troops; the Templars were the first uniformed force in the new Europe, and were subject to strict regulations in battle. The main task of the Hospitallers was always the maintenance of the great Hospital at Jerusalem, which had first charge on their revenues and was the first European body of the kind to retain a permanent medical staff. It has been suggested that by this route the superior Arab knowledge of medical care was channelled to the west, but at this time every western city was providing hospitals; it was just that circumstances made the Hospital of S. John at Jerusalem much the greatest and most advanced of all.

In spite of the contribution which these two orders made to the Latin possessions in the east, they (and especially the Templars) were subject to criticism. This is partly to be explained by resentment at the wealth and privileges which they had rapidly assembled, and to the involvement of the Templars in international banking. Before the end of the century Walter Map was complaining that 'nowhere except at Jerusalem are they in poverty'.[21] Behind this, however, was contemporary unease at the confusion of ideals which they represented, since, being at once monks and knights, they posed the question of militarism in its most acute form. The Templars were conscious of their ambiguous status as followers of 'this new kind of religion, that is that you mix knighthood with religion'.[22] Bernard of Clairvaux addressed himself to the problem in the pamphlet which he wrote at the request of the Templars some time before 1135, *In Praise of the New Militia*. It is true that this is in many ways the most aggressive statement of militant Christianity written: 'in the death of the pagan the Christian glories, because Christ is glorified in it.'[23] But Bernard is clearly aware of the need to defend the standing of an order formed of men who were both monks and killers, and other writers, including John of Salisbury, William of Tyre, and Walter Map, continued to be very critical. The Templars were never unambiguously accepted as champions of Christendom.

The Latin population of Syria consisted largely of Franks, together with Italians in the trading posts which had been conceded to them in the ports in return for naval assistance in the conquest. Residence in a society of many faiths and languages was an unfamiliar experience to them, and they reacted by a firm assertion of Latin supremacy. Antioch and Jerusalem immediately received Latin patriarchs, and the traditional boundary between them was altered to correspond with the northern frontier of the kingdom of Jerusalem. Greek bishops were replaced by Latins, and new Latin bishoprics created. On the other hand the Syriac churches remained relatively unaffected since they were regarded as separate and schismatic organizations, and the great majority of Greek local churches in the countryside must have remained undisturbed. There was, indeed, no occasion to create a Latin parochial system covering the conquered territories, because the immigrants resided mainly in cities and in castles. There are some instances of the creation of purely western villages, especially in the kingdom of Jerusalem, which is much the best

---

[21] M. R. James *et al.* (eds.), *Walter Map, De Nugis Curialium* (Oxford, 1983), i.20, p. 60.
[22] H. de Curzon (ed.), *La règle du Temple* (Paris, 1886), c. 57, p.58. It is not clear when this phrase was accepted into the Rule.
[23] Bernard, *De Laude novae Militiae*, iii.4 (*Opera*, iii.217).

documented of the states; but they were certainly not numerous. We would be safe to think of the Latin church as consisting of bishoprics, some monasteries, city parishes, and castle chapels, surrounded by Greek and Syrian Christians whose liturgical life was probably not much disturbed by the new rulers.

We know much less than we would wish about everyday life in Outremer ('Overseas') as the Franks were inclined to call it, but the dominant picture has changed greatly since the days when historians saw in its society the basis for a Franco-Syrian nation. R. C. Smail and Joshua Prawer have taught us to see the Latins as a highly privileged group, retaining in their hands almost all powers of government and the vast majority of estates. They were intolerant towards the Moslems, many of whom had in any case been killed or fled during the period of the conquest. Moslems and Jews were not normally permitted to enter Jerusalem, which was a holy city for all three religions, and there is virtually no evidence of functioning mosques during the crusader occupation. Villages of Moslem peasants retained their own headmen and presumably observed the daily prayers and other basic duties of Islam. The pattern of Latin dominance and exploitation was so strong that Frankish Syria has been described as the first example of western colonialism.[24] In substance this picture must be the correct one, but it is important not to draw it in too simplistic a fashion. There must have been a large population of mixed race derived from marriage between Frankish men and Syrian Christian women; if they do not appear clearly in the sources, the most probable explanation is that they were assimilated to the Latins for legal purposes. Moreover Bernard Hamilton has pointed out that relations between the various Christian communities were more amicable than is sometimes recognized. The Greeks were certainly regarded as part of the true church, and the rulers continued to tolerate divergences of customs which were becoming increasingly questioned in the west. There was a good deal of mutual admiration between Armenians and Latins. Eastern Christians were ready to look to the Franks for protection in times of danger, but ultimately there was no real identity of interest, and native Christians did not necessarily prefer Latin rule to that of a tolerant Moslem ruler such as Saladin.[25]

[24] J. Le Goff, *La civilisation de l'occident médiéval* (Paris, 1964), 98; and J. Prawer, *The Latin Kingdom of Jerusalem: European Colonialism in the Middle Ages* (London, 1972).
[25] B. Hamilton, *The Latin Church and the Crusader States* (London, 1980), chs. 7–8.

The brilliant successes of the early years were followed by a long period of stability. Tyre, the last Moslem port in central Syria, was taken with Venetian assistance in 1124, and Ascalon in 1153. The failure to maintain the Christian position in the second half of the century has been variously explained, in particular by an insufficient number of settlers and inadequate aid from the west. The underlying truth was that the resources of the Frankish states, although considerable, had obvious restrictions. There was a shortage of good agricultural land, and much of the income from the developing trade went to the privileged Italian cities whose naval strength had made the conquest of the coast possible. The number of western settlers was probably large, but there was no prospect of attracting enough immigrants to westernize the region entirely.[26] The society would have been secure against anything other than a sustained offensive by a large Moslem power, and there was initially little reason to fear this. The first grave warning came when in 1144 Zengi overran Edessa, the most exposed of the principalities. More serious still in a sense was the character of his propaganda, with its revival of the old Koranic idea of *jihad*, holy war, now directed against the Franks as occupiers of the holy city of Jerusalem. The idea became a central plank in the political platform of his successor Nureddin, whose aim it was to assemble an Islamic confederation large enough to overthrow the Frankish states. This was in fact achieved under Saladin, who had extinguished the Fatimite caliphate in Egypt, and by 1183 had brought Cairo, Damascus, and Aleppo under his government. Although a bitter political conflict within the kingdom of Jerusalem made Saladin's task easier, it was fundamentally this achievement of Moslem unity which made the position of the Franks untenable. On 4 July 1187 a large Christian army was completely overwhelmed at the Battle of Hattin, and on 2 October Jerusalem capitulated. The Christian population found Saladin a more merciful conqueror than the crusaders had been in 1099.

To both of the major crises the west responded by sending a large expedition. The Second Crusade, which was an answer to the loss of Edessa, was the occasion for an international recruiting campaign by Bernard of Clairvaux, and large French and German forces set out under Louis VII and Conrad III. The survival of the earliest crusading songs gives us a clear idea of the motivation of the recruits,

---

[26] M. Benvenisti, *The Crusaders in the Holy Land* (Jerusalem, 1970), 18 and 215.

or at least of what the song-writer thought they would find an acceptable ideal. The first vernacular one is *Chevalier, mult estes guariz*, which invites the knight to accept the opportunity of forgiveness, to avenge the wrong done to God by His enemies, and to follow his noble leader, Louis:

Chevalier, mult estes guariz,	Knights, now is this your healing hour
Quant Deu a vus fait sa clamur	When God to you has made His plea
Des Turs e des Amoraviz,	Against the Moors and Turkish power
Ki li unt fait tels deshenors.	Who treated Him dishonourably.
Cher a tort unt ses fieuz saisiz;	They wronged Him and they took His fief,
Bien en devums avoir dolur,	And we must feel the deepest grief,
Cher la fud Deu primes servi	For there God first was served and then
E reconuu pur segnuur.	Was recognized as Lord by men.
Ki ore irat od Loovis	If you with Louis will arise
Ja mar d'enfern avrat pouur,	You will not need to fear hell's sword.
Char s'alme en iert en pareis	Your soul will go to paradise
Od les angles nostre Segnor.[27]	With the angels of our Lord.

The expedition was a disaster. The German army was almost destroyed, and the French army weakened, during the crossing of Anatolia, and the remaining strength of the French army was wasted by political wrangling and misjudgements in Syria. Its failure sent waves of shock throughout western Europe. Saint Bernard, who had been so closely associated with its preaching, was fiercely criticized, and Eugenius III who had authorized it described the catastrophe as 'the most severe injury of the Christian name which the church of God has suffered in our time'.[28] In the 1170s concern was rekindled when a series of appeals from Syria warned western Europe about the grave danger threatened by Saladin, but they led to no effective action until the shocking news arrived that Jerusalem had fallen and almost all the kingdom, with the exception of the port of Tyre, was in the hands of Saladin. The impact of this news in the west was profound. It is one of the few events of the period which appears in chronicles in every country, and innumerable laments on the fall of the Holy City, and recruiting songs for a next crusade, were written. Gregory VIII's appeal for the crusade, *Audita tremendi*, struck a new note in blaming its loss on the sins of Christendom as a whole: 'not only the sins of its inhabitants but also ours, and those of the whole

---

[27] J. Bédier and P. Aubry (ed.), *Les chansons de croisade* (Paris, 1909; repr. Geneva, 1974), no. 1, pp. 7–12.
[28] Eugenius III, ep. 382 to Abbot Suger of Saint-Denis, PL 180.1414C.

Christian people'.[29] For the first time the institution of reforms in the church was associated with the crusading enterprise.

The preaching was conducted so successfully that the largest of all the crusades set out, its armies led by the three senior rulers in the west, the Emperor Frederick Barbarossa and the rival kings Philip Augustus of France and Richard of England. It was a formidable expedition, but was gravely damaged by the death of Frederick Barbarossa in crossing the river Saleph on 10 June 1190. In the early summer of 1191 the forces of Philip and Richard arrived by sea in Syria and rapidly succeeded in recovering the important port of Acre, thus bringing to an end a long and bitter siege. Without the emperor, however, the personal hostility between the two kings jeopardized the progress of the expedition, and when Philip went home at the end of July Richard continued the campaign alone. He then confronted the strategic problem which Saladin's conquest had left: the fortresses which had protected Jerusalem from the south, Kerak and Montréal, along with Ascalon and its encircling castles, had fallen into Moslem hands. Even if Jerusalem were retaken, it would be effectively undefended against an attack from Egypt. Richard's preferred objective for the campaign was Ascalon, where he could sever the main communications between Cairo and Damascus and threaten Egypt itself, but in the event he failed to secure Ascalon permanently or to take Jerusalem. He left the east in October 1192 with a three-years' truce, and probably an intention to return. The former Frankish possessions had been transformed: they now consisted of the island of Cyprus, seized by Richard on his way to Syria, and of a string of ports and coastal castles as far south of Jaffa. The problem of how to recapture and defend Jerusalem remained, and was to dominate the planning of the thirteenth-century crusades.

Meanwhile the image of the Saracen as a monster of iniquity had been widely disseminated in the west. The parody in the *Song of Roland*, with its idolaters and image-worshippers, had been taken into later songs and poems which circulated among the military classes. How generally the opprobrious lives of Mahomet composed by such writers as Guibert and Embricho were known, is less clear.[30] Another version had been added with the *Otia de Machumete* of Walter of Compiègne in 1137, and this was put into French much

---

[29] See E. Siberry, *Criticism of Crusading* (Oxford, 1985), 81–3.
[30] For earlier versions of this material, see ch. 6 above.

later by Alexander of Villedieu in 1258. Thereafter, it circulated freely, but it is not possible to say with confidence whether these stories were shaping opinion before then. In contradiction to this general western view a handful of scholars was arriving at a better understanding of the Moslem religion. In 1142 Peter the Venerable, in the course of a visit to Cluniac abbeys in Spain, sponsored a series of translations from Arabic, most notably a version of the Koran by the English scholar Robert of Ketton. On the basis of this information, he wrote his 'Book against the Sect or Heresy of the Saracens'. The title is significant, for it contains the implication that Islam is an aberrant version of Christianity, not a monstrosity, and the intention was the eirenic one of resorting to reason instead of force. Yet it made little impact, and a further introduction to Islam was provided by William of Tyre. About 1184, shortly before his death, William was engaged in completing two histories, the *History of Outremer*, which is our major source for the kingdom of Jerusalem, and the *History of the Princes of the East*. Much has been claimed for this latter work; William, a native of Jerusalem, is said to have read widely in the Arabic sources, and produced a unique work, a serious Christian history of Islam, which was subsequently used by scholars and preachers in the next century, including Oliver of Paderborn, James of Vitry, William of Rübrück, and Raymond Lull. It may well be, however, that the great merit of the book lies in its disappearance; William's knowledge of Arabic is not confirmed by occasional mentions of the language in the *History of Outremer*, and there is no clear evidence that he was doing more than rehashing, with some material derived at second hand from Christian Arabic sources, the accepted western ideas. Nor is it certain that the later writers really did derive their knowledge of Islam from William's book. In the long run, in any case, this study of Islam fell on stony ground: the book was not of sufficient interest to be widely copied, and all its manuscripts have now disappeared. The serious attempt to understand the enemy was confined to a tiny group of academics and enthusiasts, and even they studied it with doubtful effect. Meanwhile, the first indications were reaching the west that in the depth of Asia there were pagans, and even Christians: there was something beyond Islam. But the consequences of that discovery lie in the thirteenth century, and we shall return to it then.

12

THE MESSAGE OF THE CHURCHES

i. *Towards a Christian Society*

However active the concern for the defence and extension of the boundaries of Christendom, a still greater task faced the church at home: to build a Christian society among those (the overwhelming majority of the population) who professed the name of Christ. Both inside and outside the Christian frontier, pastoral endeavours were directed to the same end: to create temples where the name of the true God would be honoured. A modern student is likely to ask whether the Christian convictions of the population were nominal or real. A contemporary, at the beginning of our period, would have found such a question difficult to understand, for it would have seemed to him that a community which had been baptized and which worshipped according to a Catholic liturgy was by that fact a Christian community. Prayer was a communal activity according to set forms, and private prayer was no more than an overflow of communal worship, as when a monk would recite the whole psalter as an act of daily piety. Prayer was, moreover, the special function of monks, so that when a layman received 'an excellent missal' as part of a transaction, he naturally gave it to the monks of St Victor, Marseille, with a request to use it in praying for his family and himself. The foundation of a church was the path to virtue: 'let every one build a church, that he may be sure of receiving the kingdom of heaven'.[1]

In the course of the twelfth century we can discern significant changes in this cultic approach. The policy of the papal reformers provided the foundation for some of them. They had emphasized the need for purity in worship, which must not be offered by priests defiled by simony or intercourse with women. This was essentially a demand for ritual cleanliness, but the reformers had gone further. In spite of the monastic influence at Rome, Gregory VII had been

---

[1] *Cartulaire de S. Victor, Marseille*, ed. M. Guérard (Paris, 1857), I, nos. 413 and 269.

conscious of the pastoral responsibilities of the episcopal office. In a pontifical from his time the new bishop is admonished, 'you have undertaken a great weight of labour, that is the burden of the government of souls', and the papal household encouraged the writing of lives of model bishops such as Peter of Anagni, Berard of Marses, and Bruno of Segni. Another feature of the Gregorians' programme had been the ordering of the liturgy. Gregory was concerned to secure the general adoption of the Roman rite, which he assumed was the practice of the primitive church, and there was a major revival of liturgical scholarship. Works such as the *Micrologus* of Bernold of Constance, Ivo of Chartres's *Sermones de Ecclesiasticis Sacramentis*, and (later) John Beleth's *Summa de Ecclesiasticis Officiis* were widely read, and provided the foundation for a way of celebrating the liturgy which survived into the twentieth century.[2] The growth of the regular canons, which the papal reformers had done much to foster, brought into being an influential force committed to cure of souls as part of their philosophy. The Gregorian concern to define the duties of the order of clergy led to a determination to extend the observance of righteousness to the ranks of the laity also, and hence to define the right form of marriage (seen as the special feature of the lay order) and to prescribe the duties of the various estates as society became increasingly diversified. In some groups the movement towards a distinctive lay religion went further. Although the task of living the apostolic life was, in respectable circles, regarded as the duty of monks, the eremitical movement had already opened it to laymen, and lay groups were increasingly attracted by this heady prospect. This 'reform of the laity' will be considered in the succeeding chapters. Finally, the cultic approach was being eroded by an increasingly interior religion, of which the Cistercians were the champions. While the desire for confraternity with traditional monasteries continued to be felt, lay nobles were less content with the simple knowledge that they were associated in the liturgy of the house, and required specific rites and institutions to provide for their needs, including prayer for the departed members of their family. The combination of this concern for interior purity, the partial weakening of ancient solidarities, and the definition of the duties of the various 'orders' of laity led to the

---

[2] See R. E. Reynolds, 'Liturgical Scholarship at the Time of the Investiture Controversy', *Harvard Theological Review* 71 (1978) 109–24.

development of a new, and much more personal, discipline of penance.

These new movements gave a very different atmosphere to the twelfth century, but they did not lead directly to an awareness of the need for an active ministry towards the population as a whole. If we were anachronistically to apply post-Tridentine standards of pastoral ministry, we would find the twelfth century extremely defective. The work of the local clergy received little support, or even notice, from the hierarchy. Scholars gave them scant attention and bishops still had no proper structures of administration, and the changes which were modifying the cultic approach applied to an élite of monks, nobles, and academics, and had not reached the mass of the population. In some circles responsibility for pastoral care was dismissed altogether. Rupert of Deutz held that the apostolic life did not demand a pastorate to ordinary people: 'preaching, baptizing and working miracles do not make an apostle'.[3] Rupert's point was a theological one, but the bishop of Senlis had more secular assumptions in mind when about 1180 he issued a revealing statement about the unsuitability of pastoral work for canons of his cathedral:

For it is most unworthy that a person who in the cathedral church has been assigned to the holy altar in his due turn according to his dignity as a canon, should be tied to a parochial cure. It is foreign to the dignity of a canon to bless marriage beds, purify women after childbirth, refer to the bishop the brawls and contentions of the people and be subject to the rural dean; and that he should be counted among local and lower-class priests who, because of the dignity of his office, is entered in the roll of the church among those who are great in the church.[4]

As a consequence of this sort of assumption, there is almost complete silence in our sources about the weekly devotions of ordinary people, and unhappily this can be interpreted in different ways. A practice may not be mentioned because it did not exist, or because it was so commonplace and uncontroversial that it did not seem worth mentioning. Needless to say, the picture of twelfth-century religion is changed greatly by the decision which of these assumptions to make. At least, however, our starting-place is secure. The prevailing cultic approach implies that we must begin with the provision of

---

[3] Rupert of Deutz, *De Vita vere apostolica* ii.16 (PL 170.631–2).
[4] *Gall. Christ.* X, Appendix no. 76, pp. 436–7.

places for worship: of great churches where multitudes assembled, and local ones for the worship of each village.[5]

ii. *The Great Churches*

To say that the great church was an invention of our period would be an exaggeration, but a pardonable one. There had been large churches in the past, including some of the Roman basilicas and the greater Carolingian abbeys, but there is no earlier parallel to the number and size of the churches which now began to be constructed throughout Europe. Some of these have been mentioned in an earlier chapter: Monte Cassino completed in 1071, the abbey churches of Norman England, and the greatest example of all, Cluny III. The design of these churches was marked by regional characteristics. In Normandy and England a distinctive style emerged which is now usually called 'Norman' and which expresses the piety and the imperial pretensions of the Norman race. South of the Loire there were many churches with domes, such as Fontevraud; and on the great pilgrim road which led from France to Spain a network of great churches was built, catering specially for the needs of pilgrims and echoing the architecture of the basilica which was their final goal, St James of Compostella.

One of these regional schools provided the seed-bed for the second phase in the building of the medieval great church. Northern France had produced relatively few major buildings during the century after 1050, but the reconstruction of Saint-Denis by Abbot Suger in the 1140s initiated a wave of activity. It was not completely distinct in style from existing architecture: Durham and Laon, for example, have a good deal in common. Nevertheless the French style, exaggerated and refined, rapidly began to be imitated in other countries, at Canterbury as early as 1174, and it provided the basis for the architecture which we now strangely know as Gothic. There is no single reason for its emergence and its subsequent influence. Part of the explanation is utilitarian. Architects were anxious to provide their churches with stone roofs as a precaution against the fires which frequently destroyed the older 'Romanesque' buildings,

[5] The changes mentioned in this section have been briefly set within the wider developments in the introduction to Part II of this book. In the study of popular religion, one important question is the nature of popular beliefs and customs and their adaptation to official Christian culture. This will be considered in a later chapter; the centre of interest in ch. 12 is the attempt by the authorities of the church to provide for the needs of a Christian society.

and this made ribbed vaults essential and pointed arches advantageous to support them. The Gothic style also may be explained by the desire to produce exceedingly high churches, of which the thirteenth-century cathedral at Beauvais is a grotesque example, and these required a battery of flying buttresses to support them and long, pointed windows to light them. The development of the new style was encouraged by the growth of the cities and their desire for a church which would express their grandeur, for Gothic, although certainly employed by monastic builders, was more characteristically the language of the cathedrals. It also expressed a new attitude to decoration: the message of the building was addressed to worshippers through stained glass and statues, art-forms introduced or reintroduced in the early twelfth century. It is not a coincidence that Suger, intent upon a particularly complex symbolism in the windows and statues of his church, arrived at the first approximation to the new style. There have been varied interpretations among historians of the motive force behind the design of the new Gothic churches. One school has emphasized the symbolic character of the buildings, seeing them as images of heaven, radiant with God's light which streamed through the great windows; others have seen the church as a machine for worshipping in, its design being prescribed by the needs of the liturgy as well as the practical requirements of building in stone. Both considerations were present in the minds of the master masons of the age; in this chapter, I shall concentrate primarily on the way in which the needs of worship helped to shape the plans of the great churches.

The enthusiasm for vast buildings and the Gothic style was in any case not universal. The city of Rome was unaffected: when San Clemente and Santa Maria in Cosmedin were rebuilt about 1100 the traditional basilican design was adopted. There were criticisms of the new magnificence, notably Bernard's attack on the Cluniacs in his *Apologia ad Guillelmum* and the complaint later in the century, by Peter the Chanter at Paris, about the excessive provision of churches and chapels.[6] Italy was resistant to Gothic, and its buildings, if richly decorated, were of moderate size until the thirteenth-century preaching churches of the friars. There was sometimes conservative opposition, such as Suger encountered from those who reverenced the old building. At Anagni the population complained about the

---

[6] Peter the Chanter, *Verbum Abbreviatum*, 29 (PL 205.107AB).

cost of rebuilding the cathedral; at Reims and Paris they preferred to finance new parish churches, leaving the canons to find the resources for the cathedral. In spite of these reservations, it is clear that there was a lot of lay enthusiasm. Donations came from all social levels, from the royal houses who financed Cluny III to the swineherd of Stow, who contributed his mite to St Hugh's new cathedral at Lincoln. There were even occasions when the building was the centre of a religious revival: at Chartres in 1145 nobles and people pulled cart-loads of stone, singing hymns on their way.

The cost of these buildings was prodigious. Some were funded by the profits of conquest: the cities in England were marked by the close combination of cathedral and castle, which we can still see at Durham, Rochester, and Lincoln, and the resources for some northern French cathedrals came from the French conquests in Normandy and on the Albigensian Crusade. Then as now, money was raised for church buildings by direct appeals. The inducements are set out in the appeal for the cathedral at Aix-en-Provence about 1070:

We have begun the construction of a larger church, in which you and other visitors will have space enough to stand . . . We ask each of you to give what he can, so as to receive from God and us a full remission of his sins, and have a portion and association in all the advantages of the community of St Saviour's. For everything you give, you will receive a hundredfold from the Lord in the day of Judgement.[7]

It became customary to give a formal indulgence to contributors to a building fund, as Urban II did at Figeac in the south of France in 1092. Offerings by pilgrims were an important source. At Canterbury in the late twelfth century more than a quarter of the treasurer's income came from the shrine of St Thomas, and in 1220, the year of the dedication of the new shrine, the offerings reached the then vast figure of £1,142. Sometimes a Fraternity of the Fabric was established, a medieval equivalent of Friends of the Cathedral, whose members were enrolled and remembered at mass.

The great churches were of different kinds: cathedrals, abbeys, and collegiates. Probably most were open to the laity, at least for the main festivals. The inordinate size was not intended to hold a large Sunday congregation. It was partly to facilitate access to the relics for

---

[7] V. Mortet, *Recueil de textes relatifs à l'histoire de l'architecture en France au m.a.*, 2 vols. (Paris, 1911–29), no. LXV p. 203.

the crowds on the patronal festival, and also to provide a processional space. The great procession at high mass took place in the nave, and sometimes the people were kept out of the nave and admitted instead to the galleries or to a westward extension or Galilee 'where the laity stand so as not to impede the processions'.[8] In a sense, the church was conceived as a theatre. The comparison would not have been natural at the time, because the theatre as such did not exist, but the scholarly M. Honorius, who was familiar with the classical theatre, saw the celebrant as a 'tragic actor' in front of the Christian people.[9] The shrine of the saint was a centre of power within the church, and was one of the main influences on its design. Under the pressure of growing crowds of pilgrims the relics were, in one church after another, brought up from the crypt into the main sanctuary, where they stood on the high altar or in a shrine behind it. By popular demand, the relics became the centre of the plan. In Roman tradition the bishop's throne stood in the centre of the apse, facing the people across the altar. It still occupies this position in a number of churches at Rome, and there are vestigial traces of the arrangement elsewhere, for instance at Canterbury and Norwich. With the arrival of the saint's shrine, the bishop had to be moved out of the way, usually to the north side of the sanctuary, where his throne might be impressively decorated, but was without a liturgical function. It was also necessary to provide a system for overcoming the problems of the traffic flow and allowing the crowds to be shepherded past the shrine. The favourite plan on the continent was the ambulatory, curving round the apse and allowing orderly access to the shrine.

The great church was not planned as a building, but as a series of liturgical spaces. Even in earlier centuries, the choir or *schola cantorum* was separated by a low enclosure from the laity, and this continued in the neighbourhood of Rome. In the north, and especially in England, a much clearer division was adopted. A great screen or *pulpitum* was built across the church, normally to the west of the tower crossing; it seems to have existed already at Beverley in the 1060s and at Canterbury in Lanfranc's time. The *pulpitum* developed into a heavy stone barrier, which allowed no communication except through side-doors which led into the aisles of the choir. Other requirements led to further fragmentation. There were more masses,

[8] Mortet, *Recueil*, 23.
[9] Honorius, *Gemma Animae*, i.83 (PL 172.570AB).

and hence a need for more altars, which were often provided in a series of chapels radiating from the ambulatory at the east end. An increasing demand for marriage ceremonies and for the transaction of business led to the creation of a sheltered north porch, like the splendid one at Wells (*c.*1210), a handsome room of considerable dimensions. The great church was not so much a building as a set of buildings, shaped by the needs of its resident clergy and those of a wider lay public.

iii. *The Local Churches*

Visits to great churches would have been formative experiences, but regular worship depended on the local church. Bishop Herman of Ramsbury, visiting Rome in 1050, boasted that England was full of churches. Domesday Book and associated records suggest that he was right. In the diocese of Rochester the *Textus Roffensis* preserves a list dating from about 1100 which records 124 parish churches and 28 dependent chapels, much the same as the provision for Anglican worship in 1800. The picture in northern France was similar. The deanery of Lille included 64 parishes in the late twelfth century, as against 80 in the same geographical area at the end of the Middle Ages. It is probable that most were already there in 1090, when we first encounter the deanery as a unit. In Lotharingia, Michel Parisse has emphasized the continuity of the parish as a phenomenon more striking than the new foundations and subdivisions which took place from time to time. These were densely populated regions where village churches had been provided well before the beginning of our period.

Elsewhere the position was different. The Domesday evidence suggests that in the north and west of England a single church, with a staff of clergy, would serve a large district including several small villages. The process of making additional provision was still continuing, even in an 'old' area like Worcester, where Bishop Wulfstan (1062–95) 'established churches throughout his diocese on his own estates and encouraged their provision on those of others'.[10] For the really underdeveloped areas we have to look eastward. When the diocese of Bamberg was created in 1007 to cover a large part of central southern Germany, there seem to have been only 39 churches

---

[10] *Vita Wulfstani*, iii. 10, ed. R. R. Darlington (Camden Soc. iii. 40, 1928) 52. For detailed references for this section, see the local studies listed in the bibliography.

there. The Fichtelgebirge on the eastern border was without a church at all until the foundation of one at Hof some time in the twelfth century. It is not possible to be sure about the date of new foundations in the diocese, but it is probable that the original 39 were increased by 30 during the twelfth century and 34 in the thirteenth, building up to a total of 203 parishes by the end of the Middle Ages. In Silesia the provision of churches followed the large-scale German settlement in the thirteenth century: church buildings can be found in 24 places in 1200, and in 146 by 1270. All over Europe these would initially be simple wooden buildings. At Ranworth in Norfolk a lengthy lawsuit was occasioned when in the disorders under King Stephen (1135–54) a local lord stole the church, removing it physically into his own fief. At Sutton in Lincolnshire a donor provided a site for a stone church in the late twelfth century, explaining that 'my wish is that the earlier wooden church . . . shall be taken away and the bodies buried in it shall be taken to the new church'.[11] Before 1200 even stone churches were often of a basic design, single-celled or double-celled with a tiny chancel opening off a larger nave.

In most eleventh-century towns there was a small number of churches forming one ecclesiastical unit, with the provost of the major churches appointing clergy to serve at the others, as was the practice at Sens, Tournai, and Arras. Lille offers us a model of conservative expansion to meet the needs of a rising population. It had three churches in 1066, the canons of the mother-church having the right to designate priests at the other two. In 1144 a fourth church was added, St Sauveur, and the situation remained static until 1233, when two more parishes appeared, with a seventh by 1273. This sort of growth is typical of its region: at Ypres there were four parishes, at the very large city of Cologne thirteen parishes by 1172 and nineteen by 1300. These examples must represent a fairly balanced proportion of churches to population, but in other cities churches proliferated at an astonishing speed. At Paris the population grew rapidly after 1100, and the parochial system more rapidly. In the eleventh century Notre Dame was the only mother-church on the small island which formed the heart of the city, but when in 1183 Bishop Maurice de Sully reorganized the parishes there were already twelve churches in this tiny area. The building of a greatly extended

[11] D. Owen, *Church and Society in Medieval Lincolnshire* (Lincoln, 1971), 5.

city wall by Philip Augustus led to the creation of additional parishes for those whom it had separated from easy access to their former place of worship. The multiplication of churches appears in an extreme form in England, where it began early. Lincoln had thirty-five churches by 1100, and nearly fifty by 1200, although by continental standards it was not a large city. By 1200 London had well over 100 parishes.

As we noticed in Chapter 1, the ministry in a region had often begun with a team of clergy operating from a 'mother-church'. The building of additional churches involved the transfer of rights from the mother-church to them, thus creating the parochial system in its enduring form. There was still no precise term for the village church, which was endowed with a full ministry to the population within its limits. It could indeed be called a parish (*parochia*), but this really meant an area of jurisdiction and was commonly used for a diocese. It was also known as a 'title' (*titulus*), a term which has survived with special meanings: the cardinals' churches at Rome or a qualification (title) for ordination. Although the terminology was fluctuating there was a clear recognition of the rights involved in parochial status. These were defined as tithes, baptism and burials; or, less commonly, as baptism, burial, and visitation of the sick, which were described in Saxony as 'the custom of the mother churches'.[12] The most important element was baptism. A church which had no right of baptism could not have a proper Easter liturgy, since the baptismal ceremony was an integral part of this, and with the Easter liturgy came Easter communicants, Lent confessions, the Maundy Thursday chrism, and therefore the anointing of the sick. The dominant position of Easter in the twelfth-century liturgy can be appreciated from a book of offices composed for the cathedral of Volterra (Tuscany) about 1170, where the section on Easter contains a huge amount of material from canon law on baptism, penance, and ordination. From the eleventh century onwards churches were being provided with stationary fonts, and after that the definition is simple; we can recognize a parish by its font. In most places the duty of regular ministry passed completely to the parishes from the mother-church, which was simply left with some financial and ceremonial rights. In Kent about 1100 village priests had to collect and pay for the chrism at twelve minsters, and in Saxony a little later village

[12] M. Erbe, *Pfarrkirche und Dorf* (Gütersloh, 1973), 50.

churches had to pay synodal dues to the mother-church and contribute to the maintenance of its fabric. In Picardy parishioners visited the mother-church on its feast day in a *croix banale* or *bannkreuz* ('church parade' would be a fair translation). In Italy the development was different. The cathedral retained its position as the baptismal church, and we can still see the impact of this in the separate baptisteries which continued to be built throughout our period—Florence and Pisa are magnificent examples, but there are many others. They were the sole or main place of baptism, and were dear to the citizens of these great urban centres. At Parma the *carroccio*, the command centre for the communal army, was kept in the baptistery, and Dante remembered with affection the baptistery of Florence, *il mio bel San Giovanni*. But Italy is an exception. In most of Europe there was a steady movement towards a system of parish churches, each provided with its own right to baptize, bury, and dispense the sacraments. The growth of this network was connected with a change which we have already observed in another context: the growing control of the bishop over the routine administration of his diocese.[13] While it would be rash to give a date for a process which was progressive and which inevitably varied between different regions, its culmination may be seen in the canon of the Fourth Lateran Council in 1215 requiring all adults to confess to their 'own priest' (*proprius sacerdos*), thus assuming the existence of a uniform system of discipline throughout most of the Latin world.

iv. *Learning through Worship*

There were formidable problems involved in communicating the faith to the mass of the population. Most people were unable to read, and only the rich had access to books. Worse still, the liturgy was celebrated in a language which, at least outside Italy, was incomprehensible to the congregations. True, there was a lot of popular interest in the major ceremonies of the church. People dated their lives (when they had need of dates) by the saints' days, and there was a vast gathering when one of the great pilgrimage churches celebrated its festival. It can also be said that some of the ceremonies were of a kind whose significance could not easily be missed: the adoration of the cross on Good Friday, and on Easter Day the

---

[13] See ch. 9. iii above.

kindling of the new fire, which in some regions was taken into the homes of each parishioner, would seem to carry their own message. Nevertheless, it remains true that there was little attempt to use the liturgy proper as a medium of instruction. It would be more accurate in the twelfth century to describe the changes taking place as a withdrawal of the liturgy from the people.

One reason for this surprising development was the insistence on the separation of clergy and people in both life and worship, which had the effect of focusing the attention of the hierarchy upon the liturgy of the clergy. Some lay reforming movements, such as the *Patarini* of Milan, shared the same assumptions: they demanded greater clerical purity, not greater lay participation. At a more fundamental level, changes in the liturgy were merely catching up with a change in the nature of the local Christian community. The worship of the early church had been that of believers who had confessed the faith in baptism and assembled for the common meal in the weekly eucharist, and who required training and support for their task of upholding the Gospel in a pagan world. The local congregation had, by the twelfth century, assumed a quite different form, with universal child baptism and very infrequent communion in a society which officially accepted a monolithic Christian world-view. It is not surprising that elements in the traditional rite which expressed the participation of the whole congregation, but which for long had been a dead letter, were removed in the revisions which took place at this time. What is more, the whole understanding of the sacraments was shifting. The originally communal character of baptism and the eucharist had become incomprehensible and contemporaries were looking for a new way of defining their meaning. They found it in a place characteristic of medieval society: in the significant gesture. A sacrament was an action which transformed the recipient. St Augustine had provided the basis for this understanding when he defined a sacrament as the sign of a sacred thing, a definition taken up, although scarcely in its original sense, by Hugh of St Victor.[14] The assimilation to contemporary ideas went further in the supposition that a sacrament involved a physical object. Hugh defined it as containing 'a bodily or material element'.[15] In an age when land was transferred through a physical

---

[14] Hugh of St Victor, *De Sacramentis*, I.9.2. (PL 176.317B): 'sacramentum est sacrae rei signum.'

[15] *De Sacramentis*, I.9.2, 'corporale vel materiale elementum' (317D).

token it was a natural way to understand the meaning of a gesture. The advent of this idea of a sacrament had the effect of transforming some of the rituals: in confirmation, the laying on of hands was abandoned, since anointing seemed to be the vital thing; in ordination the priest received delivery of chalice and paten (*porrectio instrumentorum*) and this came to seem more important than the imposition of the bishop's hands. Even where the form of the ceremony was not altered, the congregational significance was diminished: the application of water and the consecration of bread and wine, accompanied by the correct formula, were the essence of baptism and the communion. As on so many medieval occasions, the community had become witnesses rather than participants.

The final collapse of the old rite of initiation took place in the thirteenth century, and the process is therefore discussed in Chapter 19, ii below. As to the mass, it remained the central act of worship, but what had begun as a celebration of Christian community, in which president, deacons, readers, and the choir had each performed their distinctive part and which culminated in the communion of the people, had ceased to exist in the old form. The assumption now was that the mass was a mystery or miracle which won God's blessing as a result of the cultic acts of the priest. The most crucial, the consecration, began to be performed in a way which made it visible to the congregation, and it was supposed that the mass could be offered for many mundane purposes. Bishop Odo of Cambrai wrote about 1113 that 'we pray at the time of the sacrifice against the peril of fire, for our homes; against drought or tempest, for our crops; against sickness, for our animals; against other losses, for everything else'.[16] For several centuries it had been customary to multiply private masses either to secure benefits for sponsors or because penitents had been ordered to pay for masses as a penance. The process continued in the twelfth century, in part in response to the demand for masses by guilds and confraternities. The main mass of the community itself began to be interpreted in terms of private masses, as if these were the norm. We find for the first time about 1140 the instruction that the celebrant was to say *sotto voce* the readings and antiphons which were being performed by the lectors and choir, as if the whole liturgy was essentially a solo by the priest. The community celebration was being seen as a mere variant of the private one—an exact reversal of the original situation.

[16] Odo of Cambrai, *Expositio in Canonem Missae* (PL 160. 1058A)

At the same time, efforts were made to make the mass a vehicle of instruction, although by means which would have astonished earlier centuries. It was treated as an allegory which conveyed a message. There were various ways of interpreting it, but the dominant one was as the story of the life of Christ from the Nativity to the Ascension. The connections were artificial, and could only have been made in a society with a strong allegorical sense, and they perhaps echo the technique of memory in which ideas were recalled by their association with a familiar scene or illustration. In the ninth century Amalarius of Metz had glossed the liturgy in this way, and in the twelfth the tradition was renewed by Hugh of St Victor, Rupert of Deutz, Sicard of Cremona, and Cardinal Lothar of Segni, the future Innocent III. The system must have been designed to form the spirituality of clergy, for it required a close familiarity with the ceremonies, combined with a recollection of their complex meanings. About 1175 a simplified version was made available in *The Lay Folk's Massbook*, originally composed in French in Normandy, but this is not so much a lay spirituality, as a clerical one reduced for laymen.

The collapse of a common liturgy, and the failure to use it as a means of communication with the laity, was balanced by a growth of subsidiary ceremonies which were designed to present the Biblical message in a more simplified form. We are not sure, in most cases, to whom they were directed, and it would be rash to assume that they were predominantly designed for the laity. There were plenty of monks, minor clergy, and boys to appreciate something more comprehensible than the mass allegories. One of the most direct ways of providing this was the development of a series of music dramas. The earliest was a simple telling of the visit to the empty tomb on Easter morning, the *Quem quaeritis*, which was widely known in the tenth century but never attained much elaboration. In the course of the eleventh century a range of these liturgical dramas developed, such as a more complex Easter play, one on the story of the shepherds (*officium pastorum*), and one on the Magi (*officium stellae*). Such plays remained within the church building but acquired an increasingly popular air. The rubrics sometimes stress the importance of the gestures used, which would have conveyed the meaning to a congregation ignorant of Latin. The adoration of the Virgin and child by the Magi, or the display of the grave-clothes of the risen Christ, would have been comprehensible even to the simplest bystander. In France in particular the clergy ceased to perform in liturgical garments and adopted suitable costumes and properties: wings for angels or a star on the end of a string for the Magi. The twelfth-century plays contained a number of comic scenes, and a few had a large mixture of buffoonery: the feast of the ass, in which the Christ-child was carried by a girl on a donkey to shouts of 'Hee-haw!' from the congregation, was celebrated at a number of cathedrals in northern France. One particular composition about 1150 pointed the way into the future: the *Play of Adam* was written in French and was apparently designed for performance outside the church building, in the cloister or the public square. The plays were musically interesting, and a vigorous argument continues about whether they had a rich instrumental accompaniment.

In general, music may have been an important way of appealing to congregations who could not follow the words. The clergy, at least, thought that 'by the sweet modulations of the cantor the people is fired by pious devotion and divine love, and thus runs to the Lord and is made one body in Christ'.[17] It is impossible to be sure whether great churches designed their music to have congregational appeal, but it has been plausibly suggested that the development of polyphony by Perrotin and his colleagues at Notre-Dame, Paris, about 1200 was intended to attract large audiences, and that it made use of well-known tunes. We are on surer ground in supposing that songs were an important influence on lay culture:

In the mouth of the laity who fight for Christ the praise of God is growing, because there is nobody in the whole Christian realm who dares to sing dirty songs in public, but as we have said the whole land rejoices in the praises of Christ, in songs in the vernacular as well, especially among Germans, whose language is more suitable for good songs.[18]

Gerhoh was optimistic about the dirty songs, the demand for which remained buoyant, but he is good evidence for the pious hymns as an expression of popular devotion.

The music dramas were associated with another aspect of popular worship: the use of images. The *officium stellae* ended with the adoration of the image of the Virgin and child, which was probably placed on the altar for the occasion. The aim of the older statues was to depict the dignity of the subject, and some, such as the golden

---

[17] John of Avranches, *De Officiis Ecclesiasticis*, ed. R. Delamare (Paris, 1923), 13.
[18] Gerhoh of Reichersberg, cited U. Müller, *Kreuzzugsdichtung* (Tübingen, 1969), no. 7.

Virgin of Essen or Ste Foy at Conques, were covered with precious metal. In the course of the eleventh century simple wooden statues became more common, painted in natural colours, and they seemed very lifelike to worshippers, so much so that at Aurillac the peasants believed that the statue of St Gerard nodded in answer.[19] Their value in stirring up devotion was recognized from the beginning of our period:

The block of wood is not being worshipped, but through that visible image the inner mind of man is stirred, in which the passion and death which Christ endured for us is, so to speak, written upon the parchment of the heart, that every one may recognize within himself how much he owes to his redeemer.[20]

The most common images were those of the Virgin and child. The iconography was conventional, with the Virgin seated on a throne and the Christ-child sitting upright, like a tiny adult, on her lap. The image was sometimes called the 'majesty' and almost every sizeable church must have possessed one, because 200 survive, mostly from the twelfth century. Apart from its use in the play, it was placed on an altar, or on a pillar behind, as a focus for devotion, and was carried in procession on festivals.

Another important image was the crucifix. In the later Middle Ages the great rood was the most prominent feature in the furnishing of the churches in northern Europe, and its rise to prominence was achieved between 1050 and 1200. It was a time of keen interest in the passion of Christ, and pilgrims returning from the Holy Land brought relics of the passion to their favourite churches. Their arrival encouraged the dissemination of liturgical customs associated with the death of Christ: the processional use of the cross and reading of the passion on Palm Sunday; the 'entombment' of Christ, represented by the sacrament or by the cross; and the adoration on the feast of the holy cross on 14 September. In the past, the use of a great cross in church decoration had not been prominent, and it often did not carry an image of the crucifixion: when before 1035 King Cnut gave a cross to Winchester it appears to have been plain and accompanied by images of Mary and John. The interest in the crucifix proper was encouraged by the development of pilgrimage to Lucca, where the Santo Volto was thought to preserve Christ's authentic appearance.

[19] A. Bouillet, *Liber Miraculorum S. Fidis* (Paris, 1897), i.13, p. 47.
[20] Synod of Arras 1025, canon 14 (Mansi xix.455).

It was said that the rood-cross in the English abbey of St Albans was modelled on it, after it had been seen by Abbot Leofric on his way to Rome in about 1050. It seems from the miracles related by William of Malmesbury that there was a rood at Winchcombe in 1091, and in Germany the great crucifix had appeared a century earlier when Archbishop Gero had one carved for Cologne cathedral. By 1200 it was normal to find a large crucifix in a church, and the Limoges enamellers were turning out smaller models in great numbers to meet the demand for private devotion. Perhaps even more important was a change in the portrayal of Christ on the cross. In ancient tradition, he had been shown alive, beardless and young, but from the ninth century we begin to find (especially in imperial monastic circles) first drawings and then statues of the Lord as a dead man. It was an evocative change in church decoration which brought before the eyes of all the faithful the suffering humanity of Jesus and thus marks an important turning-point in the history of Christian piety.

Romanesque churches were painted from floor to ceiling. The effect can still be seen in a few French churches, such as Tavant and St Savin-sur-Gartempe, and more clearly in the mosaics at St Mark's Venice and at Monreale outside Palermo. Village churches, too, were vividly painted: there are substantial survivals of the decorative effect at the tiny church of Vic in central France, whose paintings were rescued by Georges Sand, and in a group of Sussex churches under the patronage of the Cluniac priory of Lewes, of which Hardham is the best surviving example. The twelfth century saw some dramatic changes in decoration. Stone sculpture was very rare indeed before 1100, but thereafter it developed rapidly and great churches were provided with sculptural themes on the capitals of the arcades and on the west front. The sculpture was profusely painted and must have made a dramatic impact. With Suger's work at Saint-Denis in the 1140s stained-glass windows came to be very important. They certainly existed before then, and one or two accomplished fragments survive from previous centuries, but it is unlikely that any previous church had been decorated with a complete scheme of windows, and certain that none had been designed with as much window space.

It is difficult to be sure of the purpose of this rash of decoration: was it to educate the laity, aid the devotion of the clergy, or simply to glorify God through the beauty of His temple? All of these purposes were probably present in different buildings. The spoken

word and significant gesture were for most people the primary way
of understanding; the modern desire to 'have it in writing' was
anticipated only by a small group of intellectuals towards the end of
our period. For monks and clergy a series of pictures with captions
would be more evocative than a text, and there are indications that
this was the audience to which much decoration was directed. Abbot
Suger's complicated scheme of typology, his long Latin inscriptions
and enamelled great cross, which could rarely if ever have been seen
in detail by visiting pilgrims, leave one doubtful whether there was
any design to instruct the laity. Indeed, he seems to say at one point
that the symbolism was only comprehensible to the literate.[21] As a
medium, stained glass achieves high marks for splendour but few for
comprehensibility. There are certainly some subjects easy to follow,
like the sequence of Old Testament figures at Canterbury c. 1180, but
many windows are hard to identify or even to see, and this is not
only the result of the disruption of the design which is so common in
early windows. The 'dean's eye' at Lincoln of c. 1240 is still in its
original setting and largely intact, but it is, and must always have
been, very difficult to decipher. Such decorations may have revealed
God's splendour to the visiting laity, but are unlikely to have
conveyed much information. The problems are illustrated in the
great Romanesque churches of the Auvergne. They contain capitals
with Biblical subjects carved with tenderness and power, but at
Issoire these are in the choir, where they would have been only
partially visible to the laity; while the nave capitals are mostly
grotesques, with beasts and acrobats of the kind which St Bernard
criticized at Cluny. The pattern is different elsewhere: at Besse, some
twenty miles away, a nave capital has four dramatic representations
of the story of Dives and Lazarus, presented in a way which would
almost certainly have spoken to the laity. The great pilgrimage
church of St Benoît-sur-Loire has capitals which are iconographically
strange. Hardly any of them display the miracles of St Benedict,
while there are several in honour of the monk Hugh of Sainte-Marie
(perhaps the historian Hugh of Fleury). The decoration seems to
commemorate inappropriately some internal power-crisis at the end
of the eleventh century. The evidence suggests that church decor-
ators before Suger's work at Saint-Denis could not or did not
construct a coherent programme presenting the faith to either clergy
or laity.

[21] Suger, *De Rebus in sua Administratione Gestis*, 23 (PL 186.1233C).

Nevertheless evidence remains of an intention to instruct the laity. Gregory the Great's famous statement that 'what writing presents to the literate, pictures do to the ignorant who see them' was still quoted. Gratian referred to them as the 'literature of the laity', and a regular canon, Hugh of Fouilloi, in criticizing the decoration of monastic churches in 1153, made a significant exception: 'if this is permissible for any one, it is for those who are established in cities or towns, to whom a great mass of people flow, so that their simplicity may be attracted by the charm of painting, although they cannot enjoy the subtlety of Scripture'.[22] Romanesque art was essentially poster art, designed to present bold subjects in an eye-catching way. Sometimes the upper ranges of painting were huge out of all proportion and garishly coloured to make them visible. The main characters in a scene were larger than the subsidiary ones, the gestures were flamboyant and, in a style reminiscent of the modern strip-cartoon, pictures might include events distinct in space and time. The names of characters were provided in a few simple words, and so were scrolls containing a few crucial remarks, which could easily be read to a group by one of its members who had a smattering of letters. The designs and text might be attractively informal: a wall-painting at San Clemente, Rome, probably painted shortly after 1084, contains our first record of vernacular Italian. The subjects of sculpture seem to have been closely related to the music dramas: the charming picture of the angel waking the three kings at Autun is unmistakably based on the scene in the play. We have almost no direct information about the extent to which ordinary people understood the decoration, but some of it at least was certainly addressed to them.

v. *Preaching*

The twelfth century was a golden age of learned preaching. Few sermon collections survive from the preceding period, although one would have to note the Old English homilies of Wulfstan and Ælfric and the sermons of Peter Damian as exceptions. Before that, the Carolingian homiliaries consisted predominantly of patristic material, and recent study has suggested that they were intended as much for

---

[22] Gregory I, letter to Bishop Serenus of Marseille (PL 77.1128C); Gratian, *Decr.* de consec. D. III, c. 27 (1360); Hugh of Fouilloi, *De claustro animae*, ii.4 (PL 176.1053C). For other references, see M. Camille, 'Seeing and Reading', *Art History* 8 (1985), 26–49.

personal meditation as for reading in church. It has been bluntly said that 'the preachers of the twelfth century had to start again'.[23] Many of the surviving sermons come from monastic sources, for the daily routine allowed a substantial place for preaching. The most outstanding monastic preachers are to be found among the Cistercians, above all the great Bernard of Clairvaux. He had disciples who were themselves distinguished preachers, including Guerric, abbot of Igny (1138–57) and Isaac, abbot of l'Étoile (died 1169). The Augustinian abbey of St Victor at Paris also was an important centre of preaching, and sermons survive from several of its leading scholars. Outside the monasteries preaching was specially the task of the bishop, and increasingly also of the *scholasticus* or head of the cathedral school. Hildebert of Lavardin (died 1133) and Geoffrey Babion, who is probably to be identified with Geoffrey du Louroux, archbishop of Bordeaux 1135–58, are examples of preachers who were both masters and bishops. From this scholastic background there sprang a remarkable tradition of preaching at Paris. Its exponents included Peter Lombard, who died in 1160 after a short time as bishop, and a series of chancellors: Odo of Soissons, who died in 1172 as a Cistercian and a cardinal; Peter Comestor (died 1178), whose sermons were the most widely circulated of all; and Hilduin (died 1193). They put their theology into sermon form, and in particular stressed the obligation to personal morality. The hearer was urged to form himself by meditation upon the example of Christ: 'every action of Christ is a lesson for the Christian'.[24] In line with this moralizing tendency was a strong association between preaching and the confessional. The masters moved away from the traditional exposition of the liturgy for the church's year, and in particular of the Gospel for the day, and concentrated on the analysis of single texts, whose full meaning (indeed, more than the full meaning) was extracted by a series of distinctions and classifications. The convention of beginning with a text, which has been so influential in modern preaching, has a continuous history from the time of the Paris masters.

The Paris school was of epoch-making importance because it led directly to the popular preaching movement championed by the

---

[23] P. Tibber, 'The Origins of the Scholastic Sermon' (unpublished University of Oxford D.Phil. thesis), 2.

[24] J. Longère, *Oeuvres oratoires de maîtres parisiens au XIIe siècle*, 2 vols. (Paris, 1975), ii.77 n. 36.

Paris masters of the early thirteenth century and by the friars. This concern was becoming apparent by about 1190, and it must be considered in a later section in connection with the pastoral revolution which was to follow. But before then Paris sermons were specifically scholastic, designed for audiences of students or clergy. We have to look elsewhere for popular preaching, and it is hard to know how much there was, or whether the hierarchy had much interest in providing it. One thing cannot be doubted: there were preaching campaigns on special occasions outside the parochial framework. The new hermits, champions of poverty and preaching, conducted tours in northern France around 1100 in which they gave popular sermons. Among them we may list Robert of Arbrissel, Vitalis of Savigny, Bernard of Tiron, Odo of Tournai, Peter the Hermit, and Norbert of Xanten. These popular advocates of poverty, whose message was critical of the established order, might spill over into an open breach with the church, as did Tanchelm of Antwerp, Henry of Lausanne, and Arnold of Brescia. Some preaching tours were officially sponsored as an answer to heresy, like Bernard's visit to southern France in 1145, but these were rare in the twelfth century. The crusades called into being mass recruiting campaigns by Peter the Hermit in 1095–6 and Bernard in 1146–7. Celebrations at the consecration of a new church or altar, and the patronal festival at major centres, would be marked by sermons.

These are all infrequent occasions, and while individual preachers could have dramatic effects they could have contributed almost nothing to the general level of instruction in the population as a whole. It would be interesting to know whether bishops and *magistri* provided regular courses of sermons for lay audiences at cathedrals and other great churches. The main difficulty in supposing that they did lies in the almost total absence of sermons which are clearly directed to a lay audience, but there are hints that this sort of provision was being made, at least in some places. Gerhoh of Reichersberg attached great importance to providing instruction for the people, and sermon techniques sometimes suggest that an uneducated audience is in the preacher's mind. Geoffrey Babion's style is simple and clear, and the use of illustrative tales or *exempla*, which did not appear at Paris until after 1200, is quite widespread in twelfth-century sermons elsewhere. Direct applications to secular life can be found early in the century in the sermons of Ivo of Chartres, and in Honorius Augustodunensis lessons are drawn for different social classes: an anticipation of a method of addressing special audiences which was to become of great importance and which is known as *ad status* preaching. The cities also give us examples of laymen who are both pious and well-informed, such as the charitable Werimbold of Cambrai, and, more remarkably, Valdes of Lyon, who had a good knowledge of the vernacular Scriptures and also (to believe a later account) consulted a local theologian about his crisis of faith. The matter cannot be conclusively resolved, but it is quite likely that urban populations, especially their more privileged members, were receiving some regular instruction from the clergy of their principal church.

It is at first sight disconcerting that very few vernacular sermons survive from before 1200, but this is an apparent rather than a real problem. The evidence is overwhelming that when sermons were preached to the laity (and possibly also to *conversi*, nuns and parish priests) they were in the congregation's own language. We know of prelates who had a reputation for being able to preach well in more than one language, including Archbishop Hildebert of Tours, Bishop Gerard of Angoulême, and Abbots Odo of Battle and Samson of Bury St Edmunds. There are instances of preachers struggling with an unfamiliar language or needing a translator, including Norbert at Valenciennes; Arnulf and Bernard of Clairvaux at the time of the Second Crusade; Archbishop Baldwin of Canterbury at the time of the Third; and Patriarch Godfrey of Aquileia in 1189 at the consecration of an Italian monastery. There are also notes in some Latin sermons which indicate that they were designed to be used as a basis for vernacular preaching. Latin was the language of record, but sermons for the 'illiterate', that is those without Latin, were delivered in the common tongue.[25]

If vernacular preaching was being provided at great churches, that would have helped to create an instructed urban patriciate and laid the foundation for later pastoral developments. Even on optimistic assumptions it would only have touched a tiny part of the population, most of whom were dependent on their country priests. It is not even clear that parish priests were supposed to preach, for there were conflicting assumptions about their responsibilities which go back to the days of the early church. The dominant view in our period was that preaching was an episcopal prerogative. It was never

---

[25] Many of the references for this section are in M. Zink, *La prédication en langue romane* (Paris, 1976), 85 ff.

listed among the duties implicit in cure of souls, and at the Fourth Lateran Council a canon which was designed to extend the provision for preaching spoke only in terms of the bishops and their assistants.[26] It is inconceivable that a regular preaching programme was taking place in country churches in the twelfth century. Few parishes would have possessed a collection of sermons for the priest to use. An instance in southern Germany in the eleventh century shows how acute the famine of books could be. A copy of the *Cura Pastoralis* of Gregory the Great was donated to a group of priests. The manuscript, which was already 200 years old, was divided into two sections and read in two separate assemblies, the parts being interchanged each year. Presumably they could not afford an additional copy, and the cumbersome procedure illustrates the difficulty of access to a basic pastoral text.[27] Even in the rare cases where a parish owned a homily book of the Carolingian type, the material would be unsuitable for ordinary parishioners, and the sort of straightforward exposition of the Gospels which survives from late in the twelfth century has left few or no examples earlier.

There was, however, another route by which a priest might teach his parishioners. It was an obligation for all members of the church to know the Creed and the Lord's Prayer. Both Gerhoh and Honorius stressed the duty of priests to help people learn them, and the possibility of teaching through their medium. There was quite a widespread practice of including within the mass a vernacular section, sometimes called the prone, which might consist of a summary of the Gospel, some intercessions and the teaching of these basic texts.[28] We have no solid information about how universal the custom of the prone was, or how effectively parish priests took the opportunity which it provided; but it is possible that the simple teaching of the Creed and the Lord's Prayer was fairly common. It was a very elementary basis for the understanding of Christianity, and it does not modify the general conclusion that the people of the time were witnesses of a ritual rather than the holders of a faith.

---

[26] Canon. 10 (Alberigo, 215). The alternative view was based on Jerome's teaching that 'it is the office of the priest to give answer according to the Law'. The sentence was quoted by Bonizo of Sutri as part of the exposition of 1, Tim. 3: 1–7 which he largely took from Jerome: E. Perels (ed.), *Bonizo: Liber de Vita Christiana* (Berlin, 1930), ii.6, p. 37.

[27] H. Maurer, 'Die Hegau-Priester', *ZSSRGkA* 92 (1975), 37–52.

[28] Most of the evidence for the prone is from the thirteenth century, and is therefore considered later. For the Lord's Prayer and Creed with explanation, see Honorius, *Speculum ecclesiae*, PL 172.819–20 and 823–4.

vi. *Ceremonial and Society*

Ritual and religion were not bounded by the walls of the church, but came out into the surrounding society, invading its space and shaping its perception of the calendar. Ceremonial literally emerged from the church in processions, the most important of which circumambulated the town. The processions for the papal 'stations' or masses were part of the calendar of Rome, and those for Rogationtide were major social events each year. At Bamberg, where they can be traced back to the twelfth century, all the churches took part, the relics of the cathedral were carried, and on each of the three Rogation days a different route was taken through the town. The Palm Sunday procession also went through the town, taking with it the 'palm ass' and culminating in the adoration of the cross in the churchyard. In such ceremonies the laity participated with the clergy in what was essentially a civic event: in some German towns the schoolchildren had an allotted role, and at Mainz, at least late in the Middle Ages, each household was represented by one of its adult members. Elsewhere, it was customary to arrange processions round the parish boundary to keep alive the memory of its location. The date of the origin of these ceremonies of 'beating the bounds' is uncertain, but it is reasonable to suppose that they go back to the original settlement of the division, often in the twelfth or thirteenth century. The *Bannkreuz* of Flanders, an annual procession to the mother-church, commemorated its status as the origin of the parishes. The response to a crisis was often to institute a procession: in preparation for a crusade or even (at Jerusalem in the closing weeks of the First Crusade) to prepare an assault. The impact of these processions should not be judged by the refined ceremonial of the modern church; they represented the power of ritual to intervene in and regulate secular space, and their effect was, according to their purpose, more like the demonstration, or church parade, or Lord Mayor's Show of our own day.

Prominent in the organization of lay society were the guilds, confraternities, or charities (for all these names, and others, were used). Their origin lay in the Germanic past, and we know from Hincmar and other Carolingian sources that their purposes already included many of those found later. The central event was a regular confraternity supper, and they offered support for sick and needy members, funeral arrangements and prayers for the departed, participation in the offertory, and support for their guild altar in the parish church. The balance of social and charitable activity varied from one confraternity to another, and some came close to being simple dining-clubs; one Italian peasant confraternity became proverbial by its discovery, at the end of its supper, that it had exactly a halfpenny left for other purposes. In the eleventh century, the monastic confraternities were very powerful. These were not local ones but fellowships which admitted a priest or lay noble to participation in the spiritual privileges of Cluny or other abbeys. With the growing energy of urban life, we soon find associations of clergy and laity in the cities, such as the Grand Fraternity at Paris or the one at Rouen founded in 1072. Most continued to have the traditional range of functions, but some were created for specific purposes. Bishop Arnulf of Lisieux and others founded gilds to raise funds for the building of their cathedrals, and there were confraternities for all the purposes dear to the twelfth century: to provide bridges and maintain roads, to fight infidels and heretics and ransom captives, even to compose poems dedicated to Our Lady. Hospitals and leper-houses were run by confraternities. A group founded as a confraternity might later adopt the Rule of a monastic order or a congregation of canons. Conversely, there was no firm line between pious and professional associations. The first mention of the merchant guild at Arras refers to its function of maintaining lights at one of the altars at the abbey of St Vaast, and some confraternities played a crucial part in the running of their town. A notable example was that of the Holy Spirit at Marseille, which in the thirteenth century effectively formed the city government, while having statutes similar to those of any other pious association.

Like the chameleon, the confraternities (or at least those of which we hear most in the sources) took their colour from the surrounding society. Associations linked to great abbeys were specially characteristic of the beginning of our period, when society was marked by a strong sense of traditional solidarities and prayers for the departed, and other spiritual benefits, were seen as given by membership of a community. These groups were supplemented or replaced in the twelfth century by ones with a strong commitment to practical works of charity or embodying the devotion of particular trades or professions. Then, in the thirteenth, there emerged groups linked with the friars and associations of the growing numbers of local clergy. The confraternities seem to have expressed the religious and social aspirations of ordinary people. It is interesting to find that these, while not being dictated by the hierarchy, underwent an evolution markedly similar to the ideals of the influential groups of the church as a whole.

While processions and confraternities were linking local life with worship, pilgrimage influenced the organization of regional and international society. We saw in Chapter 1 that pilgrimage, which in the past had been an activity limited to small numbers, was changing its character. As a movement, it was becoming more clearly defined. Not only did the word *peregrinus* come to mean 'pilgrim' instead of exile or foreigner, but the pilgrim obtained a special status in the eyes of the churches. The Vich missal of 1083 contains one of the earliest masses for pilgrims, a *missa pro fratribus in via dirigendis*, and from about 1100 the staff and wallet, signs of pilgrimage, were being blessed liturgically. Meanwhile the great shrines were producing emblems which pilgrims could wear to indicate that they had completed the journey; a system which worried the popes, who were conscious that tokens could easily be bought anywhere on the way. Although pilgrimage could be enjoyable it was, like all medieval travel, dangerous. The Roman Church extended its protection in the First Lateran Council of 1123, which imposed excommunication on all those who stole from 'travellers to Rome and pilgrims to the shrines of the apostles and those visiting the oratories of other saints'.[29] This basic protection was widened to include other privileges. Pilgrims were permitted to have dealings with excommunicates when it was necessary to trade with them on the journey, and clergy were exempted from the canons excluding them from taverns and requiring them to wear clerical dress. Grants of indulgences by popes and bishops expressed their approval of a shrine and gave a further inducement to those visiting it.

The vast numbers brought onto the roads by pilgrimage needed places to stay. These were provided in part by the development of commercial taverns and inns, but much more by the creation of a network of hostels. Since the medieval hostel was an all-purpose building catering for many needs, there is no way of estimating how much of this development was directly a response to demand from pilgrims, but the location of the new hostels is significant. Those acquired by the Hospitallers in Mediterranean ports by 1113 must

---

[29] Canon 14 (Alberigo, 169) = Gratian, *Decr.* C. XXIV, q. 3, c. 23 (996–7).

have been designed for the Jerusalem pilgrims, and the development of the large hospital at Altopascio on the lower Arno and of a string of hostels two or three miles apart along the roads through Lucca strongly suggests that provision was being made for the journey to Rome, and perhaps also to Italian ports for embarcation to the Holy Land. The pilgrim traffic, like the tourist trade nowadays, was as important in the development of communications as was the growth of commerce.

The artistic impact of pilgrimage was highly significant. We have already noticed the way in which church plans developed to make the shrines accessible to visitors, and it is striking to find a great number of churches of basically similar design in southern France and Spain, strung out along the way to St James at Compostella; a 'regional group' constituted, not by a region, but by a road. Some of the finest artistic work in the period was devoted to reliquaries such as the superb housing for the relics of the Three Kings at Cologne, the arm-reliquary of St James at Aachen, and the head 'made in the likeness of the emperor' given by Frederick Barbarossa to his godfather, Count Otto of Cappenberg, between 1156 and 1171, to contain a fragment of the head of John the Baptist; all of them combining, in various ways, piety, art, and imperial ideology. The arrival of reliquaries from Byzantium, especially after the Fourth Crusade, tended to create waves of influence, with their artistic ideas imitated by nearby craftsmen. In literature, pilgrimage produced guide-books (notably to Compostella and the Holy Land) and collections of miracle stories of the saints, designed to advertise their healing power to potential customers. It also influenced western thinking at a deeper level, particularly through the symbolism of Jerusalem. The crusades themselves were a variant of pilgrimage, using similar terminology and developing alongside the great pilgrimages to other shrines. It also affected the contemporary understanding of the spiritual universe. We shall have to look later at the complex scene of eschatological expectation, but one of its features was a movement away from the traditional expectation of the coming of Jerusalem out of heaven, and its replacement by a sense of quest, the search of the human soul for Jerusalem and the sense of the whole life of man as a pilgrimage to the heavenly city. Like confraternity, pilgrimage was not just an institution. It was part of the soul of man:

Now in the meantime, with hearts raised on high,

We for that country must yearn and must sigh,
Seeking Jerusalem, dear native land, Through
our lone exile on Babylon's strand.[30]

The purpose of pilgrimage was usually to pay a visit to the shrine of a saint. The purpose of that in turn might be merely to honour the saint, or because a local pilgrimage had become a convention or obligation; but often it would be to seek healing. Such healing ministries were centred on the shrine in which the relics were kept or a place where a marvel had occurred. The launching of a successful cult often began with such a marvel, which might be great or small: the murder of a noble lady by her husband (St Godelième at Ghistelles, Flanders *c.*1070) or of a churchman (St Thomas of Canterbury 1170), or conversely the death of a horse near a tomb (Guy of Anderlecht *c.*1060) or even (Guibert of Nogent complained) the mere fact of a death on Good Friday. When an account of the miracles was written in sufficient detail we can sometimes trace the wave as its spreads out from the shrine, its power rapidly fading into the distance. It was assumed that a saint, like a low-powered radio transmitter, would only be effective over a limited range; it could be said that St Eutropius could not help because he was 'more than ten leagues away'.[31] Distant healings by invocation of a saint were not unknown in the twelfth century, but they were rare, and on the whole the closer the supplicant could approach the relics, the better his prospect of success. Shrines were built with pierced holes so that it was possible to touch or see the reliquary inside (St Osmund, Salisbury; at St Menoux in central France the presence of a shrine into which the head could be placed eventually gave it a reputation for healing the mentally ill). The faithful drank water or wine, *vinagium*, into which dust from the tomb or wax from candles had been mixed, or they drank from sacred springs at or near the church. Many of the healings took place among those who spent the whole night beside the saint's tomb.

All of this was an extremely social experience. Villages would organize a pilgrimage together led by a cantor, with the sick carried with them on carts. News of miracles spread from one group of pilgrims to another; we have several cases of people who set out for one shrine but were 'captured' by news of a good miracle at another.

---

[30] Peter Abelard, *O quanta qualia*, F. J. E. Raby (ed.), *The Oxford Book of Medieval Latin Verse* (Oxford, 1959), no. 169; *English Hymnal*, no. 465.

[31] Cited P.-A. Sigal, *L'homme et le miracle dans la France médiévale* (Paris, 1985), 61. These paragraphs are largely based on this important work, which should be consulted for details.

Healings were greeted enthusiastically by the crowds, and checked and proclaimed by the wardens of the shrine; songs were sung in the vernacular of the life and miracles of the saint, especially at the time of his annual feast. Prayers were both communal and crude. Strikingly we rarely hear before 1200 of advice to confess; more typically devotions seem to be led by the clergy with the laity joining in as best they might (and sometimes, for good measure, singing highly secular songs to match the psalms of the clergy). The primitive assumptions of the worshippers cannot escape the notice of the modern reader, and educated contemporaries were aware of them. As we have already seen, some attempt was made to check the authenticity of healings which were claimed and formal evidence taken from witnesses, while Guibert of Nogent's book on *The Relics of the Saints* (*De Pignoribus Sanctorum*) satirized ill-documented relics and popular cults. Yet the great sanctuaries were not relics of a more primitive past, but were being built up with the expansion of society. Specialization in one particular disease was beginning in the twelfth century. Perhaps the earliest instance was the treatment of leprosy at the tomb of St Hubert in the Ardennes, but such concentration on a particular clientèle tended to grow, echoing the increasing specialism in trades in society as a whole. Several shrines catered particularly for women's diseases, both physical and psychological. Scepticism about the efficacy of the saints belongs mainly to a post-critical age, and should not be used as a basis for our assessment of twelfth-century society. The growth of sanctuaries can more correctly be seen as forming part, along with hospitals and leper-houses, of the attempt to offer remedies for sickness and misfortune in a general policy of expanding charitable provision, to which we must turn in the next chapter.

13

CHRISTIANITY AND SOCIAL IDEAS

i. *The Basis of Christian Social Action*

The formation of Christendom did not only mean the building of more, and more splendid, churches for worship; it also involved the making of moral directives to shape the life of society. The twelfth century saw a sustained attempt to apply Christian principles to the conduct of social affairs in a way unparalleled since the days of Ambrose and Augustine. It represented a development of the ideals of the reforming popes, with their concern to purify priesthood and worship. The thinking about the ethics of lay action during the twelfth century forms a bridge between the cultic concerns of the Gregorians and the personal pastoral aspirations of the thirteenth century. The Gregorians themselves provided a starting-point for the new development by their definition of the duties of the clerical order and its separation from the laity, for this almost necessarily involved a redefinition of the duties of lay people within the kingdom of God. We shall see shortly that a sharp, even extreme, separation between clergy and laity was characteristic of medieval social thinking, which in that important sense remained in the Gregorian tradition. A further reason for the new thinking was the growth of differentiation between lay functions and careers and the greater self-awareness of laymen with their new specialist skills. In addition, the study of canon law and the emergence of skilled theologians and administrators made contemporaries much more aware of the social teaching which was to be found in patristic writing. The picture sometimes drawn of medieval society as neglecting questions of poverty, violence, family life, or commercial morality is frankly absurd: although the suppositions and possibilities of twelfth-century people were different from those of our own century, they were clear-minded about social problems and determined in the application of solutions.

A more serious concern about lay ethics was promoted by a new spirit of humanism, which was strikingly illustrated in the work of Bishop Ivo of Chartres (1091–1115). Ivo found that human society had value in the eyes of God and wrote of 'the dignity of the human condition'—an idea which it is difficult to find in Gregory VII or his close associates. He held that need might overrule religious edicts, so that the prohibition of swearing in Matthew 5: 34–7 did not apply to 'human contracts', and it was permissible to have dealings with excommunicates for the sake of humanity. He strove to secure peace between *regnum* and *sacerdotium*, 'without whose concord human affairs cannot be secure'. The word 'humanity', after 500 years in which it had mainly referred to the impotence of man in face of the majesty of God, reappeared in Ivo's works in a good sense, shaped by its old classical meaning of 'philanthropy'. This was, of course, a Christian, not a secular humanism, shaped by the conviction that 'honour or maltreatment of the poor refer to Christ'.[1] With widened sympathies and improved techniques of study, the church sought to instill the principles of Christian conduct in a broad range of human affairs.

There was, none the less, a serious difficulty. Since the end of the Ancient World there had been a gap between the culture of the clergy, whose skill was with words, and the unlearned laity. The church had for a long time tried to persuade its ordinary members that if they attended more carefully to the Word they would order their affairs better: 'If only the sons of men would make use of me they would be the safer and the more victorious, their hearts would be bolder, their minds more at ease, their thoughts wiser: and they would have more friends, companions and kinsmen.'[2] In the twelfth century the gap between the two cultures became wider rather than narrower, as clerical education became more specialized and orientated to canon law and theology, while more structured ways of life developed in the cities and in the courts of princes. The attempt to make real the Gospel in the ordinary affairs of men could look very like an attempt to subject laymen to codes of conduct devised by the clergy.

It was recognized that the church, in the exact sense of the word,

---

[1] Rule of Aubrac 1162 in L. Le Grand, *Statuts d'Hôtels-Dieu* (Paris, 1901), 17. The reference is to Matt. 25: 40: 'as you did it to one of the least of these my brethren, you did it to me.' For the theology of Christian humanism, see ch. 15.ii below.

[2] K. Crossley-Holland, *The Exeter Book of Riddles* (Harmondsworth, 1979), no. 26, p.47. The answer is 'book' or 'Scriptures'. The manuscript is of *c.* 1150, but there is no way of dating the riddle.

included all the baptized. 'The church (*ecclesia*) is properly so named because it calls all men to itself and gathers them into one.'[3] This definition by St Isidore was often quoted in the twelfth century. Within the one body were orders with special functions. In the Carolingian period a threefold division was the most popular one, and it was succinctly expressed by Abbo of Fleury shortly before 1000: 'There are three grades or orders, of which the first is of laymen, the second of clerks, and the third of monks.' Of these grades, he said, 'the first is good, the second better and the third best'.[4] In our period, this was largely superseded by a twofold scheme which was rooted in the desire of the papal reformers to make a clear separation between the way of life of clergy and laity, and obtained its classic expression in the text *Duo sunt genera Christianorum*:

There are two kinds of Christians. There is one kind which, being devoted to God's business and given up to contemplation and prayer, should refrain from all activity in worldly affairs. These are the clergy and those devoted to God, that is the converted *(conversi)* . . . The shaving of their head shows the putting away of all temporal things. For they should be content with food and clothing and have nothing of their own among themselves, but should have everything in common. There is also another kind of Christians, who are laymen. For *laos* means 'people'. These are allowed to possess temporal goods, but only to the extent that they make use of them . . . They are allowed to take a wife, to till land, to judge between man and man, to conduct lawsuits, to place oblations upon the altar, to pay tithes, and thus they can be saved if they avoid sin by well-doing.[5]

This remarkable text welds together two concepts of the clergy: a juridical one (they include all who have been tonsured) and a spiritual one (they live in community without private property and attend to prayer). The lay state is allowable, but that is the most one can say for it, and secular clergy outside communities have no part in the scheme at all. The inclusion of the passage in Gratian's *Decretum* gave it authority for the future, and by about 1160 the canonist Stephen of Tournai had developed the separation between the two orders with startling clarity. He began by asserting that there was one city (the church) and one king (Christ), but he then continued: 'there are two

---

[3] Isidore, *De Ecclesiasticis Officiis*, I.i.2 (PL 83.739–40).

[4] Abbo of Fleury, *Apologeticus* (PL 139.463B).

[5] Gratian, *Decr.* C. XII, q. 1, c. 7 (678). His ascription of this text to Jerome is certainly wrong, and it was probably composed within the circle of the papal reformers. The thought is an exaggerated form of that in Urban II's bull to Rottenbuch.

peoples; two orders in the church, clergy and laity; two lives, spiritual and carnal; two authorities, the *sacerdotium* and the *regnum*; a twofold jurisdiction of divine and human law.'[6] Thus the seamless robe of Christendom was torn in two. There is plenty of evidence in canon law of the suspicion in which laymen were held. It was a principle that laymen should have no standing (*nulla facultas*) in the determination of ecclesiastical affairs. A decretal of pseudo-Isidore declaring that laymen 'are altogether hostile' to the bishops became the basis of regular complaints about lay oppression, which show us the clergy in a state of siege, striving to maintain the service of God amid laity who are the spokesmen of a sinful world.

This absolute contrast could not be sustained. Gregory VII knew very well that there were righteous rulers as well as unrighteous, but his test of righteousness was obedience to the injunctions of the see of Rome. The clergy had the directive authority in matters of morals. On this assumption, however, they were willing to recognize the various walks of life which were developing as lay society became more specialized. About 1090 Bonizo of Sutri in his *Liber de Vita Christiana* discussed the duties of merchants, craftsmen, and farmers. It was the first in a series of affirmations that the layman is well-pleasing to God if he performs faithfully the duties pertaining to his rank. Abbot Bernard of Clairvaux asserted that every class (*genus*) had its own distinctive work and pleasure, and he understood the Pauline prophecy that the dead will rise 'each in his own order' (1 Cor. 15. 23) to mean that they would be grouped as knights or merchants or farmers.[7] Gerhoh of Reichersberg held that all Christians lived under rule: 'Every order and every profession without exception has in the catholic faith and the doctrine of the apostles a rule suited to its quality, and whoever lawfully fights under it can receive a crown.' In the same spirit James of Vitry, shortly after 1200, described all Christians as 'regulars', a term normally reserved for monks.[8] A long tradition of Protestant historiography, going back to Martin Luther, criticized the medieval church for giving no place to the lay professions within the divine purpose, but this criticism is not well founded.

Nevertheless lay walks of life were never really seen in the same

---

[6] J. F. von Schulte (ed.), *Die Summa des Stephanus Tornacensis* (Giessen, 1891), prol. p. 1.

[7] Geoffrey, *Declamationes ex S. Bernardi sermonibus collectae*, 10 (PL 184.444A).

[8] Gerhoh, *De Aedificio Dei*, 43 (PL 194.1302D); James of Vitry, *Historia Occidentalis*, 34, ed. J. F. Hinnebusch (Freiburg, 1972), 165.

light as clerical ones. Jacques le Goff has drawn attention to the abandonment of the concept of the three 'orders' of society and the use instead of more secular expressions such as 'profession' or (especially in the thirteenth century) 'estate'.[9] The layman did not serve God in the same direct sense as a priest, and the right of canon law to regulate lay society rested upon the special occasions when the layman came under the direction of the church by marrying, taking a vow, or making a will, or because his business was in danger of leading him into sin. It was a halfway concept. The medieval church did not believe in a secular society, but neither did it think of one Christendom under its uniform government.

ii. *Provision for the Poor*

'The bishop ought to be solicitous and vigilant concerning the defence of the poor and the relief of the oppressed and the protection of monasteries.'[10] In these words Gratian about 1140 summed up the traditional duty of care for the poor. According to the Fathers and the early councils the revenues of the church were designed for the use of the bishop, the clergy, the fabric, and the poor, and these principles were incorporated by Gratian into his collection of canons and reasserted by such writers as Peter Damian: 'Do you not know that this is why lands were bestowed on the church, so that the poor may be supported from them, the needy fed, and so that from them the widows and orphans might receive aid?'[11] While the principles were traditional, the way in which charity was dispensed underwent some important changes during the period under consideration.

In late Carolingian times it is probable that there was not much institutional care provided. The main responsibility for caring for those in misfortune fell upon their kindred and neighbours. We have no real idea how effective this system was, but it was certainly not adapted to dealing with those groups created in a climate of greater social mobility who moved into the cities, settled marginal land in the forests, and crowded onto the roads between the major centres of pilgrimage. They had left the traditional structures of support and they were more exposed to famine, of which we begin to hear a good deal more in the eleventh century. In a few special circumstances,

---

[9] J. Le Goff, *La civilisation de l'occident médiéval* (Paris, 1964), 325.

[10] Gratian, *Decr.* D. 84, ante c. 1 (294).

[11] Peter Damian ep. IV.12 (PL 144.322A). Cf. Placidus of Nonantula, *De Honore Ecclesiae*, lxxi (MGH LdL ii.598): 'res pauperum, id est possessiones ecclesiarum.'

societies reacted to the new situation by reinforcing the old arrangements: when tithes were introduced into Iceland in 1097 they were made available to the *hreppr* or local organization to subsidize the expenditure on poor relief. But in most of Europe, there was a growing reliance on institutional care. The responsibility for this in canon law rested with the bishop, but, like so many ecclesiastical obligations, it had come to be discharged primarily by monasteries.

The Rule of St Benedict required monks to give special attention to the needs of the poor and pilgrims, and this duty had been incorporated into the liturgical round. A certain number of poor men were maintained in large abbeys as pensioners. Far more were fed in specially endowed meals on feast-days and in commemoration of the departed. The provision for their souls included not only masses, but also charity to the poor, sometimes on a very large scale. The poor offered an opportunity for the monks to achieve salvation for themselves and others by exercising charity, and the system had the merit of building charitable care into the life of an abbey. There was, so to speak, a divine economy of charity, which was clearly explained to the knights on the First Crusade by Bishop Adhemar of Le Puy: 'None of you can be saved if he does not respect the poor and succour them; you cannot be saved without them, and they cannot survive without you.'[12] The signs are that many monasteries took their responsibilities seriously. The excavations conducted by K. J. Conant at Cluny suggest that about 1050 there were four buildings designed for those in need: the infirmary of the monks (the best of the buildings, it must be admitted), a hospice for the poor near the gate, a guest house for rich travellers, and a small almonry for resident pensioners. Abbeys responded to the growing need by putting the poor under the care of a special officer, the almoner. Lanfranc's monastic customs followed those of Cluny in requiring that the almoner be a man of active charity, and we have a description of such an almoner in Gerald of St Chaffre (Velay, central France) who shortly before 1100 established the work for the poor there and ministered to vast crowds who came for relief.[13]

There are striking examples of abbots who provided abundantly for the poor. One such was Æthelwig of Evesham (1058–77):

Since our father Benedict in his Rule bids that 'the table of the abbot should

[12] *Gesta Francorum*, ed. R. Hill (Oxford, 1979), 74.
[13] D. Knowles (ed.), *The Monastic Constitutions of Lanfranc* (Edinburgh, 1951), 89; M. Mollat, *Les pauvres au Moyen Âge* (Paris, 1978), 68–9.

be with pilgrims and guests' this abbot always gave bountiful provision from his table to thirteen poor men daily. In addition, until the day of his death, whether at home or abroad, he maintained twelve poor men according to the commandment (*ad mandatum*) with food and clothing in all respects the same as a monk's. He or his prior, who had special charge of this under him, loved with all humility daily to wash the hands and feet of these men with warm water. Some of them were lepers, but Aethelwig washed and kissed their hands and feet exactly as he did those of others . . . Every year four or five days before Christmas and between Palm Sunday and Easter Day a great army of poor and pilgrims used to come to Evesham; all these Aethelwig succoured both in person and by means of monks and faithful laypeople, giving bountiful alms, accompanying the Lord's command by washing their feet, giving clothes to some, boots to more, and money to many others.[14]

This sort of help was valuable at times of famine. In 1069–70 Æthelwig supplied the needs of refugees from William I's harrying of the north, and in 1095 Abbot Odo of St Martin at Tournai exhausted the food supply of the house in trying to cope with the needs of the starving population. Abbeys would liquidate their treasures on such occasions, as when St Benoît-sur-Loire in 1146–7 sold a fine silver crucifix, and at about the same time Abbot Geoffrey of St Albans stripped off the silver plate which had only recently been added to embellish the shrine of the patron saint.[15] The needs of the involuntary poor were also remembered by hermits who had embraced a voluntary poverty for themselves. Robert of Arbrissel is a notable example. To a noble correspondent he sent a lengthy exposition of the duty of almsgiving: 'Be merciful to the poor, but especially to the very poor, and even more to those who have left the world for God.'[16] The assumption continued throughout the twelfth century that charity was particularly the business of the monks, an idea which is illustrated by the marked tendency to place hospitals in cities under the care of nearby abbeys.

Nevertheless it was becoming clear that the contribution of the monasteries was not sufficient. The instances of charity which have been mentioned are impressive, but were recorded because they were

---

[14] W. D. Macray, *Chronicon Abbatiae de Evesham* (RS 29, 1863) 91–3. The reference to commandment is from John 13: 34: 'A new commandment I give to you, that you love one another.' The word *mandatum* in this context gave us the word Maundy for the day on which foot-washing and alms were particularly observed.

[15] Hermann, *Liber de Restauratione S. Martini Tornacensis*, c. 76 (MGH SS XIV.311); H. T. Riley, *Gesta Abbatum S. Albani* (RS 28, 1867), i.82.

[16] Letter to Ermengarde, published in *Bibliothèque de l' École des Chartes* 5 (1854), 234.

exceptional. We hear also of complaints that abbots were greedy and negligent, or even that they actively oppressed the poor. There was also a topographical problem. A large part of the problem of poverty now lay in the towns, and there the monasteries could not easily provide assistance on the scale that was needed; the Cistercians in particular were both physically and in sympathy distant from the cities. Something else was needed.

The texts quoted in Gratian's *Decretum* called attention to the bishop's duty to provide for those in need, but the position of the bishop had changed. He no longer disposed of all the ecclesiastical property in his diocese, for much was controlled by local churches and even in the cathedral the revenues were often received individually by the canons. The clergy as a whole were still under an obligation to make provision for those in need, and we have no grounds for supposing that all relief of the poor had completely stopped, but it was a matter of personal charity, which was not mediated through institutions and which has left no historical evidence. In the past there had been hospices in cathedral cities, but these may not have been functioning in the early eleventh century, and cathedrals did not appoint almoners until late in the twelfth century. The impetus for change probably came from the papal reform movement, with its emphasis on the proper ownership and use of church revenues. Bishop Peter of Anagni (1062–1105) will serve as an example of these ideals in action. He was appointed to his central Italian see by the favour of Gregory VII and an account of his life was prepared by the ultra-Gregorian Bruno of Segni. When he rebuilt the cathedral and surrounding buildings, Peter provided himself with a room immediately above the place for pilgrims and guests, 'and thus visited assiduously the guests and the poor by a staircase'. [17] The initiatives of the bishops were complemented by the laity. There was nothing new about instructing the laity in the duty of almsgiving, which was a normal part of the expenditure of a great household, but it was innovatory to apply it to the needs of the rising cities. An illustration of the new urban ethic in action is provided by Werimbold of Cambrai. Werimbold was a member of the patriciate, born about 1080. He accumulated great wealth and built himself a handsome house of stone. He was converted, it seems, by the sermons on avarice which he heard at church, and the whole family decided to retire from the world into religious life.

[17] *Vita B. Petri episcopi*, 2, *AASS* Aug. I.237B.

They were moved, we are told, by fear of judgement, but much more by the maxims of the Gospel and the friendship of Christ:[18]

Exhortati per plurima	Encouraged by the numerous
scripturae predicamina	Appeals that the Bible has expressed,
pro Christi amicitia	They, for the friendship of the Lord,
cuncta relinquunt propria.	Abandoned all that they possessed.

Werimbold lived in an area imbued with the spirit of the poor preachers, for Odo of Tournai, Robert of Arbrissel, and Norbert of Xanten had all worked not far away, but unlike those later converts from the urban patriciate, Valdes of Lyon and Francis of Assisi, he apparently did not attempt evangelism among the poor, but provided benefactions for their benefit. He bought up a toll which was causing them much distress, and handsomely rebuilt and supplied the old hospice of Holy Cross, which had fallen into disrepair.

The principal way of providing poor relief in the city was the hospital, a building which might cater for the poor, the sick, or travellers, or for all three together. It was thus more like a modern hostel or group home, and it was not a new idea. Such hostels or *xenodochia* had been provided in the late Roman period and an attempt had been made by the Carolingians to revive the system. What was new was the large scale on which this was done in the twelfth century. A number of local studies suggest that the founding of hospitals on a substantial scale began about 1100, and that the largest number was being founded in the late twelfth and early thirteenth centuries. Even by 1150 Narbonne had adopted the logical arrangement of two hospitals and two leper-houses, divided between the old city and the suburb across the river. Paris had a long-established hospital, of which there is an isolated mention in the ninth century, and which was either revived or greatly expanded in the twelfth. It grew into the Hôtel-Dieu, one of the largest hospitals in western Europe, on a site which it was to occupy until the replanning of the city by Haussmann in the nineteenth century. At Genoa the hospital of San Giovanni was founded between 1163 and 1186 under the auspices of the Hospitallers. It became the favourite good cause of the citizens in their benefactions, and in the next century produced one of the first saints of the order in Ugone (died 1233), revered for his labours for the poor and sick. Establishments

---

[18] Metrical life of Werimbold, *Gesta Burchardi Episcopi Cameracensis* c. 6 (MGH SS XIV.216).

of any size, and even some of the smallest, were run by confraternities governed by a Rule. When about 1220 James of Vitry described the hospital system as a whole, he assumed that all were run by communities and wrote of 'the congregations without any estimate or definite number in all the regions of the west, who humbly and devoutly minister to the poor and sick'.[19] He was critical of houses which were slack or misused their revenues, but he also mentioned good ones at Paris, Noyon, Provins, and Brussels, and other excellent establishments which were the centre of whole groups, such as Holy Spirit (Rome), St Samson (Constantinople), St Antoine (near Vienne), and Roncevaux (Pyrenees). The international order of the Hospitallers, in addition to its work in the Holy Land, ran a considerable number of hospitals in the west. Nursing the sick was probably one of the functions of hospitals from the beginning, but at first the emphasis was on spiritual ministrations and the laying on of hands. Gratian quoted the disapproving text, 'the precepts of medicine are contrary to the divine decree'.[20] The movement towards the acceptance of medical practice during the next few generations was part of a more general willingness to take the sciences seriously, but given the severe limitations of medical practice the element of custody and care must always have been large.

Alongside the hospitals were institutions of a different type, which were also being rapidly founded: leper-houses or *ladreries*. Leprosy was giving rise to concern because of the greater ease with which it could spread in the crowded cities. Old Testament texts were understood to imply that the disease carried with it a ritual impurity, but the reason for isolating lepers in a house outside the walls was to avoid contagion, of which (although this is sometimes denied) contemporaries were well aware. Leper-houses were founded by abbeys and by civic benefactors, and they sometimes originated in self-help when a wealthy leper withdrew with a group of fellow-sufferers. The motivation of a rich donor might be a recollection of the story of Dives and Lazarus, or more generally a spirit of social responsibility, as in the foundation of the house of la Madeleine at Saint-Omer in 1106:

Since at the castle of S.-Omer the disease of leprosy was springing up in an unprecedented way, and it was very harmful to live unsegregated with such

---

[19] James of Vitry, *Historia Occidentalis*, 29, pp 146–7.
[20] Gratian, *Decr.* de consec. D. V c. 21 (1417).

men, the charity of God inspired a certain rich man called Winred, who undertook at his own expense to contruct a remote dwelling, suitable for men possessed by this disease.[21]

Lepers were regarded as forming confraternities, with whom healthy men or women may sometimes have been associated, and in 1179 the Third Lateran Council legislated on behalf of 'lepers who cannot live with healthy people or attend church with them' and allowed leper-houses a church and cemetery of their own.[22]

The houses were normally situated outside the cities, and a small fragment of a twelfth-century leprosery which still survives near Périgueux indicates that the rooms faced inwards onto a courtyard with only slit windows looking onto the road outside. The impression is of a decent, even comfortable, provision by the standards of the time.

Did all this constitute, within the possibilities open to a pre-industrial society, an effective response to the problem of poverty? Statistically, we have no means of answering that question. It must be remembered that the issue facing contemporaries was not that of raising the total standard of living, an undertaking which would have appeared, and indeed would have been, impossible. They had to set themselves more limited objectives: to prevent the exploitation of ordinary people by profiteering (a topic to which we will return shortly) and to care for the poor and sick who had moved beyond the assistance of the kindred. There is no doubt that care was sometimes given in a miserly fashion and that some people found the responsibility irksome or repulsive, but at least one modern attitude is not found among them: the assumption that the poor are responsible for their own misfortunes and do not deserve help. On the contrary, there was a real attempt to safeguard the dignity of the poor. The almoner was to be a monk noted for his compassion; orphans were to be given dowries to enable them to marry according to their rank; those caring for the poor must not wear fine clothing which would shame them; and a variety of minor benefactions speak of consideration for personal dignity, such as the rent of forty pence a year to provide head-coverings for those shaven for ringworm.[23] It

---

[21] A. Bourgeois, *Psychologie collective et institutions charitables: lépreux et maladreries du Pas-de-Calais* (Arras, 1972), 301–2.

[22] Can. 23. (Alberigo 198–9).

[23] Rule of Hospitallers in L. Le Grand, *Statuts d'Hôtels-Dieu*, 8, often adopted by other orders; and British Library MS Cotton Tib. C xii f.135v dated 1175/96 (reference supplied by Dr Joan Wardrop).

is also clear that a large institutional effort was being made to solve the problems; it was not a mere matter of exhorting people to be generous, but of creating hospitals and leper-houses on a scale previously unknown.

iii. *Marriage*

Throughout much of European history there has been an accepted idea of marriage as a lifelong union to which both parties have consented and which excludes all forms of subsidiary marriage or concubinage. This was the pattern which for many years was imposed by the courts of western Europe and which still is esteemed by people of traditional outlook. It was very largely the creation of the twelfth century.

The picture before then had been one of entrenched marriage customs among the laity which were little affected by clerical ideas without a clear practical application. We know very little of marriage among the peasantry at this time, and our picture has to be drawn from the conduct of royal houses and the aristocracy. Marriage was pre-eminently negotiated by families and designed for the continuance of their lineage. The relationship began with a formal betrothal, which took place in the family's home and included a property settlement even when, as was not unusual, the intended partners were still small children. The ceremony proper would include the endowment of the bride and her solemn removal to her new household, including sometimes the installation of bride and groom in the marriage-bed. It is likely that the participation of the priest was valued as a protection from malign influences which might render the union infertile: Guibert of Nogent, describing the early married life of his parents, accepted that his father's initial impotence was the result of magic.[24] The function of the priest varied from one area to another: in some regions the nuptial mass had been long in existence, although we do not know how much it was in demand, while elsewhere the priest's main duty seems to have been to bless the bridal chamber. Lay opinion took marriage seriously, but there was little objection to a second marriage during the life of the first wife. There was a *cause célèbre* in the 1090s produced by the French King

---

[24] G. Duby, *The Knight, the Lady and the Priest* (Harmondsworth, 1983), 141–2; but see the important review by John Gillingham in *JEH* 38 (1987), 275–7, in which he argues against too sharp a distinction of lay and clerical models, and in particular rejects Duby's interpretation of the affair of Philip I's marriage.

Philip I when he repudiated his wife Bertha, put her in possession of her dower, and married Bertrada of Montfort, the wife of Count Fulk of Anjou. The king insisted on the status of this union as a second marriage and most bishops accepted his view. Nevertheless the affair caused a scandal, less perhaps because of the divorce than because of the seizure of the wife of another great prince and the relationship of Philip and Bertrada within the prohibited degrees of marriage, and the canonist Bishop Ivo of Chartres stirred up papal intervention against the supposed marriage. The primary duty of a great lord was to provide an heir, and to this end 'serial polygamy' was practised, as in the case of Geoffrey Martel, count of Anjou, who died, still childless, in 1060.[25] Secondary marriage or concubinage was still fairly common in the eleventh century among both laity and clergy. The reaction of ecclesiastical authority to this situation varied. There was a general assumption that chastity was in all circumstances better than marriage, and this could issue in readiness to bless any union accepted by lay convention. Clergy were habitually more worried about close family relationships within marriage than breach of the marriage vow; as late 1164, it could still be said that 'incest is worse than adultery'.[26] Carolingian churchmen had set out a programme of rules for marriage at the council of Paris in 829, which was taken up in the writings of Jonas of Orléans and Hincmar of Reims, but of this more positive approach there was little sign at the beginning of our period.

Marriage had always come within the jurisdiction of the church, for its ceremonies might involve the participation of the clergy and its laws were prescribed, however briefly, in the Scriptures. The twelfth century saw an enormous expansion in the degree of control which the church courts exercised in matrimonial cases, under the impulse of several different forces. The papal reformers, while being primarily concerned with the right ordering of the clergy, also held that the laity should live in their own proper order, that is in matrimony. Gregory VII accordingly wrote to Genoa to complain that 'we learn that . . . the sacrament of marriage, protected by laws and precepts, is being viciously profaned among you'.[27] A positive approach to the value of marriage now became more apparent, as when the saintly Arnulf, a Flemish noble who had become a hermit

---

[25] Duby, *Knight, Lady, and Priest*, 89–92.
[26] S. Bertin Genealogy 12 (MGH SS IX. 320).
[27] Greg. VII. *Reg.* i.48 (74).

near St Médard, Soissons, prayed successfully for heirs for barren marriages and provided advice to families about the problems involved in forming suitable matrimonial links.[28] The hierarchy was also encouraged to formulate a coherent teaching about marriage by the emergence of challenges to the institution within heretical groups. Already in 1022 heretics at Orléans were arguing that the church should take no part in the blessing of marriages; a century later, Henry of Lausanne asserted that marriage contracts were purely the business of the laity; and by the later twelfth century Catharists were rejecting marriage completely as evil. It was at first difficult to agree on an approach: when between 1089 and 1098 the monk Ernulf was consulted in a divorce case by Bishop Walkelin of Winchester he began his reply with a discouraging quotation from Augustine: 'I am aware that no cases are more obscure or perplexing that matrimonial ones'.[29] To produce a coherent theory of marriage was the task begun by Bishop Ivo of Chartres, who led a protest against Philip I in the Bertrada affair which culminated in a sentence of excommunication by the pope at Clermont in 1095, continued by Gratian in his *Decretum* about 1140 and Peter Lombard in his *Sentences* before 1160, and subsequently by a series of decretal letters by Alexander III.

The success of the canonists in securing the general acceptance of norms of marriage cannot be explained by any obvious agreement between lay interests and ecclesiastical ideals. The prohibition of divorce, the insistence on consent of the parties, and the condemnation of close-kin marriage all contradicted accepted practices, and there were innumerable clashes over marriage policies, for instance with successive French kings. Undoubtedly, pious laymen were attracted by a doctrine which saw them as an order marked by the sacrament of matrimony for the service of God in the world. There was also an element of cynical compromise. The degrees of prohibition were drawn so widely that many marriages were made within them, and as a result marriages could be dissolved at the will of the parties on a plea that they were improperly contracted. A theory which excluded close-kin marriage and divorce therefore coexisted with a practice which admitted both, and the frequent complaints that lawyers made their fortunes out of the break-up of marriages make it clear that contemporaries were well aware of the situation.

[28] G. Duby, *Knight, Lady, and Priest*, 127–30.
[29] F. Barlow, *The English Church 1066–1154* (London, 1979), 168–9.

Strangely, the idea of marriage formulated during the twelfth century was a long way from the teaching of the Scriptures. It consisted rather of Biblical elements shaped by the thought of the Fathers and by new perceptions recently introduced. It was based on three affirmations. The first was that marriage is indissoluble. Provided that the marriage had been valid in the first place, there were no circumstances in which it was right to put away a partner and marry another. Divorce in the modern sense was impossible in law and morality. The permanence of marriage was in line with earlier canon law, but the fully developed doctrine went well beyond that of the past in its rigour and consistency. Never before had there been such a review of possible grounds for divorce (insanity, sterility, misrepresentation of social status) ending in the refusal to countenance any of them. The 'Matthaean exception' of adultery was explained as permitting separation but not remarriage.[30] Moreover, indissolubility was linked with the Pauline doctrine that marriage is a sacrament which 'means Christ and the church' (Eph. 5: 32). Plainly, if this is its significance, it would be absurd to permit the break-up of the union. Gratian expressed the idea clearly: 'As long as life lasts a certain conjugal bond remains, which neither separation nor coupling with another can destroy; just as the apostate soul, withdrawing so to speak from marriage to Christ, even when it has lost its faith does not lose the sacrament of faith which it received in the font of regeneration.'[31]

The second principle was that marriage was created by the consent of man and wife. The necessity of consent had been taught by Roman law, and with the revival of legal studies at Bologna writers became aware of Ulpian's dictum that 'marriage is not made by intercourse but by consent'. Canonists went much further, however, in insisting on full and free consent as a constituting element in marriage. The consent theory received its extreme formulation in the Paris theologians, and notably in Hugh of St Victor and Peter Lombard, who declared that 'the effective cause of marriage is consent'.[32] Under Alexander III the papacy adopted the theory, except on one or two points, in a thoroughgoing way. No one could be married against his or her will, and a promise entered into by

---

[30] This was how the words of Christ in Matt. 5: 32 were interpreted: 'every one who divorces his wife, except on the ground of inchastity, makes her an adultress.'

[31] Gratian, *Decr.* C. XXXII, q. 7, c. 28 (1147).

[32] Peter Lombard, *Sentences* iv.27.3 (PL 192.910). So also Innocent III in Greg. IX, *Decretals*, X IV.1.25 (670).

children had no validity—an important ruling in view of the use of child marriage in pursuit of political advantage or property.[33] The only ceremony required was a profession of intent before witnesses: 'I, A. take thee, B. to wife.' Alexander and subsequent popes urged, as a matter of discipline, that vows should be sworn at a public ceremony, but he conceded that nothing was strictly necessary except the promises of the couple. Religious ceremonies and even the presence of witnesses were in the last resort optional extras. This formulation had the advantage of accepting the validity of marriages contracted according to a great variety of local customs, but it achieved this within an extreme doctrine of consent which had no basis in Scripture, went far beyond the teaching of the civil law, and shifted the responsibility for the union from the families to the couple themselves.

The third principle governing the new marriage system was the prohibition of matrimony within a wide group of blood relations. Earlier canon law defined this as the seventh degree of consanguinity, but there were two systems of computation. Under Roman law grades were calculated by counting up to the common ancestor and back again, so that cousins would be related in the fourth degree. The Germanic practice was to count by generations, cousins thus being in the second degree of consanguineity. The question of computation was discussed by Peter Damian in *De Gradibus Parentele* and then regulated by Alexander II. His decision was cited at length by Gratian.[34] Alexander found for the calculation by generations, which had the effect of including a vast range within the seven prohibited degrees. These inevitably extended far beyond recorded family links and, if taken seriously, would have made it hard for the aristocracy to find wives. The rule could not have been enforced, and in 1215 the Fourth Lateran Council limited the prohibition to the first four degrees. Even this was far wider than the incest bars imposed by the Bible or accepted in modern society, but at least it was within manageable limits.

Permanence, consent, and the prohibition of marriage within the kin were the three foundations of the new law of matrimony. Gratian, Peter Lombard, and Alexander III thought of themselves as reviving the teaching of the Scriptures and the ancient canons, but the traditional *dicta* had to be fashioned into a consistent legal system

[33] Greg IX, *Decretals*, X IV.2.5 and 8 (673–6).
[34] Gratian, *Decr.* C. XXXV, q. 5, c. 2 (1271–4).

which could be enforced by the courts, and this in itself introduced some major innovations. For the first time the courts of western Europe were applying a law which excluded the possibility of divorce and remarriage; and it became accepted that marriage, being one of the seven sacraments, creates a relationship which cannot be destroyed. It is not clear whether an attempt was being made to to give marriage a more human face. The theory of consent was being stated in terms which tended to weaken the hold of the family, but can we conclude from this that canonists and theologians were striking a blow for human dignity? To believe so is not absurd: this was a time which valued individual choice, as for example in the recruitment of mature candidates by the new monastic orders, and there are several signs of a more humane approach. Hugh of St Victor and Peter Lombard wrote of marriage as a 'union of minds' and a 'conjugal society', and when Gratian and Alexander III spoke of 'marital affection', they may have had the same idea, although in the civil lawyers the phrase probably only meant an intention to fulfil the duties of the married state. The French church adopted early in the century a form of marriage which expressed the consent theory. It took place in the church porch, and included solemn questions about the existence of impediments, especially relationship within the forbidden degrees. These were followed by the contract between the parties and the giving of a ring and a blessing. It was the direct ancestor of the marriage service which is familiar today. The affirmative view of marriage was subsequently stated in the numerous thirteenth-century sermons on the topic, which presented it as ordained by God in paradise, honoured by the presence of Christ at Cana in Galilee, and as being the first established of religious orders. The reality was very far from that imagined by some modern historians, of a 'virulent hostility to marriage' in the teaching of the medieval church.[35]

iv. *Commercial Morality: the Question of Interest and Usury*

The ethics governing marriage and charity applied to a very wide section of society, for it was assumed that all laymen would be married and all rich laymen would care for the poor. It was more characteristic of this period to discuss the norms, not for people in

---

[35] For the teaching of the sermons, see D. d'Avray, 'The Gospel of the Marriage Feast of Cana', *SCH* Subsidia 4 (1985), 207–24.

general, but for particular social groups. The first positive affirmation of the duties of knights appears in the work of the Gregorian Bonizo of Sutri, who defines their duties as 'to obey their lords, not to seize booty, not to spare their lives in protecting their lord, and to fight to the death for the good of the commonwealth, to suppress heretics and schismatics, to defend the poor and widows and orphans, not to violate their sworn faith nor ever to swear falsely to their lords'. A generation later the *Elucidarium* of Honorius had a chapter 'on the various estates of the laity', but this was still negative in its ideas of the lay state, and ended with the conclusion, 'it seems that there are few who are saved'.[36]

The church faced the development of a commercial economy with initial hostility. The Bible originated in a rural society where the principal concern was to prevent the exploitation of the poor, and the late Roman Empire had been opposed to entrepreneurial values. Twelfth-century writers were familiar with Leo I's view that 'it is difficult for sin not to intervene in transactions between sellers and buyers', and with the proposition that 'a merchant is rarely or never able to please God'.[37] Early councils had prohibited clergy from the practice of usury, citing the psalmist's description of the righteous man, 'he who does not put out his money at interest' (Ps. 15: 5). The initial impact of the revival of the cities was to cause ecclesiastical authorities to sharpen these condemnations of merchandise and usury, and to extend them to all profit-making activities. Avarice was promoted to be the gravest of all vices, 'the root of all evil' as Peter Damian quoted from 1 Timothy 6: 10. Merchants were thought to have little chance of salvation, because their profit comes from fraud, lies, and selfishness.[38] Usury was repeatedly equated with theft. Gratian preserved the traditional condemnations and treated buying and selling for profit as usury, and Eugenius III and Alexander III condemned as usurious the practice of mortgage, which allowed the lender to retain an estate and its revenues until the loan was repaid. The Third Lateran Council in 1179 took the important step of prohibiting the laity, and not only the clergy, from the practice of usury—yet one more example of the hierarchy's determination to extend Christian moral standards throughout

---

[36] E. Perels (ed.), *Bonizo, Liber de Vita Christiana*, iii.28, pp. 248–9; Honorius, *Elucidarium* ii, Y. Lefèvre, *L'Elucidarium et les lucidaires* (Paris, 1954), 427–9.

[37] Cited Gratian, *Decr.* de pen. D. V, c. 2 (1240) and Ia pars D. LXXXVIII, c. 11 (308).

[38] Peter Damian, ep.i.15 (PL 144.234B); Honorius, *Elucidarium* ii, Lefèvre, *L'Elucidarium et les lucidaires*, 428.

society.[39] In the middle of the twelfth century the attitude of authority fitted the modern interpretation of the medieval church as inherently hostile to economic enterprise and the growth of capitalism.

Usury continued to be condemned throughout the Middle Ages. The taking of unlawful interest upon a *mutuum* or loan remained an offence whose gravity placed it in the direct jurisdiction of the bishop. Already in the generation after Gratian, however, usury was being redefined so as to permit interest in normal commercial transactions. The decretists Rufinus and Huguccio took the first steps in defining circumstances in which it was legitimate to make a charge for loans, and by the time of Hostiensis at the end of our period the number of exceptions had grown to thirteen, including recompense for damage sustained by the creditor through the non-availability of his money and compensation for the risks he was taking. Co-operative enterprises and associations, which Gratian had included within the prohibition of usury, were easily defined so as to avoid the implication that there was a direct loan at interest from one partner to another. Although the circle of Peter the Chanter was engaged in a vigorous campaign against usury around the year 1200, these scrupulous moralists accepted some of the qualifications which were being introduced. Another important step was the issue of Urban III's decretal *Consuluit*.[40] For the first time this quoted Luke 6: 35: 'lend, expecting nothing in return'. Although this is a stringent rule it located the sin in the intention of the lender and was frequently cited in support of the contention that there is no offence in straightforward commercial transactions. It thus reflected the new values of an age which stressed intention as an important measure of morality and which provided the confessional as a remedy. The taking of gain, since it lay in the conscience of the financier, had become a matter for the confessional rather than the courts, a sin which could be purged by restoration or by charitable works, and even (as the doctrine of purgatory offered a further opportunity) remedied after death. Among medieval thinkers the merchant rarely achieved the dignity of the priest, the utility of the craftsman, or the honesty of the peasant, but the shameful trade of usurer was now limited to a group of pawnbrokers and money-lenders who manifestly exploited the unfortunate. The capitalist could hope for

---

[39] Third Lateran can. 25 (Alberigo 199).
[40] Greg. IX, *Decretals*, V.19.10 (814).

salvation as long as he arranged his affairs wisely. All he needed was a good confessor.

v. *Chivalry*

The emergence of chivalry is the best-known instance of the impact of the church's thinking upon secular society, and there is no doubt that the old ethic of the Germanic warrior underwent profound changes in this period. Familiar literary descriptions such as that in Chaucer's *Canterbury Tales* suggest that a simple ideal of the perfect, gentle knight became a norm for the aspirations of warriors, but the reality in the twelfth century was a great deal more complex. Out of developing social conditions there came new ideas both among the warriors themselves and among the clergy. There was much interplay between the two patterns of thought, but it may be helpful to consider them separately.

In Chapter 2. iv I remarked upon the emergence of the castle as one of the most important social and military changes of the period. With the weakening of royal leadership and of the general levy of freemen, the household warriors based on castles were the most effective force. The warrior (*miles*) began to be contrasted with the peasant (*rusticus*), whose military significance was rapidly diminishing. At the same time technical developments were making the cavalry the dominant force on the battlefield. By 1100 the heavy lance had replaced the spear, and a Greek writer could remark with awe that 'a Frank on horseback would go through the walls of Babylon'.[41] The word *miles* already in eleventh-century France was used for a horseman since he had now become the élite warrior. In classical Latin it had meant a footman, and the French *chevalier* or German *Ritter* were more exact terms. For a time, the *milites* formed a middle group between the nobles and peasants, but progressively the nobles began to call themselves knights. The transition took a long time, and both usages can be documented in the abundant literature of the First Crusade; but by the late twelfth century the identification of nobility and knighthood was universal. Although there was a vast social difference between a great lord and one of his household knights, a cameraderie of arms grew up between them, for they were fighting with similar weapons as well as living in one closed community. Initially, and throughout most of the twelfth

[41] Anna Comnena, *Alexiad*, tr. E. R. A. Sewter (Harmondsworth, 1969), 416.

century, chivalry was a profession, not a class: a privileged profession whose skills were highly prized by the nobility and whose equipment was expensive. The granting of arms to a knight came to be an increasingly elaborate ceremony. The young Prince Louis of France (later Louis VI) was 'ordained' to knighthood in 1098, and in 1128, on a particularly splendid occasion, Henry I of England knighted Geoffrey of Anjou and thirty of his followers with him.

In the eyes of some of its practitioners, chivalry also should be a civilized profession. The romance *Alexandre* (*c.*1130) presented in Alexander's education a new ideal which combined *clergie* and *chevalerie*, for Alexander studied the seven liberal arts as well as knightly skills. No doubt he was a special case, but knights increasingly came to value good manners and the ability to compose songs and to engage in the elegant arts of love. There was thus an opening for churchmen to instruct them in higher ideals, but these aspirations were not universal in the twelfth century. They are represented in the romances such as those of Chrétien de Troyes, which were probably more popular among the ladies in the chamber than among the warriors in the hall. The examination of a group of *chansons de geste* from the later twelfth century reveals that they contain few of these more elegant aspirations, and that the values which they esteemed were the more obvious military ones of courage and prowess.[42] The poets who were writing for the laity had different views about true chivalry; Bertrand of Born's glorification of violence may be a deliberate contradiction of Bernard of Ventadour's belief in the primacy of love.

Towards the knights, as towards the merchants, the official teaching of the church originally reflected almost total hostility. Traditionally the defence of the Christian people was the responsibility of the anointed king, and the emergence of an élite of warriors was regarded with disapproval, especially as so many of them maintained themselves by levies upon the monasteries and the poor. The assumption was that the only road to salvation for a warrior was to become a monk. Geoffrey III of Sémur, brother of Abbot Hugh, expressed this clearly in 1088:

I, Geoffrey of Sémur, have heard the Lord say in the gospel, 'whoever does not renounce all that he has cannot be my disciple' (Luke xiv.33), and recognize the enormity and the profound abyss of my sins. I have chosen

---

[42] J. Flori, 'La notion de chevalerie dans les chansons de geste', *MA* 81 (1975), 211–44, 407–45.

rather to be lowly in the house of God than to dwell in the tents of the wicked, and having taken off the belt of worldly service (*militie secularis*) in which I gravely offended God, to submit myself . . . to the service of God, whose service is perfect freedom.[43]

The profound opposition to men of violence, which treated the knights as the medieval equivalent of gangsters, continued for a long time: the revealing pun *militia–malitia* is found in many twelfth-century writers. But the pope and bishops needed the knights. In France it was necessary to come to terms with the failure of royal government, which had led to an increasing level of violence, and in the empire the Roman Church was looking for forces which it could use against imperial policy. Before the end of the eleventh century there had been three distinct attempts to enlist the knights in God's service. The initiation of the Peace of God coincided with the early development of the new-style *milites* and helped to give rise to the idea of a knighthood which would refrain from violence against the weak and would serve the cause of justice. A much more specific appeal to the military classes was Gregory VII's concept of a militia of St Peter in which the nobility were enlisted to defend the Roman Church against the emperor, although here we are probably still dealing with a rather more old-fashioned type of military class, for the distinctive features of French *chevalerie* were only slowly entering Germany and Italy. We have already noticed that in Gregorian circles Bonizo of Sutri produced the first list of the duties of knights, which included the suppression of heretics and schismatics. Immensely the most influential for the future was the appeal to the knights to participate in the crusades. Guibert of Nogent, reflecting in 1108 on the significance of the First Crusade, saw it as the point at which God had lifted His embargo on the military order and opened the door to salvation:

In our time God has instituted holy warfare so that the knightly order (*ordo equestris*) and the unsettled populace, who used to be engaged like the pagans of old in slaughtering one another, should find a new way of deserving salvation. No longer are they obliged to leave the world and choose a monastic way of life, as used to be the case, or some religious profession, but in their accustomed liberty and habit, by performing their own office, they may in some measure achieve the grace of God.[44]

This way of thinking is already implicit in the use during the crusade

---

[43] J. Richard, *Le cartulaire de Marcigny-sur-Loire* (Dijon, 1957), no. 15, pp. 15–17.
[44] Guibert, *Gesta Dei per Francos* i, RHC Occ. IV.124.

itself of *milites Christi* as a standard term for the members of the expedition. An expression which until then had been the monopoly of monks had been extended to knights, and the idea was further developed in the foundation of the Templars and the pamphlet *In Praise of the New Militia* by Bernard of Clairvaux.

The enlistment of knights for the Peace of God, the militia of St Peter, and the crusades provided a basis for a wider programme of sanctifying chivalry. Long before, liturgical forms had been provided for the blessing of arms when they were delivered to the anointed king, and by 1100 these had been adapted for use in the making of a knight. We do not know how often this was accompanied by religious ceremonies. A comparison of the wholly secular festivities at the knighting of Geoffrey of Anjou in 1128 with the ritual prescribed by John of Salisbury in 1159 suggests that those were the years of crucial change, but this may be misleading, for John's description looks like an elaborate programme which need not have been put into practice. The recognition of knighthood as an 'order', which we have already noticed, gave it religious as well as social status. Ideas of ethical conduct were formulated for the knights. Their duties were first described by Bonizo, then by Honorius, and the authors of romances were usually clerks themselves and often had a training in the schools, which influenced the way they thought about chivalry. By 1200 a knight could choose from a variety of models of chivalry, some of them strongly influenced by Christianity. Yet the opposition to violence remained, and with it an ambiguity in the church's attitude, reflected in the widespread dislike of the order of Templars as a mixture of warfare and religion, and in the advice given by the hermit Stephen of Muret:

It shows admirable knowledge, and is very pleasing to God, when a man who is involved in an evil enterprise restrains himself from evil. It can be done like this. If a knight is setting out on an expedition for the sake of his secular lord, to whom he cannot refuse obedience, if he wishes to be faithful to God, let him first speak thus in his heart: 'Lord God, I will go on this expedition, but I promise that I will be your knight there, wanting nothing in it except to be obedient to you, to eliminate evil and to seek what is good on every occasion as much as I can.'[45]

The way of salvation was open; but knighthood, like merchandise, was never completely baptized.

---

[45] Stephen of Grandmont, *Liber de Doctrina*, lxiii.1, ed. J. Becquet, *Scriptores Ordinis Grandimontensis*, CC(CM) (*1968*), 33.

14

DISSENT

The last few chapters have been concerned with the building up of Christendom, that is with the growing consciousness of participation in a society directed by obedience to God and regulated by his representatives, the clergy. This development had a corollary in increasing hostility to groups who were seen not to be part of Christendom. Although to our eyes Christian society was more securely organized in 1200 than it had been in 1050, it was also much more aware of the threats which were posed by Islam, Judaism, heresy, and sorcery. These forces were 'demonized', seen as a conspiracy by the devil to destroy the faith. Sometimes they were literally thought to be conspirators, an idea which can be found as early as Raoul Glaber's report that the Jews of Orléans had advised Caliph Hakim to destroy the church of the Holy Sepulchre in 1009; more usually they were all seen as servants of the devil, and features of one group were transferred quite wrongly to the others. This chapter will be concerned with the emergence of religious opposition within western European society.

i. *The Beginnings of Heresy (1050–1140)*

'The catholic faith has fought and has crushed, conquered and annihilated the blasphemies of the heretics, so that either there are no more heretics or they do not dare to show themselves.' The triumph of catholicism seemed complete and was celebrated in these words in a sermon of Bishop Herbert Losinga of Norwich (1091–1119).[1] Scholars still had a theoretical knowledge of the great heresies of the patristic period listed by Isidore of Seville, but were ill-informed as to their content, and it was so long since they had been living movements that the word 'heresy' no longer had a clear meaning. The heresy of which most was heard in the period of papal reform had little to do with erroneous belief: 'simony was the only survivor

---

[1] Herbert of Losinga, Sermon 14, ed. E. M. Goulburn and H. Symonds (Oxford, 1878), 418.

of the ancient heresies'.[2] The identification made by Gregory I
between heresy and simony was decisive in the history of both
concepts, and the standard use of 'heresy' in the late eleventh century
was in polemic against bishops who either practised simony or
supported the imperialist pope.

Even apart from this problem of terminology, the profile of heresy
in the first half of our period is a strange one. Before 1050 we can
identify several scattered groups whose ideas brought them into
conflict with authority, such as those at Orléans in 1022 and
Monforte in 1028. There is little sign of communication between
them, and with the emergence of the papal reform movement we
enter a period where the hierarchy largely reserved the term 'heresy'
for the champions of simony, so that the old sort of heretical groups
vanish from the records for a period. The Gregorian movement itself
was the cradle which nursed the emergent heretical ideas of the
twelfth century, for several of its features anticipated later dissenting
programmes. One was the rejection of the ministry of simoniacal
priests, which was such an important element in reforming policy.
The trouble which this could cause was shown in the fierce divisions
at Milan between the *Patarini*, supported by the papacy, and the
clergy and laity who adhered to the traditional values of the Milanese
church; and in Flanders by the case of Ramihrd of Esquerchin in
1077. Ramihrd was a preacher from the region of Douai who was
questioned 'about the catholic faith' before Bishop Gerard II of
Cambrai. His answers were satisfactory, but he refused to receive
communion because the clergy present were incriminated in simony.
He was thereupon denounced as a heresiarch and burned by the mob
with the co-operation of some of the bishop's officers. Ramihrd had
opened a division among the authorities: Gregory VII saw his
rejection of the sacraments as obedience to the policy of boycotting
polluted clergy, but the local church and people saw him as a
heretic.[3] Another feature of Gregorian policy which was a source of
later dissenting movements was the advocacy of the 'apostolic life'. It
could involve itinerant preaching and the creation of new forms of
community. It was often possible for a *modus vivendi* to be reached
with the hierarchy through the acceptance of a recognized form of
monastic life, but some enthusiasts persevered in their eccentricity.
At Hérival in Lotharingia a certain Engelbald founded a community

---

[2] *Chronicon Affligense* 1, MGH SS IX.407.
[3] R. I. Moore, *The Birth of Popular Heresy* (London, 1975), nos. 6–7.

where 'against the custom of the church he decreed that no church should be built there, no mass celebrated and no communion administered, nor should psalms be sung according to the rite of the church'. This was a decidedly unusual version of catholic worship, and in spite of the efforts of two successive bishops of Toul, Engelbald maintained it until shortly before his death about 1110.[4] It appears that the Gregorian programme provided an umbrella under which a variety of reforming groups could shelter, and there were broad similarities of structure among them. All tended to combine a new sense of community, an ascetic master or leader, and a message based on an attempt to restore the church to New Testament simplicity. In this sense we may agree with Brian Stock in seeing them as text-based groups, founded on a knowledge of the Scriptures, although at first this knowledge was probably mediated through the master, who was very often a priest or monk.[5] It is significant that in the early twelfth century attacks by the authorities were almost always directed against a 'heresiarch', a word which is more common in the sources than 'heretic'. It was the erring master with his followers, rather than an alternative programme of belief, which originally roused the anxieties of authority.

It is difficult to be sure whether the official attacks on new teaching, which became evident in northern France about 1100, were motivated by genuine novelties in the message of the dissenting leaders. Probably this was an element in the situation: Robert of Arbrissel, for example, disquieted even bishops who in general admired him by the originality of his ministry to women and the vehemence of his attack on clerical corruption. The growth of urban communities in northern France provided a ready audience for criticism of this type and opened France to the sort of tensions which already existed in the Italian cities a generation earlier. The Gregorian revolution also was inherently unstable, for the popes were at once inciting people to reject corrupt priests and claiming the direction of ecclesiastical affairs for the clergy. It is not surprising that preachers such as Henry of Lausanne complained, for example, of the growing clericalization of marriage. Soon after 1100 we find that the heresiarchs were securing an enthusiastic following by attacking

[4] J. Musy, 'Mouvements populaires et hérésies au XIe siècle en France', *Revue Historique* 253 (1975), esp. 68–70.

[5] B. Stock, *The Implications of Literacy* (Princeton, 1983), 88–151. For the question as a whole, see R. I. Moore, 'New Sects and Secret Meetings: Association and Authority in the Eleventh and Twelfth Centuries', *SCH* 23 (1986), 47–68.

accepted features of catholic belief, or at least (and it is hard to be sure which is the correct statement of the case) that such attacks were being ascribed to them by hostile propaganda. Tanchelm of Antwerp (died *c.*1115) provides us with a good example of a Gregorian who became a threat to the hierarchy. He seems to have begun in the service of a Gregorian sympathizer, Count Robert II of Flanders, and his message was rigorist: 'He said that the efficacy of the sacraments proceeded from the merits and holiness of the ministers . . . This blasphemer urged the people not to receive the sacraments of the body and blood of Christ, and not to pay their tithes to the ministers of the church.' Our sources add that Tanchelm took to demagogic excesses, including golden raiment, a large armed escort, ceremonies of marriage to the Virgin, and the distribution of his bath water to drink, but these stories (even if true) can be paralleled from other popular preachers, and they do not prove that his teaching was bizarre.[6] Another teacher with an anti-sacramental message was Henry of Lausanne, a former monk and a man of some learning. In 1116 he came to Le Mans where in the absence of its scholarly Bishop Hildebert he 'turned the people against the clergy with such fury that they refused to sell them anything . . . and treated them like gentiles and publicans'. At this stage, Henry may have simply been an anti-clerical reformer like Erlembald of Milan before or Arnold of Brescia after him, but more radical views were beginning to circulate in southern France, where Pope Calixtus II at the council of Toulouse in 1119 condemned those who 'reject the sacrament of the body and blood of Christ, the baptism of children, the priesthood and other ecclesiastical orders, and condemn the ties of legitimate matrimony'.[7] Henry of Lausanne, having been expelled from Le Mans, preached in a series of southern cities, and we last hear of him in Toulouse in 1145. By this time his teaching was similar to that condemned at the council. He may have been influenced in a more radical direction by Peter of Bruis, the priest of a country parish in the Hautes-Alpes who was expelled about 1119 and for the next twenty years preached in southern France until he was burned, apparently in a popular tumult. Peter rejected infant baptism, the mass and prayers for the departed. He recognized that Christ had offered mass before his Passion, but held that he had made no provision for its continuance; and he taught that it was wrong to

---

[6] Moore, *Birth of Popular Heresy*, nos. 8–9.
[7] Ibid., nos. 11 ff; C. of Toulouse can. 3 (Mansi xxi.226–7).

reverence the cross, which was the shameful instrument of Christ's suffering. By this time the threat of unorthodox teaching had become serious enough to require attention, and the first substantial treatise against it, *Contra Petrobrusianos*, was composed by Peter the Venerable about 1139, to be followed a few years later by a preaching campaign by Bernard of Clairvaux.

The source of these new ideas was partly the improving level of education, which made it possible for clergy to make up their own minds about the meaning of the Scriptures and to apply rigidly the Gregorian policy of condemning the sacraments of unworthy ministers and glorifying the poverty of the apostolic church. It was paradoxically easy to move from an ultra-Gregorian position to the denial of hierarchical authority when this was perceived as failing in its duty of uprooting simony. The heresies of the early twelfth century are thus explicable in terms of the development of western ideas, but there is also a possibility of eastern influence. In the Byzantine empire there were organized churches structured round a spiritual élite and based on a dualist mythology which rejected the world as inherently evil. There is no doubt that ideas were entering the west from this source from 1140 onwards, but historians have long argued whether they can be found earlier. Only one account between 1050 and 1140 is unambiguous: Guibert of Nogent's description of a group near Soissons about 1114 makes clear their radical dualism, but it is possible that Guibert had wrongly identified them as Manichees and was writing up their beliefs from the pages of St Augustine. Peter of Bruis is a more likely connection, with his systematic and reasoned rejection of traditional sacramental practice and his objection to the use of the crucifix, but his views could have been drawn from an idiosyncratic reading of the New Testament. The connections are not strong enough to justify us in assigning the widely scattered anti-sacramentalism of the period to eastern influence, but the situation was to change rapidly with the definite arrival of Balkan heresies just after 1140.

Up to this point the hierarchy had taken little repressive action. There had been few decrees or treatises: Toulouse 1119 and *Contra Petrobrusianos* are almost the only ones. The very few burnings were the result of the action of the populace, either against the wishes of the bishop's officers (Soissons 1114) or with their collusion (Ramihrd 1077). Teachers as influential as Bishop Wazo of Liège and Abbot Bernard of Clairvaux condemned the execution of heretics. Gratian quoted authorities both for and against the punishment of heretics, and at first sight he appears to support the use of force: 'when Jerome denied that the church should persecute any one, that should not be taken to mean that the church may persecute no one at all, but that the church should persecute no one unjustly'.[8] But Gratian was thinking mainly of simony and of the need for the church to defend itself against it. The repression of those with deviant opinions was not at the forefront of his mind; nor were contemporaries keenly aware of it. While enthusiasts of orthodoxy were anxious to control theological innovation by such men as Berengar of Tours or Peter Abelard they had little idea of the investigation and control of popular opinion. It is sometimes supposed that in the century after 1140 the church moved from persuasion to coercion.[9] But before then bishops were not very good at either, and they had little thought of doing more than resist direct attack. If they were to move towards a serious effort to control opinion, new methods of preaching, controversy, and repression all had to be developed.

ii. *Cathars and Waldensians (1140–1200)*

In about 1143 Everwin, provost of Steinfeld near Cologne, wrote to Bernard of Clairvaux about some heretics in the region. There were two sects, one of which held views we have already encountered, condemning infant baptism, the mass, and prayers for the departed. The other group struck a new note. They were aware that their beliefs had been preserved in Greece; they not only rejected infant baptism, but replaced the sacraments by the laying on of hands; and they abstained from meat and all food produced by intercourse. They observed a division between 'elect' and 'hearers'. These features were characteristic of Balkan dualism. Everwin's description is the first clear account of the Catharist heresy, to adopt the name by which it is usually known. He knew nothing of its underlying theology or mythology: either the adherents did not know it themselves or they were concealing it. There is a mention at Liège of a similar group which also had elect and hearers and taught that 'marriage leads to damnation'.[10] By the 1160s the new believers were well established near Cologne, where about 1163 Eckbert of Schönau

---

[8] Gratian, *Decr.* C. XXIII, q. 4, dictum ante c. 37 (916).
[9] R. Manselli, 'De la *persuasio* à la *coercitio*', CF 6 (1971), 175–97.
[10] Moore, *Birth of Popular Heresy*, nos. 22–3, giving the date 1144/5. G. Despy (see bibliography) has argued for 1135.

preached the *Sermons against the Cathars* which provide the first coherent account of their beliefs. Although some of his ideas may be borrowed from St Augustine's account of the Manichees, he had a good personal knowledge of the sect. He discovered that the refusal to eat meat was based on the conviction that 'all flesh is made by the devil' and that they believed that Christ 'did not truly have human flesh, but a kind of simulated flesh'. He explained that 'in Germany they are called *cathars*, in Flanders *piphles* and in France *tisserands* because of their connection with weaving'.[11] The *piphles* or *publicani*, assuming these to be the same group, appeared at Arras in 1163, in England shortly afterwards, at Vézelay in 1167 and at Reims soon after 1176. It is tempting to think that their variant names were derived from the Paulician movement in the Balkans, but that is only a guess. It has been suggested that the spread of heresy and the emergence of stable communities in place of the heresiarchs of the early years of the century represents an 'organizational' phase not unlike the growth of structured monastic orders after the first hermit experiments.[12]

It was in the south of France, however, that Catharism was to become established. Henry of Lausanne and Peter of Bruis had won considerable support there in spite of a preaching tour against them by Bernard of Clairvaux in 1145. Nothing is known of the relationship between these earlier heretics and the Cathars who succeeded them, but by 1165 Cathar influence was so alarming that the archbishop of Narbonne held a council at Lombers, near Albi, to question suspected heretics. The meeting had little success. Shortly afterwards (the precise date is uncertain, but may be 1174) the Cathars received a visitation from Nicetas, an emissary of the Dragovitsan church in the Balkans. He was received at an assembly at St Félix de Caraman in the presence of three Cathar bishops, and the meeting agreed to appoint three more. It may have been Nicetas's mission which introduced into western Catharism a more radical dualism: the creation of the physical world was no longer seen as the result of the Fall, but as the act of an evil god, the equal and opposite of the good deity. In 1177 Count Raymond V of Toulouse reported that the heretics 'worst of all, have introduced two principles'.[13] Meanwhile, by the time of Nicetas' visit, the Cathars

[11] Moore, *Birth of Popular Heresy*, no. 29.
[12] Moore, 'New Sects and Secret Meetings', *SCH* 23 (1986) 57–8.
[13] Eckbert of Schönau in 1163 attributed absolute dualism to the Cathars of Cologne, but this may have sprung from his identification of them with the Manichees in St Augustine.

had already established themselves in Italy. During the last quarter of the century their influence was moving southwards through the peninsula: by the 1170s there was a group at Orvieto, where in 1199 its sympathizers murdered Peter Parenzo, the catholic prefect appointed to control it. Catholics were lamenting that 'cities, suburbs, villages and castles are full of false prophets of this kind'.[14]

The term most often used for the Cathars in southern France was Albigensians, and in Lombardy *Patarini*, thus continuing the old term used for the reformers who had been allies of Gregory VII, although it is far from clear that there was any link between them. The Cistercian Caesarius of Heisterbach recalled about 1220 that 'the error of the Albigensians grew so quickly that in a short length of time it had infected as many as a thousand cities, and if it had not been reduced by the swords of the faithful, I am sure it would have corrupted all Europe'.[15] In parts of Languedoc and Italy it had secured its position as an alternative religion. Its adherents could meet with impunity and its leaders or 'perfects', readily identifiable by their black robe, travelled widely and without much danger of arrest. In Languedoc they were not firmly established in the larger cities— Narbonne remained almost wholly catholic and in Toulouse the heretics were a small minority—but they had the sympathy of the lesser nobility. In small towns in the lands of the count of Toulouse or the Trencavel vicomtes of Béziers and Carcassonne a great part of the population was infected with heresy. At Verfeil, it was said, few died without receiving the Cathar 'baptism' or *consolamentum*; at Laurac, the whole population turned out to hear and revere the perfects. In Italy the heretics appear to have been firmly based in the cities. Although they had some friends among the nobility, their support came mostly from the suburbs, working-class areas where the friars would also make their settlements.

The distinction between perfects and hearers was fundamental to the Cathar community. The perfects had been admitted to the *consolamentum* or laying on of hands, and thereafter were bound by the laws of perfection: they lived austerely, refraining from sexual intercourse and abstaining from meat and milk, which were the fruits of coition. Although there were horror stories about obscene practices in private gatherings it is likely that the perfects did live in purity and discipline. James Capelli, a Franciscan observer of the sect

---

[14] Bonacursus, *Manifestatio heresis Catharorum*, PL 204.778B.
[15] Caesarius, *Dialogus miraculorum*, v.21, ed. J. Strange (Cologne, 1851), i.300–3.

in Italy, later admired their way of life and the love which bound them together. The hearers lived in ordinary society, with the obligation to receive visiting perfects and perform the solemn reverence or *melioramentum* before them. It was the aim of the hearers to receive the *consolamentum* on their death-bed. The movement therefore offered the prospect of a normal life, combined with an élite whose position rested on personal sanctity. The hearers saw themselves as followers of the 'pure' (Greek *katharoi*, hence Cathars). This purist approach to religion had its perils: there was no place for repentance after the *consolamentum* and it was held that a sinner could not 'console' others validly. Italian Catharism in particular fragmented into sections, each offering a rival *consolamentum* and paying anxious visits to the Balkans to be consoled anew. 'Hence', wrote a converted heretic about 1250, 'all Cathars labour under very great doubt and danger of soul.'[16] Many, although not all, adherents believed in two equal and opposite principles of good and evil, and had thus abandoned the fundamental catholic idea of monotheism. In their own eyes, however, their religion appeared as a pure and original version of Christianity, cleansed from the distortions introduced by the catholic clergy. They had little interest in the nicer points of theology and professed a spiritualized Christianity. A Cathar of Toulouse, who was engaged (as he thought) in a friendly conversation with a relative, explained that he was unsure whether there were two gods or not, but believed that 'nothing of these visible things is good'. He also believed that 'matrimony was prostitution', that capital punishment was murder, and 'that mass was not celebrated in the church up to the time of the blessed Sylvester, nor did the church own property up to that time'. This believer, Peter Garcias, had a Cathar father and Waldensian mother, and his views, with the mention of the ruin of the church at the time of its endowment by the Emperor Constantine and Pope Sylvester, represent an amalgam of the two systems which may not have been uncommon in southern society.[17]

The Waldensians had originated about 1174 with the conversion of Valdes, a rich citizen of Lyon. Unfortunately the accounts of this

---

[16] Rainerius Sacconi, *Summa de Catharis*, 13, cited W. L. Wakefield and A. P. Evans, *Heresies of the High Middle Ages* (New York, 1969), 336.

[17] Testimony against Peter Garcias, tr. W. L. Wakefield, *Heresy, Crusade and Inquisition* (London, 1974), 242–9. This is a later report dated 1247, but it is likely that similar views were held in 1200.

conversion are late, and may be largely legendary.[18] Like Francis of Assisi thirty years later, Valdes resolved to undertake a ministry of poverty and preaching, and at the Third Lateran Council in 1179 he appeared before Alexander III, who is said to have welcomed his vow of voluntary poverty but forbidden him to preach except at the request of priests. The anxiety of authority was presumably the result of Valdes's lack of theological training: his knowledge of the Bible depended on vernacular translations, which he was active in commissioning. Shortly afterwards Abbot Henry of Clairvaux, as papal legate, secured an orthodox profession of faith from Valdes, who declared his intention to live in poverty and to obey the precepts of the gospel as commands. Soon the followers of Valdes were expelled from Lyon, apparently for unauthorized preaching, and at the council of Verona in 1184 the 'poor men of Lyon' were listed as a heretical sect and condemned for preaching without permission.[19] There followed a remarkable dispersion of Waldensian preachers. Before 1200 they had appeared at Béziers, Narbonne, Carcassonne, Toul, and Metz and had founded a group in Milan. We do not have an early Rule for the new society, but it seems that emphasis was placed on the dignity of the preachers, who observed apostolic poverty, and the basis of devotion was the vernacular Scriptures. Valdes had seen himself as an obedient son of the church, and this tradition was continued by Durand of Huesca, whose *Liber antiheresis*, directed mainly against the Cathars, was composed shortly after 1190. On the other hand the emphasis on the Bible led to the abandonment of priestly confession, prayers for the departed, and the taking of oaths, and there was a demand for sacraments from Waldensian ministers. The followers of Valdes, like the disciples of John Wesley many centuries later, slowly evolved away from the parent body to form a denomination of their own. The Lombard group took the lead in this and in 1205 they divided from their more conservative French brethren.

The proliferation of heresy presented the hierarchy with a new set

[18] The Laon account of the conversion is translated in Moore, *Birth of Popular Heresy*, no. 34, and the problems raised by the source are considered in M. D. Lambert, *Medieval Heresy* (London, 1977), 67–9 and 353–5. Stephen of Bourbon in the mid-thirteenth century ascribed Valdes's conversion to evangelical poverty to his reading of vernacular translations of 'many books of the Bible and many authorities of the saints'.

[19] But there are problems: the Verona decree is badly worded and may not be intended to condemn the 'poor men of Lyon', nor is it certain that preaching was the issue. Surprisingly there was no mention of preaching in Valdes's profession of faith. See G. Gonnet, 'Le cheminement des vaudois vers le schisme et l'hérésie (1174–1218)', *CCM* 19 (1976), 309–45.

of problems. It was difficult for a bishop to discover heretics, uncertain what was the proper procedure for examining them and hard to prevent itinerant preachers from moving on to deliver their message elsewhere. The pope's position was ambiguous, for in one sense he was the natural leader of resistance against heresy, but it was also his task to hear appeals against grievances. The Arras affair of 1162 and the case in 1175 of Lambert le Bègue, who had been expounding the vernacular Scriptures to his parishioners, illustrate the concern of both rival popes, Alexander III and the imperialist Calixtus III, to restrain the local powers. Inevitably, however, attitudes were changing, and in 1148 at the council of Reims Eugenius III issued a general anathema against the heretics of Gascony and Provence and condemned the followers of the Breton Eon de l'Étoile, a bizarre personality whom the council assumed, probably rightly, to be insane. At the council of Tours in 1163 Alexander was a little more precise about the procedure: heretics were to be excommunicated and separated from the community 'that when all the consolations of humanity are withdrawn they may be compelled to repent of their error'.[20] From this time secular and ecclesiastical authorities in northern Europe were working together against heresy. In England Henry II dealt with brutal efficiency with some immigrant *publicani* and followed his actions with a clause against them in the Assize of Clarendon 1166, the first anti-heretical legislation by a lay ruler for many centuries. In 1183–4 Archbishop William of Reims joined Count Philip of Flanders in ordering the burning of several heretics. The position was very different when the lay power was ineffective. In 1177 a letter from Raymond V of Toulouse to Abbot Henry of Clairvaux urged that it was necessary for the kings of France and England to intervene. This appeal was probably the origin of the preaching mission of Cardinal Peter of St Chrysogonus in Languedoc in 1178, and thus of canon 27 of the Third Lateran Council. It was directed against heretics and *routiers* (mercenaries) in southern France and it reaffirmed their exclusion from Christian fellowship. It also offered an indulgence and other crusading privileges to those who would take up arms—an important innovation.[21] The immediate practical consequences were slight.

Third Lateran had been addressed to the needs of Languedoc, and

---

[20] Council of Tours can. 4, Mansi xxi. 1178.
[21] Third Lateran can. 27 (Alberigo 200–1).

in 1184 it was followed by the council of Verona under Lucius III and Frederick Barbarossa, which was designed for the other critical region, Lombardy. Its decree *Ad abolendam* was in a sense the foundation of later legislation against heresy, because for the first time it formulated a procedure by bishops, who were to obtain sworn denunciations by laymen, and it demanded oaths from lay authorities to co-operate in the extirpation of heresies. It also formally condemned a list of modern heretics, to match the long-obsolete list in Isidore of Seville: Cathars, *Patarini*, Humiliati, Speronists, and the 'poor men of Lyon'. Movements with clearly unorthodox beliefs were condemned along with others which merely practised unauthorized preaching, and as a result enthusiasts of the apostolic life were separated from the church. The pressure of legislation continued after Verona: the bishop of Toul in 1192 demanded the arrest of Waldensians, the council of Montpellier 1195 re-enacted some of the Verona provisions for Languedoc, and the kingdom of Aragon imposed the death penalty for heresy. The actual effect of all this was not great, and the alienation of the Waldensians strengthened the force of the waves of heresy which were threatening southern France and Italy. By the end of the twelfth century little had been achieved by the hierarchy in the struggle against heresy.

iii. *Sorcery*

Heresy was one way of disobeying the commandments of God. Another was sorcery. The Ancient World had known a great variety of magic arts. There were astrologers who used the heavenly bodies to foretell the future; those who examined omens or texts (*sortes*) as an aid to prophecy or to discover lost goods; and others who claimed by their rites to affect the weather, win favour, or inflict damage. The subsequent history of magic was shaped by St Augustine's rejection of the entire body of its practices as impermissible for Christians. Having listed a wide variety of them, he concluded:

All such arts, belonging to superstition which is either trivial or harmful, and which is constituted on the basis of a vicious association of men and demons, indeed through a treaty of faithless and deceitful friendship, are to be competely repudiated and avoided by the Christian.[22]

The rejection is fundamental: magic arts derive their power from

---

[22] Augustine, *De Doctrina Christiana*, cited Gratian, *Decr.* C. XXVI, q. 2, c. 6 (1022).

negotiation with demons. The most influential teacher of the medieval world had given an unambiguous ruling. In the patristic and medieval discussion of magic, scepticism about its effectiveness was at most a secondary element; it was generally accepted that sorcerers could foretell the future, influence events and produce illusions, but their opponents said they did so by the power of the devil. Magic as a whole came to be known as *maleficium*, which originally meant 'ill-doing'.

We know only a little about the practice of magic between 1050 and 1250. Some of the descriptions were so strange that it has been thought that magicians only appeared in the fevered imaginations of their enemies, but modern study has established the existence of learned magic as a reality. In eleventh-century Italy it was already a subject for anecdotes and accusations. Anselm of Besate made it the centre-piece of his *Rhetorimachia* about 1050; a story grew about the magic arts of the learned Gerbert (Pope Sylvester II); and the synod of Brixen accused Gregory VII of practising magic which he had learned in a school which Gerbert had founded at Rome. With the twelfth century, scholars began to obtain access to Arabic magical treatises, and the increasing effectiveness of the courts of kings and princes provided patronage for people interested in magic and medicine (which, however distinguished its future, hardly had more scientific basis at this time than did sorcery). John of Salisbury in the *Policraticus* (1159) was disturbed by the practice of magic in the court, while anecdotes by Walter Map and Gervase of Tilbury testify to the courtiers' interest in the subject. By 1200 there was an abundance of magical texts available in the schools, and William of Auvergne was shortly to comment on the number he had encountered as a student at Paris. The tradition of learned magic can thus be traced from the stories of eleventh-century Italy, through growing attempts to make it a subject of study, to the serious practice of court magic in the thirteenth century. Viewed from the modern world, it was all an exercise in futility, but it was not at that time clear that magic had an insecure basis in comparison with medicine or psychology, which were also developing at the same time.

When Gratian or John of Salisbury discussed magic, what they had in mind was the learned practice of the fourth or fifth centuries. Gratian discarded from earlier collections of canons almost all texts which described Germanic practices, preserving only the *Canon episcopi*, which owed its retention to his erroneous belief that it had been issued by the early council of Ancyra.[23] Given the attention paid to learned magic, it is not surprising to find the emergence of a mixture between it and older popular superstitions. The wondrous women who in Germanic legend had the power of night-flight were now believed to fly with Diana or Herodias; and we occasionally hear of divination and augury being practised by the clergy. In whatever form, the magic of the countryside must also have survived throughout our period. It is recorded in traditional spells, in occasional mentions in sermons and later in the manuals of confessors from the end of the twelfth century onwards. Although the documentation is poor, we must assume the continuation of a living tradition of popular spells and magic, mixed with ideas derived from learned magic and from the ceremonies of the church.

As compared with other disciplines and practices, magic had a fatal flaw. The problem was not that it did not work, but that it worked only with the help of demons. This Augustinian position was affirmed by Hugh of St Victor, who in his *Didascalicon* denied magic any proper place in a scheme of learning: 'Sorcerers are those who . . . by the co-operation of the devils and by evil instinct perform wicked things.'[24] The reality was less cut and dried than these views suggest, because a simple equation of magic with demonic dealings could not in fact be sustained. Astrology depended on the observation of the heavenly bodies and received partial acceptance as a science, and several writers distinguished between rites which involved demonic converse and those which did not. These partial reservations were not enough to save magic. The prevailing view remained that of Augustine: magic was wrong because it enlisted the aid of demons.

The sorcerer came to be increasingly associated with other representatives of dissent, and witch, heretic, and Jew came to be confounded together as worshippers of demons and addicted to unnatural vice. The command of Exodus 22: 18, 'You shall not permit a sorceress (*malefica*) to live among you', was interpreted in the standard gloss as meaning that *heretics* were to be excommuni-

---

[23] Gratian, *Decr.* C. XXVI, q. 5, c. 12 (1030–1). The text first appeared just after 900 in Regino of Prüm, and is probably a Carolingian capitulary or an amalgam of extracts from capitularies.

[24] J. Taylor (tr.), *The Didascalicon of Hugh of S. Victor* (New York, 1961), vi.15 (p. 155). The fact that this section is a note appended by Hugh may indicate that interest in magic was quickly developing in educated circles after the completion of the work some time in the late 1120s.

cated. As early as the heresy of Orléans in 1022 it was alleged that the sectaries met at night to invoke the presence of the devil. When he appeared in the form of an animal, they put out the lights and engaged in sexual intercourse, even with their mothers and sisters. Children thus conceived were burned, and their ashes collected to give to the sick as a last sacrament.[25] For two centuries there was a trickle of similar descriptions of meetings of heretics, including those of Guibert of Nogent, Walter Map, and Alan of Lille. The same things had been said about the early Christians, who had turned the accusations back against their persecutors. Since medieval writers believed that they were faced by a recrudescence of early heresies, it was natural to seize on such descriptions, modified by a new stress on demon-worship, and to produce stories which are probably confections by scholars (although they later entered popular awareness) rather than a reflection of what ordinary people were saying about heresy.

The abuse directed against heretics contaminated the Jews as well. There is a strong belief in Jewish sorcerers, in devil-worship and (as we shall see shortly) atrocious stories about infanticide. The confusion of the three sorts of dissent is illustrated by the use of the word 'synagogue' to describe the illicit gatherings of the *publicani*. It originated with Walter Map and became the standard term for an assembly of heretics, and later (until it was replaced by 'sabbath') of witches, for it was the witches who ultimately became the victims of this propaganda.[26] The witch-craze belongs to a later stage of European history. Between 1050 and 1250 sorcery was certainly a crime and there were legends of weird women with the power to fly by night, but witches produced much less anxiety than heretics and were the focus of less hostility. It is important to notice, however, that the concepts had already been shaped which later made the witch-craze possible. Sorcery had been identified with devil-worship. The synagogues of heretics had been imagined as combining obscene behaviour with the worshipping of the devil in the shape of a beast. The attacks on heretics had formed an image of the diabolical dissenter which could, in a sense with more appropriateness, be transferred to the witch, whose essential character was that of someone who traded with the devil. In 1250, none the less, this further development was still some way in the future.

[25] Paul of St Père of Chartres in Moore, *Birth of Popular Heresy*, no. 2.
[26] M. R. James *et al.* (eds.), *Walter Map, De Nugis Curialium* (Oxford, 1983), i.30, p. 118.

iv. *The Jews*

The alienation between Christians and God's ancient people, the Jews, had deep roots. The writers of the gospels had been anxious to show that the primary responsibility for the death of Christ lay, not with Pilate and the Roman military jurisdiction, but with the Jews: 'His blood be on us and on our children!' (Matt. 27: 25). Although the reasons for this emphasis were remote from medieval concerns, such passages formed the image of the Jews as a deicide nation. They were seen as doing the will of the devil (John 8: 44) and their assemblies were 'synagogues of Satan' (Rev. 2: 9 and 3: 9). The policy of the Christian emperors and the popes after the triumph of the church was to tolerate Jewish worship but deprive the Jews themselves of social and legal privileges. In the mid-eleventh century they were still in the position of a reluctantly tolerated minority and were present in almost every country in the west, having entered England for the first time in the wake of the Norman conquest. By this time their communities were largely urban, and they took advantage of the rise of the cities to achieve an enviable position of prosperity and learning. They did not differ from their neighbours in dress or language, for Hebrew was used for religious purposes only and their daily speech was the vernacular. The Jewish schools of the Rhineland and northern France paralleled, or rather anticipated, the rise of the Christian schools, and in Rashi (died 1105) the community of Troyes had one of the greatest Jewish scholars of all time. Christian Biblical scholars co-operated with them, and the influence of Rashi and his school can be seen in the Old Testament commentaries of Hugh of St Victor and his pupil, Andrew, with their strongly literal interpretation of the text. Peter Comestor, although no Hebraist, was master of the school of Troyes and knew their work, and Herbert of Bosham (later theological adviser to Archbishop Thomas Becket) took the opportunity to become the best Latin Hebraist of the Middle Ages. The controversy between Christians and Jews was lively, but was not a mere matter of invective. Gilbert Crispin, abbot of Westminster and friend of Anselm of Canterbury, wrote his *Disputatio Iudei et Christiani* about 1093 on the basis of friendly conversations with a visiting Jew from Mainz, and this relatively eirenic work became the main handbook of Christian polemics. It was widely circulated in its own right, and used as the basis for a collection of excerpts which provided Alan of

Lille with material for the Jewish section of his *Summa Quadripartita* of perhaps 1190/4. This in turn was found in many libraries in the next century. The Jews were protected by both ecclesiastical and secular authorities. A succession of popes issued a charter of protection, *Constitutio pro Iudeis*, at least from the time of Calixtus II in 1120, prohibiting forced baptism, interference with Jewish festivals, and any form of violence against Jews. Princes also attempted to stop attacks on the Jews, as Henry IV did in 1096 and Louis VII at Blois in 1171. The change of policy by the authorities, which coincided with the turn of the century and with the mounting of much more severe attacks on heresy, was to alter the position of the Jews profoundly in the thirteenth century.

But dark clouds were already gathering, dark enough for many historians to date the beginning of the continuous persecution of Judaism to 1096. There were problems of two kinds. One was a change in the social and political position of the Jews. They began to acquire a special and very unpopular function: that of money-lenders. The mid-twelfth century, with its growth of the money economy, saw an increasing need for loans; it was also the time when usury, understood in a very extended sense, was being prohibited to laymen as well as to clergy. It was therefore convenient to have a group of licensed usurers whose activities were not restrained by law. Deuteronomy 23: 19–20 had prohibited lending at interest to a brother, but permitted it to a foreigner. Rashi of Troyes taught that 'a man shall not lend to Gentiles for interest, when he is able to get a livelihood in any other way', but Rashi, whose own income came from his vineyards, lived in a more open society in which his co-religionists were landowners and merchants. Increasingly the Jews were constrained by their exclusion from other economic opportunities to resort to usury. Two generations after Rashi, Rabbi Eliezer ben Nathan explained that 'in the present time, where Jews own no fields or vineyards whereby they could live, lending money to non-Jews for their livelihood is necessary and therefore permitted'. This growth of money-lending was associated with a much greater dependence on the secular ruler. The extreme case was Angevin England, where the Jews were treated as a machine for usury, living by exploiting others and exploited in their turn by the Crown, which claimed ownership of all their property. They could count on royal protection for the collection of their debts and for their personal safety, but by the time of Henry II (1154–89) this protection had become a claim to monopoly of exploitation. In Germany it was similarly said that Jews 'belong to the *camera*' or treasury. They were becoming a group increasingly alienated from society, dependent on political masters, their very means of livelihood a sin.

With the growing sense of the solidarity of Christendom, and the odious social role of the Jews, it was inevitable that they would be 'demonized' and treated as a subhuman people. Peter the Venerable said as much: 'Really I doubt whether a Jew can be human, for he will neither yield to human reasoning, nor accept the authorities which are both God's and his own.'[27] Guibert of Nogent, writing about 1115, provides an early example of the identification of the Jews with other out-groups such as sorcerers, heretics, and with the devil himself. He tells of a monk who had fallen ill and consulted a Jewish physician, who was also skilled in magic and who acted as a mediator with the devil, with whom the monk made a pact. He also gives a vivid description of Count John of Soissons 'a judaizer and a heretic'.[28] The accusations of malignity and sorcery produced tales about Jews who had plotted to take the lives of Christians, and to these was added the new charge of ritual murder. The story was that Jewish worship required that each year, somewhere in Christendom, a Christian child should be crucified for the celebration of Passover. The first occurrence of the charge known to us was at Norwich in 1144, where a boy called William was said to have been the victim, and this was followed by the case of Harold of Gloucester in 1168. In France there was Richard of Pontoise in 1163, and then a case at Blois in 1171, where the charge of murder could not even be supported by the production of a body. It seems that at Norwich the accusation began as a simple one of murder, and that a few years later the clergy and a converted Jew confected the much more 'theological' accusation that the purpose had been to re-enact the crucifixion. Somewhat surprisingly, most of these charges of ritual murder did not lead to any loss of life among the Jews, but there was a serious exception at Blois, where more than thirty Jews were burned in 1171.

The relative absence of pogroms suggests that the demonization of the Jews was still developing only sporadically, and that the authorities were able to make their protection effective. But there

[27] Peter the Venerable, *Tractatus contra Judaeos* 3, PL 189.551A.
[28] E-R. Labande (ed.), *Guibert de Nogent, Autobiographie* (Paris, 1981), ii.5, p. 252.

was one context in which accusations easily circulated and led to persecution: the crusades. There was a curtain-raiser as early as 1063, when a French expedition to Spain launched attacks on local Jews on its way, but the first large-scale massacres took place at the hands of the First Crusade. Significantly, the atrocities were not the work of the main princely contingents but of armies assembled by preachers or minor nobles, the worst offender being Count Emicho of Leiningen. The bishops and imperial officers in most cases tried to defend the Jews, but found it difficult to do so, and in Speyer, Worms, Mainz, Trier, Cologne, and Prague the Jewish communities suffered many casualties. The unfortunate Jews of the Rhineland suffered again at the time of the Second Crusade in 1146, when Bernard of Clairvaux intervened energetically for their protection, and on the brink of the Third Crusade the massacres extended to England and Normandy, where not even the authority of the Angevin government was able to afford adequate protection. These experiences entered deeply into Jewish tradition and spirituality, which venerated as martyrs those who killed themselves and their families rather than accept baptism, but they cannot be said to have destroyed the prosperity and learning of the Jews as a whole, and their effects, however terrible, were local. They were indicators of the growing alienation of the Jews from the society around them which was to reach its fatal consequences in the following century when the protection of popes, bishops, and princes was withdrawn.

15

THE FORMULATION OF THE FAITH

i. *The Growth of Theology*

The years after 1050, and still more after 1100, saw an immense increase in the discussion of the Christian faith. After a period of almost two centuries in which there had been little theological writing its volume grew to be greater than at any previous time, and its importance to be unequalled since the fourth and fifth centuries. The shape of later medieval Catholic belief, and hence the Protestant and post-Tridentine systems which arose from it, rested upon foundations laid by the theologians of the twelfth century. Matters of doctrine became the subject of interest in streets and market-places. The anxiety of officialdom to silence the teaching of Berengar of Tours about the eucharist reflected the concern that the question 'has so filled the land that not only clerks and monks, whose office it is to concern themselves with such matters, but also the very laity discuss it in the streets'. At much the same time Peter Damian was expressing his dismay that peasants were arguing (in front of women, too) about the teaching of Scripture, and later Bernard of Clairvaux complained that discussions were going on in front of the general public in towns, villages, and castles.[1] Scholars were respectful of the teaching of the Fathers, but they were also conscious of their own originality, so that Abbot Rupert of Deutz—a conservative in his general approach to the subject—could claim that 'the broad field of the Holy Scriptures is common to all the confessors of Christ, and the liberty to discuss them cannot rightly be denied to anyone as long as, subject to the faith, he dictates or writes what he thinks'.[2] Confidence in the new studies was expressed in the idea that the learning which once found its home in Greece and Rome had now come to France, and Otto of Freising thought that

---

[1] M. R. James, *Catalogue of Manuscripts of Aberdeen* (Cambridge, 1932), 36; Peter Damian, ep. v.1 (PL 144.337AB); letter of French bishops in Bernard ep. 337 (PL 182.540C).

[2] Rupert, *In Apocalypsim*, prol. (PL 169.827–8).

this 'translation of studies' had taken place 'in the time of the illustrious masters Berengar, Manegold and Anselm'.[3]

Given the cultural prominence of the monasteries, it is not surprising that many of the outstanding theologians were monks. Lanfranc of Pavia, who had come to France for study, joined the newly founded monastery of Bec in Normandy about 1042 and subsequently became its head. He was an internationally famous teacher, author of an important tract against Berengar of Tours, *De Corpore et Sanguine Domini*, and a commentary on the Epistles of St Paul, and he ended a distinguished career as archbishop of Canterbury (1070–89). Still more outstanding was his protégé Anselm, also a north Italian, who succeeded him at both Bec and Canterbury. Two of Anselm's books occupy a special position in the history of Christian thought: *Proslogion* (1078), which provided the so-called ontological proof for the existence of God, and *Cur Deus Homo* (completed 1098), a major reassessment of the doctrine of salvation. Another important figure in monastic theology was Rupert, a monk of St Lambert of Liège and abbot of Deutz from about 1120 to 1130. He wrote a vast range of Scriptural commentaries and other works and was a vigorous opponent of the methods being adopted in the urban schools. The most influential teaching, however, came less from abbeys of traditional observance than from the new orders, and above all from the spiritual theology of the Cistercians. Towering above all others was Bernard of Clairvaux, but there were also William of St Thierry, Ælred of Rievaulx, and a host of others, most of them basing their thought on Bernard's.

There are important common features among all those who were doing theology in the twelfth century. They began from the same set of traditional commentaries, and most of them shared a concern for the practical application of their studies in the worship and discipline of the church. Leading Cistercian thinkers had been students, and sometimes masters, in the schools. Moreover the gulf between the monasteries and the city schools was bridged by the regular canons. The outstanding school of these was St Victor, founded at Paris by William of Champeaux about 1113. Hugh of St Victor, who entered the house about 1115 and remained there until his death in 1141, was one of the most influential theologians of the century, and his work

---

[3] Otto, *Chronicon*, v. prol., tr. C. C. Mierow, 323, referring to Anselm of Laon. The choice of scholars is odd, and Richard Southern has suggested that it was intended to indicate the declining standards of the modern age.

included the *Didascalicon* (a major educational treatise) and the fullest
exposition so far of sacramental theology, *De Sacramentis Christiane
Fidei* (1130–7). Later works from the school included the *De Trinitate*
of Richard of St Victor (prior 1162, died 1173) and the literalist
Biblical commentaries of Andrew (died 1175). The canons regular
were a diverse movement who as a whole do not represent a single
school of thought, but some similarities of emphasis many be found.
Scholars such as Gerhoh, provost of Reichersberg (1132–69) and
Bishop Anselm of Havelberg (died 1158) were well acquainted with
the work of the schools, but their interests were less in critical
questions of theology than in the philosophy of history, a subject
which was prominent in the work of Hugh of St Victor, in contrast
with most city masters whose approach was quite different.

Nevertheless, we have to distinguish sharply between different
schools of thought or, perhaps more exactly, between different
contexts of thinking. One of these was the cathedral schools, in
which theology increasingly emerged as (in our terms) an academic
discipline, shaped by the technical requirements of teaching and
learning. Beside this we must place a much wider area of thought
devoted to human relationships, in which theology was fed by
devotion and personal experience: a humanism which was distinctive
of, but by no means confined to, the new religious orders. Practical
issues relating to the penitential system and the sacraments (and
hence the doctrine of salvation and atonement) provided another area
of activity; and there was the group of mainly German thinkers who
saw the key to the understanding of the contemporary world in
history and eschatology. It is tempting to pick out one of these
schools as specially significant for the future, but this would be to
misrepresent the variety of approaches which existed in the twelfth
century.

ii. *The Science of Theology*

Among the masters of the rising schools, the first to make an
important contribution to the history of doctrine was Berengar, who
was *scholasticus* at Tours from about 1032 and taught there for much
of his life until he died in 1088. A brilliant logician, he applied the
new dialectical techniques to theology, but his most famous role was
in formulating Eucharistic ideas which gave rise to a long-running
controversy. A generation later M. Anselm of Laon (died 1117) was

establishing many of the theological methods to be used in the schools, and his Biblical commentaries became the basis of the later standard or 'ordinary' gloss. Increasingly, however, it was to be Paris which was the centre of theological teaching. Before 1100 there was already Manegold, the 'master of modern masters', and soon afterwards William of Champeaux, a pupil of Anselm of Laon. About 1113 Peter Abelard began to teach at Paris; like Berengar, he had been trained as a logician and applied its methods in theology.[4] He was a man with a talent for trouble, and twice found himself condemned by authority, at the council of Soissons in 1121 and, as a result of action by Bernard of Clairvaux and William of St Thierry, at Sens in 1140. His works (notably the *Theologia Christiana*, the *Ethics* and the *Sic et Non*) are among the most original and stimulating of the period. Another major Paris teacher was M. Gilbert of Poitiers (de la Porée), an immensely learned man whose doctrine of the Trinity provoked Bernard to arraign him at the council of Reims in 1148. By this time there was an increasing number of senior churchmen who had lectured or studied in theology at Paris, including the English scholars Robert Pullen (papal chancellor 1144–6), Robert of Melun (bishop of Hereford 1163–7), and John of Salisbury (bishop of Chartres 1176–80). Peter Lombard was at Paris from about 1134, and formulated the methods and conclusions of Paris theology in his *Four Books of Sentences* (1155–8). The collection generated a good deal of controversy, but was accepted as the standard text in the schools; at the Fourth Lateran Council in 1215 under Innocent III, a Paris theologian himself, Lombard's work was mentioned as authoritative. Almost as influential as Lombard was his pupil, Peter Comestor, who came to Paris from his native Troyes shortly before 1158 and who specialized in the production of 'aids to study' which summarized existing scholarship and were immensely popular. The most famous was the Biblical history, the *Historia Scholastica*, which he completed shortly after 1170.

Alongside these masters was a rather distinct group founded by Bernard and Thierry of Chartres. Bernard, whose works do not survive, was a famous master of the early years of the century and

---

[4] If we are to believe his autobiography, the *Historia Calamitatum*, Abelard had no proper theological training before he began to lecture and was contemptuous of the approach of Anselm of Laon. There are serious questions about the authenticity and reliability of this entertaining work.

was outlived by his younger brother Thierry, who died some time after 1150. Their pupil William of Conches (died c.1154) was a voluminous writer in the same tradition, the influence of which is evident in Bernard Silvestris and—combined with ideas drawn from Gilbert of Poitiers—in Alan of Lille (died 1202). This approach was for a long time ascribed to the cathedral school of Chartres, but it is now questionable whether this is correct, or whether we have here another group of Paris masters with a distinctive outlook. They were Platonist in approach and had a strong interest in cosmology and in the account of the creation in Genesis, which Thierry interpreted in the light of Plato's *Timaeus*. The idea of Nature as a force of order, working in accordance with God's plan, was a favourite theme. The attempt to restate Neoplatonist concepts from Macrobius, Boethius, and others involved them in a number of major intellectual problems, because Platonic ideas did not sit happily with the Biblical image of God, nor with the Aristotelian logic which was an indispensible tool in the teaching of the schools. John of Salisbury, in spite of his personal admiration for Bernard of Chartres, unkindly observed that they tried to bring Plato into agreement with Aristotle and 'worked in vain to reconcile after death those who disagreed throughout their lives'.[5]

The study of doctrine which these scholars pursued was a rational, at times almost a rationalist, activity; and thereby hangs a paradox. It was an age in which most people accepted without question the formularies of the faith and scholars were governed by the authority of the Bible and the Fathers, yet doctrine was analysed, defined, and codified in a way for which there is no previous parallel. There is no puzzle about the starting-point in this process. It had always been recognized that the Christian should not rest content with blind affirmation, but should strive to understand his faith. A key text was Isaiah 7: 9, 'Unless you believe, you will not understand,' which both Anselm of Canterbury and Peter Abelard used as a justification of their methods: 'I do not seek to understand in order to believe, but I believe in order to understand.'[6] Both claimed to be writing in response to requests for explanation, and it is likely that the desire to understand was stimulated by an awareness of the low level of basic

    [5] John of Salisbury, *Metalogicon*, ii.17 (PL 199.875D).

    [6] Anselm, *Proslogion*, i, ed. Schmitt, i.100. The text is also cited in Abelard, *Theologia Christiana*, iii.51, ed. E. M. Buytaert, CC(CM) xii.2 (1969) 215. It was quoted in the Old Latin version, which differed from the Vulgate but was known from Augustine's quotation of it.

comprehension in society as a whole. William of Conches complained that some people 'do not want us to inquire beyond what is written, but to believe simply like a peasant'.[7] But a rational approach to religion did not necessarily rest on this elitist basis: some works were specifically designed to demonstrate the truth of the Christian faith to unbelievers, who did not accept the same Scriptures but might be persuaded by rational argument. Anselm's two great works, the *Proslogion* and *Cur Deus Homo?*, were of this kind, and so was Abelard's *Dialogue between a Jew, a Christian and a Philosopher*. The most obvious targets for such apologetics were the Jews, but it is has been argued by some scholars that they were also designed as an appeal to Islam.

It was accepted that secular learning should be applied in the elucidation of Biblical teaching or, to use the technical terms of the time, the *artes* were to be used in studying the *sacra pagina* or sacred page. This had been Augustine's plan in his *De Doctrina Christiana* and the principle was not challenged. In the schools of northern France, however, the arts had come to be dominated by logic or dialectic, which provided the masters with an array of arguments, questions, and distinctions which the Fathers could not have anticipated. Terminology drawn from logic invaded the study of doctrine, and some scholars saw in it the key which would give access to the mysteries contained in the Scriptures. The use of the resources of logic to order theological masterial is a central theme in the emergence of theology as a discipline, and its influence can be observed in the approach to a number of major issues.

The first was the conflict of authorities, as scholars brought to life books whose teaching created difficulties. On the whole it was not a matter of discovering previously unknown works, although these became increasingly important late in the century, but of the more intensive study of available texts. The interest of the so-called Chartres school in Neoplatonic ideas opened a wide range of issues, and the controversy over the Trinity, in which Gilbert of Poitiers became involved, was partly the result of his devotion to the teaching of St Hilary of Poitiers, whose trinitarian doctrine had been shaped in the east and was more Greek than Latin. Even at the time, it was realized that there was a difference between the Eucharistic teaching of Ambrose and Augustine. The analysis of contradictory

[7] *Glossa in Boetium*, cited M.-D. Chenu, *Nature, Man and Society* (Chicago, 1968), 12 n.

authorities was a task to which logic was well adapted, and the introduction to Abelard's *Yes and No* (*Sic et Non*) was a model exposition of the methods which should be used. The scholar had to ensure that the text was authentic, and that its meaning had been rightly understood in context. The weight of conflicting authorities should then be compared, since some (and most of all the Scriptures) were of much greater force than others. It was a programme which in fact was not followed. Abelard simply left his readers with the conflicting statements, yes and no, without providing a resolution, and those who followed him failed to see the force of his approach. The *Sentences* or collections of authorities were to be the basis of study in the schools, but they were almost all marked by inaccurate texts, misattributions, misunderstandings, and the failure to determine the force of a particular authority.

This introduces us to the second feature in the emergence of theology as a discipline : the provision of techniques for study to satisfy needs which were now quite different from the reflective meditation which had been developed by the monks. True, the new methods grew from the traditional root of commentaries on the Biblical text. In the previous century the commentaries of Lanfranc and of Bruno of Cologne had been a compilation of patristic quotations, but increasingly this method was succeeded by original discussion of the literal and symbolic meaning of the text. The favourite parts of the Scriptures for comment were Genesis, the Psalms and, above all, the Pauline epistles, to which in monastic circles the Song of Songs was added, and these preferences reflected the range of interests in theology, cosmology, and spirituality. Biblical commentaries provided a nursery for new ways of study. From early in the twelfth century commentators isolated one or two difficult problems and discussed them more extensively as 'Questions', whose function was similar to that of the 'Appendices' in a modern commentary. As time went on the Questions came to occupy more space than the comment, and finally the comment was dropped altogether: the process may be seen, for example, in the commentary on Paul by Robert of Melun (1145/55). The Question provided the opportunity for the logical analysis of a statement in the text, and it also helped to satisfy another concern, the provision of a wider range of opinions from the Fathers. Such compilations of Sentences, arranged around the discussion of a series of questions, culminated in the authoritative one by Peter Lombard. By the later part of the century a solid foundation of textbooks had been provided in the so-called 'ordinary gloss', the *Sentences* of Peter Lombard and the *Historia Scholastica* of Peter Comestor.

The topics to which this material was addressed were often practical, as in the case of Peter Abelard's *Ethics* or the *De Sacramentis* of Hugh of St Victor; but they could also be highly speculative. The doctrine of the Trinity was a matter of central interest in the works of both Abelard and Gilbert de la Porée. There were all sorts of reasons for its prominent position on the agenda. Because of the *filioque* dispute it had become an issue between east and west, and was prominent at Urban II's Council of Bari in 1098. The Trinity was necessarily an important issue in controversies with Judaism; and a new sense of the humanity of Christ raised problems about the sense in which he was God, and therefore about the character of the Trinity. But the most exciting feature, from the point of view of speculative thinkers, was the possibility that the relationship between the three Persons could be clarified by dialectical methods. A series of thinkers tried to apply the concept of substance, which was fundamental in philosophy, to the comprehension of a God who was three Persons in one substance.

It was much the most controversial of the new methods, and conservatives who were not necessarily opposed to the use of the *artes* strongly objected to the use of logic to elucidate the mystery of the Trinity. This was the battle-ground in many of the clashes of the period, notably the controversy between Rupert of Deutz and Anselm of Laon before 1117 and the confrontations of Bernard of Clairvaux with Abelard and Gilbert. The objectors had much justice on their side, because there was a serious difficulty about the logic of the attempt. God is pure Being, subject to no attributes and qualities, and in those circumstances the accepted rules of logic were inapplicable. Boethius had recognized the existence of a separate area of thought, which he termed 'theology', distinct from the conditions of change and contingency to which logical analysis could be applied. In the strictest sense, the question was whether it was possible to say anything about God at all, or whether He could merely be apprehended by faith and love. The answer of Peter Abelard in his *Theologia Christiana* was the doctrine of analogy. We can use images of God, which have a certain resemblance to him, but are nevertheless susceptible of logical treatment. 'Whatever we assert about this highest philosophy we profess to be the shadow, not the truth, and as it were a certain likeness, not the thing itself.'[8] By the time of Alan of Lille's *Regulae Theologicae* about 1160 the analysis had become more subtle, and the rules defined with some precision what types of analogy could be used of God and in what senses qualities could be attributed to him. Alan's work was widely read in later centuries, but the validity of this approach still did not satisfy everyone, and a different line of argument was to be employed by Aquinas in the next century. Nevertheless, the effect of these changes was already, by the later part of the twelfth century, to constitute theology as a discipline of study. It had its own name (Abelard's *Christian Theology* was one of the first instances of its use to describe an academic discipline), its proper subject-matter, and its text-books. It was an important stage in the history of the Christian faith.

iii. *The Theology of Humanism*

For the first time in centuries, the church had a non-monastic theology designed for men who would eventually occupy important public offices. Even the Cistercian teaching, which was directed to monks and included an element of conscious rejection of the work of the schools, was addressed to hearers who had been brought up in the world and educated outside the monastery, and the Cistercians more than anyone were champions of new patterns of piety. There are a few instances where an innovation in worship was rejected out of simple conservatism: Anselm of Laon criticized the over-emotional ceremonies which were developing on Good Friday and Bernard of Clairvaux refused to countenance the feast of the immaculate conception of Mary. But the prevailing tendency was towards a theology sensitive to contemporary aspirations.

The pattern of education formed in theologians a degree of optimism about humanity. In their days as students of the *artes* they had a chance to absorb something of classical humanism, and in theology they were taught to use human analogies as an approach to the nature of God. Although Bernard rejected Abelard's analogies, he did not do so on the ground that there was no point of contact between God and man, but rather that Abelard was looking in the wrong place, to reason instead of love. Richard of St Victor used the experience of human love to illuminate the nature of the Trinity: 'the proof of perfect charity is to wish to share with another the love we receive'.[9] It is therefore not surprising to find in the theology of the time a new sense of the dignity of man. Christian doctrine contains an ambiguity about humanity, which had been expressed by Peter Damian: 'All things are truly man's, if man himself is truly man. For it is possible to be a man in name alone, and also to be really and truly a man.'[10] Accordingly the word 'humanity' had both a good and a bad sense in Christian tradition. It did not wholly lose the idea of philanthropy which it had possessed in classical usage, but the dominant sense was that of frailty, stated by Gregory the Great: 'Holy Scripture is accustomed to include all those who seek the things of the flesh under the name of humanity'.[11] From Ivo of Chartres onwards we find a powerful statement of respect for humanity which was not confined to redeemed mankind, whose dignity had never been in doubt, but was directed also to man in the natural order. As William of St Thierry wrote about 1130, 'the upright form of man, stretching toward heaven and looking upwards, signifies the imperial and royal dignity of the rational soul'.[12] Peter Abelard stated this in a brilliant hymn for Saturday mattins:

Fit omnium novissimus	Man was made last of everything
homo, qui presit omnibus.	and over all was set as king.
Ad hunc cuncta	The rest was planned
spectabant terminum	for this alone.
tamquam finem	Creation's purpose
cunctorum unicum.	is made known.
Summus creatur omnium,	Man is created as the best,
in quo summa stat operum.	and is the sum of all the rest.
In hoc omnis	For in this one
expletur termino	and final name
consilii	God's wisdom has
divina ratio.	achieved its aim.

---

[9] Richard, *De Trinitate*, iii.11, ed. J. Ribaillier (Paris, 1958), 146.

[10] Peter Damian, *De brevi Vita Pontificum Romanorum*, 5 (PL 145. 479), commenting on 1 Cor. 3: 22–3, 'all things are yours . . . and you are Christ's'.

[11] Gregory, *Moralia in Iob*, xviii.54.92 (PL 76.94D). The 'philanthropy' meaning may be found in the decretals of pseudo-Theodore, where it is permitted to reconcile an excommunicate on his deathbed *propter humanitatem* (xx.12, cited in *Leges Henrici Primi* 70.17, ed. L. J. Downer (Oxford, 1972), p.224). There is an excellent discussion of the subject in R. Sprandel, *Ivo von Chartres* (Stuttgart, 1962), 24–8. For humanism as a basis for Christian social action, see ch.13.i above.

[12] William of St Thierry, *De Natura Corporis et Animae* (PL 180.714B).

Hoc unum plasma nobile	This single noble being here,
in quo resplendes, domine,	Lord, is the place your light shines clear.
illud tue	The beauty of
decus imaginis	your image he.
et gloria	Your likeness now
similitudinis.[13]	the world can see.

Humanism issued in a new sense of the value of human love. As far as our evidence goes, this appeared quite suddenly in the opening decades of the twelfth century, and it spread throughout many forms of literature, including the lyrics of the troubadours and trouvères and the romances. Religious authors shared the same high view of love. It is striking to read in the works of a monk of an austere order that 'the art of arts is the art of love, whose teaching nature has reserved to herself, and God the author of nature . . . For love is the force of the soul, bearing with it a natural bias towards its place and end.'[14] The idea of a continuum of experience between the love of men and the love of God was a fundamental of Cistercian spiritual teaching. William of St Thierry used the term 'fleshly love', which in the past had been an evil to be avoided, in the affirmative sense of natural affection, the love of family which is the start of the soul's ascent to God. For Bernard, this was the secret psychology of the incarnation: 'I think that this was the main cause why the invisible God wished to be seen in the flesh, and as man to converse with men: so as to draw all the affections of fleshly men, who could only love in a fleshly way, to the saving love of his flesh, and thus by stages to lead them to a spiritual love.'[15] Both of these writers saw in love the central mystery of the universe: 'What is so like to God as love? God, in fact, is love.'[16] In his *Paraclete Hymnbook* Abelard, who had a talent for expressing new truths in an awkward form, pointed the analogy between the growth of a man's body and of charity in the soul, and provided Heloïse, his former mistress and wife, with some remarkable sentiments to sing every Thursday at lauds:

Virtutum caritas	All virtues charity
est consummatio,	consummates truly,
virilis virium	as man's ability

---

[13] J. Szövérffy, *Peter Abelard's Hymnarius Paraclitensis* (New York, 1975), ii. 32–4.
[14] William of St Thierry, *De Natura et Dignitate Amoris*, 1, PL 184.379C.
[15] Bernard, *Sermo 20 in Cant.* 6 (*Opera* i. 118).
[16] Bernard, *Sermo 69 in Cant.* 6 (*Opera* ii. 205).

aetas perfectio.	time perfects duly.
Ut corpus hominis	Just as the body fills
hoc implet viribus	with manly power,
sic mentem caritas	love consummates our wills
consummat moribus.[17]	with virtue's flower.

The assertion of a close connection between human love and the love of God rested on traditional ideas which were being used in a new way. St Augustine had held that every human mind is led by the love of certain things, which impart to it a weight or bias. William of St Thierry adopted the same idea, while giving it a warmth which it had previously lacked. By *amor* Augustine had only meant direction or inclination, whereas the Cistercians took it to be natural affection or love. Another starting-point was the Song of Songs, whose erotic symbolism had traditionally been understood as expressing the love of Christ for the church or for the individual soul. Interest in the Song of Songs was already growing in the eleventh century, for a German translation had been dedicated to Henry IV and about 1084, in the circle of the Countess Matilda, John of Mantua had written a commentary. The outstanding meditation on it was to be the series of sermons by Bernard of Clairvaux, which formed a large body of spiritual teaching still incomplete at his death in 1153 and was followed by commentaries by other Cistercians.

All the same, distinctions had to be made. There was no inclination to see personal relations outside the monastery as being as valid as those within it. The word *amor* stood for any kind of love, or more precisely according to Augustinian psychology any object of desire, but there was a separate word for that love which was divinely given: *caritas*. As Ælred of Rievaulx wrote, 'it is plain that charity is love, but is is not less plain that not all love is charity'.[18] There was also another word which helps to underline this difference, *amicitia*. We translate it as 'friendship', but that does not convey the overtones which it had for the men of the time, who were aware that it is cognate with *amor*. In French the word *amis* could be used of a lord, a lover in the modern sense, or a friend, and all were spoken of in deeply emotional terms. Ælred's lament over his dead friend Simon is a lover's cry of anguish:

You were the example by whom I lived, the guide whom I followed—

---

[17] Szövérffy, *Hymnarius*, ii.66. The word *virilis* is not as overtly sexual as 'virile' in English, but the thought is not far away.

[18] Aelred, *Speculum Caritatis*, iii.7 (PL 195.583D).

where have you gone? Where are you now? Where shall I turn? Whom shall I take for my guide? How are you torn from my embrace, rent from my kisses, hidden from my eyes? I will embrace you, dear brother; not with the flesh, but in the heart. I will kiss you, not with the touch of the lips, but with the affection of the mind.[19]

As in most of their thought about social relationships, monks and scholars based their understanding of friendship upon the rediscovery of the past. Christian friendship was discussed by some of the Fathers, notably Ambrose and Cassian, and Carolingian scholars were keenly interested in the idea. The friendship cult of the twelfth century was directly influenced by classical models, as set out in the letters of Seneca, some poems of Horace, and above all Cicero's treatise on friendship, the *De Amicitia*, the best-loved book by a non-Christian author. From these sources was derived a small stock of texts and images. There was the definition of Cicero: 'Friendship is nothing other than a common mind (*consensio*) in divine and human things, with benevolence and charity.'[20] This provided a classical parallel to the description of the apostolic community in Acts 4: 32, which was so influential in monastic thought. Also from the Scriptures came the model friendship of David and Jonathan and the teaching of Christ that the disciples were his friends (John 15: 15). These references made it natural to think of the relationship between members of a monastic community in terms of *amicitia*. The supreme practitioner of this sort of friendship was Aelred of Rievaulx, who said that as he moved through his monastery he felt himself in paradise, bound to all his brethren by bonds of friendship. Particularly notable were his treatises *The Mirror of Charity* (*c.*1143) and *Spiritual Friendship* (completed 1165), and a long letter on Christian friendship from Bernard of Clairvaux to William of St Thierry. The concept of *amicitia* makes it clear that the pursuit of the apostolic life was intended to create a community within which true personal relations could flourish.

Amicitia also had another important feature. It operated over a distance. Much of the writing about it is to be found in the letter collections which were assiduously assembled at the time, including those of Anselm of Canterbury, Hildebert of Lavardin, Bernard of Clairvaux, and Peter of Blois. One could make a 'treaty' of friendship with a distant colleague, and a letter from a friend would

---

[19] Aelred, *Speculum Caritatis*, i.34 (col. 543BC).
[20] Cicero, *De Amicitia*, vi.20, ed. W. A. Falconer (London, 1923), p. 130.

be highly valued as a token of esteem whose cost in parchment, composition, and transport made it a handsome present. These friendship networks were one of the ways in which scholars, administrators, and monks, the directing powers in the contemporary church, were able to keep in contact, and they immensely increased their political effectiveness. The policies of Gregory VII and Urban II were disseminated through such connections, and in 1130 and 1131 the north of Europe was won for Innocent II by their use. The methods of friendship overlapped those of diplomacy, which operated by sending a letter with a suitable bearer, and as is shown by Odo of Ostia (Urban II) on his visit to Germany in 1085 a representative might build up personal links of lasting importance. Friendship, in the reality of the time, was at once an emotional satisfaction, a manifestation of the apostolic life, and a mode of political action.

iv. *Sin and Redemption.*

The new-found respect for man was also shown by the shaping of the penitential system into a more humane form. The eleventh century had inherited an external discipline. Penance was primarily a public exercise designed for the correction of major sins, and bishops relied on lists such as the *Corrector* of Burchard of Worms, specifying a 'tariff' of penances suited to the offence and circumstances. The penances imposed on the warriors of William the Conqueror in 1067 to atone for the men they had killed or wounded are a proof that these ideas were still in force. Monastic tradition was, however, well aware of the distinction between inner sorrow and the performance of penitential actions, and this was increasingly taught to the laity. An important, perhaps decisive, moment was the preaching of the First Crusade in 1095, when Pope Urban dispensed participants from all penances, provided they went for devotion alone and made a full confession of their sins.[21] The legislation of the Carolingian period had urged the faithful to confess to their local priests, and this teaching was now renewed. We do not know how common regular confession was before the Fourth Lateran Council imposed it as an annual obligation. A reference at Acre in Syria suggests that

---

[21] Urban, letter to Bologna, Sept. 1096, H. Hagenmeyer, *Die Kreuzzugsbriefe aus den Jahren 1088–1100* (Innsbruck, 1901), no. 3; R. Somerville, *Decreta Claromontensia* (Amsterdam, 1972), 74.

confession in Holy Week was usual there in the second half of the century, but Hugh of St Victor had earlier suggested that the laity were inclined to argue about it. The stress on personal repentance seems to have preceded the general adoption of the confessional, but it rapidly came to be seen as the vital element in forgiveness, just as consent had become the essential cause of marriage: 'sin is remitted by contrition of heart'.[22]

This change had wider implications than may be immediately apparent. It coincided with the conviction that in ethics what mattered was the intention. This was a sharp alteration in the assessment of human actions, for previous generations had been remarkably insensitive to motive. The long-established Benedictine practice of oblation, by which children were dedicated to a monastery by their parents, was a powerful witness against the significance of personal decision, and it is startling to modern understanding to discover that these boys were often supposed to make the best monks. The new emphasis on intention was commonly expressed in the school of Laon, and Guibert of Nogent saw the assessment of intention as a major concern of the historian and a key issue in preaching.[23] Abelard presented quite an extreme statement of the position in his book, significantly entitled *Ethics, or Know Yourself*, and Heloïse observed that 'an offence lies not in the consequence for the sufferer but in the intention of the actor.[24] The concern with motive was fundamental to the spiritual theology of the Cistercians. They saw the whole devotional life as a progress in motivation, a change from loving God for our own sake to loving ourselves for the sake of God: 'O holy and chaste love, O sweet and gentle affection, O pure and undefiled intention of the will . . . To be thus disposed is to be united with God.'[25] This strong concern with inner dispositions lies behind the revival of interest in psychology, which at first took the form of a close analysis of what were called the 'affections'. An early instance was Anselm of Canterbury, whom Guibert of Nogent heard teaching on the subject. There followed some important studies by the Cistercians, notably William of St Thierry's *The Nature and Dignity of Love*

[22] A. M. Gietl (ed.), *Die Sentenzen Rolands* (Freiburg, 1891), 249. Hugh of St Victor, *De Sacramentis*, ii.14.1 (PL 176.549D), reported that people, when urged to confess, used to demand 'give your authority'.

[23] For Guibert's views see PL 156.21B and 27B.

[24] Héloïse, ep. ii.5, PL 178.186A.

[25] Bernard of Clairvaux, *De diligendo Deo*, x.28 (*Opera* iii.143: *sic affici, deificari est*).

(*c*.1120) and *The Nature of Body and Soul* (*c*.1135) and Ælred of Rievaulx' *Mirror of Charity* (*c*.1143) and *The Soul* (*c*.1165).

These new interests were associated with a change in the character of the theology of the atonement. In many writers the emphasis is on the change of human affections: the work of Christ was a lesson in humility and, above all, an appeal to love. Here the writings of spiritual theologians were akin to the changes in popular worship, such as the greater prominence of the crucifix and the portrayal in it of the sufferings of Christ. In one of his sermons, Bernard presented a theory of the atonement as an appeal by God to mankind, in which he tried first threats, then the offer of eternal life, but all in vain.

Seeing it was no use, God said, 'There is just one thing left. Within man there is not only fear and greed, but also love, and nothing motivates him as strongly as that.' And so He came in flesh and showed himself so lovable, and extended to us that love than which no man has greater; for He gave up His life for us.

The thought is close to that of Abelard: 'our redemption is that great love awoken in us by the passion of Christ.'[26]

It would, however, be wrong to conclude that this concern for the individual and subjective had abolished any idea that the atonement had objective implications for humanity. In Abelard, indeed, it may have done so, but William of St Thierry attacked him on the point and asserted that one must recognize in Christ the 'mystery of redemption' as well as the lesson in humility and love. The most famous contribution to atonement theology in the period, moreover, is thoroughly objective in character. In his *Cur Deus Homo* Anselm of Canterbury rejected the prevalent theory that man, having sinned, was subject to the rights of the devil, and that his liberty had to be 'redeemed' or bought back. Anselm was brisk in his dismissal of this time-honoured view, and in its stead he argued that God's honour had been gravely disparaged by man's sin. It would be contrary to justice for this to be merely disregarded, but tragically man could no longer offer to God an atoning sacrifice. The problem was solved by God's love, for he came himself as man to offer the satisfaction which justice demanded. It was a literal rendering of the words of St Paul, 'God was in Christ reconciling the world to himself' (2 Cor. 5: 19). The theory is different from much twelfth-century thinking,

---

[26] Bernard, *Sermo 29 de Diversis*, 2–3 (*Opera* vi.211–2); Abelard, Commentary on Romans, PL 178.836B.

and whatever its later importance its immediate impact was limited—Bernard, for example, continued to accept the 'rights of the devil' theory. But although Anselm's work was distinctive, it has many features of the period around 1100. It rests wholly upon the passion, the resurrection having little place within it. It sees Christ essentially in human terms, his sacrifice being an offering from man to God, and it takes the assumptions of 'tariff' penance (that God has to be repaid as a condition of forgiveness) and uses them to account for the reconciliation of mankind with God in Christ.

In the twelfth century the sacraments were for the first time identified as a distinct field of study. Hugh of St Victor's *De Sacramentis* was an early attempt to see them as a whole, and it was a feature of the school of Abelard to divide the study of doctrine into faith, charity, and sacraments. The eucharist was normally regarded as the greatest of the sacraments, as baptism would have been in the patristic age, and our period began with the controversy associated with Berengar of Tours over the nature of Christ's presence in the bread and wine. It was a development of a difference of emphasis in Carolingian theology between Paschasius and Ratramnus, but it contained some features which were important for the future. One was the wide public interest in the affair, on which several of the participants commented. Another was the action of the popes in a series of councils in support of a very simple assertion of the physical presence of Christ. At Rome in 1059 Berengar was forced to read a statement affirming that

the bread and the wine which are placed on the altar are not only a sacrament after consecration, but the true body and blood of our Lord Jesus Christ, and physically (*sensualiter*) not only in sacrament but in truth are touched and broken by the hands of the priest and ground by the teeth of the faithful.[27]

The episode is curious. It is an early date to find the Roman Church acting as the policeman of general orthodoxy, and the crude statement does not correspond with the views which Lanfranc had been arguing. Both features clearly belong to the context of reforming thought among the leaders at Rome, with their passionate emphasis on the need for cultic purity in the priesthood whose task it was to handle the body and blood of Christ, and Cardinal Humbert may have been responsible for the immoderate draft of the

---

[27] The document is translated in full in A. J. Macdonald, *Berengar* (London, 1930), 130–1.

statement. The argument also saw the introduction of a new technical terminology. The use of the word 'substance' and its cognates was not totally new, but previous instances were rare and untechnical. Now the terms were employed by Berengar himself and one of his opponents, Guitmund of Aversa, and in a more moderate formula which Berengar accepted in 1079:

> the bread and wine which are placed on the altar, through the mystery of the consecrating prayer and the words of our Redeemer, are converted sustantially into the true body and proper life-giving flesh and blood of Jesus Christ our Lord'.[28]

By the 1140s we find M. Roland and Stephen of Autun using the word 'transubstantiation'. [29] It would be wrong, however, to think that the main concern of twelfth-century theologians was to establish the correct terms for defining the mode of Christ's presence. Their concern was more precisely to understand the way in which the eucharist offers salvation to the faithful. The relatively crude approach of Berengar's opponents was refined by Anselm of Laon and Hugh of St Victor, who thought in terms of an encounter between Christ and the individual communicant, one which could quite effectively take the form of the new practice of 'mystical communion'. Later in the twelfth century a wide range of writers, including Peter Lombard, moved to a new approach: the eucharist expresses the unity of the church in faith and love. In a sense, this was a revival of an old patristic understanding, but it was characteristic of the period to give it a new, more juridical form. As one writer depressingly remarked, 'sacramental reception is necessary at least once a year because it unites the church, remits sin, and defends against sin'. Underlying these theologies was the view (which dominated popular piety) that the eucharistic body was no other than the historical body of Jesus. It was this which underlay the anger that it should be handled by impure priests, and the desire to see the consecrated elements at a time when communion was infrequent. The elevation of the host in the later sense was introduced in the thirteenth century, but before that the elements had been held up to the people, probably during the actual words of

[28] Macdonald, *Berengar*, 192.
[29] A. M. Gietl, *Die Sentenzen Rolands* (Freiburg, 1891), 231; Stephen of Autun, *De Sacramento Altaris*, 13–14 (PL 172.1291–3), in the form of the verb *transsubstantiare*. The attribution of the term to Peter Damian, which is sometimes found, rests on a false ascription.

consecration, and there are reports of miracles in which the celebrant was seen to be holding a child in his hands.

The formation of a coherent list of sacraments did not at first seem a hopeful undertaking. Baptism, communion, penance, confirmation, ordination, marriage, and extreme unction are so divergent in character that their inclusion on a common basis may appear a triumph of system over sense. There was originally no agreed list, but the *Sentences of Divinity* about 1145 brought together the seven which were subsequently adopted by Peter Lombard and became standard. The process was an example of the determination of scholars to reduce awkward phenomena to order, but there was more to it than that. The definition of the seven sacraments was a recognition that the grace of God attends mankind from cradle to grave, from baptism to unction. Divine grace stood at the entry to each order, lay or clerical, married or ordained. There was also an attempt to establish the basis of authority on which the sacraments rested. Some writers were content to ascribe different sacraments to different sources, as Hugh of St Victor did, but in others each was ascribed to a specific act of foundation by Christ. Similarly there was a growth in interest in the so-called ordinals of Christ in which each order (major or minor) was established by a word or work of Jesus. This concern was characteristic of another feature of twelfth century theology: it was profoundly Christ-centred, and its image of Christ was that of the historical Jesus, as he was perceived in a pre-critical age.

Devotion to the crucified humanity of Christ was prominent in monastic spirituality in the twelfth century, and particularly in circles with hermit connections; we find it in Peter Damian, in Anselm of Canterbury, and in its most fully developed form in the Cistercians. The adoration of the wounds of Christ figured prominently in the meditation of Anselm of Canterbury on the Passion, and reflection on the five wounds occurs several times in the devotions of Peter Damian: 'Lord, by the five wounds of your most holy body you have healed all the wounds which were inflicted on us by the five senses of our body.'[30] The same type of meditation may be found in Bernard of Clairvaux, and in the Cistercian writers as a whole the growth of an affective relationship between the believer and Christ was prominent, as in Ælred's attractive book, *When Jesus was Twelve Years Old*. The Cistercians appear deliberately to have promoted the

---

[30] Peter Damian, prayer for Good Friday, PL 145.927–8.

devotion to the crucified humanity as an appropriate path for simple Christians to follow, and in doing so they made a rather startling adjustment to Biblical teaching. For St Paul, the great division lay between the unbeliever and the converted: 'to know Christ after the flesh' (2 Cor. 5: 16) meant to think of him in a worldly way, as Paul had done in his days of unbelief. William of St Thierry and others seized on the phrase to describe the condition of the beginner in the monastic life. The monk was intended to go further, progressing on the path of meditation and purification to union with the Eternal Word, but this teaching of a highly interior spirituality was not designed for the laity, and probably not for the *conversi* within the monastery.

There is at this point an unmistakable link between the learned and the popular worlds. The devotion to the historical Jesus was spreading among the faithful as a whole in such forms as reverence for his body in the eucharist, a growing attachment to the cult of his mother the Blessed Virgin (on which more will be said in a later chapter), pilgrimage to the relics of the apostles, and devotions before the crucifix. It is hard to be sure how the connection was made between the monastic and popular forms of this quest for the historical Jesus. In part, there was a time-lag. Many of the devotional practices of the late Middle Ages were introduced under the influence of the Franciscans, who thus popularized the spirituality which they had learned in religious circles. But that is not the whole story. Obscure as is the evolution of popular worship in the twelfth century, there was unquestionably a growing use of the crucifix and reverence for Mary and for Christ's sacramental body. Crusaders were certainly inspired by a desire to associate themselves with the suffering of their Lord, to walk in his path and visit his sepulchre, and to follow him as their personal master, and veneration of the five wounds can be found in crusading circles: as early as the First Crusade Peter Bartholomew, the protagonist in the affair of the holy lance, had a vision of the five wounds of Christ. Indeed, we must not exclude the possibility of the influence of lay devotions upon monasteries: the Cistercians and other new orders were recruited from those who had grown up in the world, and it may be that the starting-point of the Cistercian pilgrimage (Christ according to the flesh) was precisely the piety of the lay aristocracy, with their love of the Saviour as their personal Lord in an almost feudal sense.

Whatever the truth is about the relationship of monastic and lay piety, we cannot escape the presence in twelfth-century society of the desire to be close to the historical Jesus. It was expressed in the reverence for the body of Christ in the eucharist, and hence in the demand for a priesthood which would celebrate it worthily; and in the decoration of churches. It lay behind the crusading movement, with its desire to be where the Lord once walked. Radical reformers could find in the teaching of Christ and in the New Testament as a whole a witness to a way of life opposed to the established order of society. Here again there was a link between the learned and popular worlds: new hermits, Catharists, Waldensians, and satirists saw the poverty of Christ as calling into question the splendours of a triumphalist church. To some authors the recovery of the values of the ministry of Jesus indicated the dawn of a new historical period; to others, the gap seemed so wide that it presaged the end of the world and the return of Christ.

v. *The World to Come*

The character of a society is determined as much by its expectation of the future as by its past. In this period conservative thinkers anticipated no transformation of the world order, for the process of history had essentially completed its course. St Augustine had largely drawn the sting of eschatological expectation. He saw humanity as living in the sixth age of history which would stretch from Christ to the end, and no new age was due, only the appearance of Antichrist to bring the historical process to its conclusion. The New Testament had spoken of a thousand years during which Satan would be bound and the martyrs would reign with Christ (Rev. 20: 2–4), but Augustine interpreted this as the present age in which the church serves and worships God. The great majority of thinkers in our period adhered to the Augustinian scheme and assigned a very short timetable to the whole history of creation. Since they believed that the world was only about five thousand years old, it was common sense, not eccentricity, which suggested that the end of the world would not be long delayed. It was none the less unusual to suppose that it was an immediate prospect. It was assumed that everybody now living would die, and a prophecy produced in Matildine circles about 1085 postponed the coming of Antichrist to a distant future.[31] True, some people thought otherwise. Norbert of Xanten suggested to Bernard of Clairvaux that Antichrist would come in their

---

[31] Rupert of Deutz, *In Apocalypsim*, ix.16 (PL 169.1126A); and C. Erdmann, 'Endkaiserglaube und Kreuzzugsgedanke im 11 Jh.', *Zeitschrift für Kirchengeschichte* 51 (1932), 384–414.

generation (although Bernard was unconvinced) and in 1147 Gerard of Poehlde calculated that less than 200 years remained.[32] But there was no authoritative teaching about the length of time left, and rarely any fever of expectation.

It was the fate of the departed to remain in the tomb until the last day. The only exceptions were saints and martyrs, who were thought to behold the face of God in heaven where their intercessions could avail for their brethren on earth. Ordinary Christians did not expect to go to heaven when they died, and did not console themselves with the thought that they would shortly be rejoining loved ones who had died before them. The state of the departed was represented by the legend of the sleepers of Ephesus, who were awoken after two or three hundred years to refute a heretic who denied the resurrection of the dead. The position was starkly expressed in a poem attributed to Hildebert of Lavardin:

Ad mortis diem veniam,	For there is nothing I can do
Postquam nil quibo facere	When I arrive at death's last day
Quo poenas passim fugere,	To turn my punishment away.
Sed consumar in cinere	I shall be turned to ash and must
Dissolvarque in pulvere.[33]	Be finally dissolved in dust.

No room is left in these lines for purgatory or the continued life of the soul. The reality to which death is the gate is the final judgement, for until then the individual soul will be asleep or kept in cold storage, *refrigerium*.

Although Augustine had no expectation of a perfect life on earth as a result of a historical change, he did think that in this present age the faithful could participate by foretaste in the heavenly experience. In his language, we can in the sixth day enter by anticipation into the joys of the seventh. Monastic tradition sought to make this possible by contemplation, and it underlay the devotion to the heavenly Jerusalem which developed rapidly in the eleventh and twelfth centuries. The character of this devotion is reflected in its hymns. There was only one of major importance before 1050, *Urbs beata Jerusalem*, which pictured Jerusalem 'coming down out of heaven from God' (Rev. 21: 2).[34] From 1050 Jerusalem-hymns strike a

---

[32] Bernard, ep. 56 (PL 182.162); B. McGinn, *Visions of the End* (New York, 1979), 113–14.

[33] Hildebert, *Lamentatio* (PL 171.1339–40).

[34] F. J. E. Raby (ed.), *The Oxford Book of Medieval Latin Verse* (Oxford 1959), no. 63. The well-known English version by J. M. Neale (*English Hymnal*, no. 169) must be read with care, as the translator was unclear whether the heavenly city was going up or down. The original is not ambiguous.

different note. It is we who are going to Jerusalem, not the city which comes to us, and it is a long way from our present discontents. In his *Hymn to the Trinity* Hildebert could only salute Jerusalem from afar, *de longinquo*, and Peter Abelard produced the classic description of pilgrim humanity:

> Nostrum est interim mentem erigere
> Et totis patriam votis appetere,
> Et ad Ierusalem a Babylonia
> Post longa regredi tandem exsilia.

> Now in the meantime, with hearts raised on high,
> We for that country must yearn and must sigh,
> Seeking Jerusalem, our native land,
> Through our long exile on Babylon's strand.[35]

The solidity of the membership of the heavenly city has disappeared and been replaced by a sense of distance. The contrast with the original Christian confidence is remarkable.

This sense of distance and note of longing spread in lay society too. We hear it in verse, for instance in Jaufré Rudel's 'distant love', and the search for Jerusalem is reminiscent of the quest theme so beloved in chivalric literature, while the crusades were an acting out on a prodigious scale of the pilgrimage to Jerusalem. The same awareness of alienation began to influence the ceremonial of death. Safety no longer seemed to lie in membership of a community; on the contrary, those who could afford it now provided special ceremonies for the salvation of themselves and their families. The change in the course of two generations can be illustrated by the prayers for two Frenchmen of royal birth. When Philip I of France died in 1108 in the great Benedictine abbey of Fleury he was clothed in a monastic habit and was commemorated within the liturgical ceremonies of the house, whereas on the death of Duke Geoffrey Plantagenet of Brittany in 1186 Philip Augustus had him buried in Notre-Dame at Paris and appointed four priests to celebrate mass in perpetuity for the departed. Earlier gifts had been made to a monastery without condition in anticipation of burial and commemoration there: now the conditions were spelled out, and a donor would give a sum 'for celebrating his anniversary'. The demand was for individualized services, for the *annuale* (a mass celebrated

---

[35] A. B. Scott, *Hildebertus: Carmina Minora* (Teubner, 1969), no. 55; J. Szövérffy, *Hymnarius* ii, p.78; *English Hymnal*, no. 465.

regularly for a year after death) or the anniversary (yearly on the day of death), and the conditions were sometimes listed in full contractual detail. This desire for special commemorations reflects the growing ambition of the nobility for ceremonial outside a religious community which would bring their family prestige; it also expresses the sense that the individual must provide for his own salvation, which cannot come simply from membership of a sacred community.[36]

Looked at from another point of view, this new pattern of commemoration was part of the extension of the church's control over death outside the walls of the monastery, part of that Christianization of society which we have already discerned in so many fields. The church was taking over death just as it was taking over marriage. This was happening even in terms of physical space. The old custom of burying the dead away from the habitations of the living lingered only in remote areas, as when in 1128 the bishop of Saint-Brieuc in Brittany prohibited burial at the foot of the cross at crossroads.[37] Burials now normally took place in the cemetery or churchyard. The space originally used in the court or *atrium* of the church rapidly became full, and it was necessary to dig up the dead regularly and store the bones in charnels, which sometimes took the form of sheds erected round the *atrium*. Elsewhere larger cemeteries were established and also functioned as social centres for markets, residences, and even games. The dead were kept in an intimacy with the living which would be offensive to the modern mind. The presence of the church as the major influence at the deathbed was also becoming more evident in the twelfth century, although the definition of a standard procedure involving extreme unction, absolution, and will-making was primarily the work of the synods of the thirteenth century.

The essential message was of the connection of death with judgement, since there would be no subsequent opportunity to make amends. The theme became common on the west front of cathedrals, especially in France, where the last day was no longer seen as a manifestation of Christ's glory, but as a time of judgement. At Beaulieu in the Dordogne and Conques in the Auvergne there are two early examples of a transitional imagery which includes both

---

[36] For the evidence, see M. M. McLaughlin, 'Consorting with the Saints' (unpublished Stanford University Ph.D. thesis 1985), ch. 7.
[37] H. Morice, *Mémoires . . . à l'histoire civile et ecclésiastique de Bretagne* (Paris, 1742), i. 559.

elements. On the great west front of Saint-Denis completed *c.*1140
by Abbot Suger the theme of judgement is paramount, with Christ
specifically labelled as 'Judge' and imagery drawn from the parables
of the sheep and the goats (Matt. 25: 31–46) and the wise and foolish
virgins (25: 1–13). The west front of Saint-Denis is reticent about the
pains of hell and still gives much of the space to the heavenly session
of Christ amid the angels, elders, and apostles, but the message of
judgement is urgent and unavoidable. The confidence in the
salvation of the whole Christian community has vanished. Only
those will be saved who can make a good answer on the day of their
death. This stark presentation was, however, modified by one
important feature. For a long time, visions of the other world had
spoken of a 'purgatorial fire' where the departed might purge their
sins with a punishment which fell short of the eternity of hell. Bishop
Adhemar, the papal legate who died on the First Crusade, was seen
in torment for having doubted the authenticity of the Holy Lance
found at Antioch; his place of punishment seems to have been hell,
but he was only there for a short visit. The Paris theologians from
about 1170 onwards formalized this concept into a separate place,
purgatorium. The word had previously existed only as an adjective,
especially in the phrase 'purgatorial fire'. The theologians may have
been preceded in this concept by the Cistercians, but it was a
significant change which must be considered further in a later
chapter. Death, penitence, and judgement formed a nexus of motifs
which originated in traditional monasticism and had now been
adapted for Christians in general. Some of these ideas had entered lay
circles already. One of the more refined of the new penitential
concepts, the importance of a pure intention, became a commonplace in Chrétien of Troyes and other writers of romances. Another
quite common theme was that of meditation on a corpse as a means
of banishing the love of the flesh. Anselm recommended the practice
to Gunhilda, daughter of King Harold of England, and it was used in
Innocent III's famous treatise *The Misery of the Human Condition*.[38]
This type of meditation was not necessarily as macabre as it sounds:
in the German poem *Von des todes gehugde* meditation upon the body
of the beloved includes a regretful mention of his expanded
waistline, and is primarily a satire on newly fashionable courtly
ideals.

This nexus of spirituality pointed the individual to his own death

[38] See R. W. Southern, *Saint Anselm and his Biographer* (Cambridge, 1963), 185–8.

as the key to eternal life. But what of humanity as a whole? The Fathers had laid down little about the details of the end of the world, and theologians were slow to attempt formulation. From Peter Lombard onwards an eschatological tract appeared in major theological handbooks, but the Lombard's treatment of the subject was hesitant and left several major issues to one side. There were a few indications in the New Testament which all were bound to accept. Before the last day the figure of Antichrist would appear; he was an amalgam of the 'son of perdition' in 2 Thessalonians 2 with Satan in Revelation 20 and the beast in Revelation 13. Before him there would be premonitory signs, one of which would be the final end of the authority of the Roman emperor. It was a bleak picture of human history and it gave so little information that it was of no use as a guide to action. Eschatological thinkers strove both to discover more material and to give a more meaningful role to human action in history.

There was already a legend of the last emperor, derived from Byzantium and made familiar in the west by the works of Adso of Montier-en-Der. It was foretold that he would overcome his enemies, restore Christian rule at Jerusalem, and rule in peace until the coming of Antichrist. A hope was thus extended in a framework quite different from the old millenial expectations. It was to take place before the coming of Antichrist; it was deeply conservative since it consisted in the completion of the existing order; and it rested on no Biblical authority. 'Last emperor' speculations were naturally most popular in imperial and royal circles. A Sibylline prophecy was used to encourage support for Louis VII on the Second Crusade, and Frederick Barbarossa, at whose court the *Play of Antichrist* was performed, may have been inspired by such ideas on the Third. In theological and monastic circles a different amendment to the Augustinian scheme was being canvassed, moved by the existence of Biblical prophecies which seemed to have no place for fulfilment within it. The Bible offered a slight foothold for this sort of speculation in a curious space of forty-five days in Daniel 12: 11–12 which could be read as offering a pause in events after the defeat of Antichrist. The ordinary gloss, Honorius Augustodunensis and Otto of Freising made various uses of this remission: it was to be for the conversion of Israel, or the conversion of the peoples, or (in line with developing ideas of penitence) an opportunity for repentance at the last.

These amendments to the Augustinian scheme still left the course of Christian history looking empty, for they offered no scheme for understanding the activity of God since the resurrection and no pattern of expectation for his future action. The Paris theologians were content with this situation. Their interest in history and eschatology was slight, and they found the key to doctrine in the ordering of the statements of the Bible and the Fathers with the aid of the rules of logic. Nevertheless, this approach did not satisfy the aspirations of some of the most effective men of the time. Enthusiasts of the new monastic movement looked to God's intention to renew (*renovare, reformare*) the church to its former state, and some thinkers endeavoured to give weight to this in their view of the universe. History was taken seriously in the school of St Victor: Hugh adopted a historical approach in his *De Sacramentis* and insisted on a historical methodology in Biblical exegesis: 'The foundation and beginning of sacred doctrine is history . . . When you begin to build, first lay the foundation of history.'[39] The fullest development of a new approach to history and eschatology was, however, left to a number of German writers.

The most famous was one of the greatest of medieval historians, Otto bishop of Freising, a member of the imperial house, a Paris man, a Cistercian, and an imperial bishop. His *Two Cities* or *Chronicle* (1143–7) was a conscious reworking of the historical scheme of St Augustine, but it included some important amendments. Otto assumes that the Roman Empire will continue to the end of time, but glosses this view by pointing to the 'translation' of authority and learning which has already taken place in the successive ages of history. His interest in eschatology was keen, and he provided his history with an eighth book, a 'history of the future' dealing with the end of the world and the condition of the future life. Perhaps because of the condition of the empire when he was writing, the *Two Cities* is basically a pessimistic work. His later book, *Gesta Friderici*, showed some of the new confidence generated by Barbarossa's reign; but for a positive affirmation of the creative possibilities within human history we have to turn to some other German writers. It is perhaps exaggerated to speak of a German 'historical' school, for there are great differences between them, but they had in common a hostility to the French dialectical theology and the use of a

---

[39] J. Taylor (tr.), *The Didascalicon of Hugh of S. Victor* (New York, 1961), vi.3, p. 138, adapted from Gregory the Great.

rich, not to say florid, symbolism in Biblical interpretation. They also showed a degree of optimism about the working out of God's plans in the historical present and future, and through the influence of monasticism they hoped for an age of improvement, if not of perfection, before the coming of Antichrist. The keynote was struck by Rupert of Deutz in his book, *The Holy Trinity and His Works*, completed in 1117. He believed in the thorough involvement of the Trinity in the historical process:

The work of the same Trinity is tripartite from the foundation of the world to its end. The first part is from the dawn of the first light to the fall of the first man; the second, from the first man's fall to the passion of the second man, Jesus Christ the son of God; the third, from his resurrection to the consummation of the world—that is, the general resurrection of the dead. The first work is proper to the Father, the second to the Son, the third to the Holy Spirit.[40]

The most balanced of these writers was the Premonstratensian Bishop Anselm of Havelberg, who wrote his *Dialogues* at the request of Pope Eugenius III about 1150. The first book, *One Faith in Many Forms*, was addressed to the question, 'Why are there so many novelties in the church of God? Who can count so many orders of clergy? Who does not wonder at so many kinds of monks?'[41] He was not alone in arriving at the eirenic conclusion that the various forms of monks and canons performed a function in the divine purpose— the Liège treatise *Libellus de Diversis Ordinibus* had done the same— but Anselm struck a distinctively optimistic note about God's work in the world: 'first good things were planned, then better, and finally the best of all'.[42] Accordingly he subdivided the Christian era into a series of stages represented by the opening of the seven seals in the book of Revelation and arrived at a theology not of stasis, but of development. The regular canon Gerhoh of Reichersberg and the abbess and visionary Hildegard of Bingen both were gravely concerned aout the crisis through which the church was living in its conflict with the empire, but they too saw a measure of hope in a time of renewal which would be brought about by religious reform. This German tradition has until recently been underestimated as a force in the medieval church. It is not surprising that this should be so, for the Paris scholars were the forerunners of Thomas Aquinas

[40] H. Haccke, (ed.), *Ruperti Tuitensis de Sancta Trinitate et operibus suis*, CC(CM) 21, prol., i.26.
[41] G. Salet, *Anselme de Havelberg, Dialogues I*, SC 118 (1966), prol. p. 34.
[42] Salet, *Dialogues I*. 13, p. 116.

and the great theologians whose ideas were so long to be authoritative, whereas Rupert of Deutz and his followers pointed along a quite different line of development. Later thinkers were going to take their ideas much further.

16

PROPERTY, PRIVILEGE, AND LAW

Since the time of the late Roman Empire the clergy had enjoyed extensive legal privileges. One of the striking features of the period from 1050 to 1200 was a determined attempt to extend their rights and revenues, an enterprise undertaken not only by the self-seeking, but by reformers and spiritually minded men. In part this policy rested on a misunderstanding. Their expectations were shaped by the canons composed in the ninth century by pseudo-Isidore, which we know to be an imaginative statement of ecclesiastical claims but which they believed to be the law of the early church. Behind this lay the belief that Christ's work in the world was essentially the business of the clergy, and if they were to direct the ambitious programme for Christendom which we have been studying in the last few chapters, the need for resources was enormous. There had to be revenue to provide and maintain magnificent great churches and numerous local ones, and there had to be legal safeguards if the clergy were to do justice and maintain equity in a world of powerful lords. Ecclesiastical privilege was insufficient to prevent the arrest of the pope by the emperor in 1111 or the murder of the archbishop of Canterbury by the king's knights in 1170, and the combined cost of the building programme, poor relief, and the maintenance of the community exhausted the impressive revenues of Cluny in the 1120s. Even the radically minded Gerhoh of Reichersberg admitted that he was worried about a policy of unilateral disarmament; as he put it, if the church too readily took off its purple robe (of imperial majesty) it might also lose its white robe (of priestly dignity).[1] It was only a short distance to a further idea, namely that Christ was honoured when honour was shown to his ministers; triumphalism, which valued the worldly glory of the churches, was never far from the medieval mind. The abundant revenues, the legal protection, and the authority of canon law all appeared to popes and bishops as a divine gift and not as the arrogant claim of a privileged corporation.

[1] Gerhoh, *De Novitatibus huius Temporis* (MGH LdL iii.297).

i. *Ownership and Distribution*

In 1200 something like one-fifth of the land in western Europe was in the hands of ecclesiastical institutions, who also had the right of receiving tithes, in effect a tax of 10 per cent on all incomes. In addition there were other smaller, but considerable, sources of income. By any comparison with the patristic or modern situation it must at once seem that the medieval church was absurdly over-endowed, but the reality was not altogether favourable. If the income was large, so were the expectations: the cost of the cathedrals was always (and not only in the twentieth century) a financial headache. Moreover, the resources were maldistributed. Some dioceses and parishes were much richer than others, and the inequality was often not related to pastoral responsibilities. The diocese of Lincoln, stretching from the Humber to the Thames, retained throughout the Middle Ages the absurd dimensions resulting from the collapse of two bishoprics which had not been restored after the Danish invasions. The expansion of the authority of the Roman Church was not accompanied by a proportional growth in its revenue, and its attempts to improvise resources for itself were to become a major source of dissension and scandal. Bishoprics as a rule were well endowed with estates, but they relied to a great extent on lands for which secular service had to be performed, and this left its imprint on their character. The prince-bishop was not (or not only) produced by original sin, but by the structure of ecclesiastical property. The income of cathedral and collegiate churches was divided among the canons into individual stipends. Land, and to a still greater extent tithe, had been appropriated by lay lords and was not in practice available to the clergy. It is tempting to speculate on what might have been achieved if this vast income had been available for allocation according to pastoral and charitable need, but in fact ecclesiastical revenue did not exist as a coherent whole; it is merely a term for the sum of the income of institutions and individuals.

Contemporaries were aware of the situation. At the council of Rome in 1078 Gregory VII decreed that the bishops should be in charge of the administration of revenues. The measure applied to tithe, but the policy was capable of extension to other income:

Canonical authority demonstrates that tithes were provided for religious purposes, and by apostolic authority we forbid their possession by laymen.

Whether they have received them from bishops or from kings or from somebody else, if they do not return them to the church they are to know that they are committing the crime of sacrilege and stand in danger of eternal damnation . . . We decree that these tithes should be at the bishop's disposal, so that he who presides over others may distribute them justly to all. He is not to show special favour to anyone by which others might feel aggrieved, but everything shall be held in common, because it would appear wrong for some priests to be wealthy and others to be at a disadvantage. As there is one catholic faith, so it is necessary that the one who is charged with making provision in a locality, even if there are many churches, shall make distribution faithfully to all.[2]

Gratian discussed the whole question of ecclesiastical property in one of his most interesting sections, *Causa* XII, in which he gave a general application to Gregory's principles. With a multitude of authorities he demonstrated that 'the common life should be observed by all clergy'. The property of the church was at the disposal of the bishops, who should allocate resources to those living the common life according to their need. Clergy should not retain their personal property after ordination, and if they did they were unworthy of the name of clerk. The division of the common fund of a church into separate prebends was improper.[3] Gratian's position was both radical and rational, but it was a blueprint which had little basis in past or present practice. The most persuasive texts which he deployed were inauthentic, and a large proportion of revenue was in fact divided among individual clergy as prebends or benefices. Gratian half-heartedly admitted that there were circumstances in which prebends may be allocated, but it is clear that we are in the presence of two different ideas of ownership. The radical policy of Gregory and Gratian demanded a redistribution of resources which would have altered the history of the medieval church, but which was never put into effect.

ii. *Tithes*

According to contemporary thinking, God had made provision for the upkeep of the clergy by the institution of tithes. The Old

---

[2] Greg. VII, *Reg.* VI. 5b (404–5) = Gratian, *Decr.* C. XVI, q. 7 c. 1 (800). The second half of the quotation is not in the Register, nor in the collections of Ivo or Anselm; it is not clear whether it comes from a fuller version of the canons or is a later gloss.

[3] Gratian, *Decr.* C. XII q. 1, c. 2, 16 and post c. 25 (676, 682–3, 686).

Testament recorded the divine command to pay one-tenth of the produce of the land for the use of priests and Levites, and Alexander III held payment to be compulsory 'since tithes were instituted not by man but by God himself'.[4] The major problem facing ecclesiastical authority was not so much refusal to pay tithe as the fact that the right to receive it had fallen into the hands of the lay aristocracy, and Gregory VII's decree in 1078 was directed to its recovery. This remained the papal policy on tithes for a long time, and in particular lay ownership of tithes continued to be condemned. Gratian preserved a text denouncing as heretics and antichrists those bishops who simoniacally granted tithes to laymen; the council of Reims in 1148 echoed Gregory's decree and asserted that laymen holding tithes were guilty of sacrilege; and in 1151 the court of the commune of Genoa accepted that the possession of tithes by laymen was 'contrary to the sacred canons and the ordinances of the Holy See'.[5] As in the case of lay ownership of churches, with which the claim to tithe was closely connected, this pressure produced a significant movement of tithe from lay to ecclesiastical possession. At Ferrara there was a massive transfer of churches and tithe in the pontificate of Paschal II, and at Liège, where the process has been studied over a number of centuries, the retrocession of tithes seems to have begun after the Concordat of Worms. In France it had started earlier, from about 1040 for example at Le Mans, where there was a further boost given to lay generosity by the visit of Urban II in 1096. The success of the restitution programme must not be exaggerated. A great deal of tithe was recovered by purchase rather than by pious surrender and there was even a worry that the repurchase of tithe, which was a spiritual revenue, might be regarded as simony. Moreover, a great deal of tithe remained in lay hands. When about 1143 Archbishop Siro of Genoa prepared an inventory of the revenues of his see (the only almost complete list of tithes which survives from the period), the parish churches mostly held a quarter of the tithes, but much of the rest belonged to laymen.[6] There was also a counter-current carrying tithes from churchmen to laymen. It was in the time of Alexander III that the compromise with reality began. The Third Lateran Council prohibited 'laymen who hold tithes at the peril of

---

[4] Greg, IX, Decretals, III.30.14 (561); see Paschal II in Gratian Decr. C. XVI, q. 1, c. 47 (775).

[5] Gratian, Decr. C. XVI, q. 7, c. 3 (801); C. of Reims can. 8 (Mansi xxi.716); C. E. Boyd, Tithes and Parishes in Medieval Italy (Ithaca, 1952), 131.

[6] Boyd, Tithes and Parishes, 134–5.

their souls from transferring them to other laymen in any way. If anyone receives them and does not return them to the church he shall be deprived of Christian burial.'[7] This can hardly be said to be favourable to lay proprietors, but it conceded that they had legal security by prohibiting not the ownership, but the transfer, of tithes. Innocent III followed this implied precedent and recognized the tenure of tithes held by laymen before 1179, the *decimatio antiqua*.[8]

The attack on lay tenure of tithes, although maintained for a century, thus ended in a compromise which in defiance of their spiritual character left a large part of the revenue at the disposal of the lay nobility. The claim that tithes should be controlled by the bishop was never pursued with the same determination, for it encountered two difficulties in canon law. One was the provision, already formulated in the Carolingian period, that tithes should be paid at the baptismal church, an idea much more realistic in large dioceses than the 1078 rule that they should be distributed by the bishop. Gratian noted that there were two different regulations and, in spite of the importance which he ascribed to the episcopal control of revenue, he supported the right of baptismal churches, holding that tithes were due to the parish church where the payer resided. The idea of episcopal distribution left its mark only in Italy, where there was a widespread custom that the baptismal church received its *quartese*, a quarter of the tithes, while the other three-quarters was at the bishop's disposal. Even so, the bishops in practice found it difficult to recover their portion of the tithe from lay holders. The prerogative of the bishop survived generally in canon law in the weakened form of a right of consent before tithe could be transferred from a parish to any other ecclesiastical institution, and especially to a monastery.[9]

As in the case of the restitution of parish churches, the tithes returning to ecclesiastical ownership were mostly granted to monasteries. Various claims were made on the monks' behalf: that they were entitled to the tithe which they had been granted, or to receive it on behalf of the parish churches which they had received, or again to be exempt from the payment of tithe on their own lands. At the same time Cistercians and regular canons denied the right of monasteries to receive tithe, since they should not be exercising a

---

[7] Greg. IX, *Decretals*, III.30.19 (562).
[8] Greg. IX, *Decretals*, III.30.25 and III.10.7 (564, 504).
[9] Gratian, *Decr.* C. XVI, q.1, part VI (778).

pastoral office. Not surprisingly, papal policy fluctuated in face of these varying pressures. Alexander III admitted that 'we would not wish to hide from you that our predecessors of holy memory conceded to almost all religious the tithes of their labours', but recorded that Hadrian IV had restricted this privilege.[10]

The result of the failure of the policy of Gregory VII and Gratian was therefore to continue the dissipation of tithe income into a multitude of property rights held by particular parishes, monasteries, cathedrals and lay interests. The popes nevertheless strove to maintain the productivity of tithe, and issued a series of decrees designed to extend it. Tithe must be paid before deducting such expenses as the wages of labourers. Tithes (*novales*) must be levied on land newly brought into cultivation, and new developments were matched by a requirement to pay an appropriate tithe, for example on the profit of windmills, an invention of the late twelfth century. The principle was firmly announced by Celestine III (1191–8): 'the faithful man is obliged to pay tithes on everything which he can acquire lawfully.'[11]

iii. The Structure of Ecclesiastical Property

It would be interesting to know how much income the churches received from their landed endowments, but no such information is available for the twelfth century. With the major exception of Domesday Book in England in 1086, no survey was prepared of sufficient scope and exactitude to give us the figures we require. Apart from the lack of the administrative skill needed for such elaborate exercises, there was a further difficulty: church property in this century fluctuated greatly in extent and assumed many divergent forms. A recent examination of papal confirmation charters to the churches of northern France has revealed that different institutions had wholly different attitudes to the type of rights which they wished to include in a list of their possessions; there was no uniform concept of ecclesiastical property which could be applied on a standard basis to bishoprics, cathedrals, and old and new monasteries.[12] In spite of these difficulties, David Herlihy has found an

---

[10] Gratian, *Decr.* C. XVI, q. 7, c. 2 (800). This is a *palea* or insertion, and the interpolator clearly intended it to apply to tithes as well as to other rights.

[11] Greg. IX, *Decretals*, III. 30. 13 and 21–3, 26, 28, 30, 33 (559–68).

[12] D. Lohrmann, *Kirchengut im nördlichen Frankreich* (Bonn, 1983).

ingenious way of estimating the extent of ecclesiastical holdings as a proportion of cultivated land. The custom of defining an estate by mentioning the contiguous landowners allows us to observe what proportion of the latter were ecclesiastical institutions.[13] The picture which emerges is that the high point of church ownership of land was in the ninth century, when one-third of land was in ecclesiastical hands, and that thereafter the proportion steadily diminished. The beginning of the process no doubt was connected with the disorders of the post-Carolingian period, but it is striking that the proportionate decline continued. In the twelfth century ecclesiastical institutions appear as owners of 16 per cent of settled land in Italy, 32 per cent in northern France, and 13 per cent in southern France, where there was a large drop from the eleventh century (31 per cent). These figures do not provide precise information, because an estate held from a church by a lay tenant can be defined by its neighbours variously as belonging to the church or the laymen. But this uncertainty is itself of interest since the description reflects the way in which contemporaries perceived the balance of interest in the estate. It is probable that the declining proportion of clerical property reflects the creation of more solidly based noble and knightly families which gave their neighbours confidence in their permanence. Even so, the presence of the church as a landowner remains impressive. In England, Domesday Book (in spite of considerable technical problems in its interpretation) brings us closer to a grasp of the revenue from church lands. In 1066 the monastic lands were valued at about a sixth of the total valuation of the whole country. The archbishop of Canterbury was the greatest landowner in the kingdom with a landed income of some £1,150. The bishopric of Winchester received about £920, Lincoln £660, and Chichester, one of the poorer dioceses, £142. For purposes of comparison, there were about a hundred landowners with an income of over £100.

Even if we could define the boundaries of ecclesiastical estates with great precision it would not mean very much, because church land, like charity, covers a multitude of sins. Domesday Book sometimes made a sharp distinction between land reserved for the maintenance of the monks (*dominium, ad victum monachorum* or *ad vestitum monachorum*) and land used for knights (*terra militaris*). This is relatively clear, but there were many ambiguous situations. Abbeys

[13] D. Herlihy, 'Church Property on the European Continent 701–1200', *Speculum* 36 (1961), 81–105.

were sometimes reluctantly obliged to place a knight on what legally was *dominium*. On other occasions they might lose control of a piece of property which was formally theirs, but where the bailiff had made himself hereditary or secured possession for an invariable rent. This grey area was specially important in France, where very large estates belonging to the older monasteries had effectively been taken over by their lay advocates. With the growth of the seigneurial system, lords in any case did not derive their revenue directly from agriculture so much as from *haute justice* or monopolies on mill and oven, salt and wine; it was lordship, not ownership, that mattered. At the same time cathedral chapters such as Notre-Dame, Paris, grew rich on house rents and market tolls. The churches were inescapably involved in all the complexities of feudal tenure and commercial finance.

In the middle of the eleventh century gloomy views were expressed about the condition of ecclesiastical revenues. The preface to the decrees of the Council of Pavia in 1022 lamented the impoverishment of the church, which had been so well endowed in the past by pious kings and emperors.[14] The problem, as the papal reformers perceived it, was not precisely that the churches had been deprived of estates, although that had certainly happened, but rather that revenues intended for common use had been appropriated by both clergy and laity, and a campaign was launched, parallel to those for the restitution of local churches and tithes, to recover ecclesiastical estates. In 1056 the synod of Toulouse, held under the presidency of a papal legate, revived an ancient concept when it said that *res ecclesiastice* were not to be detained by laymen. These were defined as 'the office of abbot over monks or archdeacon over clerks, or a provostship or the honour of a priest, a sacrist or schoolmaster, or any honours pertaining to the aforesaid right'.[15] *Res ecclesiastice* remained an important concept until about 1160, when canonists began to formulate the concept of *spiritualia*. Even as late as this, it was uncertain to what extent the lands of the church were appendages of the office, and Gregorian legislation in particular was so concerned about the avoidance of simony and misuse of *res ecclesiastice* that they said less about the defence of church lands than did the earlier Peace of God synods.

---

[14] MGH Legum IV. Const. I.72, no. 34. The complaint was particularly about the appropriation of the revenues of the church by the families of clergy.
[15] Toulouse can. 8 (Mansi xix. 848).

Nevertheless, the restoration of the episcopal estates was one of the duties of a reforming bishop. Gregory VII, writing in 1074 about the vacant see of Fermo, stressed the need 'to recover and put in due order those properties of the church which have been dispersed and put into confusion'. The Gregorian model bishops of central Italy, Peter of Anagni, Berard of Marses, and Bruno of Segni, were actively engaged in restoring the bishop's rights, the *episcopium*, in reorganizing estates, building mills, and repopulating deserted *castra*.[16] One bishop notable for his struggle for episcopal rights was Hugh of Grenoble (1078–1132), patron of monastic reform and friend of the Carthusians. He found that the episcopal estates had largely fallen into the grip of the powerful Albon family, and after a series of fierce conflicts accepted a compromise by which some were recovered and others allowed to stand as fiefs held by lay tenants. A significant feature of Bishop Hugh's policy was the importance which he attached to providing a written record in the form of an elaborate cartulary. He also made inventories of the income of the see—a form of record which, as far as our evidence goes, was still very rare.

Another instructive example is the diocese of Lucca, which had a series of outstanding bishops from 1056 onwards in Anselm I (Pope Alexander II), the canonist Anselm II, and Rangerius, and which benefited from the patronage of Countess Matilda. The new lordship which emerged was quite different from the old. The episcopal estates in the neighbourhood of the city had been conceded by formal grant or *livello* to noble families, and were almost irrecoverable. Episcopal rights within the city were largely transferred to the churches there, especially San Martino, the cathedral. The new structure was based mainly on groups of local lordships some way from Lucca, for example around Montecatini and in the Val di Serchio, and the bishop may have been assisted by the commune in building up these *castelli*, since they defended the regional frontiers. This history of the episcopal lands was probably repeated in other Italian cities, and it represents a pattern of development in which the secular power of the bishop had become subordinate to the commune, for he did not hold large rights within the city, which was the real centre of authority, but was allowed to build up his estates on the periphery where they were useful to the government.

[16] Greg. VII. Reg. ii. 38 (174); P. Toubert, *Les structures du Latium médiéval* (Rome, 1973), 807 ff.

It must be remembered that the secular importance of the bishop extended further than the area of his estates. In England the bishop of Durham held 'palatine' powers, and in northern France the dioceses of Reims, Beauvais, Noyon, Langres, and Le Puy, among others, held counties and several bishops had the right of coinage. The clearest signs of the development of 'prince-bishops' were to be found in southern France before the Albigensian Crusade and in Germany. The bishops of Agde, Lodève and Béziers were all energetically advancing their secular authority in the later years of the century, and in 1188 the bishop of Lodève bought from the vicomte the lordship of the whole diocese for 40,000 sous. In Germany, bishoprics had been handsomely endowed by the emperors with revenues and counties before 1050. Even the most energetic rulers continued this close commitment, because some bishoprics were the only basis for royal influence in their region. Thus by the time of Frederick Barbarossa (1152–90) there was little royal land in Lotharingia, and ducal authority had largely collapsed after the death of Godfrey le Bossu in 1076. In 1081 Bishop Henry of Liège issued a peace for his diocese which was regarded as an exercise of delegated royal authority. When in 1144–5 Bishop Henry II reissued the peace, he did so on the specific ground that there was no other authority to maintain order. By the late twelfth century the bishop had in effect become the duke within his diocese. The bishops of Liège were mostly faithful to their traditional loyalty to the emperor, but they were territorial princes with a very large revenue and a thousand knights to protect their interests.[17] Similarly in 1157 Frederick I issued at Arbois a bull to Archbishop Heraclius of Lyon, which granted, in confirmation probably of an existing situation, 'all regalian rights throughout his whole archbishopric on this side of the Saône . . . over counties, courts, combats, markets and mints'.[18]

One change in episcopal estates which took place almost universally was the separation of the lands of the bishop and chapter. The cathedral canons had originated as a group of clergy resident in the bishop's household and supported from his estates, and even in 1050 in many parts of Europe there was no clear separation between the lands of the cathedral and those reserved for the bishop's own use. Between 1050 and 1200 there was a general tendency to divide the

---

[17] For references, see J-L. Kupper, Liège et l'église impériale (Paris, 1981), pt. 4.
[18] Cited H. J. Légier, 'L'église et l'économie médiévale: la monnaie ecclésiastique de Lyon', Annales 12 (1957), 564 n.

chapter property from that of the bishop and also to separate the chapter estates into individual holdings or prebends. These processes took place at different times and were subject to reversals and exceptions. During the revival of diocesan life in eastern Germany after the Concordat of Worms the communities of canons remained under strict episcopal control, while in England monastic cathedrals such as Canterbury and Winchester were controlling their own estates by about 1135 but were never divided into prebends. One major influence on the development of the chapters was the bishops' increasing need for legal advisers and administrators. Towards the end of the twelfth century the chapters were ceasing to be a body serving the liturgical needs of a great church and were becoming a resource to reward the officers of the diocese. The common life in church, refectory, and dormitory was progressively abandoned, at first in those cathedrals which had always allowed private property, and then in those served by regular canons, and the bishop's estates were clearly and finally separated from those of the cathedral church all over Europe.

iv. *Clerical Privilege*

'Touch not my anointed ones, do my prophets no harm' (Ps. 105: 15). Long before the twelfth century it had been established in canon law that it was an act of sacrilege to assault, murder or rob a clerk. This reflected the conviction that unholy hands should not misuse the servants of God and was also a necessary piece of lawmaking in a violent world where the clergy were debarred from carrying arms. The contribution of the twelfth century was not to assert the principle but to provide a new sanction. This had caused problems in the past, because it was not realistic to leave action to the lay power: if the state were effective, the assault would be punished in any case. The solution, finally promulgated at the Second Lateran Council of 1139, was to impose a spiritual sanction, but one of particular weight:

if anyone by the persuasion of the devil shall incur the guilt of sacrilege in that he lays violent hands upon a clerk or monk, he shall be subjected to the bond of anathema and no bishop shall presume to absolve him except in urgent peril of death until he has presented himself to the pope in person and received his mandate.[19]

---

[19] Gratian, *Decr.* C. XVII, q. 4 c. 29 (822).

There were few offences thus reserved to the pope's personal decision, and the gravity of the crime was underlined by a rule which imposed the onerous duty of a journey to the pope's presence.

The bishop had long had a special responsibility for the property of the church and the discipline of his clergy, but it is not clear how far in the eleventh century this was regarded as giving the clergy exemption from the action of royal courts. Lay and ecclesiastical jurisdiction had become confused. In France powers which in theory belonged to the bishop were being exercised by lay lords. This was a particularly intractable problem in Normandy, where even after 1150 the archdeacon of Bayeux was complaining that 'certain laymen are usurping to themselves ecclesiastical and episcopal jurisdiction and summoning before them both clerks and laymen to answer even in cases which belong to ecclesiastical justice'.[20] In England the shire and hundred heard causes belonging to both royal and ecclesiastical law until William I reserved certain areas of jurisdiction to the bishop and archdeacon. The main concern initially was not to extend the area of clerical exemption, but to secure the surrender by laymen of ecclesiastical justice which they had annexed. Thus in 1116 Count Hugh of Grenoble allowed the bishop jurisdiction over the clergy unless they held land of him. A similar principle was applied elsewhere: the English Crown proceeded against Odo, bishop of Bayeux in 1082 and William of St Calais, bishop of Durham, in 1088 for offences committed specifically as barons.

In the twelfth century the development of the law was complicated by a technical misunderstanding. Late Roman laws contained a provision that if a clerk were deprived or abandoned his office, he should be 'surrendered to the court', *traditur curiae*. The original meaning was apparently that he came under the administrative *curia* and was henceforth subject to normal civil duties and taxation. In the ninth century the Isidorian forger found this penalty among the texts which he was adapting and imposed it on clergy conspiring against their bishops.[21] So far it had nothing to do with the right of the lay power to try clergy, but Bishop Ivo of Chartres misunderstood it as meaning 'handing over to the lay court' and thereafter the question of clerical criminals was usually discussed in terms of *traditio curiae*. Gratian's conclusion was that a clerk must answer in a civil case before a civil judge, but 'in a criminal case . . . a clerk should be

---

[20] Cited R. Généstal, *Le privilegium fori en France* (Paris, 1924), II, p. xxv n. 2.
[21] Généstal, *Privilegium fori*, II, p. xxiv n. 3.

examined only before the bishop . . . In a criminal case no clerk may be brought before a civil judge, except perhaps with his bishop's consent. When however they are found incorrigible, then after they have been deprived of their office they are to be surrendered to the court.'[22] The canonists who followed Gratian regarded it as normal for a clerical criminal to be deprived of his orders and surrendered to the lay court for punishment. This was certainly the procedure defined by the Constitutions of Clarendon (1164), which were asserted to represent English practice. The treatment of criminous clerks was a particular issue in Archbishop Thomas's resistance to the demands of the king, and his stand was given weight by his martyrdom in 1170. In about 1178 Alexander III's decretal *Et si clerici* officially adopted the programme of clerical liberty for which Thomas had fought. Clergy were not to be tried before lay judges. If found guilty of a serious crime, a clerk should be degraded from his order, but should not then be transferred to the lay power for a similar penalty.[23] It is interesting to observe that the settlement of 1176 had already recognized some exceptions to this extreme claim in England and that subsequent popes did not sustain it. When in 1209 Innocent III's decretal *Novimus* was issued to clarify the law he made provision for the surrender to the lay power of a clerk who had been found guilty of a serious crime in an ecclesiastical tribunal. The privilege of clergy remained large. They were answerable to their own tribunals, even for offences against the law of the land; they could clear themselves of charges by oaths with relative ease; and if they were found guilty *Novimus* provided that the spiritual power should ask that the clerk should not be executed after the *traditio curiae*. Clerical liberty had come close to offering, not so much protection to the innocent, as easy terms for the guilty.

The question still remained what groups should be regarded as clergy for legal purposes, for there were many people on the margin of clerical status: lay brethren or *conversi*, members of hospital confraternities, those in minor orders, and those who had been tonsured but not ordained. There was also doubt how far clergy could claim the benefits of their order if they did not accept its discipline, for example if they married, wore secular dress, or carried weapons. If it was difficult to define which groups of people enjoyed clerical status, it was equally problematical what matters fell within

---

[22] Gratian, *Decr.* C. XI, q. 1, post c. 30 (635).
[23] Greg. IX, *Decretals*, II.1.4 (240). The decretal occurs also under the title *At si clerici*.

the jurisdiction of church courts, and the resolution of this inevitably depended on the effectiveness of the lay power in a given region. In England the Constitutions of Clarendon in 1164 claimed a wide range of business for the royal courts, including the patron's rights in a benefice (advowson, *advocatio*). The canonists never conceded this particular claim, but in practice the Crown retained the greater part of advowson litigation. On the other hand it left to the church courts testamentary causes, which were not necessarily part of the spiritual jurisdiction and elsewhere were dealt with by lay authorities. Between one country and another there continued to be considerable differences in the range covered by the ecclesiastical courts, but soon after the middle of the twelfth century it had been established that there would be a separate set of tribunals administered by the ecclesiastical authorities, far more active than in the past and co-ordinated by a canon law which was systematically defined.[24]

v. *The Growth of Canon Law*

The programme of the reforming papacy had stimulated the study of canon law. The work of the school of Constance, Deusdedit, and Anselm of Lucca added much new material and took its classification further than any previous collection. But these Gregorian writers were polemic and selective in their interests, and undervalued the synods of Spain and Gaul which had provided a great part of the material which Burchard knew. The way was open for a collection which would combine the new methods with the laws of the earlier medieval church. This was the achievement of Ivo of Chartres. He was probably a native of Chartres and had studied at Bec as pupil of Lanfranc and fellow-pupil of Anselm. He was closely associated with the developing movement of regular canons, first as a canon of St Martin-des-Champs, Paris, and then from about 1079 as provost of St Quentin, Beauvais. He became bishop of Chartres in 1091 and was probably responsible for three collections: *Tripartita*, *Decretum*, and *Panormia*. The last of these, which was completed just after 1094, became the principal manual of canon law during the first half of the twelfth century. Its success was due to its wide coverage and to the high quality of the arrangement, for it was ably adapted to practical use and well provided with summaries or headings. Its supremacy

---

[24] For the general framework in which these conflicts of jurisdiction arose, see ch. 9. iv above.

was only terminated by the publication an even more remarkable work, Gratian's *Concordia Discordantium Canonum*, which was finished about 1140.[25]

This was one of the finest works of scholarship during the whole Middle Ages, but we know little about its author. The few factual statements which have been made about him have dissolved in the acid of recent criticism, and it is far from certain that the *Concordia* as it now exists is the work of one hand. Nevertheless Gratian (as we must call the author for convenience) produced a collection which superseded all others and became the textbook of the traditional law of the western church. Its main source was Ivo's *Panormia*, and it presented a rich collection of materials in a form suited to academic or forensic lawyers who wanted to look up particular issues. It was designed as a harmonization of authorities, a *Concord of Discordant Canons*. The need had been evident for over fifty years, and the principles to be followed in the conciliation of conflicting texts had been set out by Bernold of Constance in his *De Excommunicatis Vitandis* some time after 1084, and about the same time by Alger of Liège in his *Liber de Misericordia et Iustititia*.[26] Ivo had written a short treatise on the subject, probably designed as a prologue for *Panormia* but in wide circulation as an independent work, and about 1120 there was Peter Abelard's scintillating introduction to *Sic et Non*. Ivo and Abelard, however, had left it to their readers to carry out the work of harmonization for themselves, whereas Gratian provided an ordered discussion of a wide range of topics. The editing was careless, bad even by twelfth-century standards. Not only were there, inevitably, numerous inauthentic texts from pseudo-Isidore, but not infrequently sentences were misquoted, sometimes in a way which altered their meaning entirely. In spite of these defects, Gratian was sensitive to legal principles and practical needs, and his discussions provided a firm basis for later commentators.

Bologna was already becoming an international centre of legal studies. Probably the *Concordia* was written there; certainly it was used there as the textbook for further work. Already in the 1140s Paucapalea's *Summa* and Roland's *Stroma* or 'Jottings' were based upon it. During the next two decades Rufinus and John of Faenza

---

[25] The title now conventionally used, *Decretum*, was a later one and is in fact not very meaningful, although I have retained it in references as it is the accepted form. The question of dating is re-examined by G. Fransen, 'La date du Décret de Gratien', *RHE* 51 (1956), 521–31.

[26] On the date of Alger's treatise, see N. M. Haring, 'A Study in the Sacramentology of Alger of Liège', *MS* 20 (1958), 41–78.

each completed a *Summa*. Gratian's collection was meanwhile being expanded by additions or *Paleae*, as they came to be known.[27] For the rest of the century canonists teaching at Bologna continued to use Gratian as their basic text and produced a series of commentaries, the most outstanding being the *Summa* of Huguccio just after 1188. The international standing of Bologna ensured that the influence of *Concordia* would spread to other countries. It is evident in France in 1160 or shortly afterwards, both in the *Summa Parisiensis* and in the *Summa* which Stephen, canon of Orléans (later bishop of Tournai) wrote on his return from Bologna. Distinct canonistic schools emerged in France and the Anglo-Norman lands, influenced by Bologna but having features of their own. Rome, too, was influenced by the new styles of law. During the chancellorship of Haimeric (1123–41) the great Bologna teacher Bulgarus wrote an introduction to Roman law for his use, and we can in fact find a case in about 1125 in which Haimeric made use of Roman law in its adjudication. Shortly before 1150 Bernard of Clairvaux was complaining about the influence of Roman law at the curia. Nevertheless, there is a contrast between Bologna and Rome after the middle of the twelfth century. Gratian's compilation was the final statement of the old law, collected from the canons of councils, from papal letters and from the Fathers. Conversely at Rome, especially from the time of Alexander III (1159–81), the law was being defined by the issue of decretal letters. The contrast was concealed until recently by the belief that Alexander III was to be identified with the Bolognese canonist Roland, but there is no reason to think that they are the same man, and no evidence that Alexander ever studied law. By training he was a theologian, not a lawyer.[28] The link between the Gratian-based teaching at Bologna and the decretal-based administration at Rome is still not clear.

The more the church strove to regulate and to sanctify the life of the faithful, the more it was necessary to provide a mechanism for guidance, and this was the decretal letter. There are 12 decretals surviving from the 6 years of Eugenius III, 8 for Hadrian IV's 5 years, and 713 from the 22 years of Alexander III.[29] We have seen

---

[27] The name *palea* was perhaps derived from Paucapalea as the first scholar to expand the text, but its origin is disputed.

[28] See 8.iii above and the references in the bibliography there.

[29] The figures, which need slight adjustment from more recent research, are those in W. Holtzmann, 'Über eine Ausgabe der päpstlichen Dekretalen des 12 Jhs', *Nachrichten der Akad. Wiss. Göttingen* (1945), 34.

(Chapter 9.ii above) that such letters were indispensible tools in the construction of a system of appeals: they gave judgements in their own right and rarely referred to the earlier authority on which they were based. They also had the special feature of being issued not of the pope's mere volition but in response to a request from an ecclesiastical judge in a particular case, and thus represented the adoption at the curia of the rescript style of government, characteristic of the later part of our period.[30] The procedure showed a strong influence from Roman civil law, as did some of the decisions themselves, in contrast with Gratian's conservatism in admitting such material into his collection. Some canonists were uneasy about what was happening: Stephen of Tournai complained to the pope about the way theologians neglected the Fathers in favour of new-fangled commentaries, 'and, if we turn to judgements which are made under canon law, either under your commission or by ordinary judges, there is offered for sale an inextricable forest of decretal letters, supposedly in the name of pope Alexander of holy memory, and the earlier sacred canons are rejected, thrown out and despised'.[31] Nevertheless they made their peace with the new order and altered the basis on which the canon law rested. Gratian had attached equal weight to the canons of councils and papal decrees, which were authoritative provided they contained 'nothing contrary to the decrees of earlier Fathers or the precepts of the Gospels'. A decretal letter in Gratian is any authoritative utterance of a pope, and is the same thing as a decree. Now the phrase 'decretal letter' came to refer specifically to responses to applications for guidance. This narrower type of document was recognized as having decisive authority, so that towards the end of the century Huguccio held that a decretal letter overruled earlier canons if they were in conflict. The normal method of amending canon law was now the use of a type of papal letter which had barely existed at the beginning of the century, and by the end of Alexander's pontificate the process of assembling collections of decretals was under way. Within fifty years it would bring into being a new body of canon law, which differed from the old in character and content and in the authority on which it rested— a sort of New Testament to the Old Testament of Gratian.

---

[30] Stephen of Tournai defined a decretal letter as one sent by the pope 'to any bishop or other ecclesiastical judge who is in doubt about any case and has written to consult the Roman Church': J. F. von Schulte (ed.), *Die Summa des Stephanus Tornacensis* (Giessen, 1891), prol. p. 3.

[31] Stephen of Tournai, ep. 251 (PL 211.517BC).

vi. *The Critics*

The expansion of endowments, privileges, and law was an expression of what may be called triumphalism. It was accepted that it was the duty of the hierarchy to provide for mankind's spiritual well-being, and that honour to God should be reflected in honour to the church, its worship, and its clergy. Yet there was a paradox here, because it was one of the aims of the reformers to restore the purity of the primitive church, in evident contrast with much that was happening in the twelfth century. There was a tradition going back to Jerome that with the recognition of the church by the Christian emperors 'it became greater in power and riches indeed, but poorer in virtues', and in the twelfth century it was supposed that Constantine and pope Sylvester were immediately responsible for the change.[32] The basis for a radical criticism of clerical privilege could be found in the policy of the reforming papacy, in its insistence that clergy should live in community with no private property and that they should be free from the obligations of secular service. Imperialist critics pointed to the inconsistencies in the outlook of the Gregorian popes, to their desire to retain *regalia* while abolishing service and their arrogant claim to authority: 'The Lord Jesus allowed himself to be reproved, saying "If I have spoken wrongly, bear witness to the wrong" (John 18: 23), but they say, "The lord pope is judged by no one" '.[33] In both papal and imperial circles there was room for criticism of the triumphalism of the church after the Concordat of Worms. There were three groups of critics who demand our attention.

The first were those critics who, although much divided among themselves, were associated with the agonized discussion of these issues in the Roman curia in the middle years of the century. There were many reasons why they came to a head then: the continued uncertainty in some circles about the nature of the settlement with the lay power in the Concordat of Worms; the revival of Hohenstaufen propaganda against clerical corruption; the influence of the new reforming movements of the Cistercians and the regular canons; the creation of a secular city government at Rome in opposition to the papacy; the appearance at the curia of a new legalism; and the hostility in some circles to the new theology of the schools of northern France, which had strong sympathizers within the curia.

---

[32] Jerome, *Vita Malchi*, i (PL 23.55B).
[33] *Tractatus de Investitura Episcoporum*, MGH LdL ii.502.

The uncertainties of the radicals may be summed up in three striking figures: Bernard of Clairvaux, Gerhoh of Reichersberg, and Arnold of Brescia.

Bernard of Clairvaux wrote his *De Consideratione* about 1150 at the request of Eugenius III, and in it protested strongly against contemporary developments in the curia such as the splendid ceremonial and the growth of legal business. His complaint that more was heard there of the law of Justinian than of the law of Christ was an early indication of the influence of civil law, and he objected to the pope's involvement in property suits and to the fees which were being charged. In contrast he presented the ideal of a papacy designed for service and not for dominance:

Consider first of all that the holy Roman Church at whose head God has placed you is the mother and not the ruler of all the other churches. It follows from that, that you are not the lord of the bishops but one of them, the brother of those who love God and companion of them who fear Him.[34]

Eugenius III himself, a Cistercian and disciple of Bernard, showed considerable sympathy with these ideals, and was thought by Gerhoh of Reichersberg to embody them: 'after him', he remarked later, 'no one was found like him in the apostolic see to observe the law of the Most High'.[35]

Gerhoh was a leading member of the regular canons of southern Germany with their loyalty to the ideas of Gregory VII. In his earliest work, *De Edificio Dei* (1128/9), Gerhoh argued that a clerk who held a benefice was automatically excommunicate, because he was appropriating to his private use what rightfully was the common property of all—a total rejection of the way the church was developing. Gerhoh also claimed that ancient authority allowed 'no one to minister at the altar or baptize or preach unless he is living an apostolic and common life'.[36] He pressed a number of popes to excommunicate all simoniacal clergy and those living with women and to declare their sacraments invalid. With similar stringency he wished to secure a clear separation between worldly and spiritual obligations, and attacked the juridical development of Rome and the new-fangled use of the term curia to describe it: 'if we examine the

---

[34] Bernard, *De Consideratione*, iv.7.23 (PL 182.788A).
[35] Gerhoh, *Commentary on Ps.65*, MGH LdL iii.493.
[36] Gerhoh, Letter to Innocent II, MGH LdL iii.211.

ancient writings of Roman pontiffs, we nowhere find in them this word *curia* as a designation of the holy Roman Church'.[37] This radical approach to the relationship of church and state was rooted ultimately in the Gregorian programme of an earlier generation, and criticized at once the security of a beneficed clergy and the new legalization of the church. It is when we hear an authentically Gregorian voice like Gerhoh's that we realize how unsatisfactory the wide use of 'Gregorian' is as a description of the later twelfth-century papacy.

Like Gerhoh, Arnold of Brescia was a regular canon. Unfortunately none of his writings survives, and we have to reconstruct his views from the works of his opponents. Arnold was the abbot of a house of regular canons at Brescia in Lombardy, where in the absence of his bishop he stirred up the laity against the propertied clergy and as a consequence was deposed by Innocent II and exiled in 1139. He went to France, where in 1140 he supported Abelard at the council of Sens and earned the hostility of Bernard, who succeeded in having him expelled from the kingdom by Louis VII. He then preached in the diocese of Constance, probably at Zurich, whither Bernard's indignation and letters pursued him. Nevertheless, he seems to have had sympathizers in high places: in 1143 he was in the company of Cardinal-deacon Guy, the papal legate to Bohemia (with whom Gerhoh also travelled) and in 1146 he was reconciled with Eugenius III at Viterbo. Arnold travelled to Rome, where by 1148 he had joined forces with the commune in rebellion against the pope and attacked the exercise of political power by the clergy. For several years Arnold was a leading figure in revolutionary Rome, and he seems to have helped to shape a policy in which the senate attempted, in vain, to ally with the emperor against the pope. Eventually Hadrian IV secured his expulsion from the city, and with Frederick Barbarossa's help he was handed over to the prefect of Rome and subsequently executed by him. His body was burned, and the ashes thrown into the Tiber, to prevent the populace from venerating his remains as relics. The official papal story was that the execution had been the act of the prefect alone, without collusion from the curia, but Gerhoh and others suspected that the pope was involved. As to the principles of action which lay behind this stormy career, we can probably accept the summary of Otto of Freising: 'he said . . . that clerks who have property, or bishops *regalia*, or monks possessions,

[37] Gerhoh, Letter to Cardinal Henry (1158), MGH LdL iii.439.

can in no way be saved. All these things belonged to the prince, by whose beneficence they ought to be granted to the use of laymen alone.'[38] This presumably means that, like Gerhoh, Arnold wished to put outside the church clergy who held benefices and monks who owned private property. He differed from Gerhoh in the total condemnation of the holding of *regalia* by bishops and in his readiness to invoke lay action against the clergy and hence to co-operate with the emperor in dispossessing the Roman Church of its property and privileges.

The differences between these three reformers must in no way be overlooked, but they shared a common opposition to the political and legal involvements of the papacy and the greed and wealth of the church. They were not alone in these attitudes in the twelfth century. Apart from the direct disciples of Arnold, whose activity can be dimly perceived in a number of Italian cities, we find a link with such men as Henry of Lausanne who, beginning from a position of radical hostility to the corruptions of the clergy, ended by adopting doctrinal heresies and separating from the church altogether. There is not much sign that Arnold went as far (although there were a few accusations that he had done), but these groups represent a common hostility to the trimuphalism of the church. In circles which were impeccably orthodox the learned John of Salisbury complained to his friend Hadrian IV about the greed of the curia for gold; and in 1179, by then bishop of Chartres, he entered a protest against the legislation proposed at the Third Lateran Council in 1179: 'God forbid that we should issue new rules, or dress up some of the old and reissue them! . . . What we need to do is to proclaim and strive for the keeping of the Gospel, because there are few people who obey it now.'[39]

These complaints by reformers in the middle years of the century gave rise to a series of criticisms from poets and writers who had been trained in the schools. Their satires were not dovetailed into a coherent policy of church reform such as we find in Bernard and Gerhoh; indeed, some of them were not reformers at all. They were, however, furious at the invasion of the church by lawyers, particularly because this denied the prospect of promotion to well-educated arts men:

---

[38] Otto, *Gesta Frederici* ii. 10, ed. F-J. Schmale (Berlin, 1965), p. 340.
[39] Peter the Chanter, *Verbum Abbreviatum* 79 (PL 205.235C).

Et magister appellatur	Now you can become a master
hic, qui numquam conabatur	if you never have got past a
ad 'Fraternas acies'.	little bit of Latin prose.
Perierunt in eternum	Now you need no longer worry
et descendunt in infernum	over type and category,
genera et species.	you can say, 'to hell with those'.
Sic heredes Gratiani	Gratian's heirs are all-demanding;
student fieri decani,	they would like an abbot's standing
abbates, pontifices;	or a dean's or bishop's place.
cathedrantur ut electi,	They're enthroned as if elected,
set per manum sunt provecti,	for promotion they're selected
ad pastoris apices.[40]	for a gift of hands is grace.

The satires are not only funny, but contain the awareness of a tragedy. The order of the church has been perverted by the lawyers:

> Now the pastor's seat is turned
> into a tribunal.[41]

Finally, behind these satires against the lawyers' take-over of the church runs a tradition of almost universal complaint about the greed of the Roman Church. Its authors were people aggrieved by the cost of litigation, or the writers who entertained them; and sometimes they were the mouthpieces of lay powers seeking an occasion against the clergy. Even at the beginning of the century we have blasphemous parodies such as the liturgy for the feasts of St Albinus and Rufinus (silver and gold) or the *Gospel according to the holy Mark*, which turns out to be a mark of silver. The complaints never cease. Gerald of Wales included a chapter in his *Speculum Ecclesiae* filled with quotations from attacks on the curia, including the acid comment 'Roma manus rodit; quos rodere non valet odit': (Rome bites your hand; and what it can't bite it will hate).[42] They are voiced by the literary figures of the Goliards or 'Bishop Golias', who act as the symbols of wandering clerks who rage against the establishment of the church. And they shape the writing of history: when the courtier Walter Map late in the century recalled the life of Arnold of Brescia he made of him a good man who was a victim of the greed of

---

[40] K. Strecker, *Moralische-Satirische Gedichte Walters von Châtillon* (Heidelberg, 1929), no. 1, stanzas 18* and 21*, p. 9 n. These verses occur only in a manuscript of English origin.

[41] T. Wright (ed.), *Latin Poems attributed to Walter Mapes* (Camden Soc., 1841), 41.

[42] Gerald of Wales, *Speculum Ecclesiae*, iv.15, ed. J. S. Brewer, RS 25 (1873) iv. p. 291.

the Roman clergy. The existence of this general dissatisfaction, which was to grow into an even greater torrent in the next century, is a disquieting sign of the failure of the policies of the reformers to remedy the problems posed by the new order of things at Rome.

PART III

THE THIRTEENTH CENTURY

INTRODUCTORY

Most historians, if asked to choose the two outstanding popes during the centuries covered by this book, would point to Gregory VII and Innocent III. The two form a striking contrast both as personalities and as representatives of their times. Living in a society with undeveloped administrative structures, Gregory had pursued his aims by means of propaganda, exhortation, and symbol rather than by systems of control which would have been inconceivable to his contemporaries. Nor could the detailed regulation of the life of the faithful have any part in his aims. He desired that the church should be 'catholic, chaste and free', that is that the priesthood should be liberated from the ritual impurities of simony, concubinage, and lay control. His own positive achievement was very limited. His extreme policies had divided his supporters and forced him into exile from Rome, and the victory of his ideals, in so far as they were adopted, was the result of the skilful government of his successors.

Government by exhortation is a necessary part of the work of any pope and forms the ultimate basis of all papal authority. Nevertheless the development of society provided Innocent III with mechanisms for the consistent application of policy of which Gregory could not even have dreamed. A well-organized college of cardinals and central administration, a developing system of appeals to the curia and a canon law which looked to the Roman Church as the supreme arbiter were reinforced by other institutions which could be pressed into papal service: the international religious orders, the concept of the crusade, and the emergent universities were among them. By 1200 a major development anywhere within the western church was almost certain to require some reference to Rome. Innocent showed remarkable skill in the use of these resources and deployed them to meet the three external menaces to the Roman Church of which he was acutely aware: the loss of Jerusalem, heresy, and the Hohenstaufen dominance in central Italy. He was also convinced that the first two of these threats at least demanded as a response the thorough reform of the western church and the creation of a pastoral system which would provide instruction and guidance to the faithful. The problems and the administrative resources would have been there, whatever pope had been in office; the authority and vision were distinctive to Innocent.

For all his governmental skills, Innocent was an initiator rather than an achiever. He wrote the agenda for his successors in a way which has been rare in the history of any governing institution. The Fourth Lateran Council bequeathed to the church an ambitious reforming programme which councils and bishops attempted to apply for the next thirty years, and the plans for a great papally directed crusade. His sympathy for apostolic poverty and dealings with Francis and Dominic provided a basis for the creation of two great orders which he did not himself live to see. His use of crusading against heretics and legislation against them were the raw material from which the inquisition was to be forged. Trained as a theologian, he imported into his decretals a rhetoric of papal supremacy which was to form the thought of the canonists of the next generation.

Because of the wide range of his activity Innocent's policy expressed, and bequeathed to his successors, the profound ambiguities which marked the medieval papacy. He was at once a man with a sincere love of apostolic simplicity; a reforming administrator who pressed upon the hierarchy the discharge of its pastoral authority; and a triumphalist pope who proceeded ruthlessly and by all available means against the enemies of the Roman Church. The contradictions engendered by these divergent ideals marked the history of the thirteenth-century church, and to them were added two other pressures. The rising tide of eschatological expectation which is particularly associated with Joachim of Fiore sounded a note which had scarcely been heard in the twelfth century. At the opposite extreme of thought, the immensely influential Paris theology, whose pastoral ideals had helped to shape Innocent's reforming policy, was overtaken by a new wave of metaphysical speculation based on the works of Aristotle, which (just after the end of our period) was to produce the most polished statement of medieval scholasticism in the works of Aquinas. In the past a school of Catholic historians and theologians, of whom Étienne Gilson is a distinguished example, was inclined to treat the middle of the thirteenth century as the golden age of the medieval church and papacy. The view has something to be said for it. By then all the great innovations which the papacy had created or encouraged were in being: regular canons, monastic orders, friars, crusades, universities, canon law, papal supremacy, the system of appeals. It is difficult to think of anything which the papacy was to create on this scale before the sixteenth century. It is also true that a new ideal of pastoral care, which was to be profoundly influential in the later history of the church, had by then been formulated.

The new pastoral approach was also associated with another very important development, which is quite specific to the thirteenth century: the rapid growth of records. Perhaps it is only chance which denies us the registers of papal correspondence before 1198 (other than that of Gregory VII), for the indications are that most popes kept one; even so, the very impressive registers of Innocent III and his successors would seem to mark a new level of efficiency. Closely associated with this was the codification of the many papal decretal letters on legal affairs into a coherent volume of law, undertaken by a series of canonists and culminating in the edition by Raymond of Peñafort in 1234 which effectively provided the canon law with a second volume of material, the decretals, to match the collection of canons which Gratian had put into order almost a century previously. This drive towards record and order spread widely throughout the church. We know of no episcopal register of institutions to parishes before 1200, whereas by 1250 they were standard, at least in England and France. These records were consciously intended by bishops devoted to the pastoral ideals of the Fourth Lateran as means of improving the efficiency of the parishes, but in practice the thirteenth century was to bequeath to the later medieval church not a regenerated clergy but a vastly improved machinery of bureaucratic control.

The sense of a golden age of papal monarchy and of the growing efficiency of the control of the hierarchy may carry with it an Augustan sound of serene achievement. This would however be an absurd misconception. The first half of the thirteenth century saw a new savagery in the behaviour of the church as crusades were directed against the Greeks, against heretics, and against the political enemies of the papacy in central Italy, and as inquisition and persecution played an increasing part in the life of wide areas of western Christendom. Lands which had been relatively prosperous were depopulated as armies with papal authority incessantly ravaged the Languedoc or brought a baptism of fire to Prussia; in Italy, accustomed as it was to warfare, the conflicts with Frederick II seemed peculiarly savage. Moreover, a new tone was added to these wars by the new eschatological speculations, because the participants saw themselves in contending roles in the apocalyptic drama which was being played out in their days. Perhaps of no other period in the history of the church has the motto been so true, that *la civilisation est une fleur carnivore.*

17

THE PONTIFICATE OF INNOCENT III (1198–1216)

In the spring of 1216 a German observer wrote home about the recently concluded Fourth Lateran Council. He reported that

it is beyond my power to describe to you everything at Rome which seems worthy of, indeed beyond, admiration; but I tell you that *no eye has seen, nor ear heard, nor the heart of man conceived* so many different languages, so many ranks of distinguished people, from every nation which is under heaven, who have gathered at present at the apostolic see: *Parthians and Medes and Elamites,* with those who dwell at Jerusalem.[1]

The Council was the most dramatic expression of the monarchical power of the medieval papacy. Under the presidency of the pope there were representatives from all the ancient patriarchates as well as a huge attendance from the churches of the west, and the business done there covered many aspects of ecclesiastical and political life. The reform of the pastoral ministry, the definition of the faith, the uprooting of heresy, the settlement of southern France after the Albigensian Crusade, the civil conflicts in England, and the succession to the empire, were all topics for discussion and papal enactment. Innocent's policy closed one chapter and opened another in many aspects of papal history. The change was the more striking because it followed the period of twenty years in which the popes had been overshadowed by Hohenstaufen power. In looking at this pontificate, we must however beware of an optical illusion. Innocent is the first pope since Gregory VII whose register survives almost complete, and if we had access to a fuller range of his predecessors' correspondence we would be able to judge better the breadth of vision which they brought to the papal office and the extent of the change under Innocent. Yet, this warning being noted, the importance of the years after 1198 in the history of the western church is unquestionable. The papacy was given an unique opportunity with the collapse of German rule in Italy, and its powers were in the hands of a remarkable man.

[1] S. Kuttner and A. Garcia y Garcia, *Traditio* 20 (1964) 123, citing 1 Cor. 2: 9 and Acts 2: 9.

i. *The New Pope*

Lothar of Segni was born in 1160 or 1161. His father was an important landowner in the Roman Campagna and his mother from the Scotti family had many connections with the patriciate of the city. Lothar was brought up and educated at Rome and then went to Paris to study theology. His Paris training was important to him and he remembered it with affection. Peter of Corbeil, who taught him, received rapid promotion to the bishopric of Cambrai and the archbishopric of Sens, and Lothar used Paris men in his service, notably Stephen Langton and Robert of Courson, who were probably his fellow-students. Paris theology in the late twelfth century was no longer shaped by the speculative pursuits which had been evident in the days of Abelard, Gilbert of Poitiers, and Peter Lombard with their interest in dialectic and Trinitarian theology. The most influential master was Peter the Chanter, who concentrated on practical issues such as preaching and penance, for which moral and sacramental theology was the appropriate intellectual preparation. This influence may be seen in Innocent's outlook. He embodied two of the greatest forces in the medieval church, the Roman nobility and the Paris intelligentsia.

Lothar remained in France until 1187. It has been supposed in the past that he then studied law at Bologna under the great Huguccio, but at the most he spent two years there and there is no proof that he had any formal training as a canonist. Although Innocent was to enjoy a great reputation for judicial wisdom, so that he was somewhat satirically nicknamed Solomon III, his skill may have been derived from practical experience in the curia. The evident influence of Paris on his thought, the fact that his own writings were entirely theological, and the introduction of non-canonistic ideas into his definition of the papal office all warn us not to attach too much importance to his Bologna training. In 1189 or 1190 he was made cardinal-deacon of SS Sergius and Bacchus. The belief, held by many historians, that he was largely excluded from the business of the curia under Celestine III has been shown to be mistaken, for he was a frequent subscriber to papal acts and was active in administration. He also wrote two works of devotional theology which were among the most influential books of the Middle Ages. His *Mysteries of the Mass* (*De missarum mysteriis*, 1195/7) reflected a continuing element of his piety: he was subsequently noted for his care in saying mass, and his legislation stressed the reverence with which altar furnishings and vessels should be maintained. The book was absorbed almost wholesale into the standard liturgical textbook of the later Middle Ages, the *Rationale divinorum officiorum* of Durandus (*c.* 1290). Cardinal Lothar's other major work was *The Misery of the Human Condition* (*De miseria humane conditionis* or *De contemptu mundi*, *c.* 1196) which survives in almost 700 manuscripts. Its title adequately describes its contents, and it is in modern eyes a strange work to have been written by so active a pope. Although Lothar suppressed or generalized his own experiences in it, there are good reasons for seeing it as the work of a curialist designed to warn himself and his colleagues of the perils of exercising authority. It does not recommend withdrawal from active life, as did most works in the 'contempt of the world' tradition, and it might look very different if Innocent had written his intended sequel on the dignity of human nature, which one supposes fell a victim to his election as pope on 8 January 1198.

We do not know why he was chosen; only that he received a majority on the first ballot and the required vote of two-thirds on a subsequent one. Celestine had hoped to be succeeded by Cardinal John of St Paul, but there are no grounds for the judgement that a politician had been preferred to a man of devotion. Although people were worried about his youth—at 37 he was probably the youngest man who has ever been elected pope—his administrative ability, piety, and record of distinguished publication spoke for him. The cardinals (who were mostly good Romans) wanted a firm stand against German power, and Lothar, a Roman noble with a Paris education and thus doubly an opponent of the Hohenstaufen, must have seemed the man for the job. At his election he took the name Innocent III.

The new pope was small in stature, pleasing in appearance, and clear in speech. Personal reminiscences of him indicate that he had a liking for scholarly conversation, was able to find time for leisure among his many occupations, and when hearing judicial cases he was inclined to the occasional *bon mot*. He showed liking and understanding for men of sanctity and welcomed reformers and critics, whom he was concerned to avoid driving out of the church. His policy bore marks of personal concern for the unfortunate, such as prisoners and orphans. There is also another side to him. One of his opponents in the city at Rome shouted at him, 'Your words are God's words, but your works are the works of the devil', and he was remarkably ruthless in face of opposition. From the beginning of his pontificate he was ready to use force in central Italy and Sicily and, although there had been militant popes before him, none perhaps had boasted of military triumphs in the way Innocent did in some of his early letters.[2]

ii. *The Papal State, Sicily, and the Empire.*

'The heir to Henry VI was Innocent III.' There is truth in Ranke's comment, at least as applied to central and southern Italy. The strong personality which had directed Hohenstaufen policy for almost a decade was removed, with dramatic results for the three lands which he had governed: in Germany there was a disputed election, in Sicily the succession of a small child, and in central Italy a power vacuum. The papal claims there included the Campagna, southern Tuscany, Umbria, the march of Ancona, the Exarchate of Ravenna, and the Matildine lands, and for the legal basis of his policy of 'recuperation' Innocent used the diplomas of Carolingian and later emperors and not the Donation of Constantine. He was claiming 'the lands named in many imperial privileges from the time of Louis (the Pious)'.[3] The Campagna and southern Tuscany had long been subject to papal influence. In the more distant provinces papal rights had not been applied in practice and had not even figured prominently in negotiations with the empire, but they were being carefully documented by papal chamberlains during the latter years of the twelfth century. With the death of Henry VI they came out of the archives into political life.

It was a response to the harsh rule which the Hohenstaufen had, for the first time, imposed on the area. The imperial tax or *fodrum* had been collected, imperial officers had been established in the Duchy of Spoleto (Conrad of Urslingen) and the march of Ancona (Markward of Anweiler), and Henry's brother Philip of Suabia had invaded papal rights in Tuscany. The Roman Church, the cities, and the landowners therefore had a common interest in furthering a reaction against German rule which had already begun before the death of Celestine III. The ancient donations provided a legal basis on which the provinces could reject imperial authority in favour of

---

[2] For references see H. Tillmann, *Pope Innocent III* (Amsterdam, 1980), 289–315.
[3] Ibid., 104–5.

papal overlordship. The policy of recuperation was already a going concern when Innocent became pope early in 1198, but it was he who shaped its further development during the decade from 1199 to 1209 when there was no effective German presence in central Italy. His propaganda emphasized the need to act against Hohenstaufen oppression, and there is every reason to suppose that he strongly shared the dislike of the German invaders. He claimed in contrast to offer an unexacting lordship and was fond of quoting to his subjects the text, 'my yoke is easy and my burden is light' (Matt. 11: 30). His power always rested on its acceptability. He did not attempt to impose a close control and, as he found at Narni in 1213 and elsewhere, he had difficulty in disciplining even the smaller towns. Much depended on the support of the nobility, and Innocent's influence in the Campagna was advanced by his own family, especially his brother Richard of Segni who came to control large territories south of Rome and across the frontier in the Regno (the kingdom of Sicily and Apulia). The establishment of papal governors or rectors, usually cardinals, proved possible only in the Campagna and the Tuscan patrimony.

This is not to say that Innocent was content with a merely nominal authority. In the city of Rome itself he had a more secure control than any pope since the rise of the commune. With the help of his connections among the nobles he weathered a period of conflict in 1202–5 and thereafter the single Senator, the senior officer of the city government, was drawn from his own supporters. The revenue from the Papal State was greatly increased by the collection of the *fodrum* and by tribute from cities which had formerly paid the pope little or nothing. We cannot evaluate this income, but it enabled Innocent to spend freely in Rome in poor relief and in rebuilding and redecorating churches. Innocent held that the authority of the pope in his territories was analogous to that of any other secular ruler and thus gave the papacy a juridical basis which had not previously been defined. Its character was symbolized by the parliament of Viterbo in 1207, an assembly of bishops, abbots, barons, and representatives of the communes which expressed the fact that a new political unit had come into existence. Innocent was the creator of the Papal State. The term is anachronistic, but it is a useful description of the area of papal lordship in central Italy, whose frontiers were to continue with only limited changes for over 600 years. The Roman Church had always been keenly aware of its temporal interests, but it had now become a territorial power in a more precise sense than before, a state among other Italian states. The existence of this political unit was of doubtful advantage to subsequent popes because it contained no firm basis for central control and was not strong enough to resist outside pressure. It was more of a tribute to temporary imperial weakness than to the strength of the apostolic see. The Papal State was created on the battlefields of Sicily and Germany.

When Innocent became pope the situation in Sicily appeared favourable to the interests of the Roman Church. Constance, the widow of Henry VI, had taken over as regent for her young son Frederick II and was anxious for the support of the pope as overlord of the kingdom. The situation changed with her death on 28 November 1198. Innocent claimed the regency on the grounds of his rights as suzerain, the terms of Constance's will, and his duty to protect orphans.[4] Meanwhile Markward of Anweiler, the embodiment of the good old Hohenstaufen cause, shifted his attention to Sicily and Innocent resolved to combat him by every possible means. Mercenaries were sent to Palermo and a crusading indulgence offered to those who opposed Markward, since he had allied with the Sicilian Moslems and 'become a worse infidel than the infidels'. In practice nothing came of this appeal, but in principle it was the first of the political crusades of the thirteenth century. Innocent also encouraged Walter of Brienne to invade the Regno. It is true that none of these devices was unprecedented: previous popes had levied war, used spiritual censures against political enemies, and made alliances based on self-interest. But Innocent's intervention in Sicily between 1199 and 1201 combined these strategies in an intensive way for which there were few previous parallels and which was designed to enforce a secular claim, his right to exercise the regency. The accidental death of Markward in summer 1201 eased the pope's difficulties but did not solve them. It was only in 1206 that Innocent was generally recognized as having the effective powers of regent. Technically he had emerged as successful, but the success was mainly negative, in preventing Hohenstaufen agents from using Sicily as a base for interfering with the process of recuperation in the Papal State. This success was bought at a great price: a large expenditure of papal resources, the use of spiritual sanctions for secular ends and grave damage to the royal position, for which as regent he was

---

[4] O. Hageneder and A. Haidacher (ed.), *Die Register Innocenz' III*, i (Cologne, 1964), no. 555, p. 807.

responsible. Innocent often in his correspondence wrote of his pastoral duty to maintain peace. It would be unjust to blame him for the outbreak of the civil war in the Regno, but he can hardly be said to have acted there in the cause of pacification.

In Germany the consequence of Henry VI's death was a disputed election. Since it was no longer realistic to support the infant Frederick the Hohenstaufen supporters turned to Duke Philip of Suabia, Henry VI's brother, and elected him on 8 March 1198. The princes of the Rhineland, encouraged by Archbishop Adolf of Cologne, elected the Welf Otto of Brunswick on 9 July 1198. It was an unequal contest, for the Welf party had only regional support and 'the whole strength of the empire supported Philip'.[5] There were also international implications, for Otto was supported by his uncle Richard I of England and Philip by the French King Philip Augustus. It is probable that Innocent favoured Otto from the start, but the breach came from the Hohenstaufen side. In spring 1199 Philip's supporters drew up a statement of their position which Philip approved at Speyer on 28 May. The Declaration of Speyer had a distinguished list of signatories and constituted 'a sharply worded ultimatum'.[6] It claimed that by his election Philip had already received imperial authority and demanded that the pope should not interfere with the rights of the empire and should give his support to Markward. It was a reassertion in new circumstances of the policy of Henry VI, and Innocent flatly rejected it in his reply. It was probably at this point that he had the correspondence enrolled in a special volume, the *Registrum super negotio Romani imperii* whose creation showed how seriously the question was viewed in the curia. Early in January 1201 at a secret consistory Innocent adjudicated the rival claims of the candidates. This *Deliberatio*, a careful piece of legal reasoning, found in favour of Otto, and the pope offered to recognize him subject to certain guarantees. These were given at Neuss on 8 June, and included the acceptance of the territorial claims of the Roman Church in central Italy and its overlordship in Sicily. The papal recognition of Otto IV was published by Innocent's legate on 3 July. A further protest by the Hohenstaufen party against this invasion of the electoral rights of the princes produced in response

[5] Arnold of Lübeck, *Chronica Slavorum*, vi.2 (MGH SS XXI.213).
[6] F. Kempf, *Papsttum und Kaisertum bei Innocenz III* (Rome, 1954), 26. There is considerable uncertainty about the dating of some of the negotiations and hence about the sequence of events leading to the final decision. The view in the text largely follows the dating proposed by Kempf.

the decretal *Venerabilem* at the end of March 1202. *Venerabilem* asserted the right of the Roman Church to concern itself with the election of an emperor. In case of a disputed election the pope had the duty of adjudicating the dispute, and in all cases he had the authority to inquire into the suitability of a candidate to receive imperial coronation. *Venerabilem* completed the process of defining the constitutional rights of the papacy towards the emperor-elect. Innocent had analysed his claims with unprecedented care. Behind the conflict of political interest there were opposing constitutional views about the nature of the imperial coronation, the character of papal territorial claims, and the status of the Sicilian kingdom, with the Hohenstaufen view expressed in the Declaration of Speyer and the papal position in the renunciation of Neuss, the *Deliberatio*, and *Venerabilem*.

Papal recognition strengthened Otto's position only temporarily. In the course of 1204 it collapsed, and on 6 January 1205 Philip was crowned at Aachen by Archbishop Adolf of Cologne, who had abandoned Otto's cause. Negotiations were resumed between Innocent and Philip for his recognition. By the spring of 1208 the basis had been laid for an agreement, which included a guarantee of the integrity of the Papal State in return for imperial coronation. The prospect of a new order in Italy was frustrated by the murder of Philip in a purely private quarrel on 21 June 1208. To Innocent it appeared a God-given confirmation of the rightness of his championship of Otto, who was accepted by all the princes at the Diet of Frankfurt on 11 November 1208. There followed a honeymoon period during which the new king enjoyed good relations with both Rome and the princes. Otto expressed his gratitude to the Roman Church and on 22 March 1209 at Speyer he issued a diploma incorporating the concessions accepted at Neuss, and added to these the abandonment of important royal rights over the German churches. In the summer of 1209, even before Otto entered Italy, there were indications of deteriorating relations with the curia, and by the time of the imperial coronation on 4 October 1209 the tension between Otto and Innocent was obvious to all. The matter came to a head when an appeal was received from the Regno for the emperor's intervention there. In October 1210 he crossed the frontier, and his invasion met only feeble opposition.

Otto's power seemed formidable, with a strong army and a united Germany behind him, and his alliance with his uncle John of

England, two monarchs united in hostility to the Roman Church, was disturbing. To Innocent he seemed like Goliath; and the only alternative was to reverse his whole policy and sponsor the young Frederick. Even if this were successful, it was a desperate expedient because it threatened to restore the union of Sicily and the empire in Hohenstaufen hands. It was only when Otto proved obdurate that Innocent published his excommunication on 31 March 1211. He did not promulgate a sentence of deposition, but the excommunication was a signal to the reviving German opposition, whose sympathy Innocent cultivated, and they elected Frederick of Sicily at Nuremberg in September 1211. The papal legates were authorized to depose bishops who continued to support Otto. Frederick, in the role of papal protégé, issued the Golden Bull of Eger on 12 July 1213 in which he renewed the concessions made by Otto at Speyer in 1209. He surrendered rights over vacant churches, recognized freedom of the election of bishops and abbots without royal participation, permitted the right of appeal to the curia and promised his assistance in the suppression of heresy.[7] Eger established a new basis for the rights of the German churches, replacing the Concordat of Worms with a settlement far less favourable to the Crown.

Innocent's volte-face enjoyed rapid success in Italy, where German control depended on the continued presence of a large army. The Regno and Papal State were soon out of Otto's control. In Germany the two parties were more evenly balanced until the defeat of Otto IV by Philip Augustus of France at Bouvines on 27 July 1214. The battle was decisive for the struggle in Germany and placed the northwest entirely in Frederick's hands. He was crowned at Aachen in July 1215 and took a crusading oath. In spite of protests by Otto's remaining partisans the Fourth Lateran Council found in favour of his claim to the imperial title. On 1 July 1216 Frederick, still faithful to his alliance with papal interests, undertook at Strasburg that after the imperial coronation he would hand over his young son Henry to be a ward of the Roman Church as king of Sicily and allow him to be controlled by a papal nominee. Innocent had died before the news of this oath reached him, but in the closing months of his life he could have felt that his policy had been a success: his final candidate was secure and was on the path to giving a guarantee against the dreaded *Unio regni ad imperium*, the union of kingdom and empire.

Such an impression would have been superficial. Innocent had

[7] MGH Legum IV Const. ii, nos. 46–7.

claimed the right to intervene in a disputed imperial election and to examine the suitability of any candidate. He had for years sustained the cause of Otto IV, a minority candidate who in the time of success had proved to be a deadly enemy of papal interests in Italy. Innocent did not live long enough to discover that he had done the same thing a second time by raising the formidable Frederick II to the imperial throne. In deciding whether a candidate was qualified, moreover, the prime test appeared to be the territorial interests of the papacy: broader considerations of the welfare of the empire or even of the church as a whole seemed to have small part. It was a dangerous inheritance to have left to his successors.

iii. *Innocent and the Lay Power.*

The relations of the Roman Church with the empire were dominated by political and historical claims. Throughout most of Europe the popes were involved in their capacity as rulers of the Christian community at large, but this general authority was complicated by a number of special relationships. Hungary, Poland and Aragon, as well as Sicily, traditionally acknowledged the pope as their overlord, and it has been suggested that Innocent wished to extend his supremacy to other countries and thus create a general political supremacy for the apostolic see. It is true that he warmly welcomed the submission of England in 1213, but it would be a mistake to see such relationships as the basis for a system of universal papal authority. The arrangement transferred to Rome a titular overlord-ship with a limited number of rights and in particular the receipt of an annual tribute. Where Innocent was overlord, he was inclined to intervene more actively than usual in support of royal authority or in exhorting the king to perform his duties justly, but (specific and limited rights apart) he did not behave in a fundamentally different way in tributary kingdoms from other countries, and usually justified his interventions on the same general moral principles as he applied elsewhere.

Innocent often gave expression to his universal responsibility for the maintenance of good government. We may suspect that his application of high principles was frequently shaped by political interest, but of his belief in the principles there is little doubt. He acted for the preservation of peace, sometimes in the interests of crusading but also on general grounds: 'we who are, however unworthily, the vicar of Christ on earth, following his example and imitating the custom of of our predecessors, wish and are obliged to attend to the restoration of true peace and concord between those who are in dispute.'[8] Here Innocent stoof firmly in the tradition of ecclesiastical activity since the Peace of God movement, and he also intervened on the side of the powerless and oppressed, ordering the release of captives in Sicily in 1198 and protecting the claim of the young Ladislas of Hungary in 1203 on the grounds that 'we are required by the office of our apostolate to care for the fatherless, because we are the vicar on earth, however unworthy, of him to whom it was spoken by the prophet, *You shall be a helper to the fatherless*'.[9] Innocent's whole conception of royal authority stressed the religious duties of the king, as we can see in the oath taken to him by Peter II of Aragon: 'I will defend the catholic faith; I will persecute heresy; I will respect the liberties and immunities of the churches and protect their rights. Throughout all of the territory submitted to my power I will strive to maintain peace and justice.'[10] This is typical of Innocent's approach, which focused on the maintenance of peace, the defence of the Holy Land, and the protection of churches. These were not the whole of a ruler's duties (indeed, some were inclined to treat them as optional extras) but they bulked large in the pope's mind. A great part of his dealings with the secular power was directed to safeguarding the privileges of the church: in Poland he supported a former Paris colleague, Henry Kietlicz archbishop of Gniezno, against the attempts of Grand Duke Wladislaw to maintain the old tradition of strong lay control, and in Norway, where King Sverre had been engaged in a fierce conflict with the church, Innocent ordered the excommunication of his followers and the proclamation of an interdict on their lands.[11]

With the growth at once of royal government and of the canon law, the issues requiring settlement became ever more complex. Thus in Innocent's early years problems arose in England as diverse as the complaint of a Berkshire rector about the conduct of royal officers, the king's custody of the lands of the archbishop of York, and the pressure of Richard I upon the Canterbury monks during an interminable dispute between them and Archbishop Hubert Walter.[12]

---

[8] Reg. i. no. 355, p. 530, letter to Philip Augustus, summer 1198.
[9] Reg. viii.39 (PL 215.597 A) Apr. 1205.
[10] Reg. vii.229 (PL 215.550 C).
[11] Reg. i. no. 82, pp. 577–9, 6 Oct. 1198.
[12] For references see C. R. Cheney, *Pope Innocent III and England* (Stuttgart, 1976), *passim*.

Other conflicts were produced by breaches of the marriage law. In 1193 Philip Augustus of France had married Ingeborg of Denmark, but had immediately renounced her. Having secured an annulment from the French bishops he married Agnes of Meran in 1196 and kept Ingeborg in strict custody. Innocent maintained that the marriage with Ingeborg was the true one and made energetic attempts to reconcile them, and on his failure imposed an interdict on the royal demesne in 1200. The dispute illustrates the acute difficulty of disciplining a determined monarch. Philip quickly agreed to separate from Agnes and to acknowledge Ingeborg, thus escaping from the interdict, but in reality negotiations continued over the years until in the spring of 1213 Philip was finally reconciled with the wife he had married twenty years before. The danger of a direct confrontation had been avoided by a long stalemate in which neither side had secured a satisfactory solution.[13] From all this we do not derive the impression of the even application of the moral law throughout Europe. Innocent always had to bear in mind the dangers for the churches which would arise from an open breach with the lay power; and in any case the machinery of the curia was better adapted to responding to petitions than to the equal application of general principles. Thus when in England Archbishop Hubert Walter resigned the important office of justiciar it was rumoured that this was the result of a papal intervention, but it was followed by no general attempt to exclude the clergy from political activity. The pope's action, while strictly in line with the canons, was probably a response to pressure by Hubert Walter's political opponents.[14]

The classic confrontation between church and state during the pontificate followed Hubert Walter's death on 13 July 1205. A disputed election followed, and in Innocent's presence at Rome a delegation of the monks elected Stephen Langton, an English scholar who had for a long time been a distinguished teacher in Paris. It was a provocative choice, because the king had not been consulted and was unlikely to welcome a resident of the capital of his enemy, the king of France.[15] Innocent consecrated the new archbishop at

---

[13] It is often suggested that Innocent failed to pursue the matter of the Ingeborg marriage effectively because politically he could not afford the hostility of Philip Augustus. H. Tillmann argues in *Pope Innocent III*, excursus 2, that the pope did not intend any connivance but was simply unable to resolve an unsatisfactory situation.

[14] Cheney, *Pope Innocent III and England*, 19.

[15] The whole affair is admirably discussed in Cheney, *Pope Innocent III and England*, pt. III. Common sense leads one to suppose that Langton was the nominee of Innocent, who had known him at Paris. We have no evidence to confirm this, and it must be admitted that the pope showed little confidence in his old colleague's judgement.

Viterbo on 17 June 1207 and an escalating conflict began. King John refused to admit Langton to England and expelled the monks from Canterbury. The pope in turn imposed an interdict upon England in March 1208, and John retorted by ordering the confiscation of the possessions of all clergy who refused to celebrate divine service. In response the pope finally excommunicated him in November 1209. Further than that he did not go; the rumours circulating in 1212 that he had deposed John and released his subjects from their oath of allegiance were untrue. The indications are that the interdict was widely observed, and in large parts of the country the only rites available were the baptism of infants and the absolution of the dying. But strikes are an uncertain way of influencing public opinion, which was probably inclined to blame the church rather than the king. At this stage, the church had sustained more damage than it had inflicted: many leading churchmen were in exile on the Continent and their revenues were in royal hands.

The Achilles' heel in the armament of the English king was the hostility of France and dissatisfaction among his own subjects. The discovery of a baronial plot in the spring of 1212 shook John's confidence, especially as there were signs of a combined front against him by the rebel barons, Stephen Langton, and the French king, who on 8 April 1213 declared his intention of invading England. It is not clear that Innocent was involved in these plans, but nevertheless John decided that he must settle his quarrel with Rome. The king met the papal legate Pandulf at Dover on 15 May 1213 and accepted Innocent's terms: Stephen Langton would be admitted and full restitution made to the churches for their financial loss. John was intent on far more than a simple peace treaty and over the next two years he made a series of striking concessions to the pope, designed to change hostility into close alliance. He began by informing the legate that he surrendered the Crowns of England and Ireland into the hands of the pope, to hold them as a fief of God and the Roman Church, for which he would do liege homage and pay a tribute of 1,000 marks sterling each year. John also asked for a legate *a latere* to be sent to England. The following year he issued a charter granting to all cathedral and monastic churches the right of free election, thus at a stroke ensuring that, in theory at least, there would be no repetition of the Canterbury affair. Finally, on 4 March 1215 John took the cross. From being an oppressor of the church, he had become the executor of Innocent's policy. The papal success was brilliant, but it had its price in the pope's willingness to become

John's uncritical protector. The renewal of baronial opposition in 1214–15 met with condemnation, the attempts of Stephen Langton to secure a settlement led to his suspension, and the grant of Magna Carta was annulled by papal letters. The pope's authority was now intimately involved in the troubled politics of England, but it had been placed at the disposal of the king, and was moreover uncertain in its operation because of the delays involved in consulting Rome. In England and in the empire Innocent seemed to have triumphed, but he still depended on the goodwill of men whose purposes were different from his own. It remained to be seen after his death whether the papacy had created a secure basis for authority, either in the structure of politics or in the hearts of men.

Innocent III involved himself in political actions to a greater extent than previous popes, in the sense both that he issued more instructions about secular affairs (whether it was to obey the Crown in England or Hungary or to make peace in France) and that he pursued policies such as the recuperation of papal lands, the exercise of the regency in Sicily and intervention in the imperial election. To speak of 'political' action is to use a modern term, but it corresponds to the impression formed by contemporaries. The question is whether these features were the reflection of a new theory of papal supremacy, or of the application of accepted doctrine in a new political situation. The claims made on behalf of the papacy by Bernard of Clairvaux, or by Bishop Rufinus at the inauguration of the Third Lateran Council, were already large. Did Innocent extend them or merely apply them? He was both a theorist and a politician, and it is wise to remember that his declarations were responses to particular situations, so that *Venerabilem* in 1202 contained a careful statement of the electoral rights of the German princes which had been missing from the *Deliberatio* of 1200. It is therefore not surprising to find a certain incoherence in his contribution to the development of papal theory. On the one hand he added to its rhetoric, creating new combinations of images which were powerful but imprecise; on the other his decretals contained specific definitions which assisted the analysis of technical issues by later theorists.

Innocent denied, in a statement at the highest level of authority, any wish to invade the jurisdiction of the lay power:

We do not desire laymen to usurp the rights of clergy. In the same way, we are concerned to prevent clergy from appropriating the rights of laymen. For this reason we forbid any clerk, under pretext of ecclesiastical liberty, to extend his jurisdiction at any future time to the prejudice of secular justice. Let everyone content himself with the written constitutions and customs hitherto approved. Thus *the things that are Caesar's* will be *rendered to Caesar* and *the things that are God's to God* according to the dictates of justice.[16]

There was thus no overt challenge to the classic division between the rights of clergy and laity, but this did not exclude the redefinition of their areas of responsibility. Some passages, indeed, ascribe almost no limit to the power of the pope. In a sermon on the anniversary of his consecration, he asserted that

it was said to me in the prophet, *I have set you over nations and over kingdoms, to pluck up and to break down, to destroy and to overthrow, to build and to plant* (Jer.i.10). . . . Others are called to the role of caring, but only Peter is raised to fullness of power. Now therefore you see who is the servant who is set over the household, truly the vicar of Jesus Christ, the successor of Peter, the Christ of the Lord, the God of Pharaoh; established in the middle between God and man, lower than God but higher than man; less than God, but greater than man; who judges all, and is judged by none.[7]

That this supremacy was not confined to ecclesiastical affairs is made clear by the statement that his marriage to the Roman Church had brought to him 'a dowry precious beyond price, that is the fulness of spiritual and breadth of temporal powers, both of them great and manifold'.[18] He had a special sense of enjoying divine authority for his actions: in connection with quite routine ecclesiastical business he announced that 'by the common counsel of our brethren, we have proceeded as was divinely revealed to us'.[19] Of previous popes only Gregory VII is known to have felt the same intensely personal conviction of speaking on God's behalf, and even then with a different nuance. Gregory saw himself as the agent of Peter and Paul, charged to strike down iniquity in high places, while Innocent acted under the privilege by which Christ 'left to Peter the government not only of the church but of the whole world'.[20] Although Bernard was a source for some of Innocent's terminology, the accent is markedly different, for Bernard was concerned to reduce the amount of worldly business in the papal household.

Innocent made important changes in the discourse of papal political theory. In particular he combined new imagery from the

[16] Fourth Lateran, canon 42, citing the standard text Matt. 22: 21 (Alberigo 229).
[17] *Sermo 2 in consecratione* (PL 217.657–8).
[18] *Sermo 3 in consecratione* (col.665 AB).
[19] Reg. i.485 (PL 215.453 A) and i.435 (415 BC), both to Richard I of England in 1198.
[20] Reg. ii.209 (col.759 CD).

Bible with accepted concepts to provide more elaborate ideological statements. He was fond of Old Testament passages which elevated the position of the priesthood such as Deuteronomy 17: 8–11, where the Israelites were ordered to submit difficult questions to the priests. Jeremiah 1: 10 had long been used to justify the correction of errors and uprooting of vices, but was now seen as bestowing power to regulate the political order and was quoted as justification for the grant of the Crown to the ruler of Bulgaria.[21] These ideas were brought into combination with the traditional Petrine texts, the authority to bind and loose, the fullness of power and the title of vicar of Christ, to create a powerful nexus of ideas which shaped the thinking of later popes and canonists. Like so many large statements of ideology, Innocent's are not always clear in precise content. Even verbally, they are not consistent: the claim to the government 'not only of the whole church but of the whole world' does not seem to tally with the distinction between the fulness of spiritual power and the breadth of temporal power. In an attempt to achieve consistency some scholars have argued that to Innocent fulness of power (*plenitudo potestatis*) referred strictly to supreme spiritual authority, and that the claim of power over the whole world was also spiritual in content: it indicated universal authority in contrast with the restricted jurisdiction of all other prelates. Such claims would then be consistent with a concern not to invade the rights of laymen. Undoubtedly Innocent did sometimes use the terminology in this sense, but even the few passages quoted here suggest strongly that his claims sometimes included the secular sphere. Few statesmen have ever limited their aspirations to a rigorously consistent scheme, and Innocent was not one of them.[22]

Alongside this elaboration of papal rhetoric there were some specific contributions to the definition of church–state relations. Innocent's statement of papal rights over the imperial election was a subtle and precise one which became normative in canon law, and which for the first time officially adopted the theory that the papacy had translated the empire from the Greeks to the Franks. The decretal *Novit*, issued to the French bishops probably in April 1204 to justify his intervention in the warfare between Philip of France and

---

[21] Reg. vii. 1 (col. 277 C).
[22] For the arguments see Tillmann, *Pope Innocent III*, 22–4 and notes; Kempf, *Papsttum und Kaisertum bei Innocenz III*, 296 ff.; and J. A. Watt, 'Theory of Papal Monarchy', *Traditio* 20 (1964), 273–4. A further complication is the uncertainty whether a given passage refers to political rights within the Papal State or a general supremacy in secular affairs.

John of England, introduced the important distinction between the king's judgement of feudal tenure (*iudicare de feudo*) and the church's decrees about sin (*decernere de peccato*). In *Per venerabilem* to the count of Montpellier Innocent argued that while he did not normally exercise authority in secular affairs, he could intervene on occasions, *casualiter*. Some of his other decretals made a start in defining what these occasions might be, and later canonists analysed them carefully. This important element in his thought forbids us to define Innocent's doctrine as a crudely hierocratic or monarchical one which claimed that all secular power was inherent in the papal office; nor, conversely, was it a consistent theory of two independent powers. He produced an elaborate rhetoric of the papal office which was adopted into canon law, and he left behind him a variety of legal definitions of major technical importance. More important still was the practical use to which these theories were applied. Innocent left to his successors a forceful exercise of papal authority which few earlier popes had approached and a resolute enforcement of his secular claims within the empire. His government helped to shape the policy of the thirteenth-century papacy, and the way in which its powers were understood.

iv. *Reform*

'Among all the good things which our heart can desire, there are two in this world which we value above all: that is to promote the recovery of the Holy Land and the reform of the universal church.' These were the priorities declared by Innocent III in *Vineam domini sabaoth*, in which he summoned the Fourth Lateran Council.[23] Developing the idea enunciated by Gregory VIII on the eve of the Third Crusade, he came to see the failings of the west as responsible for the loss of Jerusalem and its purification as the necessary condition for restoration of the city by God's blessing.

The reform policy was set out systematically in the Fourth Lateran decrees, and many of its elements are found in the pope's correspondence throughout the pontificate. One of his concerns was the obvious one, pursued by successive popes, of remedying misconduct among the clergy. In spite of the many instances of disciplinary action it would be useless to attempt a statistical survey of clerical misbehaviour. The registers tell us of a few intractable

[23] Reg. xvi.30 (PL 216.824 A).

offenders even among the bishops, whose sins ranged from the appointment of under-age relations through the sale of offices and open unchastity to the manslaughter of servants and killing of peasants in war. Such bishops may indeed have been reported because their behaviour outraged public opinion, but often the complaints arose in the course of disputes with their clergy; and they concern exaggerated versions of normal conduct, for bishops commonly advanced their families and, when necessary, employed militias to defend the rights of their sees—Innocent was active in doing both. It is hard to define 'corruption' in this context, and still harder to estimate how widespread it was. Nevertheless it was an important step to present a coherent policy of reform in place of the sporadic interventions which, as we saw in an earlier chapter, had been characteristic of energetic bishops in the twelfth century. An equally significant change was the sharpening of the cumbersome machinery of inquiry into serious offences. This had required a formal accusation by an accuser who was himself subject to penalties should his case fail. It is true that if there was a widespread report of misbehaviour (a 'defamation' in technical language) the ecclesiastical superior had a duty to take action, but his authority did not extend to examining witnesses, only to requiring an oath of innocence (a 'purgation') with supporting oath-helpers. Only in the case of heresy could the bishop use his own initiative and carry out an investigation. The system had been designed to favour the defendant and to protect clergy from malicious charges by powerful men whom they might have offended. Innocent authorized the extension of the inquiry procedure or 'inquisition' from heresy to other charges, and defined it in canon 8 of the Fourth Lateran Council. There were still protecting clauses: it could only be invoked if there was persistent defamation and it required the formal recording of a complaint. In that case, the bishop or other authority had the duty of investigating and of questioning witness. This became the basic pattern of disciplinary action during the later Middle Ages.

Innocent's concern with the correction of abuses extended also to monasteries. In canon law responsibility for monastic discipline belonged to the bishop, but many large and wealthy abbeys were exempt from episcopal authority and directly subject to the Roman Church. The Premonstratensians and Cistercians, for whom Innocent had a particular respect, had an internal system of discipline by means of their general chapters and the supervision of daughter-houses by the founding community. Some Benedictines were becoming interested in the Cistercian structure, and there were proposals to create general chapters in Denmark in 1205 and in the province of Rouen in 1210. Canon 12 provided for the practice to be extended to every province, in the first instance with Cistercian advisers who were experienced in operating it. The project was as a whole unsuccessful, but it was applied in England in particular as a result of the conciliar decree.

Another major concern at the Council was the improvement of the administration of the church. The procedure in elections was defined (canon 24), as was that in cases of excommunication (canon 47). A full record was to be kept of the documents in litigation before church courts—an important measure which completed the shift from the old oral pleas to a written procedure based entirely on record (canon 38). Clergy were strictly prohibited from involvement in the shedding of blood. They were not to write letters dealing with executions, not to command archers or *routiers*, not to be surgeons nor to bless the instruments for use in the ordeals of hot or cold water or hot iron (canon 18). These ancient practices were slowly disappearing from the European legal system. The withdrawal of clerical participation was not universally observed, but it stopped the use of ordeals in England and hastened their decline elsewhere. They were unpopular with some clerical thinkers because they appeared irrational or because they were unknown in Roman law, but it must be said that the Council's legislation against them does not read like a piece of enlightened reason but sets the prohibition firmly in the context of the taboo on blood-shedding.

There were other problems within the administration of the church to which Innocent gave his attention. One was the creation of a clerical proletariat by granting applicants minor orders without an appointment or 'title' to provide them with a means of support. From the beginning of the pontificate papal letters insisted on the duty of bishops to provide for such clergy if they found themselves destitute. The policy met with stubborn opposition from the bishops. Stephen of Tournai complained that they could not afford it and had no record of the names involved, and it was reported that the bishop of Poitiers took an oath from 200 ordinands that they would not expect any support from him. The absence of any mention of the question in the canons suggests that the pope could not carry the bishops with him at the Council or even that he had despaired of doing so.[24] A financial question of still more importance was the support of the Roman curia, which had insufficient revenues for its widened responsibilities in the western church. The situation encouraged curialists to maintain themselves by exorbitant charges or actual fraud, and at the Council Innocent made a proposal to assign to the curia a revenue from every cathedral (one-tenth or one of the prebends) with the objective of ending the extortion. Not surprisingly the idea did not win acquiescence and had to be dropped. One consequence of this failure was the continued development of 'provisions' or the assignment of canonries to clerks nominated by papal letters. The author of Innocent's biography wrote of the number of learned and worthy clerks for whom he thereby secured advancement, and this was certainly part of the story.[25] It none the less represented an important increase in the patronage of the Roman church which was to prove capable of enormous extension.

Much the most striking feature of the Lateran decrees was, however, the stress on the pastoral responsibilities of the clergy. The groundwork for such a development was laid in the twelfth century, with the increasing concern to define the special function of ranks within the laity and the growth of preaching. We shall also see, when we discuss in more detail the distinctive pastoral approach of the thirteenth century, that a very active concern with preaching, the confessional, and practical ethics can be traced to Paris shortly before 1200, and it is tempting to suppose that Innocent absorbed the new ideas during his time there. He was concerned to set a personal example, giving counsel to visitors to the curia and preaching assiduously: we have about seventy-eight of his sermons, some of them collected for publication by Innocent himself. The keys to his pastoral strategy were preaching, confession, and the mass, and canonists regarded as perhaps the most important Lateran decision canon 21, *omnis utriusque sexus*, which commanded every adult to make his or her confession once a year, to perform the penance enjoined, and to receive the sacrament of the Eucharist at Easter. The publication of the decree implies that annual confession and communion were not universal, and the requirement to publish it

---

[24] See Tillmann, *Pope Innocent III*, 198–200. The increase in the number requesting minor orders presumably reflected the growing career prospects for clerks through study in the schools and service in administration or medicine.

[25] *Gesta Innocentii*, c. 147 (PL 214.ccxxv A): 'ubique per orbem in ecclesiasticis beneficiis provideri.'

frequently and to enforce it upon pain of suspension from entry to the church and prohibition of Christian burial strengthens the impression that a new requirement was being imposed. The decree emphasized that priests must be skilled to give advice and instruction in the confessional. We should beware of supposing that this was intended to be counselling of a subtle kind: in one of Innocent's own sermons there is a dialogue in which a priest urges a penitent to try to give up consorting with prostitutes, and this may well have been the rather basic norm. The canons of Fourth Lateran also contained concrete plans for the improvement of preaching. It was observed (canon 10) that bishops were unable to dispense sufficiently the word of God, 'specially in huge and scattered dioceses' (an unusual recognition of a major problem) and they were therefore instructed to provide competent men to preach, hear confessions, and give penance. These were to visit the people, and were clearly thought of as a sort of diocesan missioner. Canon 11 prescribed that in every metropolitan church there would be an appointment made 'to teach Holy Scripture to priests and others, and especially to form them in things which concern the cure of souls'. The devotion to the eucharist was built up, not only by a definition of its theology, but by instructions to maintain the sanctity of churches and of the sacred vessels, and to keep the host under lock and key (canons 19, 20). Another aspect of pastoral concern was shown in the reform of the marriage law. The reason was the 'danger for souls' presented by the older rule which prohibited marriage within seven degrees of relationship—a range so absurdly wide that it involved many people in unconscious breaches of the rules of the church and made it possible to obtain what in practice was divorce at will. The Council consciously amended this and restricted the range of prohibition to the fourth degree (canons 50–2).

We can only evaluate the success of the ambitious reform programme formulated at the Fourth Lateran by examining its application during the following generation, but some preliminary points may be made now. As one would expect from a large enterprise, it was not completely original: some of its elements were derived from developments widespread in the twelfth century and others (its more distinctive features) owed a great deal to Paris thinking during the preceding twenty-five years. The hope was to apply the new approach to the western church as a whole. Some of Innocent's policies were not adopted by the Council. These included the attempt to provide finance for the curia and to enforce episcopal responsibility for those in minor orders (two major problems in the later medieval church). Other provisions, like the governmental reform of Benedictine monasticism and the abolition of the ordeal, had only a very limited effect. Nevertheless the decrees performed an important function both of definition and of innovation, and they provided a starting-point and inspiration for later ecclesiastical reform. The most striking feature was the advance from older ideals of cultic purity of the clergy to a demand for an active pastorate directed towards the faithful as a whole. That is not to say that the Council envisaged the possibility of a radically new lay spirituality. The intention for the laity was a disciplinarian one: they were to be instructed in right belief and right action in sermons and the confessional. There was little in the decrees about ways in which lay devotion was actively expressing itself (pilgrimage, processions, confraternities) or about the ideals of apostolic poverty which were beginning to acquire a new life among the followers of Francis of Assisi and parallel movements. The prohibition of the creation of new religious orders may have been directed precisely against such ideas, and may also be another instance of the triumph of the opposition over the more radically minded pope. Whatever the reason, what emerged was essentially the programme of the Paris pastoral school. Like good schoolmasters, the bishops were anxious that laymen should be instructed in their duties and should take their proper place in the life of the church by performing them scrupulously. They also thought it was the job of the laity to do precisely what they were told.

v. *The Christian East*

Innocent III was the heir to Henry VI, not only in central Italy and Sicily, but in the crusading movement. Henry's death put an end to his projected expedition to the east, and Innocent was ready to accept the responsibility, which he regarded as properly belonging to the Roman Church, for the recovery of the holy places. His first crusading appeal was issued on 15 August 1198 and his plans incorporated two important new features. One was the assumption that the direction would be in the hands of the pope and not, like the Third Crusade or that of Henry VI, of lay rulers, and the second was the institution of a general papal tax on the western churches. In

December 1198 Innocent required clergy to pay one-fortieth of their ecclesiastical revenues.[26] It is not clear how much was raised. There was no specific sanction for non-payment, and years later the pope was still complaining that some bishops had not yet made the proceeds available to the Holy Land.

In spite of his determination to supervise the planning of the Fourth Crusade Innocent rapidly lost control. The time-scale was unrealistic and by March 1199, when the participants should have been assembling, little had happened. The real origin of the Crusade lay in the passionate preaching of Fulk of Neuilly in France, and in the initiative of Count Theobald of Champagne who from November 1199 began to gather a powerful group of French nobles around himself.[27] Their preparations seem to have progressed independently of the pope. It is doubtful if he knew in advance of their agreement with Venice in spring 1201 to provide naval transport and supplies, and it is unlikely that he was consulted in the election of a new leader after Count Theobald's death, for his successor Boniface of Montferrat was a supporter of Philip of Suabia. Without a major power to direct it, the Crusade drifted from its original purpose. The Treaty of Venice had seriously overestimated the number of participants, and when the crusaders assembled there in the summer of 1202 they were unable to find the promised payment. The Venetians offered transport on condition that the crusaders would assist in the capture of Zara, an Adriatic city which had fallen into Hungarian hands. In November the Franco-Venetian force therefore took a Christian city whose lord, the king of Hungary, had himself taken the cross. A much larger diversion was to follow. The Byzantine emperor, Alexius III, had secured the throne by deposing his brother, and his nephew, also called Alexius, had made his way to the west. In the course of 1202 young Alexius made the crusading leaders an offer which they could not refuse. In return for his establishment on the imperial throne, he would subject the Greek church to the authority of Rome and would contribute on a handsome scale to the recovery of the Holy Land. The terms were accepted and in July 1203 he was enthroned as co-emperor with his

---

[26] Reg. ii.270 (PL 215.828–32); English translation in L. and J. Riley-Smith, *The Crusades: Idea and Reality* (London, 1981), no. 34, pp. 144–8. For the question whether this was really the first general tax on the church see D. E. Queller, *The Fourth Crusade* (Leicester, 1978), p. 2 n.7.

[27] The dates are far from clear, and it has been suggested that the activity of Count Theobald should be placed in late 1198, when it would be more clearly a response to Innocent's appeal. See E. John in *Byzantion* 28 (1958), 95–103.

deposed father under the threat of a Frankish army and fleet outside the walls of Constantinople. In reality there was little prospect that he, a puppet of the hated Latins, would be able to assemble the troops and money which he had promised. He was overthrown by his own subjects, and the crusaders stormed the city. It fell (for the first time in 900 years) on 13 April 1204, and its fall was marked by a sack of horrifying proportions. The Latin capture of Constantinople was a disaster for Christendom. To the Greeks it was an unforgettable outrage. In place of the Byzantine emperor there was now a Latin emperor of *Romania*, as the Greek territories were called, but his position was always insecure, resented by its subjects, and challenged by Greek successor states in outlying parts of the empire.

Innocent almost certainly did not intend the Fourth Crusade to undertake the restoration of Alexius, let alone create a Latin empire, which nobody had originally foreseen. Yet the pope is not clear of all responsibility: he had already planned a crusade against Christians in Sicily, had threatened military action if Alexius III did not assist in the recovery of Jerusalem, and his reaction to the attack on Zara was not as stringent as it might have been. The dilemma which faced everybody, the pope included, was that the Franks could only secure shipping by agreeing first to the attack on Zara, and then to the diversion to Constantinople. The pope could not take a firm line without bringing the crusade to an end, and this he was unwilling to do. Even before 1204 Innocent had shown himself more inclined to treat the Byzantines as rebels against Rome than any previous pope, and it is therefore understandable that, although he was horrified at the news of the sack, he expressed his delight that the kingdom of the Greeks had been 'changed by God's just judgement from proud to humble, from disobedient to faithful, from schismatics to catholics'.[28]

The creation of a fragile Latin rule at Constantinople evoked bitter resentment from the Greek church, as well as constituting a serious distraction from the western effort in Palestine. Innocent failed to recognize either of these problems. He gave unwavering support to the Latin empire and proceeded on the assumption that the eastern churches were subject to Rome in the same sense as those of the west, demanding oaths of loyalty from the bishops. In practice this implied the imposition of a Latin hierarchy, which was in any case the intention of most of the conquerors. By his own lights Innocent was concerned to secure a satisfactory church settlement in the east.

[28] Reg. vii.153 (PL 215.455 C), Nov. 1204 to Emperor Baldwin

He recognized the continued use of the Greek rite, which for that matter the Frankish rulers had no interest in disturbing. He also resisted the attempts of the conquerors to exploit the churches and expropriate their lands. In particular, Innocent fought a long battle against the Venetians' attempt to dominate the patriarchate of Constantinople and the chapter of St Sophia. It is difficult to see how the pope could have found a satisfactory policy after 1204, but he showed an astonishing lack of perception of the problem. He continued to assume that the Latin conquest had provided a definitive solution to inter-church relations and made no serious attempt to seek for new initiatives in the Lateran Council. A similar lack of realism marked his hope that the expedition might be continued from Constantinople to Jerusalem. His first response had been to order all members of the army to assist the new Emperor Baldwin of Flanders 'for the defence and retention of the empire of Constantinople, by aid of which the Holy Land can be more easily freed from the hands of the pagans'.[29] He retained this comforting illusion for some time and was furious when in 1205 his legate Peter of Capua took the realistic step of dispensing the crusaders from their vow to go to Jerusalem.

When it became apparent that there was no hope that the Crusade would continue to the Holy Land, the pope's attention was distracted by the outbreak of the campaign against the Albigensians in southern France and by the Spanish war, which he supported by an indulgence and which led to a decisive victory over the Moors at Las Navas de Tolosa in 1212. The proclamation of a new expedition to the east did not take place until the encyclical *Quia maior* in April 1213.[30] This left the final arrangements to the Lateran Council but introduced a carefully planned programme of preaching and liturgical propaganda, which included monthly processions and the singing at every mass of Psalm 79, 'O God, the heathen have come into thy inheritance'. The plans were completed by the Council's decree *Ad liberandam* on 30 November 1215.[31] The army was to gather for transport in the kingdom of Sicily on 1 June 1217, and Innocent would be there in person. A tax of one-twentieth for three years was imposed on clergy, a much larger levy than before and this time with the full authority of the Council. The whole project was designed to

[29] Reg. vii.153 (col.455 B).
[30] Reg. xvi.28 (PL 216.317–22); English translation in Riley-Smith, *The Crusades*, no. 28, pp. 118–24.
[31] English translation in Riley-Smith, *The Crusades*, no. 27, pp. 124–9.

avoid the problems which had plagued the Fourth Crusade: it had longer planning, better finance, the promised participation of three kings (Frederick II, John of England, and Andrew of Hungary), and tighter papal control.

Innocent was dead by the appointed date, and a judgement of his crusading policy must turn on our speculation about the probable success of the Fifth Crusade under his leadership. Its prospects were undoubtedly weakened by his death. His direction would have been more forceful than that of his successor, Honorius, and he was much more likely to secure the participation of Frederick, who in the event absented himself from the expedition. Yet the basic difficulties would have remained. In spite of a hint at the Lateran Council, it is unlikely that Innocent would actually have travelled with the army, and the attempt to control a distant expedition through a legate would have been as awkward as it actually proved to be. The military situation in the east, moreover, was too unfavourable to hope for permanent success from a single expedition which depended on a very long line of communication. Innocent had been correct in believing that only some new ingredient, such as massive Byzantine support, could alter the situation in Syria; where he had for a time been wrong was in his belief that the Latin conquest of Constantinople would make it available.

vi. *The Struggle with Heresy*

In the repression of heresy, as in so many other areas, the accession of Innocent saw a new initiative. From the beginning he threatened the use of force against heretics and their supporters. His first encyclical to the bishops of Languedoc announced that 'on no occasion do we intend to be stricter in judgement than in the eradication of heretics', and those who acted against them were offered the same indulgence as pilgrims to Rome or Compostella.[32] This looked back to the canon of Third Lateran. More original was the decretal *Vergentis in senium* addressed to Viterbo on 25 March 1199, in which he equated heresy with the crime of treason in civil law and applied the same penalties, confiscation of the offender's property and disinheritance of his descendants. It was initially addressed to a city under the pope's temporal lordship but was quickly extended outside the Papal State. It offered to catholic princes the prospect of a secure title to the

---

[32] Reg. i. no. 94, p. 137, 21 Apr. 1198.

lands of heretics whom they conquered. Warfare and secular penalties alike required the assistance of the lay power, which was fundamental to Innocent's plans. As he wrote to Philip Augustus of France,

For the protection of his spouse, the universal church, the Lord instituted priestly and royal dignity, the one to care for its children and the other to combat its adversaries; the one to build up the life of its descendants by word and example . . . , the other to exercise the material sword *to punish those who do wrong and to praise those who do right*, and to protect with arms the peace of the church.[33]

Innocent was even more concerned with the use of peaceful persuasion, especially in winning back champions of poverty and preaching. He defined his approach when a group of Waldensians was discovered at Metz in 1199: 'The depravity of heretics must not be tolerated, but at the same time the religion of simple people must not be undermined. Otherwise our tolerance will make the heretics bolder or our excessive intolerance will confuse the simple and they will leave us and go astray and turn into heretics.'[34] The Lombard sect of Humiliati, which had been condemned at Verona in 1184, was reconciled when in 1201 Innocent authorized the practices of three groups within it: a community of men living under Rule, another of women, and a 'third order' of laymen living with their families. He conceded that within this lay fellowship those who were 'wise in faith and expert in religion' could teach and exhort the others, presumably on the principle that, while the theological exposition of the more obscure passages of Scripture was the preserve of the clergy, laymen could expound the literal text of the Gospels and the Epistle of St James. The Waldensian movement had by this time travelled beyond the point of no return, but it proved possible to recover its more conservative members including the theologian Durand de Huesca, who was reconciled after a disputation at Pamiers in the south of France and whose programme or *propositum* for the society of 'Catholic Poor' received papal approval in 1208.

This conciliatory policy also enabled new movements to emerge under the protection of the church, and not in opposition to it. The most remarkable figure was Francis, the son of a rich merchant of Assisi. He had been born about 1182 and at first lived as a well-to-do

[33] Reg. vii.79 (PL 215.361 CD), 28 May 1204, citing 1 Pet. 2: 14.
[34] Reg. ii.141 (PL 214.695–8).

young citizen. He had little formal learning, with probably a smattering of Latin acquired at a parochial school. In about 1205 he turned his back upon warfare and trade, his inherited way of life. His primary purpose was the literal following of the Gospel. By this he understood complete poverty and an itinerant ministry of witness and preaching, which was however combined with a strong reverence for the authority of the church. He began his public ministry by repairing with his own hands San Damiano and other decrepit church buildings near Assisi, and soon afterwards, at mass in the little chapel of the Portiuncula, he was struck by the Gospel command: 'Preach as you go, saying 'The kingdom of heaven is at hand. . . . Take no gold, nor silver, nor copper in your belts, no bag for your journey, nor two tunics, nor sandals, nor a staff' (Matt. 10: 7–10). Since Francis saw himself as living directly under the commands of the Gospel, he did not envisage his followers as requiring a Rule in the ordinary sense, and the one which he submitted to Innocent III in 1210 probably took the form of a simple collection of Gospel texts. After some hesitation the pope gave his approval, insisting that the brethren should preach only with Francis's permission. By the end of the pontificate these followers had grown in number and included a group of nuns, of which the young Clare was the first member. We must not exaggerate the significance of the movement in 1215. It was small compared with the parallel movement of the Humiliati, with their 150 houses in the neighbourhood of Milan. The explosion was still to come.

Innocent was convinced that preaching and reform were integral to the struggle with heresy and was sensitive to the charge that heretics were provided with easy targets by the corruptions of the clergy. As his agents in Languedoc he looked initially to the Cistercians, whose connections with the region went back to Abbots Bernard and Henry of Clairvaux, but the most striking development of the Languedoc mission was the result of the intervention of two Spanish clergy. Their distinctive contribution perhaps reflected the circumstances of their homeland, for they came from a territory which had only recently been a missionary area. Bishop Diego of Osma had been sent on a diplomatic embassy in 1203 and had taken as travelling companion Dominic of Caleruega, an able young man who had read theology at Palencia and become an Augustinian canon. On their journey they encountered Cathar believers for the first time. In the course of a second embassy in 1205 they resolved to visit Rome in the hope of obtaining the pope's permission to preach beyond the frontiers of Christendom.[35] On their way back to Spain they met the Cistercian legates in southern France and heard their laments about the difficulty in converting the Albigensians. Diego produced a revolutionary solution: instead of appearing as officials of high standing they should travel in poverty and simplicity, as the Cathar 'perfects' did. It would be interesting to know whether this project had been discussed with Innocent at Rome, but we have no evidence on the point. We only know that a papal letter of 17 November 1206 gave his support: 'We ordain and prescribe . . . that you take proved men, suitable for the purpose, not afraid in imitating the poverty of Christ who was poor to approach the humble in lowly garb and with fervent spirit.'[36] The new mission was fully constituted by the spring of 1207, when Arnold Amaury, abbot of Cîteaux, appeared with a considerable staff of Cistercians to join the two Spaniards. A summer of hectic travelling and disputations followed, and the effort had some success: Cathars were converted, a house for women converts was established at Prouille, and the Waldensian Durand of Huesca was reconciled with the church. The mission, however, was essentially temporary; it could be little else with a personnel mainly of Cistercian monks. It broke up in autumn 1207, leaving Dominic to continue a ministry of preaching based on the nunnery at Prouille.

In any case events were moving in the direction of force. The Albigensian Crusade was not only a response to an emergency but was rooted in Innocent's earlier policies. He had begun his pontificate with an indulgence to those who acted against heretics, and he had appealed to Philip Augustus in May 1204 and early 1205 to 'eliminate heretics from the kingdom of France'. In November 1207 he renewed his pressure. The leading noble of the south was Count Raymond VI of Toulouse, who was treated by northern propagandists as a friend of Cathars. This is probably not true, but nor was he an effective persecutor. In several places within his county Cathars lived undisturbed under the protection of sympathetic local nobles, and they were even more secure under the Trencavel vicomtes of Béziers and Carcassonne. The uncompromising legate Peter of Castelnau pressed Count Raymond to support

---

[35] The details of their travels and objectives are obscure; see M. H. Vicaire, *S. Dominic and his Times* (London, 1964), ch. 4.

[36] Reg. vii.185 (PL 215.1025 AB).

political action against heresy, and when he failed to secure his agreement he excommunicated him. The crusade appeal of November 1207 drove Raymond to renewed negotiations, which ended in an angry quarrel. When on 14 January 1208 Peter of Castelnau was murdered it was natural to suspect Raymond, although there were many in the south with good reason for fearing the legate. The murder redoubled Innocent's determination to launch the crusade, for which he offered an indulgence and a tax on the French clergy. Philip Augustus remained stubbornly uninterested, but enough northern bishops and barons enlisted to assemble a considerable army on the Rhône in summer 1209.

The natural target was the excommunicate Raymond VI, but at the eleventh hour he submitted, promised reparation, and joined the crusade himself. The army marched instead against the lands of Raymond-Roger Trencavel. It was a logical decision because of the number of Cathars there, but it meant that the campaign was directed against territories which had made no preparations against attack. Béziers fell on 22 July 1209 and many of its inhabitants were massacred. The story was later told that Arnold Amaury was asked how to distinguish heretics from catholics and replied, 'Kill them all! God will know his own.' If the story is a myth, it is a true myth: Arnold did nothing to restrain the conquerors. On 15 August Carcassonne capitulated, and its inhabitants had to leave carrying (observed a northern chronicler pleasantly) nothing but their sins. Simon of Montfort was elected lord of the conquered dominions. A series of attempts was made to reach a settlement with Raymond of Toulouse, but the immigration of Cathars into his county from the former Trencavel lands made it even more difficult for him to satisfy the demands of the legates in 1211 than it had been in 1207. When war broke out Simon's smaller army defeated the joint forces of Count Raymond and Peter II of Aragon at the battle of Muret in August 1213.

By 1215 Simon held most of the county of Toulouse as well as the Trencavel lands, and power was being exercised by men committed to the destruction of heresy. Two of the major sees were held by northern abbots who had come with the crusade, Arnold Amaury (Narbonne) and Guy of Vaux-de-Cernay (Carcassonne), and Toulouse was in the hands of an ardent catholic, Bishop Fulk of Marseille. Legislation had been introduced to facilitate the discovery of heresy: at Avignon in 1209 it was required that in each parish a priest and two or three laymen should take an oath to report heretics, and Simon's statute of Pamiers on 1 December 1212 protected the privileges of the church. Important centres had been eliminated with burnings of substantial numbers of perfects. It seems that after Béziers indiscriminate slaughter was quite rare, but selected executions of leading heretics took place at Minerve (140 burnings), Lavaur (300), and Cassès (60). The Cathar position in the south was seriously threatened, but two problems remained. One was political instability. The great majority of catholic southerners deeply resented the rule of Simon of Montfort, and he did not command the resources to impose his control outside a limited number of centres. The other difficulty was the absence of any machinery either to win the goodwill of the population by preaching or to track down heretics whom many southerners were not willing to denounce. One immediate initiative was taken by Bishop Fulk of Toulouse. He invited Dominic to the city in 1215 to organize a preaching mission. Fulk's charter echoed the methods of Bishop Diego's old campaign, but it also pointed forward: Dominic was now established with a few followers living in a religious community, and the commission to preach was directed to the group as a whole. It was a small body designed to work in one diocese, but in principle it was the foundation of the Order of Preachers.

vii. *The Fourth Lateran Council*

At the first plenary session of the Fourth Lateran Council on 11 November 1215 Innocent preached to a congregation of over 400 bishops and 800 abbots, deans, and others. Cathedrals and collegiate churches had sent representatives and there were clergy also from the eastern patriarchates, to form the largest council yet held in the history of the church. His address was based on Luke 22: 15: '*I have earnestly desired to eat this passover with you before I suffer*, that is to say before I die.' The last words are curious in view of Innocent's death a few months later, but it is a romantic fiction to suppose that he was voicing a premonition. The 'passover' which he desired was not the council, but a threefold 'passage': the bodily journey to recover Jerusalem, the spiritual journey from corruption to reform, and the eternal journey from earth to the glory of heaven. The address was designed as a programme for the council and, as at all good conferences, the text was made available for those who could not hear the pope's words in the crowded church. There were three plenary sessions on 11, 20, and 30 November. In addition there were separate discussions of major issues, some of them amounting to full-dress debates. Much of the legislation was an expression of policies which Innocent had followed throughout his pontificate, but the council was no rubber stamp. There was a good deal of redrafting, for instance in the crusading decree *Ad liberandam* (canon 71), and at times the pope had to make considerable concessions. The deprivation of Raymond VI of Toulouse was contrary to his own wishes; he was obliged to withdraw his proposal for a tax on cathedral churches; and the prohibition of new religious orders 'lest too great a variety of religions create confusion in the church of God' (canon 13) looks like a conservative protest against such experiments as the Humiliati and the Catholic Poor.

The legislation about reform and crusade has already been considered in earlier sections. Equally important was the definition of the faith and the struggle with heresy. It was a very long time since the church had produced a new creed (canon 1). It was directed against the wave of heresy and reflected the terminology and sacramental teaching of the Paris masters. It is significant that a definition of doctrine, issued at the highest level of authority, could incorporate non-Biblical language which earlier councils avoided in declarations of the faith:

There is one universal church of the faithful, outside which no one at all is saved, in which Jesus Christ is at once priest and sacrifice; whose body and blood are truly contained in the sacrament of the altar under the species of bread and wine, the bread being transubstantiated into the body and the wine into the blood by the power of God . . . And this sacrament no one can perform except a priest who has been duly ordained according to the keys of the church, which Jesus Christ himself granted to the apostles and their successors.[37]

The impression of Paris influence is strengthened by the spirited defence of the Trinitarian doctrine of Peter Lombard against Joachim of Fiore (canon 2). Canon 3 provided the most thorough statement so far of a programme of action against heretics. Their goods were to be confiscated, and secular powers required to take an oath to drive them out. Catholics helping to exterminate heresy would receive the same indulgence as those who aided the Holy Land; unauthorized

[37] Alberigo 204.

preaching was prohibited; and bishops were instructed to inquire after heretics, taking testimony in cases of defamation and demanding purgation by oath. The council expressed its good will towards the eastern churches: 'we wish to care for and respect the Greeks, who in our days are returning to obedience to the apostolic see, and to maintain as far as the Lord allows their customs and rites' (canon 4). The striking thing, however, is what the Council did not say. No effort was made to create conditions for unity or to discuss outstanding issues, and although almost all who attended from the eastern empire were Latins it was assumed that the process of unification was complete. Canon 5 was supposed to reaffirm the rights of the eastern patriarchs, but it demanded that they receive the pallium from the Roman pontiff and take an oath of obedience to the Roman Church, which could hear appeals from them and send legates. This was to treat them on the same level as western archbishops, and accordingly a disputed election at Constantinople was finally settled by papal decision. The idea, which the Gregorian Deusdedit had still expressed, that the patriarchs should co-operate in preserving the faith had been lost. The whole church was to be directed from Rome.

Alongside these religious issues political controversies were regulated. Frederick II was recognized as emperor, in spite of a passionate statement on behalf of Otto IV, and the baronial opposition was condemned in England and Archbishop Stephen Langton suspended from office because of his sympathy with them. A settlement was attempted in Languedoc by the deprivation of Raymond VI of Toulouse and the recognition of Simon of Montfort, the claims of the young Raymond VII being limited to the family territories east of the Rhône. Bishop Fulk of Toulouse and Dominic had come to the Council in the hope of confirmation for their novel order of preachers. Their ideas may well have influenced the decree on episcopal preaching (canon 10), but the pope, presumably in deference to the decree against new religious orders, urged them to formulate their customs by selecting from bodies already in existence. Dominic's aspirations were still close to those of the regular canons and he could therefore find what he wanted within the elastic Rule of St Augustine.

While attempting to bring to settlement at the Council the issues which were already confronting him, such as the matter of the empire and the Albigensian Crusade, Innocent also provided an ambitious programme for the next phase of his pontificate: the recovery of the Holy Land, the reform of the church, and the further prosecution of heresy. Its implementation was left to his successor, for he died at Perugia on 16 July 1216. His was the longest pontificate in our period after that of Alexander III. He was an unusually able man, equipped by birth and training to direct the affairs of the church. Circumstances gave him an unusually free hand, and he was confident of his ability to govern. We must therefore ask how far Innocent's personal ideals fashioned the changes in the church which were to make the thirteenth century very different from the twelfth. For all his masterful approach, his policy was inevitably influenced by his predecessors and advisers. The programme of 'recuperations' in Italy had been initiated by Celestine III, the first steps towards the repression of heresy taken by Alexander III, and the details of his decretals must have owed a great deal to legal experts in the curia. He also died at a crucial moment, after initiating new projects at the Council, so that he did not have to face the difficulties in which his policies became enmeshed through the stubborn resistance of Raymond of Toulouse or the ambitions of Frederick II. Nor could he have foreseen the spectacular success of the friars as international agents of the papacy. Fate had tricks and treats in store of which Innocent had no conception in 1216.

Among these uncertainties it is still possible to identify some of Innocent's personal contributions, and they are striking. He devoted himself to the needs of Christendom, by which he understood crusade, reform, and the correction of heresy. He originated the Fourth and Fifth Crusades and formulated a reforming programme for the next generation. He was not afraid to challenge ancient institutions such as the ordeal or the prohibition of marriage within the seventh degree. He restored the link between the Roman Church and the apostolic poverty movement, which his predecessors had broken, and his sympathy for Francis and Dominic was crucial in the prehistory of the friars. He put into action on a large scale the use of indulgence and crusade against heresy for which his predecessors had provided precedents. He was determined in his defence of the political rights of the Roman Church, effectively creating the Papal State and involving papal authority in the internal politics of the empire and of England and other kingdoms. His pursuit of these policies sat uneasily with his attempt in the decretals to distinguish between royal rights and ecclesiastical ones, and it left the Roman

Church with a tradition of fierce defence of its political claims in the Italian peninsula. The potential conflict between his political and ecclesiastical aims was partly concealed from Innocent by his conviction of his special position between God and man. He left an enriched vocabulary for the papal fullness of power, but did not clearly discern the practical and theoretical limits to its exercise.

The language of unlimited authority did not describe reality. Although the growing power of the curia had eroded the rights of national churches, kings too had at their disposal an improved machinery of government, and bishops and abbots retained resources in revenue and influence which meant that they were far from being mere subjects of papal monarchy. Rome did not possess the machinery to direct in detail the affairs of the western churches, nor the revenue to finance its enterprises, which often had to depend on self-interested allies and out-of-date information. At times Innocent's policies followed strangely circular routes: in England a long struggle to install Stephen Langton as archbishop ended in his suspension by the pope, and in the empire he stubbornly resisted one Hohenstaufen only to sponsor another in whose person the union of Germany and Sicily was renewed. Innocent is a test case for papal monarchy, because no pope in history was so fitted by talent and cirumstances to make it workable. The language became progressively more absolute, but rhetoric had outstripped reality. The curia could respond to outside pressure, exert moral influence, and enlist the sympathy of interested parties; but only rarely could it command.

18

FRIARS, BEGUINES, AND THE ACTION
AGAINST HERESY

i. *The Growth of The Friars*

At the death of Innocent III, Francis of Assisi and Dominic of Caleruega were at the head of small religious fellowships. Dominic had about sixteen followers resident at a house in Toulouse as preachers in the diocese; Francis had a larger body of disciples in Umbria, living under the simple rule or 'intention' approved by Innocent in 1210. These two societies were to become the most innovative force in the thirteenth-century church.

There is much contemporary material about Francis, including his own brief reminiscences in the *Testament* and the two versions of his life written by Thomas of Celano in about 1228 and 1245. All these works bear the marks of controversies which began in his own lifetime, and it is hard to distinguish between accurate reporting, coloured recollection, and propaganda. The impact of Francis was so great that it is tempting to see him as radically original, especially as this is confirmed by his own belief that he had received a message from God which was to be carried to the whole of humanity: 'no one showed me what I ought to do, but the Most High himself revealed to me that I ought to live according to the form of the holy Gospel'.[1] In this confidence he addressed himself 'to all Christians, religious, clerks and laity, men and women, all who live in the whole world'.[2] Yet his message was also shaped by the society in which he lived. People were leaving the cities of Umbria to live as penitents in the wilderness, and the first stage in his ministry was to join their ranks: 'the Lord caused me, brother Francis, to begin doing penance in this way'.[3] His conviction that he was called 'to live according to the form of the holy Gospel' had been anticipated by hermits and

---

[1] Francis, *Testament* (SC 285, p. 206).
[2] Francis, *Epistola ad fideles*, ii. 1 (p. 228).
[3] Francis, *Testament*, 1 (p. 204).

preachers, among them Stephen of Muret and Rainier of Pisa, and in another way by Waldensians, Humiliati, and Cathars.[4] The severity of Italian hermit orders such as Camaldoli was echoed in Francis's life-style and he rejected any suggestion that he should follow the Rules of Augustine and Benedict, those two great moderators of monastic extremes. Like a number of the radical preachers in the twelfth century, Francis at first probably had an ambition to include women within the sphere of his ministry. He may well have taken the initiative in persuading the young Clare of Assisi in 1212, at the age of 17, to take a vow to follow the path of Gospel perfection. In the early days Clare and her small group of followers, based at San Damiano just outside the walls of Assisi, seem to have followed a life which included a practical ministry to the poor outside the convent walls.

It was, indeed, the special genius of Francis to be immoderate. No one has ever been less disposed to compromise, nor affirmed the underlying paradoxes of the Gospel with so little desire to find a middle way. The basis of his thinking was a combination of Gospel texts and simple images, and gives us a glimpse of a lay piety of which we know too little. It did not provide him with the means of recognizing contradictions or resolving them. His consciousness of a universal mission went hand in hand with the rejection of the means which would make an international ministry possible: he wanted no papal exemption, no formal education, in a sense no Rule. His conviction that his little brothers (*fratres minores*, friars minor) must be obedient to all, especially to the authority of the church, was absolute; so was his affirmation that no friar was bound to do what he thought was unlawful.[5] He saw the natural order as a reflection of God's glory, and combined this world-affirmation with the denial to the brothers of even the most basic securities of religious orders: they were to live by labour and by begging, to have no corporate revenues and never handle money. Francis saw this spirituality of obedience and freedom as a reflection of the life of Christ. His piety revolved round the Nativity and the Passion in a way which reminds us strongly of the Cistercians before him. A vision before the crucifix at San Damiano had been a decisive stage in his conversion, and at

---

[4] For Rainier, see J. Sumption, *Pilgrimage* (London, 1975), esp. 173 ff.

[5] *Regula non Bullata*, v.2, (p. 130): 'if any of the ministers commands anything to any brother which is against our life or against his soul, he is not obliged to obey him.' The clause occurs in a weaker form in *Regula Bullata*, x.3 (pp. 194–6).

Greccio in Christmas 1223 he brought the crib scene into popular devotion. His programme contained profound insights into the Gospel, and it is easy to understand why men were inspired by it. It is equally plain that it was a recipe for trouble.

The rapid growth in the number of Francis's followers led to a decision in 1217 to send missions north of the Alps and to appoint provincial ministers to improve the supervision of the growing movement. The missions were wretchedly planned: the brothers, unprotected by papal recommendations and, in Germany, unable to speak the language, won little sympathy and were even taken for Cathars. As a result in 1219–20 proposals were put forward to change the friars into something more like a traditional order, to adopt a version of the Benedictine or Augustinian Rule, and to secure papal protection. When he heard what was happening Francis, who was in the eastern Mediterranean, hastily returned.[6] The growth of the order had brought to the surface the incoherence which underlay Francis's mission, and he never again exercised direct control, appointing Peter Catani as vicar-general and then, on his death on 10 March 1221, Elias of Cortona to succeed him. Francis withdrew to the mountains, especially to his beloved Rieti valley, where he spent much of his remaining years in seclusion with Leo and a few other companions. The culmination of this time of withdrawal was the experience at La Verna on Holy Cross day, 14 September 1224, when a vision of the crucified Christ left him with the stigmata, the marks of the wounds on his feet, hands, and side. The episode was concealed during his lifetime, but there is little reason to doubt its historicity.

Meanwhile the society was pursuing an unsteady course towards normalization. The first papal privilege, *Pro dilectis filiis*, was issued on 29 May 1220 and ordered bishops to permit friars to preach in their dioceses. Attempts were made to draw up a rule which would embody the original inspiration of Francis while rendering the order governable, but the drafting proved highly controversial. The *Regula Non Bullata* of 1221 contained strong elements of Francis's radical message of freedom, and was not adopted. The final version, the *Regula Bullata*, was revised by the sympathetic Cardinal Hugolino, an admirer of Francis and protector of the movement, and received the approval of Honorius III on 29 November 1223. It remains the

---

[6] There is uncertainty about the sequence of events as the general chapters for these years cannot be securely dated. See K. V. Selge, 'Franz von Assisi und die Römische Kurie', *Zeitschrift für Theologie und Kirche* 67 (1970), esp. 151–7.

definitive Rule, and by traditional monastic standards it was a very radical document, even if the pronouncements of liberty in its predecessor had been toned down. Its character may be illustrated by the provision that 'the friars shall appropriate nothing to themselves, not a house nor a place nor anything else'.[7] This statement of absolute poverty opened the door to a compromise: the friars could use the premises of their patrons, and once they received papal protection for these the position was only formally different from ownership. Hugolino, who perhaps introduced the clause, was to move the friars several stages along this path when he became pope as Gregory IX. The approval of the Rule was not the end of the matter, for on his deathbed Francis produced his *Testament*, a moving statement of the inspiration of the early days. Its authority was difficult to determine: he stressed that he was not attempting to supersede the Rule but nevertheless commanded that both should be observed together.[8] When he died on 3 October 1226 Francis left behind him a strange situation. He was the founder of a great movement, a man of tremendous magnetism and revered as a saint in his lifetime. Conversely he had lived in retirement, was unknown to most of the recruits to the expanding society, and left behind him a document which imposed a distinctive interpretation upon the Rule.

We do not know whether Francis and Dominic ever met. The theme inevitably attracted writers and painters to put forward their best inventive talents, but there is only one account which carries much conviction, the description in Thomas of Celano's second *Life* of an encounter at Rome in the house of Cardinal Hugolino. Neither the date nor the reality of the meeting of the two founders is certain, but there is a temptation to place it late in 1216 and attribute to it the sharp change of course which Dominic followed in the following year. Before that, he had responded to Innocent's invitation at the Lateran Council by adopting the Augustinian rule with a particularly severe set of customs selected from the Premonstratensians. The community was to own no property, but only revenues—an unusually strict policy, but far from the style of poverty advocated by Francis.[9] This was the programme approved by the new pope,

---

[7] *Regula Bullata*, vi. 1 (p. 190): *Fratres nihil sibi approprient nec domum nec locum nec aliquam rem.*

[8] Francis, *Testament*, 24–6, 34–9 (pp. 208–10).

[9] Our knowledge of early Dominican legislation is based on the constitutions accepted by the general chapter of 1228. The problem is then to distinguish, with the aid of Jordan of Saxony's chronicle, between the customs of 1216, the legislation of 1220 and the additions of later years. See M-H. Vicaire, *S. Dominic and his Times* (London, 1964), app. V, and R. B. Brooke, *The Coming of the Friars* (London, 1975), 189–200.

Honorius III, in *Gratiarum omnium* on 21 January 1217. The text contains little beyond an exhortation to the 'prior and brothers of St Romain, preachers in the region of Toulouse' to continue their work there, but it thereby gave authorization to a whole community to exercise the right of preaching. This was effectively unprecedented because preaching, as Fourth Lateran had recently reaffirmed, was an episcopal function, and its exercise depended in each case on the bishop's commission.[10] With *Gratiarum omnium* the Dominicans were recognized as a special form of regular canons, with the right to preach vested in the community as a whole.

In any event on Dominic's return from Rome he revealed new and far-reaching plans. No contemporary gave an adequate account of the reason for the abrupt change, but it is natural to suppose that it had been formulated early in 1217 at Rome, where it could have been discussed with Francis and authorized in principle in *Gratiarum omnium*. It was probably at Pentecost 1217, precisely when the Franciscans were agreeing to send missions outside Italy, that Dominic announced his intention to disperse his followers. Some would go to Paris, others to Spain, while a few remained at Toulouse and Dominic himself would return to Rome. The brethren understandably 'were all astonished when he pronounced the decision to which he had come so suddenly', and it was opposed by Bishop Fulk and Count Simon.[11] Dominic also began to press his brethren to give up their assured revenues and live by begging. In spite of the strongly Franciscan overtones of these proposals there remained important differences. Dominican expansion was protected by papal privileges, which Francis was reluctant to invoke, and it was focused on the universities. The largest group was sent to Paris, and a house soon established at Bologna under the canonist Reginald of St Aignan. The legislation of the general chapter of 1220 confirmed the change, showing no further dependence on the customs of regular canons and embodying the principle of communal poverty: 'on no account may possessions or rents be received'. It was provided that

[10] There was a distant precedent in Gregory VII's grant of power to preach and hear confessions to Provost Odfrid and the canons of Watten in Flanders in 1077, but that was motivated by the need to replace the ministry of a simoniacal bishop. Innocent's recognition of the Humiliati and Franciscans did not go further than the right of lay brothers to exhort others. *Gratiarum omnium* was essentially original, and it was subsequently understood as conveying a universal power to preach, not merely in the diocese of Toulouse. See the excellent discussion by J.-P. Renard, *La formation et la désignation des prédicateurs au début de l'Ordre des Prêcheurs* (Freiburg, 1977).

[11] Jordan c. 47 (Brooke, *Coming of the Friars*, 170).

the general chapter was to be held alternately in Paris and Bologna, and that the study of theology should be given precedence among the activities of the brothers.[12] The declaration that 'our order is recognized to have been founded especially for preaching and the health of souls, and our zeal should be chiefly and ardently directed to the end that we can be useful to the souls of our neighbours' breathed the spirit of *cura animarum* characteristic of regular canons, but now refined by the sense of spiritual direction which was becoming widespread.[13] It also indicated that a man joined the Order of Preachers not for his own good, but out of a calling to serve others. Dominic only survived the first Bologna chapter by a year or so, dying on 6 August 1221 at the house of St Nicholas at Bologna, but the main principles of the order had been firmly established.

By 1228 the order had formulated a new system of government. At each level of administration (convent, province, and order) a superior was elected, but the government was not then left in his hands. The chapter in each province was attended by large numbers of friars and legislation was placed in the hands of the provincial prior and four elected diffinitors. The general chapter had a double form. Every third year it consisted of the provincial priors, but in the other two years its membership was the master general together with one diffinitor from each of the eight provinces. New measures required the consent of each of the two types of chapter. Some elements in this system were drawn from the Cistercians and other orders, but it was radically original, as the Dominicans were well aware. It abandoned the old principle of obedience to the abbot, which was no longer applicable in an order where the members regularly moved from one convent to another, and it provided for the community as a whole to deliberate on policy. This constitution belonged to the world of guilds and estates, in which representation was beginning to appear at both the urban and national levels, but its adoption by the Dominicans at this early stage must have helped to establish it in secular society. It was the remote ancestor at once of modern techniques of representation and of such complex structures as the government of republican Venice. In all this the Dominicans owed nothing to the Franciscans, who were in a state of crisis long after their fellow friars had provided themselves with a secure and balanced scheme of administration.

[12] *Constitutions*, XXVI.1, XIII.2, and XXVIII-IX (Brooke, *Coming of the Friars*, 197–9).
[13] *Constitutions*, prol.2 (191) which may have originated in 1216 or 1220.

The new system of government had to serve (or, in the case of the Franciscans, failed to serve) the needs of two orders which were expanding at astonishing speed. Shortly after 1260 Brother Jordan of Giano looked back over forty years of Franciscan mission: 'When I consider my own lowly state, and that of the others who were sent with me to Germany, and when I consider the present state and glory of our order, I am astounded and praise the divine mercy in my heart'. [14] By 1250 there were houses of friars in every part of western Christendom. The Preachers had about 20 houses at Dominic's death; by 1234 they had almost 100, and by 1277 over 400. Italy was the main centre for both orders, but they were expanding rapidly everywhere. By the middle of the century it is possible to count 38 houses of Preachers in Germany and over 100 of Minors, and in England Thomas of Eccleston counted 1,242 brothers minor in 49 places there in 1255, thirty-two years after their first arrival. [15] In direct contrast with the Cistercians, whose expansion had anticipated theirs, the friars founded their houses in the cities. Recent studies have indicated that they were very responsive indeed to urbaniz-ation. In Germany their first settlements were on the Main and lower Rhine, where the major cities were located, and they moved south and east as the wave of urban growth preceded them. The choice of the cities as their centre of activity was scarcely a conscious one. The Franciscans had been formed in the world of Italian communes, and from 1215 the Dominicans were centred in cities and found most of their recruits there. Their way of life was adapted to the city. Communities could only live by mendicancy in large centres of population, and as establishments became larger they tapped urban sources of revenue and came to derive a modest security from donations and bequests by townsmen. The Dominican Humbert of Romans explained the advantage of a city-based ministry: there are more people in cities, and they are therefore the best places to preach; there are more sins there and more need of repentance; and the region around the city is influenced by its standards. [16] Also important was the presence of schools. After the dispersion of 1217 Paris and Bologna became the Dominican centres, and a decade later Jordan of Saxony, on a visit to Oxford, reported his 'ample hopes of a good

[14] H. Boehmer (ed.), *Chronica Fratris Jordani* (Paris, 1908), prol. p. 2.

[15] A. G. Little (ed.), *Fratris Thomae de Eccleston De Adventu Minorum in Anglia* (Manchester, 1951), ii. p. 11.

[16] Cited and discussed by J. le Goff, 'Ordres mendiants et urbanisation', *Annales* 25 (1970), 929–30.

catch' among the students.[17] Although the Franciscans began as a lay and unlearned order they began to recruit in the schools during Francis's lifetime. Their first outstanding scholar was in a sense an accident: Antony of Padua was a regular canon who in 1220 encountered a mission in his native Portugal. Soon after this, students and masters began to join on an important scale. At Paris four doctors, among them the Englishman Haymo of Faversham, were recruited in 1225, and they were later followed by Alexander of Hales, the university's most respected theologian. At Oxford the Franciscans established an outstanding theological school under the headship of the secular master Robert Grosseteste.

While the ministry of the friars was distinctively urban, it had a wide significance. They offered preaching where the ordinary clergy were unskilled and adaptability where traditional monks were tied to one house: they could be used in disputing against heretics and investigating them, in the struggle against Frederick II and in missions beyond the frontiers of Christendom. The most spectacular illustration of their impact came in the revival which swept the cities of Lombardy in 1233, which came to be known as the Great Devotion or the Alleluia. It was described by a witness at the canonization process of Dominic in 1234, who spoke of the saint's enormous influence,

as is plain by its effect on the cities of Lombardy, in which a great many heretics have been burned, and more than 100,000 people who did not know whether they ought to support the Roman Church or the heretics have been converted sincerely to the catholic faith of the Roman Church by the preaching of the Friars Preacher . . . And almost all the cities of Lombardy and Marche handed over to the friars their acts and statutes for adjustment and amendment according to their will, to erase, add, subtract and change as seemed appropriate to them. And this they did to end the warfare and make and establish peace among them, and to restore usury and wrongful acquisitions and hear confessions and many other good things which would be too long to report.[18]

At the Ghibelline city of Verona the Dominican John of Vicenza was actually given power as *rector* or *podestà*, basing his actions on the support of the people and thus anticipating the later despots. The high tide of enthusiasm soon receded: the general chapter forbade

---

[17] Jordan, *Letter to Diana Dandolo* (Brooke, *Coming of the Friars*, 188).
[18] *Acta canonizationis S. Dominici*, ed. A. Walz, *Monumenta Ordinis Fr. Praedicatorum Hist.* 16 (Rome, 1935), 158–9.

this type of involvement and Gregory IX disowned John of Vicenza. Yet it was only an extreme example of a general trend. The friars exercised their influence by their preaching and living, by counsel, and in some cases through inquisition into heresy. They did not join the traditional establishment, at least in the time of Gregory IX, who was sensitive to their ideals. If we omit the special case of missionary bishops, no Franciscan received episcopal office in his time, and few Dominicans did. Things were to change in the 1240s under Innocent IV. At the beginning of his pontificate he confirmed the nomination of the Franciscan Leo dei Vavassori as archbishop of Milan, and by 1261 we can count nineteen Franciscans who had been bishops in Italy alone, and the true number must be larger.

The first convents of friars were very modest. On arrival the Franciscans were ready to move into any rooms or undercrofts which were put at their disposal. Dominican requirements were slightly more complex because as canons they required a church in which to say the offices, but they were concerned that the provision should only be simple. The general chapters of 1220 and 1228 both legislated against building lofty churches and convents, and at Florence for example they received a small eleventh-century church, Santa Maria Novella, which had a tiny chapel attached which could be used as a chapter-house. In the first twenty years of expansion the two orders produced just one building each of any architectural pretensions. At Bologna the church of St Nicholas delle Vigne, which contained the tomb of St Dominic, was greatly enlarged; this is now the church of San Domenico, but has been changed beyond recognition in later centuries. Much more dramatic was the vast basilica planned at Assisi as a shrine to St Francis. Otherwise major building began after 1240 and then proceeded apace. Growing numbers meant larger accommodation, and the popularity of the friars' preaching demanded larger churches 'to take people for sermons', as it was said at Antwerp in 1243. Quite often there was insufficient room on the original site and the convent had to move, as the Dominicans did at Limoges in 1241. This increased the tendency to establish their houses in the working-class areas of the suburbs, where sites were cheaper and audiences closer at hand. Attracting the laity by their preaching and confessional skill, binding them by pious confraternities, the friars were on the way to creating a supplementary parochial ministry which at times dominated the old: well before 1300 the friars' churches at Florence, Santa Maria Novella and

Santa Croce, were bigger than the old cathedral. They were designed as great auditory chambers for addressing the people, but they brought with them growing display and increasing concern for revenue.

From the beginning the friars hoped to carry out a supplementary ministry with the agreement of existing churches, and bishops all over Europe from Robert Grosseteste at Lincoln (1235–53) to Federigo Visconti at Pisa (1254–77) were delighted to have their help. Inevitably a flow of complaints began from the secular clergy about the pastoral activity of the friars, who were interfering with their duties and deflecting the offerings of the laity. The friars defended themselves by papal privileges, in spite of Francis's original reluctance to obtain them, up to the time of the issue of the crucial general bull *Nimis iniqua* on 28 August 1231. The full-scale conflict was to arise just after 1250, with a fierce controversy at Paris and a series of changes in papal policy, but the tension between friars and seculars had already become apparent.

The transition from a small band of brothers to an international society with great responsibilities and privileges had taken place in a lifetime: several of Francis's closest companions, including Clare, Giles, and Leo, outlived the middle of the century. Among the Dominicans there were some who looked back with regret to the old simplicities, but the impact upon the Franciscans was far greater. One reason for this was the unsatisfactory nature of their constitution, which meant that they had no effective way of reaching a decision which would command general obedience. An additional strain was imposed by the place which the friars came to occupy in the church. What the hierarchy valued was help which could best be provided by scholars and clergy. These were the recruits for whom the Order of Preachers had always been designed, but the clericalization of the Franciscans had drastic effects on the original conception of the order. Imposed on the tensions already generated by Francis's distaste for any existing rule, for papal privileges, and for property or assured revenues, it created deep divisions within the society. Although historians do not agree on the matter, it is probable that the crises which shook the order were not produced by distinct issues on each occasion, but by the seismic fault which lay beneath its foundations. The tensions had been apparent in 1219–20, and again in Francis's *Testament*. After the saint's death the Pentecost chapter of 1227 chose John Parenti as minister-general in preference to Elias,

Francis's own choice as vicar in 1221. Elias was given responsibility for the construction of the great basilica at Assisi which was to be the resting-place of the saint's body and an international pilgrimage centre of the first rank. In July 1228 Pope Gregory IX, who as Cardinal Hugolino had been Francis's friend and protector, visited Assisi to proclaim the canonization of Francis, commission his *Life* from Thomas of Celano, and lay the foundation stone of the great church. Two years later in the bull *Quo Elongati* of 28 September 1230 he clarified two of the uncertain points in the government of the order: the *Testament* was said to have no binding authority and permission was given for buildings and property to be owned by friends of the order and made available for its use. All these decisions under papal authority between 1228 and 1230 may well have commanded the support of most friars, even if they were little to the taste of brother Leo and his circle or Clare at her convent of San Damiano. In 1232 the party of Elias, who was enthusiastically championed by the Italian lay friars, put such pressure on John Parenti that he resigned and left the way open for Elias to become minister-general. Elias is a tragic figure in Franciscan history. He had been close to Francis and had expressed his veneration through the planning of the basilica, but his time as minister was a disaster. He governed autocratically and was accused of living in luxury. The opposition was led by the *magistri* of the northern provinces, who had not known Francis and were impatient of government by uneducated laymen. Elias was deposed in 1239 and tarnished his reputation further by entering the service of Frederick II. He was succeeded by the first priest to be minister-general, Albert of Pisa (1239–40), and then by the first theologian, Haymo of Faversham (1240–4). The position of the general chapter was strengthened and recruiting restricted almost completely to educated clergy. The fall of Elias ended the experiment of a society run by laymen with a distinctive piety yet with papal approval. The most hopeful attempt to break through the clerical monopoly of religion had been abandoned.

ii. *Religion for Women: the Rise of the Beguines*

At that time there were some people, in Germany especially, who described themselves as religious and received a religious habit, but not strictly. They were of both sexes, but mainly women. They professed continence and simplicity of life by a private vow, but not bound by the rule of any saint, nor were they confined in any cloister. Their numbers increased so much in a short time that two thousand were to be found in the city of Cologne and its neighbourhood.[19]

Thus the English Benedictine Matthew Paris described the Beguines. As he indicated, it was primarily a women's movement, and it can only be understood in the light of the inadequate provision made for women in earlier generations.

Medieval society was dominated by males. The few women who exercised enormous influence, among them Countess Matilda the staunch ally of Gregory VII, Agnes of Blois the protector of Ivo of Chartres, and Blanche of Castile the regent of France for her son Louis IX, are exceptions in a world where political authority was in the hands of men. Women were still more completely excluded from authority in the church, and there were not even many opportunities to become a nun, because the number of convents for women was small and places were normally reserved for noble families. The modern balance of sexes in religious orders, with far more nuns than monks, is the reverse of the medieval situation. Many writers saw women primarily as a source of temptation, and this conviction was fortified by the dominant physiological theory that women were by nature more lecherous than men—an interesting example of the shaping of science by the dominant group.

In a number of ways the twelfth century had seen a more positive attitude to the social position of women. It characteristically identified interest groups or 'estates' and provided for their needs: the growth of cities, courts, and schools enabled such groups to advance their claims and the process of Christianization shaped an ethic for them. What applied to knights and merchants also affected the position of women. The recognition of marriage as an honourable estate, and legal provisions which protected the weaker partner, did something to assist their status. A different route to the same destination was offered by the conventions of courtly love, *fin'amors* or, in German, *Minne*. Many versions of this were anathema in the eyes of moralists, but there is no one code of courtly love. It could, as in Chrétien of Troyes's *Knight of the Cart* or *Lancelot*, glorify adultery, but it also offered a vocabulary of respect which was

[19] Matthew Paris, *Chronica Majora*, RS 1877, iv.278. In modern convention the term 'Beguine' has come to be used entirely for women, with 'Beghard' reserved for men. Thirteenth-century writers included both *beguini* and *beguine* in the word.

widely used in aristocratic society. A few writers came to speak positively of women's social role: in the thirteenth century, Archbishop Federigo Visconti of Pisa criticized those who interpreted the sin of Eve as excluding women from grace, and was careful to speak of 'Christian men and women', *christiani* and *christiane*.[20]

Attention has often been drawn to the enormous growth in reverence for the Virgin Mary and its potential for the dignity of women. The development in the cult of the Virgin and its expansion to wider social strata during the twelfth century is unquestionable. The use of the Hail Mary spread rapidly and by 1210 a synod at Paris was requiring its knowledge by all believers along with the Creed and the Lord's Prayer.[21] The antiphon *Salve regina* passed quickly into liturgical use. Legends of Our Lady were collected to disseminate knowledge of the miracles she had performed, and her shrines rose in the league table of popular pilgrimage, among them Rocamadour in central France, where the body of her servant Amadour was discovered in 1166 and gave rise to many miracles. Love for the Virgin was expressed in feudal style: 'the spouse of our Lord is our mistress, the spouse of our king is our queen; therefore let us serve her'.[22] The supreme new artistic expression of this theme was her coronation in heaven. Its first surviving occurence may be on a capital of Reading Abbey, but this is of uncertain date; and it was magnificently depicted just after 1140 in a mosaic on the west front of Santa Maria Trastevere at Rome. It is natural to suppose that the elevation of Mary would bring with it the elevation of women, but the matter is more complicated than that.

One difficulty was the failure to produce a coherent account of Mary's role. While doctrines of Christology and the eucharist were in process of formulation Mariology remained in chaos. Conservatives sought to stay within the guide-lines of the past. Bernard of Clairvaux reprimanded the canons of Lyon for observing the increasingly popular feast of the immaculate conception, and his theological works were almost completely Christ-centred in their thinking. Peter Lombard and most of the schoolmen declined to accept the immaculate conception; the Victorines were reserved in

---

[20] A. Murray, 'Archbishop and Mendicants in Thirteenth-century Pisa' in K. Elm (ed.), *Stellung und Wirksamkeit der Bettelorden* (Berlin, 1981), 35–7.

[21] For details of the spread of the Hail Mary, see H. Graef, *Mary: a History of Doctrine and Devotion*, i (London, 1963), 229–31.

[22] Aelred of Rievaulx, *Sermo* xxi (PL 195.324 A).

their references to Mary, and some scholars refused to commit themselves to belief in the bodily assumption. On the other hand there was little attempt to control popular ideas and some writers (among them St Bernard and Peter of Celle) were cautious in their more serious works but expressed themselves floridly elsewhere. Popular devotion followed divergent paths. The *Lives* of Mary and the Passion plays taught the faithful to associate themselves with Mary in her sufferings. This tradition, which later obtained its finest expression in the *Stabat mater*, was associated with the desire to be close to the historical Jesus. The other road led towards the replacement of Christ by Mary. She was often decribed as the universal ruler, and already in the twelfth century we find the contrast between Christ as judge and Mary as the merciful intercessor. The rhetoric could take startling forms. Peter of Celle once speculated whether Mary might be seen as a Quaternity with the other persons of the Godhead, and shortly before the middle of the thirteenth century Richard of St Laurent's *De laudibus Sanctae Mariae* repeatedly applied to Mary Biblical statements about the work of Christ.[23] It was an incoherent scene, and it was quite rare for writers to argue from the greatness of Mary to the dignity of women in general. For the liberation of religious women we must look elsewhere.

Traditional nunneries had been few in number (there were perhaps nine in England in 1066) and were monopolized by the aristocracy, for whom also the houses of secular canonesses were mainly designed. New religious foundations were steadily added, such as Messines in Flanders, established by Count Baldwin V and his wife Adela in 1060 for the daughters or widows of the nobility. The ladies of the upper classes were also liable to capture houses founded for other purposes, as they did at Fontevraud shortly after 1100. Most of these institutions did not satisfy the more exacting standards of a new age. They paid no attention to apostolic poverty, and some of them were so relaxed as to draw criticism from authority; the nuns of Messines and Denain, for example, attempted to become secular canonesses at a time when the whole thrust of ecclesiastical policy was to establish communities upon a more regular basis. One option for women who had no access to existing nunneries was to become a recluse. There seem to have been far more women than men living in

[23] Peter of Celle, *Sermo* xiii (PL 202.675): 'et si ullo modo Trinitas illa quaternitatem externam admitteret, tu sola quaternitatem compleres'.

partial withdrawal from the world, and they ranged from those following a strict regime of poverty through widows acting as caretakers of churches to people who in effect had secured a leisurely retirement, like Ermengarde of Harzé, countess of Montaigu, who in 1067 attached herself to the canons of St Feuillen, made frequent pilgrimages and retained a comfortable income. Recluses were common in Lotharingia, the later home of the Beguines, and we know of a number of outstanding ones in England. Women like Christina of Markyate, while they were retired from society, attracted visitors and developed a considerable practice as advisers in spiritual and other affairs. They also had links with traditional monasticism. Christina, who had joined the hermit Roger around 1118, developed close relations with Abbot Geoffrey of St Albans (too close, censorious tongues observed), made a form of profession as a nun there in 1131, and by the end of her life was in charge of a priory.[24]

The first sustained attempt at a ministry to women can be found among preachers such Robert of Arbrissel, Odo of Tournai, and Norbert of Xanten, who attracted crowds of women followers. These men, Robert in particular, have been greeted as champions of women, but there were severe difficulties in the way of any real equality of treatment. It was hard to secure adequate endowments for nunneries and they required a great deal of care to supervise. Contemporaries were impressed by the perpetual danger of immorality. 'To be always with a woman', observed St Bernard, 'and not to have intercourse with her, is more difficult than to raise the dead', and Robert's practice of sleeping between his men and women followers was thought to require heroic sanctity as a 'new and unheard-of martyrdom'.[25] Such considerations explain why interesting experiments such as double monasteries tended to be abandoned by the authorities who had initiated them. In 1141 the Premonstratensian abbots ordered that women should be accommodated in separate houses at some distance from those of the men, and by the end of the century they had 'decided by common consent that we will henceforward receive no more sisters'.[26] In the English order of Sempringham it was alleged that the segregation of men and

---

[24] On the twelfth-century hermits and their relation to recluses, see ch. 10. i above.
[25] Bernard, *Sermones in Cantica* 65.4 (PL 183.1091 B); Geoffrey of Vendôme, letter to Robert (PL 157.183A).
[26] See P. F. Lefèvre (ed.), *Les Statuts de Prémontré* (Louvain, 1946), p. 114 and n.

women, strict in theory, was lax in practice, and Ælred of Rievaulx told the scandalous story of the nun of Watton who was seduced by a lay brother of the house. The Cistercians made no official provision for nuns, although some women's houses adopted Cistercian customs and Stephen Harding himself founded the nunnery of Tart, which recruited from the same Burgundian noble families as did Cîteaux itself.

An upsurge of women's piety began in the late twelfth century. More women were venerated as saints and the ideal of female sanctity came to be less withdrawn and more involved in the caring ministries. The tendency was not confined to any one region: in central Europe, for example, the ruling families produced women saints, including Elizabeth of Thuringia (died 1231) the daughter of King Andrew II of Hungary and Agnes of Prague, daughter of King Ottokar I of Bohemia and fervent follower of Clare of Assisi. Women were also prominent as witnesses in the canonization processes for mendicant preachers in Italy. This marked change in their overall spiritual position went along with better provision in religious orders. Cistercian abbots began to show active sympathy for the women's movement. Abbot Walter of Villers (1214–21) founded nunneries in the Low Countries with the support of the dukes of Brabant. The Cistercian house of Aywières became an important centre for holy women, including the mystic Lutgard. The general chapter continued to sound a note of caution and in 1228 decided to accept responsibility for no more nunneries, but in practice exceptions were frequent and foundations proceeded apace: in Germany, where there had been only 15 in 1200, a further 150 had been created by 1250. James of Vitry commented that 'the order of Cistercian nuns has multiplied like the stars of heaven and grown to a huge size'. Dominican policy was basically similar, in that general chapters showed reluctance to adopt any nunneries apart from two for which Dominic himself had been responsible, San Sisto at Rome and Prouille, but in practice numerous convents were founded in Germany and the Low Countries. In southern Europe the sisters of St Clare (Clarisses or Poor Clares) spread widely. After initial hesitations they adopted strict seclusion, but they did not follow any one rule and in most cases were not dissimilar to the nunneries of the older orders. In spite of Clare's fierce determination to maintain the principles of St Francis and to live in total poverty, Gregory IX and Innocent IV insisted on a Rule for the order which was quite relaxed, and which was Benedictine in character rather than Franciscan. Only Clare's own house, San Damiano, and one or two others followed the strict regime of the so-called 'privilege of poverty'.

Closely related to the nunneries was the movement which we know as the Beguines. Its founder and place of origin are alike uncertain. An early tradition traced it to Lambert le Bègue, a priest of Liège who was an active reformer in the 1170s, but his involvement is not clearly established. The most prominent figure in the early stages was Mary of Oignies, who about 1191 retired from the world to live near a small leper-house. About 1207 she moved to the Augustinian priory of St Nicholas at Oignies, where she was the centre of a group of like-minded women. Her reputation reached Paris, and attracted James of Vitry to come to the Low Countries. James was an outstanding preacher who formed wide connections and eventually became bishop of Acre (1216–27) and a cardinal. When he went to Italy in 1216 he may well have been hoping to secure a rule, but have been defeated by the Lateran Council decree against the foundation of new orders. He had to be content with formal permission for religious women to live in common and assist each other by mutual exhortation. The movement spread rapidly: we hear of them at Cologne in 1223, and about the same time in northern France. By the 1230s they were being called Beguines, a name whose meaning is uncertain. James of Vitry's travels in southern Europe awoke his awareness to the international dimensions of what was happening: everywhere there were pious confraternities arising, inspired by apostolic ideals but outside the strict bonds of monasticism. In the north as well as the south the impetus was primarily urban and recruiting was mainly among women of the propertied classes.

The permission to live in community granted in 1216 accelerated the formation of houses of Beguines. In some areas there was a tendency towards very large Beguinages which contained substantial communities and formed exempt parishes. It was some time before anything like the present Beguinage at Bruges came into existence, but the first steps can be seen in several cities before 1250. Eventually the movement came to provide a decent and useful life for ladies, but in the earliest days the spirit of apostolic poverty was strong. It was only in the later thirteenth century that institutions which had once provided an exacting challenge became places of leisured retreat, and even then they never lost a genuinely spiritual character. The spirituality of the Beguines was drawn from many sources. Women prominent in the movement sometimes began as recluses, like Ivetta of Huy, or had associations with the Cistercians (Lutgard of Aywières), Premonstratensians (Ivetta), Augustinians (Mary of Oignies), or Dominicans (Margaret of Ypres). There was probably an influence from the German mystical writers: Hildegard of Bingen had had close associations with the abbey of Villers in the 1170s. The description by James of Vitry stresses both their love of poverty, extending even to a desire to live as mendicants, and their intense orthodoxy. Mary was a keen supporter of the Albigensian Crusade and the whole movement had a strong devotion to the eucharist which culminated in a campaign by Juliana of Cornillon for a new feast in honour of the sacrament. In 1246 Bishop Robert of Thouroute at Liège resolved to institute this, and his archdeacon James Pantaleon subsequently became pope as Urban IV and in 1264 authorized the feast of Corpus Christi for general observance in the church.

The Beguine mystics represented a change of course in the current of medieval piety. Their devotion was a vernacular one, nourished by the visionary tradition of the recluses and by a straightforward reading of the Gospels. Even learned women such as Hadewijch of Antwerp attached importance to vivid personal experiences, which could be valued more than works of charity, as when Lutgard asked for her gift of healing to be taken away because it deprived her of solitude. This was a different approach to spiritual life from the monastic writers of the past who were shaped by liturgy and learned exegesis. The Bernardine devotion to the crucified humanity of Christ lay behind many of the new ideas. But when they meditated on the crucifix, as Ælred of Rievaulx had recommended, what had originally been a symbol became a visionary experience. The Lord showed them his wounds, placed his arm round them, kissed them mouth to mouth, and marked the worshippers with his own wounds. In these tendencies the Beguines were part of a larger movement, with an important overlap with the Franciscans. The stigmata appeared in saints in both Italy and the Low Countries. Some writers saw the coming of interior religion as the inauguration of a new age. The sense that God had brought into being a new work was strong among Franciscans and Beguines and by the end of our period it was being linked with the teaching of Joachim of Fiore about a coming age of the Holy Spirit. Hadewijch was full of anticipation:

At the new year
We hope for the new season
That will bring new flowers
And new joys manifold.[27]

The Beguines had powerful champions. They were supported by
James of Vitry, protected by Gregory IX in his bull *Gloriam
virginalem*, and praised at Oxford by Robert Grosseteste and at Paris
by Robert of Sorbon. They also caused anxiety by their lack of a rule
and by their teaching. James of Vitry was aware of the need to defend
their orthodoxy, and a Beguine was apparently executed for heresy
in northern France in the 1230s. The French satirist Walter of
Coincy, a Benedictine with a traditional outlook, dismissed them as
hypocrites, while in Germany about 1250 the Franciscan Lamprecht
of Regensburg regretted their lack of moderation. Like the Franciscans themselves they had strained the limits of the acceptable, so that
both movements were perceived in the later thirteenth century as
containing elements outside the bounds of orthodoxy.

iii. *The Repression of Heresy*

The movements which we have been discussing were born into a
world of heresy and were conscious of the problems which it
presented for the church. The origin of the Dominicans was the
Albigensian mission; the followers of Francis would have been
familiar with heresy in the Italian cities, although their polemic
against it was not as open; and Mary of Oignies was devoted to the
cause of orthodoxy. Even by 1230 only very limited progress had
been made in the campaign against Cathars and Waldensians. The
scene of most of the action had been the south of France, but the
attempt of the Fourth Lateran Council to impose a settlement by
depriving the family of Saint-Gilles of its estates west of the Rhône
was met by strong resistance. Many loyal catholics were opposed to
the imposition of northern rule. Their voice is heard in the second
part of the *Chanson de la Croisade*, composed anonymously about
1228. The author represented Innocent III as complaining that Simon
of Montfort 'has ruined the catholics as well as the heretics', and
agreed sarcastically that Simon should be venerated as a saint,

If killing men and shedding blood,

[27] C. Hart (ed.), *Hadewijch: the Complete Works* (London, 1981), 144.

And causing loss of souls and massacres
Is in this world to conquer Jesus Christ. [28]

The decree of the council led to a widespread reaction in the course of which Simon was killed in the fighting on 25 June 1218. Although his son Amaury succeeded him, his death was a severe blow to the northern cause, and by 1224 Raymond VII had retaken almost all his family's lands and most of the southern aristocracy had returned to power.

Raymond VII was interested in recovering his lands and protecting his supporters, and had little sympathy for Catharism. Pope Honorius III, however, made no distinction between political and religious resistance and gave uncritical support to the Montfortian cause. He complained in 1218 that 'the people of Israel are oppressed by Pharaoh'; in October 1221 he officially deprived Raymond VI of all his dominions, and on his death in the summer of 1222 he denied him Christian burial. This policy was in part simply a stubborn defence of the Lateran settlement, but it was also the result of disquiet at the revival of heresy. As the traditional nobility recovered its lands the perfects also reappeared, often in the very places where they had been influential before, and in 1225 an assembly of about 100 'good men' agreed to create a new Cathar bishopric at Razès. The new French King Louis VIII (1223–6) was by then ready to undertake a full-scale crusade in the south. Amaury had surrendered to him the Montfortian lands, and Louis required stringent terms from the papal legate to make clear that the crusade was a royal enterprise. A large expedition assembled at Lyon in June 1226. After being held up for three months at Avignon it rapidly recovered most of the former Montfort lands. Louis's death on 8 November 1226 left Raymond VII in possession of Toulouse and enabled him to strengthen his position once more. He was, however, convinced of the need for a settlement, which was finally ratified at the Peace of Paris on 12 April 1229. The wide territories of Béziers and Carcassonne were recognized as royal possessions and Raymond agreed to marry his daughter Jeanne to a member of the Capetian family with the prospect of succession after his death.

Up to that point only a limited amount had been achieved by the papal programme against heresy. The support of the lay power had been doubtful precisely in the regions where the danger was greatest.

---

[28] See Y. Dossat, 'La croisade vue par les chroniqueurs', *CF* 4 (1969), esp. 252–7.

In Languedoc the traditional nobility had temporarily reasserted its power. In Italy Frederick II had issued laws against heresy, but his quarrel with the papacy after 1226 reduced their effect, and the powerful cities were reluctant to adopt anti-heretical provisions into their statutes. The machinery of inquiry into heresy was still inadequate. By 1230, however, there were possibilities of new initiatives. The Peace of Paris, agreement between pope and emperor, and the expansion of the friars established the preconditions for the official persecution of heresy. Its most obvious feature was the appearance of the papal inquisition, but the significance of this must not be overstated. It was not an organization: the word *inquisitio* did not mean 'the Inquisition', but an inquiry by an investigator with papal authority. Nor did the system of inquiry have an unbroken history thereafter. It met with a great deal of opposition and by 1250 papal commissions of inquiry had largely been abandoned throughout Europe. It was only one of the weapons against heresy, although an effective one which had been newly forged.

The inquisition was created by a policy decision by Gregory IX. In February 1231 he issued a general condemnation of heresy in the bull *Excommunicamus*, which was based on *Ad abolendam* of 1184 but with an up-dating of the penalties. Those convicted of heresy were to be transferred to secular judgement 'to be punished by the appropriate penalty', *animadversione debita puniendi*.[29] In the *Liber Augustalis* of 1231 Frederick II had provided that heretics 'should be burned alive in the sight of the people', and that may have been the punishment which Gregory had in mind. The issue of *Excommunicamus* was soon followed by the appointment of inquisitors, often Dominican friars, in many parts of Europe. Hannibal, senator of Rome, issued statutes against heretics discovered there 'by inquisitors appointed by the church'.[30] The first surviving inquisitorial commission was issued to Conrad of Marburg in Germany on 11 October 1231, soon followed by instructions to two Dominicans of Regensburg to preach and to seek out heretics 'according to our statutes against heresy recently promulgated'.[31] In southern France the work of papal inquisitors

---

[29] L. Auvray (ed.), *Les registres de Grégoire IX* (Paris, 1896), no. 539, p. 351. See J. M. Powell (tr.), *Liber Augustalis* (Syracuse, 1971), 9.

[30] Auvray, *Les registres de Grégoire IX*, no. 540, p. 353.

[31] A. Patschovsky, 'Zur Ketzerverfolgung Konrads von Marburg', *DAEM* 37 (1981) 641–93, for discussion and references. (It is now generally accepted that an earlier commission to Conrad in 1227 was an instruction to bring heretics before episcopal tribunals and thus different from the 1231 commission.) See also E. Peters, *Heresy and Authority in Medieval Europe* (London, 1980), no. 38.

was instituted by bulls in April 1233, and on 19 April 1233 Robert the Little, or *le Bougre*, a converted Cathar who had become a Dominican, was instructed to undertake the extirpation of heresy from La Charité sur Loire and the surrounding regions.[32] In Lombardy we soon hear of inquisitors, but the main contribution of the friars was to secure the inclusion of anti-heretical measures in communal statutes. The simultaneous introduction of the new procedure into so many countries confirms that it was the result of a decision taken within the papal curia.

Historians have found it difficult to arrive at agreement about the character of the inquisition in its first twenty years. Our main information comes from descriptions of the work of inquisitors among the Albigensians, supplemented by a few surviving registers of cases and by accounts of the bloodthirsty careers of Robert le Bougre in northern France and Conrad of Marburg in the Rhineland. There has been a reaction against the sweeping liberal condemnation of the inquisition, and it has been stressed that it was an orderly institution which was penitential in character, was inclined to be more merciful than lay powers, and only rarely surrendered the accused to the death penalty. Almost certainly the great majority of sentences was for the lighter penances, the wearing of a cross on the garments or the undertaking of a pilgrimage. These could lead to opprobrium or inconvenience, but at least they were much more frequently imposed than indefinite imprisonment and surrender to the secular arm for burning. The scattered records from the Midi in the 1240s suggest that over 90 per cent of those sentenced received the less stringent penances.[33] It is also true that the vocabulary of the time is liable to mislead a modern reader. The term *persecutio* did not mean persecution in the modern sense, but any sort of programme against heresy including peaceful preaching, and in the language of the inquisition the word 'heretic' was the technical expression for a Cathar perfect. It was against this relatively small group that the full rigour of the procedure was turned, whereas their hearers or *credentes*, as well as Waldensian preachers, could expect more merciful treatment. This no doubt accounts for the the low incidence of extreme penalties. It has also been suggested (although here the argument takes a more tendentious turn) that the most savage

---

[32] Auvray, *Les registres de Grégoire IX*, no. 1253, p. 707.
[33] See the survey of the evidence by Y. Dossat in *CF* 6 (1971), 253–72 and 361–78. The nature of the surviving records means that we have no real knowledge of the number of burnings ordered by inquisitors before 1250 in the normal course of their operations.

campaigns do not represent the church's official policy. In the Rhineland Conrad of Marburg provoked wide anger and opposition, resulting in his murder in 1233, and in northern France Robert le Bougre's violent activities culminated in the burning of 180 Cathars at Mont-Aimé in May 1239; but both men have been seen as untypically savage, even perhaps insane. Conrad was not replaced, and Robert was disgraced and imprisoned. On this argument, the regular operation of the inquisition must be contrasted with these occasional outbreaks of savagery, and not blamed for them.

This may be fair comment on the intentions of many of the Dominicans who served on the tribunals, but it misses the point. The inquisition marked the effective introduction on an international scale of procedures of inquiry which dispensed with the existing ideas of legality. Roman law and canon law were traditionally tender towards the rights of the defendant: he was called to answer only an express accusation by a named accuser, and witnesses against him must be of good standing. This legal protection had been eroded by anti-heretical measures from *Ad abolendam* onwards and it was now stripped away entirely. The accused was not told the names of witnesses, who might themselves be involved in heresy or otherwise of ill repute. He could call no witnesses on his own behalf, and in practice had no way of rebutting the charge. The archbishop of Mainz complained that Conrad's tribunal uncritically accepted the statements of witnesses, so that 'the accused was given the option either to confess and live or to swear his innocence and be burned on the spot', and this appears no more than an exaggerated application of standard inquisitorial procedure.[34] Contemporaries were also shocked because the same procedures were directed against the upper classes, whose privileges were ignored. What was happening in practice was that a normal system of justice was being replaced by inquiries designed to identify the names of the perfects or hard-core heretics. When a group of perfects was located, the severity of the inquisitors increased at once: they were certainly involved in questioning the prisoners at Montségur in 1244 and the massacre which followed may well have had their approval. On less special occasions the arrival of the inquisitors would be marked by a public sermon, which was accompanied by an offer of easy reconciliation to those who would confess and who would supply information. The use of informers, the negation of the legal rights of defendants, and,

[34] Chronicle of Alberic of Troisfontaines, s.a. 1233, MGH SS XXIII.931.

after Innocent IV's decree *Ad extirpanda* in 1252, the use of torture give the whole procedure an unpleasantly twentieth-century ring. The fact that the tribunals were manned not by lawyers, but primarily by friars whose training was in preaching and the confessional, does not necessarily imply amiability; it may just as easily indicate a willingness to override the rules of law. The procedure provoked opposition from people who had no brief for heresy. The first complaints were directed against Conrad of Marburg's 'monstrous and unheard-of judgement' in 1231–3, but there is no reason to think that his approach was much different from that of other inquisitors elsewhere. In the Midi the Dominicans were expelled from Toulouse for a time in 1235 by the consuls of the city, and civil disorders were provoked in Narbonne by the activities of Friar Ferrier. Raymond VII several times complained about Dominican activities and urged the pope to restore to the bishops their jurisdiction over heresy. In the face of such opposition the early history of the inquisition was a chequered one. There was no really active papal inquisition in northern France or Germany after Robert and Conrad, and in the Midi the functions of the inquisitors were first suspended by Gregory IX, then interfered with by Innocent IV, and finally subordinated for a period to the bishops. In the mid-thirteenth century it was not clear that the inquisition would prove to be more than a temporary expedient in the campaign against heresy.

By that time the effectiveness of the Cathar movement had been much reduced. In northern France we hear little of it thereafter, and we know that there were 150 French perfects living in exile near Verona. In the Rhineland, too, the Cathars who had once been well established there seem to have disappeared after the fierce onslaught by Conrad of Marburg.[35] In the Midi the power of the heresy had been much more formidable, but there too it had been gravely weakened. The southern aristocracy, on whose support it had depended, had finally been undermined after an ineffective rebellion in 1242. Raymond VII had increasingly been obliged to follow the lead of the dominant Capetian power and in 1249 his death put his estates in the hands of Alphonse of Poitiers, the younger brother of King Louis IX. The perfects, who were of crucial importance to the

---

[35] It has often been supposed that the Rhineland Cathars had already disappeared and that Conrad's persecution was directed against a different sect, whether real or imaginary, called Luciferians. Patschowsky has, however, demonstrated that this group is identical with the Cathars.

continuance of the sect, were greatly reduced in number. They had been obliged after the Peace of Paris to take refuge in a small number of fortresses, of which the most important was Montségur. In 1241 the garrison of the castle was rash enough to carry out a raid and murder an inquisitor at Avignonet. After a delay this gave rise to a determined siege and the fall of the castle in March 1244. The massacre of over 200 heretics probably removed a substantial part of their remaining strength. Only in Italy was Catharism largely intact and in a position to provide refuge for those fleeing across the Alps. The continuing conflicts between Frederick II and the papacy and the spirited independence of the communes worked against co-operation in pursuit of heresy, and it was only in the 1240s that inquisitors such as Peter of Verona and Rainier Sacconi became really active. There were districts in many of the major cities which had well established networks of *Patarini*, as the movement was generally known there.

The collapse of Catharism north of the Alps must in part have been due to the preaching of the friars. They offered the witness of holy men, as did the perfects, along with orthodoxy. There was a more clearly defined doctrine, and an attempt at better popular preaching; the Franciscans taught a warm devotion to creation through the Christ-child and the cross and thus powerfully countered the Cathars' rejection of the created order. The university of Toulouse was founded in 1229 and provided local training for the clergy. It is natural to suppose that these new forces sapped away the strength of the Cathars, but it is not easy to demonstrate it in detail, and there is a serious counter-argument: in northern Italy, where the friars were strongest, the Cathars held their position best. It is easier to see the effects of persecution. Groups of exiles from northern France and Languedoc provide clear evidence of the force of repression in their native lands. The fortunes of the Albigensian heretics were closely associated with those of the local nobility, so that they shared their failures, successes, and final collapse. The disappearance of the movement in Germany seems closely associated with the career of Conrad of Marburg. The contribution of preaching and witness may well have been very significant, but the forces which can most readily be seen at work are those of repression, of crusade and inquisition, which by 1250 were well on the way to overcoming Catharism everywhere north of the Alps.

The attacks on Catharism, and to a lesser extent on the Waldensians, were the most important steps in the growth of religious repression in the thirteenth century. There was also a significant deterioration in the position of the Jews. True, the tradition of papal protection, provided that they remained in an inferior position within Christian society, still continued. Gregory IX stated the important principle, 'the same kindness should be shown by Christian to Jews, that we wish to be shown to Christians resident in pagan lands'.[36] Innocent IV in his *Lacrimabilem Judaeorum* of July 1247 strongly defended the Jews from the charge of ritual murder, which was still being levelled against them. Nevertheless hostility to the Jews was not solely a popular phenomenon. The Fourth Lateran Council had codified legislation against them, including the provision that they were to wear distinctive dress. It must be remembered that this was a society which expected rank and station to be distinguished by appropriate clothing: it was not the equivalent of the Nazi imposition of the star of David as a badge of Judaism. But later popes interested themselves in its enforcement, and it marked a further stage in the marginalization of the Jewish community. This was increased by an attack upon the Jewish law code, the Talmud. It had already been criticized in the twelfth century by Peter Alfonsi and Peter the Venerable, but now repressive action was taken against it. A Jewish convert, Nicholas Donin, complained to Gregory IX about its contents, and on 9 June 1239 the pope issued an instruction to confiscate all Jewish books the following March and hand them to the friars for examination. Any containing doctrinal error were to be burned. The consequence was the burning of twenty-four wagon-loads of manuscripts at Paris in 1242. At the same time, the custom began in France and in Aragon of obliging rabbis to hold disputations with the friars under the chairmanship of a member of the royal family, and of forcing Jewish communities to listen to sermons. The attack on the intellectual liberty of Jews was reaching a new level, and was to have great significance for the future.

[36] Auvray, *Les registres de Grégoire IX*, no. 1216, p. 692 (6 Apr. 1233).

19

PROCLAIMING THE FAITH

i. *Crusade and Mission*

The first half of the thirteenth century was the golden age of crusading. After the loss of Jerusalem to Saladin in 1187 a major expedition set out to the eastern Mediterranean in every decade. Crusades were used as a solution to every sort of problem, and were directed against the pagans of the Baltic, the Greeks, the Spanish Moslems, Cathars and the political enemies of the papacy. It is not an accident that the widest extension of crusading coincided with the greatest effectiveness of the papal monarchy, for the crusade put at the disposal of the Roman Church privileges which it could employ to promote military action against its enemies. The process of defining the rights of crusaders, which had begun in the twelfth century, was taken much further. The decree of Fourth Lateran, *Ad liberandam*, was the fullest statement so far of a crusading plan, and the clarification was completed in the works of the great canonist Hostiensis. The crusader bound himself by a vow, which was enforced by canonical sanctions unless it was commuted for a money payment or some other undertaking. He wore the cross as his badge and received an indulgence, the forgiveness of all sins and release from the penance which would otherwise have been due. His lands and rights were protected by the church, and the expedition might be financed by papally authorized funding. Strangely, this formidable machinery for the promotion of holy wars did not have a name. The term 'crusade' barely existed, although such expressions as the French *croiserie* or the Latin *crucesignati* are sometimes found. More commonly the members of the expedition continued to describe themselves by the undifferentiated term 'pilgrims'. Historians have been anxious to give a precise definition to the word 'crusade', but it is important to remember that this was not a thirteenth-century problem. As far as the Roman curia was concerned, it had at its disposal a body of privileges which could be granted, in whole or part, to those who would support the expeditions which they sponsored.

It is probably true that Jerusalem was the goal of every crusade to the eastern Mediterranean, but thirteenth-century crusaders seemed keen to fight for it anywhere except in Palestine. The balance of power had changed since the first Frankish conquest had been facilitated by the fragmentation of Moslem Syria and the political decay of Egypt. The Ayubid empire established by Saladin and his brother al-Adil (1200–18) presented a formidable opposition to any attempt to take Jerusalem by direct assault. Nor did the surviving Latin possessions offer a natural base for operations in southern Palestine. The second kingdom of Jerusalem, as it had been left at the end of the Third Crusade, was very different from its predecessor. It consisted of a string of coastal cities and castles, and owed its continued existence to the military orders and to an aristocracy which drew most of its resources from the newly acquired island of Cyprus. The city of Ascalon and the fortresses of Transjordan, essential to any secure Christian occupation of Jerusalem, had been lost. The west had to recognize that, as Villehardouin put it, 'in Syria you can do nothing . . . The land of Outremer will be recovered, if recovered it is, by the land of Babylon [Egypt] or by Greece.'[1] This argument had already justified the deflection of the Fourth Crusade to Constantinople; the next major effort was to be made against Egypt.

The crusade proclaimed at the Fourth Lateran Council had lost its originator with the death of Innocent III, but military operations began as planned in 1217. When the expedition reached the east it was decided to direct it against Egypt, and a landing was made near the port of Damietta at the end of May 1218. For most of the next three years overall control was in the hands of the papal legate, Cardinal Pelagius of Albano. The Fifth Crusade was more completely under ecclesiastical leadership than any other in the Mediterranean, and it was weakened by divisions between the legate and the lay commanders, especially John of Brienne, the titular king of Jerusalem. Damietta fell after a long siege on 5 November 1219, but the Christian army was kept inactive throughout 1220. An offer to cede Jerusalem in return for withdrawal was rejected because the Templars and Hospitallers argued that it could not be defended, and also because Pelagius was confident that Egypt could be conquered.

[1] G. de Villehardouin, *La Conquête de Constantinople*, ed. E. Faral (Paris, 1938), i.96.

His conviction was increased by the appearance of prophecies which announced the coming victory of the crusaders and promised them the help of a great Christian king in the east. In 1221 Pelagius advanced with disastrous consequences: the whole expedition was cut off in the Nile delta and obliged to negotiate terms of surrender. On 8 September the Sultan al-Kamil re-entered Damietta and the crusade was at an end.

Pelagius had accepted that, since Jerusalem could not be held securely without Egypt, the crusaders must invade that country. Frederick II drew the opposite conclusion and settled for an insecure tenure of the city. In 1225 he had married Isabella, the daughter of John of Brienne, and assumed the title of king of Jerusalem. He had also inherited the Hohenstaufen interest in prophecies of the last emperor, who was to wear the crown at Jerusalem and govern the earth in peace, and the manifesto which was read at his coronation claimed that he had been raised up as the deliverer of the Christian people. On the Moslem side, the Ayubid empire was beset by succession problems, and al-Kamil was more interested in compromise than warfare. Finally, Frederick found himself in the anomalous position of an excommunicate crusader, conducting an expedition under the disapproval of the pope. He had taken the cross in 1215 but the long Damietta campaign had come and gone without his personal participation. Eventually he promised to leave in August 1227 on pain of excommunication. In that month he assembled a large army at Brindisi, but returned to port almost at once on a plea of sickness. The illness may well have been genuine, but the new pope Gregory IX would listen to no more excuses and excommunicated the emperor. Frederick nevertheless sailed in June 1228 without receiving absolution. All the circumstances favoured a rapid agreement rather than a long campaign, and the treaty of Jaffa was signed on 18 February 1229. The Christians received Jerusalem, Lydda, and Bethlehem, protected by a ten-year truce. The Moslems retained the Temple area, which contained the Dome of the Rock and the Aqsa mosque. To the modern reader this may seem a sensible solution to a vexatious quarrel, but the treaty was fiercely criticized, in particular because it offered no security of tenure. This was certainly true: there was no protective ring of castles, and the city itself was not refortified. This unusual crusade ended with the crown-wearing by the excommunicate Frederick in the church of the Holy Sepulchre, followed by his rapid return to the west.

The truce lasted its full ten years, and at its end expeditions by Theobald of Navarre and Richard of Cornwall (1239–41) secured further territorial concessions from the deeply divided Moslems. The kingdom of Jerusalem on the map was now looking quite like its pre–1187 self, but the reality was different, for it was still without the southern fortresses which had once defended it. Its precarious character was shown in 1244, when war broke out between the Ayubid rulers of Egypt and Syria. As-Salih, the sultan of Egypt, and his allies swept into Jerusalem and on 17 October 1244 the Syrian-Christian alliance was wholly defeated near Gaza. Jerusalem was not to return to Christian rule until Allenby's armies entered it in 1917. It is reasonable to suppose that the news of the loss of the city influenced the decision of Louis IX of France to undertake a crusade, although there is no clear proof of it. Louis's was perhaps the best planned of all the crusades. The French army has been estimated at 15,000 men, and the total expenditure of about 1.5 million *livres* of Tours was enormous, amounting to more than ten times the annual royal revenue. The strategy rested on the rejection of the appeasement policy of the previous twenty years. Louis's goal was the conquest of Egypt; his charter for the archbishopric of Damietta showed every sign of envisaging permanent occupation. The expedition began brilliantly. After wintering in Cyprus the ships arrived at Damietta on 5 June 1249, and within twenty-four hours the city, which had resisted Pelagius for so long, was in French hands. The advance was not resumed until early the following year and was then held up at Mansurah, where a costly attempt to break through the Egyptian positions failed on 8 February 1250. This time the campaign proved even more disastrous than that of Pelagius, for Louis allowed himself to be cut off from Damietta and on 6 April he had to capitulate with his entire army. It was agreed that the captives would be released in return for the surrender of Damietta and a very large ransom. Louis spent some years in Palestine, occupied both in negotiating the release of prisoners and in strengthening the fortifications of the surviving castles and cities. They were thus enabled to resist for another generation, but no expedition on a similar scale was to be mounted to come to their relief.

Holy war against the unbelievers had never been confined to Syria. The First Crusade had been preceded by campaigns against the Saracens in Spain, and these remained part of papal strategy. Spain was one of the great crusading successes, for with the victory of Las

Navas de Tolosa in 1212 Christian supremacy was secured, and by 1250 almost all the peninsula had been incorporated into the Christian kingdoms. In the Baltic the missionary effort had already been reinforced by crusades, and the thirteenth century saw their extension into Livonia and Prussia. In Livonia the period of conquest effectively began with the appointment of Albert of Buxtehude as bishop in 1198. He was a canon of Hamburg-Bremen, the centre of the northern mission, and founded the city of Riga in 1201 and located the cathedral there. By 1212 the Livs in the Dvina valley had accepted his lordship, and after a series of ruthless campaigns had subjugated southern Estonia the country was partitioned in 1222 between Bishop Albert and the Danes who had occupied the northern coast. The conquest of Prussia began later. There the Cistercian Bishop Christian (1215–45) had initially been successful in securing conversions, and the intervention of the military orders was perhaps a political conquest of peoples who were already in the process of adopting Christianity.[2] Christian himself turned to the use of force, but his leadership was superseded by that of the Teutonic Knights, who in 1230–1 began to establish a chain of strongpoints along the river Vistula, and thence along the coast to Elbing (1237) and Königsberg (1254). The conquest of the Baltic provinces was by no means a story of unbroken success. Lithuania was increasingly organized as a centre of pagan resistance after annihilating an invasion at Siauliai in 1236, and was to remain pagan for centuries. The encounter of the invading Germans with the Russian princes also re-enacted the rivalry of Latin and Greek Christianity in the far north, and culminated in a major war in 1240–2 and in the famous victory of Alexander Nevsky over the western knights on the ice of Lake Peipus. Nevertheless by 1250 the later frontiers of Livonia (Latvia) and Prussia had been approximately drawn, and they had been incorporated into Latin Christendom.

The sources oblige us to see the conquest of Livonia and Prussia largely through the eyes of the military orders. As they present it, it was a particularly pure example of holy war. The principle that baptism was a matter for free choice was almost abandoned, so that the chronicler Henry of Livonia, although himself a mission priest, simply assumed the rightness of spreading the faith by force. The new provinces were in ecclesiastical hands. Bishop Albert was

[2] For this view see K. Gorski, 'Probleme der Christianisierung in Preussen, Livland und Litauen', in K. Nowak, *Die Rolle der Ritterorden* (Torun, 1983), 9–34.

recognized as a prince of the empire in 1207, and at Fourth Lateran he secured the exemption of the bishopric of Riga from Hamburg-Bremen. It became an archbishopric in 1253. In Prussia the Teutonic Knights secured a similar position of dominance. The Golden Bull of Rimini in 1226 granted their master, Hermann of Salza, the status of prince of the empire for his prospective conquests, and in 1234 the territory of the Knights was recognized as a papal fief. A series of legates, especially Bishop William of Modena between 1225 and 1242, supervised the setting up of a diocesan organization. The legates also attempted, with very limited success, to preserve the rights of converts against oppression. As Gregory IX wrote in 1239, 'men signed with the mark of Christ must not be worse off than they were as limbs of the devil'.[3] The spearhead of the conquest was provided by the knights. Bishop Albert founded the Livonian Sword-Brothers (or the Brothers of the Militia of Christ) in 1202. In Prussia Bishop Christian founded the Knights of Dobrzyn in 1228 but the effective conquest was the work of the Teutonic Knights, who founded an order at Acre during the Third Crusade in imitation of the Templars and Hospitallers. The defence of the Holy Land was always its top priority, but it early showed an interest in the frontiers of Europe. When he undertook the conquest of Prussia the grand master Hermann of Salza used his influence with Frederick II to ensure that he had a free hand. In Livonia the Sword-Brothers were intended as an arm of episcopal power, but after the death of Bishop Albert in 1229 they became uncontrollable and their indiscipline led to their absorption into the Teutonic Knights in 1237. Much of the fighting was done by crusaders, largely German, who came in a series of frequent expeditions. In 1245 Innocent IV granted indulgences to all who went to Prussia, even without a specific papal appeal. The Baltic crusades offered the opportunity to obtain an indulgence without undertaking the tedious journey to the eastern Mediterranean, and provided a better prospect of acquiring territory than Palestine. The main pattern of landholding of the later Prussian nobility was founded in these crusades. The operation was controlled by Germans, and was a formative chapter in the *Drang nach Osten*. Its success was based on the superiority of western technology: on the stone castle, the heavy cavalry, and the crossbow; on the cog, the large merchant ship which maintained commercial and naval links between Lübeck and Riga; and on the successful creation of German

---

[3] Cited E. Christiansen, *The Northern Crusades* (London, 1980), 125.

cities and villages. The original population, although sometimes atrociously treated, survived, but the price of survival was the acceptance of German settlement and culture and a Latin religious establishment.

While the popes were sponsoring expeditions to recover Jerusalem, they were also directing crusades against a variety of enemies, including Greeks, heretics, and political opponents in Italy. The crusade against Christians has often been seen as a new phenomenon which, by alienating public opinion, led to the discrediting of the movement as a whole. This view must be formulated with some care, because there was nothing new about the use of warfare against the enemies of the church within western Europe. The campaign of Leo IX against the Normans and the use of 'knights of St Peter' by Gregory VII had been precedents for the First Crusade, so that it might almost be said that the war against Islam was a by-product of the holy war at home. One can find a few examples in the twelfth century: the offer of indulgence made by Urban II in 1095 was repeated at the council of Pisa in 1135, this time to those who would fight against Anacletus II, and again at Third Lateran in 1179 for participation in operations against the Albigensian heretics. These measures, however, led to virtually no consequences, and in reality there had been few crusades against Christians. There had been no use of crusading privileges against the Greeks, or in practice against heresy, and although Alexander III had employed political measures against his imperialist enemies he had held back from any offer of indulgences. The political crusades of the thirteenth century came as a novelty to contemporaries.

From Innocent III onwards the use of crusades within Christendom became ever more significant in papal policy, until by the middle of the century the reaction of the Roman Church to almost any threat was to direct a crusade against it. Innocent sponsored the first and largest of the crusades against heretics. He was at least the *de facto* founder of crusades against the Greeks, and the Fourth Crusade led to attempts to buttress the crumbling position of the Latin emperor at Constantinople. Gregory IX was convinced that the defence of the Latin empire was a crucial stage in the recovery of the Holy Land, and supported a clumsy project for a joint expedition against the Greeks by Bela IV of Hungary and the Emperor Baldwin II. The most striking development was, however, the use of crusading privileges against the Hohenstaufen, who were primarily political enemies of the Roman Church. The first clear example was Innocent's action against Markward of Anweiler in Sicily, which had little practical effect. It is often suggested that in 1228 Gregory IX avoided turning his conflict with Frederick II into a crusade, but he issued an indulgence to his supporters and made an international appeal for money and men. In any event, he promulgated a full-scale crusade against Frederick in 1239, and his example was followed by Innocent IV and later popes.

While the crusading movement was increasingly diversified another approach to the unbeliever was developing: peaceful preaching. The first half of the century saw the beginning of major attempts to proclaim the Gospel outside Europe and to formulate a theory of mission. The fact that this missionary activity was in the long run unsuccessful should not lead us to neglect it, because the ideas which shaped it eventually influenced the expansion of the church initiated by Atlantic exploration in the fifteenth century. Gregory IX's decretal of 1235 *Cum hora undecima* 'contained the basic statement of the church's missionary function', and in the amplified form issued by Innocent IV it was repeatedly copied in later centuries.[4] Innocent IV was also responsible for the first developed statement of the relationship between the church and the non-Christian world in his commentary on the *Quod super his* of Innocent III. The idea of conversion was of course not new in the thirteenth century, and had appeared in crusading propaganda; but it was now transformed under the impact of major changes in the way western Europeans understood the world. The most obvious reason for the new missionary initiative was a technical one. With the growth of the military orders, and much more with the emergence of the friars, there were groups of men available to go where they were needed. Missions outside Europe were undertaken largely by Franciscans and Dominicans, and they were well placed to keep the mission field before the eyes of the Roman curia. More fundamental in creating a change of view was the radical thinking about poverty and simplicity. This helped to stimulate the so-called Childrens' Crusade of 1212, which probably consisted not of children but of shepherds, household servants, and the poor. It seems to have been a spontaneous movement among those who believed that God would restore Jerusalem to humble men when he had withheld it from the mighty; and it succeeded in going no further than Genoa. A far more

---

[4] J. Muldoon, *Popes, Lawyers and Infidels* (Liverpool, 1979), 36.

effective expression of the ideal of poverty was to be found in the friars. Both Francis and Dominic saw their mission as extending beyond the boundaries of Christendom: 'I say to you in truth that the Lord chose and sent the friars for the profit of the souls of all men in the whole world, and they are to be received not only in the lands of the faithful but also of the infidel.'[5] Francis himself paid his famous visit to Sultan al-Kamil to preach to him at the time of the Fifth Crusade in 1219. The message was incorporated into a new vision of the end of the world, which took seriously the prophecy that 'this gospel of the kingdom will be preached throughout the whole world, as a testimony to all nations; and then the end will come' (Matt. 24: 14). Given the information which was becoming available about the extent of the missionary task the crusades no longer seemed relevant to it. Joachim of Fiore seems to have regarded them as of little significance, and the *Commentary on Jeremiah* (a work in Joachim's tradition and written under his name) was fiercely critical of the use of force. It was unusual in seeing crusades and missions as contradictory; some people, like Gregory IX and Innocent IV, were keen advocates of both.

The friars did not expect immediate success; on the contrary, many went in the hope of martyrdom. Nevertheless, the changing situation in Africa and Asia held out a prospect that the gospel could be preached to unbelievers. The victory of the Spanish Christians in 1212 opened the way to preaching to the Moors of Spain and created the possibility of a Moroccan mission. The first Franciscans were martyred there in 1220. They were followed by others, and the Dominicans also made Spain and north Africa a target for missionary activity. Innocent IV corresponded with Moslem rulers to protect the friars' freedom to preach and threatened diplomatic or commercial reprisals if they were persecuted. The amount of liberty remained very restricted, but the mission in Spain was secure, and the Moroccan mission was at least a possible area of growth.

More striking was the change in western ideas about Asia. The assumption that Christianity and Islam occupied most of the surface of the planet was disturbed by the discovery that in Asia, behind the Islamic barrier, there was a network of Nestorian churches and great populations to whom the faith could be brought. Western interest in further Asia had already been shown in the twelfth century by the

[5] Francis of Assisi to Cardinal Hugolino, as reported in *Scripta Leonis Rufini et Angeli sociorum*, ed. R. B. Brooke (Oxford, 1970), 233.

popularity of legends of Alexander. The first recorded visit by an Asian bishop to Rome took place in 1122, but the details are extremely imprecise. Then in 1145 news of Prester John arrived for the first time, brought by the bishop of Gabala in northern Syria. The report was almost certainly based on the defeat of the Seljuk Sultan Sanjar in 1141, which rumour ascribed to a great Christian monarch. The real impact of Asiatic affairs upon Christendom began, however, with the rise of the Mongol empire. The Mongol tribes had been united by the military genius of Temüjin, whom they recognized in 1206 as Genghis Khan (Universal Ruler). In 1219 a Mongol army overran Persia and ravaged its cities. Until then, Christendom had been aware of two worlds, Islam and itself; now for the first time the Third World was beginning to write the agenda. The Mongols were devoted to world conquest, but they were also potential allies against Islam and a rich field for missionary enterprise. The first information to arrive was thoroughly confusing. The warfare inspired the story that a Christian King David, a relative of Prester John, had come from India and overrun the Persian kingdom. It was this report which misled Pelagius at Damietta, and subsequently Honorius III. The possible implications of the Mongol empire only became apparent when about 1235 the great khan Ogödei sent a huge army westwards under his general Batu. It took Kiev in December 1240 and defeated western armies in Hungary and Silesia in April 1241. The whole of eastern Europe was overrun by the Mongols, but in the spring of 1242 their armies withdrew eastward, leaving Poland and Hungary. The occasion was the death of Ogödei and the prospect of a succession dispute, in which Batu was interested, at the capital Karakorum. Europe was left to speculate on the likelihood that they would return.

It was Innocent IV who undertook the collection of information from the east. One of the major purposes of the assembly of the council of Lyon in 1245 was 'to find a remedy against the Tartars and other despisers of the Christian faith'.[6] Innocent received accounts from survivors of the Hungarian catastrophe and promised papal aid in the event of a renewal of the Tartar offensive. He also sent friars to establish contact with the Mongol rulers. The most remarkable of these missions was that of the Franciscan John of Pian di Carpine, whose report was the first great narrative of Asiatic travel by a

---

[6] Letter to archbishop of Sens 3 Jan. 1245: H. Wolter and H. Holstein, *Lyon I et Lyon II* (Paris, 1966), 250–1.

westerner. Leaving Lyon in April 1245, he arrived in Mongolia in July 1246, in time to be present at the assembly which elected the new khan. He had carried two letters from the pope, one an exposition of the Christian faith and the other a protest against the invasion of Christian kingdoms. The great khan's reaction was disquieting. He sent a hostile reply in which he demanded papal recognition of his supremacy and claimed that the kings who resisted him were opposing God's will. Friar John warned the pope that 'it is the intention of the Tartars to bring the whole world into subjection if they can'.[7] Other envoys received similar responses, but there were a few meetings with Nestorian officials which gave some grounds for a slender hope. The ground, at least, had been prepared for the great missionary journeys to central Asia and China which were to follow.

The position of crusading within the western church during the first half of the thirteenth century was paradoxical. Crusades had never before been so prominent in papal policy or Christian consciousness. Historians have supposed that widespread disillusionment with crusading arose because of persistent failure, the increasing weight of taxation required to support expeditions, and resentment against the political misuse of the movement. Certainly, this became a commonplace of satirists' complaints:

> Rome, to Saracens you turn the other cheek.
> All your victims are Latin or else Greek.
> In the pit of hell, Rome, is your true location,
>
> Sitting in damnation.
> God knows I want none
> of your pilgrims' dispensation
> if their stated destination
> is at Avignon!
>
> Rome, you understand that my words are biting,
> Since with tricks against Christians you are fighting.
> Tell me in what text do you find it written,
>
> Christians should be smitten?
> God, who are true bread
> for us every day,
> bring down what I pray
> on the Romans' head.[8]

---

[7] C. Dawson (tr.), *The Mongol Mission* (London, 1955), 43.

[8] Guilhem Figueira, *D'un sirventes far*, R. T. Hill and T. G. Bergin (ed.), *Anthology of the Provençal Troubadours* (Yale, 1941), no. 122, pp. 178–9.

We must not place this anti-crusading feeling too far back in time, for crusades enjoyed a great deal of sympathy, and only limited criticism, between 1187 and 1229. In this context the defeat of Louis IX may have been decisive. Its impact is described by the English chronicler Matthew Paris:

All of France was filled with grief and confusion, and clergy and knights lamented bitterly and would not be consoled . . . Driven distracted by anguish of mind and great sorrow they accused God of being unjust, in words of blasphemy which sounded like those of apostates or heretics. And the faith of many began to waver. The most noble city of Venice and many cities of Italy, whose population is only half Christian in any case, would have fallen into apostasy had they not been strengthened by the consolation of bishops and holy religious men, who rightly said that the slain are now reigning in heaven as martyrs . . . This quietened some people's indignation, but not everybody's.[9]

These words are often seen as the obituary of the great crusades. Popular shock at the pious king's failure, resentment against taxation, the anger of imperialists and troubadours at the launching of crusades against Christians, created an atmosphere in which the great endeavour could not be successfully renewed.[10]

ii. *The Pastoral Revolution*

The thirteenth century saw a sustained effort to instruct and discipline the faithful. As it was enunciated by councils and applied by bishops, this programme was quite specific. It aimed at the use of the confessional as a means of counselling and teaching; at the instruction of the laity in Christian belief and conduct; and at the education of the parish clergy as a step towards these objectives. This is the movement which has in recent years been identified as 'the pastoral revolution', and it incorporated some new assumptions about the mission of the church.

Earlier reformers had not been much interested in ordinary people. The papal reform movement had aimed at the cultic purity of the

---

[9] Matthew Paris, *Chronica Majora* (RS 57) v. 169–70.

[10] For another view, see Elizabeth Siberry, *Criticism of Crusading 1095–1274* (Oxford, 1985), where it is argued that the critics were largely self-interested and not necessarily representative of public opinion, and that the shock at the defeat of Louis IX was no greater than that at the failure of the Second Crusade, which was not fatal to the movement. The point is an interesting one; the test is the ability of the west to recover from the setback, which lies outside the scope of this volume.

church, at freedom from simony, clerical concubinage, and lay control. Monastic and eremitical leaders had sought to create communities living the apostolic life. The later years of the twelfth century saw a reassessment of the place of the laity. Theologians began to show an interest not only in great saints and sinners, but in the fairly good and the fairly bad, the *mediocriter boni et mali*. A classic sermon of Innocent III set out schematically the range of human vice and virtue and located the sorts and conditions of men within it.[11] The growing awareness of the needs of the mediocre was reflected in the emergence of a much firmer idea of purgatory. It had been accepted for a long time that holy men might experience a fire of purification after their death, and might purge particular sins by a short residence in the upper parts of hell; but from about 1170 the Paris theologians began to speak, not merely of 'purgatorial fire' or 'purgation', but of purgatory as a noun and a place. 'Paradise', we are told, 'receives the spirits of the perfect; hell, the very bad; the fire of purgatory, those who are neither very good nor very bad.'[12]

The beginnings of a shift in pastoral perspectives may be observed already in the twelfth century. The concern to provide an ethic for groups in lay society in such areas as chivalry and marriage was a stage on the way to a general ministry to all men. So was the growth of episcopal responsibility for the local clergy. When bishops began to institute the parish priests, to protect their income from the lay patron and to keep records of their admission to livings (although such lists must have been extremely rare before 1200), it was a natural step to become concerned for their discipline and training. These were presages of the new approach, but perhaps the things which crystallized it most clearly were the threat of the Saracens and the heretics. In face of the loss of the Holy Land, repentance was incumbent on all Christians, as Gregory VIII had insisted in *Audita tremendi*. In face of the rise of heresy, simple laymen were defenceless if they had no understanding of the faith, especially when they encountered those who claimed to be living in accordance with the New Testament. It was these considerations which probably led Innocent III, a Paris graduate who had learned the new theology there, to formulate it as a policy for the western church as a whole in

---

[11] Sermon 27 on the Assumption of the Blessed Virgin (PL 217.578–90).

[12] For references see J. Le Goff, *The Birth of Purgatory* (London, 1984). The use of the noun *purgatorium* seems to go back before 1170 to the Cistercian writers, and it occurs in a sermon of Bernard of Clairvaux whose authenticity there is no reason to doubt; but the development of the concept took place in the Paris theologians.

the decrees of the Lateran Council. The drive to implement it was a
co-operation between four of the most powerful forces in the church:
the Paris theologians, the ecumenical authority of a great council, the
friars, and the diocesan bishops especially in France and England.[13]

The discipline of the confessional was formally established in the
western church by canon 21 of Fourth Lateran, *Omnis utriusque
sexus*, which has been called with pardonable exaggeration 'perhaps
the most important legislative act in the history of the church'.[14] It
was intended to enact at the highest level of authority a discipline
which was being actively developed in the preceding decades. The
old tariff-penance, under which each sin carried a prescribed penalty
of fasting, was superseded by a confessional of the modern type, in
which a priest would impose a penance and give absolution
immediately after confession. The transaction was private, without a
public penance or public reconciliation. Penances were at the
discretion of the priest or, as it was technically expressed, were
'arbitrary'. Although manuals continued to list tariffs as a guide, the
emphasis was that the penance should be appointed in the light of the
situation of the penitent. Such a discipline gave a lot of responsibility
to the confessor, and parish priests were poorly trained to discharge
it. Manuals were therefore produced to assist them. They had at least
one precursor about 1160, *Homo quidam*, an anonymous Norman
tract which breathes something of the new spirit, but the production
of textbooks really began about the end of the century in close
connection with Paris. They included Alan of Lille's *Liber Peniten-
tialis* (first edition *c.*1191); Robert of Flamborough, canon of St
Victor (1199 onwards); Thomas of Chobham, a former Paris master
(*c.*1215); and another Victorine, Peter of Poitiers (*c.*1215). The
Fourth Lateran decree encouraged the writing of many more such
works, and the *Summae Confessorum*, as they came to be known,
became an influential branch of literature. Some of them were major
theological compositions, such as the *Summa de casibus penitentie*
(*c.*1225), a foundation text for the study of moral theology by the
Dominican Raymond of Peñafort. At the opposite extreme were

---

[13] For details of developments mentioned in this summary paragraph, see ch. 13 (ethics);
Ch. 9.iii (diocesan administration); and ch. 17.iv (Fourth Lateran reforms).
[14] H. C. Lea, *A History of Auricular Confession* (London, 1896), 230. The development of the
penitential system is complicated by the double change from public to private penance and
from tariff to arbitrary penance. The extent of private penance in the twelfth century is difficult
to determine. In the text I have been content with the common-sense assumption that the
Lateran Council was aiming at an immense increase in its use. See also ch. 15.iv.

simple texts for the guidance of priests circulated in some English dioceses, and books in the vernacular like the widely circulated *Manuel des Péchés* of c.1260.[15] The efforts of local clergy were supplemented by the expertise of the friars, and by 1200 bishops were already appointing penitentiaries to receive confession of those graver sins which had to be referred to episcopal authority.

The establishment of the confessional meant more than the provision of annual visits by reluctant parishioners to their local priest. Counselling had to rest upon teaching about cases and problems, and thus gave a secure place to moral theology in clerical education; it has been suggested that the work of Robert Grosseteste in translating Aristotle's *Ethics* was the result of his concern as bishop of Lincoln for penitential discipline. Confession was also a parable of ecclesiastical authority enacted at a level where it could be seen by every Christian. The participation of the community had been stripped away; in normal cases there was no public penance or reconciliation. The one-to-one relationship of priest to penitent raised a question about the source of the forgiveness which was bestowed. The predominant twelfth-century view, expressed by Anselm of Canterbury, Peter Abelard, and Peter Lombard, was that the act of confession itself was the basis of forgiveness provided that there was true sorrow for sin. This was superseded by an increasing tendency to stress the authority of the priest, who could draw on the power of the keys and the treasury of merit created by the suffering of Christ and his saints. This in turn influenced the rite, and the first occurence of the authoritarian formula, *Ego absolvo te*, can be traced to about 1200. Ultimately the confessional was the enlistment of every lay person into the service of God. It was not enough to participate in ceremonies; the laity had to be committed by self-examination and will. It belongs to the 'piety concerned for immediacy to God' which some writers have seen as a new feature of the thirteenth century.[16] Its effect, however, was not to give liberty, for the key to the exercise was discipline. The laity were expected to accept the rules formulated by the clergy, who now secured dominion even in the internal forum of the conscience. The *Summae confessorum* functioned as an organ of social control. Social control, however, is a complex matter, and the confessional had unexpected

---

[15] For the texts circulated in English dioceses see F. M. Powicke and C. R. Cheney, *C&S* II.ii.220–6, 305.

[16] W. Pannenberg, *Christian Spirituality and Sacramental Community* (London, 1984), 4.

results. It made it difficult to dismiss whole ways of life, for it was necessary to counsel merchants, money-lenders, and others who were exposed to constant temptation. Like purgatory, it was a facility designed for the not-so-good and forced the church to say what was the minimum of acceptable behaviour. The entrepreneurial spirit was legitimized from the confessor's chair.

The new discipline was both an individual one which required all adults to answer for their personal sins, and a recognition of the variety of social ranks into which the population, especially in cities, was now divided. The element which had largely disappeared was the sense of a general Christian community in each place, and its loss can be seen in the disintegration of the old baptismal ceremony, about which significantly the Lateran Council had little to say, for it had largely disappeared from the centre of pastoral attention. In the eleventh century the standard rite was still the old Roman one, which prescribed baptism for two major occasions each year, Easter and Pentecost. The bishop presided and the candidates received baptism by water, the laying on of hands, and first communion. Adult baptism was rare, but infants were baptized according to the same rite and councils stressed that they should receive communion, normally in the form of wine alone. The whole occasion must have been a noisy and vivid expression of the local community, assembled to celebrate a major festival and incorporate its new members. Even by this time there were two elements of disintegration. Infants whose life was in peril (no doubt a significant proportion) received baptism and communion without waiting, and because of the large size of dioceses in most of Europe it was necessary for priests to conduct the Easter ceremony and to reserve the laying on of hands ('confirmation') for the bishop.

The collapse of the originally unitary ceremony proceeded throughout the period from 1050 to 1250. One important solvent was the pressure to baptize infants without waiting. This had become usual for those in poor health, but after 1050 theologians and synods increasingly demanded immediate baptism. There was a conflicting attempt to keep the observance of the old liturgical times, on which the legatine council of London still insisted in 1237, but before the end of the thirteenth century they were being used only for a few newly born infants, or even for no one at all. The dissolution of the ceremony was taken further by the abandonment of the practice of giving communion to children, which probably took place in the course of the thirteenth century and may well have been connected with the refusal of the cup to the laity, since this was how infants received. The decision to restrict communion to adults may have been a deliberate one by the Lateran reformers. Bishop Odo of Sully prohibited child communion at Paris, and *Omnis utriusque sexus*, with its rule about confession and communion for those of years of discretion, implicitly excluded children. By the end of the period the communal rite of initiation had collapsed. Children were being baptized within a few days of birth and confirmed subsequently when and if the bishop could be found, and did not receive communion until they were old enough to confess. The new situation expressed the new pastoral ideal of ministry to individual souls.

These souls had to be instructed in the faith, and this instruction took two different forms. It is natural to refer to both as preaching, but they had essentially different functions. The basic teaching was now normally defined as the Apostles' Creed, the Lord's Prayer, and the Hail Mary, all to be learned by heart.[17] Bishop Grosseteste of Lincoln about 1239 prescribed a more ambitious programme: priests were to expound regularly the Ten Commandments, the seven deadly sins, and the seven sacraments and were to ensure that the people knew the formula for baptism in English.[18] There was provision for other teaching too, such as the need to care for very young children and the learning of prayers for various times in the day. No clear indication was given when such instruction took place, but it is reasonable to assume it was at the Sunday mass in association with the reading of notices and bidding prayers (the 'prone') which in the thirteenth century—and possibly earlier—were in the vernacular. Just after the end of our period the Franciscan Bonaventure pointed out how much basic understanding could be derived from the services when he said that laymen were

obliged to believe explicitly in those things which are opened to them, not only in preaching but also in the use and custom of the church. For instance, in the Unity and Trinity: this they can know from making the sign of the cross, because they sign themselves in the name of the Father, and of the Son and of the Holy Spirit. Also in the birth, passion and resurrection and in the remission of sins: these they can learn from the ceremonies performed by the church and the actions of the priests.[19]

[17] Statutes of Salisbury, I (1217/19) c. 5 (*C&S* II.i.61).
[18] Statutes of Lincoln, c. 1 (i.268).
[19] Bonaventure, *Liber III Sententiarum*, D. 25, art. 1, q. 3 (*Opera Theologica Selecta* iii (Quaracchi, 1941), 535).

This elementary instruction was supplemented by explanation of the readings for the day. Canon 10 of the Fourth Lateran Council had called on bishops to provide themselves with assistants for preaching, and there seems already to have been a new wave of preaching around Paris about 1200. Bishop Maurice of Sully provided homilies for parish clergy, in Latin and French; a parish priest, Fulk of Neuilly, preached repentance and the Fourth Crusade; Stephen Langton and Robert of Courson are said to have carried out brilliant preaching tours; and of James of Vitry it was later reported that 'his words moved France, as never in the history of man a preacher had moved it'. The advent of the friars rapidly increased the manpower available for popular preaching, and the thirteenth century abounds in large collections of sermons by friars and seculars alike. In France for example there were those of William of Auvergne, bishop of Paris 1228–49, and of two outstanding Dominicans from the house of Lyon, Stephen of Bourbon and Humbert of Romans. In Italy there were Antony of Padua and Federigo Visconti, archbishop of Pisa, with innumerable other collections by Preachers and Minorites.

The sermon collection was in much more demand than handbooks on how to preach, but nevertheless the author might provide an introduction about methods. The only previous instance of this in our period had been the introduction provided by Abbot Guibert of Nogent in 1084 to his commentary on Genesis, but now they appeared in a steady supply. Alan of Lille's *Summa de Arte Predicandi* contained instructions about the preparation of sermons with seventy-four sketches of homilies. These included addresses of a relatively new type designed for different social groups, the *sermones ad status*. James of Vitry likewise published a large collection of sermons with reflections on the art of preaching, and Honorius III provided encouragement by donating manuscripts of his own sermons and urging the recipients to make them available to others. Handbooks on preaching methods were followed by other works of reference. William of Auvergne produced a treatise *De faciebus mundi* (*Aspects of the World*) which listed at dismaying length ways in which natural objects could be presented as symbols of divine truth. Biblical commentaries were designed for the reference of preachers: Archbishop Federigo Visconti of Pisa prepared his sermons with the *Postilla in totam Bibliam* of Hugh of St Cher by his elbow. Other authors collected *exempla*, stories from history, the life of the saints, nature, and experience. They were part of the new style of simpler, more approachable preaching, their punch-lines sometimes recorded in the vernacular as a pun or snappy phrase. Their use in preaching to laymen was strongly recommended, and their collection culminated in Stephen of Bourbon's immense work which contains almost 2,900 *exempla* and was still incomplete at his death in 1261. The popular sermon also had an impact on the design of churches. The first stone pulpits, which were in Dominican churches, were probably built after 1250, but the tendency to treat the nave as a separate lay church, with a great screen isolating it from the choir, was in part related to the growth of sermons for the laity. There is no certainty about the availability of regular homilies in local churches, but the quality of popular preaching had improved through the use of friars and other trained personnel, and one of the aims of the reform was to educate the parochial clergy as confessors and instructors. The methods used must be considered later: our next task is to assess the impact of the pastoral revolution upon the state of popular religion.

iii. *Popular Religion*

To present an anatomy of popular religion in a short space is an impossible task. For one thing, we do not have the information. The illiterate have left no account of their faith, and the literate acquired not only skill in writing but with it a culture which made them untypical of most of society. We do not even have many accounts of the faith of the people seen from outside by the clergy. There is some information about it in the sermons and inquisitorial records of the thirteenth century; the most obvious example, a detailed inquiry at the village of Montaillou in the Pyrenees with a great deal of verbatim material from witnesses, has been made famous by E. Le Roy Ladurie, but falls considerably after the end of our period.[20] Confessors were undoubtedly concerned with the legends and customs of the countryside, but did not often record them. The best sources (and even they are not very informative) are the *Corrector* of Burchard of Worms before our period and the *Liber de officio Cherubyn* of Friar Rudolf after its end.

The concept 'popular religion' has also been used by some writers in a strangely free way. There was not one lay culture but many: the expression of a great noble's religion was very different from that of a citizen or a peasant, while peasant cultures were locally rooted and varied very much across the face of Europe. Worse than that, the

---

[20] E. le Roy Ladurie, *Montaillou* (London, 1978).

concept suggests that there was a distinctive type of religion characteristic of the laity, and this is broadly untrue. The *populus* does not appear as an autonomous cultural group, but as the recipients, eager or reluctant, of ideas handed down by their social and spiritual superiors. Deference remained strong: only one non-noble layman was canonized in the thirteenth century, Homobonus of Cremona by Innocent III, and the saints who received most popular support in the Italian cities tended to be not ordinary fellow citizens, but members of the mendicant orders. In the religion of the people we see the ritual and teaching of the church in reflecting or distorting mirrors, which moreover were touched at different times by different rays of light. Remote villages would escape the network of ecclesiastical supervision, like the peasants who only knew it was a feast-day because there was an old man who made a hobby of the calendar and always dressed up for the occasion: 'Master Gosselin has his red shoes on.'[21] At the opposite extreme were city-dwellers whose contacts with regular canons or friars would enable them to keep up with recent developments and hear a series of good sermons. There were laity moved by the apostolic poverty movement and the words of Christ to become Cistercian lay brothers, friars, Beguines, or Waldensians; while others learned deference and discipline from the pulpit and the confessional. Sections of the urban population seem to have been sceptical of established religion in general. In rural society it was more usual for religious practice to be shaped by cults of holy places, stories of the saints, and legends woven round the Biblical narrative. A recent school of French historians would prefer to speak not of popular religion, but of *culture folklorique*, which is a better description at least of part of the spectrum. They have shown that the common assumption that we are dealing with only two elements, a pre-Christian culture which was being reshaped by a coherent Christianity imposed by the church, is far too simple. True, there are features preserved from ancient Germanic religion—the days of the week are still named after pagan deities—but much of the *culture folklorique* was supplied by the ceremonies of the church and was being introduced precisely in the period we are now studying. A book by J.-C. Schmitt illustrates the variety of influences which could play upon a local community. Stephen of Bourbon was dismayed to find, only thirty miles from the large city of Lyon, that country people were bringing their children for healing to the well of

[21] A. Lecoy de la Marche, *La chaire française au moyen âge* (Paris, 1886), 424.

St Guinefort, who on inquiry turned out to be a greyhound who had saved his master's child from a serpent and then been slain himself. This remarkable story, apart from the starring role given to one of the few pet animals admitted to the order of the saints, seems to display four influences: reverence for holy wells, the Germanic practice of exposing sick children, the cult of the saints, and the story, originally from classical literature, of the faithful hound. It is mystifying how the villagers had come across this last piece of learning (could it have been a preacher's *exemplum* which went wrong?) but the episode shows how a deeply rooted custom could be reinterpreted by new influences.[22]

By 1250 most people in western Europe had a parish church easily available. True, in mountainous or thinly populated regions the church might still be a long way away, and in Poland it was still quite common to have ten or twenty villages associated with a mother-church. In most of the west, this phase had been left a long way in the past. Estimates in both France and England indicate that there were between 100 and 300 adult laity in an average parish. In England and Wales the *Taxation* of Pope Nicholas after the end of our period listed 8,085 churches, and it is certainly not complete. It had become normal for the church to form the centre of the village, the natural place to meet for gossip and a strongpoint for the deposit of valuables. The bell provided the measure of time for the villagers. Every child had to be taken there for baptism, and within a year, an English synod optimistically prescribed, should be taken to the bishop for confirmation.[23] The Lateran Council assumed that everybody had an 'own priest', *proprius sacerdos*, to whom he might go for confession. The reality of the baptismal link is illustrated by the spread of Christian names derived from the Bible or the saints in place of traditional German or Slavonic ones. The process has only been studied in detail in a few places, but it was a marked feature of these centuries, and interestingly it sometimes took place more rapidly in lower-class society: the aristocracy was more wedded to its old family names. Christian symbolism insinuated itself into the details of everyday life . It was common to make the sign of the cross and to possess a small personal cross, even at a time when the image of Christ on the great crucifix remained a distant and royal one.

[22] J.-C. Schmitt, *The Holy Greyhound* (Cambridge, 1983). For methods of transmission of such ideas, see the interesting article by A. Boureau, 'Narration cléricale et narration populaire', in. J.-C. Schmitt (ed.), *Les saints et les stars* (Paris, 1983), 41–64.

[23] Statutes of Canterbury, I (1213/4) c. 37 (*C&S* II.i.32 and n.).

Amber crosses have been found alongside hammers belonging to the storm-god in deposits at Gdansk in Poland which date back to the period of the conversion in the eleventh century. The symbols and names of the Christian religion permeated everyday life. But what sort of religion had emerged from it?

Its first feature was ignorance. Most people knew little about the Christian faith. It was the ambition of most legislators in the thirteenth-century church that the people should know the Lord's Prayer, the Creed and the Hail Mary, and that this was close to the maximum attainment is indicated by the almost invariable recommendation that they should be used as prayers at various times in the day. We hear also of cases where they had been learned in Latin by people who could not understand them, and of a Dominican novice at Bologna who 'had never fasted except on Good Friday, had hardly ever abstained from meat except on Fridays, had never been to confession and knew nothing of the prayers which are said in church except the Lord's Prayer'.[24] Even the friars, with their concern for the poor, accepted ignorance as a fact of life and were relatively untroubled by it. Humbert of Romans cited the text, 'the oxen were ploughing and the asses were feeding beside them' (Job 1: 14) with the crushing gloss, 'the asses, that is the simple, ought to be content with the teaching of their betters'. Even Gregory the Great had been less authoritarian in his comment.[25]

The learning of the basic formulae was treated, in fact, as one of the duties which the ordinary believer owed to God, for the peasant was bound in a network of services which dominated his religious and secular duties. The two were closely connected: 'You should believe and understand that you owe to your earthly lord dues and tallages, fines, services, carriage, transport and escort. Render them all in full at the proper time and place.'[26] Dues to God and the church were similarly defined in formal terms, with an emphasis not on spiritual enlightenment but on the avoidance of sin. There was no shyness about insisting on the payment of tithes. On the contrary, to withhold them was presented as a particularly terrible offence: the miracles of Rocamadour, written about 1172, told of a man who was possessed by a demon because he despised the clergy and failed to pay tithe. Instructions about the confessional have a plodding air

[24] S. Tugwell, *Early Dominicans: Selected Writings* (London, 1982), 126.
[25] See A. Murray, *Traditio* 30 (1974), 298 n.
[26] Homilies of Maurice of Sully, cited M. Zink, *Prédication en langue romane* (Paris, 1976), 180.

about them. Bernard of Clairvaux told of a lay brother who spent the night in vigil and lamented the next morning that 'I was thinking in the vigil about a monk in whom I counted thirty virtues and cannot find even one of them in myself'. Bernard recommended this dreary exercise as a 'sublime meditation'.[27] It was a religion of dues and services which enmeshed the simple believer as the tenurial system did.

The disciplinarian approach was motivated by the fear that even basic duties were in danger of being left unperformed. Parts of the population seem to have been almost wholly neglectful of religion. Humbert of Romans lamented that 'the poor rarely come to church or to sermons, and therefore know little of what pertains to their salvation'.[28] The comment is far from unique, and the possibility exists that, while great churches and shrines would be crowded on important occasions, the local churches were not, and some people scarcely ever came. The inclusion of foolery in the ceremonial of major festivals was a concession to attract people to them. Reformers disliked such ceremonies as the procession of the ass, customary in northern France at the Epiphany, in which the donkey was greeted by cries of 'hee-haw', or such chaotic institutions as the lord of misrule or the boy bishop. Thomas of Chobham remarked unhappily that they were tolerated because 'otherwise many men would not come to such feasts if they could not play games'.[29] We have virtually no statistical information about church attendance, and it is unsafe to assume that it was high. There was no machinery for compelling the indifferent to attend, and the requirement of one confession and one communion a year speaks volumes for what might be expected. Thirteenth-century observers thought there were many unbelievers, particularly in Italy, of which the comment is made most often. Matthew Paris said that the Italians were only half Christian, and preachers spoke of the 'chill of unbelief' which they found there.[30] The doubt most frequently expressed was over the presence of Christ in the eucharist: the relative frequency of proof-miracles and visions at the consecration confirms the existence of these doubts, and in addition the doctrine of the Eucharistic presence was under attack from heretical groups. There was also scepticism, recorded by Antony of Padua and others, about the future

[27] Bernard, *Sermones per annum, Opera* v.214–6.
[28] Cited A. Murray, *Traditio* 30 (1974) 301. See also his article in *SCH* 8 (1972), 93–4.
[29] F. Broomfield (ed.), *Thomae de Chobham Summa Confessorum* (Louvain, 1968), 268.
[30] Matthew Paris, *Chronica Majora* (RS 57) v.169.

resurrection of the dead. More often, popular unbelief was practical rather than doctrinal, and people simply took no notice of the church's teaching in their ordinary lives. Preachers commented on the prevailing sexual immorality, and the survival of an older sexual ethic was an obstacle to the new rules. Although the church had significantly reshaped the law and ceremonies of marriage, it was conventional in many peasant groups to postpone the church ceremony until pregnancy or even after childbirth, and many entered into clandestine marriages without a priest or even witnesses. The growing cities brought their own temptations with them. Fulk of Neuilly, following the example of Robert of Arbrissel and Peter the Hermit, collected funds for the dowries of prostitutes and founded the Cistercian convent of St Antoine on the outskirts of Paris as a refuge for them. Peter the Chanter's rigorist position on homosexuality initiated the repressive attitude which, in the thirteenth century, succeeded the more relaxed approach which had previously prevailed towards the gay scene at Paris. Preachers passionately criticized usury, even if confessors were also engaged in a more delicate definition of what it was.

It would be a simplification to say that the church was threatened by worldliness in the cities and superstition in the country, but there is truth in the statement. The countryman's year necessarily followed the cycle of nature, and the ceremonies which marked its turning-points retained such connections with the ancient past as the leading of the plough round the fire on Plough Monday and the May Day games. Most important phases of human life (childbirth, sickness, love) were protected by rituals and charms, and their complexity is illustrated by the German confessional treatise *De Officio Cherubyn*. They included the invocation of ancient powers, the *Waldfrau* or woman of the wood, Holda queen of heaven, and the *stetewalden* or spirits of the house. The countryman lived in a world filled with contending spirits and mysterious forces, including the spirits of the dead. In remote districts the custom continued in the Carolingian period and even later of depositing grave-goods for the dead and digging pits for their spirits. Official church-teaching launched a vigorous attack upon 'superstition', as this whole world of practices was termed. Maurice of Sully warned his hearers, in line with orthodox thinking about magic, that to employ spells was to invoke the powers of darkness and was contrary to the creed. Bishops investigated pilgrimages to holy wells or groves and canonization

came under papal control, although in practice locally revered saints
continued to emerge. More positively, the liturgy offered access to
better magic than that of the old charms. The power of God was
dispensed by his priests as they blessed weapons, ornaments,
implements for the ordeal, and holy water. A Christian presence was
asserted in the farming year through the blessing of the fields at
Rogationtide and of the plough. By the eleventh century the charms
used by Anglo-Saxon healers were far more Christian than pagan in
terminology. The power of the saints, concentrated in their shrines,
was opened to crowds of pilgrims, and provision was made for the
dead through the creation of parish cemeteries and through requiem
masses and purgatory. We have spoken already of the conversion of
Europe, but almost equally important was the exorcism of Europe:
the expulsion of evil spirits, the grant of repose to the restless dead,
and the presence of an army of saints to fight for the faithful. The
process is difficult to trace, but the indications are that by 1250 a
Christian cosmology had made a deep impression on the cycle of the
year and the ancient world of spirits.

This success was bought at a price, for it was partly due to the
marvels and legends which were embodied in the Christian system.
It is impossible to distinguish clearly between Christian and pagan
magic. The peasants of Montaillou held beliefs about charms and
spirits which cannot be labelled as belonging to any one world-view.
Aleksander Gieysztor has emphasized that much of the magic in late
medieval Poland had been imported from the west with the Gospel,
which offered at first exorcism and later healing at such shrines as
that of St Stanislas. Biblical stories became entangled in a web of
fantasy. The tendency is still apparent in modern versions of the
Christmas story, but in the Middle Ages every Biblical event and
personage carried a baggage of myth. Learned culture in earlier
centuries had been conservative in its resistance to the marvellous
and the bizarre, but in the twelfth and thirteenth centuries it was
much more ready to accept them. Often these strange stories came
from outside Christendom: from the east (where the Alexander
legend was set, with its many wonders) or 'the matter of Britain',
Celtic stories which formed the basis of the Arthurian romances.
There are also signs of the adoption of popular stories into the lives
of saints, such as the taming of *la Tarasque*, the dragon of Tarascon,
by St Martha. One supposes that the dragon in such a story is a
survivor of pre-Christian myth, but that may not be so in all cases,

for the association of legends of dragons with cities in the late Middle Ages hints that they were being invented or at least transformed during the period of rapid urban growth. Compositions such as the vernacular life of Mary Magdalen, written in the late twelfth century and designed for recitation to the crowds, occupied a strange no man's land between history and legend. B. Cazelles has pointed out that there is an extraordinary gap between saints officially promoted by the church and those whose lives were most popular in thirteenth-century France. The latter group was remote from the contemporary world, and most of them did not exist historically: Jean Bouche d'Or had no connection with St John Chrysostom but the name. They took the hearers to a world of fable, where the extraordinary could come to the resue without the restraints of everyday reality.[31]

The reduction of the saints to legend jeopardized the attempt which was being made, in all sorts of ways, to bring the believer into the thought-world of the New Testament. It was abundantly illustrated on the walls of churches, but unfortunately there is very little evidence whether these paintings were understood by ordinary worshippers. Sites with New Testament links ranked among the most popular pilgrimage centres: Rome, Compostella, Vézelay , and above all the Holy Sepulchre at Jerusalem. By these means was conveyed to lay groups a spirituality which went beyond the picture of dues and burdens, of marvels and miracles, which has been drawn so far. Laymen formed confraternities which, even if the prayers they learned were very simple ones, absorbed something of the spirituality of their directors: Franciscan tertiaries, for example, were unpopular with the Italian communes because of their commitment to peace and opposition to bearing arms. Preachers spoke of following Christ in poverty and humility, and in their sermons this appeal sat uneasily beside the demand for dues and services: 'if we desire to come to the glory of God, we must follow his way in humility, obedience and suffering.'[32] The early Waldensians and Franciscans reveal the existence of a lay piety based on the reading of the Gospels. True, the capture of the Friars Minor by an educated leadership after the fall of Elias led to a hierarchical stress upon the duties of belief and conduct, but Francis's own spirit also survived in simple teaching through the Christmas crib, hymns, or lauds and the naturalistic painting styles developed by Giotto. There was a

[31] B. Cazelles, *Le corps de sainteté* (Geneva, 1982).
[32] Raoul Ardent, PL 155.1847D.

growing sense of Christ as a loving Lord, to whom a believer owed his loyalty. The word *fideles* meant both 'believers' and 'sworn men', and it was easy to amalgamate the two. The change was reflected in the adoption of a new position of prayer, kneeling with hands together, which is that of a man doing homage to his lord. Papal portraits adopted the attitude in the thirteenth century, but official iconography was probably conservative and the new style was apparently spreading before 1200. The ordinary Christian might therefore in his imagination occupy one of three different worlds: that of dues and services; of sorcery and marvels; and of the Gospel history, simply understood. Many, one suspects, occupied all three at once.

20

REASON AND HOPE IN A CHANGING WORLD.

In the preceding chapters a good deal has been said about the pastoral commitments of the church. Through preaching and the confessional, through the example of friars and the repression of heretics, the faith and morals of the laity were to be purified. This was not pastoral care in the modern spirit, for the preachers were strong on discipline and weak on lay leadership, but it represented a pattern of ministry which cannot be paralleled in earlier centuries and which had influential champions. It affected intellectuals and administrators, but they also had other concerns, and the next two chapters will examine the forces which shaped scholarship and governmental structures.

i. *A New Pattern of Learning: the Universities*

A *universitas* is a guild, a type of organization widely developed in medieval society. The recognition of the privileges of a 'university' of masters, which freed it from control by local ecclesiastical or civic authorities, created a new type of higher education in Christendom. That is not to say that it was an abrupt break. The three most outstanding universities in the thirteenth century all had a previous history as centres of study before they acquired their new privileges shortly after 1200, and the other city schools continued to function effectively. In spite of the number of masters teaching at Paris in 1170, the evidence that there was already an organized guild there is tenuous; but by the time of Innocent III the masters formed a body with its own regulations, and in 1215 the issue of statutes by Robert of Courson, papal legate and former master in theology, marked the definitive emergence of the university. In April 1231 the bull *Parens scientiarum*, which has been called the Magna Carta of the new university, adjudicated the continuing disputes with the bishop's chancellor. By the middle of the century the main outlines of the constitution were clear, with a rector, proctors, faculties, and a subdivision into nations. The formalization of the structure corresponded with a much clearer definition of subjects and syllabuses. Twelfth-century scholars had moved fairly freely from one type of study to another: it is easy to find writers (such as John of Salisbury, Gilbert Foliot and Peter of Blois) who were men of letters, and at the same time had a good grasp of philosophy, canon law, and theology. By the thirteenth century a clearer dividing-line had emerged between the disciplines. The aspiring scholar would first read a degree in the basic faculty of arts, and then proceed to the higher faculties of law, medicine, or theology. While arts always preserved an atmosphere of omnium gatherum about it, specialists in law had to proceed to a further qualification, and at Paris we begin to find a relatively new phenomenon, the arts man who has little interest in the interpretation of Scripture. The changing structures gave rise, as we shall see, to a revival of speculative philosophy at Paris after a period when study had been directed to practical and pastoral matters. Another formative feature at Paris was the suppression of civil law by Honorius III in 1219. The purpose of this measure is uncertain, but it may have been a response to pressure by Philip II of France, who wanted to protect French customary law from erosion by the civil code. In any event, its effect was to inhibit the growth of the law faculty. Paris had four faculties, of which arts (which provided the foundation course) was much the biggest, and theology enjoyed the highest reputation as an international centre of excellence. The importance of Bologna had already been marked by the privilege *Habita*, granted to foreign students in Lombardy by Frederick Barbarossa in 1158, but the first indication of a university in the formal sense was contemporaneous with similar developments at Paris. In 1215 we hear that the *Rhetorica antiqua* of Buoncompagno was read 'before the university of professors of canon and civil law'. The structure of Bologna was quite different from that of Paris. The presence there of law students who were already relatively senior men with families led to a high degree of student control and to a lay spirit alien to Paris, although the importance to the university of papal privileges guaranteed a substantial degree of ecclesiastical control. While Oxford did not have the same international importance as Paris and Bologna, it made a distinctive contribution to learning, and its origins were rather similar to theirs. Its growing importance was marked by a charter from the papal legate in 1214, defining the clerical status of members of the university and mentioning for the first time its new head, the chancellor. This office seems to have been filled by the eminent scholar Robert Grosseteste.

The establishment of university constitutions at Paris, Bologna, and Oxford was quickly followed by other foundations. Some were already important schools in the twelfth century (Orléans, Montpellier); some arose from secessions from existing universities (Padua, Cambridge); while others were created by a specific decision (Naples in 1224 by Frederick II; Toulouse in 1229 as a centre of orthodoxy amid the Albigensians; the *studium curiae* about 1244 for clergy of the papal curia). These foundations did not achieve the international standing of Paris and Bologna, which attracted students of many nationalities: the list of Paris theologians in the thirteenth century contains more foreigners than Frenchmen.

Seen in the context of ecclesiastical policy, the emergence of the universities presents a paradox. They attracted the patronage of the papacy and other members of the hierarchy because of their potential for training a new generation of leaders of the clergy. By their very constitution, however, the universities separated the most talented teachers from the normal responsibilities of church government and placed them in independent corporations. Christian tradition had vested the office of teaching in the bishop, and it is no accident that in the past so many of the greatest theologians had come from the ranks of the episcopate. A second source of doctrine had been the monasteries, for the heart of monastic prayer was the reading of Scripture, *lectio divina*, which formed the basis for the exposition of the Bible. In the thirteenth century the schoolman replaced the bishop and the abbot as the typical exponent of doctrine. The syllabus in theology and law was mainly controlled by the masters, and the arts course came to be shaped not so much by the needs of pastoral training as by technical considerations, including the needs of the higher faculties. That is not to say that universities were isolated from the government of the church. The *magistri* hoped for, and often obtained, influential promotion and popes could intervene in the shaping of the syllabus. What had happened was that the masters had emerged alongside the bishops and the abbots as formative influences in the life of the church. As a source of doctrine, they had indeed superseded them.

The thirteenth century saw the triumph of scholasticism. In spite of the ridicule which was directed against it at the Renaissance, the work of the greatest schoolmen, and most of all of Thomas Aquinas, has continued to influence the thought of the church up to the present time. It would be idle to look for a precise definition of the term 'scholastic'. Basically it refers to the distinctive methods of study in the schools or universities. The development of the 'question' method of discussion generated a great deal of literature in the form of Sentences and *Summae*, systematic expositions of theological issues which had effectively no parallels in the earlier history of doctrine.[1] In all fields of study it was accepted that the text was authoritative, and its close examination was not directed to discussing whether it was true, but to clarifying its meaning in the light of other authorities which seemed to contradict it. These methods were in use before 1200, and in that sense we can speak of Paris scholasticism as already existing then. Normally, however, to use the word 'scholastic' we ask for something more: an extremely refined use of logic, developed in the arts course, and a strongly philosophical base. The schoolmen did not subject their texts to verification in the modern manner, but they did scrutinize them with rigorous analysis and assess their place within a total philosophy. These methods were being shaped in the first half of the twelfth century, but (as we shall see in the next section) interest in a philosophical foundation actually waned in Paris in the following period. The full development of scholasticism was to take place in the thirteenth century.

One of the marked changes in the educational system was the reduced importance of grammar and rhetoric, and the consequent diminution in that wide reading of the classics which had been undertaken as part of those subjects and had provided the basis for the Renaissance of the twelfth century. Grammar now became a means of acquiring enough Latin for further study, and was taught mainly at a pre-university level by means of textbooks newly composed for the purpose, such as the *Doctrinale* of Alexander of Villedieu (1199). The reason for this change lay in the increasingly technical character of further studies. Ambitious students wanted to move as quickly as possible to the profitable study of law or medicine, or at least to the *ars dictaminis*, which offered training in composition and secretarial duties and which had become popular in many schools by 1200. Within arts faculties intellectual interest centred on logic or dialectic, which had grown much more technical with the arrival of the 'new logic', the previously unknown works of

---

[1] The emergence of the *questio* in twelfth-century schools is mentioned in ch. 15.i above.

Aristotle. These had become available at Paris by about 1150, and logic had progressively expanded at the expense of the rest of the arts syllabus. The structure of study increasingly rested upon this Aristotelian logic, conceived as a way of handling propositions derived from authority. Grammar was being abandoned in the interests of philosophy and law:

Artes diu floruerunt,	Once the arts men were in clover;
et, ut leges regnaverunt,	now that law has taken over
artes sunt inutiles;	arts no longer seems to pay.
leges sedent super thronum	Law is sitting on the throne
et eructant verbum bonum	belching out good words alone
omni die septies.[2]	seven times in every day.

Conservatives were increasingly disquieted by the way the new masters, 'neglecting the rules of the arts and abandoning authoritative texts, catch flies of empty verbiage like spiders in their webs'.[3] There was a real fall in the literary quality of the works of the *magistri*: to turn from John of Salisbury or Gerald of Wales to the publications of the mid-thirteenth century is a shock to the system. It has even been called 'the century without Rome', a desert in which the streams of classical humanism, so fruitful in the twelfth century, dried out until their renewal in Italy in a succeeding age.

The change was important, but its nature should not be misunderstood. Apart from the fact that a good knowledge of the classics was far from unusual in the thirteenth century, a literary change does not necessarily imply the abandonment of humane values. Interest in nature could be better sustained on the basis of the 'natural books' of Aristotle, now becoming available, than of older materials, and Sir Richard Southern has emphasized that the reality was not so much a flight from humanism as an engagement with more technical studies, which could no longer be contained in a pleasing literary format.[4] In the twelfth century *natura* had been personified as the handmaid of God, and the properties of natural objects were examined because they were thought to convey truths to mankind. There was little investigation of natural causes, and only

---

[2] K. Strecker, *Moralische-Satirische Gedichte Walters von Châtillon* (Heidelberg, 1929), 8, with a reference to Ps. 95: 1. It is an addition in one manuscript and not, I suspect, by Walter himself. The resentment of arts men at the promotion of lawyers in the hierarchy has been mentioned above, ch. 16. vi.

[3] Bishop Stephen of Tournai, cited L. J. Paetow, *The Arts Course at the Medieval Universities* (Champaign, 1910), 31 n.

[4] R. W. Southern, *Medieval Humanism and other Studies* (Oxford, 1970), 31 ff.

rarely was knowledge based on observation. There was, in other words, no 'science' as we understand it.

The development of scientific disciplines was to take many centuries, but the thirteenth century made a significant start, which can be ascribed to three influences. The first was the arrival of translations of the works of Aristotle and his commentators, which not only provided information about the natural order (for example on magnetism), but offered a coherent philosophy of motion and causation. Oxford and Paris reacted differently to the new material. In matters of theology Oxford was conservative, continuing to base its teaching firmly upon Biblical glosses, and showing relatively little interest in the philosophical issues presented by Aristotle, Avicenna, and Averroës. Conversely the 'natural books' of Aristotle continued to be expounded at Oxford when they were prohibited at Paris, and Oxford scholars showed a keen interest in obtaining material from Greek and Arabic. The outstanding figure was Robert Grosseteste, master of the schools and then bishop of Lincoln until his death in 1253. The basis of his philosophy was the theory that the universe is ultimately composed of light, and he initiated some significant experimental work in optics. He learned Greek and produced a new translation of pseudo-Dionysius and the definitive verson of the *Ethics* of Aristotle, and his pupil Roger Bacon pursued the themes of translation, experiment, and observation. Such studies were not confined to the universities: after Frederick II returned to Sicily in 1220 he conducted an energetic scientific programme. His protégé Michael Scot translated the works of Averroës, and Frederick corresponded with Islamic rulers about astronomy and mathematics. In addition to the pervasive influence of Aristotle there was an increasing interest in mathematics, based on other Arabic texts: an important supplement to Aristotle, who had not given it priority in his scientific works. There was a strong mathematical influence at Oxford, but the most creative thinker was Leonardo Fibonacci of Pisa, whose *Book of the Abacus* (1202) was not equalled for several more centuries in its grasp of theory. Alongside this was a third influence upon natural studies: the detailed work of practitioners. Accurate observation is much more evident in thirteenth-century writing than previously. Famous examples are the careful descriptions in Frederick II's *Art of Falconry* (*De arte venandi cum avibus*), and the medical writing of William of Saliceto at Bologna (1215–80). Frederick's specific objective in his book was stated as the description of things as they really are, and he criticized the great master Aristotle for his failure to found his views on observation.

It is tempting to see these developments as laying the foundations of modern science, but there are serious obstacles to doing so. Experiment remained a very minor element, and progress was to be hampered for a long time by studies which ultimately were discovered to be pointless, in particular astrology, which was an important discipline at Bologna and to which Frederick II attached great weight. There are therefore difficulties in seeing Robert Grosseteste or Roger Bacon as the remote ancestors of modern science. Nevertheless, the achievements are significant: scholars had a far clearer sense of causation and of the value of observation in controlling and supplementing what could be learned from authority. A new sense of natural regularity and causation had been achieved by the middle of the century, and it was to have very varied effects in the following decades. It can be perceived in the growth of ideas of natural law and in a stronger awareness of the state and of political necessity; in the more natural and biographical approach to the saints, whose lives were no longer a collection of miracles; and in the naturalistic painting which followed in the work of Giotto. These assumptions asked severe questions of the theologians, and can be seen behind the Thomist system, with its recognition of the autonomy of the natural order and its clear subdivision of the universe into natural and supernatural, nature and grace. They also nurtured a real scepticism, which was expressed in the so-called Averroism of the 1270s and subsequently in the logic of Occam. It would be much too much to say that by 1250 man had come of age; but he was beginning to find his feet and explore the world around him.

ii. *Theology: from Pastoral Care to Speculation*

The thirteenth century was one of the most creative periods in theology. It saw the promulgation of a definition of the faith with universally binding authority, the creation of scholastic theology, and the reception of Aristotle into Christian thought. Its greatest achievements lie just after 1250, with the innovative work of Albertus Magnus, Thomas Aquinas, Bonaventure, and Siger of Brabant, and this section will be concerned with preliminary stages behind their work.

The declaration of faith in canon 1 of the Fourth Lateran Council was regarded as fully authoritative by subsequent synods, and sometimes described as *symbola*, the standard word for 'creed'. It was to be explained to clergy and set out 'in ordinary speech' to their parishioners.[5] The teaching of twelfth-century theology about the Trinity, Christology, eucharist, and sacraments had thus been adopted by the highest authority for universal dissemination. It is significant that the expression 'article of faith' (*articulus fidei*) began to supersede the older and more general term 'rule of faith' (*regula fidei*). The idea that faith was the acceptance of a series of statements or articles promulgated by authority was beginning to shape the teaching of the church and the progress of scholasticism.

In 1200 Paris theology was pastoral theology. That had not always been the case: the more speculative style of Abelard and Gilbert de la Porée was once a source of worry to those of a more conservative cast of mind.[6] In the later part of the twelfth century this approach had gone out of fashion, especially in the teaching of Peter the Chanter (died 1197), an outstanding representative of the pastoral approach. He was strenuously opposed to controversial writing based on philosophical divergences: 'the schools of theology should be the house of unity, and we should walk with consent in the house of God. Some people make divisions in them as in secular letters, realists and nominalists'. He included preaching as one of the three functions of a theology professor, along with lecturing and disputing.[7] His works were designed to provide a basis for sermons: he was the first master to compose a commentary on the whole Bible, with brief glosses of a literal kind, and his notes were directed towards practical issues of morality and penance. This attitude had foundations in earlier Paris tradition, in the Victorines, to some extent in Peter Lombard, and in Peter Comestor's *Historia scholastica*; and it enjoyed enormous influence under the favour of Innocent III. Its continuation seemed to be guaranteed by the settlement at Paris of the Franciscans and Dominicans, who had been drawn there for training in preaching and the refutation of heresy, and certainly not for philosophical instruction—in 1228 the Preachers were forbidden to study the books of the Gentiles and the philosophers.[8] True, this is

---

[5] Statutes of Salisbury I c. 3 (1217/9) and Exeter, I c. 1 (1225/37), *C&S* II.i.61, 228. For the character of the creed itself see ch. 17.vii.

[6] For Paris theology before the middle of the twelfth century see briefly in ch. 15.i above.

[7] J. W. Baldwin, *Masters, Princes and Merchants* (Princeton, 1970), ii.69, 91–2.

[8] H. Denifle and A. Chatelain (ed.), *Chartularium Universitatis Parisiensis* (Paris, 1889–97), i.57.

not the whole story of Paris theology at the beginning of the thirteenth century. In the preceding decades the Porretani, followers of Gilbert, had maintained more speculative interests, making extensive use of Boethius, welcoming new Greek material in translation and attempting to define the nature and methodology of theological knowledge. This Gilbertine outlook could not be wholly lost, for a good deal of it was incorporated in the authoritative *Sentences* of Peter Lombard, but it had few continuators after 1200. Alan of Lille died far away from Paris in 1202, and the brilliant dialectician Simon of Tournai died in 1201, a career failure who had gained little preferment and who was the target of anecdotes about his arrogance. There was a long road to travel from the conservative dominance of 1200 to the innovating spirit of fifty years later.

It must be noted, none the less, that even scholarship designed for practical ends became increasingly technical. One of the first of the massive aids to preaching was the collection of key-words or *Distinctiones* to clarify Biblical images and concepts, and these catalogues were arranged alphabetically or thematically. Early examples were the much used *Distinctiones Abel* of Peter the Chanter (*c.* 1190) and the *Liber in distinctionibus* of Alan of Lille (before 1195). The most outstanding worker in this field was Hugh of St Cher, who held one of the two Dominican chairs of theology at St Jacques from 1230 to 1236 and who became a cardinal in 1244. He produced glosses or postills on the Bible which were in enormous demand. He also collaborated with other Dominicans in the preparation of an alphabetical concordance to the Bible, which was followed soon after 1250 by similar reference books to the works of the Fathers. The use of material of this kind required a standard text and conventional divisions, and the system of chapter enumeration in the books of the Bible which is now in use made its appearance, probably in the later works of Stephen Langton. This type of technical apparatus was designed for both scholars and preachers. About 1220 Cardinal Peter of Capua explained that he had written the *Alphabetum* to help the scholars of Paris in their studies and the clergy of Rome in their preaching. It must have been far above the heads of the majority of the clergy and of value only to those with a university training and access to a good library. Moreover, because it was one of the purposes of postills to provide a large volume of earlier material, authors found it difficult to express clearly their own point of view. It is striking that the mendicants Hugh of St Cher, Alexander of Hales, and John of La Rochelle were actually less demanding in their call to obey the Gospel than had been Peter the Chanter before them. The friars were caught up in the technicalities of work in the schools until the decisive breach between them and the secular masters, shortly after 1250, raised more fundamental issues.

The structure of the Paris theology course, moreover, did not allow even the most cautious master to exclude philosophical speculation entirely. Peter the Chanter listed disputation as one of the duties of a master, and the discussion of difficult issues outside the framework of a set text could be wide-ranging, especially as the tendency to separate the questions from the commentary proper gained strength. The emergence of the new discussions for all comers, *disputationes quodlibetales*, which had a free agenda, allowed still more room for radical questions. Students in theology, moreover, had read the arts syllabus, and were bound to import into theology problems which were by origin philosophical. Peter the Chanter had complained about this, and John of St Giles echoed him in remarking that when masters of arts 'come to the faculty of theology, they can scarcely be detached from their (profane) knowledge, as some of them show, who in their theology cannot be separated from Aristotle, . . . posing philosophical questions and opinions'.[9] However much some masters might deplore it, their criticisms show that there was elbow-room for a speculative approach. This was given real significance by the arrival at Paris of the works of Aristotle.

Certain logical treatises of Aristotle had been known to western scholars for centuries, and his other logical works, forming the so-called 'new logic', had been available at Paris since about 1150. By 1200 a large new instalment of his writing had arrived, the books of natural philosophy or 'natural books'. These included the *Physica*, *De anima*, *De caelo*, *De generatione*, and *Meteora*. The appearance of these works was the consequence of activity by translators in southern Europe, where it was possible to gain access to the manuscripts of the originals. Leaders of the movement were James of Venice and Burgundio of Pisa (died 1193) from Greek, and a team at Toledo translating from Arabic, led by Gerard of Cremona (died 1187) and Dominic Gundisalvi. The history of Aristotle's impact on western thought would be easier to understand if straightforward translations of his works had arrived, but this was far from being the case. One influential text, the *De causis*, was attributed to Aristotle but was really by Proclus, a thorough Neoplatonist whose philosophy was of a very different kind. The commentaries of Avicenna, which arrived in the same wave of translation, were designed to set Aristotle's works within a Neoplatonist scheme. By 1240 another important set of commentaries was reaching Paris, those by Averroës in the version of Michael Scot, with a much more materialist, indeed atheistic, interpretation than that of Avicenna. The impact of all this material was bound to be great, because up to this time western philosophy had been almost wholly dominated by logic. With few exceptions thinkers had known little about the Neoplatonic philosophy of being, and even less about Greek concepts of the natural order. The unfamiliarity of the new scheme of learning is indicated by the use of the generic term 'natural books' in implicit contrast with the logical literature which they already possessed. To call this material 'Aristotle' is at best a convenient shorthand, for it contained a mass of natural and philosophical speculation, some of it diverging widely from the true positions of Aristotle.

We can see something of the effect of the new learning in the decree of the synod of the province of Sens, meeting at Paris in 1210, which condemned the teaching of Amaury of Bène and David of Dinant and ordered that 'neither Aristotle's books of natural philosophy nor the commentaries shall be read at Paris in public or in private'.[10] The conservatives who dominated the theology faculty had clearly become alarmed and moved to suppress the arts lectures on the natural books and Avicenna. Not much is known of the occasion for the ban. Amaury of Bène was a master of arts who, before his death c.1206, had won converts to his views around Paris, but his doctrine was an extreme pantheism which could hardly have come from Avicenna. David of Dinant, on the other hand, was a knowledgeable Aristotelian who had arrived at firmly materialistic conclusions from his study. If, as is reasonable to suppose, he was teaching arts at Paris, he offers a remarkably early illustration of the possibility of shaping a coherent non-Christian philosophy from the natural books. The conservatives secured the assistance of papal authority: Robert of Courson as legate renewed the ban in 1215, and in 1231 Gregory IX appointed a commission with the formidable task of removing the errors from the prohibited books. Unsurprisingly it never reported and the books remained banned until Roger Bacon began to lecture on them in 1245. It seems that the ban was

[10] *Chartularium*, i. 11,12.

designed to prevent lectures on the books in the arts faculty at Paris and that they continued to be lectured on at Oxford and in the highly orthodox university of Toulouse. The regulation had the paradoxical effect that until after 1250 we must look for the impact of the new Aristotle on Paris theology and not on arts.

As one would expect, the conservatives in the early years of the century were not welcoming to Aristotle, and rarely quoted his works. He was used much more by the Porretan masters Alan of Lille and Simon of Tournai, the latter of whom treated the word 'philosophy' as synonymous with 'the teaching of Aristotle', although it is not clear whether the references in his *Disputations*, which must have been completed well before 1200, show knowledge of the natural books. The conservative polemic is well represented in a sermon of James of Vitry:

> We can take some things from the philosophers which contribute to our own interests. Boethius, indeed, in *De consolatione* is thoroughly catholic and moral. The others however said much that is false and vain, like Plato who said the planets were gods and Aristotle who laid down that the world was eternal. So there is much to beware of in the natural books, as they are called, and we are in danger of error from too much inquiry . . . Since therefore theological books are enough for a Christian, it is not appropriate of him to be too much occupied with the natural books.[11]

This reactionary attitude did not persist, and theologians' writing between 1220 and 1240 began to show marked influence from the ideas of Aristotle and Avicenna. The earliest example is William of Auxerre, whose *Summa Aurea* (two recensions between 1215 and 1229) contains a hundred quotations from Aristotle and shows a discreet use of his ideas. The Dominican master Roland of Cremona's *Summa Theologica* (1232/4) drew heavily on William of Auxerre, but also quoted Aristotle abundantly—surprisingly, in view of the Dominican prohibition on the use of pagan authors. A more original use of the new learning can be found in the *Summa de Bono* of Philip the Chancellor (1228/36) and the *Magisterium divinale ac sapientale* of William of Auvergne (1223/36), and in Alexander of Hales, whose *Summa* was incomplete at his death in 1245. These theologians were addressing a range of philosophical issues which had previously not been under discussion, except in a limited way among followers of Gilbert de la Porée. It has often been said in the past

---

[11] James of Vitry, *Sermo ad scolares*, cited FM 13, 194 n.

that western thought was dominated by the philosophy of St Augustine until that came under attack from Aristotelian thought in the thirteenth century, but it is nearer the truth to recognize that thinkers before 1200 did not possess a coherent natural philosophy, nor the means of constructing one. The influence of Augustine was enormous, but it was theological and doctrinal. It is a matter of opinion whether Christianity in the west has been enriched or damaged by the attempt to set it within a specific philosophical framework, but it is a fact that the continuous history of this attempt goes back to the reflections of the Paris theologians on the natural books in the years after 1220. The issues which were raised there were numerous, but they were arranged round a central theme. The coherent statement of Neoplatonism which they encountered in the *De causis* and in Avicenna saw the universe as an ordered hierarchy of being, stretching from the pure being of the Godhead to the physical universe, which was subject to fluctuation, contingency, and the operation of regular causation. Such a world-view posed questions of Christian thinkers at almost every point: about its correlation with the Biblical revelation; about the source of human knowledge and the nature of the 'active intellect' which made it possible to formulate general statements; and about the relationship between the observable universe and the ideas or forms which underlie it. These discussions in turn generated attempts to provide an account of the reasons for belief in the existence of God and of the character of theology as a subject. In William of Auvergne it is clear that these issues had become central concerns for the theologian. Although critical of Aristotle, he used the new ideas extensively and showed heavy dependence on a Spanish philosopher, the Jewish scholar Avicebron (died *c.*1058), whom he described as 'the noblest of all philosophers'.

While William of Auvergne and Philip the Chancellor had begun to use the new learning in the formation of scholastic theology, their thought is still only in the ante-room of the great systems of the later Middle Ages. In particular, they used Averroës so little that it is doubtful whether they knew his work at first hand. His reductionist view of Aristotle's philosophy stripped away a good deal of the metaphysical speculation which surrounded it in Avicenna and brought it closer to the original. For the next generation of thinkers the knowledge of the authentic Aristotle was increased by translation work of high quality such as the version of the *Ethics* by Grosseteste and the *Politics* by the Dominican William of Moerbeke. Aquinas was much closer to a genuine understanding of the ideas of Aristotle than had been possible for his predecessors, and with it the new synthesis of Thomism became conceivable. The first theologian to be strongly influenced by Averroës was the Dominican Albertus Magnus, who was at Paris from 1242 to 1248. His early works showed a genuine grasp of Averroism but had not yet arrived at a new synthesis. Albert moved, with his pupil Thomas Aquinas, from Paris to Cologne in 1248, and the new philosophical theology was shaped after that date.

iii. *Joachim of Fiore: a New Eschatology*

While Paris theologians were developing their speculations about the natural order and the place of revealed religion within it, other thinkers rejected their philosophical approach and sought in the Scriptures a guide to the past, present and future of the world. The crucial figure was Joachim of Fiore. He had been born some time after 1135, and by 1177 he had become abbot of the Benedictine house of Corazzo in southern Italy. Attracted by the Cistercian way of life, he applied to have his abbey affiliated to the order, and in 1183–4 he was staying in the Cistercian abbey of Casamari to receive training in its customs. Soon afterwards, however, he withdrew in pursuit of contemplation to the remote Sila plateau and founded the abbey of San Giovanni da Fiore. In 1192 the Cistercian general chapter was threatening him with action as a 'fugitive' monk, but Joachim continued as abbot of Fiore until his death in March 1202.

Joachim's career as a prophet began with an experience at Casamari when he received 'a revelation of the fullness of the Apocalypse and of the complete agreement of the Old and New Testaments' and a vision of the nature of the Trinity.[12] Shortly after this he began to compose his major works, the *Concord of the Old and New Testament*, the *Exposition of the Apocalypse*, and the *Ten-stringed Lute*.[13] His announcement of a coming eschatological crisis made him famous, and he was interviewed by some of the most powerful men of the time, including Popes Lucius III and Urban III, the Emperor Henry VI and, during his Mediterranean crusade, Richard I

---

[12] Cited B. McGinn, *Apocalyptic Spirituality* (London, 1979), 99
[13] The *Concordia novi et veteris Testamenti*, *Expositio in Apocalypsim*, and *Psalterium decem chordarum* were all written and rewritten between 1182 and 1200.

of England. Contemporaries regarded him as a prophet, but he saw himself essentially as an interpreter of the Scriptures, and told the Cistercian Abbot Adam of Persigny that he had no prophecy nor conjecture nor revelation about future events, but that God had given him the spirit of understanding, to comprehend all the mysteries of Holy Scripture.[14] Joachim redefined the accepted methods of Biblical interpretation. Most commentators were concerned to discover the moral and spiritual truths which underlay the Scriptural letter, truths which were necessarily the same from one generation to another. Joachim, on the other hand, saw the power of the Spirit as manifested not in unchanging truths, but in the transformation of the historical order. It was an established method of interpretation to seek for concords or types, similarities between the Old and New Testament; such a method had governed Suger's ambition scheme of decoration at Saint-Denis. Joachim's originality was in their use as a method of understanding the future. He saw them as landmarks: 'every traveller who goes forward until the route ahead is unclear finds the correct way to proceed by looking backward'.[15] His thought was pictorial, not logical in structure. It is expressed most vividly in a collection of diagrams, the *Book of Figures*, which was probably assembled by his followers but is close to Joachim's thinking. The function of these images was not to formulate dogma but to elucidate God's operations in history. Joachim saw himself as studying a 'living order' or 'the transfer of grace from people to people and one kingdom to another people'.[16] Religious teachings were of value according to the historical context in which they were set; they were, in a phrase which contrasts dramatically with the ideas of the Paris theologians, 'good in their time'.[17]

The historical order, evolving under the direction of the Spirit, was now reaching the time of crisis. Joachim saw this as an immediate one. His calculation of forty-two generations from Christ would point to 1260 as the time of Antichrist's coming, but there are signs that he regarded the crisis as closer than this. His concept of the coming new order was still more striking. He did not expect, as in earlier tradition, that the overthrow of Antichrist would bring the Last Judgement and the end of the world. On the contrary, he

---

[14] See M. Reeves, *The Influence of Prophecy in the Later Middle Ages* (Oxford, 1969), 13.

[15] B. McGinn, *Apocalyptic Spirituality*, 123.

[16] *Tractatus super Quatuor Evangelia*, ed. E. Buonaiuti (Rome, 1930), 309.

[17] *Psalterium decem chordarum* (Venice, 1527), 265 b.

thought that it would usher in a new age of history. Human history was to consist of three *status* or ages, which he classified variously as those of Father, Son, and Holy Spirit; Old Testament, New Testament, and spiritual understanding; laity, clergy, and monks. Where St Augustine had seen a single historical period, the 'sixth day', as extending from Christ to the end of the world, and Gregory the Great thought of the church as identical with the kingdom of heaven, Joachim regarded the 'seventh day' as a solidly historical period, shortly to be reached by the renewal of the church.[18] The church of Peter was to be replaced by the church of John, the clergy by monks, the New Testament by spiritual understanding or by 'an eternal Gospel to proclaim to those who shall dwell on the earth' (Rev. 14: 6). This age would be introduced by signs which caught the imagination of contemporaries, including those who did not accept the scheme as a whole. Joachim believed that he could read the time of the approaching crisis from events such as the loss of Jerusalem in 1187 and the death of Frederick Barbarossa on the Third Crusade. These he interpreted within a rigorous system of parallels between the chronology of Old Testament history, and that of the New Testament and the church. He anticipated the coming of two new religious orders with a special task of preparing the way and envisaged a heroic role for a pope. The papacy had not hitherto figured much in eschatology, and this element in Joachim is the beginning of the later hopes of an angelic pope who would return the church to righteousness and humility.

These ideas distanced Joachim from many of the influential movements in the contemporary world. His alienation from Paris theology was expressed in a sharp attack on Peter Lombard's doctrine of the Trinity and resulted in the rejection of Joachim's criticism by the Fourth Lateran Council. The episode was a shock to his followers in spite of a personal tribute to him which sweetened it. His expectation of a monastic age embodying the perfection of the church separated him from the universities and the papal curia, two of the dynamic forces of the period. It was almost a reversion to the age and the ideals of St Bernard. Joachim felt a strong sympathy for movements of poverty and simplicity, but he was not close to the urban pressures which were to give rise to the friars; contemplation, rather than either poverty or preaching, lay at the heart of his thought. He even stood at a distance from the Cistercians. There is

[18] For the view of Gregory the Great, see PL 76.104 A.

little in his work reminiscent of the Bernardine experience of God's presence at an individual level: Joachim's gaze is fixed on the new order. He was a backwoodsman, in touch with few of the ideas which were dominant in society, but he was a radical backwoodsman whose dislike of what was happening led him to modify Augustinian eschatology, with its near identification of the present church with the kingdom of God, and to propose an original alternative. Joachim was the first medieval thinker to have a clear idea of a great social transformation to take place within history. The source of this new perception is not clear. Greek and Jewish ideas were readily accessible in southern Italy, but it is hard to see that their contribution was more than marginal. There is a clearer connection with the German 'historical' school represented by Rupert of Deutz, Anselm of Havelberg, and Gerhoh of Reichersberg. Joachim shared their awareness of progress within the history of the church, their flamboyant use of imagery and their distrust of the French *magistri*. His exegesis is his own, however, and he believed that it had been shown him by God. It would be a mistake to erode the large area of originality within Joachim's thinking.

Radical thinkers, especially among the Franciscans, were soon to use these ideas for their own purposes. In the discontinuity between the second and third *status* they saw the overthrow of existing institutions and their replacement by a church guided by the Spirit into all truth. Historians have disagreed over whether Joachim intended these revolutionary implications. Marjorie Reeves has argued that a more conservative reading would be nearer to his thinking. In particular it is characteristic of his use of symbols that each age is not severed from the others, but continues to embody their characteristics. The replacement of the church of Peter by the church of John would thus represent the purification of the papacy rather than its abolition and would be consistent with Joachim's readiness to submit his works to papal approval. He left unclear the relations between the emerging monastic order and the clergy and laity in the third age, but he does not seem to be talking about the equal sharing of the Spirit among all believers, the ultimate spiritual democracy which appeared about the same time among the followers of Amaury of Bène . Moreover, the agent of the change is the Holy Trinity. We are a long way from a revolution attained by huuman effort. Yet, while accepting these qualifications, it is right to insist on the revolutionary character of Joachim's thought. It may be significant that his *Treatise on the Four Gospels* stressed the radical elements in the expectation of the third age. It is a summary work, which makes more evident the cutting edge of his thought, and with a probable date between 1200 and 1202 it seems to represent his final view on the subject. Joachim also contributed to the vocabulary of revolution. Up to his time the word and its cognates (*revolutio, revolvere*) had been used to describe the revolution of the stars in their courses. Joachim gave it a solidly historical meaning by using it to describe the turning of the pages of sacred history, and he is reasonably consistent in this usage: semantically, the language of revolution is more common in his pages than the language of reform. God's purpose in history is *revolvere* not *reformare*. The gap between Joachim and the Spiritual Franciscans is large, and the distance to travel before there is any thought of a man-made revolution very much larger. But a watershed is crossed here: God is seen as the agent of change, which is implicit in his very nature as Father, Son, and Holy Spirit; and the technical term for this change is 'revolution'.

iv. *The Influence of Joachim*

Thirteenth-century Italy was filled with eschatological excitement, in part because the events themselves seemed laden with apocalyptic meaning: the loss of Jerusalem in 1187, the new religion of the friars, the bitter dispute of empire and papacy which finally erupted in 1239, and the coming of the Tartars. The special importance of Joachim was to provide a scheme which made these events comprehensible, and in particular to identify them as pointing to the coming of Antichrist and the subsequent renewal. It was to be prepared by two orders, one of preachers, 'perfect men, preserving the life of Christ and the apostles', and the other 'of hermits imitating the life of the angels'.[19] Their identification as Dominicans and Franciscans proved irresistible, and there was also some basis in Joachim for the presentation of the emperor as Antichrist as papal propaganda demanded. The early history of his influence is obscure, but some channels can be traced. One was the order of Fiore. Joachim had founded two major houses, San Giovanni da Fiore and Fonte Laureato, and the order spread until by 1250 it was close to its maximum of fifty houses, all in southern or central Italy. Many were

---

[19] Cited B. McGinn, *Visions of the End* (New York, 1979), 136.

not new foundations but Benedictine or Basilian houses which had adopted the Florensian rule. At first there were great hopes for the order, and in 1234 Gregory IX's bull *Fons sapientie* mentioned the Florensians side by side with the Benedictines and Cistercians. Perhaps because of the rival attractions of the friars, expansion stopped and no houses were founded north of Tuscany. There was also a wider circulation of his ideas, which within twenty years of his death in 1202 were being mentioned by writers north of the Alps. In all these cases he appeared primarily as a prophet of the arrival of Antichrist, without any mention of the third age, and his image was inevitably tarnished by the condemnation of his ideas on the Trinity at the Lateran Council.

A more specific, and in the long run more important, area for the operation of his ideas was the Franciscan order. The chronicler Salimbene tells us of the arrival of a Florensian abbot at Pisa shortly after 1240, bringing with him manuscripts of Joachim, and by 1248 Salimbene knew of an influential circle of Joachites at Hyères in Provence led by Hugh of Digne, the friend of John of Parma, minister-general 1247–57. There is still no mention of 'third-age' thinking, and the evidence strictly interpreted suggests that Joachite influence on the friars came late and in a conservative form. This, however, may be an understatement. There is no reason to suppose that the Pisan connection was the only one, and in 1247 we find brother Giles welcoming the election of the Joachite John of Parma as minister-general, a hint of alignment between Joachites and the original followers of Francis. By 1254/5 an aggressive interpretation of Joachism in the *Introduction to the Eternal Gospel* of Gerard of Borgo San Donnino was causing a scandal at Paris. There was also a *Commentary on Jeremiah* which emphasized the radical features of Joachim's thought: the need for the reform of the present church, the expectation of the third age and the stress on the persecution of spiritual men as a sign of the end. The book was ascribed to Joachim, but was certainly written after his death, probably betwen 1238 and 1243. Its ideas later exercised a strong influence on the Spiritual Franciscans, but scholars are not agreed whether the book was written in Franciscan circles or by followers of Joachim among the Cistercian or Florensian monasteries. It therefore remains uncertain whether radical Joachism can be traced back among the Franciscans before 1250. Of its later importance there can be no doubt.

The final area where Joachim's influence can be traced was the controversy between Frederick II and the papacy. After the second excommunication in 1239 the dispute was waged in apocalyptic language on both sides, in a way for which there is no previous parallel. It was not all Joachism, by any means. Frederick's language was based on the old Last Emperor tradition, heightened by panegyric designed to present him as a renewer of the world order, and his birthplace Jesi as a second Nazareth. On the papal side the emperor's interest in scientific learning and his collaboration with Islamic advisers formed the basis for accusations which, supported by Frederick's own exaggerated language, made it possible to present him as Antichrist. This was the theme of the extraordinary manifestoes of Cardinal Rainer of Viterbo in 1245, in which Frederick appeared as 'the corrupter of the world' and 'the disturber and the hammer of the whole earth'. The extent to which a knowledge of Joachim contributed to this propaganda is questionable, but there are some signs of the involvement of clearly Joachite groups in the conflict. The Dominican Arnold in Suabia in 1248–50 was looking forward to a third age which would be inaugurated by Frederick II and the Dominicans—the first unambiguously political use of the 'third age' concept. On the other side the *Commentary on Jeremiah*, in spite of its critical attitude to ecclesiastical authority, cast Frederick II as Antichrist. His failure to survive until the crisis year of 1260 was a blow to these new Joachites, and Salimbene recorded that it was one of his own reasons for abandoning Joachism. By this time the foundations of a new eschatology had been laid and its acceptance was spreading among radicals.

There were other intellectual forces which pointed thirteenth-century men towards a sustained attempt to predict the future. They had, or thought they had, new sources of information. Earlier centuries had taken seriously the utterances of the classical Sibyls, and these were now supplemented by the prophecies of Merlin and the study of astrology. Once the accurate observation of the movements of planets and stars became available through Arabic learning, it seemed possible to arrive at precise predictions based on scientific observations. Frederick II and other rulers allowed the timing of their decisions to be dictated by the advice of astrologers: Frederick was counselled by Michael Scot, the translator of Averrroës. Astrology and the prophetic texts were not popular absurdities, but the legitimate concern of learned men, and belong to the history, not of superstition, but to that of discredited science.

Shortly after the middle of the thirteenth century the English scholar Roger Bacon was arguing for a serious programme of research on such materials, in order that the future might be known and impending evils circumvented.

The new structure of hope propounded by Joachim, the keen anticipation of the Last Day, and the use of materials which might be considered scientific were all new features of the thirteenth-century scene. There were also large parts of society which were unaffected by these trends, and who fixed their hopes not on the cosmic deliverance shortly to come, but on the delivery of the individual in face of judgement. Essentially this was the Augustinian scheme, with two important modifications which had already appeared in the twelfth century but which now were taken further. One of these was a more interior piety, among laity as well as clergy. The believer was urged to place himself in the presence of his judge, and to reflect on the answer he must make there. Whatever prehistory the *Dies Irae* may have had before 1200, it attained its classical shape and popular dissemination in the thirteenth century. The Apocalypse was translated into French verse in several versions and provided with a prose commentary which originated in the second quarter of the century. The stress was upon Christian discipleship and austerity (*âpreté de vie*), with almost no attempt to use contemporary events as a basis for future expectation. The concentration on the individual soul and its salvation was also apparent in the definition of the new deathbed ceremonial in the synodal constitutions of the time. They included confession and the making of the will, which would include a commendation of the soul to God and legacies to the church. Extreme unction was recommended in legislation, but was not in general use. The prescriptions for a pious death for the layman were now clear, and relatively easy to achieve; a great contrast with the uncertainty of the lay situation at the beginning of our period.

The other modification was the increasing importance attached to the doctrine of purgatory. It was expounded by the Paris theologians, including William of Auvergne and Alexander of Hales, and began to figure as a specifically Latin position in controversies with the Greeks. On 6 March 1254 Innocent IV, writing to his legate in the east, Odo of Châteauroux, stressed the need for the Greeks to accept the doctrine of purgatory. This already indicated its official adoption, and it was to be approved at the Second Council of Lyon in 1274. The effect was to make eschatology even more individual

than it had been in the theology of Augustine, for the soul was now
thought of as being assigned at death to heaven, hell, or purgatory.
The Last Judgement continued to be depicted in churches, but its
significance was now to represent the choice facing the individual at
death. The thirteenth century therefore saw the dissolution of the
consensus about the church's expectations which had, by and large,
marked the previous period. There were now groups who looked for
an end within a generation, and who sometimes hoped for a future of
a revolutionary kind, while the Augustinian tradition not only
remained the dominant one in the church as a whole, but had been
developed to a point where all expectation was fixed upon the
moment of death. It is hardly an exaggeration to say that, under the
influence of this development, the great majority of christians was
ceasing to have any eschatology at all.

21

THE STRUCTURE OF GOVERNMENT

i. *The Bishops*

After I had been appointed bishop, I reflected that I was a bishop and shepherd of souls, and that I was obliged . . . to show every diligence in visiting the sheep which had been committed to me, as Scripture disposes and commands. I therefore undertook to tour my bishopric and all its rural deaneries. I had the clergy of each deanery in order summoned for a set day and place, and the people warned to come then and there with children for confirmation, to hear the word of God and to confess. When the clergy and people had assembled, I myself frequently expounded the word of God to the clergy, and one of the Friars Preacher or Minor to the people. And four friars thereafter heard the confessions and imposed penances. Children were confirmed on the same day and subsequently, and all the time my clerks and I were engaged in inquisitions, corrections and reforms, as is required by the work of inquisition. On my first tour some people came to me and said in criticism of what I was doing, 'Sir, you are doing something new and unaccustomed'. I replied to them: 'Every new thing which establishes, forwards and perfects the new man is bound to corrupt and destroy the old. So blessed is the new, and altogether acceptable to Him who comes to renew the old man with his own newness'.

This manifesto for the pastoral revolution was presented in a memorandum to the pope and cardinals in 1250 by Bishop Robert Grosseteste of Lincoln.[1] Its agents above all were bishops, friars, and scholars, and in Grosseteste the three groups came together, for he was an outstanding scholar and close associate of Franciscans and Dominicans. The question which faces us now is the character of the thirteenth-century episcopate and the extent to which it embodied the new style of pastoral ministry.

The method by which these men were appointed had by this time been regularized. As in so many areas Innocent III's pontificate was the crucial one, for he secured the recognition of freedom of election in Sicily, Germany, and England, the very areas where royal

---

[1] *C&S*, ii.264–5. For the full text see S. Gieben in *Collectanea Franciscana* 41 (1971), 340–93.

influence had been greatest in the twelfth century, and thereafter the ruler's official part throughout most of Christendom was limited to the granting of a licence to elect and subsequent approval of the candidate. Meanwhile the electoral assembly had been defined. In Chapter 9 above it was observed that in the twelfth century the right of election had been progressively restricted to canons of the cathedral to the exclusion of other clergy and laity. It did not prove easy to complete the removal of laity, especially in Germany where the *ministeriales,* the military and administrative servants of the bishopric, had always been involved in episcopal assemblies and were increasing in power from the later twelfth century onwards. Even after 1220 we still find them intervening in the choice of bishops at Paderborn and elsewhere. In a few places, too, the rights of the clergy of the diocese survived for a time, as at Cologne, where a college of *priores* embodied the views of senior clergy. But the formal position was now clear in canon law: when the Fourth Lateran Council prescribed the procedure in elections it only took the canons into account. In the thirteenth century the normal and legal method of appointing a bishop was election by the cathedral chapter. The arrangement makes the period unique in the history of the western church.

The committing of election to a precisely constituted body was new, at least outside the special circumstances of the monasteries, and required the development of new terminology. In the time of Alexander III we first hear of the cathedral canons as the 'college' or 'chapter', the term which was to become standard. The definition of types of election by the Fourth Lateran was probably a tidying up of practices which already existed.[2] In law the chapter's freedom of choice was now well established, but outside voices had no difficulty in making themselves heard. If the local nobility could no longer attend the election, their families were on the cathedral chapters and nothing could prevent a display of strength on the day of decision in the city streets. The king had a natural opportunity to make his opinion known when the licence to elect was requested, and in practice chapters sometimes had to accept the lay ruler's nomination. In England, where there was a tradition of royal control, John's charter of 1214 reduced, but did not abolish, the Crown's influence. He reserved the right to refuse assent if there were reasonable and lawful grounds, and at Bangor he actually named the new bishop

---

[2] IV Lateran canons 23–6, cited Greg. IX, *Decretals,* I.6.41–4 (88–9).

when he granted the licence to elect. In 1257 the clergy of the province of Canterbury included among their grievances a complaint of improper royal pressure upon electors, who were overawed by the king's requests or found that their choice was rejected.[3] Paradoxically, however, it was the papacy, which had done so much to achieve freedom of election, which was the primary agent in undermining it. The pope could intervene in the electoral procedure for a number of reasons, the most important being to adjudicate a disputed election, and in addition, from Innocent III onwards, the Roman Church claimed that by virtue of its fullness of power it could set aside the rules and proceed to an appointment by its own authority. The right was used only rarely in the first half of the century, but in 1246 Innocent IV, in face of his conflict with Frederick II, instructed German chapters that they should not proceed to elect to any vacancies, but consult his legate. This measure seems to have been a temporary response to a political crisis, for in 1252 he ordered the procedure for canonical election to be followed in future. It therefore remains the case that the overwhelming number of bishops were elected by their cathedral chapters; but the normal working of the system required frequent reference to Rome, and there had been disquieting signs that the liberty could be revoked in the interests of the papacy.

What sort of bishops were appointed by these procedures? It is easy to point to outstanding examples of great scholars, nobles, or administrators, but in many cases we know little of the education or earlier career of bishops. There had already been a considerable group of *magistri* among twelfth-century bishops, but the period after 1200 saw the most distinguished promotions of scholars, especially in England and northern France, and among them were the leaders in the new pastoral methods. It was natural that Paris should have a series of bishops drawn from the university since at least the time of Peter Lombard (1159–60). In the thirteenth century these included Odo of Sully (1196–1208) and the theologian William of Auvergne (1228–49). Another Paris master who joined the Franciscans and subsequently became a bishop was Odo Rigaud, archbishop of Rouen (1247–76). In England one of the most influential was Stephen Langton (1207–28), and two scholar-bishops were canonized as saints, Edmund of Abingdon at Canterbury (1234–40) and Richard Wych at Chichester (1245–53). Alexander

---

[3] Complaints of the clergy c. 3–4 (*C&S* ii. 540).

Stavensby of Coventry and Lichfield (1224–38) had taught theology at Toulouse, and Robert Grosseteste of Lincoln (1235–53) at Oxford. The impact of scholars upon the Italian episcopate was less significant because of the small size of many bishoprics and the attractions of employment at the curia. Royal clerks probably provided fewer bishops in the first half of the thirteenth century, but there are still some prominent examples. In France the Hospitaller Guérin was a close friend of Philip Augustus and described as 'second only to the king'. He became bishop of Senlis in 1213 and was favoured with a series of grants from Philip, whose donations to the church were usually parsimonious. He was a commander at the victory of Bouvines in 1214 and assisted in the establishment of the abbey of La Victoire as an act of thanksgiving. In England we find such royal agents as the financier Peter des Roches (Winchester 1205–38) and the chancellor Ralph Nevill (Chichester 1224–44) who was such a perpetual absentee that his precentor had to write to invite him to the Easter ceremonies.

The twelfth-century pattern of aristocratic bishops continued, and included some who had nothing to commend them except their high birth. In England Henry III's appointments included his half-brother, Aylmer of Lusignan, whom he pressed on the electors at Winchester in 1250 in spite of his evident unsuitability, and the queen's uncle Boniface of Savoy (archbishop of Canterbury 1245–70) spent a great deal of time outside the country in support of his own interests. In Germany the waning of imperial influence left sees increasingly in the hands of the local nobility. Thus Speyer broke away from its close union with imperial interests and passed into the hands of the Leiningen-Eberstein family, descending from uncle to nephew with only two exceptions between 1237 and 1336. Local nobles are not bound to be bad bishops, but some of these emphatically were: Henry of Geldern, whom Innocent IV appointed to Liège before 1247 was well under age, left his diocese to be administered by papal legates, and remained a subdeacon in order to devote himself to the pursuit of papal political interest. In many parts of the western church, bishops continued to be predominantly chosen from the local community, often from one family. The bishopric of Clermont in France will serve as an example. All the bishops whose origin is known during the twelfth and thirteenth centuries were from the Auvergne, and the see descended from uncle to nephew for almost a century between 1195· and 1286 in the influential family of La Tour du Pin. While this was an important power locally, it owed its success to royal service: Bishop Robert (1195–1227) assisted Philip II to establish the control of the Crown in the region, Hugh (1227–49) died fighting on Louis IX's Egyptian crusade, and strong pressure was exercised by the court to secure the election of Guy (1250–86). In this instance Crown, nobility, and church were locked together into a particularly stable system. The increased independence of the chapters gave a particular character to these local links, for they had a marked tendency to elect people with experience in ecclesiastical administration, either from their own ranks or from nearby dioceses, and the choice of deans or archdeacons as bishops helped to confirm the control of dominant families in some bishoprics. The family interests may have expressed themselves in rather different forms from those of two hundred years before, but they were no less strong.

By 1200 the 'new episcopalism' which had been developing throughout the previous century was arriving at a much clearer conception of the bishop's office.[4] Drawing from the concepts of Roman law, the canonists defined the powers of the bishop as 'ordinary jurisdiction'. This embraced almost everything involved in the well-being of the church in his diocese, and was expressed by Honorius III as including 'canonical obedience, subjection and reverence, institution and deprivation, correction and reformation, and ecclesiastical censure; also jurisdiction over all causes lawfully pertaining to the ecclesiastical forum, penances and . . . also annual visitation'.[5] However much the popes might intervene, they did not doubt that bishops were the proper rulers of their dioceses, and the amount of business before the bishop was increasing rapidly. The strictly legal terminology which was introduced strikes harshly on modern ears. We would more readily speak of the bishop's function in administration and use the analogy of the civil service, but medieval society, with its insistence on public government and the open transaction of business, thought in legal terms and regarded the bishop as ordinary judge. While it is true that diocesan tribunals heard a great number of cases about tithes and wills, the pastoral significance of the bishop's legal powers was not lost, as can be seen from Grosseteste's account of his visitations with which this section opened. Without the bishop's newly defined position as ordinary the

[4] See ch. 9.iii.
[5] Greg. IX, *Decretals*, I.31.16 (193).

strenuous attempt to discipline the local clergy could scarcely have been conceived.

In 1200 canon law contained few prescriptions about the administrative structure within which the bishop's jurisdiction should be exercised, and one of the achievements of the first half of the century was the creation of a regular system by the reconstruction of the bishop's staff. In England and France the term 'official', originally a general term for an administrator, came to be applied to a specific group with supervisory authority in diocesan affairs, for example at York in a long vacancy from 1181 to 1191 and at Canterbury in the frequent absences of Archbishop Hubert Walter (1193–1205). It then was used for a single officer in charge of the bishop's spiritual jurisdiction, the later 'official principal'. By 1210 such an official existed in most dioceses in England and northern France, and subsequently the practice spread to the Rhineland and southern France. The official's fortune was finally made by Innocent IV's decretal *Romana ecclesia* in 1246 which, while it did not require such an appointment in all dioceses, provided a pattern which was widely followed except in Italy. The adoption of the Romano-canonical procedure had already begun to shape the pattern of diocesan courts. It involved for each case numerous appearances or court days and the keeping of a full written record, and the old system was unable to incorporate it. In the past major pleas had been heard before the bishop in his synod (in England and Germany), or (in France) in an assembly of senior clergy and lay tenants in the bishop's court. The change did not involve an abandonment of synods; indeed, as we shall shortly see, they had an important, but quite different, role in the thirteenth century. Perhaps we should allow ourselves a moment to mourn the passing of the synod as a major tribunal: for centuries trial before fellow-clergy had been the primary guarantee of a fair hearing, and its replacement by a professional tribunal, with a right of appeal to superior authority, was an important organizational change. Even in 1200 it was possible to use the word 'synodical' as a synonym of 'legal', but in the thirteenth century it is rare to hear of the adjudication of cases in the diocesan synod. Instead they went to the bishop's auditory, staffed by his legal advisers, which in the course of the first half of the century came to be known by its later name of consistory, with the official as its regular president. The process was embodied in *Roman ecclesia* in 1246, where Innocent IV defined officials as those 'who generally take cognizance of causes pertaining to the forum' of the bishops and should be deemed to constitute 'one and the same auditory or consistory with the bishops'.[6]

The discipline of the diocese depended on the development of an effective system of visitation. In his memorandum to Innocent IV Robert Grosseteste showed his awareness that he was innovating in extending visitation beyond the monasteries to the secular clergy and laity. Visitation records are rare for the mid-thirteenth century, those of Archbishop Odo Rigaud at Rouen being much the best preserved, and we cannot be sure of the details; but in the minds of some bishops the visitation was the northern equivalent of the inquisitions which were being held in southern France. Indeed, canonically it *was* an inquisition, directed against abuses rather than heresies. In the nature of things visitation by the bishop in a large diocese was a rare event, and a great deal depended on the efficiency of the archdeacons in pursuing more regular inquiries. Well before 1200 (in England at least) the archdeacon was being assisted by a vice-archdeacon or official; with a few exceptions he could hear any case which fell within the bishop's jurisdiction and had primary responsibility for the institution of clergy in their parishes. How efficient the archdeacons were, and how far they should be blamed for the unsatisfactory state of the parochial clergy, it is hard to say. They had a poor press, and academics amused themselves with the question whether an archdeacon could be saved; but the absentee archdeacon was not as common a figure as he later became, and in any case his functions were largely executed by his official. The system did, however, create a clumsy duplication. The archdeacon was the agent of the bishop, but so was the bishop's official, and the same ordinary jurisdiction was being administered twice. It was an awkward arrangement which created tangles in practice and conflicts between bishops and archdeacons.

The synod, which was no longer a major centre for pleas and litigation, came to fulfil another purpose. It was chosen as a vehicle for the pastoral instruction of the clergy, at a variety of levels from the Fourth Lateran Council through provincial assemblies to diocesan synods. These were steps in an international system of information, and far more of their concern than in the past was directed to the daily responsibilities of the parochial clergy in baptizing, saying mass, hearing confessions, and instructing their

[6] *Sext.* II. 15. 3 (Friedberg ii. 1015).

people. There were a few earlier instances of diocesan statutes: at
Saintes the Second Lateran decrees were reissued locally just after
1139, and the decrees of Lincoln survive from 1186. The new
tradition really began with the lengthy statutes which Bishop Odo of
Sully issued for Paris shortly after 1203. They were used as a quarry
for decrees by later councils. In 1213 Robert Courson as papal legate
held a major reforming council at Paris which provided material for
Fourth Lateran. In England Hubert Walter had already held a
provincial council at Westminster in 1200, and Fourth Lateran was
followed by the legislation of Bishop Richard le Poore for Salisbury
diocese in 1217/8 and of Stephen Langton for the province of
Canterbury at the council of Oxford in 1222. In both France and
England diocesan synods reissued this legislation for their own
clergy and incorporated it in a synodal book along with teaching for
parish priests about confession, moral theology, and the faith as a
whole. Such a book was prepared by William of Beaumont, bishop
of Angers, in 1216/9 and was widely adopted in western France,
while some dioceses required a copy of their statutes to be available
in every parish.

This sustained and serious attempt to instruct the local clergy was
accompanied by better keeping of records. The first steps were taken
in the later twelfth century, but they have left few traces and progress
becomes evident in the thirteenth. Archives and files were beginning
to be kept on a large scale. The continuous history of surviving papal
registers begins with Innocent III in 1198, and the first episcopal
registers are those of Hugh of Wells at Lincoln (1209–35) and Walter
de Gray at York (1215–55). This was not only the product of a
passion for order, but reflected the concern of Fourth Lateran for the
condition of the local churches: institutions to benefices and the
endowment of vicars are prominent in the earliest registers. Another
form of record was a description of parishes and their revenues, a
sort of ecclesiastical Domesday which in France is known as a *pouillé*,
of which an example survives for the diocese of Lyon from about
1190, prepared by Archbishop John Bellesmains. This movement
towards record-keeping was characteristic of churches all over
Europe, but Italy had its own version. The most literate of all
Christian nations, it already had a service of public notaries working
in the cities, and the bishops rarely developed their own records.
They employed registrars who had notarial training or simply used
the local notaries as the need arose. With few exceptions episcopal

archives in Italy consist of copies of deeds and grants, differing considerably from the administrative files which were beginning to be assembled in bishops' chanceries north of the Alps.

The distinctive features of Italian dioceses have been mentioned more than once, and are an illustration of the way in which national churches were pursuing their own lines of development. All had been influenced by the new pastoral ideals, but were expressing them in different ways. In England and France the bishops had taken the lead in applying the Lateran policy, strengthening their administration, disseminating instruction in synods, and using friars as preachers and confessors. The influence of Paris and Oxford was strong. In southern France the same ideas were being applied with the very important difference that the bishops there were largely concerned with the repression of heresy and depended on inquisitions conducted by friars under papal authority. Germany presents a different pattern: the bishops were particularly influential in politics, princes on a scale which in England only Durham could partly match. Nobles rather than scholars, they were much less interested in pastoral innovation, which they left to the friars, who along with the Beguines were creating a new spiritual atmosphere in the cities. Contemporaries were well aware of the contrasts. A clerk from Paris commented that 'almost all the German bishops wield both the spiritual and secular swords. And since they make judgements of blood and wage war, they are better suited to being soldiers than attending to the salvation of souls committed to their care.'[7] In Italy, especially in the centre and south, the bishops stood out much less prominently among the clergy; communities of canons were important in the urban churches; there was a strong link between the church and the rulers of the city communes; and the new spirit was again expressed by the friars, who however were less scholarly and more given to popular enthusiasms than their brethren in the north. Even Archbishop Federigo Visconti of Pisa, whose ideas in many ways matched those of his French colleagues, reminds us of the special features of Italy in his close association with Pisan political interests, his connections with St Francis and the central position given to personal preaching in his ministry. In all countries there were of course good bishops and bad, faithful servants and perpetual absentees. All of them found it formidably difficult to alter the conditions of life of the local clergy.

[7] Caesarius of Heisterbach, *Dialogus miraculorum*, ii.27, ed. J. Strange, i.99.

ii. *Parishes*

In the eyes of reforming bishops the parish church was the keystone to ecclesiastical discipline, in a sense which had not been true in the past. The Fourth Lateran Council had required the faithful to confess to their own priest, *proprius sacerdos*; northern French synods insisted that people from outside the parish should not be allowed to receive marriage, burial, or purification after childbirth there, nor even be permitted to attend mass; and southern synods saw the parish as a unit for inquiry into heresy.[8] The new assumption is illustrated in a document of Bishop Alberic of Chartres, who in 1241 discovered to his dismay that pastoral responsibility for the canons and junior clergy of Blois and their families had not been formally allocated. Remarking that 'considerable danger often arose from this uncertainty', he held an inquiry into local customs and carried out a division of souls among the churches there.[9]

This shift of emphasis at once posed a problem, because the revenues of the church were not concentrated in its parishes. The older canons which Gratian revived gave stewardship of tithes and landed revenues to the bishop, not to the individual country churches, and in distributing them priority was given to the support of monks and regular canons. When a new emphasis was placed on the parish it was found to be underfunded. The problem was not primarily the lay patron. True, local nobles had often managed to keep hold of tithes, but at least their ability to tap ecclesiastical revenues in the future had been strictly limited. The threat to parochial revenues came primarily from the communities to which they had been transferred during the process of restitution in the eleventh and twelfth centuries. Provided that an abbey simply acted as patron and presented its nominee to the bishop this did not have direct implications for the revenue, but often the abbey had retained the whole income for its own use, leaving the service of the parish to temporary and ill-paid substitutes. At Bourges around 1200, for example, there was constant tension between the archbishop and the abbey of Déols over the administration of its parishes. At about this time clear legal expression was being given to the position of monasteries which had absorbed the parish into their community resources. The decretals of Innocent III wrote of 'conferring in

[8] On the earlier development of the parish church, see ch 12.iii above.
[9] *Gall. Christ.* VIII, Instr. pp. 432–3.

perpetuity vacant baptismal churches' and recognized that in certain cases 'religious are permitted to convert their churches to their own use'.[10] The process was soon to be known as incorporation or appropriation, and its essence was that the monastery did not *present* the rector; it *became* the rector and received his income. In many countries the first formal acts of appropriation are found shortly after 1200, but they were essentially extending or confirming a state of affairs already customary. The problem which faced the bishop was to secure provision for an adequate ministry in such a parish, and this was achieved by insisting on the appointment of a vicar with a secure income. The first clear statement of this policy was at the Council of Reims in 1148, which required that the *proprius sacerdos* should have a revenue assigned to him.[11] The same policy appeared in canons issued at Avranches in 1172 and York 1195, and specific instances of the ordination of vicarages can be found from the 1150s onwards.[12] The arrangement was generalized by canon 32 of the Fourth Lateran Council, which criticized the 'vicious custom' by which priests serving parishes were left without a sufficient portion. This decree has been described as the Magna Carta of the parish priest and was followed, particularly in England, by a campaign for the ordination of vicarages.

Appropriation was not the only way in which resources were deflected away from the parish. Another major problem was the number of rectors who did not perform their pastoral duties. The fragmentary evidence of institutions in England before 1250 suggests that some 80 per cent of those appointed rector had not yet been ordained priest. They were pressed to proceed to the priesthood as soon as possible and to reside in their benefices, but even if they did so it remains true that bishops who were endeavouring to build up the pastoral ministry were normally obliged to appoint men without experience, who had never presided at mass, heard a confession, or preached a sermon. One suspects that inactive or non-resident rectors who left the work to their vicars were common in thirteenth-century England. Their ranks were increased by the ability of influential clergy to accumulate benefices to an extent which cannot be demonstrated for earlier periods; a man such as John Mansel, one of Henry III's confidential advisers, could build up what amounted

---

[10] Greg. IX, *Decretals*, III.10.8 and V.33.19 (505 and 865).
[11] Mansi xxi.716.
[12] Mansi xxij.139; *C&S* i.1049.

to an empire of ecclesiastical posts. Although canon law prohibited such pluralism it was easy to obtain papal dispensations, and privileged clergy could increase their incomes by obtaining one of the growing number of papal provisions, to which we must turn later.[13] A great deal of the actual work was undoubtedly done by perpetual vicars, chaplains, or others, who were maintained out of only a small proportion of the income of the parish. Did the bishops succeed in securing for such junior clergy a sufficient income to discharge their offices properly? There is a good deal of evidence from thirteenth-century England about the assessment of the incomes of those serving parishes. In the diocese of Chichester, where there were many vicars, over half the parish priests had an income assessed at more than £7. This was roughly the same as the wage of a skilled craftsman and would have made the priest one of the richest men in the village. What is more, these figures come from assessment lists for taxation and are likely to be understated. Beyond this point all is uncertainty, and historians have reached very different conclusions about the adequacy of the endowments. John Moorman's view was that 'with one or two notable exceptions the clergy of England in the thirteenth century were poor men'.[14] Conversely Brian Tierney thought that the parochial clergy had a sufficient income to maintain themselves adequately and in addition to perform their duty of poor relief, which may have been better provided than at any other time before the twentieth century.[15]

In many lands there were signs of vitality in parish life which confirm that, from whatever source, there was income available. In spite of much later rebuilding it is still easy to see the contribution of the first half of the thirteenth century to the architecture of local churches. The extension of chancels reflected the development of a more complex liturgy. Clergy were more numerous—a large parish was supposed to have the assistance of a deacon, subdeacon, and clerk in minor orders—and were provided with their own entrance directly into the chancel from outside, and ambitious parishes were beginning to build rood screens and Easter sepulchres. Lay initiatives were more frequent. In the large cities of Italy laymen began in the

[13] Pluralism was prohibited in Third Lateran can. 14 (Alberigo 194 = Greg.IX, *Decretals*, III.5.5 (465)) and. with the significant exclusion of influential and learned people, in Fourth Lateran can. 29 (Alberigo 224 = Greg. IX, *Decretals*, III.5.28 (477–8)).

[14] J. R. H. Moorman, *Church Life in England in the Thirteenth Century* (Cambridge, 1945), 154.

[15] B. Tierney, *Medieval Poor Law* (Berkeley, 1959), 109.

twelfth century to administer the fabric fund in important churches. The division of responsibility for the building between rector and people is difficult to date, but it was common in the first half of the thirteenth century and obviously implied that the financing of the nave (the people's part of the church) was coming under the supervision of laymen. Shortly after 1250 we begin to encounter the first signs of wardens (the later churchwardens) at a few places in England. In some regions the community as a whole secured the right to elect its priest. It is not surprising that the governing classes in Italian communes did so, but more striking to find that in the German countryside, when a new parish was separated, it was not uncommon to give the inhabitants the right to present the name of the incumbent to the bishop. Amid all the regional diversity there is a common pattern: the parish church was a more lively place in 1250 than in 1150 and the laity contributed to its activities more than they had done in the past.

It would be satisfying if we could end this sketch of parochial life with a comparison of the local clergy in 1050 and 1250, but any such attempt would be hazardous. We do not have the sort of evidence needed to reach precise conclusions; our knowledge is impressionistic and anecdotal. Moreover, it would be misleading to attempt a straightforward comparison between 1050 and 1250, because the nature of the church's presence in the countryside had greatly changed. In almost every district there were more parish churches (sometimes many more) and they were larger, better built, with a more numerous staff of clergy. Even more striking was the increased number of houses of monks and regular canons in the countryside and towns. There were also more recent changes, which still had to take full effect, designed to raise the level of discipline and understanding among the laity through the confessional, visitations, confraternities, and preaching. Some of the practices attacked by the Gregorians had almost disappeared. It is significant that when the Fourth Lateran complained about simony, it assumed it was being practised in secret—a dramatic change from the eleventh century. The direct inheritance of livings from father to son, which in some places was still quite widespread in the later twelfth century, was finally eradicated as a result of the episcopal control of institutions to livings. Lay patrons had almost disappeared in some regions, and in others their ability to exploit their churches was under control. Other evidence, however, suggests that the problems had changed their form rather than been solved. While synods condemned the levy of undue charges by clergy for their ministry and sacraments, they also insisted that 'just as we command that wrongful exactions must not be made from (laymen), so we command laudable customs must be maintained'.[16] This appears to concede the maintenance of established charges for the sacraments, and in fact parochial accounts show a significant income from customary dues at mass, confession, churchings, and marriage, though rarely at baptism. The prohibition of simony had been diluted until it merely forbade new charges. The campaign against clerical marriage had undoubtedly reduced the number of married priests, perhaps almost to vanishing point, but in consequence it had produced a great deal of sexual immorality. When Archbishop Odo of Rouen visited the deanery of Eu in January 1249, he found eight priests who were reputed to be incontinent. Several of them were suspected of having relations with more than one woman, while the rural dean, appropriately to his higher status, was having an affair with the wife of the knight of the village. There are plenty of similar reports, and the impression is confirmed in detail by the visitation records from Kent in 1292. The opponents of the Gregorian reform seem to have been right in their pessimistic prophecies about the result of denying marriage to the clergy; indeed, people were still making the same complaints againt Innocent III:

> Non est Innocentius, immo nocens vere
> qui quod Deus docuit, studet abolere;
> jussit enim dominus feminas habere,
> sed hoc noster pontifex jussit prohibere.[17]

> Innocent by name, but not innocent in deed,
> trying to abolish rules which God has decreed.
> For the Lord provided a woman for a man,
> but it's been prohibited by a papal ban.

There were other complaints about the parochial clergy, too, in particular drunkenness, which seems to have been widespread, and ignorance. Although there was a steady permeation of graduates from the universities, they were coming in at the level of rectors, whose impact on the actual quality of ministry was not necessarily great. The evidence points clearly towards the conclusion that the

---

[16] Statutes of Salisbury, c. 17 (1217/9), *C&S* ii.66, based on IV Lateran canon 66.
[17] T. Wright (ed.), *The Latin Poems attributed to Walter Mapes* (Camden Society, 1841), 172.

bishops were faced with almost insuperable problems and had failed to secure a reasonable standard of ministry in many local churches. When the radical Franciscan Salimbene looked back to the Fourth Lateran Council, it seemed to him to have achieved nothing worth reporting, and he omitted it 'for weariness and the avoidance of prolixity'.[18] It is a cruel judgement on the endeavours of Innocent III, but undeniably a significant one.

iii. *Monasteries and Cathedrals*

Some observers in 1200 saw the monastic establishment as the finest product of medieval society and as full of hope for the future. The number of monasteries was enormous. When Louis VIII of France made his will in 1225 he provided benefactions for 60 Premonstratensian abbeys, 40 Victorine, 60 Cistercian, a further 20 Cistercian nunneries, 200 hospitals, and 2,000 leper-houses, and this was to make no mention of the many Cluniac and black-monk houses, most of them surrounded by satellite cells.[19] Innocent III turned to the Cistercians for action against the Albigensians and for leadership in monastic renewal, and Abbot Joachim, with his perceptive if eccentric feel for contemporary events, looked forward to the new age as a sort of republic of monks. By 1250 these hopes had been disappointed. Historians of monasticism have tended to link the thirteenth century with the later Middle Ages and have seen it as the introduction to a long decline, but the reality was more mixed. There were important success stories, including the expansion of Joachim's order of Fiore in southern Italy and the flowering of nunneries associated with the Beguines in the Low countries and the abbeys which directed them: Thomas of Cantimpré called Afflighem 'the most regular of all the monasteries of this order'.[20] Yet these were exceptions. Taking Europe as a whole the central themes of the period were the problems afflicting black-monk houses; the failure of the Cistercians to maintain the initiative which they originally possessed; and the halting progress of the reforms promoted by a series of popes.

One of the signs of decline which was to become evident in the fourteenth century was a fall in the number of monks, but it is not

[18] O. Holder-Egger (ed.), *Cronica Fratris Salimbene de Adam*, MGH SS XXXII 22.
[19] M. Bouquet *et al.* (eds.), *Recueil des Historiens des Gaules et de la France* (Paris, 1738–1904), XVII.310–1.
[20] *Vita S. Liudgardis* ii.2.24 (*AASS* June iii.249).

clear that communities had fallen to an unsatisfactory size before 1250: figures ranging from 35 to 100 monks can commonly be found in important abbeys. The monastic establishment remained stable throughout the thirteenth century. Although there were few new foundations, few monasteries disappeared. In England not a single house was abolished apart from a handful of dependent cells whose monks were relocated by the parent abbey; in Italy and Germany dispersions were few in proportion to the total number of houses. Yet there were disquieting signs. Some abbeys, often with papal approval, defined a quota of monks which must not be exceeded—a financial precaution rare before 1200. New foundations aimed at a low admissions target: when Hayles Abbey in Gloucestershire was opened in 1251 its founder, Richard of Cornwall, told the chronicler Matthew Paris that he had spent 10,000 marks on building the church, yet the abbey had only twenty monks.[21] The unit cost of a monk was very high. We can also observe the closure of an important source of recruits. In 1221 Stephen of Lexington left the schools at Oxford and went with several companions to the Cistercian abbey of Quarr on the Isle of Wight. He was a distinguished capture, who was to become abbot of Cîteaux, but he was one of the last of the great scholars attracted by the order. From then onward they took to joining the friars. In 1150 there had been a Cistercian pope, Eugenius III, and a roll-call of scholars and politicians would have to include Bernard of Clairvaux, Otto of Freising, Arnold of Brescia, Anselm of Havelberg, Suger of Saint-Denis, Aelred of Rievaulx, Gilbert Foliot, Henry of Blois, Peter the Venerable and many others from the monks and regular canons. In 1250 it is hard to think of any contribution of similar quality in any field other than the writing of history. The divorce between monasteries and universities was expressed in Robert Grosseteste's warning to the friars to persist with their studies, otherwise 'it will surely happen to us as it has to other religious, whom we see (alas) walking in the shadows of ignorance'.[22] Stephen of Lexington attempted to remedy this state of affairs by founding the college of St Bernard at Paris in 1246 and other orders soon followed his precedent, but the basic structure of monastic life inhibited commitment to universities, popular ministry or even involvement in political affairs—concerns to which the flexible organization of the mendicants was admirably suited.

[21] Matthew Paris, *Chronica Majora*, ed. H. R. Luard (RS 1880) v.262.
[22] Thomas of Eccleston, *De adventu* xv, ed. A. C. Little (Manchester, 1951), 91.

Many abbeys were in debt, often to a very serious extent. In 1196 St Bénigne at Dijon borrowed 1,700 *livres* from a Jewish usurer, and by 1207 the debt amounted to 9,825 *livres* and had to be paid as an act of charity by the countess of Champagne. By 1255, according to Matthew Paris, Christchurch Canterbury was more than 4,000 marks in debt.[23] Perhaps we should not attach too much importance to this, because for medieval monasteries as for modern football clubs indebtedness was a way of life, and their underlying endowments were large. Nevertheless the administration of many houses inhibited by its extreme fragmentation the wise use of resources. The abbot had sole control of a great part of the estates, and there was no proper check on his use of the revenues. The complication of Benedictine landholding required managerial skills far beyond many abbots. Jocelin of Brakelond provides a description of Bury St Edmunds under Abbot Hugh, who let the finances fall into such a state that Jewish money-lenders were dunning the monks for repayment.[24] Some abbots employed the income for the benefit of their relations: in 1256 it was reported that the abbot of Mont St Michel had given dowries to several nieces, maintained a nephew at university, and bought him a handsome book of canon law.[25] In addition each major officer or obedientiary had his own estates from which he derived the income with only a minimum of co-ordination. In the late twelfth century this inept administration faced changing circumstances. In the agrarian economy production was increasingly directed to the market for cash profits, while prices began to rise. This posed acute problems for authorities whose income came from rents, and black-monk abbeys were poorly placed to secure direct control of their estates. In the long run they could hope for some spin-off from the rising profitability of agriculture, but it came to them too slowly and late to counter the effects of price inflation. The exception to this picture was England, where monasteries were able to recover direct control over their estates, and Winchester Cathedral priory, Peterborough, and Christchurch Canterbury became improving landowners on a large scale. There was also a contrast between the position of the Benedictines and Cistercians, whose direct exploitation of their estates under the administration of *conversi* enabled them to take advantage of the new economic opportunities. Gerald of Wales remarked that the Cluniacs would create want out of

---

[23] Matthew Paris, *Chronica Majora*, v. 502.
[24] H. E. Butler (ed.), *The Chronicle of Jocelin of Brakelond* (Edinburgh, 1949), 3–4.
[25] *Register of Eudes of Rouen*, tr. S. M. Brown (New York and London, 1964), 274.

plenty, while the Cistercians could bring wealth out of a wilderness.[26]

It is disconcerting to find, nevertheless, that Cistercian abbeys were also caught in the toils of indebtedness. This suggests that poor administration and a changing economy were not the whole story. One difficulty which all monasteries faced was the pressure of lay government. Increasingly in the thirteenth century they were subject to taxation, and individual houses were threatened by many kinds of oppression. Hirsau, once the standard-bearer of the Gregorian cause in southern Germany, was obliged to surrender much of its land to the emperor in 1215 and accepted him as its advocate in 1225, and at Monte Cassino the monks were driven out in 1239 so that Frederick II could fortify its strategic site. Perhaps the most important element in increasing indebtedness was greater display and luxury. Abbots kept magnificent households, whose cost was a great burden on monastic finances. The monks expected more comfort in line with the assumptions of a more luxurious age: private rooms, wainscotting, cubicles in the cloister, financial allowances (the *peculium*), and facilities for meat-eating and conversation all made for a relaxed life and greater expenditure. Building continued to demand large sums, sometimes with much outside help (as in Henry III's rebuilding at Westminster), sometimes required by the collapse of the fabric (the great tower at Saint-Denis) and sometimes by the growing ambitions of the abbey itself (east end at Rievaulx). By 1250 the abbeys had travelled a long way down the road towards becoming hugely expensive institutions, which could only gain a sort of financial stability by severe restrictions upon the numbers of their monks.

The process of decay was opposed by the reforming programme promoted by Innocent III. The Fourth Lateran Council required the holding of triennial chapters in each kingdom or province, initially with the advice of Cistercian abbots, who were accustomed to the system. The chapters were to appoint visitors to supervise the houses, and the popes encouraged visitation, both by their own legates and diocesan bishops.[27] The popes pressed upon abbeys the need for regular audits and the appointment of single treasurers to receive all the income of the house. Instructions issued by papal legates were designed to bring the abbot back into the community

---

[26] Gerald, *Itinerarium Kambriae* i.3 (*Opera*, ed. J. F. Dimock, RS 1868, vi. 45). For the Cistercian economy see ch. 10.ii and iii above.

[27] Fourth Lateran can. 12 (Alberigo 216–17).

and to require the consent of the chapter for land-grants. In Italy in particular, decayed monasteries were transferred to other communities, notably the Cistercians and the Florensians. Transfers of this sort, unknown in England, were a common feature of the Italian scene. The reforming programme was embodied in statutes formulated by Gregory IX in 1235 and 1237, and it had some limited effect. General chapters continued in existence in some countries in spite of opposition and absenteeism, and diocesan visitation of monasteries had become general by the second half of the century. Better financial methods were adopted, and some highly un-Benedictine practices such as the *peculium* were held in check. The fight for an effective monastic order was thus still in progress in 1250, but there were reasons for pessimism. Innocent IV granted exemptions from Gregory's statutes in order to secure financial and political support against Frederick II, and behind that setback lay a more fundamental difficulty: black-monk houses were not really susceptible to control by the machinery provided by the papal initiative. The new chapters were a shadow of those of the white monks, for they did not have the same power to legislate and visit; and the great exempt houses behaved as if they were answerable to no one. Moreover no system of organization could meet the fact that the stream of piety was flowing into new channels. The battle for a restored monasticism had not been lost by 1250, but it was going to be.

The cathedral chapters were richer and more influential than most monasteries, and with them must be counted the highly endowed collegiate churches which were numerous throughout western Europe.[28] By this time the constitution of cathedrals displayed every conceivable combination between the living of the common life and the individual endowment of the canons, but they all showed a steady movement towards private endowment, which proceeded at different speeds in different places. At one extreme were the monastic chapters, which lived a fully communal life, at least in the modified form which was fashionable in contemporary monasticism. In England almost half the cathedrals were monastic, but elsewhere this was rare. Monreale, founded in 1183 near Palermo, was Benedictine, and some of the cathedrals of eastern Germany were Premonstratensian. The opposite type of secular foundation is well represented by Salisbury, Lincoln, and York, but the sole survivor of their early constitution, the statutes of Bishop Osmund

---

[28] For the development of communities of canons in the twelfth century, see ch. 10.ii above.

at Salisbury, is probably a compilation based on the usage there in
the second half of the twelfth century, and there is no solid reason to
suppose that the separate residences and endowments (or 'prebends')
went back, as is sometimes thought, to 1091–2. Most cathedrals
followed a path between common life and individual prebends. At
Exeter, where Bishop Leofric had founded a community in 1051
based on the common life, even the dean and chancellor only
received separate prebends in 1225. At Chartres the property of the
church was finally assigned as prebends in 1171, but there were
regular redistributions in order to keep the salaries roughly equal;
and at Cologne and Bamberg the canons of the cathedral were still
using the common refectory in the late twelfth century. Once
prebends were allotted, some non-residence was inevitable, because
the canon had to attend to the parish church and property from
which he drew his income; and with the growth in the scale of
endowments this pressure became irresistible. The property of
cathedral chapters expanded quickly, partly because of their success
in establishing a claim to a share of the bishops' estates: in 1179,
when Bishop Manasses of Langres received a grant of the county
there, he gave one-third of the revenue to his chapter, and German
chapters were particularly successful in the drive to turn themselves
into great landowners. Some canonries were enormously valuable:
the highest in England was Masham Vetus (York), taxed at 250
marks a year. An appointment of this kind, especially as it was not
held to involve the cure of souls, would attract any royal or papal
clerk, and canonries were the earliest and most obvious objective for
papal provisions. It came to be accepted that a canon could opt
whether to be resident or non-resident. Sometimes (as at Exeter and
Hereford) prebends were not large enough without a share in the
common fund reserved for residentiaries and thus obliged most of
the canons to reside, but in the thirteenth century it was more typical
for the residentiaries to be only half the total body.

At the same time the importance of the cathedral chapters was
growing in the administration of the diocese. Apart from their own
jurisdiction they were being recognized as providing a council for the
bishop. Alexander III wrote to the patriarch of Jerusalem in 1168 that
'as you and your brothers are one body, so you are regarded as the
head and they as the members. Therefore it is not proper for you to
ignore the members and employ the advice of others in the business

of your church'.[29] What this meant varied in practice, for the rights of the chapter were defined in imprecise terms such as advice, consent, and subscription. When under Frederick Barbarossa the imperial consent was required, the part of the canons was nominal; but their importance was growing rapidly. By the early thirteenth century they were recognized as the sole electors of the bishop, and chapters successfully claimed the power to administer spiritual affairs during a vacancy in the see. They began to assume that they were the church, of which the bishop was the proctor or representative, and they began to demand concessions from candidates before electing them to the bishopric. Such 'electoral capitulations' were contrary to canon law, but in Germany they became common and elaborate. The main sequence began at Verdun in 1209 and continued with Hildesheim in 1216, Würzburg in 1225, Mainz in 1233, Worms in 1234, and Paderborn in 1247. Powerful chapters also began to restrict their recruitment to members of exclusively noble descent. It is true that such men might be qualified in theology or law, but the effect was to close the upper reaches of the German church as a career open to the talented.

This growth in wealth and power made the cathedrals the target for papal provisions. They were not the only one, for provisions might also be issued for parishes with cure of souls, but as Maitland rightly declared, 'canonries were the staple commodity of the papal market'.[30] Interference in appointments in other churches was, among the powers exercised by the thirteenth-century papacy, the one which had the least basis in custom. The first case on record is a request by Innocent II in 1137 for the archbishop of Compostella to confer a benefice on a clerk named Arias, and the practice developed quickly. We know of four instances under Eugenius III (1146–53), including a request in support of the theologian Peter Lombard, and a year or two later the practice was so common that it appears regularly in the correspondence of Provost Ulric of Steinfeld in Germany and of the royal chancellor, Hugh of Champfleury, in France.[31] Under Alexander III papal nomination or provision was a frequent method of appointment, and the number continued to grow until the floodgates really opened under Innocent IV (1243–54). We

[29] Greg. IX, *Decretals*, III.10.4 (502).
[30] F. W. Maitland, *Roman Canon Law in the Church of England* (London, 1898), 67 n.
[31] For references see H. Baier, *Päpstliche Provisionen* (Münster, 1905), 6–8.

can only outline the rising numbers vaguely, but it is significant that the registers of Innocent III mention twenty-five mandates of provision by his predecessor Celestine III, probably only a minute proportion of those issued. By the death of Innocent IV it was recognized that the situation was out of control. Cathedrals had providees queueing up for canonries, as at Acre, where there were ten clergy with mandates and no vacancies, and providees were employing agents to listen for news of dead men's shoes. In 1255 Alexander IV had to try to restore order by revoking existing mandates in his constitution *Execrabilis*. The rising tide of protest confirms the impression of increasing numbers. For a long time the only opposition was the simple failure of the bishop or other patron to act upon the mandate, but in 1232 there was an angry movement in England protesting against the grant of benefices to foreign clergy and against papal taxation generally. In Matthew Paris's chronicle provisions had become a major grievance; Bishop Robert Grosseteste complained angrily about the provision of unsuitable candidates, especially those who plainly had no intention of residing, and took his opposition to extremes: he presented a searing memorandum to the pope and cardinals in 1250 and refused to accept a mandate in favour of the nephew of the pope himself.

Paradoxically the Roman Church was rarely able to appoint to a specific benefice, for the simple reason that it did not know that there was a vacancy until the local patrons had had ample time to fill it. The first letters were therefore general requests to provide a clerk with a benefice, but they became more specific through the grant of an 'expectancy' or 'expectative' which gave a claim to the first vacant canonry in a named church and often a pension to sweeten the time of waiting. Contemporaries found this a distasteful practice, because it created a vested interest in another person's death, and it was prohibited by a decree of the Third Lateran Council in 1179.[32] The effect of this was to make expectatives in law a papal monopoly, since only the pope could dispense from the decree. A further device was reservation, the declaration that a benefice should not be bestowed until the pope had been consulted. The first reservation of which we know dates from the beginning of Innocent III's pontificate, but the full development falls after our period with the appearance of the 'general reservation', which required a whole class of benefices to be left vacant for papal decision. It is likely that the

---

[32] Third Lateran can. 8 (Alberigo 191).

main impetus behind the development of provisions was the pressure of petitioners rather than a deliberate policy of expanding papal influence, and we can discern four main classes of beneficiaries. The first consisted of those with a training in the schools: it is no accident that Peter Lombard is one of the first names we encounter. Then there were officials of the papal curia, whose needs were openly recognized by Hadrian IV: 'we ought to reward such persons with ecclesiastical benefices when we conveniently can'.[33] Clerks in royal service figured among the beneficiaries of provisions from an early stage, for the pope was thus enabled to gratify influential men at somebody else's expense. Finally, even clergy who were seeking preferment within their own diocese began to see provision as a more direct and expeditious way of obtaining it.

The first letters of provision were requests, or something between a request and a mandate expressed in such phrases as *rogando mandamus*. Even before 1160 if the bishop ignored the request the pope applied pressure, and by the thirteenth century popes were beginning to appoint 'monitors' and 'executors' to enforce them. Innocent IV issued such additional letters at the same time as the provision, thus completing the system in its later form. Geoffrey Barraclough has insisted that the mandate of provision was never a purely administrative act but was simply an instruction to collate which could be resisted on legal grounds such as the unsuitability of the nominee. This is an important point, and is quite correct in law. On the other hand, provisions explicitly rested on the right of the apostolic see, by virtue of its fullness of power, to dispose of any ecclesiastical office. A papal dispensation could free the candidate from many of the objections which could be urged against him, such as non-residence, plurality of benefices, or being under age, and thus leave the local church with no legal grounds to resist a provision which was clearly a pastoral abuse. The system was a response to a new situation in which able clergy were entering the universities and government service in church and state. It was natural for them to look for preferment to international authority, and the Roman Church performed a valuable function in meeting this need. All systems are open to abuse, but provisions perhaps more than most, for careerists were able to use them to create large incomes from local benefices whose functions they had no intention of performing.

[33] Cited Baier, *Päpstliche Provisionen* 8.

22

THE ROMAN CHURCH AND THE LAY POWER IN
THE THIRTEENTH CENTURY

i. *Papacy, Kingdoms, and City States*

It is often said that the thirteenth century saw the rise of the nation state. At first sight this may seem a paradox, since national sovereignty was inhibited by the claims to universal jurisdiction made by both empire and papacy. Frederick II asserted that God 'has set us above kings and kingdoms', and the canonist Johannes Teutonicus held that 'the emperor is above all kings . . . and all nations are under him'.[1] Such views, however, had little impact outside the territories of the empire, and the teaching of Innocent III's decretal *Per venerabilem* that the king of France 'acknowledges no superior in temporal affairs' was incorporated into canon law.[2] The international authority of the Roman Church posed a more complex question and its significance will be considered further in this chapter. We must not in any event concentrate too much on the nation states. The process of their formation was still in its early stages in 1250 and was in progress only in parts of the west. In Germany, Italy, and Poland the opposite was happening: power was being devolved from the centre to princes, communes, and duchies. These governments, however constituted, were functioning within a political system which had changed with the enormous conquests by the French Crown in the old Angevin lands and the southern provinces, which had made the Capetians the leading national monarchy. The decisive period was a short one, because the battles of Las Navas de Tolosa, Muret, and Bouvines between 1212 and 1214 marked the overthrow of the old order and the creation of the balance of power characteristic of the new century.

The first change which can be observed in European government

---

[1] MGH Legum iv Const ii, no. 197, p.263; Johannes Teutonicus, *Gloss* (1215/20) cited Gaines Post, *Studies in Medieval Legal Thought* (Princeton, 1964), 457.
[2] Greg. IX, *Decretals*, IV.17.13 (715).

(ecclesiastical as well as secular) was a great increase in activity. The availability of lawyers and secretaries trained in the universities made it possible to regulate the life of the community in greater detail through the development of legislation and lawbooks, including Frederick II's lawcodes in Sicily, the works of Glanvil and Bracton in England, the ordinances of Louis IX in France, and the huge development of the civil law and the compilation of the *Decretals* authorized by Gregory IX. Another area of government initiative was taxation. Governments were requiring from their subjects not only the traditional feudal dues, but levies based on a proportion of the value of their movable wealth or income. The issue of secular taxation of the church was initially faced at the Third Lateran Council of 1179 as a result of levies made by city governments in Italy. Such charges were wholly forbidden 'unless the bishop and clergy observe that there is such necessity and utility that, to relieve the common necessities, where the resources of laymen are not sufficient they consider without coercion that subsidies should be granted by the churches'.[3]

Whereas in the past jurisdiction had belonged to a number of different owners whose interests were defined by custom, there was now a marked tendency to see all significant rights as vested in a single authority. For the civil lawyer this was embodied in the principle 'the will of the prince has the force of law', a tag much quoted in the thirteenth century.[4] It did not work only to the benefit of the emperor. At Milan and in other Italian cities it was claimed that all imperial rights had been transferred at the Treaty of Constance in 1183, and in Germany Frederick II issued a series of concessions. The *Privilege in favour of the Ecclesiastical Princes* (April 1220) and the *Constitution in favour of the Princes* (January 1231, confirmed 1232) transferred to the princely territories almost all the powers of government. In the western kingdoms general supremacy came to be vested in the Crown. Bracton wrote that the king 'should have no equal, let alone a superior', and in France by 1283 Beaumanoir could describe the king as *souverains* because he had 'the general guard of all his kingdom'.[5] The sovereignty which was thus

---

[3] Third Lateran can. 19 (Alberigo 197) = Greg. IX, *Decretals*, III.49.4 (654–5); Fourth Lateran can.46 (231) = Greg. IX, *Decretals*, III.49.7 (656). The latter canon included the significant gloss, 'because of the imprudence of some people, they shall first consult the Roman pontiff, whose business it is to provide for the common good'.

[4] *Digesta* 1.4.1, ed. Th. Mommsen (Berlin, 1962), 14.

[5] Bracton, *De legibus Angliae*, III.9.3, ed. T. Twiss, RS 70, vol. 2, p.172; Beaumanoir, *Coutumes de Beauvaisis*, ed. A. Salmon (Paris, 1899–1900), xxxiv.1043.

emerging was normally not absolutist. Medieval societies were complex, including within themselves organizations accustomed to local liberty. Barons, townsmen, and corporations of clergy did not think of themselves as equal before the law but as groups with guaranteed privileges. Hence there arose the paradox that a time of growing government was also a time of growing consultation. Brian Tierney has stressed the unusual character of these corporate states or *Ständestaaten* in the perspective of world history. Society was moving in the direction of the idea formulated by Marsilius of Padua: 'royal monarchy is a temperate government in which the ruler is a single man deferring to the common good and to the will or consent of his subjects'.[6] This qualified character of royal authority is shown in the stress on the special duty of the ruler to provide for the common defence of the realm in times of peril, as if his powers were designed for emergencies rather than for normal circumstances. 'Urgent necessity' was accepted by the church as grounds for the taxation of the clergy. Rulers also needed the consent of subjects for taxation, legislation, and other measures. The most famous guarantee of this was the issue by John of England of Magna Carta in 1215, which in its original form required that taxation should be approved by the 'common counsel of the realm'. In Hungary the Golden Bull of 1222 by Andrew II contained even larger guarantees of the privileges of the magnates, while Duke Wladislaw of Great Poland in a charter of 1228 conceded 'just and noble laws according to the counsel of the bishop and barons'. In 1231 an edict of King Henry (VII) obliged German princes making new laws for their territories to have the consent of 'the better and greater of the land'. Consent was a mark of the new style of government.

Bishops and barons could be consulted personally, but communities such as cities, cathedrals, or monasteries required a system of representation. Mandates summoning representatives rarely survive from before 1250, but experiments were certainly being made. There had been a few instances in the twelfth century of assemblies including members from the towns, notably at Frederick I's Diet of Roncaglia in 1158, but a new period opened when the Roman-law concept of the 'proctor' was adapted to the practice of representation. In Roman law, the proctor belonged essentially to civil litigation, for he was the nominee empowered to act for the principal in a suit. The office was adopted in church courts as a way of speeding up business

[6] Marsilius, *Defensor Pacis*, ed. R. Scholz, MGH Fontes, 38.

and was expected to be given full power (*plena potestas*) to bind his principal. In constitutional terms the important innovation was to use the same idea for the appointment of representatives in public business. Gaines Post suggested that Innocent III was largely responsible for this step. In 1200 he summoned proctors with full power from six cities in the march of Ancona to meet with his curia, and in 1207 he met city representatives from the Papal State generally. In 1214 the council of Lerida, over which one of his legates presided, was perhaps the first Spanish assembly to include proctors from the cities and in 1215 the Lateran Council was attended by representatives of cathedral chapters and monasteries. After Innocent's death the Dominicans rapidly developed their distinctive system of representation, and in 1231 Frederick II was the first secular ruler to summon representatives with full power from the cities. Meanwhile the pressure for both papal and royal taxation was beginning to lead to clerical assemblies which met for financial business and included proctors of cathedral chapters and other clergy.

The movement was away from directly personal lordship and towards institutional government. The word state (*status*) was still not normally used in the modern sense, although it does occur about 1228.[7] The main terms were *civitas* in Italy and *regnum*, which was coming to be used for the territorial kingdom in its later sense. National identities were strengthening with a standardization in the forms of language. The troubadours wrote a fairly consistent version of *langue d'oc*, and the dialect of the Paris region was coming to be regarded as correct French. Histories and laws began to appear in the vernacular, which was now uniform enough to be widely understood. Villehardouin's *Conquest of Constantinople*, Frederick II's Landpeace of Mainz in 1235, and the works of Alfonso the Wise of Castile are milestones in the emergence of national cultures. The growth of these new political entities has been seen as a reaction to ecclesiastical claims: 'the Gregorian concept of the church almost demanded the invention of the concept of the state.'[8] This is at best a half-truth. The development of the state was primarily a response to changing social, economic, and educational conditions. The new states were not secular organizations in any obvious sense of the

---

[7] Accursius, gloss *Ad Digest.* 1.1.1.2, cited B. Tierney in *Comparative Studies in Society and History* 5 (1962–3), 386 n.

[8] J. R. Strayer, *On the Medieval Origins of the Modern State* (Princeton, 1970), 22. For the custom of royal healing, see F. Barlow, 'The King's Evil', *EHR* 95 (1980), 3–27.

word, and thirteenth-century rulers had no doubt that their authority came from God. Frederick II went further than his predecessors in claiming a divine purpose for his government and the Capetians rejoiced to be anointed with chrism which had, it was said, been brought from heaven. Although there had been a few scattered precedents for the custom of royal healing of scrofula by touch, it is probable that it became an established custom in France and England in the course of the thirteenth century. Nor were rulers careful to avoid involvement in ecclesiastical affairs. If their direct control had been reduced by concessions, they insisted on their remaining regalian rights and pressed the pope to further their interests and appoint their nominees.

The sense that the ruler was not only a personal lord, but the head of a society, was expressed in the Roman-law theory that the prince had initially derived his power by delegation from the people. The developed awareness of community created problems for the clergy, who in the twelfth century had secured large exemptions from royal jurisdiction. In matters of taxation and justice it was hard to see them as part of the same society. In the Lombard cities the administration was largely in lay hands, and measures were sometimes taken to exclude the clergy from power and to invade their privileges. In northern Europe the process was slower, because there was not the same tradition of lay education, but things were moving in the same direction. By the middle of the century many civil servants in France and England were laymen, and others were only technically clergy and were inclined to marry and to return to the lay state. More than in the past, the clergy appeared as a privileged group within a society governed predominantly by laymen. Hence there arose a current of popular criticism against the hierarchy, which remained strong throughout the thirteenth century. The love of apostolic poverty, the dissatisfaction of radical Franciscans and the eschatological speculation of the time made it possible to construct a fierce polemic against the papal curia. Whereas the popes of the eleventh century had been champions of a new order, it was possible now for Frederick II to present himself as God's agent in purging the church and restoring it to apostolic simplicity. Troubadours such as Peire Cardenal and Guilhem Figueira wrote searing attacks on the papacy. Figueira's *D'un sirventes far* has already been quoted for its attacks on the misuse of crusading. It also attacked the pretensions of the clergy to political power:

Tant voletz aver   You want so much to be

del mon la senhoria . . .[9]   the lords of all the world . . .

In the more sober circles around Louis IX it was the practice to contrast life at the royal court with the corruption of the papacy. On the whole governments steered clear of heresy, even if they exacted a price for assisting in its repression, but there are some contrary examples: the followers of Amaury of Bène may have enjoyed protection inside the Capetian court, and there was a significant Catharist presence in the cities of north Italy, where the aggressive attitude of some communes towards the clergy may reflect sympathy with heresy. A searing sermon of James of Vitry accused communes of subverting ecclesiastical liberty and protecting heretics.[10]

Two coherent jurisdictions, temporal and spiritual, now confronted one another. The picture at the beginning of our period had been one of franchises and rights which depended more on custom than on a consistent theory. Such franchises often survived into the thirteenth century, but they came to exist within a pattern of law which reached into everyday life. As the settlers had cleared the forests, so the lawyers had brought definition to ordinary affairs. Marriage and will-making were subject to detailed regulations, property was taxed and its conditions of tenure defined. The fact that this extension of law-making was being carried out by not one, but two, sets of judges, tribunals, officers, and legislators carried with it the risk of enormous confusion: but before we examine the conflict of laws it is necessary to look briefly at the men who were at the head of secular government.

France and England, the two greatest western kingdoms, were held by two men who succeeded in boyhood and remained king for many years, Louis IX (1226–70) and Henry III (1216–72). Louis' character is not easy to read with confidence. We have personal reminiscences of him, especially the biography by Joinville, but they were mainly composed after his canonization in 1297 and under the influence of a reputation for sanctity. The indications are that he changed considerably after his absence on crusade from 1248 to 1254 and became more given to lengthy personal devotions and readier to accept the guidance of the friars and to further the political schemes

---

[9] R. T. Hill and T. G. Bergin (eds.), *Anthology of the Provençal Troubadours* (Yale, 1941), no. 122, pp. 178–9.

[10] James of Vitry, *Sermo ii ad burgenses* in A. Giry, *Documents sur les relations de la royauté avec les villes* (Paris, 1885), no. 20, p. 58.

of the papacy. Before the crusade he had been heavily influenced by his mother, Blanche of Castile, and continued the style of government she adopted during the minority. Louis was a conscientiously Christian king. He was an upholder of the church against heresy, and the generosity of his donations contrasted with the parsimonious ways of his grandfather Philip Augustus. The royal accounts survive only in a fragmentary form, but it appears that grants to churches consumed over a quarter of the expenditure in the summer of 1248, as compared with only one-fifteenth in 1202–3. His building projects included the Cistercian abbey of Royaumont, founded in 1228 as a memorial to Louis VIII and dedicated in 1236; the Sainte-Chapelle at Paris, designed to house the crown of thorns acquired from Constantinople in 1239; and the reconstruction of Saint-Denis (about 1237–54), accompanied by the design of new tombs for Louis's predecessors. These buildings were magnificent statements of the splendour of the Capetian house and its devotion to God. All of this did not make Louis subservient to the papacy. He defended the rights of the crown in spiritual as well as secular matters. He stands in a long tradition of Christian kings, convinced of their responsibility for the church in their realms. Henry III of England, his contemporary and close relative by marriage, shared many of Louis's assumptions and was influenced by him: the rebuilding of Westminster abbey which he began in July 1245 followed the projects at Saint-Denis and the Sainte-Chapelle and was conceived in a French architectural style. Henry, however, was much less able to dominate his baronage, among whom a pattern of constitutional opposition was emerging, and was heavily dependent on papal support. This had been invaluable during the minority, when the legates Gualo and Pandulf had helped to establish his position in face of French invasion, and thereafter Henry regarded the pope as an ally and was inclined to leave the barons and bishops unsupported in their complaints about papal exactions.

The collisions between the jurisdiction of church and state were limited by flexibility on both sides. The secular authorities were willing to concede a good deal to canon law: almost everywhere matrimonial and testamentary litigation was left to church courts in spite of the property issues which might be involved. It is true that in Lombardy marriage could be registered before a public notary and the civic authorities were inclined to assert an interest, and in England the barons at Merton in 1236 refused to adopt the canonical rule that bastards were legitimized by subsequent marriage: 'we do not want to change the laws of England'.[11] Yet these were the exceptions to a general willingness to recognize the church's jurisdiction. Another example of flexibility was the application of the rules governing criminous clerks. Alexander III's decretal *Et si clerici* had made this a matter for the bishop's court, and this ruling was accepted in England under the impact of Becket's murder. In France a royal ordinance of 1205 maintained the old practice under which the bishop would hand over guilty clergy for punishment by the secular arm, and this custom was accepted in part by Innocent III's decretal *Novimus* in 1209. Thereafter France adopted the practice of *Et si clerici*, as contained in a canon of the council of Château Gontier in 1231.[12] The eventual French practice interpreted clerical privilege more generously than did canon law.

Similarly the hierarchy did not expect to secure the full acceptance of its juridical claims. As Innocent III put it, 'many things are tolerated out of patience, which if they were brought to judgement should not be tolerated within the demands of justice'.[13] Litigation over patronage or advowson was a matter for the royal courts in England from the Constitutions of Clarendon onward, and they increasingly insisted that suits between clergy on secular matters should be heard before them. The expansion of ecclesiastical justice brought with it the issue of more sentences of excommunication, the effectiveness of which depended on the support of the lay power. Some governments were prepared to give unconditional support: in 1220 Frederick's *Privilege in favour of the Ecclesiastical Princes* promised to enforce such sentences, and in 1229 Blanche of Castile issued the ordinance *Cupientes* to support the prosecution of heretics in the southern provinces. But elsewhere Blanche and Louis IX opposed the indiscriminate use of excommunication: Joinville tells us that when Bishop Guy of Auxerre complained that excommunication was being widely disregarded, the king promised to apply sanctions against excommunicates 'provided that he were given full knowledge of the sentence in each case, so that he might judge whether it was just or not'.[14] Obviously, the more novel the claim, the more resistant the lay power tended to be: when Bishop Grosseteste, intent on stepping up the efficiency of visitation, began to demand sworn

---

[11] Discussed by F. M. Powicke, *King Henry III and the Lord Edward* (Oxford, 1947), 150–1.
[12] Mansi xxiii.237 can.20. [13] Greg. IX, *Decretals*, III.5.18 (471).
[14] Joinville in M. R. B. Shaw, *Chronicles of the Crusades* (Harmondsworth, 1963), 332.

testimony from laymen on a large scale, the king prohibited any such practice.

It was money—the exploitation of the national churches by papal taxation and provisions—which caused most trouble. Papal taxation did not have much of a prehistory.[15] The crusading taxes of 1199 and 1215 were followed in England by requests for subsidy issued by Honorius III in 1217 and 1225, both of them however for the assistance of the king. These few levies were succeeded by a heavier burden of taxation under Gregory IX and Innocent IV, and the problem was made worse by the fact that it was designed to support unpopular policies. The tenth of 1228 was to be used in the war against Frederick II, and it may have been matched in 1229 by a request for a subsidy from English laymen. The subsidy proposed for the eastern empire in 1238 was followed by another against Frederick II in 1239, and the papal-imperial conflict led to a fresh bout of demands in France and England in 1244–5. The clergy had reason to think they were faced with an unprecedented pressure, and this was strengthened by other forms of papal exaction. Innocent III had secured an annual tribute of 1,000 marks from England in 1213, and it continued to be paid by Henry III. He had also tried in 1205–7 and 1214 to secure the full proceeds of Peter's Pence in place of the sum of 300 marks which had become conventional. In 1225 Honorius III made a large proposal to the western churches generally: he offered to abolish all charges at the Roman curia and offer a free service in return for a grant of a prebend in every cathedral church, a fixed income from monasteries and collegiate churches, and perpetual gifts from the bishops. It was the most ambitious of the series of attempts to relieve by agreement the chronic underfunding of the Roman Church, but it was rejected by the French clergy at Bourges in November 1225 and the English at London in May 1226.

The growth of papal intervention was not necessarily in conflict with the interests of the Crown. Henry III was so dependent on papal support that he is said to have remarked in 1239, 'I neither will nor dare to oppose the lord pope in anything', and in France Louis was able to use the papal influence in episcopal appointments as a convenient way of advancing his own nominees.[16] The unpopularity

---

[15] For twelfth-century requests for subsidies see ch. 9.ii above. Presumably 1217 and 1225 were the application of the Fourth Lateran decision that papal consent was required for a clerical subsidy to the lay power.

[16] Henry's remark is recorded in Matthew Paris, *Chronica Majora*, RS, iv. 10.

of papal demands after 1238 had the effect of focusing national resentments against taxation and provisions. Matthew Paris, the great chronicler of St Albans, was an exemplar of conservative English attitudes, resentful of anything which took English money to Rome. He collected protests against Roman exactions, including a forceful memorandum by the rectors of Berkshire in 1240 in opposition to a proposed tax against the emperor. Secular weapons, they argued, may only be used against heretics; the Roman Church has its own patrimony and other churches have theirs, by the gift of kings and princes, in no way tributary to Rome; the churches belong to the care of the pope, not to his dominion and ownership.[17] Bishop Grosseteste, while he deplored many papal decisions, felt constrained to obey them, whereas the rectors simply dismissed papal demands upon their income as *ultra vires*. The spirit of the French opposition is contained in the protest made to the pope on behalf of Louis IX in 1247. It was an angry statement, objecting at length to both provisions and taxation. Innocent IV was rebuked for destroying the happy relations which had existed between the papacy and France, and it was argued that the endowments of the churches were the gift of kings and princes, at whose disposal they are in case of need.[18] Our period ended with serious tensions between the papacy and the western kingdoms, which foretold the conflicts of the last years of the century.

ii. *Frederick II*

There are striking similarities between the three major secular rulers in thirteenth-century Europe. All ascended the throne as minors, partly under the protection of papal legates, and reigned for many years. All were concerned with the reconstruction of government in their kingdoms. Two of them, however, Louis IX and Henry III, had the reputation of being devout members of the church, whereas Frederick II came to be regarded as its enemy. The contrast is the more remarkable in that there were obvious common interests between pope and emperor: Frederick's candidature to the empire had been promoted by Innocent III, and the Roman Church was anxious to have imperial support against heresy and in the defence of the Holy Land. The bitter quarrels which took place between

[17] *C&S* ii.288–92.
[18] Matthew Paris, *Chronica Majora*, RS, vi.99–112.

Frederick and the papacy were not the result of some inevitable law of nature. Some historians have found the cause of dispute in the originality of Frederick as a thinker and statesman. He has been perceived as the first modern man, a sceptic in religion and the designer of an absolutist state which left only a secondary place for the spiritual power. The brilliant and eccentric book by Ernst Kantorowicz presented Frederick as a man 'who had taken on himself a new mission'.[19] Sober assessment is made difficult by the exaggerated rhetoric of Frederick's contemporaries. Gregory IX had put a Dominican, James Buoncambio, in charge of his chancery and the former sober language was replaced by flaming encyclicals which bore the marks of mendicant enthusiasm. Innocent IV's chancery followed a more moderate style, but wild accusations were still current, especially in the circle of Cardinal Rainer of Viterbo. This group may have been the source of the pamphlet *Eger cui lenia* (end of 1245), an extreme statement of papal claims which was put into the mouth of Innocent IV. Meanwhile the imperial chancery under Peter della Vigna wrote cautiously in reply to these criticisms, but also on occasions employed a full-blown rhetoric developed at Bologna and imported new ideas into the presentation of the imperial office. The problem of distinguishing propaganda and reality is acute.

One famous accusation, that Frederick had denied the Christian faith, was always tentative. Gregory IX's letter of excommunication on 20 May 1239 merely indicated that action on such charges was being considered. On 12 July the pope wrote that Frederick had said the world had been deceived by three impostors, Christ, Moses, and Mahomet, and also that only fools believe in the virgin birth. Frederick at once denied having said anything of the sort, and the charge was not repeated by Innocent IV. Innocent's sentence of 12 July 1245 included heresy among the reasons for deposing the emperor, but claimed no more than solid grounds for suspicion, and the details he gave had little force. It is true that Frederick, more than most princes of the time, was interested in scientific and astrological learning, and that he sponsored translations from Arabic, including the work of Averroës. There is, however, no sign that he drew from them a system of sceptical beliefs, or that his own personal convictions were any different from conventional catholics of his day. His anti-heretical legislation, which was more severe than that

---

[19] E. Kantorowicz, *Frederick II* (NY, 1931), 607. The phrase is used here to describe a new phase in Frederick's policy, but Kantorowicz also stressed the consistency of the whole.

of other rulers, and his repeated offers to prove the orthodoxy of his belief, can be taken at face value.

This does not dispose of the possibility that the emperor, while his personal faith was conventional, had as his objective the realization of a new political ideal. New concepts were certainly exploited in the implementation of Frederick's programme. The *Liber Augustalis* of 1231 was designed to provide a coherent body of law which would unite the diverse customs within the kingdom of Sicily. He presented himself as legislating as emperor within the Regno—a marked change in the traditional position. Although the collection contained references to existing custom and to statutes of his predecessors, the greater part consisted of new edicts by the 'Augustus' himself, and he drew freely on the civil law expounded at Bologna. The book is a much more coherent piece of political philosophy than Bracton. The Roman law provided Frederick's advisers with new methods of glorifying the imperial office, including the idea that it existed to serve the cult of justice—a theme which deepened the ethical and religious content of secular government and which was worked out in the design of the monumental bridge-gate begun at Capua in 1234. Moreover in the current atmosphere of eschatological expectation Frederick was presented as the recipient of Biblical promises and the appointed deliverer of the Holy Land. These ideas first clearly surfaced in the address at the crown-wearing at Jerusalem and were actively promoted after his return to Italy in 1229. The claim that he desired to restore the church to apostolic simplicity won the sympathy of some groups of mendicants, including Elias of Cortona. We cannot be sure how seriously Frederick took these innovations in the presentation of the imperial office, but it would be a mistake to imagine that he stepped in one stride from the medieval to the modern world. If he was a long way from the world of Frederick Barbarossa, he was equally far from that of Marsilius of Padua, let alone Machiavelli. When he defined the relationship between spiritual and temporal powers, his language was conventional. Papacy and empire, he wrote in 1239, are like sun and moon, so that 'the greater communicates its brightness to the lesser'.[20] He acknowledged, at least under pressure, 'the full power in spiritual affairs granted by the Lord to the bishop of the holy Roman see'.[21]

[20] J. L. A. Huillard-Bréholles (ed.), *Historia Diplomatica Friderici Secundi* (Paris, 1857), V. 348.

[21] MGH Const ii. no. 262, p. 362.

These statements seem to be confirmed by his practice. The *Liber Augustalis* protected clerical exemption from lay courts and the rights of vacant churches; Sicilian clergy such as Archbishops Berard of Palermo (1214–51) and James of Capua (1225–40) were among his closest advisers; and he was ready to offer the Roman church generous terms in peace negotiations. His officials knew the canonists and used them to imperial advantage in arguing that the cardinals had an authority co-ordinate with that of the pope. The language of the imperial chancery may have alarmed papal supporters and exacerbated the quarrel, but its origins cannot be found in a design by Frederick to subvert the spiritual power.

The cause of the bitter series of conflicts appears to be not Frederick's advocacy of a new religion or a new state, but the collision between papal and imperial political interests. At the heart of the matter was the union of Sicily and the empire. When Innocent III had decided to support the cause of the young Frederick as emperor, he had attached the condition that he would transfer Sicily to his infant son Henry. Frederick had followed the opposite policy. He attached great importance to the imperial dignity, which he ascribed to 'the creator of all things . . . through whom we are guided to the summit of empire'.[22] So far from envisaging the separation of kingdom and empire, he looked towards their closer union and legislated in the Regno by imperial authority. His objective was to retain Sicily under his own control and to provide for the succession of his son to the empire. This was achieved in 1220 when the princes accepted Henry (VII) as king of the Romans, or successor, and the *fait accompli* was reluctantly recognized by Honorius III when he crowned Frederick on 22 November 1220. The early years under papal tutelege had left a scar. While popes congratulated themselves on the protection which the apostolic see had given him as an orphan, Frederick saw things very differently, complaining 'that the church had sent enemies into Apulia in the guise of protectors' and that 'the church had rejected him instead of protecting him as his guardian, and had placed in his father's house a stranger [Otto IV] who was not content with the empire and had aspired to the kingdom as well'.[23] Frederick saw the union of the two

---

[22] Letter of 10 Feb. 1221, Huillard-Bréholles (ed.), *Historia Diplomatica Fridenci Secundi*, ii.123.

[23] Letter of Honorius III early May 1226, discussed R. W. and A. J. Carlyle, *A History of Medieval Political Theory in the West*, v (Edinburgh, 1928), 236–7 n.

titles as his by divine gift and the Roman Church as a conspirator against this right.

The union of kingdom and empire intensified the conflicts which for thirty years had remained consistent elements in papal–imperial relations. One was the Papal State. Frederick had recognized its territorial integrity, including the duchy of Spoleto and march of Ancona. By and large he was faithful to this assurance until the final split of 1239, when he ordered its occupation, but the situation was always delicate because the Papal State formed a barrier across his communications and was in such disorder that imperial agents were tempted to intervene. A more acute problem was the character of Frederick's administration in the Regno and in particular his alleged invasion of the rights of the churches. There was ample scope for conflict. The position of the papacy as overlord, the need to recover royal rights which had been acquired by bishops and barons during the minority, and the promotion of royal servants in spite of the concession of freedom of election, all generated complaints. The most serious problem, however, was presented by the Lombard cities. Their success against Barbarossa had been followed by a whole generation in which there had been little of an imperial presence in Lombardy. The cities reacted violently to any type of intervention, while Frederick saw them as an unholy combination of heretics and rebels. He himself said that the Lombards were the main reason for his final breach with the papacy in 1239. Initially the cities, with their invasions of clerical privilege and protection of heretics, were not obvious allies of the papacy. The curia may have feared that if the Lombards were subjugated the emperor would turn against the Papal State, but it is hard to find documentary support for this suggestion. A more immediate pressure was the anger of the popes at the deflection of effort from the crusade. In 1226 the emperor's operations in Lombardy threatened to put off once more his much postponed expedition, and in 1236 they prevented him from offering the pope help in the east or at Rome. Honorius and Gregory seem to have had no sympathy for the imperial attempt to recover long-lost rights in Lombardy; when they functioned as arbitrators their whole thrust was to prevent war between Christians and obtain forces for the crusade from both sides.

At first there seemed little reason to suppose that these issues would lead to catastrophic conflict. Innocent III's successor Honorius III was a member of a family of the middle Roman nobility, the

Savelli, and had been a highly efficient chamberlain in the curia of Celestine III and the compiler of the *Liber Censuum*. He has sometimes been presented as a pale and senile shadow of Innocent, but in reality he was probably little older than his predecessor (and therefore in his fifties when he became pope) and he had not been one of the in-group who had advised Innocent and executed his policy. Nevertheless his priorities were much the same, as they were bound to be: the crusade, action against heresy, and the protection of papal territory. The personal union which Frederick had secured between Sicily and the empire in 1220 could not be undone, but the pope at least received an undertaking that his overlordship over Sicily was not in question. Frederick had emerged into international politics as the favourite son of the Roman church, and in spite of difficulties the spirit of co-operation survived for most of the pontificate of Honorius. It was shaken in 1226 when Frederick, having reasserted his authority in Sicily, was actively preparing his crusade, and summoned an imperial Diet to settle affairs before his departure. His choice for a venue, Cremona, one of the most fiercely imperialist of the Lombard cities, was provocative. Milan, the champion of Lombard liberties, felt threatened and secured the renewal of the League. The emperor, who had not expected so violent a reaction, requested the pope's mediation, and a compromise settlement seemed close when Honorius died on 18 March 1227. There had been other signs of tension in his last year: Frederick was levying military service from the Papal State, and a formal complaint from the pope about the mistreatment of the Sicilian church produced, for the first time, a really acrimonious correspondence.

The next day Cardinal Hugolino of Ostia was elected with the title Gregory IX. He was a close relative and associate of Innocent III, and very different from his immediate predecessor. Gregory was a man of ardent spirituality, an early friend of the friars, had formed close contacts in Lombardy as legate there in 1221, and shared to the full the suspicions of the emperor which were developing in the curia. When Frederick, struck down by illness, failed to set out on crusade, Gregory would tolerate no delay and pronounced a sentence of excommunication on 29 September 1227. He refused even to hear the apologies of the emperor's envoys, issued a tendentious encyclical to the Christian world on 10 October, and renewed Honorius's complaint about the Sicilian church. Instead of seeking a settlement Frederick left for the crusade while still excommunicated.

This provoked a papal invasion of the Regno at the beginning of 1229. The return of Frederick to Brindisi in June 1229 led to the rapid collapse of the invasion, and after lengthy negotiations peace was concluded at San Germano on 23 July 1230. Frederick, although he was the victor on the field of battle, agreed to guarantee the freedom of the Sicilian church from taxation, secular jurisdiction, and royal intervention in episcopal elections.

There followed some years of normal relations between empire and papacy. In 1234 and 1235 they were even allies. Frederick needed support against the rebellion of his son Henry in Germany and Gregory was hoping for help against the Romans, who had exiled him from the city. There was a friendly meeting at Rieti; the pope proposed a marriage between Frederick and the English royal house; and the emperor advertised his sympathy for mendicant piety by a well publicized visit to the shrine of his relative, St Elizabeth of Hungary, at Marburg. The renewal of the quarrel was the result of Frederick's determination to proceed against the Lombards, who had been Henry's allies. Attempts by the pope to dissuade him were unsuccessful, and on 23 October 1236 Gregory wrote a letter which made unrestrained use of the Donation of Constantine. He argued that the emperor received the power of the sword in his coronation, but that the pope did not surrender the substance of his jurisdiction. The letter has been seen as an attempt 'to shift the ground of the conflict from the Lombard question to the broader issue of world dominion', but it seems to be little more than a transient effort to find a theoretical ground for interference in political affairs.[24] The emphatic defeat of the League at Cortenuova on 27 November 1237 left Milan looking for peace terms, but the emperor's demands were too high, and the failure of the imperial army to capture Brescia gave new heart to the resistance. From the later months of 1238 Gregory was moving towards an open breach, in spite of Frederick's appeals to the cardinals to prevent it. On Palm Sunday, 20 March 1239 the pope excommunicated the emperor for the second time. Most of the charges related to the affairs of the Sicilian church, and the Lombard communes were not even mentioned. The excommunication generated an immediate pamphlet war, with both sides appealing for the support of the European princes, and the mendicants pressed into service as propagandists for the papacy. On the whole public opinion was on Frederick's side. In the winter of 1239-40 much of the Papal

---

[24] T. C. van Cleve, *The Emperor Frederick II of Hohenstaufen* (Oxford, 1972), 396.

State was occupied and put under imperial administrators. Rome itself seemed about to fall, but on 22 February 1240 the aged Gregory staged a grand procession with Rome's most precious relics, the heads of Peter and Paul, and rallied the population. The German princes and Cardinal John Colonna were active in mediating, but Gregory undermined their efforts by summoning a general council to meet at Rome at Easter 1241. The bull which summoned it made clear Gregory's idea of its function, for he spoke of 'the one pastor possessing fullness of power, and the others given the part of solicitude as members in the head'.[25] On 3 May 1241 the Sicilian fleet attacked the convoy carrying bishops to Rome and captured several of them along with two cardinals. On 21 August 1241, unable to leave the unhealthy city in the heat of summer, Gregory IX died.

By this time the cardinals' college was much depleted in number. There were only nine cardinals at Rome, in addition to the two in captivity and John Colonna with the emperor outside. Even this group was divided, and only proceeded to an election when isolated in atrocious conditions by the anti-papal Roman senator—the first, and one of the most uncomfortable, of the papal conclaves. The new pope, Celestine IV, lived for less than three weeks. Most of the cardinals hastily left Rome, and a long vacancy followed until 25 June 1243, with the election of Cardinal Sinibaldo Fieschi, an outstanding canon lawyer and member of a Genoese family, as Innocent IV. The long negotiations which followed reached agreement on Holy Thursday, 31 March 1244. The emperor agreed to satisfy the Roman Church on every point, including the restoration of the Papal State. Even so the peace broke down at the last moment as a result of a dispute over the terms for papal arbitration in Lombardy and over the timing of Frederick's absolution. There is no reason to think that Innocent was not in earnest in attempting to reach a settlement, but he regarded the emperor's attitude with extreme suspicion. The events of the past few years had deepened the uneasiness of even moderates in the curia, and one group led by Cardinal Rainer of Viterbo was anti-imperial beyond all restraint. Innocent decided that peace was unattainable and on 7 July 1244 he fled from Italy to take refuge at Lyon, an imperial city close to the French frontier.

There followed a state of total war between empire and papacy. A general council of some 150 prelates opened at Lyon on 26 June 1245.

[25] Cited by van Cleve, *The Emperor Frederick II*, 447 n.

The council proceeded to a definitive sentence of excommunication and deposition. The charges reflected recent events: wilful perjury, violation of the peace, sacrilege by the capture of cardinals, and suspicion of heresy. Innocent was able to shake the fabric of Frederick's power more significantly than his predecessor had done: an anti-king was elected in Germany, substantial parts of Frederick's support there dissolved, and there was an alarming assassination plot among the imperial advisers. The war in Lombardy was still in progress, however, when Frederick died on 13 December 1250. In a sense, it left the papacy victorious, if only by default. The union of Sicily and the empire was in effect dissolved; but even this was only a partial success. The animosity between the popes and the Hohenstaufen had become so deadly that the Roman church could not feel safe while there was a Hohenstaufen state in existence in southern Italy. The attempt to remove the remaining threat bound the popes to a new cycle of political, military and financial effort, and eventually to the acceptance of Capetian protection.

The conflict had arisen, not from any great effort by Frederick to supplant the existing constitution of the church, but from that range of mixed political and religious concerns which is so prominent in the history of the medieval papacy. Frederick must certainly share responsibility for the outbreak of the quarrel. He had united the kingdom and empire in defiance of his own undertaking; his repeated postponement of his crusade was damaging and exasperating: he may (the matter is not clear) have given grounds for offence by his exploitation of the Sicilian church; above all, his operations against the Lombards in 1226 and 1236 alarmed the papacy because they amounted to a rejection of the policy of co-operation in the cause of the crusade. Nevertheless the dangers to the papacy of a total war were great. The effort could only be sustained by the exploitation of the spiritual headship of the popes and a great increase in taxation, provisions, and indulgences. The aim was not the defeat of the infidel, but warfare against Christians, and Italian writers commented that the war was a particularly savage one. The mid-thirteenth century saw a marked change in the character of the medieval papacy. Since the time of Leo IX, whatever the scope of their political involvements, most popes had been patrons of reform and renewal, and the Fourth Lateran Council had produced an impressive programme to this end. The council of Lyon in 1245 issued no canons at all for the spiritual welfare of the church, although there was a good deal of technical legislation about the hearing of causes. Perhaps this was an extreme case, but it is hard to think of later popes who were leaders of international reform in the old style. Although the changing character of the papacy had a number of causes, the total war with Frederick II was perhaps the most immediate one.

iii. *The Papal Monarchy in the Thirteenth Century*

The thirteenth century was the high point of the papal monarchy. Innocent III had intervened with far more energy than the twelfth-century popes in the affairs of the empire, and Innocent IV took the struggle against the emperor even further. The theoretical structure which upheld the papal dominance was given far more solidity. Innocent III imported into his letters a range of concepts which had hitherto been little used to support the dignity of the pope: vicar of Christ, fullness of power, priest-king like Mechizadek. The canonists moved sharply in the direction of papal sovereignty, and the letter *Eger cui lenia* was a complete statement of papal authority over the world. Only *Unam sanctam*, the product of a later and more desperate crisis, equals it in the range of its claims.

It is this situation which has led historians such as Walter Ullmann to present the period as the fullest statement of the hierocratic theory, which saw the papacy as the source of all authority upon earth and denied the old, dualist division betweeen the two powers of church and state. It can be readily agreed that there are some statements which present the hierocratic theory without reservation, but a broader look at the evidence reveals the same pattern of qualification or incoherences which we have encountered in earlier statements of papal theory. *Eger cui lenia* is untypical, and displays marked contrasts with the more measured teaching of Innocent IV as a canonist in his commentaries. We do not know how such a conflict arose: the most probable explanation is that *Eger cui lenia*, although written in Innocent's name, was really a product of Cardinal Rainer's passionate propaganda. The commentaries reflect the ambiguities which had always been apparent in the treatment of the papal office in canon law. Canonists were not political philosophers but lawyers concerned with the application of texts to particular problems. Hence it is that Innocent IV stood in the tradition of Innocent III in insisting on the rights of secular governments. The theory that the

Roman Church may intervene on special occasions (*casualiter*) was given firmer shape by the detailed discussion of the grounds for such intervention. There were times when Innocent even insisted on greater independence for the secular power. His concern for the world outside Christendom led him to insist that the political authority of unbelievers was authentic and lawful—a position questioned by other canonists.

Even with regard to papal authority within the church, the canonists continued to insist that it had limits. These were the articles of the faith, the common good of the church, and the obligation not to create scandal to the brethren. Hostiensis declared of the pope that '*all things are lawful* to him, provided that he does not act against the faith . . . and provided that he does not offend God by mortal sin'. Accordingly, the pope should take great care in the issue of provisions to benefices, in hearing causes, and in the grant of privileges.[26] These were real limitations, but they existed in a framework of emphatic declarations about the wide scope of papal sovereignty, many of which were elaborations of language introduced by Innocent III, whose borrowings from theology and rhetoric produced a permanent distortion in the previous thinking of the lawyers. Thus the idea of the pope as the vicar of Christ (a rare concept in law before 1198) was interpreted as granting to him all the powers which belonged to Christ on earth. Innocent IV elaborated this notion by a vision of human history as consisting of a series of governments provided by the providence of God for the regulation of human affairs, of which the authority of the papacy was the last. In this respect the statement in *Eger cui lenia* that 'we exercise on earth the general legation of the king of kings' was in line with papal thinking.[27] It is therefore impossible to categorize papal doctrine in the simple terms 'hierocratic' or 'dualist'. Canonists were in no doubt that different powers had been ordained for the government of the church and the state. The very dignity of the spiritual power, which ultimately meant that it was the superior, also meant that it should not be debased by the decision of merely human affairs. Within the church, too, however great the authority of the apostolic see, no one supposed that it was the only dignity appointed by God, and it is rare even to find a systematic argument that all other

[26] L. Buisson, *Potestas und Caritas* (Cologne/Graz, 1958), 90 n. The reference is to 1 Cor. 6: 12.

[27] P. Herde in *DAEM* 23 (1967), 517.

dignities derived their authority from the pope. The ambiguities of canon law were not self-contradictions but attempts to formulate legal doctrines appropriate to a complex reality. In that sense they bear a distant similarity to modern constitutional theories which attempt to reconcile the authority of the state with the guarantee of individual or regional liberties.

The combination of autocracy with corporate power is illustrated by the cardinals. Already in the twelfth century they had become the electors of popes, their advisers, the auditors of causes in the papal curia, and the usual source of legates. With growing centralization of authority in the thirteenth century the link between the cardinals and the popes came to be more closely defined. Admittedly different popes had different styles in their dealings with the cardinals. Innocent III relied upon a small group of favoured advisers, among them Peter of Capua, Robert of Courson, and Hugolino, the later Gregory IX. Other cardinals were pushed to the periphery of influence, and Innocent did not hesitate to abandon favourites when he disapproved of their conduct of policy. In 1216 there was a sharp change with the accession of Honorius III, himself one of the cardinals who had lost power under his predecessor. He used almost the whole college in the business of the curia, and only one or two members were of special significance. No pope, however, made a deliberate effort to escape from the power of the cardinals, whom they regarded as indispensible agents. For most of the first half of the thirteenth century they were a small group, numbering eighteen at the accession of Gregory IX and only twelve in the electoral crisis after his death. The smallness of the college helped to reduce tensions with the popes: Innocent IV was able to provide himself with advisers to his own mind by nominating no less than twelve new cardinals on 28 May 1244, thus swamping any dissent. The growing emphasis on papal authority had the effect of increasing the status of the cardinals. In 1225 the *Summi providentia principis* of Honorius III imposed severe penalties for offences against them in terms which implied that they participated in the majesty of the pope himself. Innocent IV, responding to the problems which had become manifest in the recent papal election, drafted a measure, *Quia frequenter*, which would have given the power of immediate election to those cardinals present at the curia at the death of a pope—a striking amendment to the 1179 electoral decree which in the event was never implemented. He also bestowed on them the right to wear the red hat as a symbol of office. By the middle of the century we hear from the canonist Hostiensis that the cardinals were 'commonly and generally known as the sacred college'. It came to be accepted that their office rested upon divine ordinance. This may be the meaning of the decretal *Per venerabilem* of 1202, where the cardinals are apparently regarded as descended from the Levitical priests, but there is nothing else in the letters of Innocent III which bears out such an interpretation.[28] The Biblical authority of the cardinals next appeared in a letter of Frederick II on 10 March 1239, which described them as successors of the apostles.[29] This is confirmed by Gregory IX's reference to them in 1241 as 'lawful successors of the apostles'.[30] The assumption was also growing that pope and cardinals shared the same authority, the college being 'united by God with the pope, because it is one and the same with him'.[31] Utterances about the universal authority of Rome are by no means equivalent to assertions of papal authority; as canonists noted, the title 'Roman Church' might mean the whole catholic church, or the pope and cardinals, or the pope alone.

Immensely more business was now being brought from all parts of Christendom before the curia, which was obliged to restructure its organization accordingly. In a way typical of the contemporary style of 'rescript government' the papal officers were responding to public demand rather than themselves formulating new policies.[32] Already by 1192 we have a description of writers of petitions sitting at the entrance to the Lateran palace surrounded by customers.[33] The increasing level of business led to the adoption of routine. By 1180 there were signs of the distinction of two types of letters, the later letters of justice and letters of grace, although the curia was still far from the schematization of the later thirteenth century. Petitions for favours or 'graces' would be embodied in a letter to be read or checked before the pope for approval. Applications for judicial instructions were initially processed in a more routine way, but it

---

[28] See the discussion by W. Maleczek, *Papst und Kardinalskolleg 1191–1216* (Vienna, 1984), 284–5. The reference is to Deut. 17: 8–12.

[29] Huillard-Bréholles (ed.), *Historia Diplomatica Friderici Secundi* v.i. 282.

[30] Letter of Gregory IX, MGH Ep. Saec. XIII, I, no. 827, p.726 (although the reference may not be specific to cardinals).

[31] For the development of language of this type, see J. Lecler, 'Pars corporis papae', in *L'homme devant Dieu: mélanges offerts à H. de Lubac* (Paris, 1964), 183–98.

[32] On the nature of rescript government see ch. 9: ii above.

[33] R. Davidsohn, 'Das Petitions-Büreau der päpstlichen Kanzlei', *Neues Archiv* 16 (1891), 638–9.

was found necessary to provide special facilities for cases where the other party entered an objection or 'contradiction'. The *Audientia litterarum contradictarum* is first mentioned in connection with a case brought by Evesham Abbey in 1205/6. By 1216/7 it had a regular officer, the auditor, and soon its auditors included jurists of outstanding reputation, including Sinibaldo Fieschi, the later Innocent IV. Powerful bodies found it advisable to retain permanent representatives or proctors at the curia to keep an eye on petitions and appeals which might damage their interests; the first definite instance of a 'standing' proctor can be found in 1241. Originally there was no established bench of judges and each case was referred to suitably experienced cardinals or chaplains. The judges were sometimes surprisingly impermanent, and we even find Innocent III delegating a case to two bishops who happened to be visiting Rome at the time. There was still no indication of a permanent tribunal at the time of the issue of the Gregorian decretals in 1234, but under Innocent IV we find two committees of regular auditors. Even so, the principle that the pope was the judge continued to be a reality, for an auditor was normally empowered to conduct the hearings and then refer the file of proceedings to the pope for decision. The pressure of business, which was leading to the reorganization of judicial activities, was even more evident in the writing-office or chancery. Once again Innocent III appears as a major innovator; Peter Herde has referred to 'a new institution of the papal chancery, which according to everything we know was founded by Innocent III'.[34] In the twelfth century the ordinary city writers of Rome prepared petitions and the letters which were issued in response. Innocent was concerned to discover, immediately after he became pope, that there had been several cases of forgery, and this was the immediate cause of his reform of the chancery. A writers' college was established on the lines of the craft guilds frequent in Italian cities, and the office of corrector established with the special function of making sure that letters were written in accordance with the complex rules of diction, which made them difficult to imitate. The first corrector of whom we know is M. Peter Mark in 1212. The increasingly professional character of the chancery was reflected in the disappearance of the office of cardinal chancellor. This had already happened intermittently in the twelfth century, and from 1216 the chancery finally lost its titular head and was supervised by a

[34] P. Herde, *Audientia Litterarum Contradictarum* (Tübingen, 1970), 20.

vice-chancellor who actually attended to the business. By 1250 the curia had been streamlined to deal with the vast press of business and had assumed the outline which it was to retain, with few major changes, until the sixteenth century.

This hyperactive curia needed firm lines of communication with the provinces. Since the time of Gregory VII the office of legate had provided the main system of ambassadors, and this remained true until the nuncio emerged in the sixteenth century. The contribution of the thirteenth century was to emphasize the authority of the legate and to define his functions. To express the legate's power to speak in the name of the pope he came to wear a version of the papal garments. In 1213 Pelagius went to Constantinople 'dressed in red shoes and garments', and Hostiensis described legates as wearing red clothes, gilded shoes and having a horse with white reins. Gratian had been vague about legates; indeed, neither he nor the decretists who commented on him had distinguished between a legate and a judge delegate, who by the thirteenth century was recognized as quite a different animal. By the time of Gregory IX a formal distinction had been made between three legatine commissions. The legate *a latere* (from the pope's side) virtually exercised papal authority in the region to which he had been sent, and was usually a cardinal. His special status was first clearly indicated in a decretal of Gregory IX.[35] A legate with a more limited commission was known as a *legatus missus*, and was again distinguished from an archbishop who had been given a legatine status, the native legate or *legatus natus*.

The despatch of a legate was a rare and special occasion. The vast number of rescripts issued might seem to imply an elaborate postal system, but the reality was rather different. Many were delivered by the petitioners to whom they were issued and who presented them to the bishop or his officers for enforcement. In the great majority of cases the local investigation and hearing was entrusted to judges delegate. In the twelfth century they had mostly been bishops, but with the increasing number of trained canon lawyers it became possible to widen the pool. One active delegate in England was Richard of Mores, prior of the Augustinian house of Dunstable from 1212 to 1242, who was probably the author of a handbook on procedure and who can be traced as delegate in forty-eight suits. The parties continued to have the right to initiate an appeal at any stage in

[35] Greg. IX, *Decretals*, I.30.8 (185).

its progress before the local judges, not merely after an adverse decision, and the pope's status was thus that of 'universal ordinary', accessible to everyone with a grievance and money to pursue it. It was a curious system, because in the end the enforcement of the sentence of judges delegate depended on the authority of the bishop and his officers to apply it. Many of the cases heard, moreover, ended not in sentence but in arbitration—a statement which is true of almost all tribunals in medieval society. Such suits were numerous, and they included some of the most important issues as well as minor ones. Christopher Cheney has found traces of 270 lawsuits brought before the curia from England during the eighteen years of Innocent III, and estimates that these may be the survivors of an original 800. A small number was heard by auditors in the curia, but the vast majority went by commission to judges delegate in England.

Appeals to Rome continued to be an expensive way of proceeding. The initial communication cost money and the stream of complaints about charges at the curia went on unabated in the thirteenth century. Buoncampagno of Florence, writing a formulary on curial practice, included a letter to a bishop who had won his case 'by the grace of God and the merits of the blessed martyrs Albinus and Rufinus', those favourite Roman saints of silver and gold.[36] Why, if papal justice was expensive, was it in such high demand? The most obvious reason was that appellants did not like the way that a case was going in the bishop's court, or that they could not expect a favourable hearing in their own country or diocese. It was also important that the procedure began with an enormous advantage for the appellant. In most cases his own statement of his case was incorporated in the commission, which would be directed to judges whom he had himself proposed. The procedure thereafter was more fairly weighted, but it gave a good start to a party who did not fancy the local prospects. Once the procedure was in being it tended to be self-perpetuating because of the likelihood that an influential litigant would appeal; it was better to go to the papal tribunal at once rather than face the prospect of having to argue the case twice. Even if the matter was ended by agreement it would be advantageous to have this confirmed by a jurisdiction which promised a final settlement. It is more difficult to say whether the papal jurisdiction was actually more efficient. Although there was a considerable overlap in

[36] For details and examples see C. R. Cheney, *Pope Innocent III and England* (Stuttgart, 1976), 110.

personnel with the diocesan courts, it is likely that the most expert lawyers were employed as judges delegate. There are instances of litigants who said that the delegates were quicker, and in fact they do seem to have been reasonably expeditious, allowing for the time involved in obtaining the original commission from the curia. In all probability, however, what induced litigants to turn to the papal jurisdiction was the initial advantage which it offered the appellant and the inclination to use the tribunal in which the case was likely to end.

These were the attractions for litigants. The question why the papacy was willing to turn its household into a vast international lawcourt in face of critics from St Bernard onwards is a different one. Undoubtedly the fact that through this mechanism some people received a justice which would otherwise have been denied them by powerful local interests encouraged popes to extend and perfect it, and in particular it provided a means of defending the rights of the church against lay invasion. Perhaps even more significant was the way in which the extension of jurisdiction also carried with it the extension of law. The papacy had no regular means of legislation, for great councils were held only once in a generation, and the concern of the western church to Christianize society, and apply a standard system of law in such matters as marriage, took the form not of issuing statutes but of extending the accessibility of its courts. Alongside these larger questions of policy was undoubtedly the operation of self-interest. More suits meant more fees for writers, proctors, and advocates, as well as more gifts for cardinals with an elastic conscience. Whatever the motives, the litigants and the curia between them had conspired to create a system of appeals of enormous range and extent by the end of our period.

The extension of the appellate jurisdiction of the papacy was closely connected with a drastic change in the nature of canon law. The staple work of canonists in the later twelfth century had been the production of commentaries on the collection of Gratian, which embodied the traditional law of the western church, but even before 1200 a new law was appearing side by side with the old. From Alexander III onwards popes were building it up through the issue of decretal letters, defining norms of conduct and law, all by rulings upon problems individually referred. The *ius novum* was formed almost entirely of collections of decretals. Practitioners began to assemble small 'primitive' collections as aids in the hearing of cases from about 1180. Some seventy such dossiers are known, with a large proportion of English authorship. The next stage was the formation of systematic collections divided according to subject matter, the *Five ancient collections* (*Quinque Compilationes Antique*) beginning with Bernard of Pavia about 1190. Soon the pope himself began to authorize decretal collections. The *Third Compilation*, by Peter of Benevento, was made on the instructions of Innocent III, who recommended it to the masters of Bologna for use 'both in judgements and in the schools', although his concern was not the conscious shaping of a new legal system, but the provision of a body of texts of guaranteed authenticity. In 1226 Honorius III similarly authorized the *Fifth Compilation*, echoing his predessor's phrase more firmly to make it clear that there was an obligation to apply it.

The major work of ordering the whole body of decretals was undertaken by Raymond of Peñafort on the order of Gregory IX in 1230. Raymond was given wide discretion to edit the earlier collections in order to produce a single volume of letters whose rulings were to be universally applicable. The whole material was published on 5 September 1234 by the bull *Rex pacificus*. In order to give coherence to some sections Raymond was permitted to request a papal ruling on certain matters which were not made fully clear in existing decretals, and there are something over sixty such special decretals in the collection. It was known simply as the *New Compilation* or (significantly) the *Corpus Iuris*, and with it the body of canon law had almost received the form in which it was to exist until 1917. The *Decretum* of Gratian and the Gregorian compilation formed the old and new testaments of the legal revelation. While the decretal collections were being assembled legal commentaries were already appearing, provided by canonists known as the decretalists in contrast with the decretists who had worked on Gratian. The 'ordinary' gloss, which became the basis for study, was produced by Johannes Teutonicus on the *Ancient Compilations*, and then updated by Bartholomew of Brixen by the incorporation of the necessary references to the now standard Gregorian collection. True, the issue of decretals had not stopped, and more were added to the corpus of canon law, including the new provisions or *novelle* of Innocent IV; but their character had changed. They were far fewer in number, and they were not responses to consultations in particular cases but were much more like legislation of a modern kind. This had already been true of the decretals issued by Gregory IX for Raymond's guidance, and the *novelle* of Innocent IV consisted mainly of canons from the Council of Lyon and the great decretal *Romana ecclesia* in 1246, which went far beyond the case to which it was addressed and provided a series of rulings about the authority of metropolitans and the jurisdictions of bishops' officials. When Hostiensis, the greatest canonist of the middle years of the century, pointed to the authority of 'a constitution . . . which the pope pronounces by his own volition and puts in writing without the advice of his brethren', he was announcing the end of the golden age of decretals.[37] The assumptions which had brought canon law into the shape which it would retain for so long were different from that: it was the product of rescript government, the form which the papal monarchy had taken in its most influential period, which was now coming to an end.

[37] Cited G. Le Bras, *Histoire du droit . . . de l'église en Occident* VII (Paris, 1965), 150 n.

CONCLUSIONS

The period of church history which we have studied in this volume allows no facile summary with which to end. It is fair to talk about the programme of the reforming papacy, but not easy to see its consistent application in subsequent generations. In many areas of activity, we see not one change but a series of successive transformations, as Cluniacs and Cistercians and friars emerged in turn as the most admired version of the religious life, or as the pendulum of Paris theology swung from speculation to pastoral care and back again. Although the institutions of the thirteenth-century church are far more familiar to our eyes than those of two centuries before, there is no simple tale of 'modernization' to be told here. Sometimes the currents apparently flowed the wrong way: Thomas Merton could use the spirituality of the early Cistercians as a key to an understanding of our own dilemmas, but few now would feel affinity to the well-oiled order of the mid-thirteenth century. To contemporaries the changes seemed so far-reaching that German thinkers sought to find room within the conservative Augustinian view of history for a concept of real historical progress, and Joachim of Fiore came to see history as a series of ages in which revolutions were worked by the power of God. None of this points to the formulation of neat conclusions. Yet it remains true that during these 200 years the Roman Church had never enjoyed such authority in the western churches as a whole, and arguably it was never again (perhaps not even in the sixteenth century) going to display such initiative in creating and encouraging new movements. There is therefore an obligation, at the end of this long haul, to offer the reader some oversimplifications about the way in which papal direction had shaped church history.

One aspect is relatively easy to describe. The zone of control covered by western Christendom had undergone some significant changes. Within Europe only Lithuania retained an official pagan cult, and the frontiers of the Christian states had advanced to the

Mediterranean seaboard at almost all points. Sicily had been recovered early and by 1252 much the greatest part of Spain and Portugal lay under Christian rule, although Granada was to survive for another two centuries as a totally Moorish kingdom. Since the great enterprise to create a Christian kingdom of Jerusalem had by 1250 retained only a few toe-holds in Syria the effect was to draw the frontier between Christendom and Islam even more firmly along the Mediterranean. This rather obvious geographical reflection must not distract us from noticing two other features of significance. Since 1204 Latin Christendom had become dominant in the eastern Mediterranean, and Orthodoxy had faded into a politically second-ary role from which it was never, with the very important exception of Russia, fully to emerge. Moreover the ambitious plans for missions in Africa and Asia, which were to enjoy little success, nevertheless left behind them in the thinking of the church some seeds which were to fructify remarkably in the sixteenth century.

Christianity had expanded in its geographical coverage; it had increased immensely more in its impact upon hearts and minds. We may think first here of the much more interior spirituality which was developed among the Cistercians, and made popular by the Franciscans; and of the growth of a new Christian folklore and story-telling in town and country. Underlying these was a profound shift in the understanding of worship and the cure of souls. The Roman Church moved from its original cultic reform programme (if the sacrifice was to be acceptable, the priest must have his hands clean from simony and women) to an attempt to prescribe appropriate behaviour for all sorts and conditions of men, and thence to an ideal of care for individual souls, all of whom were to make their annual confession to their own priest. A network of parochial control spread throughout Christendom, and (at least in some parts of the Continent) the dioceses developed records which were no longer purely titles to property rights, but came to include information about the parochial clergy indispensible to their proper supervision. From the Fourth Lateran creed onwards, a more precise definition of the faith emerged in line with the teaching of Paris theology. While *symbolum* remained the standard term for a creed, we significantly begin to hear of 'articles' of belief: a declaration of faith was being seen less as a proclamation of a cosmic commitment and more as adherence to a set of defined propositions. This growing grasp and control rested partly upon its moral strength and acceptability, partly on the excellent legal and administrative services which the papal curia came to offer. In the last resort, however, the church became increasingly ready to turn to force. It always recognized that to enforce a decree of excommunication, or still more to repress a group of heretics, it needed the help of the secular arm. Far more strikingly than this, however, the church developed perhaps the only two effective repressive mechanisms which have ever developed from within Christianity: crusade and inquisition. In both, the role of the Roman Church was central, for Urban II proclaimed the First Crusade in 1095 and Gregory IX issued the first commissions of inquisition in the early 1230s; and crusade and inquisition both still influence our images of repression and warfare.

This pattern of care, control, and repression was an international one, and this too was a new development of our period. True, if we could visit medieval Europe we would be struck by its intense localisms. Major churches had their own liturgical customs, cities championed their own saints or protected their own heretics from among their favourite sons, and nobles ran courts of warfare, love, and piety in whatever combination they thought fit. Yet the elements of growing internationalism were powerful. The most dramatic of all was perhaps the vast struggle of western Christendom to extend its boundaries through the crusading endeavour. There were international religious orders: the Cistercians required the same daily routine to be applied from the Scottish borders to the mountains of Calabria, and the friars expected their members to be available for transfer between houses and if necessary between countries and continents. Paris and Bologna were truly international universities. At the heart of this process stood the Roman Church itself, which during these years completed the process of development from the local church of Rome to a curia which recruited personnel from many parts of the west to run an international organization, which had largely lost its local connections in Rome and which for long periods was unable to enter the city at all.

We can well understand how such developments gave rise to the rhetoric of papal lordship and even of papal monarchy. We have also seen reasons why such rhetoric should not be taken too seriously. Many canonists were aware of the qualifications which had to be made: the God-given right of the secular power to run its own affairs and the duty of the pope to uphold the faith and proper order of the entire church. Absolutist claims which ignored these limitations were rare, unrealistic, and usually the polemical product of a critical situation. As we have seen, the machinery of government was not designed to define a policy and impose it upon an unwilling society, and the enormous growth in the influence of the curia during these centuries can be ascribed mainly to two things. One was the demand throughout Europe for an organization which would offer protection, exemption, or relief to the great numbers of petitioners who addressed it, from great monasteries to distressed townswomen and communities of peasants. The other was the long tradition of alliance between Rome and creative movements in the western church as a whole. Once Leo IX had put the control of the Roman Church into the hands of the northern reformers, Rome became a natural champion for all those who were dissatisfied with conditions within their local churches. There are some remarkable examples of this championing of radicalism, ranging from the lay strike directed against simoniacal clergy to the welcome extended by the great Innocent III to the *poverello* of Assisi. Perhaps it is unfair to say that even the mid-thirteenth-century papacy had lost this natural sympathy with radicalism, for Gregory IX was devoted to the friars and Innocent IV gave Clare her longed-for privilege of poverty. It may be more correct to see the papacy as the victim of its own success. As it exploited its financial and administrative opportunities more widely (through provisions, crusade commutations, income taxes) the western church as a whole became more aware of the use of these resources for political ends in Italy. After 1250, it is hard to find the same championing of international reform or to think of great initiatives in the old style; and the tide of complaints about the curia, which had in all conscience been high enough since early in the twelfth century, rose to a mighty flood.

BIBLIOGRAPHY

The amount of publication in this field is enormous, and the purpose of this selection is to mention important works, usually recent, which will take further the discussion of subjects considered in the text. For reasons of space I have not included books which were of importance in the development of a topic if they no longer provide a natural starting-point for the student; nor have I normally attempted to cover editions of sources. English translations of modern works are shown under the date of their publication in this country. In every section I have tried to include at least one work with a substantial bibliography of its own. Some important periodicals and records series may be found in the list of Abbreviations at the beginning of the book.

GENERAL

Medieval church history. The most obvious starting-point for those interested in the detailed history of the medieval church is H. Jedin and J. Dolan (eds.), *History of the Church*: vol. iii, *The Church in the Age of Feudalism*, by F. Kempf and others; iv, *From the High Middle Ages to the Eve of the Reformation*, by H.-G. Beck and others (London, 1980). Older but still of great value are vols. vii–x of A. Fliche and V. Martin (eds.), *Histoire de l'église depuis les origines jusqu'à nos jours* (Paris, 1939–) . A valuable handbook is H. Jakobs, *Kirchenreform und Hochmittelalter* (Munich–Vienna, 1984). There is a brief survey of interest by D. Knowles and D. Obolensky, *The Christian Centuries*: vol. ii, *The Middle Ages* (London, 1969), and a brilliant one by R. W. Southern, *Western Society and the Church in the Middle Ages* (Harmondsworth, 1970). K. A. Fink's book, *Papsttum und Kirche im abendländischen Mittelalter* is intermittent in coverage but outstanding on what it does cover. For a broad introduction to medieval religious attitudes, the reader could not do better than to begin with B. Hamilton, *Religion in the Medieval West* (London, 1986). The famous collection of materials by G. G. Coulton, *Five Centuries of Religion*, 4 vols. (Cambridge, 1923–50), gives a good if selective impression of the attitudes of contemporaries in their own words.

The medieval world-view. Historians since the Second World War (and in some cases before it) have moved away from the history of events and replaced it by the study of social structures and of the way in which they are reflected in the medieval attitude to the world. Five great books which illustrate this approach are M. Bloch, *Feudal Society* (London, 1962); R. W. Southern, *The Making of the Middle Ages* (London, 1953); J. Le Goff, *La civilisation de l'occident médiéval* (Paris, 1967); W. von den Steinen, *Der Kosmos des Mittelalters von Karl dem Grossen zu Bernhard von Clairvaux*, 2nd edn. (Berne-Munich, 1967); and G. Duby, *La société aux XIe et XIIe siècles dans la région mâconnaise* (Paris, 1954), a local study of very wide interest. To them must be added other original and interesting works, among them A. Y. Gurevich, *Categories of Medieval Culture* (London, 1985); F. Heer, *The Medieval World 1100–1350* (London, 1962); and G. Duby, *The Making of the Christian West* (Geneva, 1967). There are interesting collections of studies by J. Le Goff, *Time, Work and Culture in the Middle Ages* (Chicago, 1980), and R. Fossier and others, *Le Moyen-Âge* vol. ii, *L'éveil de l'Europe 950–1250* (Paris, 1982)). R. Pernoud has written a lively attack on modern assumptions about the Middle Ages in *Pour en finir avec le Moyen Âge* (Paris, 1977), and there is a very large collection in which the attitudes prevailing in different medieval centuries are brought into interesting comparison by A. Borst, *Lebensformen im Mittelalter* (Frankfurt-Berlin, 1973). For detailed histories of government and policy one now has to turn to specialist studies, but there are interesting overviews which include this aspect by K. Hampe, *Das Hochmittelalter*, 5th edn. (Graz, 1963); H. Zimmermann, *Das Mittelalter*, 2 pts. (Brunswick, 1975–9); and J. H. Mundy, *Europe in the High Middle Ages 1150–1309* (London, 1973).

Reference lists. The classic bibliographies are L. J. Paetow, *A Guide to the Study of Medieval History* (repr. and corrected, Millwood, 1980) and G. C. Boyce, *Literature of Medieval History 1930–75*, 5 vols. (New York, 1981). Current publications are listed each quarter in a magnificent bibliography in *RHE*, and there are valuable ones also in *AHP* and *DAEM*. The standard work to consult for lists of medieval bishops is still P. B. Gams, *Series episcoporum ecclesiae catholicae* (repr. Graz, 1957), which will eventually be superseded by the large project of O. Engels and St. Weinfurter, *Series episcoporum ecclesiae catholicae occidentalis ab initio ad annum MCXCVIII* (Stuttgart, 1982–). Study of the sources must begin with the series edited by L. Genicot, *Typologie des sources du Moyen Âge* (Turnhout, 1972–). See also R. C. van Caenegem and F. L. Ganshof, *Guide to the Sources of Medieval History* (Amsterdam, 1978).

Ecclesiastical Institutions. Here the classic work is the one edited by G. Le Bras, *Histoire du droit et des institutions de l'église en occident*: vol. vii by Le Bras, *L'Âge classique 1140–1378* (Paris, 1965); vol. viii by J. Gaudemet, *Le gouvernement de l'église à l'époque classique: 2, le gouvernement local* (Paris, 1979). Le Bras is also the author of volume xii of FM, *Institutions ecclésiastiques de la*

Chrétienté médiévale (Paris, 1959–64). The book of R. W. and A. J. Carlyle, *A History of Medieval Political Thought in the West*, esp. vols. ii, iv, and v (Edinburgh, 1909–22), contains an outstanding survey of thought on the subject, even if it was written before the work of canonists and theologians had been explored. B. Tierney, *The Crisis of Church and State 1050–1300* (New Jersey, 1964), provides an excellent selection of contemporary material.

Papacy. There are good introductions to the medieval papacy by G. Barraclough, *The Medieval Papacy* (London, 1968), and H. Zimmermann, *Das Papsttum im Mittelalter: eine Papstgeschichte im Spiegel der Historiographie* (Stuttgart, 1981). There are two pungently argued works by W. Ullmann, *A Short History of the Papacy in the Middle Ages* (London, 1972), and *The Growth of Papal Government in the Middle Ages*, 3rd edn. (London, 1970). His conclusions have been widely challenged, and the issues are clarified in an article by F. Kempf, 'Die päpstliche Gewalt in der mittelalterlichen Welt', *Miscellanea Historiae Pontificiae* 21 (1959) 117–69 and the further discussion by H. Barion and Kempf in *ZSSRGkA* 46–7 (1960–1), and in F. Oakley, 'Celestial Hierarchies Revisited', *Past and Present* 60 (1973) 3–48. There is also an interesting examination of papal authority in K. F. Morrison, *Tradition and Authority in the Western Church 300–1140* (Princeton, 1969). G. B. Ladner has produced a classic study of *I ritratti dei papi nell'antichità e nel medioevo*, 3 vols. (Vatican, 1941–80), and the significance of the names of the popes is discussed by F. Krämer, 'Über die Anfänge und Beweggründe der Papstnamenänderungen im Ma.', *Romische Quartalschrift* 51 (1956) 148–88, and B. U. Hergemöller, *Die Geschichte der Papstnamen* (Münster, 1980). The development of the ceremonial involved in the creation of popes is difficult to clarify, but there are good studies by H. W. Klewitz, 'Die Krönung des Papstes', *ZSSRGkA* 61 (1941) 96–130; and E. Eichmann, *Weihe und Krönung des Papstes im Mittelalter* (Munich, 1951). Also important is H. Zimmermann, *Papstabsetzungen des Mittelalters* (Vienna, 1968).

Rome and the Papal State. L. Halphen provided a fundamental study on this subject in his *Études sur l'administration de Rome au Moyen Âge*, Bibliothèque de l'École des Hautes Études 166 (1907). There is a most interesting assessment of the cultural significance of Rome in our period by H. Schmidinger, *Roma docta? Rom als geistiges Zentrum im Mittelalter* (Salzburg, 1973); and a very sound history by P. Partner, *The Lands of S. Peter* (London, 1972). The social and religious development of central Italy is the subject of a really outstanding work by P. Toubert, *Les structures du Latium médiéval*, 2 vols. (Rome, 1973). On the first part of our period there is a helpful article by D. B. Zema, 'The Houses of Tuscany and of Pierleone in the Crisis of Rome in the Eleventh Century', *Traditio* 2 (1944) 155–75; and above all the invaluable thesis by D. R. Whitton, 'Papal Policy in Rome 1012–1124' (University of Oxford D.Phil. 1980).

Germany. For the history of Germany, which is particularly crucial to that of the medieval church, see K. Hampe, *Germany under the Salian and Hohenstaufen Emperors* (Oxford, 1973); H. Fuhrmann, *Germany in the High Middle Ages* (Cambridge, 1986); H. Keller, *Zwischen regionaler Begrenzung und universalem Horizont: Deutschland und Imperium der Salier und Staufer* (Berlin, 1986); and A. Haverkamp, *Aufbruch und Gestaltung: Deutschland 1056–1273* (Munich, 1984). Some documents are provided in translation by B. H. Hill, *Medieval Monarchy in Action: The German Empire from Henry I to Henry IV* (London, 1972). A. Hauck, *Kirchengeschichte Deutschlands*, vols. ii–iii (Leipzig, 1896–1903), is still an invaluable work because of its huge range and references to the sources.

England. Two general histories which contain a good deal of discussion of the church are F. Barlow, *The Feudal Kingdom of England 1042–1216*, 3rd edn. (London, 1972), and A. L. Poole, *From Domesday Book to Magna Carta*, 2nd ed. (Oxford, 1955). The most useful introduction to the English church as a whole is J. C. Dickinson, *An Ecclesiastical History of England: The Later Middle Ages* (London, 1979). F. Barlow's two volumes, *The English Church 1000–66; A Constitutional History* (London, 1963), and *The English Church 1066–1154* (1979), form a fine history of the English church covering much of our period. The legislation of the English church has been magnificently edited in *C&S*.

France. The starting place is now E. M. Hallam, *Capetian France 937–1328* (London, 1980), and J. Dunbabin, *France in the Making* (Oxford, 1985). The general history of the French church is best approached through the excellent volume in F. Lot and R. Fawtier (eds.), *Histoire des institutions françaises au Moyen Âge*: iii: *Institutions ecclésiastiques* (Paris, 1962), by J.-F. Lemarignier and J. Gaudemet.

PART I: THE PAPAL REFORM MOVEMENT AND THE CONFLICT
WITH THE EMPIRE

Chapter 1: Christian Society in the Middle of the Eleventh Century

i. Introduction. The continuity with the Carolingian period will be evident from a reading of M. Wallace—Hadrill, *The Frankish Church* (Oxford, 1983) in this series, and there is a brilliant analysis of unfulfilled possibilities by K. Leyser, *The Ascent of Latin Europe* (Oxford, 1986). There is also an interesting discussion by B. Bligny, 'L'église et le siècle de l'an mille au début du XIIe siècle', *CCM* 27 (1984) 5–33. See also M. Gibson, 'The continuity of learning *c*.850–*c*.1050', *Viator* 6 (1975) 1–13. The significance of increasing literacy for religion and government is explored in three important works: B. Stock, *The Implications of Literacy* (Princeton, 1983); M. T. Clanchy, *From Memory to Written Record* (London, 1979); and H. Grundmann, 'Litteratus, illiteratus', *AKg* 40 (1958) 1–65. The relationship between writing, speech, and symbol is considered in R. Crosby, 'Oral delivery in the Middle Ages', *Speculum* 11 (1936) 88–110 (mainly on the narratives of *jongleurs*); and J. Le Goff, 'Les gestes symboliques dans la vie sociale', *CISAM* 23 (1976) 679–788. On the extent to which the medieval laity ever became literate, see J. W. Thompson, *The Literacy of the Laity in the Middle Ages* (repr. New York, 1960); M. Parkes, 'The Literacy of the Laity' in D. Daiches and A. Thorlby (eds.), *The Medieval World* (London, 1973), 555–77; P. Riché, 'Recherches sur l'instruction des laïcs du IXe au XIIe siècle', *CCM* 5 (1962) 175–82; and J. T. Rosenthal, 'The Education of the Early Capetians', *Traditio* 25 (1969) 366–76.

ii. The Pattern of Divine Government. The governmental implications of the medieval reverence for the monarch are analysed in a famous book by F. Kern, *Kingship and Law in the Middle Ages* (Oxford, 1939), and are set in a wide context in a collection of studies, *Sacral Kingship: Contributions to the Eighth International Congress for the History of Religions* (Leiden, 1959). The link between kingship and the cult of the saints is explored over a long period by R. Folz, *Les saints rois du Moyen Âge en occident* (Brussels, 1984). See also T. Renna, 'The monastic tradition of kingship 814–1150', *Cistercian Studies* 18 (1983) 184–91. The ceremonial foundations of holy kingship may be studied in E. H. Kantorowicz, *Laudes Regiae* (Berkeley, 1958); G. Tellenbach, 'Römischer und christlicher Reichsgedanke in der Liturgie des frühen Mittelalters,' *Sb Akad. Heidelberg*, 1934; H. M. Schaller, 'Der heilige Tag als Termin mittelalterlicher Staatsakte', *DAEM* 30 (1974) 1–24; and in the texts edited by R. Elze, *Die Ordines für die Weihe und Krönung des Kaisers*, MGH Leges IV.9 (1960). The classic work on the royal healing power is M. Bloch, *The Royal Touch* (London, 1973), but see the comments of F. Barlow, 'The King's Evil', *EHR* 95 (1980) 3–27, where the regular adoption of the practice is placed much later. It is not surprising that there has been a vast amount of publication on the imperial ideal. Among the best works are R. Folz, *The Concept of Empire in Western Europe* (London, 1969); W. Kölmel, *Regimen Christianum* (Berlin, 1970); E. Müller-Mertens, *Regnum Teutonicum* (Vienna, 1970); G. Koch, *Auf dem Wege zum Sacrum Imperium* (Vienna, 1972); and H. Löwe, 'Kaisertum und Abendland in ottonischer und frühsalischer Zeit', *HZ* 196 (1963) 529–62. There is an interesting interpretation of the 'world lordship' of emperor and pope by O. Hageneder, 'Weltherrschaft im Ma.', *MIOG* 93 (1985) 257–78.

The immense literature on the judicial use of the ordeal may be initially approached through R. Bartlett, *Trial by Fire and Water: The Medieval Judicial Ordeal* (Oxford, 1986); P. Brown, 'Society and the Supernatural: a

Medieval Change', *Daedalus* 104 (1975) 133–51; and C. Morris, '*Judicium Dei*: The Social and Political Significance of the Ordeal in the Eleventh Century', *SCH* 12 (1975) 95–111. For the development of the cult of the saints and of pilgrimage, see under Ch. 12.vi below. On the Peace of God movement, important studies include H. Hoffmann, *Gottesfriede und Treuga Dei*, MGH Schriften 20 (1964); G. Duby, 'Les laïcs et la paix de Dieu', MCSM 5 (1968) 448–69; H. E. J. Cowdrey, 'The Peace of God and the Truce of God', *Past and Present* 46 (1970) 42–67; and B. H. Rosenwein, 'Feudal War and Monastic Peace', *Viator* 2 (1971) 129–57.

iii. The Church and the Lay powers. On the relations between the emperor and the German churches, there are excellent surveys by T. Reuter, 'The "Imperial Church System" of the Ottonian and Salian rulers; A Reconsideration', *JEH* 33 (1982) 347–74; J. Fleckenstein, 'Zum Begriff der ottonisch-salischen Reichskirche', *Geschichte, Wirtschaft, Gesellschaft: Fs für C. Bauer* (Berlin, 1974), 61–71; L. Santifaller, 'Zur Geschichte des ottonisch-salischen Reichskirchensystems', *Sb Akad. Wien* 229/1 (1964); and H. Zielinski, *Der Reichsepiskopat in spätottonischer und salischer Zeit*, i (Stuttgart, 1984). The classic studies of *Eigenkirchentum* are those by U. Stutz, *Geschichte des kirchlichen Benefizialwesens*, vol. i only (Berlin, 1895) (see 'The Proprietary Church as an Clement of Medieval German Ecclesiastical Law', tr. G. Barraclough, *Medieval Germany 911–1250* (repr. Oxford, 1961), ii.35–70); and P. Thomas, *Le droit de propriété des laïques sur les églises et le patronage laïque* (Paris, 1906). See also H. E. Feine, 'Ursprung, Wesen und Bedeutung des Eigenkirchentums', *MIOG* 58 (1950) 195–208. Studies of lay investiture, episcopal election, the personnel of the episcopate, and the work of the local churches are listed under subsequent chapters.

iv. The Beginnings of a Reform Ideology. The circumstances at Rome in the years before 1046 have been studied in detail by K-J. Herrmann, *Das Tuskulanerpapsttum* (Stuttgart, 1973); H. M. Klinkenberg, 'Der römische Primat im X. Jh', *ZSSRGkA* 72 (1955) 1–57; G. Tellenbach, 'Zur Geschichte der Päpste im X. und früheren XI. Jh' in *Institutionen, Kultur und Gesellschaft im Mittelalter: Festschrift für J. Fleckenstein* (Sigmaringen, 1984), 165–77; and P. E. Schramm, *Kaiser, Rom und Renovatio* (repr. Bad Homburg, 1962).

Chapter 2: The Pattern of Social Change

i. The Extension of Economic Activity: The Countryside. There are many studies of the development of the medieval economy as a whole; the obvious starting-points are the *Cambridge Economic History of Europe*, ed. M. M. Postan, 2nd edn (Cambridge, 1966), and the *Fontana Economic History of Europe*, ed. C. Cipolla, vol.i, *The Middle Ages* (London, 1972). There is also R. Latouche, *The Birth of Western Economy*, 2nd ed. (London,

1967), and R. Fossier, *Histoire sociale de l'occident médiéval* (Paris, 1970).
Everyday life is an increasing interest of modern historians: see D. Herlihy,
Medieval Households (London, 1985), and O. Borst, *Alltagsleben im Mittelalter*
(Frankfurt, 1983), which has a good deal of material on ecclesiastical life,
primarily in the later Middle Ages. There are two good introductions to the
history of the countryside by G. Duby: *The Early Growth of the European
Economy: Warriors and Peasants* (London, 1974); and *Rural Economy and
Country Life in the Medieval West* (London, 1968). See also M. Bloch, *French
Rural History* (London, 1966). For a lively interpretation of the mechanisms
of change, see L. White, *Medieval Technology and Social Change* (Oxford,
1962).

ii. The Cities. Good surveys are provided by the collection of essays edited
by H. A. Miskimin and others, *The Medieval City* (New Haven, 1977), and
by E. Ennen, *The Medieval Town* (Amsterdam, 1979). A very influential
account was that of H. Pirenne, *Medieval Cities* (Princeton, 1925), based on
developments in Flanders and giving a largely commercial and 'non-
ecclesiastical' account of the emergence of the city. His conclusions are now
widely challenged: see C. Verlinden, 'Marchands ou tisserands?', *Annales* 27
(1972) 396–406, and R. G. Witt, 'The Landlord and the Economic Revival
of the Middle Ages', *American Historical Review* 76 (1971) 965–88; also the
important study by J. Lestocquoy, *Aux origines de la bourgeoisie: les villes de
Flandre et d'Italie* (Paris, 1952). There is a masterly survey of the Italian cities
by J. K. Hyde, *Society and Politics in Medieval Italy* (London, 1973), and two
significant influences from religious ideas are analysed by H. C. Peyer,
'Stadt und Stadtpatron im mittelalterlichen Italien', *Zürcher Studien zur
allgemeinen Geschichte* 13 (1955), and H. Z. Tucci, 'Il carroccio nella vita
communale italiana', *QFIAB* 65 (1985) 1–104. The number of studies of
individual cities precludes any listing, but mention must be made, because
of its special relevance, of *Lucca und das Reich bis zum Ende des 11 Jhs*
(Tübingen, 1972), by H. Schwarzmaier. The broader cultural implications
of the city are considered by R. W. Southern, 'England's First Entry into
Europe', *Medieval Humanism and other Studies* (Oxford, 1970) 135–57; F.-J.
Schmale, 'Zu den Anfängen bürgerlichen Kultur im Mittelalter', *Römische
Quartalschrift* 58 (1963), 149–61; and E. Werner, *Stadt und Geistesleben im
Hochmittelalter* (Weimar, 1980).

iii. The Expansion of Education. The development of schools in the course of
the twelfth century has been the subject of some fine works, including G.
Paré *et al.*, *La renaissance du XIIe siècle: les écoles et l'enseignement* (Paris, 1933);
vol. v, *Les écoles*, in E. Lesne, *Histoire de la propriété ecclésiastique en France*
(Lille, 1910–), and P. Delhaye, 'L'organisation scolaire au XIIe siècle',
Traditio 5 (1947) 211–68. The subject is also covered in several of the
histories of universities, which appear under Ch. 20.i below. The

connection between the schools and society as a whole is particularly examined by J. Le Goff, *Les intellectuels au Moyen Âge* (Paris, 1957); H. Classen, 'Die hohen Schulen und die Gesellschaft im 12 Jh', *AKg* 48 (1966) 155–80; L. K. Little, 'Intellectual Training and Attitudes towards Reform', *Pierre Abélard, Pierre le Vénérable: colloques du CNRS* (Paris, 1975), 235–54; and A. Murray in his brilliant book, *Reason and Society in the Middle Ages* (Oxford, 1978). In a reconstruction of the history of the twelfth-century schools, the 'school of Chartres' is specially important and specially controversial. Major works on it begin with A. Clerval, *Les écoles de Chartres* (Paris, 1895), and it is reassessed in R. W. Southern, 'Humanism and the School of Chartres', *Medieval Humanism and other Studies* (Oxford, 1970) 61–85; in the same author's *Platonism, Scholastic Method and the School of Chartres* (Reading, 1979); and in *RR* 113–37, with an alternative view by N. M. Häring in *Essays in Honour of A. C. Pegis* (Toronto, 1974), 268–329. On the development of the syllabus, there is the material edited by D. L. Wagner, *The Seven Liberal Arts in the Middle Ages* (Indiana, 1983); R. W. Hunt's collected papers, *The History of Grammar in the Middle Ages* (Amsterdam, 1980); and G. Glauche, *Schullektüre im Mittelalter* (Munich, 1970). The growth of the *ars dictaminis* is the subject of an excellent article by W. D. Patt, 'The early *ars dictaminis* as response to a changing society', *Viator* 9 (1978) 133–55. The best contemporary discussion of the syllabus is available in translation in J. Taylor, *Hugh of S. Victor, The Didascalion: a Medieval Guide to the Arts* (New York, 1961) (more correctly *Didascalicon*).

iv. The Aristocracy. An enormous amount of study has recently been devoted to the growth of the nobility in this period, and some of the general books mentioned at the beginning of this bibliography have made a major contribution; see the interesting reflections of R. I. Moore, 'Duby's Eleventh Century', *History* 69 (1984) 36–49. Among many books and essays may be mentioned R. Boutruche, *Seigneurie et féodalité*: vol. ii, *L'apogée* (Paris, 1970); G. Fourquin, *Lordship and Feudalism in the Middle Ages* (London, 1976); *La noblesse au Moyen Âge: essais à la mémoire de R. Boutruche* (Paris, 1976); M. Parisse, *La noblesse lorraine*, 2 vols. (Lille, 1976); T. Reuter (ed.), *The Medieval Nobility* (Amsterdam, 1978); and *Structures féodales et féodalisme dans l'occident méditerranéen*, École française de Rome 44 (1980).

v. The Dissemination of Ideas. There is no systematic study of the way in which ideas and attitudes were exchanged in medieval society. A survey must start with J. Benzinger, 'Zum Wesen und zu den Formen von Kommunikation und Publizistik im Mittelalter', *Publizistik* 15 (1970) 295–318, and particular aspects and examples are discussed by L. C. Mackinney, 'The People and Public Opinion in the Eleventh-Century Peace Movement', *Speculum* 5 (1930) 181–206; G. Duby, 'The Diffusion of Cultural Patterns in Feudal Society', *Past and Present* 39 (1968) 3–10; C. Morris,

Medieval Media (Southampton, 1972); E. Sourdel (ed.), *Prédication et propagande au Moyen Âge: Islam, Byzance, occident* (Paris, 1983). Very relevant to this subject are the works on literacy (ch.1.i above) and on preaching and pilgrimage (ch.12 below); these contain references to studies of the road system, and to them should be added the important studies edited by H. C. Peyer, *Gastfreund schaft, Taverne und Gashaus im Mittelalter* (Munich, 1983).

Chapter 3: Monastic Growth and Change

(For a fuller bibliography, see G. Constable, *Medieval Monasticism: a Select Bibliography* (Toronto, 1976).)
i. Monastic Growth and Change. There have been several projects designed to list all abbeys and priories, with dates of foundation and affiliations, and a convenient handbook is provided by P-R. Gaussin, *L'Europe des ordres et des congrégations*, CERCOM (Centre européen de recherches sur les congrégations et ordres monastiques), n.d. The most useful general work is L. H. Cottineau, *Répertoire topo-bibliographique des abbayes et prieurés*, 3 vols. (Mâcon, 1935–7 and 1970). For France the main work is by J. M. Besse *et al.*, *Abbayes et prieurés de l'ancienne France*, a new edition of Dom Beaunier's work (Paris, 1905–). The *Monasticon Belge* begun by U. Berlière (Bruges, 1890; Maredsous 1928–9) has been resumed in several additional volumes (Liège 1960–73). For Germany, the *Germania Sacra*, Neue Folge, Berlin and New York, 1962–), is designed to give very full information about monastic and other bodies. For England, there are D. Knowles and R. N. Hadcock, *Medieval Religious Houses: England and Wales*, 2nd edn. (London 1971), and D. Knowles and others, *The Heads of Religious Houses: England and Wales 940–1216* (Cambridge, 1972); for Scotland, I. B. Cowan and D. E. Easson, *Medieval Religious Houses: Scotland*, 2nd edn. (London, 1976); and for Ireland, A. O. Gwynn and R. N. Hadcock, *Medieval Religious Houses: Ireland* (London, 1970). The *Monasticon Italiae* has begun with vol. i, *Roma e Lazio* (Cesena, 1981). Some of the most significant collections of customs were edited by B. Albers, *Consuetudines Monasticae*, 5 vols. (Stuttgart, 1900–12), and new editions are currently being published in the series *Corpus Consuetudinum Monasticarum*, ed. K. Hallinger (Siegburg, 1963–). Information about current projects may be obtained from CERCOM at St Étienne. One of the best short introductions to monastic history in this period is by M. Pacaut, *Les ordres monastiques et religieux au Moyen Âge* (Paris, 1970), and equally useful is C. H. Lawrence, *Medieval Monasticism* (London, 1984). There are good illustrated introductions to the main types of monasticism in G. Le Bras (ed.), *Les ordres religieux: la vie et l'art*, 2 vols. (Paris, 1979–80). C. N. L. Brooke and W. Swaan's handsome volume *The Monastic World 1000–1300* (London, 1974), contains a good discussion of the development of the religious orders as well as a fine treatment of the buildings. For legal and constitutional aspects, see J.

Hourlier, *Histoire du droit et des institutions de l'église en occident* 10: *L'âge classique: les religieux* (Paris, 1974). There is an outstanding survey article by J. Dubois, 'Les moines dans la société du Moyen Âge', *RHEF* 60 (1974) 5–37, and another by G. Constable, 'The Study of Monastic History Today', in his collected papers, *Religious Life and Thought* (London, 1979). There are important regional studies by B. Bligny, *L'église et les ordres religieux dans le royaume de Bourgogne* (Paris, 1960); D. Knowles, *The Monastic Order in England*, 2nd edn. (Cambridge, 1963) (a book of wide general interest); and G. Penco, *Storia del monachesimo in Italia* (Rome, 1961). Articles on the restitution of parish churches are listed under ch. 9.iii below, and there is an important book by J. Lemarignier, *Études sur les privilèges d'exemption et de juridiction ecclésiastique des abbayes normands depuis ses origines jusqu'en 1140* (Paris, 1937).

ii. The Golden Age of Cluny. The classic publications of documentary material on Cluny are M. Marrier and A. Duchesne (eds.), *Bibliotheca Cluniacensis* (Paris, 1614; repr. Macon, 1915); A. Bernard and A. Bruel (eds.), *Recueil des chartes de l'abbaye de Cluny*, 5 vols. (Paris, 1876–94); and G. Charvin (ed.), *Statuts, chapitres généraux et visites de l'ordre de Cluny*, i (Paris, 1965). A major study of eleventh-century monasticism is K. Hallinger, *Gorze-Kluny*, 2 vols. (Rome, 1950–1), although recent work has moved away from the abrupt alignment into two opposite movements: see especially J. Wollasch, *Mönchtum des Mittelalters zwischen Kirche und Welt* (Munich, 1973), and 'Neue Methoden der Erforschung des Mönchtums im Mittelalter', *HZ* 225 (1977) 529–71, where Wollasch stresses how limited is our knowledge of the self-awareness of monastic communities. To this end he has championed a new wave of publications of the mortuary rolls and 'books of life' which expressed the solidarity of the monks throughout time and space. Life at Cluny has been described by J. Evans, *Monastic Life at Cluny 910–1157* (Oxford, 1931), and N. Hunt, *Cluny under S. Hugh* (London, 1967); and daily routine and administration by G. de Valous, *Le monachisme clunisien des origines au XVe siècle*, 2 vols., 2nd edn. (Paris 1970). The economic system is admirably surveyed in G. Duby, 'Économie domaniale et économie monétaire: le budget de l'abbaye de Cluny', *Annales* 7 (1952) 155–71. Collected studies are published in *À Cluny; congrès scientifique* (Dijon, 1950); G. Tellenbach (ed.), *Neue Forschungen über Cluny und die Cluniacenser* (Freiburg, 1959); H. Richter (ed.), *Cluny: Beiträge zu Gestalt und Wirkung der cluniazensischen Reform*, Wege der Forschung 241 (1975); N. Hunt, *Cluniac Monasticism in the Central Middle Ages* (London, 1971); and G. Constable, *Cluniac Studies* (London, 1980). On the long-standing discussion about the impact of Cluny on the general reform of the church, see H. E. J. Cowdrey, *The Cluniacs and the Gregorian Reform* (Oxford, 1970); and M. Pacaut, 'Ordre et liberté dans l'église: l'influence de Cluny', D. Loades (ed.), *The End of Strife* (Edinburgh, 1984), 155–79. There is a brief description of the Hirsau movement with good illustrations by W. Irtenkauf, *Hirsau: Geschichte und Kultur* (Lindau, 1959), and its constitutional and political significance has been carefully examined by H. Jakobs, *Die Hirsauer* (Cologne, 1961); while the same author's book *Der Adel in der Klosterreform von S. Blasien* (Cologne, 1968), is of much wider interest than the title may suggest.

iii. Hermits. The hermit-ideal is surveyed in MCSM 4 (1965), *L'eremitismo in occidente nei secoli XI e XII*. The nature of the eremitical life in general is discussed by L. Gougaud, 'La vie érémitique au Moyen Âge', *Revue d'ascétique et de mystique* 1 (1920) 209–40 and 313–28; J. Leclercq, '*Eremus* et *eremita*', *Collectanea Ordinis Cisterciensium Reformatorum* 25 (1963) 8–30; and G. Constable, 'Eremitical Forms of Monastic Life', MCSM 9 (1980) 239–64. Earlier discussions of the monastic crisis are surveyed in an important article by J. van Engen, 'The "Crisis of Cenobitism" Reconsidered: Benedictine Monasticism in the Years 1050–1150', *Speculum* 61 (1986) 269–304. See the valuable collection of studies in MCSM 6 (1971), *Monachesimo e la riforma ecclesiastica*, and H. Leyser's book, *Hermits and the New Monasticism* (London, 1984). The greatest of the Italian hermits was Peter Damian, whose letters are being edited by K. Reindel, MGH Briefe (1983–). For many of his works it is still necessary to use the old edition in PL 144–5. The best studies are in P. Dressler, *Petrus Damiani: Leben und Werk* (Rome, 1954); J. Leclercq, *S. Pierre Damien, ermite et homme d'église* (Rome, 1960); *Studi su S. Pier Damiano in onore del cardinale A. G. Cicognani*, 2nd edn. (Faenza, 1970); and *S. Pier Damiano nel IX centenario della morte*, 4 vols. (Cesena, 1972). L. G. Little re-examines the evidence for the early life in 'The Personal Development of Peter Damian', *Order and Innovation in the Middle Ages; Essays in Honour of J. R. Strayer (Princeton 1976)*, 317–41; and Peter's knowledge of canon law is clarified by J. J. Ryan, *S. Peter Damiani and his Canonical Sources* (Toronto, 1956). For France there is a fine basic study by J. von Walter, *Die ersten Wanderprediger Frankreichs*, 2 vols. (Leipzig, 1903–6), and good studies of early hermits by G. Morin, 'Renauld l'érémite et Ives de Chartres', *Revue Bénédictine* 40 (1928) 99–115; H. Grundmann, 'Deutsche Eremiten', *AKg* 45 (1963) 60–90; and G. M. Oury, 'L'érémitisme dans l'ancien diocèse de Tours', *Revue Mabillon* 58 (1971) 43–92. Works on the organization of the religious orders which emerged from these hermits are to be found under ch. 10 below.

Fundamental to the programmes of the eremitical reformers was the ideal of poverty. This has been discussed in a Marxist framework by E. Werner, *Pauperes Christi: Studien zu social-religiösen Bewegungen im Zeitalter des Reformpapsttums* (Leipzig, 1956); and in a series of articles edited by M. Mollat, *Études sur l'histoire de la pauvreté*, 2 vols. (Paris, 1974). This project led to Mollat's own magisterial survey, *Les pauvres au Moyen Âge* (Paris, 1978). These three works are of major importance for the whole history of the church in this period. Also valuable are the studies in CSSSM 8 (1969), *Povertà e ricchezza nella spiritualità dei secoli XI e XII.* The question of poverty was closely connected with the desire to recover the life of the apostolic church, which is discussed by M-D. Chenu in the collected essays *Nature, Man and Society in the Twelfth Century* (Chicago, 1968); M-H. Vicaire, *L'imitation des apôtres: moines, chanoines et mendiants* (Paris, 1963); and G. Miccoli, '*Ecclesiae primitivae forma*' in his *Chiesa gregoriana* (Florence, 1966), 225–99. For the twelfth century, see ch. 10. i below.

iv. Canons. See the bibliography under ch. 10 below.

Chapter 4: The Papal Reform 1046–73

i. The Papal Reform: General. There are sound accounts of this period by J. P. Whitney in *CMH.* vol. v, ch. 1 and in his *Hildebrandine Essays* (Cambridge, 1932); but the two books which have most profoundly influenced the modern conception of the papal reform movement are those by A. Fliche, *La réforme grégorienne*, 3 vols. (Paris, 1924–37, repr. Geneva, 1978); and G. Tellenbach, *Church, State and Christian Society at the Time of the Investiture Contest* (Oxford, 1940). Both are impressive works of scholarship; of the two, the theses of Tellenbach have better stood the test of time, for later discussion has tended to dismantle some of Fliche's central contentions. On the question of the appropriateness of his concept of 'Gregorian reform', there is O. Capitani, 'Esiste un "Età Gregoriana"?', *Rivista di Storia e Litteratura Religiosa* 1 (1965) 454–81; J. Gilchrist, 'Was there a Gregorian reform movement?', *Canadian Catholic Hist. Assoc. Study Sessions* 37 (1970) 1–10; and G. Tellenbach, 'Gregorianische Reform: kritische Besinnungen', K. Schmid (ed.) *Reich und Kirche vor dem Investiturstreit. Vorträge beim wissenschaftlichen Kolloquium aus Anlass des 80 Geburtstags von G. Tellenbach* (Sigmaringen, 1985), 99–113. Further light is thrown on the question by G. Ladner's articles 'Die mittelalterliche Reform-Idee', *MIOG* 60 (1952) 31–59, and 'Gregory the Great and Gregory VII', *Viator* 4 (1973) 1–26. Local studies have also raised questions about the character of church reform in general and 'Gregorianism' in particular: the important work of E. Magnou-Nortier, *La société laïque et l'église dans la province ecclésiastique de Narbonne* (Toulouse, 1974), leads us to think more of a Gregorian crisis than of a Gregorian reform, and there are important contributions by J.-M. Bienvenu, 'Les caractères originaux de la réforme grégorienne dans le diocèse d'Angers', *Bulletin Philologique et Historique* (1968 [1971]) ii.545–60; Y. Milo, 'Dissonance between Papal and Local Reform Interests in pre-Gregorian Tuscany', *Studi Medievali* 20 (1979) 69–86; and W. Goez, 'Reformpapsttum, Adel, und monastische Erneuerung in der Toscana', VuF 17 (1973) 205–39. The discussion of the movement was continued in particular in *Studi Gregoriani* (Rome, 1947–), which is not so much a periodical as a series of collected publications; and a new synthesis is offered in the impressive work of J. Laudage, *Priesterbild und Reformpapsttum im 11 Jh.*, AKg Beiheft 22 (Cologne, 1984/5). G. Ladner, *Theologie und Politik vor dem Investiturstreit* (repr. Darmstadt, 1968), is an interesting study, and good recent surveys are provided in vol. xi of M. Greschat, *Gestalten der Kirchengeschichte* (Stuttgart, 1985). The influence of Cluniac reform on the policy of the popes has already been mentioned in ch. 3. ii above. On Monte Cassino, the other great Benedictine abbey whose history was closely linked with the papal reformers, there is H.-W. Klewitz, 'Monte Cassino in Rom', *QFIAB* 28 (1938) 36–47; R. Grégoire, 'Le Mont-Cassin dans la réforme de l'église', MCSM 6 (1971) 21–53; H. Dormeier, *Montecassino und die Laien im 11 und 12 Jh.*, MGH Schriften 27 (1979); G. A. Loud, 'Abbot Desiderius of Montecassino and the Gregorian papacy', *JEH* 30 (1979) 305–26; and H. E. J. Cowdrey, *The Age of Abbot Desiderius* (Oxford, 1983). See also the edition of the Monte Cassino chronicle by H. Hoffmann in MGH Scriptores 1980.

ii. The Beginnings of Papal Reform (1046–57). The policy of Henry III in general is described by C. M. Ryley in *CMH* iii, ch. 12, and there is an important analysis of his ecclesiastical policy in P. Kehr, 'Vier Kapitel aus der Geschichte Kaiser Heinrichs III', *Abhandlungen der Preussischen Akademie* (1930). Contemporary views of his rule are investigated by P. G. Schmidt, 'Heinrich III: das Bild des Herrschers in der Literatur seiner Zeit', *DAEM* 39 (1983), 582–90 and E. Boshof, 'Der Reich in der Krise', *HZ* 228 (1979) 265–87. The reasons for the deposition of Gregory VI have been much disputed, for example by G. B. Borino, 'L'elezione e la deposizione di Gregorio VI', *Archivio della società Romana*, 39 (1916) 141–252, 295–410; R. L. Poole, 'Benedict IX and Gregory VI', *PBA* 8 (1917) 199–228; and F.-J. Schmale, 'Die "Absetzung" Gregors VI in Sutri', *AHC* 11 (1979) 55–103. Also important in this context are H. H. Anton, *Der sogenannte Traktat* De ordinando pontefice (Bonn, 1982); and H. Vollrath, 'Kaisertum und Patriziat', *ZKg* 85 (1974) 11–44. There is no modern synthesis of views on Leo IX, in spite of his crucial importance in papal history, although there are valuable detailed studies in *S. Greg.* and important work on Leo's councils, for example by U.-R. Blumenthal, 'The Beginnings of the Gregorian Reform', in G. F. Lytle *Reformation and Authority in the Medieval and Reformation Church* (Washington, 1981), 1–13; and a good study by E. Petrucci, *Ecclesiologia e politica di Leone IX* (Rome, 1977). Cardinal Humbert was perhaps Leo's most influential adviser. The attempts by A. Michel to claim for him authorship of a great number of important tracts can now be regarded as superseded: see, for example, H. Hoesch, *Die kanonischen Quellen im Werk Humberts von Moyenmoutier* (Cologne, 1970); the introduction to the edition of *Libri tres adversus simoniacos* by E. G. Robison (unpublished University of Princeton dissertation, 1971); J. Gilchrist, 'Cardinal Humbert of Silva Candida', *ZSSRGkA* 89 (1972) 338–49; and H.-

G. Krause, 'Über den Verfasser der *Vita Leonis IX papae*', *DAEM* 32 (1976) 49–85. Two articles by J. T. Gilchrist in *Journal of Religious History* 2 (1962) 13–28, and *Annuale Medievale* 3 (1962) 29–42, give a balanced view of his significance. On another of Leo's sympathizers there is the study by B. de Vrégille, *Hugues de Salins, archevêque de Besançon* (Besançon, 1981). For Peter Damian, see ch. 3. iii.

iii. The Reformers Come of Age (1057–73). On the policy of the reformers under Nicholas II, there are articles by G. B. Borino, 'L'arcidiaconato di Ildebrando', *S. Greg.* 3 (1948) 463–516; A. Michel, 'Humbert und Hildebrand bei Nikolaus II', *HJb* 72 (1952/3) 133–61; D. Hägermann, 'Zur Vorgeschichte des Pontifikates Nikolaus' II', *ZKg* 81 (1970) 352–61; and J. Wollasch, 'Die Wahl des Papstes Nikolaus II', *MCSM* 6 (1971) 54–78. The interpretation of the election decree of 1059 has been much disputed. The modern argument begins with H.-G. Krause's influential study, 'Das Papstwahldekret von 1059 und seine Rolle im Investiturstreit', *S. Greg.* 7 (1960), and continues with articles by F. Kempf in *AHP* 2 (1964) 73–89; W. Stürner in *ZSSRGkA* 85 (1968) 1–56 and *S. Greg.* 9 (1972) 37–52; K. M. Woody in *Viator* 1 (1970) 33–54; and H. Hägermann in *ZSSRGkA* 87 (1970) 157–93. The best general study on Alexander II is undoubtedly T. Schmidt, *Alexander II und die römische Reformgruppe seiner Zeit* (Stuttgart, 1977), and there is a study of his synods by F.-J. Schmale in *AHC* 11 (1979) 307–38. The normative study of the crisis at Milan is by C. Violante, *La pataria milanese e la riforma ecclesiastica* (Rome, 1955), together with G. Miccoli, 'Per la storia della pataria milanese' in *Chiesa Gregoriana* (Florence, 1966), 101–68; H. E. J. Cowdrey, 'The Papacy, the Patarenes and the Church of Milan', *TRHS* V.18 (1968) 25–48; H. Keller, 'Pataria und Stadtverfassung, Stadtgemeinde und Reform', *VuF* 17 (1973) 321–50; and E. Cattaneo, 'La vita comune del clero a Milano', *Aevum* 48 (1974) 246–69. On the conflicts at Florence there is a good discussion in G. Miccoli, *Pietro Igneo* (Rome, 1960), and R. Schieffer's article 'Die Romreise deutscher Bischöfe im Frühjahr 1070', *Rheinische Vierteljahrsblätter* 35 (1971) 152–74, throws light on the obscure negotiations with the German church.

iv. The Principles of Papal Reform. See ch. 4. i above.

v. The Reform of the Clergy. As a basis for understanding the attack on simony the article of E. Hirsch, 'Der Symoniebegriff und eine angebliche Erweiterung desselben im 11 Jh.', *Archiv für katholisches Kirchenrecht* 86 (1906) 3–19, is still important, and other valuable general surveys are by N. M. Häring, 'The Augustinian Maxim: *nulli sacramento iniuria facienda est*', *MS* 16 (1954) 87–117, and J. Gilchrist, '*Simoniaca heresis* and the Problem of Orders', *MIC* C.subsid. 1 (1965) 209–36. Gilchrist has also analysed the important anti-simoniacal text, the *epistola Widonis*, in *DAEM* 37 (1981) 576–604 and *Authority and Power. Studies presented to Walter Ullmann* (Cambridge, 1980), 49–58. The policy of Leo IX and Nicholas II has been the subject of a series of studies, including J. Drehmann, *Papst Leo IX und die Symonie* (Tübingen, 1908); G. Miccoli, 'Il problema delle ordinazioni simoniache e le sinodi lateranensi del 1060 e 1061', *S. Greg.* 5 (1956) 33–81; and F. Pelster, 'Die römische Synode von 1060', *Gregorianum* 23 (1942) 66–90. There are two excellent modern discussions of the general history of clerical celibacy by M. Boelens, *Die Klerikerehe in der Gesetzgebung der Kirche* (Paderborn, 1968), and G. Denzler, *Das Papsttum und der Amtszölibat*, i (Stuttgart, 1973). On our period in particular there are C. N. L. Brooke, 'Gregorian Reform in Action: Clerical Marriage in England 1050–1200', in his *Medieval Church and Society* (Cambridge, 1971), 69–99; J. Gaudemet, 'Le célibat ecclésiastique: le droit et la pratique du XIe au XIIIe siècle', *ZZSSRGkA* 99 (1982) 1–31; A. L. Barstow, *Married Priests and the Reforming Papacy* (New York, 1982); and B. Schimmelpfennig, 'Zölibat und Lage der Priestersöhne vom 11 bis 14 Jh.', *HZ* 227 (1978) 1–44.

One of the most disputed questions has been about the stages by which the Roman Church moved to the prohibition of royal investiture of bishops. The issue is examined by J. Laudage (ch. 4.i above) and by R. Schieffer, *Die Entstehung des päpstlichen Investiturverbots für den deutschen König*, MGH Schriften 28 (1981). The article by G. B. Borino, 'L'investitura laica dal decreto di Nicolo II al decreto di Gregorio VII', *S. Greg.* 5 (1956) 345–59, is still of value, and so are the much older works of A. Scharnagl, *Der Begriff der Investitur in den Quellen und der Literatur des Investiturstreites* (Stuttgart, 1908), and P. Schmid, *Der Begriff der kanonischen Wahl in den Anfängen des Investiturstreits* (Stuttgart, 1926). A surviving fragment of a treatise on papal authority is assessed by W. Ullmann, 'Cardinal Humbert and the *ecclesia Romana*', *S. Greg.* 4 (1952) 111–27, and by J. J. Ryan, 'Cardinal Humbert, *de Sancta Romana Ecclesia*; Relics of Romano-Byzantine Relations', *MS* 20 (1958) 206–38, and the broader evolution of papalist theory is carefully charted by M. Maccarrone, 'La teologia del primato romano del secolo XI', *MCSM* 7 (1974) 21–122.

Chapter 5: The Discord of Empire and Papacy 1073–1099

i. Gregory VII. The amount of publication is enormous, and a most valuable introductory guide is provided by I. S. Robinson, 'Pope Gregory VII: Bibliographical Survey', *JEH* 36 (1985) 439–83. There is no single study of the pontificate which can now be regarded as normative, but R. Morghen, *Gregorio VII e la riforma della chiesa nel secolo XI*, new edn. (Palermo, 1975), provides a series of studies on Gregory's life. One line of recent research has clarified Gregory's personal spirituality, as in A. Nitschke, 'Die Wirksamkeit Gottes in der Welt Gregors VII', *S. Greg.* 5 (1956) 115–219; R. Schieffer, 'Gregor VII: ein Versuch über die historische Grösse', *HJb* 97

(1978) 87–107; W. Goez, 'Zur Persönlichkeit Gregors VII', *Römische Quartalschift* 73 (1978) 193–216; and K. J. Benz, 'Eschatologisches Gedankengut bei Gregor VII', *ZKg* 97 (1986) 1–35. Important episodes in Gregory's early career are studied by G. B. Borino, 'Invitus ultra montes cum domno papa Gregorio abii', *S. Greg.* 1 (1947) 3–46 and T. Schmidt, 'Zu Hildebrands Eid vor Kaiser Heinrich III', *AHP* 11 (1973) 374–86, and his last year by J. Vogel, 'Gregors VII Abzug aus Rom und sein letztes Pontifikatsjahr in Salerno' in N. Kamp and J. Wollasch (eds.), *Tradition als historischer Kraft* (Berlin, 1982), 341–9, and by P. E. Hübinger in his fine book, *Die letzten Worte Papst Gregors VII* (Opladen, 1973).

The classic edition of the register is the one by E. Caspar, *Das Register Gregors VII*, MGH Epist 4.2, and the unregistered letters are edited and translated by H. E. J. Cowdrey, *The* Epistolae Vagantes *of Pope Gregory VII* (Oxford, 1972). Historians have long discussed the purpose and nature of the register, which are considered by A. Murray, 'Pope Gregory VII and his Letters', *Traditio* 22 (1966), 149–202; R. Morghen, 'Ricerche sulla formazione del Registro di Gregorio VII', *Bullettino dell'Istituto Storico Italiano* 73 (1961) 1–40; R. Schieffer, 'Tomus Gregorii papae', *Archiv für Diplomatik* 17 (1971) 169–84; H. Hoffmann, 'Zum Register und zu den Briefen Papst Gregors VII', *DAEM* 32 (1976) 86–130; and H. E. Hilpert, 'Zu den Rubriken im Register Gregors VII', *DAEM* 40 (1984) 606–11. The basic study, still important, of the Dictatus Papae is by K. Hofmann, *Der Dictatus Papae Gregors VII* (Paderborn, 1933). The discovery of collections of canons similar to the D.P. has posed the question of their relationship, which is discussed by B. Jacqueline in *RHDFE* iv.34 (1956) 569–74; H. Mordek in *DAEM* 28 (1972) 105–32; F. Kempf in *AHP* 13 (1975) 119–39; and M. Wojtowytsch in *DAEM* 40 (1984) 612–21. The question how far Gregory's reform implied the overturning of the old episcopal constitution of the church is discussed by L. F. J. Meulenberg, *Der Primat der römischen Kirche im Denken und Handeln Gregors VII* (The Hague, 1965) (see also his article in *Concilium* 8/1 (1972) 65–78); J. Gilchrist, 'Gregory VII and the Primacy of the Roman Church', *Tijdschrift voor Rechtsgeschiednis* 36 (1968) 123–35; and I. S. Robinson, '*Periculosus homo*: Pope Gregory VII and Episcopal Authority', *Viator* 9 (1978) 103–31.

ii. The Breach with the Empire. Many aspects of the Investiture Contest are examined in the excellent volume edited by J. Fleckenstein, *Investiturstreit und Reichsverfassung*, VuF 17 (1973), and there are interesting surveys of the period by E. Werner, *Zwischen Canossa und Worms: Staat und Kirche 1077–1122* (Berlin, 1973) (concentrating on the social condition of Germany) and U.-R. Blumenthal, *Der Investiturstreit* (Stuttgart, 1982). There are useful brief extracts assembled by K. F. Morrison, *The Investiture Controversy: Issues, Ideals and Results* (New York, 1971). For a balanced outline of events chapters 2–3 of *CMH*, v, by Z. N. Brooke, are still reliable. On the underlying conflict of policies, there is G. Tabacco, 'Autorità pontificia e impero', MCSM 7 (1974) 123–52. The early stages of the dispute are clarified by J. Fleckenstein, 'Heinrich IV und der deutsche Episkopat in den Anfängen des Investiturstreites', *Adel und Kirche: Festschrift G. Tellenbach*, eds. J. Fleckenstein and K. Schmid (Freiburg-im-Breisgan, 1968), 221–36; and R. Schieffer, '*Spirituales latrones*: zu den Hintergründen der Simonie-prozesse in Deutschland zwischen 1069 und 1975', *HJb* 92 (1972), 19–60. The aims of Henry's religious policy are considered in H. L. Mikoletzky, 'Der "fromme" Kaiser Heinrich IV', *MIOG* 68 (1960), 250–65; A. Nitschke, 'Die Ziele Heinrichs IV' in *Wissenschaft, Wirtschaft und Technik: W. Treue zum 60 Geburtstag* (Munich, 1969), 38–63; and E. Boshof, *Heinrich IV Herrscher an einer Zeitenwende* (Göttingen, 1979).

An exploration of the abundant literature on the crisis of 1076–7 must now begin with the two books of H. Zimmermann, *Der Canossagang von 1077*, Sb Akad. Mainz (1975), and J. Vogel, *Gregor VII und Heinrich IV nach Canossa* (Berlin, 1983). The imperialist Pope Clement III is now the subject of two excellent studies of different kinds by J. Ziese, *Wibert von Ravenna: der Gegenpapst Clemens III* (Stuttgart, 1982), and I. Heidrich, *Ravenna unter Erzbischof Wibert (1073–1100)*, VuF Sonderband 32 (1985), which supersede the earlier studies, good as these were. Also valuable is the edition of materials by M.E. Stoller, 'Schism in the Reform Papacy: the Documents and Councils of the Antipopes 1061–1121' (University of Columbia dissertation, 1985). A particularly good survey of political and ecclesiastical conflicts under Henry IV is by K. Leyser, 'The Crisis of Medieval Germany', *PBA* 69 (1983) 409–43. Among the many local studies may be mentioned those in *Investiturstreit und Reichsverfassung* (see preceding paragraph); the classic by A. H. J. Cauchie, *La querelle des investitures dans les diocèses de Liège et de Cambrai* (Louvain, 1890); and the recent *Adelsopposition und kirchliche Reformbewegung im östlichen Sachsen* by L. Fenske (Göttingen, 1977).

iii. The Revival of the Gregorian Papacy 1085–99. The standard work on Urban II is now A. Becker, *Papst Urban II*, MGH Schriften 19/1 (1964). On his councils see especially R. Somerville, *The Councils of Urban II: 1, Decreta Claromontensia* (Amsterdam, 1972), and 'The Council of Clermont and Latin Christian Society', *AHP* 12 (1974) 55–90. On a crucial question of Urban's idea of his authority there is a valuable article by S. Kuttner, 'Urban II and the Doctrine of Interpretation; a Turning Point?', *S. Grat.* 15 (1972) 55–85. We need a new book on the total contribution of Countess Matilda to the Gregorian papacy, but there are articles on aspects of her policy in *Studi Matildici*, and an interesting book by R. H. Rough, *The Reformist Illuminations in the Gospels of Matilda* (The Hague, 1973), which raises wider issues than the title may suggest.

iv. The War of Ideas 1076–99. The methods by which the controversy was conducted have been splendidly surveyed in two works: the ancient classic of C. Mirbt, *Die Publizistik im Zeitalter Gregors VII* (Leipzig, 1894), and its modern successor, I. S. Robinson's *Authority and Resistance in the Investiture Contest* (Manchester, 1978). The same author has also provided two articles on the circulation of papal propaganda, 'The Friendship Network of Gregory VII', *History* 63 (1978) 1–22, and 'The Dissemination of the Letters of Pope Gregory VII during the Investiture Contest', *JEH* 34 (1983) 175–93. The issues on which the controversy focussed are examined by K. Leyser, 'The Polemics of the Papal Revolution' in B. Smalley (ed.), *Trends in Medieval Political Thought* (Oxford, 1965), 42–64, and J. Ziese, *Historische Beweisführung in Streitschriften des Investiturstreites* (Munich, 1972). The propagandist letters of Henry IV were edited by C. Erdmann, *Die Briefe Heinrichs IV*, MGH Studientexte 1 (1937) and analysed in his 'Die Anfänge der staatlichen Propaganda im Investiturstreit', *HZ* 154 (1936) 491–512. They are translated by T. E. Mommsen and K. F. Morrison, *Imperial Lives and Letters of the Eleventh Century* (New York, 1962). Among the studies of individual episodes and writers there are particularly useful ones by H. Fuhrmann, 'Pseudoisidor, Otto von Ostia und der Zitatenkampf von Gerstungen (1085)', *ZSSRGkA* 99 (1982) 52–69; I. S. Robinson, 'Zur Arbeitsweise Bernolds von Konstanz und seines Kreises', *DAEM* 34.1 Sonderdruck (1978) 51–122; W. Berschin, *Bonizo von Sutri, Leben und Werk* (Berlin, 1972); and W. Hartmann, 'Manegold von Lautenbach und die Anfänge der Frühscholastik', *DAEM* 26 (1970) 47–149.

The wider history of canon law is covered in ch. 16. v below. On the contributions made by Gregory VII and his followers, H. J. Berman, *Law and Revolution: the Formation of the Western Legal Tradition* (Cambridge, Mass., 1983), combines old-fashioned history with interesting ideas. There are very good surveys of the canonical aspects of Gregorianism by J. Gilchrist, 'Canon Law Aspects of the Gregorian Reform Programme', *JEH* 13 (1962) 21–38; H. Fuhrmann, 'Das Reformpapsttum und die Rechts-wissenschaft', *VuF* 17 (1973), 175–203; and H. Mordek, 'Kanonistik und gregorianische Reform', K. Schmid (ed.), *Reich und Kirche vor dem Investiturstreit: Vorträge beim wissenschaftlichen Kolloquium aus Anlass des 80 Geburtstags von G. Tellenbach* (Sigmaringen, 1985) 65–82. On Gregory VII's direct impact on the canons, there are articles by J. Gilchrist in *S. Grat.* 12 (1967) 1–37 and *ZSSRGkA* 97 (1980) 192–229. There is now a good deal of work on the important Constance school: the key study is J. Autenrieth, *Die Domschule von Konstanz zur Zeit des Investiturstreits* (Munich, 1956). J. Gilchrist has edited and translated the important contemporary *Collection in 74 Titles* (Vatican, 1973; and Toronto, 1980), and it has been discussed by J. Autenrieth, 'Bernold von Konstanz und die erweiterte 74-Titelsammlung', *DAEM* 14 (1958) 375–94, and H. Fuhrmann, 'Über den Reformgeist der 74-Titelsammlung', *Festschrift H. Heimpel* ii (Göttingen, 1972) 1101–20. The collection of Anselm of Lucca has been insufficiently studied; indeed, there is not even a full edition, because that of F. Thaner (Innsbrück, 1906–15), provides a rather unsatisfactory text and was incomplete at the time of the editor's death. A good introduction is by A. Amanieu in *Dic. DC* i. 567–78. The collection of Deusdedit was edited by W. von Glanvell (Paderborn, 1905); that of Atto exists in an old edition by A. Mai (Rome, 1832), which is now our only source as the manuscript is lost.

Chapter 6: Greeks and Saracens

i. The Situation in the Mediterranean World. Many aspects of this are covered in works listed in the following sections, and Spain is the subject of a separate volume. The movement of the Greek and Latin churches to their final divorce is the subject of one of Sir Steven Runciman's best books, *The Eastern Schism* (Oxford, 1955), and there are interesting discussions of eleventh-century developments by D. M. Nicol, 'Byzantium and the Papacy in the Eleventh Century', *JEH* 13 (1962) 1–20 and J. Gauss, *Ost und West in der Kirchen- und Papstgeschichte des 11 Jhs* (Zurich, 1967). The crisis of 1054 is discussed by R. Mayne, 'East and West in 1054', *Cambridge Historical Journal* 11 (1954) 133–48; E. Petrucci, 'Rapporti di Leone IX con Costantinopoli', *Studi Medievali* iii.14–15 (1973–4); and in a particularly perceptive article by W. M. Plöchl, 'Zur Aufhebung der Bannbullen von 1054', *ZSSRGkA* 88 (1971) 1–21.

ii. The Conquest of Sicily and Apulia. The classic work is by F. Chalandon, *Histoire de la domination normande en Italie et en Sicile*, 2 vols. (Paris 1907); see also his ch. 4 in *CMH* v; R. S. Lopez in K. M. Setton vol. i (section iv below), i. 54–67; and the articles edited by C. N. L. Brooke, *The Normans in Sicily and S. Italy* (Oxford, 1977). On the Moslems there is M. Amari, *Storia dei musulmani di Sicilia*, 2nd edn. (Catania, 1933–8), and A. Ahmad, *A History of Islamic Sicily* (Edinburgh, 1975). In ch. 6 of *The Arabs and Medieval Europe* (London, 1975), N. Daniel fires a powerful broadside against the picture of Norman Sicily as a tolerant land of three cultures. The policy of the Norman conquerors is surveyed by J. Décarreaux, *Normands, papes et moines* (Paris, 1974); and in the collection, *Roberto il Guiscard e il suo tempo* (Rome, 1975). The best source, the *Ystoire de li Normant* of Aimé of Monte Cassino, is edited by V. de Bartholomaeis, Fonti per la Storia d'Italia 76 (Rome, 1935). The balance which the conquerors pursued between Latinization and the protection of Greek churches is examined by H.-W. Klewitz, 'Studien über die Wiederherstellung der Römischen Kirche in Süditalien durch das Reformpapsttum', *QFIAB* 25 (1934/5) 105–57; Lynn White, *Latin Monasticism in Norman Sicily* (Cambridge, Mass., 1938, repr. 1968); L.-R. Ménager, 'Les fondations monastiques de Robert Guiscard', *QFIAB* 39 (1959) 1–116; and E. Caspar, *Die Gründungsurkunden der sicilischen Bistümer und die Kirchenpolitik Graf Rogers I* (Innsbruck, 1902). On the character of the Greek church there is an important collection of studies in *La chiesa greca in Italia*, Atti del Convegno storico interecclesiale (Bari), 3 vols. (Padua, 1973), and interesting discussions by F. Giunta, *Bizantini e bizantismo nella Sicilia normanna*, new edn. (Palermo, 1974) (mainly political in its stress), and A. Guillou, 'Italie méridionale byzantine ou Byzantins en Italie méridionale?', *Byzantion* 44 (1974) 152–90. Works on the political relationship of the new Norman state with the papacy, and the position of the ruler as apostolic legate, are listed under ch. 9 iv below.

iii. The Rise of Christian Militarism. The classic study by C. Erdmann is now available in English translation as *The Origin of the Idea of Crusade* (Princeton, 1977), and is still of great importance in spite of some amendments to its argument, for example by J. Gilchrist, 'The Erdmann Thesis and the Canon Law', *Crusade and Settlement* (see iv below) 37–45. There are some interesting studies in Murphy, *The Holy War* (Ohio, 1976). The disputed contribution of Cluny to the new militarism is considered by H. E. J. Cowdrey, 'Cluny and the First Crusade', *Revue Bénédictine* 83 (1973) 285–311, and E. Delaruelle, 'The Crusading Idea in Cluniac Literature' in N. Hunt (ed.), *Cluniac Monasticism in the Central Middle Ages* (London, 1971), 191–216. Episodes which mark the emergence of a new form of militarism are discussed by H. E. J. Cowdrey, 'Pope Gregory VII's "Crusading" Plan of 1074' in Prawer, *Outremer* (see iv below) 27–40; I. S. Robinson, 'Gregory VII and the Soldiers of Christ', *History* 58 (1973) 169–92; and H. E. J. Cowdrey, 'The Mahdia Campaign of 1087', *EHR* 92 (1977) 1–29.

iv. The First Crusade. For the bibliography of the crusades as a whole, see H. E. Mayer, *Bibliographie zur Geschichte der Kreuzzüge* (Hanover, 1960). The best general histories are by Mayer, *The Crusades* (Oxford, 1972), and J. Riley-Smith, *The Crusades* (London, 1987). There is a full narrative account by S. Runciman, *A History of the Crusades*, 3 vols. (Cambridge, 1951–4), and a long series of studies edited by K. M. Setton, *A History of the Crusades*, 5 vols. (Wisconsin, 1962–85). There are valuable studies in P. M. Holt (ed.), *The Eastern Mediterranean Lands in the Period of the Crusades* (Warminster, 1977); J. Prawer, *Crusader Institutions* (Oxford, 1980); *Outremer: Studies in the History of the Crusading Kingdom of Jerusalem presented to Joshua Prawer* (Jerusalem, 1982); and *Crusade and Settlement*, First Conference of the Society for the Study of the Crusades and the Latin East, ed. P. W. Edbury (Cardiff, 1985). The impact of the experience of the First Crusade on western thinking has been examined in a crucial article by E. O. Blake, 'The Formation of the "Crusade Idea"', *JEH* 21 (1970) 11–31, and now by J. Riley-Smith in *The First Crusade and the Idea of Crusading* (London, 1986). He has also provided an interesting introduction to the ideas underlying the crusades in *What were the Crusades?* (London, 1977), and (jointly with L. Riley-Smith) an excellent collection of translated documents in *The Crusades: Ideas and Reality* (London, 1981). See also the essays by E. Delaruelle in the collection *L'idée de croisade au Moyen Âge* (Turin, 1980). For the evolution of the western understanding of Islam, one should begin with R. W. Southern, *Western Views of Islam in the Middle Ages* (Cambridge, Mass., 1962), and M. T. d'Alverny, 'La connaissance de l'Islam en occident du IXe au milieu du XIIe siècle', SSCISAM 12 (1965) 577–602, 791–803. The tradition of lives of Mahomet in the west is lucidly traced in Y. G. Lepage (ed.), *Le roman de Mahomet de Alexandre du Pont* (Paris, 1977), and there are further studies by N. Daniel, *Heroes and Saracens: a Reinterpretation of the* chansons de geste (Edinburgh, 1982); J. Bray, 'The Mohammetan and Idolatry', *SCH* 21 (1984) 89–98; and M. Bennett, 'First Crusaders' images of Muslims: the influence of vernacular poetry?', *Forum for Modern Language Studies* 22/2 (1986) 101–22.

Chapter 7: The Conflict Renewed 1099–1122

i. *Paschal II*. The most basic recent work is that by C. Servatius, *Paschalis II: Studien zu seiner Person und seiner Politik* (Stuttgart, 1979). For a good bibliographical review, see G. M. Cantarella, 'Le vicende di Pasquale II nella recente storiografia', *RSCI* 35 (1981) 486–504. There is a valuable work on the second phase of the Investiture Contest by M. Minninger, *Von Clermont zum Wormser Konkordat* (Cologne, 1978); and (in spite of a slightly misleading title) F.-J. Schmale's article 'Papsttum und Kurie zwischen Gregor VII und Innocenz II', *HZ* 193 (1961) 265–85, is very perceptive on relations with the empire. Paschal's attitude to papal authority is examined in important studies by U-R. Blumenthal, 'Paschal II and the Roman Primacy', *AHP* 16 (1978) 67–92, and G. M. Cantarella, *Ecclesiologia e politica nel papato di Pasquale II* (Rome, 1982). The policy of the early years is illuminated by U.-R. Blumenthal, *The Early Councils of Pope Paschal II, 1100–10* (Toronto, 1978), and its further development by M. J. Wilks, '*Ecclesiastica* and *regalia*: Papal Investiture Policy 1006–23', *SCH* 8 (1971) 69–85. There are perceptive examinations of imperialist policy by A. Waas, *Heinrich V: Gestalt und Verhängnis des letzten salischen Kaisers* (Munich, 1967), and K. Leyser, 'England and the Empire in the Early Twelfth Century', *TRHS* V.10 (1960) 61–83. The crisis of 1111–12 has naturally attracted a great deal of attention from historians. Important among the analyses are P. R. McKeon, 'The Lateran Council of 1112, the "Heresy" of Lay Investiture and the excommunication of Henry V', *Medievalia et Humanistica* 17 (1966) 3–12; P. Zerbi, *Pasquale II e l'ideale della povertà della chiesa* (Milan, 1966); S. Chodorow, 'Ideology and Canon Law in the Crisis of 1111', *ICMCL* 4 (1976) 55–80; U-R. Blumenthal, 'Patrimonia and Regalia in 1111' in *Law, Church and Society: Essays in Honour of Stephan Kuttner*, ed. K. Pennington and R. Sommerville (Pennsylvania, 1977) 9–20, and 'Opposition to Paschal II', *AHC* 10 (1978) 82–98; and M. Stroll, 'New

Perspectives on the Struggle between Guy of Vienne and Henry V', *AHP* 18 (1980) 97–115.

The background of church–state relations in England before the conflict over investitures is best approached through M. Gibson, *Lanfranc of Bec* (Oxford, 1978) and also *The Letters of Lanfranc, Archbishop of Canterbury*, ed. and tr. by V. H. Clover and M. Gibson (Oxford, 1979). On the conflict itself there is N. F. Cantor, *Church, Kingship and Lay Investiture in England 1089–1135* (Princeton, 1958), and a judicious study of Henry I's government of the church by M. Brett, *The English Church under Henry I* (Oxford, 1975). R. W. Southern's *Saint Anselm and his Biographer* (Cambridge, 1963), is a really outstanding book; some of its views have been challenged by S. Vaughn in 'S. Anselm of Canterbury: the Philosopher-saint as Politician', *JMH* 1 (1975) 279–305, and 'S. Anselm and the English Investiture Controversy Reconsidered', *JMH* 6 (1980) 61–86. On France there is M. Pacaut, 'L'investiture en France au début du XIIe siècle', *Le Bras* i.665–72 and A. Becker, *Studien zum Investiturstreit in Frankreich 1049–1119* (Saarbrücken, 1955). H. Hoffmann, 'Ivo von Chartres und die Lösung des Investiturproblems', *DAEM* 15 (1959) 393–440, is important for the settlement in both countries.

ii. The Concordat of Worms. The classic history of Pope Calixtus II is still U. Robert, *Histoire du pape Calixte II* (Paris, 1891), but there are important revisions by S. A. Chodorow, 'Ecclesiastical Politics and the Ending of the Investiture Contest', *Speculum* 46 (1971) 613–40; R. Somerville, 'The Councils of Pope Calixtus II: Reims 1119', *ICMCL* 5 (1976) 35–50; and M. Stroll, 'Calixtus II: a Reinterpretation of his Election and the End of the Investiture Contest', *Studies in Medieval and Renaissance History* 3 (1980) 1–53. P. Classen, 'Das Wormser Konkordat in der deutschen Verfassungsgeschichte', *VuF* 17 (1973) 411–60, is a truly magisterial survey, and H. Büttner, 'Erzbischof Adalbert von Mainz, die Kurie und das Reich' in the same volume 395–410 is also important. W. Fritz provides a useful collection of the relevant texts, taken from the MGH editions, in *Die Quellen zum Wormser Konkordat* (Berlin, 1955).

iii. Papal Administration. Karl Jordan began a new period in the study of its development under the reforming popes in 'Die Entstehung der römischen Kurie', *ZSSRGkA* 59 (1939) 97–152, and 'Die päpstliche Verwaltung im Zeitalter Gregors VII', *S. Greg.* 1 (1947) 111–35. J. Sydow, 'Untersuchungen zur kurialen Verwaltungsgeschichte im Zeitalter des Reformpapsttums', *DAEM* 11 (1954/5) 18–73, and R. Elze, 'Das *sacrum palatium lateranense* im 10. und 11. Jh', *S. Greg.* 4 (1952) 27–54, extended his findings, while E. Pasztor reviewed the development of the papal curia in interesting articles in MCSM 7 (1974) 490–504 and *S. Greg.* 10 (1975) 317–39, where she (perhaps questionably) traces the beginnings of a curia-type structure as early as Alexander II. R. L. Poole's book, *Lectures on the History of the Papal Chancery* (Cambridge, 1915), remains a model of the exposition of complex material, and P. Rasbiskaus, 'Die römische Kuriale in der päpstlichen Kanzlei', *Miscellanea Historiae Pontificiae* 20 (1958) goes far beyond the script into the broader history of the chancery. On the papal chapel, the study by R. Elze, 'Die päpstliche Kapelle im 12 und 13 Jh.', *ZSSRGkA* 67 (1950) 145–204, has now been expanded by S. Haider, 'Zu den Anfängen der päpstlichen Kapelle', *MIOG* 87 (1979) 38–70. On finance under the reforming popes, there are two studies of particular importance: K. Jordan, 'Zur päpstlichen Finanzgeschichte im 11 und 12 Jh', *QFIAB* 25 (1933–4) 61–104, and J. Sydow, 'Cluny und die Anfänge der apostolischen Kammer', *Studien und Mitteilungen zur Geschichte des Benedikter-Ordens* 63 (1951) 45–66. D. B. Zema probably gives too much credit to Gregory VII as a financial reformer in his articles, 'Reform Legislation in the Eleventh Century and its Economic Import', *Catholic Historical Review* 27 (1941) 16–38, and 'Economic Reorganization of the Roman See during the Gregorian Reform', *S. Greg.* 1 (1947) 137–68.

The growth of the college of cardinals was worked out by H. W. Klewitz in his essential article, 'Die Entstehung des Kardinalkollegiums', *ZSSRGkA* 25 (1936) 115–221 and in his *Reformpapsttum und Kardinalkolleg* (Darmstadt, 1957); to which should be added S. Kuttner, 'Cardinalis: the History of a Canonical Concept', *Traditio* 3 (1945) 121–214. The series of studies by C. G. Fürst, *Cardinalis: Prolegomena zu einer Rechtsgeschichte des römischen Kardinalskollegiums* (Munich, 1967), does not go far into our period, but provides valuable background; and biographical information is provided in the excellent book by R. Hüls, *Kardinäle, Klerus und Kirchen Roms 1049–1130* (Tübingen, 1977). A broad discussion of the nature of the office is provided by G. Alberigo, *Cardinalato e collegialità: studi sull'ecclesiologia tra l'XI e il XIV secolo* (Florence, 1969); to which M. Fois puts forward an alternative interpretation in articles in *AHP* 10 (1972) 25–105 and 14 (1976) 383–416.

iv. The Achievement of the Papal Reform Movement. The assessment of this has to be based on works already mentioned, and others listed in the next section.

PART II: THE GROWTH OF CHRISTENDOM (1122–98)

In addition to the general works mentioned at the beginning of the bibliography, there are good surveys of this period by S. R. Packard, *Twelfth-century Europe: an Interpretative Essay* (Amherst, 1973), and P. Zerbi, *Tra Milano e Cluny: momenti di vita e cultura ecclesiastica nel secolo XII* (Rome, 1978). It was the book of C. H. Haskins, *The Renaissance of the Twelfth Century* (Cambridge, Mass., 1927), which established this concept as an historical category, and its development in modern scholarship is recorded in the magnificent collection edited by R. L. Benson and G. Constable, *Renaissance and Renewal in the Twelfth Century* (Oxford, 1982). C. Brooke has provided a more popular survey in *The Twelfth Century Renaissance* (London, 1969), and there are other collections by M. de Gandillac and E. Jeauneau, *Entretiens sur la renaissance du XIIe siècle* (Paris, 1968), and P. Weimar, *Die Renaissance der Wissenschaften im 12 Jh.* (Zürich, 1981). The awareness of a changing culture was sometimes expressed in a contrast between 'modern' and 'ancient' writers: see the collection of studies edited by A. Zimmermann, *Antiqui und Moderni: Traditionsbewusstsein und Fortschrittbewusstsein im späten Mittelalter*, Misc.Med. 9 (Berlin, 1974), and articles by B. Smalley, 'Ecclesiastical Attitudes to Novelty *c.*1100–1250', *SCH* 12 (1975) 113–31, and M. T. Clanchy, '*Moderni* in Education and Government in England', *Speculum* 50 (1975) 671–88. On two characteristic themes of the period see E. Jeauneau, 'Nains et géants', in Gandillac-Jeauneau (above) 21–38; and A. G. Jongkees, '*Translatio studii*: les avateurs d'un thème médiéval', *Miscellanea mediaevalia in memoriam J. F. Niermeyer* (Groningen, 1967).

Chapter 8. The Roman Church and the Empire in the Twelfth Century

i. *After the Concordat of Worms.* The interpretation of the schism of 1130 as a split between old Gregorians and the new ideas of Haimeric's party was first offered in the important article of H.-W. Klewitz, 'Das Ende des Reformpapsttums', *DAEM* 3 (1939) 372–412. This view was elaborated in F.-J. Schmale, *Studien zum Schisma des Jahres 1130* (Cologne-Graz, 1961) and (with fewer reservations) in H. Bloch, 'The Schism of Anacletus II and the Glanfeuil Forgeries', *Traditio* 8 (1952) 159–264, and S. Chodorow, *Christian Political Theory and Church Politics in the mid-twelfth Century* (Berkeley, 1972); on which, see the review by R. L. Benson in *Speculum* 50 (1975) 97–106. This approach has been criticized by M. Stroll, *The Jewish Pope* (Leiden, 1987), and W. Maleczek, 'Das Kardinalskollegium unter Innocenz II und Anacletus II', *AHP* 19 (1981) 27–78. P. Classen has examined the early career of Anastasius IV in *QFIAB* 48 (1968) 36–63. F.-J. Schmale rejected the early letters of Innocent II to Germany in 'Die Bemühungen Innozenz' II um seine Anerkennung in Deutschland', *ZKg* 65 (1953–4) 240–69, but evidence to the contrary is provided in M. da Bergamo, 'Osservazioni sulle fonti per la duplice elezione papale del 1130', *Aevum* 39 (1965) 45–65 and R. Somerville, 'Pope Honorius II, Conrad of Hohenstaufen and Lothar III', *AHP* 10 (1972) 341–6. On the acceptance of Innocent in France there is A. Grabois, 'Le schisme de 1130 et la France', *RHE* 76 (1981) 593–612 and T. Reuter, 'Zur Anerkennung Papst Innozenz' II', *DAEM* 39 (1983) 395–416.

There is still much of value in H. Gleber, *Papst Eugen III* (Jena, 1936). A. Verrycken has written a stimulating article on Wibald of Stavelot, 'Au service de l'Empire ou de la papauté?', *RHE* 73 (1978); and F.-J. Jakobi a fine book, *Wibald von Stablo und Corvey* (Münster, 1979). Much the best study of Lothar's relationship with the church is now M.-L. Crone, *Untersuchungen zur Reichskirchenpolitik Lothars III zwischen reichskirchlicher Tradition und Reformkurie* (Frankfurt, 1982). The policy of Conrad III is surveyed by F. Geldner, 'Zur neuen Beurteilung König Konrads III', *Monumentum Bamburgense; Festgabe für B. Kraft* (Munich, 1955), 395–412.

ii. Frederick I and the Renewal of the Empire. The most convenient collection of studies on relevant aspects of Frederick I is *Friedrich Barbarossa* ed. by G. Wolf, Wege der Forschung 390 (Darmstadt, 1975), and the main English life is P. Munz, *Frederick Barbarossa* (London, 1969), although I have not followed his analysis of the development of Frederick's policy. The opening years of the reign are closely studied by M. Maccarrone, *Papato e impero dalla elezione di Federico I alla morte di Adriano IV* (Rome, 1959), and have more recently been discussed by O. Engels, 'Zum Konstanzer Vertrag von 1153', *Deus qui mutat tempora: Menschen und Institutionen im Wandel des Mittelalters: Festschrift für Alfons Becker* (Sigmaringen, 1987), 235–58. The imperial ideology is analysed in an important article by R. L. Benson, 'Political Renovatio: Two Models from Roman Antiquity', *RR* 339–86, and also by P. Rassow, *Honor Imperii*, new edn. (Munich, 1961). Frederick's religious convictions are examined by F. Opll, '*Amator Ecclesiarum*: Studien zur religiösen Haltung Friedrich Barbarossas', *MIOG* 88 (1980) 70–93. The affair at Sutri is the subject of a classic debate beginning with R. Holtzmann, *Der Kaiser als Marschall des Papstes,* (Berlin, 1928), and followed by E. Eichmann in *HZ* 142 (1930) 16–40, with a reply in *HZ* 145 (1932) 301–50. On Besançon, see W. Ullmann, 'Cardinal Roland and Besançon', *Miscellanea Historiae Pontificae* 18 (1954) 107–25, and especially W. Heinemeyer, 'Beneficium—non feudum', *Archiv für Diplomatik* 15 (1969) 155–236.

iii. The Alexandrine Schism. The two standard books with which to start are M. W. Baldwin, *Alexander III and the Twelfth Century* (New Jersey, 1968), and M. Pacaut, *Alexandre III: étude sur la conception du pouvoir pontifical dans sa pensée et dans son œuvre* (Paris, 1956); and more recently there is F. Liotta (ed.), *Miscellanea Rolando Bandinelli, papa Alessandro III* (Siena, 1986). On the important question of his legal education, see J. T. Noonan, 'Who was Rolandus?', *Law, Church and Society: Essays in Honour of Stephan Kuttner*, ed. K. Pennington and R. Somerville (Pennsylvania, 1977) 21–48, and R. Weigand, 'M. Rolandus und Papst Alexander III', *Archiv für katholisches Kirchenrecht* 149 (1980) 3–44. The contemporary biography of Alexander exists in English translation by G. M. Ellis, *Boso's Life of Alexander III* (Oxford, 1973). The two best studies of the origins of the schism are those by W. Madertoner, *Die zwiespältige Papstwahl des Jahres 1159* (Vienna, 1978), and T. A. Reuter, 'The Papal Schism, the Empire and the West' (unpublished University of Oxford D.Phil. thesis, 1975). The recognition of Alexander in England and France is complicated by dating problems. These may be studied in M. G. Cheney, 'The Recognition of Pope Alexander III', *EHR* 84 (1969) 474–97; P. Classen, 'Das Konzil von Toulouse 1160, eine Fiktion', *DAEM* 29 (1973) 220–3; and R. Somerville, *Pope Alexander III and the Council of Tours* (Los Angeles, 1977). There is a brilliant summary of Alexander's policy by G. Tabacco, 'Empirismo politico e flessibilità ideologica', *Bollettino Storico-bibliografico Subalpino* 81 (1983) 239–46. On the position at Rome during the schism, there is interesting material in A. Wilmart, 'Nouvelles de Rome au temps d'Alexandre III', *Revue Bénédictine* 45 (1933) 62–78, and J. Petersohn, 'Papstschisma und Kirchenfrieden: *De vera pace contra schisma sedis apostolicae* aus dem Jahre 1171', *QFIAB* 59 (1979) 158–97.

iv. The Papacy under Pressure. There is a good general survey of this period in P. Zerbi, *Papato, impero e respublica christiana dal 1187 al 1198* (Milan, 1955). The crucial events at Verona are well examined by G. Baaken, '*Unio regni ad imperium*: die Verhandlungen von Verona 1184', *QFIAB* 52 (1972) 219–97, and the background by H. Wolter, 'Die Verlobung Heinrichs VI mit Konstanze von Sizilien im Jahre 1184', *HJb* 105 (1985) 30–51. On Clement III see V. Pfaff, 'Papst Clemens III', *ZSSRGkA* 97 (1980) 261–316 and W. Maleczek in *LdM* ii.2140–1. The pontificate of Celestine III is well surveyed in V. Pfaff, 'Das Papsttum in der Weltpolitik des endenden XII Jhs', *MIOG* 82 (1974) 338–76; see also his articles in *ZSSRGkA* 78 (1961) 109–28 and 91 (1974) 121–167, L. Vones in *LdM* iii.4–7, and K. Baaken, 'Zur Wahl, Weihe und Krönung Papst Cölestins III', *DAEM* 41 (1985) 203–11. The classic discussions of Haller, Pfaff and others on the papal–imperial negotiations of 1196 are summarized and updated in G. Baaken, 'Die Verhandlungen zwischen Kaiser Heinrich VI und Papst Coelestin III', *DAEM* 27 (1971) 457–513. The dispute at Liège is discussed by R. H. Schmandt, 'The election and assassination of Albert of Louvain', *Speculum* 42 (1967) 639–60, and B. Smalley, *The Becket Conflict and the Schools* (Oxford, 1973), 208–15.

Chapter 9: The Government of the Church in the Twelfth Century

i. The Concept of Papal Authority. There are two outstanding general studies on this subject: Y. Congar, *L'église: de S. Augustin à l'époque moderne*, Histoire des dogmes (Paris, 1970), and B. Tierney, *Foundations of the Conciliar Theory* (Cambridge, 1955). In addition there are useful discussions of papal titles and prerogatives, including M. Maccarrone, *Vicarius Christi: storia del titolo papale* (Rome, 1952), and an article, which is not always given the attention it deserves, by M. Wilks, 'The *apostolicus* and the Bishop of Rome', *Journal of Theological Studies* NS 13 (1962) 290–317 and 14 (1963) 311–54. The development of the concept of plenitude of power is examined by J. Rivière, '*In partem sollicitudinis*. Évolution d'une formule pontificale', *Revue des sciences religieuses* 5 (1925) 210–31, and R. L. Benson, '*Plenitudo potestatis*:

Evolution of a Formula', *S. Grat.* 14 (1967) 193–217. The idea of the *status ecclesie* and its importance for papal theory is considered in J. Hackett, 'The State of the Church: a Concept of the Medieval Canonists', *The Jurist* 23 (1963) 259–90, and Y. Congar, '*Status ecclesie*', *S. Grat.* 15 (1972) 1–31. On the two-sword theory there is W. Levison, 'Die mittelalterliche Lehre von den beiden Schwerten', *DAEM* 9 (1951–2) 14–42; J. Leclerc, 'L'argument des deux glaives', *Recherches de Science Religieuse* 21 (1931) 299–339; and H.-X. Arquillière, 'Origines de la théorie des deux glaives', *S. Greg.* 1 (1947) 501–21. The medieval ignorance of the case of Pope Honorius, so important in later controversy, is explained by G. Kreuzer, *Die Honoriusfrage im Mittelalter und in der Neuzeit* (Stuttgart, 1975). The influential *De consideratione* of Bernard of Clairvaux has been examined by many scholars and its idea of the papacy diversely interpreted. See for example E. Kennan, 'The *De consideratione* of S. Bernard of Clairvaux and the Papacy: a Review of Scholarship', *Traditio* 23 (1967) 73–115; J. W. Gray, 'The Problem of Papal Power in the Ecclesiology of S. Bernard', *TRHS* V 24 (1974) 1–17; and B. Jacqueline, *Episcopat et papauté chez S. Bernard de Clairvaux* (Saint-Lô, 1975).

ii. The Exercise of Papal Power. The starting-point for the college of cardinals in the twelfth century is W. Maleczek, *Papst und Kardinalskolleg von 1191 bis 1216* (Vienna, 1984), which surveys the whole century and provides an excellent bibliography. The theory of the cardinal's office is examined in an interesting article by J. Lecler, '*Pars corporis papae*: le sacré collège dans l'ecclésiologie médiévale', *Mélanges H. de Lubac* (Paris, 1964), ii.183–98. The functioning of the cardinals is examined by J. von Sydow in 'Il *concistorium* dopo lo schisma del 1130', *RSCI* 9 (1955) 165–76. For other works on cardinals, see ch. 7.iii above. The emergence of delegate jurisdiction may be studied in works on some of the leading judges themselves, notably A. Morey, *Bartholomew of Exeter* (Cambridge, 1967), A. Morey and C. N. L. Brooke, *Gilbert Foliot and his Letters* (Cambridge, 1965), and M. Cheney, *Roger Bishop of Worcester* (Oxford, 1980). There are some interesting observations on the early stages by D. Lohrmann, 'Papstprivileg und päpstliche Delegationsgerichtsbarkeit im nördlichen Frankreich, *ICMCL* 6 (1985) 535–50. Although their main subject is the period after 1200, two studies are also of importance for the twelfth century: J. E. Sayers, *Papal Judges Delegate in the Province of Canterbury 1198–1254* (Oxford, 1971), and E. Pitz, 'Die römische Kurie als Thema der vergleichenden Sozial-geschichte', *QFIAB* 58 (1978) 216–359. Relations between curia and provinces are reviewed by V. Pfaff, 'Der Widerstand der Bischöfe gegen den päpstlichen Zentralismus um 1200', *ZSSRGkA* 97 (1980) 459–65.

On finance, the classic books are by W. E. Lunt, *Papal Revenues in the Middle Ages* (New York, 1934), and *Financial Relations of England and the Papacy to 1327* (Cambridge, Mass., 1939), to which should be added V. Pfaff, 'Die Einnahmen der römischen Kurie am Ende des 12 Jhs',

Vierteljahresschrift für Sozialwissenschaft und Wirtschaftsgeschichte 40 (1953) 97–118 and 'Aufgaben und Probleme der päpstlichen Finanzverwaltung am Ende des 12 Jhs', *MIOG* 64 (1956) 1–24. On the earlier books prepared by chamberlains, see W. Maleczek, 'Boso', *LdM* ii.478–9, and U.-R. Blumenthal, 'Cardinal Albinus of Albano and the *Digesta pauperis scolaris Albini*', *AHP* 20 (1983) 7–50. The standard edition of Cencius is by P. Fabre and L. Duchesne, *Le Liber Censuum de l'église romaine*' (Paris, 1910), and there are recent discussions by T. Schmidt in *QFIAB* 60 (1980) 511–22 and T. Montecchi Palazzi in *Mélanges de l'école française de Rome* 96 (1984) 49–93, where the development of the cameral literature is surveyed.

There are excellent brief introductions to councils in the period by G. Fransen, 'Papes, conciles généraux et oecuméniques', and R. Foreville, 'Royaumes, métropolitains et conciles provinciaux' in MCSM VII (1974) 203–28 and 272–315; for Third Lateran see J. Longère (ed), *La troisième concile de Latran* (Paris, 1982). The best starting-point for the study of legates is W. Janssen, *Die päpstlichen Legaten in Frankreich 1130–98* (Cologne, 1961). On the growth of papal power in canonization processes, there is E. W. Kemp, *Canonization and Authority in the Western Church* (Oxford, 1948), and R. Foreville, 'Canterbury et la canonisation des saints au XIIe siècle', *Tradition and Change; Essays in Honour of Marjorie Chibnall* (Cambridge, 1985), 63–75.

iii. The Pastorate of the Bishops. The episcopal office can be studied from general books on the institutions of the church, and there is a particularly fine collection of studies in *Le istituzioni ecclesiastiche della societas christiana dei secoli XI-XII*, MCSM 8 (1977). For the particular question of the restitution of churches it is necessary to turn to a series of local studies, among them A. Chédeville for Le Mans in *CCM* 3 (1960) 209–17; B. Chevalier for Tours in *Études de civilisation médiévale: mélanges offerts à E.-R. Labande* (Poitiers, 1975), 129–44; G. Devailly for Berry and Brittany in *Bulletin Philologique et Historique* 1968 (1971) ii.583–97; and W. Ziezulewicz for St Florent, Saumur, in *RB* 96 (1986) 106–17. Another series well worth consulting is the *Histoire des diocèses de France* directed by B. Plongeron and A. Vauchez, Paris (in course of publication). See also B. Guillemain, 'Les origines des évêques en France aux XIe et XIIe siècles', MCSM 7 (1974) 374–407. On the ideal of the bishop, see C. B. Bouchard, *Spirituality and Administration: the Role of the Bishop in Twelfth-century Auxerre* (Cambridge, Mass., 1979). Electoral procedures have been the subject of some valuable studies during the past thirty years. Notable among them are R. L. Benson, *The Bishop-elect: a Study in Medieval Ecclesiastical Office* (Princeton, 1968), who has also provided an excellent outline, 'Election by community and chapter', *The Jurist* 31 (1971) 54–80. On a series of technical aspects of the development there are good discussions by K. Ganzer, 'Zur Beschränkung der Bischofswahl auf die Domkapitel', *ZSSRGkA* 57/88 (1971) 22–82 and 58/

89 (1972) 166–97; H. Müller, *Der Anteil der Laien an den Bischofswahl* (Amsterdam, 1977); and J. Gaudemet, 'Unanimité et majorité', *Études historiques à N. Didier* (Paris, 1960), 149–62. On episcopal elections in France, see P. Imbart de la Tour, *Les élections épiscopales dans l'église de France du IXe au XIIe siècle'* (Paris, 1891); M. Pacaut, *Louis VII et les élections épiscopales dans le royaume de France* (Paris, 1957); and G. Constable, 'The disputed election at Langres in 1138', *Traditio* 13 (1957) 119–52.

iv. Churches and Kingdoms. The impact of Gregorian ideas is discussed in an excellent article by B. Töpfer, 'Tendenzen zur Entsakralisierung der Herrscherwürde in der Zeit des Investiturstreites', *Jahrbuch für Geschichte des Feudalismus* 6 (1982) 163–72. The policy of Suger is examined in M. Aubert, *Suger* (St Wandrille, 1950); G. M. Spiegel, 'The cult of S. Denis and Capetian kingship', *JMH* 1 (1975) 43–69; R. J. Braud, 'Suger and the Making of the French Nation' (University of Southwestern Louisiana D. Phil Thesis, 1977); and (on the Donation of Charlemagne) C. van de Kieft, 'Deux diplômes faux de Charlemagne au XIIe siècle', *MA* 13 (1958) 401–36. The classic discussion on Louis VII is M. Pacaut, *Louis VII et son royaume* (Paris, 1964). The control of the Sicilian kings over the church is analysed in E. Caspar, 'Die Legatengewalt der normannisch–sicilischen Herrscher im 12 Jh', *QFIAB* 7 (1904) 189–219; J. Déer, 'Der Anspruch der Herrscher des 12 Jhs auf die apostolische Legation', *AHP* 2 (1964) 117–86; S. Fodale, *Comes et Legatus Siciliae* (Palermo, 1970); and G. A. Loud, 'Royal Control of the Church in the Twelfth-Century Kingdom of Sicily', *SCH* 18 (1982) 147–60.

The transformation of the church in Ireland is covered in the first chapters of the excellent book by J. A. Watt, *The Church and the Two Nations in Medieval Ireland* (Cambridge, 1970). See also the articles by J. G. Barry, 'Monasticism and Religious Organization in Rural Ireland', *MCSM* 8 (1977) 406–15 and P. Sheehy, 'The Bull *Laudabiliter*', *Galway Arch. & Hist. Soc. Journal* 29 (1961) 45–70. The huge output of contemporary work on the Becket controversy can be consulted in *Materials for the History of Thomas Becket*, ed. J. C. Robertson, 7 vols. RS 67 (London, 1875–85). Modern historians have been equally profuse, and one can only suggest the key works of D. Knowles, *Thomas Becket* (London, 1970); B. Smalley, *The Becket Conflict and the Schools* (Oxford, 1973); and C. N. L. Brooke, *Gilbert Foliot and his Letters* (Cambridge, 1965). The criminous clerk dispute is reassessed in C. Duggan, 'The Becket dispute and criminous clerks', *Bulletin of The Institute of Historical Research* 35 (1962) 1–28, and R. M. Fraher, 'The Becket Dispute and Two Decretist Traditions', *JMH* 4 (1978) 347–68. On the consequences of Becket's death there is an overview in C. R. Cheney, *From Becket to Langton: English Church Government 1170–1213* (Manchester, 1956). M. Howell's *Regalian Right in medieval England*

(London, 1962), gives valuable information about the royal exploitation of the church.

Chapter 10: The New Monastic Orders

For general books about monasticism, see under Chapter 3 above.

i. From Hermitage to Monastery. The emergence of organized religious movements (whether catholic or heretical) from the earlier groups of hermits is the subject of a classic book by H. Grundmann, *Religiöse Bewegungen im Mittelalter* (Berlin, 1935), with a supplement in *AKg* 37 (1955) 129–82, and of a very useful survey by B. Bolton, *The Medieval Reformation* (London, 1983). In addition to relevant studies already mentioned in ch. 3.iii, there are valuable articles by P. Zerbi, 'Vecchio e nuovo monachesimo alla metà del secolo XII', MCSM 9 (1980) 3–26, and Ilarino da Milano, 'Vita evangelica e vita apostolica nell'azione dei riformisti sul papato del secolo XII' in *Problemi di storia della chiesa* (Milan, 1976), 21–72.

There are many good studies on the evolution of hermit life in our period in *L'eremitismo in occidente nei secoli XI e XII*, MCSM 4 (1965). Among the Italian hermit-orders, the classic history of Camaldoli was written by J. B. Mittarelli and A. Costadoni, *Annales Camaldulenses*, 9 vols. (Venice, 1755–), and its history has been discussed by W. Kurze, 'Zur Geschichte Camaldolis im Zeitalter der Reform', MCSM 6 (1971) 399–415. For Fonte Avellana one should now go to the publications of the Centro di Studi Avellaniti, especially vols. ii–vi (1978–83); and there is an important source published by C. Pierucci and A. Polverari, *Carte di Fonte Avellana* 2 vols. (Rome, 1972–7). On its greatest figure, Peter Damian, see ch. 3.iii above. There are good modern studies of Vallombrosa by S. Boesch Gajano, 'Storia e tradizione Vallombrosane', *Bullettino dell'Istituto Storico Italiano* 76 (1964) 99–215; D. Meade, 'From Turmoil to Regularity: the Emergence of the Vallombrosan Congregation', *American Benedictine Review* 19 (1968) 323–57; P. Di Re, *Giovanni Gualberto nelle fonti dei secoli XI-XII* (Rome, 1974); and A. Degl'Innocenti, 'Le vite antiche di Giovanni Gualberto', *Studi Medievali* iii.25 (1985) 31–91. Among the many studies of hermits whose form of life was not shaped by any rule, may be recommended G. Penco, 'L'eremitismo irregolare in Italia nei secoli XI–XII', *Benedictina* 32 (1985) 201–21; F. Cardini, *Leggenda di S. Galgano confessore* (Florence, 1982); H. Grundmann, 'Deutsche Eremiten, Einsiedler und Klausner im Hoch-mittelalter, *AKg* 45 (1963) 60–90; G. Oury, 'L'érémitisme dans l'ancien diocèse de Tours au XIIe siècle', *Rev. Mabillon* 58 (1971) 43–92; A. K. Warren, *Anchorites and their Patrons in Medieval England* (London, 1985); H. Mayr-Harting, 'Functions of a twelfth-century recluse (Wulfric of Hasel-bury)', *History* 60 (1975) 337–52; and C. J. Holdsworth, 'Christina of Markyate', *SCH* Subsidia 1 (1978) 185–204.

ii. The new orders. Only a small selection can be given from the immense volume of writing inspired by the Cistercians during the past fifty years, a guide to which may be found in R. A. Donkin, *A Check List of Printed Works relating to the Cistercian Order* (Rochefort, 1969). There is a good general introduction by L. J. Lekai, *The Cistercians: Ideals and Reality* (Kent, Ohio, 1977). The *Atlas de l'ordre cistercien* by F. van der Meer (Amsterdam, 1965), contains valuable information, but see the 'Kritische Bemerkungen' in *Analecta Cisterciensia* 22 (1966) 279–90 and 23 (1967) 115–52. There is a large volume of discussion in the Cistercian Studies series, published by Shannon Press, and including collected volumes of essays edited by M. B. Pennington (vols. iii, xii, and xiii, 1970–1). Other valuable studies were edited by K. Elm, *Die Zisterzienser: Ordensleben zwischen Ideal und Wirklichkeit* (Cologne, 1982), an Ergänzungsband in support of an important exhibition. The best editions of the Cistercian constitutional documents in their fully developed form were by P. Guignard, *Monuments primitifs de la Règle cistercienne* (Dijon, 1878), and J. M. Canivez, *Statuta capitulorum generalium ordinis cisterciensis* (Louvain, 1933–41). Since that time the discovery of earlier texts has provoked a major controversy over the origins of the order, most notably between J. A. Lefèvre and J. B. Van Damme. The best starting places are now J.-B. Auberger, *L'unanimité cistercienne primitive: mythe ou réalité?* (Cîteaux, 1986), and B. K. Lackner, The Eleventh-century Background of Cîteaux, *Cistercian Studies* 8 (Washington, 1972), and there is an excellent review of the issues by M. de Waha, 'Aux origines de Cîteaux', in *Lettres latines*, ed. G. Cambier (Brussels, 1978), 152–82. On the development of the lay brothers in their distinctive form, there is K. Hallinger, 'Woher kommen die Laienbrüder?', *Analecta Sacri Ordinis Cisterciensis* 12 (1956) 1–104; J. Dubois and J. Leclercq in two articles in MCSM 5 (1968) 152–261; and M. Toepfer, *Die Konversen der Zisterzienser* (Berlin, 1983). The expansion of the order has been the subject of many local studies such as R. Locatelli, 'L'implantation cistercienne dans le comté de Bourgogne jusqu'au milieu du XIIe siècle', *Cahiers d'Histoire* 20 (1975) 167–225, as well as articles in the collections already mentioned, and R. A. Donkin provides factual details in a useful form in 'The Growth and Distribution of the Cistercian Order in Medieval Europe' *Studia Monastica* 9 (1967) 275–86. The growth of Cistercian estates and their exploitation are examined in a wide range of articles, including the valuable survey by C. Higounet, 'Le premier siècle de l'économie rurale Cistercienne', MCSM 9 (1980) 345–68, and R. A. Donkin, 'Settlement and Depopulation on Cistercian estates', *Bulletin of the Institute of Historical Research* 33 (1960) 141–65. D. Lohrmann, *Kirchengut im nördlichen Frankreich* (Bonn, 1983), opens an interesting line of investigation into ecclesiastical property which provides a great deal of information about the holdings of the new orders.

The origins of Grandmont have been explored in a series of studies by J. Becquet; see particularly his edition of the *Scriptores ordinis grandimontensis*,

CC(CM) 8 (1968), and 'Etienne de Muret', *Dictionnaire de Spiritualité* iv.2 (1961) 1504–14. Our image of the emergence of Fontevraud has been remade by J.-M. Bienvenu, 'Aux origines d'un ordre religieux: Robert d'Arbrissel et la fondation de Fontevraud', *Cahiers d'Histoire* 20 (1975) 227–52, and *L'étonnant fondateur de Fontevraud, Robert d'Arbrissel* (Paris, 1981); and by J. Dalarun, *L'impossible sainteté: la vie retrouvée de Robert d'Arbrissel* (Paris, 1985). J. J. van Moolenbroek, *Vitalis van Savigny* (Amsterdam, 1982), is based on a good critical study of the sources. The classic study of Carthusian history is C. Le Couteulx, *Annales ordinis Cartusiensis*, ed. C. Boutrais, 8 vols. (Montreuil sur Mer, 1888). A major collection of material by M. Laporte, 'Aux sources de la vie cartusienne', unfortunately remains unpublished, but it has been used by A. Ravier, *S. Bruno: le premier des ermites de Chartreuse* (Paris, 1967), and Laporte has written on Prior Guigo I in *Dictionnaire de Spiritualité* 6 (1967) 1169–75 and edited the *Lettres des premiers Chartreux* i, SC 88 (1962). Other important materials have been edited by J. Hogg, *Die ältesten Consuetudines der Kartäuser*, Analecta Cartusiana 1 (1970), and B. Bligny, *Recueil des plus anciens actes de la Grande-Chartreuse* (Grenoble, 1958). A series of studies has been edited by M. Zadnikar, *Die Kartäuser* (Cologne, 1983), and there is a good introduction to Bruno by G. Binding in *LdM* ii.788–90.

The significance of the regular canons for the history of the medieval church has only been fully realized in the course of the last forty years. There is an introductory article by C. Dereine in *Dictionnaire d'histoire* 40.xii (1953) 353–405; and further studies in *La vita comune del clero nei secoli XI e XII*, 2 vols. MCSM 3 (1962); F. Petit, *La réforme des prêtres au Moyen Âge* (Paris, 1968), (a useful collection of texts); F. Poggiaspalla, *La vita comune del clero dalle origini alla riforma gregoriana* (Rome, 1968); C. D. Fonseca, *Medioevo canonicale* (Milan, 1970); and J. Becquet, *La vie canoniale en France aux X–XIIe siècles* (London, 1985) (collected articles). The evolution from hermits to canons is examined by L. Milis in articles in MCSM 7 (1977) 223–38 and *CCM* 22 (1979) 39–80. The underlying texts are edited by L. Verheijen, *La règle de S. Augustin*, 2 vols. (Paris, 1967). The support for canonical reform by the Gregorian papacy is well analysed by J. Leclercq, 'Un témoignage sur l'influence de Grégoire VII dans la réforme canoniale', *S. Greg.* 6 (1959/61) 173–228, and H. Fuhrmann, 'Papst Urban II und der Stand der Regularkanoniker', Sb Bayer. Akad. 1982, Heft 2. On the influence which the regular canons exercised in Germany there is an outstanding survey article by S. Weinfurter, 'Reformkanoniker und Reichsepiskopat im Hochmittelalter', *HJb* 97–8 (1978) 158–93; see also his book, *Salzburger Bistumsreform und Bischofspolitik im 12 Jh* (Cologne, 1975). The canons in England are the subject of the book by J. C. Dickinson, *The Origins of the Austin Canons and their Introduction into England* (London, 1950), and also of D. M. Robinson, *The Geography of Augustinian Settlement in Medieval England and Wales* (Oxford, 1980). The canons were subdivided into a series of groups or federations, whose history is also now under investigation. There is an excellent summary article by J. Châtillon, 'La crise de l'église aux XIe et XIIe siècles et les origines des grandes fédérations canoniales', *Revue d'histoire de la spiritualité* 53 (1977) 3–45. The fullest history of one of these families is L. Milis, *L'ordre des chanoines réguliers d'Arrouaise* (Bruges, 1969), and he has edited its constitutions in CC(CM) 20 (1970). There are useful short histories of the federations in the *Dizionario di Istituzioni di Perfezione* 2 (1975), and the Springiersbach constitutions are edited by S. Weinfurter in CC(CM) 48 (1977). The history of the Victorines was written much earlier by F. Bonnard, *Histoire de l'abbaye royale et de l'ordre des chanoines réguliers de S. Victor de Paris*, 2 vols. (Paris, 1904–8); and its *Liber Ordinis* is edited in CC(CM) 61 (1984). The most separate of the families, consituting a monastic order in its own right, was that of Prémontré. Its houses are listed by N. Backmund, *Monasticon Praemonstratense*, 3 vols. (Straubing, 1952–6 and rev. edn. of vol. i, Berlin, 1983); the statutes edited by P. F. Lefèvre and W. M. Grauwen (Averbode, 1978). On the founder there is interesting work by S. Weinfurter, 'Norbert von Xanten: Ordensstifter und Eigenkirchenherr', *AKg* 59 (1979) 66–98, and K. Elm (ed.), *Norbert von Xanten: Adliger, Ordensstifter, Kirchenfürst* (Cologne, 1984). There is a good earlier study by H. M. Colvin, *The White Canons in England* (Oxford, 1951). On the Gilbertines the basic work is now R. Foreville and G. Keir (eds.), *The Book of S. Gilbert* (Oxford, 1987).

iii. Controversy and Criticism. The links between the fall of Pons of Cluny, the papal schism of 1130, and the controversy between Cluniacs and Cistercians have been explored by H. V. White, 'Pontius of Cluny, the curia romana and the end of Gregorianism in Rome', *Church History* 27 (1958) 159–219; G. Tellenbach, 'Der Sturz des Abtes Pontius von Cluny und seine geschichtliche Bedeutung', *QFIAB* 42/3 (1964) 13–55; H. E. J. Cowdrey, 'Abbot Pontius of Cluny', *S. Greg.* 11 (1978) 177–277; P. Zerbi, 'Intorno allo scisma di Ponzio, abbate di Cluny', *Studi . . . O. Bertolini* (Pisa, 1972), ii.835–91; and A. H. Bredero, *Cluny et Cîteaux au XIIe siècle* (Amsterdam, 1985) (a revised collection of his articles). The letters of Peter the Venerable have been the subject of a splendid edition by G. Constable, 2 vols. (Cambridge, Mass, 1967). The standard biography is J. Leclercq, *Pierre le Vénérable* (St Wandrille, 1946), and there are important further studies in G. Constable and J. Kritzeck (eds.), *Petrus Venerabilis 1156–1956* (Rome, 1956); and *Pierre Abélard—Pierre le Vénérable* (Paris, 1972). The controversy is surveyed in a lecture by D. Knowles, *Cistercians and Cluniacs* (Oxford, 1955). On the *Dialogus*, an important Cistercian pamphlet, there is R. B. C. Huygens, 'Le moine Idung et ses deux ouvrages' (Spoleto, 1980).

The complicated question of the difference between monks and canons is explored by C. N. L. Brooke, 'Monk and canon: some patterns in the religious life of the twelfth century', *SCH* 22 (1985) 109–30, and also by

C. D. Fonseca, 'Monaci e canonici alla ricerca di una identità', MCSM 9 (1980) 203–22. C. W. Bynum's Docere verbo et exemplo: *an Aspect of Twelfth-century spirituality* (Missoula, 1979), is an interesting attempt to define the special characteristics of the canons. The most crucial issue between the two forms of religious life turned on the canons' claim that the cure of souls fell to them alone and that it represented a higher way of life than contemplation. The issue is explored by G. Schreiber, 'Gregor VII, Cluny, Cîteaux, Prémontré zu Eigenkirche, Parochie, Seelsorge', *ZSSRGkA* 65 (1947) 31–171; P. Hofmeister, 'Mönchtum und Seelsorge bis zum 13 Jh.', *Studien und Mitteilungen zur Geschichte des Benediktinerordens* 65 (1953–4) 209–73; F.-J. Schmale, 'Kanonie, Seelsorge, Eigenkirche', *HJb* 78 (1959) 38–63; and K. Bosl, 'Regularkanoniker (Augustinerchorherren) und Seelsorge in Kirche und Gesellschaft des europäischer XII Jhs', *Abh. Bayer. Akad.* NS 86 (1979) (but see Weinfurter's corrections in *AKg* 62/3 (1980/1) 381–95). An interesting contemporary commentary on the situation, the *Libellus de diversis ordinibus*, has been edited by G. Constable and B. Smith (Oxford, 1972).

iv. The New Orders in Twelfth-century Society. Bernard of Clairvaux stands at the centre of any modern discussion about the impact of the new orders on contemporaries, and the great volume of writing is listed by J. C. Bouton, *Bibliographie bernardine* (Paris, 1957), with a supplementary bibliography to 1970 (Rochefort, 1972). Important recent works include J. Leclercq, *S. Bernard et l'esprit cistercien* (Paris, 1975), and *Nouveau visage de Bernard de Clairvaux; approches psycho-historiques* (Paris, 1976); J. Calmette, *S. Bernard* (Paris, 1979); E. R. Elder and J. R. Sommerfeldt (eds.), *The Chimaera of his Age: Studies on Bernard of Clairvaux* (Kalamazoo, 1980); and G. R. Evans, *The Mind of S. Bernard of Clairvaux* (Oxford, 1983). The impact of the Cistercians on the Church hierarchy is discussed in articles by J. Lipkin in *The Chimaera of his Age*, 62–75, and R. Crozet in *CCM* 18 (1975) 263–8.

Chapter 11: The Christian Frontier

i. The Theory of Mission. An introductory account is provided in K. S. Latourette, *A History of the Expansion of Christianity*, vol. ii (500–1500) (London, 1938), and there is much of interest in J. T. Addison, *The Medieval Missionary* (repr. Philadelphia, 1976). J. B. Friedman, *The Monstrous Races in Medieval Art and Thought* (Cambridge, Mass., 1981), examines ideas of the world remote from western Europe, and includes a useful comment on the significance of the Vézelay tympanum. For differing views of this, see A. Katzenellenbogen, 'The Central Tympanum at Vézelay', *Art Bulletin* 26 (1944) 141–51, and M. D. Taylor, 'The Pentecost at Vézelay', *Gesta* 19 (1980) 9–15. The evolution of the idea of Christendom as a distinct culture is discussed in a number of important works: D. Hay, *Europe: the Emergence of an Idea* 2nd edn. (Edinburgh, 1968); P. Rousset, 'La notion de Chrétienté aux XIe et XIIe siècles', *MA* 69 (1963) 191–203; J. Rupp, *L'idée de Chrétienté dans la pensée pontificale des origines à Innocent III* (Paris, 1939); and (with particular reference to the growth of papal authority) J. van Laarhoven, '*Christianitas* et réforme grégorienne', *S. Greg.* 6 (1961) 1–98, and F. Kempf, 'Das Problem der *Christianitas* im 12 und 13 Jh', *HJb* 79 (1960) 104–23.

ii. Scandinavia. The most important source for the start of our period is Adam of Bremen, whose *History of the Archbishops of Hamburg-Bremen* is edited by B. Schmeidler (Leipzig 1917) and translated by F. J. Tschan, (New York, 1959). E. N. Johnson, 'Adalbert of Hamburg-Bremen', *Speculum* 9 (1934) 147–79, provides a survey of the archbishop's career, and his plan for a patriarchate is studied by H. Fuhrmann, 'Provincia constat duodecim episcopatibus', *S. Grat.* 11 (1967) 389–404. The classic account of the conversion of Norway is K. von Maurer, *Die Bekehrung des norwegischen Stammes zum Christenthume*, 2 vols. (Munich, 1855–6), which contains a great amount of useful information. For other countries there are C. J. A. Oppermann, *The English Missionaries in Sweden and Finland* (London, 1937), and D. Strömbäck, *The Conversion of Iceland* (London, 1975). The problems of organizing the northern church are examined by W. Seegrün, *Das Papsttum und Skandinavien bis zur Vollendung der nordischen Kirchenorganisation* (Neumünster, 1967); K. Haff, 'Das Grosskirchspiel im nordischen und niederdeutschen Rechte', *ZSSRGkA* 63 (1943) 1–63; B. P. McGuire, *The Cistercians in Denmark* (Kalamazoo, 1982); and K. Kumlien, 'Mission und Kirchenorganisation zur Zeit der Christianisierung Schwedens', *VuF* 12 (1968) 291–307.

iii. Eastern Europe. The best general work on the conversion of the eastern Baltic is E. Christiansen, *The Northern Crusades* (London, 1980). There are other discussions of importance in *Eastern and Western Europe in the Middle Ages*, ed. G. Barraclough (London, 1970); and F. Graus, *Die Nationenbildung der Westslaven im Mittelalter* (Sigmaringen, 1980), is a fine book with relevant material. For Poland, the best history to use is A. Gieysztor and others, *History of Poland*, 2nd edn. (Warsaw, 1979). The unpublished University of Oxford D.Phil. thesis (1972) by B. Haronski, 'Reform in the Polish Church of the Thirteenth Century', includes a very good discussion of Polish history in the preceding centuries. Still useful are P. David, 'The Church in Poland from its Origin to 1250', *Cambridge History of Poland* i (Cambridge, 1950), ch. 4, and *Les Bénédictins et l'ordre de Cluny dans la Pologne médiévale* (Paris, 1939). J. Kloczowski provides a good survey in 'La province ecclésiastique de la Pologne et ses evêques', *MCSM* 7 (1974) 437–44, and there are some outstanding essays by A. Gieysztor on the growth of culture and social structures: see, for example, *MCSM* 10 (1983) 123–45; *SSCISAM* 28 (1980) 925–61; and *Studi in onore di A. Fanfani* i (Milan, 1962), 327–67. In spite of its importance, medieval Hungary has not attracted the same scholarly attention as Poland. Its most detailed history is B. Homan, *Geschichte des ungarischen Mittelalters* (Berlin, 1940), and Z. J. Kosztolnyik has written on *Five Eleventh-century Hungarian Kings* (Boulder, 1981). Also worth consulting are G. Bonis, 'Die Entwicklung der geistlichen Gerichtsbarkeit in Ungarn', *ZSSRGkA* 79 (1966) 174–235 and G. Székely, 'Gemeinsame Züge der ungarischen und polnischen Kirchengeschichte des XI Jhs', *Annales Univ. Scient. Budapestensis* 4 (1962) 55–80.

Most of our information about the conversion of the Baltic Slavs is derived from Adam of Bremen (see above) and Helmold, *Chronica Slavorum*, ed. B. Schmeidler (Hanover, 1937), and tr. F. J. Tschan (New York, 1935). A collection of major articles has been edited by H. Beumann, *Heidenmission und Kreuzzugsgedanke in der deutschen Ostpolitik des Mittelalters*, Wege der Forschung 7 (Bad Homburg, 1963). The process of conversion has been further examined by F. Lotter, *Die Konzeption des Wendenkreuzzugs*, VuF Sonderband 23 (1977) and 'Bemerkungen zur Christianisierung der Abodriten', *Festschrift für Walter Schlesinger* ii (Cologne, 1974) 395–442. The obscurities of the 1108 appeal are examined by P. Knoch, 'Kreuzzug und Siedlung: Studien zum Aufruf der Magdeburger Kirche von 1108', *Jb. für die Geschichte Mittel- und Ostdeutschlands* 23 (1974) 1–33. The sources for the great missionary bishop Otto of Bamberg are analysed in E. Demm, *Reformmönchtum und Slawenmission im 12 Jh* (Lübeck, 1970); see also the article by J. Petersohn in *DAEM* 27 (1971) 314–72. There is a translation of some of the material by C. H. Robinson, *The Life of Otto, Apostle of Pomerania* (London, 1920). The establishment of the church in the newly converted regions is studied by K. Jordan, *Die Bistumsgründungen Heinrichs des Löwen*, MGH Scriften 3 (1939); P. David, *La Pologne et l'évangélisation de la Poméranie* (Paris, 1928); and G. Schlegel, *Das Zisterzienserkloster Dargun* (Leipzig, 1980).

iv. The Defence of the Holy Sepulchre. General histories of the crusades are mentioned in ch. 6.iv above. On the character of crusader society in Syria, there are excellent books by J. Prawer, *The Latin Kingdom of Jerusalem* (London, 1972); M. Benvenisti, *The Crusaders in the Holy Land* (Jerusalem, 1970); J. Richard, *The Latin Kingdom of Jerusalem* (Amsterdam, 1979); and R. C. Smail, *Crusading Warfare* (Cambridge, 1956). On the history of the Latin churches which they established, the best extended discussion is by B. Hamilton, *The Latin Church in the Crusader States* (London, 1980), and valuable material is assembled by G. Fedalto, *La chiesa latina in Oriente*, 2 vols. (Verona, 1973–6), and H. E. Mayer, *Bistümer, Klöster und Stifte im Königreich Jerusalem* (Stuttgart, 1977). William of Tyre's *History of Deeds done beyond the Sea* is the best single source for the history of Outremer, and has been translated by E. A. Babcock and A. C. Krey, 2 vols. (New York, 1943); there is in progress a new edition by H. C. Huygens, CC(CM) 63 (1986). On the growth of the pilgrimage to Jerusalem, see J. D. Wilkinson,

Jerusalem Pilgrims before the Crusades (Warminster, 1977); the Palestine Pilgrims' Text Society, esp. vols. iv–v (London, 1895; repr. 1971); P. C. Boeren, *Rorgo Fretellus de Nazareth et sa description de la Terre Sainte* (Amsterdam, 1980); and B. Hamilton, 'Rebuilding Zion; the Holy Places of Jerusalem in the Twelfth Century', *SCH* 14 (1977) 105–16; also G. Constable, 'Opposition to Pilgrimage in the Middle Ages', *S. Grat.* 19 (1976) 125–46.

The classic study of the military orders, still valuable, is by H. Prutz, *Die geistlichen Ritterorden* (Berlin, 1908; repr. 1968), and there is a series of studies edited by J. Fleckenstein and M. Hellmann, *Die geistlichen Ritterorden Europas*, VuF 26 (1980). D. Seward has written an English introduction to the subject in *The Monks of War; the Military Religious Orders* (St Albans, 1974); and there is an important argument by A. J. Forey, 'The Emergence of the Military Order in the Twelfth Century', *JEH* 36 (1985) 175–95. The major study of the Hospitallers is J. Riley-Smith, *The Knights of S. John in Jerusalem and Cyprus* (London, 1967). Their rule and statutes were translated by E. J. King (London, 1934; repr. 1981), and their early development reconsidered by A. J. Forey, 'The Militarization of the Hospital of S. John', *Studia Monastica* 26 (1984) 75–89. There is an outline history of the Templars in English by G. A. Campbell, *The Knights Templars, their Rise and Fall* (London, 1937), and a more recent survey by G. Bordonove, *La vie quotidienne des Templiers* (Paris, 1975). M. L. Bulst-Thiele has published a careful and scholarly account of the masters in *Sacrae Domus Militiae Templi Hierosolymitani magistri* (Göttingen, 1974), and there are articles by M. Barber in *TRHS* V 34 (1984) 27–46 and *Studia Monastica* 12 (1970) 219–40.

The dominant school of contemporary thought about warfare is examined by F. H. Russell, *The Just War in the Middle Ages* (Cambridge, 1975), and there is a survey of crusading theory by E.-D. Hehl, *Kirche und Krieg im 12 Jh.* (Stuttgart, 1980). The attitude of St Bernard is best studied in his treatise 'In praise of the new militia', which is translated in his *Treatises*, iii (Kalamazoo, 1977), and is clarified by J. Leclercq, 'S. Bernard's Attitude to War', in J. R. Sommerfeldt (ed.), *Studies in Cistercian History* ii, (Kalamazoo, 1976), 1–39. Apart from the general works mentioned above, there is a perceptive discussion of the Second Crusade by G. Constable, 'The Second Crusade as Seen by Contemporaries', *Traditio* 9 (1953) 213–79. The events leading to the fall of Jerusalem to Saladin in 1187 are being reassessed by scholars; see, as an introduction to the controversy, B. Hamilton, 'The Elephant of Christ: Raynald of Châtillon', *SCH* 15 (1978) 97–108, and studies in the volumes mentioned in ch. 6.iv. On the Third Crusade, in addition to the general works, see E. Eickhoff, *Friedrich Barbarossa im Orient: Kreuzzug und Tod Friedrichs I* (Tübingen, 1977). On the development of western knowledge of Islam, there are important studies by R. C. Schwinges, *Kreuzzugsideologie und Toleranz: Studien zu Wilhelm von Tyrus* (Stuttgart, 1977); P. Möhring, 'Zu der Geschichte der orientalischen

Herrscher des Wilhelm von Tyrus', *Mittellateinisches Jahrbuch* 19 (1984) 170–83; and B. Z. Kedar, *Crusade and Mission: European Approaches towards the Moslems* (Princeton, 1984).

Chapter 12: The Message of the Churches

i. Towards a Christian Society. There is a good introduction to the religion of the people by R. and C. Brooke, *Popular Religion in the Middle Ages: Western Europe 1000–1300* (London, 1984), but in general the discussion has been carried forward in collections of short studies. Among these are *I laici nella societas christiana dei secoli XI e XII*, MCSM 5 (1968); E. Delaruelle, *La piété populaire au Moyen Âge* (Turin, 1975); *La piété populaire au Moyen Âge*, CNSS 99 (Paris, 1977); and *La culture populaire au Moyen Âge*, ed. P. Boglioni (Montreal, 1979). There is a valuable local bibliography by P. Plongeron and P. Lerou, *La piété populaire en France: répertoire bibliographique* (Paris, 1986–). (It includes a considerable number of medieval studies, and is destined to cover other countries.) R. Manselli's book, *La religion populaire au Moyen Âge* (Montreal, 1975), is well worth reading, but the review by R. Trexler in *Speculum* 52 (1977) 1019–22 raises fundamental questions about the approach to popular religion, as does the article by J. C. Schmitt, 'Les traditions folkloriques dans la culture médiévale', *Archives des Sciences Sociales de Religions*, 52/1 (1981) 5–20. Works based on this school of interpretation are listed in ch. 19.iii below.

ii. The Great Churches. Room does not allow the listing of the many analyses of the development of architecture, and it must suffice to mention the very attractive volumes by G. Duby, *The Europe of the Cathedrals 1140–1280* (Geneva, 1966), and W. Swaan, *The Gothic Cathedral* (London, 1981). Two classic discussions of the aims of the designers are those of E. Panofsky, *Gothic Architecture and Scholasticism* (Latrobe, 1951), and O. von Simson, *The Gothic Cathedral* (London, 1956). These writers both see the great church as an image of heaven, but this assumption should be controlled by reading the important article of P. Crossley, 'In Search of a New Iconography of Medieval Architecture', *Symbolae Historiae Artium: Festchrift to L. Kalinowski* (Warsaw, 1986), 55–66. The major polemical work of the time, St Bernard's *Apologia to Abbot William*, is available in English in *The Works of Bernard of Clairvaux: the Treatises*, i, (Shannon, 1970), 3–69. On buildings of crucial importance, there is K. J. Conant, *Cluny* (Mâcon, 1968); E. Panofsky, *Abbot Suger on the Abbey Church of S. Denis and its Art Treasure* (Princeton, 1946); S. M. Crosby, *L'abbaye royale de S. Denis* (Paris, 1953); and J. Formigé, *L'abbaye royale de S. Denis* (Paris, 1960). The very distinctive art traditions of Rome are discussed by H. Toubert, 'Le renouveau paléochrétien à Rome au début du XIIe siècle', *Cahiers archéologiques* 20 (1970) 99–154; R. Krautheimer, *Rome: the Profile of a City* (Princeton, 1980); and P. C. Klaussen, *Magistri Doctissimi Romani*

(Stuttgart, 1987). On church treasures, see B. Bischoff, *Mittelalterliche Schatzverzeichnisse*, i (Munich, 1967), and H. Swarzenski, *Monuments of Romanesque Art* (Chicago, 1974). Among important studies of the financing of church building are C. R. Cheney, 'Church Building in the Middle Ages', *Bulletin of John Rylands Library* 34 (1951–2) 20–36; H. Kraus, *Gold was the Mortar: the Economics of Cathedral Building* (London, 1979); and (mostly after 1200) W. H. Vroom, *De Financiering van de kathedraalbouw in de Middeleeuwen* (Maarsen, 1981). Two informative examples have been studied by C. E. Woodruff, 'The Financial Aspect of the Cult of S. Thomas of Canterbury', *Archaeologia Cantiana* 44 (1932) 13–32 and R. Graham, 'An Appeal about 1175 for the Building Fund of S. Paul's', *Journal of the British Archaeological Association* 3. 10 (1945–7) 73–6.

The arrangement of the great churches for worship has received much less attention than their architectural design, but there are excellent introductory articles by J. Hubert, 'La place faite aux laïcs dans les églises monastiques et dans les cathédrales', MCSM 5 (1965) 470–87 and C. Brooke, 'Religious Sentiment and Church Design' in his *Medieval Church and Society* (London, 1971), 162–82. On detailed aspects of the planning of churches, there are studies by W. S. Hope, 'Quire Screens in English Churches', *Archaeologia* 68 (1916–7) 43–110; W. H. A. Vallance, *Greater English Church Screens* (London, 1947); E. Fernie, 'The Use of Varied Nave Supports in Romanesque and Early Gothic Churches', *Gesta* 23 (1984) 107–18; and C. A. R. Radford, 'The Bishop's Throne in Norwich Cathedral', *Archaeological Journal* 116 (1959) 115–32.

iii. The Local Churches. There is an excellent survey of the bibliography, extending back to the twelfth century, by J. Coste, 'L'institution paroissiale à la fin du Moyen Âge', *Mélanges de l'école française de Rome* 96 (1984) 295–326; and surveys by J. Gaudemet, 'La paroisse au Moyen Âge' RHEF 59 (1973) 5–21, and J. Avril in *Revue d'histoire de la spiritualité* 51 (1975) 289–96 and *ICMCL* 5 (1980) 471–86. Among the studies of local churches in England can be recommended W. O. Ault, 'The Village Church and the Village Community in Medieval England', *Speculum* 45 (1970) 197–215; R. Morris, *The Church in British Archaeology*, CBA Research Report 47 (1983); and articles in J. A. Raftis (ed.), *Pathways to Medieval Peasants* (Toronto, 1981), 311–33. The study of local churches in France has been particularly extensive, and includes P. Imbart de la Tour, *Les paroisses rurales dans l'ancienne France du IVe au XIe siècles* (Paris, 1900); G. Devailly, 'L'encadrement paroissial: rigueur et insuffisance', CF 11 (1976) 387–417; J. Becquet, 'La paroisse en France aux XI et XIIe siècles', MCSM 8 (1974) 199–229; and an unusual approach to architecture by J. James, 'The Uneven Distribution of Early Gothic Churches in the Paris Basin', *Art Bulletin* 66 (1984) 15–46. Among excellent local studies may be mentioned H. Platelle, 'Les paroisses du décanat de Lille au Moyen Âge', *Mélanges de science religieuse* 25 (1968)

67–88, 115–41. On Germany, there is a useful collection of texts in M. Erbe, *Pfarrkirche und Dorf* (Mohn, 1973), and thorough studies by F. Pauly, *Siedlung und Pfarrorganisation im alten Erzbistum Trier* (Trier, 1961–), and E. Guttenberg and A. Wendehorst, *Das Bistum Bamberg: ii. Die Pfarrorganis-ation*, Germania Sacra ii.1 (Berlin, 1966). For Italy see P. Toubert, 'Monachisme et encadrement religieux des campagnes en Italie', and C. Violante, 'Pievi e parrochie nell'Italia centro-settentrionale', MCSM 8 (1977) 416–41 and 643–799; and the articles in *Pieve e Parrochie*, 2 vols. Italia Sacra, 35–6 (Rome, 1984).

iv. Learning through Worship. The way in which the liturgy served the edification of the community as a whole is analysed by E. Cattaneo, 'La liturgia nella riforma gregoriana', CSSSM 6 (1968) 169–90, and 'Azione pastorale e vita liturgica locale', MCSM 8 (1977) 444–73; P.-M. Gy, 'Evangélisation et sacrements au Moyen Âge', *Humanisme et foi chrétienne*, ed. C. Kannengiesser and Y. Marchasson (Paris, 1976), 565–72; and P. Riché, 'La pastorale populaire en occident', *Histoire vécue du peuple chrétien*, ed. J. Delumeau (Toulouse, 1979), i, 195–224. The changes in the rite of initiation are discussed by J. D. C. Fisher, *Christian Initiation* (London, 1965); H. M. J. Banting, 'Imposition of hands in confirmation', *JEH* 7 (1956) 147–59; and G. Riggio, 'Liturgia e pastorale della confermazione nei secoli XI–XIII', *Ephemerides liturgicae* 87 (1974) 3–31. E. Cattaneo, 'Il battistero in Italia dopo il mille', Italia Sacra 15–16 (Padua, 1970), 171–95, and E. M. Angiola, 'Nicola Pisano, Federigo Visconti and the classical style in Pisa', *Art Bulletin* 59 (1977) 1–27 provide a valuable guide to the significance of the baptistery in Italian church life. The wide-ranging article of J. Bossy, 'The Mass as a Social Institution 1200–1700', *Past and Present* 100 (1983) 29–61, is an interesting introduction to the subject, and the account of J. A. Jungmann, *The Mass of the Roman Rite*, 2 vols. (New York, 1951–5), is indispensible. There are two excellent articles on the expansion of the private mass by C. Vogel in *Recherches de science religieuse* 54 (1980) 231–50 and 55 (1981) 206–13. The fullest study of the medieval symbolism of the mass is now R. Suntrup, *Die Bedeutung der liturgischen Gebärden und Bewegungen* (Münster, 1978). On the theology of the sacraments, see ch. 15.iv.

Music-drama has received a great deal of scholarly attention. The texts and discussion of K. Young, *The Drama of the Medieval Church*, 2 vols. (Oxford, 1933), lie at the root of more recent study, and there is a stimulating and controversial book by O. B. Hardison, *Christian Rite and Christian Drama in the Middle Ages* (Baltimore, 1965). Specific aspects are examined by H. Kindermann, *Das Theaterpublikum des Mittelalters* (Salzburg, 1980); C. Mazouer, 'Les indications de mise en scène dans les drames liturgiques de Pâques', *CCM* 23 (1980) 361–8; and W. L. Smoldon, *The Music of the Medieval Church Drama* (London, 1980). The study of medieval music lies outside our boundaries, but some scholars have brought together social and musical developments, notably A. Hughes, 'La musique populaire médiévale', *Culture Populaire* (above, i) 103–20; M. Huglo, 'La musique religieuse au temps de Philippe Auguste', R. H. Bautier (ed.), *La France de Philippe Auguste* (Paris, 1982), 1001–11; and P. Gülke, *Mönche, Bürger, Minnesänger: Musik in der Gesellschaft des europäischen Mittelalters* (Vienna, 1975). Images of the Virgin Mary are studied in a very interesting book by I. H. Forsyth, *The Throne of Wisdom: Wood Sculptures in Romanesque France* (Princeton, 1972), and the most thorough listing of representations of the crucified Christ is that by P. Thoby, *Le crucifixe des origines au concile de Trente* (Nantes, 1959). L. Gougaud collected important medieval references to the idea that pictures are 'books of the poor' in 'Muta praedicatio', *Revue Bénédictine* 42 (1930) 168–71, and H. Kraus throws light on the propaganda aspect of cathedral decoration in *The Living Theatre of Medieval Art* (London, 1967). This is not the place for a list of studies of medieval painting; one interesting group in local churches, mentioned in the text, is discussed by A. M. Baker, 'The Wall Paintings in the Church of S. John the Baptist, Clayton', *Sussex Archaeological Collections* 108 (1970) 58–81.

v. Preaching. The medieval sermon, once largely neglected by scholars, has in recent years produced work of remarkably high quality. J. Longère's book *La prédication médiévale* (Paris, 1983), is an indispensible starting-place. There are good discussions of the religious functions of sermons by L.-J. Bataillon, 'Approaches to the Study of Medieval Sermons', *Leeds Studies in English* NS 11 (1980) 19–35, and A. Vauchez, 'Faire croire: diffusion et réception du message religieux au Moyen Âge', *Les quatre fleuves* 11 (1980) 31–40. J. B. Schneyer's *Repertorium der lateinischen Sermones des Mittelalters*, 9 vols. (Münster, 1969–79), is a magnificent work of reference for the whole period. J. Longère's *Oeuvres oratoires de maîtres parisiens au XIIe siècle*, 2 vols. (Paris, 1975), is a thorough and informative study, and so is P. Tibber's 'The Origins of the Scholastic Sermon *c.*1130–1210' (unpublished University of Oxford D.Phil. Thesis, 1983). Another fine work is that by M. Zink, *Le prédication en langue romane avant 1300* (Paris, 1976). M. M. Gatch, *Preaching and Theology in Anglo-Saxon England: Aelfric and Wulfstan* (Toronto, 1977), is of wider import than the title implies.

vi. Ceremonial and Society. Processions were an important feature, but most studies are local rather than general ones. See, however, H. Niedermeier, 'Über die Sakramentsprozession im Mittelalter', *Sacris Erudiri* 22 (1974–5) 401–36, and (for a well-documented place) X. Haimerl, *Das Prozessionswesen des Bistums Bamberg im Mittelalter* (Hildesheim, 1973). On confraternities the greatest name is G. G. Meersseman, especially his *Ordo fraternitatis: confraternite e pietà dei laici nel medioevo*, 3 vols. (Rome, 1977). There are so many general books about pilgrimage that selection is really a matter of taste. I would choose P. A. Sigal, *Les marcheurs de Dieu: pèlerinages et pèlerins au Moyen Âge* (Paris, 1974); J. Sumption, *Pilgrimage: An Image of Medieval Religion* (London, 1975); and R. Finucane, *Miracles and Pilgrims: Popular Belief im Medieval England* (London, 1977). The transformation of pilgrimage at the beginning of our period is the subject of two incisive studies, L. Schmugge, 'Die Anfänge des organisierten Pilgerverkehrs im Mittelalter', *QFIAB* 64 (1984) 1–83, and R. Plötz, 'Strukturwandel der *peregrinatio* im Hochmittelalter', *Rheinische-westfälische Zeitschrift für Volkskunde* 26/7 (1981/2) 129–51. On the function of the shrines, two outstanding books: P.-A. Sigal, *L'homme et le miracle dans la France médiévale* (Paris, 1985), and B. Ward, *Miracles and the Medieval Mind* (London, 1982). P. J. Geary, *Furta sacra: Thefts of Relics in the Central Middle Ages* (Princeton, 1978) is also an instructive study, while M. Heinzelmann, *Translationsberichte und andere Quellen des Reliquienkultes*, Typologie des sources 33 (Turnhoult, 1979), is both thorough and useful. On reliquaries see E. G. Grimme, *Goldschmiedkunst im Mittelalter: Form und Bedeutung des Reliquiars von 800 bis 1500* (Cologne, 1972). The best-known critic of abuses of the cult of relics has been studied by K. Guth, *Guibert von Nogent und die hochmittelalterliche Kritik an der Reliquienverehrung* (Ottobeuren, 1970).

Chapter 13. Christianity and Social Ideas

i. The Basis of Christian Social Action. References to works on the development of humanism in the twelfth century will be found under ch. 15.iii below. There is a good short survey of thought about the laity in J. Gilchrist, 'Laity in the Middle Ages', *New Catholic Encyclopedia* 8 (1967) 331–5, and an interesting disussion of the canonical position in R. J. Cox, *A Study of the Juridic Status of Laymen in the Writing of the Medieval Canonists* (Washington, 1959). G. G. Meersseman, 'Chiesa e *Ordo laicorum* nel sec. XI', *CSSSM* 6 (1968) 37–74 is important for the background. Material on the priesthood of the faithful in medieval theology was collected by P. Dabin, *Le sacerdoce royal des fidèles dans la tradition ancienne et moderne* (Brussels, 1950). On the theory of 'orders' the best study is by G. Duby, *The Three Orders: Feudal Society Imagined* (Chicago, 1980), with further comments by E. A. R. Brown, 'Georges Duby and the three orders', *Viator* 17 (1986) 51–64. There is much stimulating discussion in J. Le Goff, *Time, Work and Culture in the Middle Ages* (Chicago, 1980). An older study in which interesting material has been assembled is L. Manz, *Der Ordo-Gedanke* (Stuttgart, 1937). Other topics are discussed in the volume edited by A. Zimmermann, *Soziale Ordnungen im Selbstverständnis des Mittelalters*, Misc.Med. 12 (1979), and G. B. Ladner, '*Homo viator*: Medieval Ideas on Alienation and Order', *Speculum* 42 (1967) 233–59. L. Prosdocimi discussed some crucial medieval texts in 'Unità e dualità del popolo christiano in Stefano di Tournai e in Ugo di S. Vittore', *Le Bras* i.673–80, and 'Chierici e laici nella società occidentale del sec. XII', *ICMCL* 2 (1965) 105–22.

ii. Provision for the Poor. In addition to the essential general works by M. Mollat (ch. 3.iii above), a volume of *RHEF*, 52 (1966), was devoted to the topic of poverty. B. Tierney, *Medieval Poor Law* (London, 1959), while being mainly concerned with England, is a very fine work with wide applications. There are two complementary studies of the organization of hospitals: S. Reicke, *Das deutsche Spital und sein Recht im Mittelalter* (Stuttgart, 1932), and J. Imbert, *Histoire des hôpitaux français: les hôpitaux en droit canonique* (Paris, 1947). The essential collection of material is by L. Le Grand, *Statuts d'Hôtels-Dieu et de léproseries* (Paris, 1901), and the social pressures which brought into being the hospital system are examined by C. Probst, 'Das Hospitalwesen im hohen und späten Mittelalter', *Sudhoffs Archiv: Zeitschrift für Wissenschaftsgeschichte* 50 (1966) 246–58. J. D. Thompson and G. Goldin, *The Hospital: a Social and Architectural History* (London, 1975), contains valuable material for this period, and so does U. Craemer, *Das Hospital als Bautyp des Mittelalters* (Cologne, 1963). The Hospitallers are discussed elsewhere, but there is an interesting discussion of their medical work (by which however I am not completely convinced) by T. S. Miller, 'The Knights of S. John and Hospitals of the Latin West', *Speculum* 53 (1978) 709–33. The medieval section of E. E. Hume, *Medical Work of the Knights Hospitallers* (Baltimore, 1940), contains useful references but is uncritical in its treatment. On the impact of leprosy on European society, see among other things P. Richards, *The Medieval Leper and his Northern Heirs* (Cambridge, 1977); S. N. Brody, *The Disease of the Soul: Leprosy in Medieval Literature* (Ithaca, 1974); A. Bourgeois, *Psychologie collective et institutions charitables: lépreux et maladreries du Pas-de-Calais* (Arras, 1972); and J. Avril, 'Le IIIe concile de Latran et les communautés de lépreux', *Revue Mabillon* 60 (1981) 21–76.

The operation of the social services may be judged from local studies, of which some excellent ones are now available. Particularly noteworthy are J. M. Bienvenu, 'Pauvreté, misères et charité en Anjou', *MA* 72–3 (1966–7); J. H. Mundy, 'Charity and Social Work in Toulouse', *Traditio* 22 (1966) 203–77; the articles collected in *CF* 13 (1978); J. Caille, *Hôpitaux et charité publique à Narbonne* (Toulouse, 1978); M. Candille, 'Pour un précis d'histoire générale des institutions charitables', *Bulletin Philologique et Historique* 1970, 117–31 (based on northern French materials); M. Rubin, *Charity and Community in Medieval Cambridge 1200–1500* (Cambridge, 1987); and a study of the system in a society where relief remained solidly the responsibility of the family, M. Stein-Wilkeshuis, 'The Right to Social Welfare in Early Medieval Iceland', *JMH* 8 (1982) 343–52.

iii. Marriage. On changing ideas of love in the twelfth century, see ch. 15.iii below. There is a guide to the literature on marriage edited by M. Sheehan and D. Scardalleto, *Family and Marriage in Medieval Europe: a Working Bibliography* (Vancouver, 1976). C. N. L. Brooke has provided good introductions to the subject in *Marriage and Christian History* (Cambridge, 1978) and there is a collection of articles edited by W. van Hoecke and A. Welkenhuysen, *Love and Marriage in the Twelfth Century* (Louvain, 1981). Sexuality in general is considered by D. S. Bailey, *The Man–Woman Relation in Christian Thought* (London, 1959), and P. Browe, *Beiträge zur Sexualethik des Mittelalters* (Breslau, 1932), which is more specialized than its title suggests but is well documented. There is an important recent survey by J. A. Brundage, *Law, Sex and Christian Society in Medieval Europe* (Chicago, 1987). The relationship between different concepts of marriage is portrayed by G. Duby, *The Knight, the Lady and the Priest* (Harmondsworth, 1985), and also in his *Medieval Marriage: Two Models from Twelfth-century France* (Baltimore, 1978). The development of the marriage rite is the subject of an excellent book by K. Ritzer, French trans., *Le mariage dans les églises chrétiennes du Ie au XIIe siècle* (Paris, 1970), which includes an excursus on the twelfth-century rite. It should be read in conjunction with C. Vogel, 'Les rites de la célébration du mariage', CISAM 24 (1977) 397–472, and with the examination of the liturgy by J. B. Molin and P. Mutembe, *Le rituel du mariage en France du XIIe au XVIe siècle* (Paris, 1974).

The doctrine of marriage in canonists and theologians is splendidly surveyed by G. Le Bras in an article, 'Mariage', in *Dic. TC* 9 (1926) 2123–316, and there is a good analysis by E. Schillebeeckx, *Marriage: Secular Reality and Saving Mystery* (London, 1965). There are thorough discussions of the subject by A. Esmein, *Le mariage en droit canonique*, 2nd edn. (Paris, 1929), and V. Pfaff, 'Das kirchliche Eherecht am Ende des 12 Jhs', *ZSSRGkA* 94 (1977) 73–131. Some radical suggestions about the motivation of the church's strategy towards marriage are put forward by J. Goody, *The Development of the Family and Marriage in Europe* (Cambridge, 1983) (mainly patristic, but with direct relevance to our period). The classic work on the acquisition of matrimonial jurisdiction by the church courts is P. Daudet, *L'établissement de la compétence de l'église en matière de divorce et de consanguinité* (Paris, 1941). The movement towards a consent theory is discussed by C. Donahue, 'The Policy of Alexander III's Consent Theory of Marriage', *ICMCL* 4 (1976) 251–81, and J. T. Noonan, 'Marriage in the Middle Ages, 1: Power to Choose', *Viator* 4 (1973) 419–34. See also Noonan's 'Marital Affection in the Canonists', *S. Grat.* 12 (1967) 479–509 and Donahue's 'The Dating of Alexander III's Marriage Decretals', *ZSSRGkA* 99 (1982) 70–124. There is material on the consequences of the new theory for social behaviour in the succeeding period in G. P. Homans, *English Villagers of the Thirteenth Century* (Cambridge, Mass., 1941), 144–94, and R. H. Helmholz, *Marriage Litigation in Medieval England* (Cambridge, 1974).

iv. Commercial Morality: Interest and Usury. There are two very good introductory books: J. Gilchrist, *The Church and Economic Activity in the*

Middle Ages (London, 1969), and L. K. Little, *Religious Poverty and the Profit Economy in Medieval Europe* (London, 1978). On usury, there is a survey article by G. Le Bras, 'Usure', *Dic. TC* 15 (1946) 2336–72, and good discussions by T. P. McLaughlin, 'The Teaching of the Canonists on Usury', *MS* 1–2 (1939–40); B. J. Nelson, 'The Usurer and the Merchant Prince', *Journal of Economic History* 7 (1947) suppl. 104–22, and the first chapter in his *The Idea of Usury*, 2nd edn. (Chicago, 1969); and J. T. Noonan, *The Scholastic Analysis of Usury* (Cambridge, Mass., 1957). J. Le Goff, 'The Usurer and Purgatory', in *The Dawn of Modern Banking* (London, 1979) 25–52, is fascinating. J. W. Baldwin, 'The Medieval Theories of the Just Price', *Trans. Amer. Philosophical Soc.* 49.iv (1959) is an important technical study.

v. Chivalry. Another favourite area for writers on medieval society. Start with three excellent introductory volumes: S. Painter, *French Chivalry* (Baltimore, 1940); M. Keen, *Chivalry* (London, 1984); and C. S. Jaeger, *The Origins of Courtliness* (London, 1985), tracing the origin of the ideals in the Ottonian court. The extent to which chivalry was influenced by the teaching and liturgy of the church is disputed. E. Curtius's view about the chivalric ethic was strongly criticized by E. Neumann, 'Der Streit um das ritterliche Tugendsystem', *Erbe der Vergangenheit: Festgabe für K. Helm* (Tübingen, 1951) 137–55. Other aspects of ecclesiastical influence have been considered more recently by C. Morris, '*Equestris ordo*', *SCH* 15 (1978) 87–96; J. Flori, *L'essor de la chevalerie* (Geneva, 1986); and G. Althoff, '*Nunc fiant Christi milites . . .*', *Saeculum* 32 (1981) 317–33.

Chapter 14. Dissent

i. Heresy: General and Beginnings (1050–1140). The important works are listed in H. Grundmann, *Bibliographie zur Ketzergeschichte des Mittelalters 1900–66* (Rome, 1967), and C. T. Berckhout and J. B. Russell, *Medieval Heresies: a Bibliography 1960–79* (Toronto, 1981). There are valuable collections of articles edited by J. Le Goff, *Hérésies et sociétés dans l'Europe pré-industrielle* (Paris, 1968), and by W. Lourdaux and D. Verhelst, *The Concept of Heresy in the Middle Ages* (Louvain, 1976). H. Grundmann has provided a scholarly factual survey in *Ketzergeschichte des Mittelalters* (Göttingen, 1963). There are two outstanding English contributions. R. I. Moore, *The Origins of European Dissent* (Harmondsworth, 1977), is an excellent book in which the likelihood of early eastern influence is rejected. The possibility is taken more seriously by M. D. Lambert in *Medieval Heresy: Popular Movements from Bogomil to Huss* (London, 1977). J. B. Russell's *Dissent and Reform in the Early Middle Ages* (Berkeley, 1965), has been largely superseded by these later works. In addition there are very perceptive surveys by C. Brooke, 'Heresy and Religious Sentiment 1000–1250', *Bulletin of the Institute of Historical Research* 41 (1968) 115–31; R.

Manselli, 'La *christianitas* medioevale di fronte all'eresia', in V. Branca (ed.), *Concetto, storia, miti e immagini del medio evo* (Venice, 1973); and E. Werner, 'Häresie und Gesellschaft im 11 Jh', Sb. Leipzig (1975). Several recent books have provided English translations with discussions of the major documents: W. L. Wakefield and A. P. Evans, *Heresies of the High Middle Ages* (New York, 1969); R. I. Moore, *The Birth of Popular Heresy* (London, 1975); and E. Peters, *Heresy and Authority in Medieval Europe* (London, 1980). Particular episodes or regions are discussed by J. Musy, 'Mouvements populaires et hérésies au XIe siècle en France', *Revue Historique* 99 (1975) 33–76; W. Mohr, 'Tanchelm von Antwerpen', *Annales Universitatis Saraviensis* III.3/4 (1954) 234–47; G. Despy, 'Les cathares dans le diocèse de Liège au XIIe siècle', *Christianisme d'hier et d'aujourd'hui: hommage à Jean Préaux* (Brussels, 1979); M. Suttor, 'Le *triumphus sancti Lamberti* et le catharisme à Liège', *MA* 91 (1985) 227–64; and in articles in *Pascua Medievalia: Studies voor J. M. de Smedt* (Louvain, 1983). See also J. Fearns's edition of the *Contra Petrobrusianos hereticos* of Peter the Venerable in CC(CM) 10 (1968).

ii. Cathars and Waldensians 1140–1200. S. Runciman, *The Medieval Manichee*, is now out of date, even in its modified reprint of 1982. The classic study of the movement as a whole is A. Borst, *Die Catharer*, MGH Schriften 12 (1953), French tr. (Paris, 1974). J. Duvernoy, *Le catharisme: l'histoire des cathares* (Toulouse, 1979), has useful material, and the changing views of catharism over the centuries are analysed in *Historiographie du catharisme*, CF 14 (1979). See also F. Sanjek, *Les chrétiens bosniaques et le mouvement cathare* (Paris, 1976). Studies on the Albigensians are listed below under ch. 17.vi. The early development of the Waldensians is obscure. It has been examined in W. Mohr, *Waldes von seiner Berufung bis zu seinem Tode* (Horn, 1970); K.-V. Selge, *Die ersten Waldenser*, 2 vols (Berlin, 1967); *Vaudois languedociens et pauvres catholiques*, CF 2 (1967); and A. Dondaine, 'Aux origines du Valdéisme: une profession de foi de Valdès', *AFP* 16 (1946) 191–235. There are two excellent survey articles by G. Gonnet, 'Le cheminement des Vaudois vers le schisme et l'hérésie', *CCM* 19 (1976) 309–45, and 'Le développement des doctrines vaudoises de Lyon à Chanforan 1170–1532', *Revue d'histoire et de philosophie religieuses* 52 (1972) 397–406. Very valuable also is his *Enchiridion fontium valdensium* (Torre Pellice, 1958). The reaction of the hierarchy to heresy in the twelfth century is discussed in important articles by R. Manselli and Y. Dossat in *Le Credo, le morale et l'inquisition*, CF 6 (1971), and B. Bolton 'Tradition and Temerity: Papal Attitudes to Deviants 1159–1216', *SCH* 9 (1972) 79–91.

iii. Sorcery. Three outstanding modern works, which relate in large part to this period, are N. Cohn, *Europe's Inner Demons* (London, 1975); D. Harmening, *Superstitio: Untersuchungen zur kirchlich-theologischen Aberglaubensliteratur des Mittelalters* (Berlin, 1979); and E. M. Peters, *The*

Magician, the Witch and the Law (Hassocks, 1978), a wide-ranging survey whose views are largely reflected in the text of this section. There is valuable material in J. B. Russell, *Witchcraft in the Middle Ages* (Ithaca, 1972), and a good collection of sources in A. C. Kors and E. Peters, *Witchcraft in Europe 1100–1700* (London, 1972). C. Vogel, 'Pratiques superstitieuses au début du XIe siècle d'après Burchard', *Études de civilisation médiévale: mélanges offerts à E.-R. Labande* (Poitiers, 1975), 751–62, presents some important material.

iv. The Jews. The best study for general reading is J. Parkes, *The Jew in the Medieval Community*, 2nd ed. (New York, 1976), and there is a thorough account in S. W. Baron, *A Social and Religious History of the Jews*, 18 vols. 2nd edn. (New York, 1952–83). A valuable survey article is that by G. I. Langmuir, 'From Ambrose of Milan to Emicho of Leiningen', CISAM 36 (1980) 313–73. Although it mostly covers an earlier period, it is worth mentioning the excellent book of B. Blumenkranz, *Juifs et chrétiens dans le monde occidental 430–1096* (Paris, 1960). Important local studies are by R. Chazan, *Medieval Jewry in Northern France* (London, 1973); G. Kisch, *The Jews in Medieval Germany* (Chicago, 1949); and *Juifs et judaïsme de Languedoc*, CF 12 (1977). There is a general account of accusations against the Jews by J. Trachtenberg, *The Devil and the Jews* (New Haven, 1943), which is useful in spite of a lack of differentiation of the period and origins of the charges. The supposed connection of the Jew with other enemies of Christendom is explored in A. H. Cutler, *The Jew as Ally of the Muslim: Medieval Roots of Anti-Semitism* (Indiana, 1986); and J. Riley-Smith, 'The First Crusade and the Persecution of the Jews', SCH 21 (1984) 51–72. B. Blumenkranz, *Le juif médiéval au miroir de l'art chrétien* (Paris, 1966), conveniently summarizes his earlier work and provides the broadest treatment of this important theme. With it should be read ch. 7 of H. Kraus, *The Living Theatre of Medieval Art* (London, 1967). The accusation of ritual murder is best studied in G. I. Langmuir, 'L'absence d'accusation de meurtre rituel à l'ouest du Rhône', CF 12 (1977) 235–49, and the same author discusses the first instance of the charge in 'Thomas of Monmouth: Detector of Ritual Murder', *Speculum* 59 (1984) 820–46. There are general studies of Christian-Jewish polemic by A. L. Williams, *Adversus Judaeos: a Bird's-eye View of Christian Apologiae until the Renaissance* (Cambridge, 1935), and H. Maccoby, *Judaism on Trial: Jewish-Christian Disputations in the Middle Ages* (London, 1982). The works of Gilbert Crispin are edited by G. R. Evans and A. S. Abulafia (Oxford, 1986). An unusual work among the polemics is that by Peter Abelard, *Dialogus inter philosophum, judaeum and christianum*. It has been edited by R. Thomas (Stuttgart, 1970), and tr. by P. J. Payer (Toronto, 1979), The general intellectual relationships of the two communities are examined by A. Grabois, 'The *Hebraica veritas* and Jewish-Christian Intellectual Relations in the Twelfth Century', *Speculum* 50 (1975) 613–34, and H. Hailperin, *Rashi and the Christian Scholars* (Pittsburgh, 1963).

Chapter 15. The Formulation of the Faith

i–ii. The Growth of Theology as a Science. Almost every significant figure in the period has been the subject of separate study, and this note will confine itself to more general works and to a limited number of themes explored in the text. Investigation of theology between 1050 and 1200 may rely upon several books of outstanding quality. The first is J. de Ghellinck, *Le mouvement théologique du XIIe siècle* (Paris, 1948). Then there is a broader survey by A. Forest and others, *Le mouvement doctrinal du XIe au XIVe siècle* (Paris, 1951) (FM vol. xiii). There are two excellent surveys of the whole field by A. M. Landgraf: *Einführung in die Geschichte der theologischen Literatur der Frühscholastik* (Regensburg, 1948) (French translation Montreal 1973); and *Dogmengeschichte der Frühscholastik*, 4 vols. (Regensburg, 1952–6). Two other brilliantly perceptive books are by B. Smalley, *The Study of the Bible in the Middle Ages*, 3rd edn. (Oxford, 1983), and M.-D. Chenu, *La théologie au XIIe siècle* (Paris, 1957), from which a good deal of material is included in *Nature, Man and Society in the Twelfth Century* (Chicago, 1968). More recent works are by D. E. Luscombe, *The School of Peter Abelard* (Cambridge, 1969), which contains material of very wide interest for the thought of the period, and J. Pelikan, *The Growth of Medieval Theology (600–1300)* (Chicago, 1978) (vol. iii of his *The Christian Tradition*). G. R. Evans' *Anselm and a New Generation* (Oxford, 1980), also covers a wide range of schools of thought. There is a convenient collection of texts in translation by E. R. Fairweather, *A Scholastic Miscellany: Anselm to Occam* (Philadelphia, 1956).

The development of theology as a subject is covered by M. Grabmann, *Die Geschichte der scholastischen Methode*, 2 vols. (Freiburg-im-Breisgau, 1909, repr. Darmstadt 1957). Modern works include G. Makdisi, 'The Scholastic Method in Medieval Education', *Speculum* 49 (1974) 640–61, and G. R. Evans, *Old Arts and New Theology: the Beginnings of Theology as an Academic Discipline* (Oxford, 1980). On one of the important new schools there is M.-D. Chenu, 'Civilisation urbaine et théologie: l'école de S. Victor', *Annales* 29 (1974) 1253–63. For the 'school of Chartres' see ch. 2.iii above, and for the career of Anselm of Canterbury ch. 7.i. D. E. Luscombe's paper *Peter Abelard*, Hist. Assoc. (London, 1979), provides a good bibliography, and there is full information about manuscripts and editions in N. M. Haring, 'Abelard Yesterday and Today', *Pierre Abélard, Pierre le Vénérable: colloques du CNRS* (Paris, 1975), 341–403. Among introductions to his career J. G. Sikes, *Peter Abailard*, 2nd edn. (Cambridge, 1946); L. Grane, *Peter Abelard* (London, 1970); and K. M. Starnes, *Peter Abelard: His Place in History* (Washington, 1981), deserve a recommendation. On exegesis one should start with B. Smalley's book mentioned above, along with H. de Lubac, *Exégèse médiévale: les quatre sens de l'Écriture*, 3 vols. (Paris, 1959–61). The concept of 'analogy' was crucial in the development of thought about God, and is analysed in R. Javelet, *Image et ressemblance au XIIe siècle de S. Anselme à Alain de Lille*, 2 vols. (Paris, 1967), and S. Otto, *Die Funktion des Bildbegriffes in der Theologie des 12 Jhs* (Münster, 1963). The theme is developed by G. R. Evans, *Alan of Lille: the Frontiers of Theology in the Later Twelfth Century* (Cambridge, 1983).

iii. The Theology of Humanism. On the twelfth-century Renaissance and allied concepts, see under Part II (before ch. 8) above. The best introduction to medieval humanism is in the title essay of R. W. Southern's collection, *Medieval Humanism and other Studies* (Oxford, 1970), 29–60. Also of great interest are R. R. Bolgar, *The Classical Inheritance and its Beneficiaries* (Cambridge, 1954); D. Knowles, 'The Humanism of the Twelfth Century', *The Historian and Character* (Cambridge, 1963), 16–30; W. von den Steinen, *Homo Caelestis* (Berne, 1965); and G. B. Ladner, *Ad imaginem Dei: the Image of Man in Medieval Art* (Latrobe, 1965). Scepticism about over-much stress on the rise of humanism is expressed by R. Bultot, *Christianisme et valeurs humaines* (Paris, 1963–), and D. Baker, 'Arabick to the People', *SCH* 17 (1981) 59–76. On the expression of the individual in contemporary writing, there is P. Dronke, *Poetic Individuality in the Middle Ages* (Oxford, 1970) and R. W. Hanning, *The Individual in Twelfth-century Romance* (London, 1977); and, more generally, M.-D. Chenu, *L'éveil de la conscience dans la civilisation médiévale* (Paris, 1969); C. Morris, *The Discovery of the Individual 1050–1200* (London, 1972); a subsequent discussion with C. W. Bynum in *JEH* 31 (1980) 1–17, 195–206; J. F. Benton, 'Consciousness of Self and Perceptions of Individuality', *RR* 263–95; and R. D. Logan, 'A Conception of the Self in the Later Middle Ages', *JMH* 12 (1986) 253–68. W. Ullmann, *The Individual and Society in the Middle Ages* (Baltimore, 1966), is important mainly for the subsequent period. For the place occupied by love in religious thought, it is best to start with J. C. Moore, 'Love in Twelfth-century France', *Traditio* 24 (1968) 429–43; J. Leclercq, *Monks and Love in Twelfth-century France: psycho-historical Essays* (Oxford, 1979); and P. Dinzelbacher, 'Über die Entdeckung der Liebe im Hochmittelalter', *Saeculum* 32 (1981) 185–208; these will give access to the immense volume of work on the concept of courtly love in literature. The cult of friendship among scholars and monks is discussed in many of the books which have been mentioned, but still awaits a systematic history. H. Legros, 'Le vocabulaire de l'amitié: son évolution sémantique au cours du XIIe siècle', *CCM* 23 (1980) 131–9, and B. P. McGuire, 'The Cistercians and the Transformation of Monastic Friendships', *Analecta Cisterciensia* 37 (1981) 3–65, are valuable introductory articles. Perhaps its greatest practitioner was Abbot Aelred of Rievaulx: his treatise *On Spiritual Friendship* has been translated by M. E. Laker (Kalamazoo, 1977), and his *Life* by Walter Daniel ed. and tr. by F. M. Powicke (Edinburgh, 1950); and the ideas of his teacher are discussed by E. C. Ronquist, 'Friendship in Laurence of Durham', *Classica et Medievalia* 35 (1984) 191–214.

iv. Sin and Redemption. The classic work of O. D. Watkins, *A History of Penance*, 2 vols. (London, 1920; repr. New York, 1961) has been supplemented by B. Poschmann, *Penance and the Anointing of the Sick* (Freiburg, 1964), and C. Vogel, *Le pécheur et la pénitence au Moyen Âge*, 2nd edn. (Paris, 1982). There are detailed studies by P. Anciaux, *La théologie du sacrement de pénitence au XIIe siècle* (Louvain, 1949), and A. Teetaert, *La confession aux laïques dans l'église latine* (Wetteren, 1926). The process of formulating the list of seven sacraments has been charted by W. Knoch, *Die Einsetzung der Sakramente durch Christus* (Münster, 1983); D. van den Eynde, *Les définitions des sacrements pendant la première période de la théologie scholastique* (Rome, 1950); and J. de Ghellinck, *Pour l'histoire du mot sacramentum* (Paris, 1924). The idea of Dominical authority for the orders of the ministry is carefully analysed by R. E. Reynolds, *The Ordinals of Christ* (New York, 1978).

The best general introduction to eucharistic theology in the period is probably the article by J. de Ghellinck, 'Eucharistie au XIIe siècle en occident', *Dic. TC* 5 (1913) 1233–1302, now supplemented by G. Macy, *The Theologies of the Eucharist in the Early Scholastic Period* (Oxford, 1984). There are important studies on the Berengar controversy by A. J. Macdonald, *Berengar and the Reform of Sacramental Doctrine* (London, 1930); R. W. Southern, 'Lanfanc of Bec and Berengar of Tours', *Studies in Medieval History presented to F. M. Powicke* (Oxford, 1948), 27–48; O. Capitani, *Studi su Berengario di Tours* (Lecce, 1966); and J. de Montclos, *Lanfranc et Bérenger* (Louvain, 1971). H. Jorissen has made an interesting contribution to the history of doctrine in his book *Die Entfaltung der Transsubstantiationslehre bis zum Beginn der Hochscholastik*, (Münster, 1965). The emergence of the ceremony of the elevation of the host has been discussed by V. L. Kennedy in *MS* 6 (1944) 121–50 and 8 (1946) 87–96, and by M. Dykmans, 'Aux origines de l'élévation eucharistique', *Zetesis: Album Amicorum aan E. de Strycker* (Antwerp, 1973), 679–94. The evolution of private masses is the subject of a lively survey by C. Vogel, 'Une mutation cultuelle inexpliquée: le passage de l'eucharistie communautaire à la messe privée', *Recherches de Science Religieuse* 54 (1980) 231–50 and 55 (1981) 206–13. There is an impressive discussion by E. Dumoutet, *Corpus Domini: aux sources de la piété eucharistique médiévale* (Paris, 1942), and material on proof-miracles was assembled by P. Browe, *Die eucharistischen Wunder des Mittelalters* (Breslau, 1938).

The study of the doctrine of the atonement can usefully begin from two books almost fifty years old, G. Aulén, *Christus Victor* (repr. New York, 1969), and J. Rivière, *Le dogme de la rédemption au début du Moyen Âge* (Paris, 1934), together with his article in *Revue du Moyen Âge Latin* 2 (1946) 100 ff.

The devotion to the crucified humanity was a particular development of this period: see works on Bernard of Clairvaux in ch. 10.iv above, and E. Dumoutet, *Le Christ selon la chair et la vie liturgique au Moyen Âge* (Paris, 1932), with the comments by C. Morris, 'Christ after the Flesh', *Ampleforth Journal* 80 (1975) 44–51.

v. The World to Come. On death, we must start with the trail-blazing if controversial book by P. Ariès, *The Hour of our Death* (Harmondsworth, 1981), and his visual accompaniment in *Images of Man and Death* (London, 1985); and there is a magnificent unpublished thesis by M. M. McLaughlin, 'Consorting with the Saints: Prayer for the Dead in Early Medieval French Society' (University of Stanford Ph.D. 1985). There are collections of articles in *Il dolore e la morte*, CSSSM 5 (1967) and H. Braet and W. Verbeke (ed.), *Death in the Middle Ages* (Louvain, 1983). The more important meditative works are discussed by G. S. Williams, *The Vision of Death* (Göppingen, 1976). The evolution of the *Dies irae* is discussed by J.-C. Payen in *Romania* 86 (1965) 48–76, and F. J. E. Raby, *A History of Christian-Latin Poetry*, 2nd ed. (Oxford, 1966), 443–52. The account of death-bed practice by K. Stüber, *Commendatio animae: Sterben im Mittelalter* (Berne, 1976), is largely focused on the thirteenth century.

B. McGinn has provided selections from eschatological writings in *Visions of the End: Apocalyptic Traditions in the Middle Ages* (New York, 1979), and *Apocalyptic Spirituality* (London, 1979), and has reviewed earlier scholarship in *MS* 37 (1975) 252–86 and *Medievalia et Humanistica* NS 11 (1982) 263–89. The figure of Antichrist is examined in a controversial book by H. D. Rauh, *Das Bild des Antichrist im Mittelalter* (Munster, 1973), and by R. K. Emmerson, *Antichrist in the Middle Ages* (Seattle, 1981). Millenarianism before Joachim of Fiore is the subject of an important study by P. Classen, 'Eschatologische Ideen und Armutsbewegungen im XI und XII Jh.', CSSSM 8 (1969) 127–62, and R. Lerner's 'Refreshment of the Saints', *Traditio* 32 (1976) 97–144, makes a contribution to the debate about Joachim's predecessors. On the links between history and eschatology see R. W. Southern, 'Aspects of the European Tradition of Historical Writing', *TRHS* V.21 (1971) 159–79 and 22 (1972) 159–80, and M. Häussler, *Das Ende der Geschichte in der mittelalterlichen Weltchronistik* (Cologne, 1980). P. Classen discussed the contribution of the German historical school in '*Res gestae*, Universal History, Apocalypse: Visions of Past and Future', *RR* 387–417, and the Premonstratensian approach is reconsidered by G. Bischoff, 'Early Premonstratensian Eschatology: the Apocalyptic Myth', E. R. Elder (ed.), *The Spirituality of Western Christendom* (Kalamazoo, 1976), 41–71. For the Paris tradition, see N. Wicki, *Die Lehre von der himmlischen Seligkeit in der mittelalterlichen Scholastik von Petrus Lombardus bis Thomas von Aquin* (Freiburg, 1954).

Chapter 16. Property, Privilege and Law

Reading for section i, Ownership and Distribution, is included in the following sections.

ii. Tithes. The two most informative books are by C. E. Boyd, *Tithes and Parishes in Medieval Italy* (New York, 1952), and G. Constable, *Monastic Tithes from their Origins to the Twelfth Century* (Cambridge, 1964), both of which are interesting on the whole development of tithes in this period. So are two older volumes by P. E. Viard, *Histoire de la dîme ecclésiastique principalement en France jusqu'au décret de Gratien* (Dijon, 1909), and a subsequent volume on 1150–1313 (Paris, 1912). Tithe restitution policy is covered in several of the studies on restitution of churches (see ch. 9.iii). C. Renardy has studied the restitution specifically of tithe at Liège in articles in *MA* 76 (1970) and *Tijdschrift voor Rechtsgeschiednis* 41 (1973) 339–60.

iii. The Structure of Ecclesiastical Property. There is some discussion of property and revenues in almost all the general histories of the church, and also in studies of particular dioceses, cathedrals, and parishes, but there have been few attempts at a systematic analysis of the policy of land acquisition. There is a great deal of information in the classic book by E. Lesne, *Histoire de la propriété ecclésiastique en France*, 6 vols. (Lille, 1910–43), and an excellent survey article by D. Herlihy, 'Church Property on the European Continent 701–1200', *Speculum* 36 (1961) 81–105. There are also some useful articles in *The Church and Wealth*, SCH 24 (1987). Of studies of the estates of bishops, it is possible to mention only a few of particular importance. These include D. J. Osheim, *An Italian Lordship: the Bishopric of Lucca in the late Middle Ages* (Berkeley, 1977); J. N. Sutherland, 'The Recovery of Land in the diocese of Grenoble during the Gregorian Reform Epoch', *Catholic Historical Review* 64 (1978) 377–97; H. J. Légier, 'L'église et l'économie médiévale: la monnaie ecclésiastique de Lyon', *Annales* 12 (1957) 561–72; H. Schmidinger, *Patriarch und Landesherr* (Cologne, 1954) (on Aquileia); A. Chédeville, *Chartres et ses campagnes du Xe au XIIIe siècle* (Paris, 1973); and K.-H. Spiess, 'Königshof und Fürstenhof: der Adel und die Mainzer Erzbischöfe im 12 Jh.', *Deus qui mutat tempora: Menschen und Institutionen im Wandel des Mittelalters: Festschrift für Alfons Becker* (Sigmaringen, 1987), 203–34. On cathedral lands, it is particularly worth looking at K. Major, 'Finances of the Dean and Chapter of Lincoln', *JEH* 5 (1954) 149–67.

iv. Clerical Privilege. There is material on this in many of the general studies of canon law, but it has attracted relatively few works as a topic in its own right. The best is a solid piece of work which covers the subject generally, R. Génestal's book *Le privilegium fori en France du Décret de Gratien à la fin du XIV* siècle, 2 vols. (Paris, 1921–4); and L. C. Gabel, *Benefit of Clergy in England in the Later Middle Ages* (Northampton, 1929), is valuable for our period also. There is a good discussion of the English situation after Becket in C. R. Cheney, 'Punishment of Felonous Clerks', *EHR* 51 (1936) 215–36.

v. The Growth of Canon Law. References are necessarily to the text published by E. Friedberg, *Corpus Iuris Canonici*, 2nd ed. (Leipzig, 1879; repr. Graz, 1959), an indispensible but far from critical edition. There is an attractive short introduction to the spirit of canon law by S. Kuttner, 'Harmony from Dissonance', in his collected essays, *The History of Ideas and Doctrines of Canon Law in the Middle Ages* (London, 1980); and some interesting remarks by J. Brundage, 'The Creative Canonist', *The Jurist* 31 (1971) 301–18. Among the general histories of the subject are the following: P. Fournier and G. Le Bras, *Histoire des collections canoniques en occident*, 2 vols. (Paris, 1931); A. M. Stickler, *Historia iuris canonici Latini: 1. Historia fontium* (Turin, 1950); W. M. Plöchl, *Geschichte des Kirchenrechts*, vol 2 (Vienna, 1955); H. E. Feine, *Kirchliche Rechtsgeschichte: die katholische Kirche*, 4th edn. (Cologne, 1964); and other works mentioned in *General: ecclesiastical institutions* above. H. Fuhrmann's *Einfluss und Verbreitung der pseudoisidorischen Fälschungen*, 3 vols. (Stuttgart, 1972–4), has transformed previous thinking about the significance of this important collection. An indispensable guide to the material from Gratian onwards is provided by S. Kuttner, *Repertorium der Kanonistik 1140–1234* (Vatican, 1937). Another useful work of reference by the same author is *Index titulorum decretalium ex collectionibus tam privatis quam publicis conscriptus* (Milan, 1977), and X. Ochoa Sanz and A. Diez have published *Indices canonum titulorum et capitulorum Corporis iuris canonici* (Rome, 1964). A more general reference work, of considerable use even if it has eccentricities, is J. A. Clarence Smith, *Medieval Law Teachers and Writers* (Ottawa, 1975). The best study of Ivo of Chartres is that by R. Sprandel, *Ivo von Chartres und seine Stellung in der Kirchengeschichte* (Stuttgart, 1962). The limitations of our knowledge of Gratian's biography have been stressed by J. T. Noonan, 'Gratian Slept Here', *Traditio* 35 (1979) 145–72. J. T. Noonan and P. Classen have disputed the existence of a formal approval of Gratian's collection in *BMCL* 6 (1976) 15–28 and 8 (1978) 38–40. For the significance of Gratian in the politics of the period, see 8.i. above. On the early relations of Bologna and Rome there is an interesting study by R. Somerville, 'Pope Innocent II and the Study of Roman Law', *Revue des Études Islamiques* 44 (1976) 105–14, and there is a useful survey of recent work by V. Piergiovanni, 'Il primo secolo della scuola canonistica di Bologna', *ICMCL* 6 (1985) 241–56.

vi. The Critics. The standard study of Gerhoh is the excellent one by P. Classen, *Gerhoch von Reichersberg: eine Biographie* (Wiesbaden, 1960). On

Bernard of Clairvaux, see ch. 10.iv, and on Arnold, G. W. Greenaway, *Arnold of Brescia* (London, 1931), and A. Frugoni, *Arnaldo da Brescia nelle fonti del secolo XII* (Rome, 1954). A. Linder's article 'The Myth of Constantine the Great', *SM* iii.16 (1975) 43–95 explores some areas of radical thought. J. A. Yunck examines the growth of satire in *The Lineage of Lady Meed* (Indiana, 1963), and its application to ecclesiastical administration is discussed by J. Benzinger, *Invectiva in Romam: Romkritik im Mittelalter vom 9 bis zum 12 Jh.* (Hamburg, 1968), and H. Schüppert, *Kirchenkritik in der lateinischen Lyrik des 12 und 13 Jhs* (Munich, 1972). R. M. Thomson has edited and translated one of the early classics in the genre, the *Tractatus Garsiae, or the Translation of the Relics of Saints Gold and Silver* (Leiden, 1973).

PART III. THE THIRTEENTH CENTURY

There are lively introductory books by L. Génicot, *Le XIIIe siècle européen* (Paris, 1968), and P. Brezzi, *Il secolo del rinnovamento: la rinascita del Duecento* (Rome, 1973).

Chapter 17. The Pontificate of Innocent III 1198–1216

i. *The New Pope.* The work with which modern readers should begin is H. Tillmann, *Pope Innocent III* (Amsterdam, 1980), a translation of the German original of 1954. There is an important collection of articles by M. Maccarrone, *Studi su Innocenzo III* (Padua, 1972). The contemporary biography of the pope, *Gesta Innocentii papae III*, lacks a critical edition but is available in PL 214.xv–ccxxviii. Much of our information comes from the magnificent series of papal registers, printed in PL 214–6. The ambitious project for a new edition under the guidance of O. Hageneder and others has so far only reached the second year (Cologne, 1965 and Rome, 1979). The basic study of the registers is F. Kempf, *Die Register Innozenz III* (Rome, 1945). The most thorough study of Innocent before his pontificate is that of M. Maccarrone, 'Innocenzo III prima del pontificato', *Archivio della Deputazione Romana* 66 (1943) 59–134. Cardinal Lothar's legal training was examined by K. Pennington, 'The Legal Education of Pope Innocent III', *BMCL* 4 (1974) 70–7. The text of his most famous writing has been edited by R. E. Lewis, *Lotario dei Segni: de Miseria Condicionis Humane* (Athens, Ga., 1978), which provides the 'received' text of the later Middle Ages, and the significance of the book is discussed by R. Bultot, 'Mépris du monde dans la pensée d'Innocent III', *CCM* 4 (1961) 441–56, and J. C. Moore, 'Innocent III's *de miseria condicionis humane*: a *speculum curiae*?', *Catholic Historical Review* 67 (1981) 553–64. The sermons (PL 217.313–688) have been examined by G. Scuppa, 'I sermoni di Innocenzo III' (Pontificia Università Lateranense, unpublished dissertation, 1961). Innocent's eucharistic doctrine is discussed by D. F. Wright, 'Albert the Great's Critique of Lothar of Segni', *The Thomist* 44 (1980) 584–96.

ii. The Papal State, Sicily, and the Empire. The 'recuperation' inevitably bulks large in the major histories of the Papal State (*General: Rome and the Papal State* above) and in D. P. Waley, *The Papal State in the Thirteenth Century* (London, 1961). The legal basis for the claims is discussed at length in M. Laufs, *Politik und Recht bei Innozenz III* (Cologne, 1980); see the review by F. Kempf in *AHP* 19 (1981) 361–7, whose views are followed in the text. The regency of Innocent in Sicily has been studied by T. C. Van Cleve, *Markward of Anweiler and the Sicilian Regency* (Princeton, 1937), and E. Kennan, 'Innocent III and the First Political Crusade', *Traditio* 27 (1971) 231–49. The basis for an understanding of the relations between papacy and empire must be the volume edited by F. Kempf, *Regestum Innocentii III super negotio Romani Imperii* (Rome, 1947), and his fine study, *Papsttum und Kaisertum bei Innocenz III* (Rome, 1954), with further reflections in 'Innozenz III und der deutscher Thronstreit', *AHP* 23 (1985) 63–91. The significance of the register has been reassessed by O. Hageneder, 'Zur Entstehung des Thronstreitregisters Papst Innocenz III', *Studien zu Ehren von H. Hoberg* (Rome, 1979), i.275–80. There are articles on specific aspects of relations with Otto IV by H. Tillmann in *HJb* 84 (1964) 34–85 and 85 (1965) 28–49; A. Haidacher, 'Über den Zeitpunkt der Exkommunikation Ottos IV', *Römische Historische Mitteilungen* 3 (1960) 132–85; and H.-E. Hilpert, 'Zwei Briefe Kaiser Ottos IV an Johann Ohneland', *DAEM* 38 (1982) 123–40.

iii. Innocent III and the Lay Power. Apart from sections in the general works already mentioned, there is a magnificent study by C. R. Cheney, *Pope Innocent III and England*, Päpste und Papsttum 9 (Stuttgart, 1976). Volumes on Innocent's relations with other countries are planned for the same series. Cheney's study rested on *The Letters of Pope Innocent III concerning England and Wales: a Calendar*, ed. C. R. and M. G. Cheney (Oxford, 1967). Still of interest, although requiring amendment in detail, is F. M. Powicke, *Stephen Langton* (Oxford, 1928). There are general views of the development of papal claims to secular authority by J. A. Watt, 'The Theory of Papal Monarchy in the Thirteenth Century', *Traditio* 20 (1964) 179–317 and B. Tierney, 'The Continuity of Papal Political Theory in the Thirteenth Century', *MS* 27 (1965) 227–45. On special features of papal theory during the pontificate, there are articles by O. Hageneder, 'Das Sonne-Mond-Gleichnis bei Innocenz III', *MIOG* 65 (1957) 340–68; B. Tierney, '*Tria quippe distinguit iudicia*: a Note on *per venerabilem*', *Speculum* 37 (1962) 48–59; M. Maccarrone, 'Innocenzo III e la feudalità: *non ratione feudi, sed occasione peccati*', *École française de Rome 44 (1978)* 475–514, and his 'La papauté et Philippe Auguste: la décrétale *novit ille*', R. H. Bautier (ed.), *La France de*

Phillipe Auguste (Paris, 1982), 385–409; and K. Pennington, 'Pope Innocent III's Views on Church and State: a Gloss to *per venerabilem*', *Law, Church and Society: Essays in Honor of Stephan Kuttner* (Pennsylvania, 1977) 49–67. H. Lanz has written on *Die romanischen Wandmalereien von San Silvestro in Tivoli* (Frankfurt, 1983), an important statement of contemporary ideas.

iv. Reform. There are important studies of the concept of papal authority within the church by K. Pennington, *Pope and Bishops: the Papal Monarchy in the Twelfth and Thirteenth Centuries* (Pennsylvania, 1984) (in which the role of Innocent III bulks large) and W. Imkamp, *Das Kirchenbild Innocenz' III*, Päpste und Papsttum 22 (Stuttgart, 1983). In spite of the reforming spirit of the pontificate, ancient abuses still lingered, and a satire on the curia is discussed and edited by P. G. Schmidt, *'Novus regnat Salomon*: une satire contre Innocent III', *Festschrift B. Bischoff* (Stuttgart, 1971), 372–90.

v. The Christian East. The diversion of the Fourth Crusade presents a fascinating detective story which has attracted many investigators, and the best place to start is D. E. Queller's *Fourth Crusade: the Conquest of Constantinople* (Leicester, 1978), with C. M. Brand's criticism in 'The Fourth Crusade: Some Recent Interpretations', *Medievalia et Humanistica* 12 (1984) 33–45, and his book, *Byzantium confronts the West* (Cambridge, Mass., 1968). The Latin intrusion into the affairs of the Greek church is reserved for another volume, but a sequence of negotiations in which the popes were much involved is examined by R. L. Wolff, 'Politics in the Latin patriarchate of Constantinople', *Dumbarton Oaks Papers* 8 (1954) 225–303.

vi. The Struggle with Heresy. For the background, see ch. 14.i–ii. The best survey of Innocent's policy is by C. Thouzellier, *Catharisme et valdéisme en Languedoc*, 2nd edn. (Paris, 1969). The approach of Innocent to the Humiliati is discussed by B. Bolton in *SCH* 8 (1972) 73–82 and 11 (1975) 125–33, with a good bibliography, and his legislation by W. Ullmann, 'The Significance of Innocent III's Decretal *Vergentis*', *Le Bras* i.729–41. The history of the Albigensian movement is surveyed by R. Manselli, 'Albigenser', *LdM* 302–7, and at full length by E. Griffe, *Les débuts de l'aventure cathare en Languedoc, Le languedoc cathare de 1190 à 1210*, and *Le Languedoc cathare au temps de la croisade* (Paris, 1969–73); and by M. Roquebert, *L'épopée cathare*, 3 vols. (Paris, 1970–86). R. Lafont and others provide a wide range of discussion in *Les cathares en Occitanie* (Paris, 1982). On the growth of repression there is J. R. Strayer, *The Albigensian Crusades*, New York, 1971); W. L. Wakefield, *Heresy, Crusade and Inquisition in Southern France 1100–1250* (London, 1974); and J. Sumption, *The Albigensian Crusade* (London, 1978). See also the studies in *Paix de Dieu et guerre sainte en Languedoc au XIIIe siècle, CF* 4 (1969).

vii. Fourth Lateran Council. The text is in Alberigo 203–47 and A. Garcia y Garcia, *Consuetudines concilii quarti Lateranensis una cum commentariis glossatorum* (Vatican, 1981), and an English translation by H. Rothwell, *English Historical Documents 1189–1327* (London, 1975), 643–75. There is useful discussion, as well as a French translation, in Foreville 227–395, and an important eyewitness is splendidly edited by S. Kuttner and A. Garcia y Garcia, 'A New Eyewitness Account of the Fourth Lateran Council', *Traditio* 20 (1964) 115–78.

Chapter 18. Friars, Beguines and the Campaign Against Heresy

i. The growth of the friars. One of the best general accounts is in D. Knowles, *The Religious Orders in England* (Cambridge, 1948), and the results of modern scholarship, with translations of important materials, are well presented in R. B. Brooke, *The Coming of the Friars* (London, 1975). The mutual influence of the two orders is discussed in an indispensible article by K. Elm, 'Franziskus und Dominikus', *Saeculum* 23 (1972) 127–47.

Franciscans. The general survey by J. R. H. Moorman, *A History of the Franciscan Order* (Oxford, 1968), is a good starting-place. The life which inaugurated a new period of scholarship was the famous work of P. Sabatier, *Life of S. Francis of Assisi* (English tr. London, 1894). Among the huge output of biographies since then we may mention J. R. H. Moorman, *S. Francis of Assisi*, 2nd edn. (London, 1963) and R. Manselli, *San Francesco*, 2nd edn. (Rome, 1981). The works of Francis have been published in several recent editions, notably by K. (or C.) Esser, *Die opuscula des hl. Franziskus von Assisi*, Grottaferrata (Rome, 1976, shortened version 1978). His text is the basis for the edition with French tr. by T. Desbonnets and others, *François d'Assise: écrits*, SC 285 (1981). There are English translations by M. Habig, *S. Francis of Assisi: Writings and Early Biographies* (London, 1979), and R. J. Armstrong and I. C. Brady, *Francis and Clare: the Complete Works* (London, 1982). There is also an edition and translation of the *Scripta Leonis, Rufini et Angeli sociorum S. Francisci* by R. B. Brooke (Oxford, 1970). All these works present difficult problems of interpretation, to which there is an excellent introduction in K. A. Fink, *Papsttum und Kirche im abendländischen Mittelalter* (Munich, 1981), 72–85. The best analysis for English readers is by J. R. H. Moorman, *The sources for the Life of S. Francis of Assisi* (Manchester, 1940). The interrelationship between the various collections is examined by R. B. Brooke, 'Recent work on S. Francis of Assisi', *Analecta Bollandiana* 100 (1982) 653–76. C. Esser has assessed the significance of Francis' work as a legislator in his *Rule and Testament of S. Francis: Conferences to Modern Followers* (Chicago, 1977), and studied the ideas of the early days in *Origins of the Franciscan Order* (Chicago, 1970). The influence of the papacy upon its development has been examined by K.-V. Selge, 'Franz von Assisi und die römische Kurie', *Zeitschrift für Theologie und Kirche* 67 (1970) 129–61; H. Grundmann, 'Die Bulle *Quo elongati* Gregors

IX', *AFH* 54 (1961) 3–25; W. R. Thomson, 'The Earliest Cardinal-protectors of the Franciscan Order', *Studies in Medieval and Renaissance History* 9 (1972) 17–80; and J. M. Powell, 'The Papacy and the Early Franciscans', *Franciscan Studies* 36 (1976) 248–62. On the conflict of ideas up to the middle of the century there is R. B. Brooke, *Early Franciscan Government: Elias to Bonaventure* (Cambridge, 1959), and M. D. Lambert, *Franciscan Poverty* (London, 1961). The wider influence of Francis is the subject of articles by E. Delaruelle, *La piété populaire au Moyen Âge* (Turin, 1975), 229–75. On his companion Clare there is R. B. and C. N. L. Brooke, 'S. Clare', in *SCH* Subsidia 1 (1978) 275–88; and *Klara von Assisi: Studientage der Franziskanischen Arbeitsgemeinschaft* (Werl, 1980).

Dominicans. The starting-point is W. A. Hinnebusch, *The History of the Dominican Order*, 2 vols. (New York, 1965–73). The standard life of Dominic himself is M.-H. Vicaire, *Histoire de S. Dominique*, new edn. (Paris, 1982) (English tr. of earlier edn. London, 1964). See also P. Mandonnet and M.-H. Vicaire, *S. Dominique: l'idée, l'homme et l'œuvre*, 2 vols. (Paris, 1938); and M.-H. Vicaire, *Dominique et ses prêcheurs* (Freiburg, 1977). There is a perceptive discussion by C. N. L. Brooke, 'S. Dominic and his first biographer', *Medieval Church and Society* (London, 1971), 214–32. The development of the Preachers is less problematical than that of the Minors, but it presents its difficulties, which are explored by G. R. Galbraith, *The Constitution of the Dominican Order* (Manchester, 1925); R. F. Bennett, *The early Dominicans* (Cambridge, 1937); and J.-P. Renard, *La formation et la désignation des prédicateurs au début de l'Ordre des Prêcheurs* (Freiburg, 1977), an excellent analysis of their standing in the history of preaching.

Expansion. The general histories of the orders naturally give a good deal of information about this, and in addition there are very many local studies. It is worth mentioning the two volumes which *Cahiers de Fanjeaux* have devoted to the friars: i (1966), *S. Dominique en Languedoc*, and viii (1973), *Les mendiants en pays d'Oc au XIIIe siècle*; and J. B. Freed, *The Friars and German Society in the Thirteenth Century* (Cambridge, Mass., 1977). Their involvement in the process of urbanization is considered in an article by J. Le Goff in *Annales* 25 (1970) 924–46, and in K. Elm (ed.), *Stellung und Wirksamkeit der Bettelorden in der städtischen Gesellschaft* (Berlin, 1981). The development of the friars' churches is discussed by G. Meersseman, 'L'architecture dominicaine au XIIIe siècle: législation et pratique', *AFP* 16 (1946) 136–90. On the advancement of the friars to positions of power, see W. R. Thomson, *Friars in the Cathedral: the First Franciscan Bishops 1226–61* (Toronto, 1975); and, on their dramatic intervention in the politics of northern Italy, A. Vauchez, 'Une campagne de pacification en Lombardie autour de 1233', *Mélanges d'Archéologie et d'Histoire* 78 (1966) 503–49.

ii. Religion for the Women: the Rise of the Beguines. The general survey by E. McDonnell, *The Beguines and Beghards in Medieval Culture* (Rutgers, 1954), if not always clear in arrangement, offers an excellent introduction. The question of social origins is discussed in O. Nübel, *Mittelalterliche Beginen- und Sozialsiedlungen in den Niederlanden* (Tübingen, 1970). There are important articles by B. M. Bolton: '*Mulieres sanctae*', *SCH* 10 (1973) 77–95; '*Vitae matrum*: a Further Aspect of the *Frauenfrage*', *SCH* Subsidia 1 (1978) 253–73; and 'Some Thirteenth-century Women in the Low Countries', *Niederlands Archief voor Kerkgeschiednis* 61, 1 (1981) 7–19. The works of an early Beguine are available in English translation in C. Hart, *Hadewijch: the Complete Works* (London, 1981), which is in fact not quite complete but provides a splendid collection based on the magisterial edition of J. Van Mierlo. Her place in the development of spirituality is examined by F. Gooday, 'Mechtild of Magdeburg and Hadewijch of Antwerp: a Comparison', *Ons geestelijk erf* 48 (1974) 305–62.

The discussion of the position of women in religious life was initiated in its classic form by C. Bücher, *Die Frauenfrage im Mittelalter* (Tübingen, 1882). The spiritual ideals presented to them are considered in an interesting book by M. Bernards, Speculum Virginum: *Geistigkeit und Seelenleben der Frau im Hochmittelalter*, *AKg* Beiheft 16 (1981), and in J. Bugge, *Virginitas: an Essay in the History of a Medieval Ideal* (The Hague, 1974). A very good collection of studies has been edited by P. Dinzelbacher and D. R. Bauer, *Frauenmystik im Mittelalter* (Stuttgart, 1985). See also G. Koch, *Frauenfrage und Ketzertum im Mittelalter* (Berlin, 1962). On medieval nunneries, the best general works are those by M. Parisse, *Les nonnes au Moyen Âge* (Le Puy, 1983), and M. de Fontette, *Les religieuses à l'âge classique du droit canon* (Paris, 1967); and there is a series of articles in J. A. Nichols and L. T. Shank, *Distant Echoes: Medieval Religious Women* (Kalamazoo, 1984). The contribution of the Cistercians is discussed by B. Degler-Spengler, 'Zisterzienserorden und Frauenklöster' in K. Elm (ed.), *Die Zisterzienser* (Cologne, 1982), 213–20, and S. Thompson, 'The Problem of the Cistercian Nuns in the Twelfth and Early Thirteenth Centuries', *SCH* Subsidia 1 (1978) 227–52; and a series, *Les moniales Cisterciennes* (Aiguebelle, 1986–), will provide a full history. For the importance in this area of Robert of Arbrissel (whose devotion to women's liberation has been exaggerated) and other new orders, see works mentioned in ch. 10.ii above. The social status of women has been the subject of much recent study, and there is a useful list of publications assembled by G. Erickson and K. Casey in *MS* 37 (1975) 340–59. Symposia include *Medieval Women*, *SCH* Subsidia 1 (1978); *La femme dans les civilisations des X-XIIIe siècles* (Poitiers, 1977); and *Women of the medieval World: Essays in Honour of J. H. Mundy* (Oxford, 1985). Books include R. Pernoud, *La femme au temps des cathédrales* (Paris, 1980) (an introductory but agreeable sketch); A. M. Lucas, *Women in the Middle Ages:*

Religion, Marriage and Letters (Brighton, 1982); and S. Shahar, *The Fourth Estate* (London, 1983).

On the cult of the Virgin Mary, the best work to consult initially is perhaps H. Graef, *Mary: a History of Doctrine and Devotion*, i (London, 1963), with good references to contemporary sources; and there is still much of value in S. Beissel, *Geschichte der Verehrung Marias in Deutschland während des Mittelalters* (Freiburg, 1909). Another good survey is by P. S. Gold, *The Lady and the Virgin: Image, Attitude and Experience in Twelfth-century France* (Chicago, 1985). On three of the important Marian devotions there is A. W. Burridge, 'L'immaculée conception dans la théologie de l'Angleterre médiévale', *RHE* 32 (1936) 570–98; P. Glorieux, 'Alain de Lille, docteur de l'Assomption', *Mélanges de science religieuse* 8 (1951) 5–18; and S. Solway, 'A Numismatic Source of the Madonna of Mercy', *Analecta Bollandiana* 67 (1985) 359–67. For an introduction to a major Marian shrine see E. Mason, 'Rocamadour in Quercy above All Other Churches', *SCH* 19 (1982) 39–54. The development of the Marian legends has been re-assessed by R. W. Southern, 'The English Origins of the *Miracles of the Virgin*,' *Medieval and Renaissance Studies* 4 (1958) 176–216, and J. C. Jennings, 'The origin of the "Elements Series" of the *Miracles of the Virgin*', *Medieval and Renaissance Studies* 6 (1968) 84–94.

iii. The repression of heresy. See also ch. 14.i–ii and 17.vi. The best handbook on the inquisition is now B. Hamilton, *The Medieval Inquisition* (London, 1981), and there are also survey works by J. Guiraud, *Histoire de l'inquisition au Moyen Âge*, 2 vols. (Paris, 1935) (see also his *The Medieval Inquisition* (London, 1929)) and H. Maisonneuve, *Études sur les origines de l'inquisition* 2nd edn. (Paris, 1960). The extent to which Dominic himself sympathized with repression is argued by M.-H. Vicaire and C. Thouzellier in *Annales du Midi* 79 (1967) 173–94 and 80 (1968) 121–38, and *CF* 6 (1971) 75–84. Important sources for the Midi were published by C. Douais, *Documents pour servir à l'histoire de l'inquisition dans le Languedoc*, 2 vols. (Paris, 1900). There is a fine recent study by E. Griffe, *Le Languedoc cathare et l'inquisition* (Paris, 1980), and for institutional history there is Y. Dossat, *Les crises de l'inquisition toulousaine au XIIIe siècle* (Bordeaux, 1959), and now the thorough study of L. Kolmer, 'Ad capiendas vulpeculas': *Ketzerbekämpfung in Südfrankreich in der ersten Hälfte des 13 Jhs*, Beiheft der *Francia* 19 (1982). E. Le Roy Ladurie's famous *Montaillou* (London, 1978), belongs to a later stage in the decline of Catharism. Practically every volume of *CF* contains material on the history of the struggle in the Midi. On Germany there is R. Kieckhefer, *The Repression of Heresy in Medieval Germany* (Liverpool, 1979); A. Patschovsky, 'Zur Ketzerverfolgung Konrads von Marburg', *DAEM* 37 (1981) 641–93 (which is of wide significance in understanding the origins of the inquisition); and P. Segl, *Ketzer in Oesterreich* (Vienna, 1984). On the career of Robert le Bougre see E. Chénon, 'L'hérésie à Charité-sur-Loire',

RHDFE 41 (1917) 299–345, and C. H. Haskins, 'Robert le Bougre and the Beginnings of the Inquisition in Northern France', *Studies in Medieval Culture* (Oxford, 1929), 193–244. The controversy with heretics is documented in the general works, but specially noteworthy is the work published by A. Dondaine, *Un traité néo-manichéen du XIIIe siècle: le Liber de duobus principiis* (Rome, 1939). On the development of repression against the Jews in the thirteenth century, there is a sober account by E. A. Synan, *The Popes and the Jews in the Middle Ages* (New York, 1965), and an important but controversial work by J. Cohen, *The Friars and the Jews* (Ithaca, 1982).

Chapter 19: Proclaiming the Faith

i. Crusade and mission. (See also ch. 11 and 17.v). There are some important studies on the thirteenth-century crusades by J. Richard which may be found in his collected studies, *Orient et occident au Moyen Âge* (London, 1976). There is a reassessment by P. Raedts of 'The Children's Crusade of 1212', *JMH* 3 (1977) 279–323, and significant new perceptions in R. T. Spence, 'Pope Gregory IX and the Crusade' (University of Syracuse Ph.D Thesis 1978). The circumstances behind the expedition of 1249 are examined in W. C. Jordan, *Louis IX and the Challenge of the Crusade* (Princeton, 1979). The Baltic war is discussed in W. Urban, *The Prussian Crusade* and *The Livonian Crusade* (Washington, 1980–1), and the activity of the military orders in H. Nowak (ed.), *Die Rolle der Ritterorden in der Christianisierung des Ostseegebietes* (Torun, 1983); H. Boockman, *Der Deutsche Orden* (Munich, 1981); G. Labuda, 'Die Urkunden über die Anfänge des Deutschen Ordens 1226–46', VuF 26 (1980) 299–316; and D. Wojtecki, 'Der Deutsche Orden unter Friedrich II', VuF 16 (1974) 187–224.

The beginning of western contact with further Asia, the story of Prester John, is excellently discussed by B. Hamilton, 'Prester John and the Three Kings of Cologne', *Studies in Medieval History Presented to R. H. C. Davis* (London, 1985) 177–92. The best introduction to thirteenth-century Asia is now D. Morgan, *The Mongols* (Oxford, 1986), and the standard work on the Mongol mission is G. Soranzo, *Il papato, l'Europa cristiana e i Tartari* (Milan, 1930). Some of the major texts, including descriptions by Franciscan travellers, are translated by C. Dawson, *The Mongol Mission* (London, 1955), and there is an intelligent survey by I. de Rachewiltz, *Papal Envoys to the Great Khan* (London, 1971). The western understanding of eastern Christians is thoroughly analysed in A. D. von den Brincken, *Die nationes Christianorum orientalium im Verständnis der lateinischen Historiographie* (Cologne, 1973), and papal involvement in Asia is examined in K. M. Setton, *The Papacy and the Levant*, i (Philadelphia, 1976), and in the first section of J. Muldoon's *Popes, Lawyers and Infidels* (Liverpool, 1979). K. E. Lupprian, *Die Beziehungen der Päpste zu islamischen und mongolischen*

Herrschern (Rome, 1981), has provided editions of the essential correspondence. E. Siberry's book, *Criticism of Crusading 1095–1274* (Oxford, 1985), challenges the picture of the decline of the movement presented by P. A. Throop, *Criticism of the Crusade* (Amsterdam, 1940; repr. Philadelphia, 1975). E. R. Daniel, *The Franciscan Conception of Mission in the high Middle Ages* (Kentucky, 1975), and G. Basetti-Sani, *L'Islam e Francisco d'Assisi* (Florence, 1975), explore the new missionary thinking in the order.

ii. The pastoral revolution. For an introductory survey, see P. Michaud-Quantin, 'Les méthodes de pastorale du XIIIe au XVe siècle', Misc. Med. 7 (1970) 76–91. A wide range of pastoral methods is surveyed in *Faire croire: modalités de la diffusion et de la réception des messages religieux du XIIe au XVe siècle*, École française de Rome 51 (1981). There is a major book by J. W. Baldwin, *Masters, Princes and Merchants: the Social Views of Peter the Chanter and his Circle*, 2 vols. (Princeton, 1970), devoted to the school of pastoral theology at Paris.

Penance. General books are listed in ch. 15.iv, and N. Beriou has written a valuable article, 'Autour du Latran IV: la naissance de la confession moderne et sa diffusion', *Pratiques de la confession* (Paris, 1983), 73–93. The development of *Summae confessorum* is surveyed by P. Michaud-Quantin in *Recherches de Théologie Ancienne et Médiévale* 26 (1959) 261–306 and in his *Sommes de casuistique et manuels de confession* (Namur, 1962); and there is a tart and original contribution in T. N. Tentler, 'The *summa* for Confessors as an Instrument of Social Control', in C. Trinkaus (ed.), *The Pursuit of Holiness in Late Medieval and Renaissance Religion* (Leiden, 1974), 103–37. There are now modern editions of most of the penitential manuals of the period. See P. Michaud-Quantin in *Sacris Erudiri* 17 (1966) 5–54; A. Morey, *Bartholomew of Exeter* (Cambridge, 1937); J. Longère (ed.), *Alain de Lille, Liber Poenitentialis*, 2 vols. (Namur, 1965); J. J. F. Firth (ed.), *Robert of Flamborough, Liber Poenitentialis* (Toronto, 1971); J. Longère (ed.), *Petrus Pictaviensis, Summa de Confessione*, CC(CM) 51 (1980); and F. Bloomfield (ed.), *Thomas of Chobham, Summa Confessorum* (Louvain, 1968). There is an interesting text and discussion in J. Goering and F. A. C. Mantello (ed.), 'The *Perambulavit Iudas* attributed to Robert Grosseteste', *RB* 96 (1986) 125–68. There are introductions to the vernacular tradition in E. J. Arnould, *Le manuel des péchés: étude de littérature religieuse anglo-normande, XIIIe siècle* (Paris, 1940), and D. W. Robertson, 'The Cultural Tradition of *Handlyng synne*', *Speculum* 22 (1947) 162–85. The debate on purgatory has made a new start with J. Le Goff's *The Birth of Purgatory* (English tr. London, 1984), and a series of articles to which it has given rise: A. J. Gurevich, 'Popular and Scholarly Medieval Cultural Traditions', *JMH* 9 (1983) 71–90; A. H. Bredero, 'Le Moyen Âge et le purgatoire', *RHE* 78 (1983) 429–52; J.-P. Massaut, 'La vision de l'au-delà au Moyen Âge', *MA* 91 (1985) 75–86; E.

Mégier, 'Deux exemples de "prépurgatoire"', *CCM* 28 (1985) 45–62; and G. R. Edwards, 'Purgatory: Birth or Evolution?', *JEH* 36 (1985) 634–46.

Preaching. (See also ch. 12.v). The best general account is probably still A. Lecoy de la Marche, *La chaire française au Moyen Âge, spécialement au XIIIe siècle* (Paris, 1886; repr. 1974). Particular aspects are examined by M. Peuchmaurd, 'Mission canonique et prédication', *Recherches de Théologie Ancienne et Médiévale* 30 (1963) 122–44, 251–76; and D. W. Robertson, 'Frequency of Preaching in Thirteenth-century England', *Speculum* 24 (1949) 376–88. Specific studies of preachers include J. M. Powell, *Speculum* 52 (1977) 522–37 and *RSCI* 33 (1979) 95–104 on Honorius III; and, on Paris preaching, P. B. Roberts, *Stephanus de Lingua-Tonante: Studies in the Sermons of Stephen Langton* (Toronto, 1968); and M. M. Davy, *Les sermons universitaires Parisiens 1230–1* (Paris, 1931). D. d'Avray has now explored the tradition of Franciscan preaching in an outstanding book, *The Preaching of the Friars* (Oxford, 1985). J. Le Goff has written a stimulating article, 'Au XIIIe siècle une parole nouvelle' in J. Delumeau *Histoire vécue du peuple chrétien* 2 vols. (Paris, 1979) i.257–79. The preachers' *exempla*, anecdotes designed to please their hearers, have delighted historians also, and the best approaches to this literature are through *L'exemplum* by C. Brémond, J. Le Goff and J. C. Schmitt (Turnhout, 1982), and the collection edited by J.-C. Schmitt, *Prêcher d'exemples* (Paris, 1985).

iii. Popular religion. For general works see ch. 12.i above: there is also a fascinating collection of studies on lay and popular attitudes in J. Le Goff, *L'imaginaire médiéval* (Paris, 1985). Several scholars have recently been turning sermon collections to good account as a basis for an understanding of the state of popular religion. Among such studies are those of R. Godding, 'Vie apostolique et société urbaine à l'aube du XIIIe siècle', *Nouvelle Revue Théologique* 1982, 692–721; and A. Murray, 'Piety and Impiety in Thirteenth-century Italy', *SCH* 8 (1972) 83–106, and 'Religion among the Poor in Thirteenth-century France', *Traditio* 30 (1974) 285–324. The cult of the saints gives a great deal of information about popular piety, and it has been splendidly explored by M. Goodich, '*Vita perfecta*': *the Ideal of Sainthood in the Thirteenth Century* (Stuttgart, 1982), and A. Vauchez, *La sainteté en occident aux derniers siècles du Moyen Âge* (Rome, 1981). There is also brilliant detective work in J.-C. Schmitt's *The Holy Greyhound* (Cambridge, 1983). B. Cazelles, *Le corps de sainteté* (Geneva, 1982), points to the striking contrast between the saints chosen for official canonization and those who were the favourite subject for lives in Old French. The articles in J.-C. Schmitt, *Les saints et les stars* (Paris, 1983), raise general issues about the subject as a whole.

There is valuable material on superstitions in A. Franz, 'De Officio Cherubyn', *Theologische Quartalschrift* 88 (1906) 411–36, and an excellent account of the husbandman's year in G. C. Homans, *English Villagers of the Thirteenth Century* (Cambridge, Mass., 1941). The greater part of our information about popular practices comes from local material, and among the mass of this we may instance the interesting information about Roman ceremonials in Benedict's *Liber Politicus* in P. Fabré (ed.), *Liber Censuum* ii (Paris, 1905), 171–4; L. Dumont, *La Tarasque* 2nd edn. (Paris, 1951); R. Hertz, 'S. Besse: a study of an Alpine cult' in S. Wilson (ed.), *Saints and their Cults* (Cambridge, 1983), 55–100; E. Pitz, 'Religiöse Bewegungen im mittelalterliche Niedersachsen', *Niedersächsisches Jahrbuch für Landesgeschichte* 49 (1977) 45–66; K. L. Jolly, 'Anglo-Saxon Charms in the Context of a Christian World View', *JMH* 11 (1985) 279–93; J. Bordenave and M. Vialelle, *La mentalité religieuse des paysans de l'Alibigeois médiéval* (Toulouse, 1973); *La religion populaire en Languedoc du XIIIe siècle à la moitié du XIVe siècle*, *CF* 11 (1976); and A. Gieysztor, 'La religion populaire en Pologne et en Bohême', J. Delumeau, *Histoire vécue du peuple chrétien*, 2 vols. (Paris, 1979), i.315–34. The practice of 'fool feasts' is briefly noted, with references, in S. Billington, *A Social History of the Fool* (New York, 1984).

Chapter 20: Reason and Hope in a Changing World

i. The universities. (See also ch. 2.iii above). A basic book, still of value, is H. Rashdell, *The Universities of Europe in the Middle Ages*, ed. F. M. Powicke and A. B. Emden (Oxford, 1936). This should now be controlled by G. Leff, *Paris and Oxford Universities in the Thirteenth and Fourteenth Centuries* (London, 1968); A.B. Cobban, *The Medieval Universities: their Development and Organization* (London, 1975); and above all by S. C. Ferruolo's very interesting book, *The Origins of the University* (Stanford, 1985). The career prospects of graduates and Paris masters are examined by J. W. Baldwin in 'Studium et Regnum', *Colloques internationaux de La Napoule* 1 (Paris, 1977), 199–215, and 'Masters at Paris from 1179 to 1215', *RR* 138–72. On the prohibition of the study of civil law at Paris, see W. Ullmann, 'Honorius III and the Prohibition of Legal Studies', *Judicial Review* 60 (1948) 177–86, and S. Kuttner, 'Papst Honorius III und das Studium des Zivilrechts', *Festschrift für Martin Wolff* (Tübingen, 1952), 79–101.

ii. Theology: from pastoral care to speculation. Basic discussions, in addition to those mentioned in Ch. 15.i above, are by M.-D. Chenu, *Introduction à l'étude de S. Thomas d'Aquin*, 3rd edn (Paris, 1974) and *La théologie comme science au XIIIe siècle*, 3rd edn. (Paris 1957). There are valuable articles on technical questions by K. J. Becker, '*Articulus fidei*', *Gregorianum* 54 (1973) 517–69, and R. H. and M. A. Rouse, '*Statim invenire*: Schools, Preachers and New Attitudes to the Page', *RR* 201–25. For the translations from Greek and Arabic, the best foundation article is by M.-T. d'Alverny, 'Translations and Translators', *RR* 421–62. On the wider philosophical issues, see *The Cambridge History of Later Medieval Philosophy*, ed. N.

Kretzmann, A. Kenny, and J. Pinborg (Cambridge, 1982); R. Klibansky, *The Continuity of the Platonic Tradition during the Middle Ages* (London, 1939); and D. A. Callus, *The Introduction of Aristotelian Learning to Oxford* (London, 1944). One of the most important studies of thirteenth-century Aristotelianism is by M. Grabmann, *I papi del duecento e l'Aristotelismo*, i (Rome, 1941). The book of R. C. Dales, *The Scientific Achievement of the Middle Ages* (Pennsylvania, 1973), is also important in this connection. On the Paris masters specifically, the reference work of P. Glorieux, *Répertoire des maîtres en théologie de Paris au XIIIe siècle*, 2 vols. (Paris, 1933–4), remains very useful, and there is a good account of the pastoral character of Paris theology at the turn of the century by J. Châtillon, 'Le mouvement théologique dans la France de Philippe Auguste', R. H. Bautier (ed.), *La France de Phillipe Auguste* (Paris, 1982), 881–904. The *Summa Aurea* of William of Auxerre has recently been edited by J. Ribaillier in *Spicilegium Bonaventurianum* 16–17 (Grottaferrata, 1982). There is an outstanding assessment of the Gospel commentaries by B. Smalley, *The Gospels in the Schools c. 1100–c. 1280* (London, 1985). On the English developments see J. J. McEvoy, *The Philosophy of Robert Grosseteste* (Oxford, 1982); S. P. Marrone, *William of Auvergne and Robert Grosseteste* (Princeton, 1983), and above all R. W. Southern, *Robert Grosseteste* (Oxford, 1986).

iii. Joachim of Fiore. Joachim is almost a rediscovery of the scholars of the past generation. The foundation of modern scholarship is the work of H. Grundmann, in particular *Neue Forschungen über Joachim von Fiore* (Marburg, 1950), and 'Zur Biographie Joachims von Fiore und Rainers von Ponza', *DAEM* 16 (1960) 437–546. These studies have been followed by three magisterial works: B. Töpfer, *Das kommende Reich des Friedens* (Berlin, 1964); M. Reeves, *The Influence of Prophecy in the Later Middle Ages* (Oxford, 1969); and H. Mottu, *La manifestation de l'Esprit selon Joachim de Fiore* (Neuchâtel, 1977). Two books which stress the revolutionary character of Joachim's 'third age' are G. Wendelborn, *Gott und Geschichte* (Cologne, 1974), and H. de Lubac, *La postérité spirituelle de Joachim de Fiore*, 2 vols (Paris, 1979–81). There is also a shorter book by Reeves, *Joachim of Fiore and the Prophetic Future* (London, 1976), and good introductions by D. C. West and S. Zimdars-Swartz, *Joachim of Fiore: a Study in Spiritual Perception and History* (Bloomington, 1983), and B. McGinn, *The Calabrian Abbot* (London, 1985). There are important collections of essays in *Prophecy and Millenarianism: Essays in Honour of Marjorie Reeves* (London, 1980), and in D. C. West (ed.), *Joachim of Fiore in Christian Thought*, 2 vols. (New York, 1975). The major works have not been edited since the sixteenth century, with the exception of the *Concordia novi et veteris Testamenti*, ed. E. R. Daniel (Philadelphia, 1983), and the newly discovered *Book of Figures*, ed. L. Tondelli, M. Reeves, and B. Hirsch-Reich (Turin, 1953), and analysed by Reeves and Hirsch-Reich, *The 'Figurae' of Joachim of Fiore* (Oxford, 1972).

The bibliography is surveyed by M. W. Bloomfield in articles in *Traditio* 13 (1957) 249–311 and in *Prophecy and Millenarianism* (above) 21–52, and the debate is reviewed by Reeves, 'The originality and influence of Joachim of Fiore', *Traditio* 35 (1980) 269–316.

iv. The influence of Joachim. Not much work has been done on Joachim's direct descendants, the Florensian order, but there is a useful introduction by C. Baraut, 'Per la storia dei monasteri Florensi', *Benedictina* 4 (1950) 241–68. M. W. Bloomfield and M. Reeves, 'The Penetration of Joachim into Northern Europe', *Speculum* 29 (1954) 772–93, and B. McGinn, 'Angel Pope and Papal Antichrist', *Church History* 47 (1978) 155–73, supply information about the evolution of the ideas. E. R. Daniel (see ch. 19.i) has argued for an authentically Franciscan eschatology, which only underwent serious influence from Joachism after our period. There is a broad discussion of the impact of apocalyptic thought on politics by H. M. Schaller, 'Endzeit-Erwartung und Antichrist-Vorstellung in der Politik des 13 Jhs', *Festschrift H. Heimpel* (Göttingen, 1972), 927–47. The polemic between Frederick II and the papacy is considered in ch. 22. The traditional attitudes which continued to prevail in large parts of the church are illustrated in B. A. Pitts, 'Versions of the Apocalypse in Medieval French Verse', *Speculum* 58 (1983) 31–59. On the development of the controversy over purgatory see R. Ombres, 'Latins and Greeks in Debate over Purgatory 1230–1439', *JEH* 35 (1984) 1–14.

Chapter 21. The Structure of Government

Apart from the general and national studies indicated at the beginning of this bibliography, there are two excellent accounts by J. R. H. Moorman, *Church Life in England in the Thirteenth Century* (Cambridge, 1945), and R. Brentano, *Two Churches: England and Italy in the Thirteenth Century* (Princeton, 1968). Both books are worth consulting on every aspect of this chapter.

i. The bishops. More general works are mentioned in ch. 9.iii above. On the controversy over the status of the episcopate see R. P. Stenger, 'The Episcopacy as an Ordo According to the Medieval Canonists', *MS* 29 (1967) 67–112, and A. McDevitt, 'The Episcopate as an Order and Sacrament', *Franciscan Studies* 20 (1960) 96–148. O. Pontal has written a good introduction to the work of bishops in supervising the 'pastoral revolution' in 'L'évolution épiscopale en France à l'époque de Philippe-Auguste', *AHC* 12 (1980) 198–204; in Germany there is P. B. Pixton, 'Watchmen on the Tower', *ICMCL* 6 (1985) 579–94; and in England the classic work of M. Gibbs and J. Lang, *Bishops and Reform 1215–72* (Oxford, 1934), retains its value. An early visitation record is available in an English translation by S. M. Brown, *The Register of Eudes of Rouen* (New York, 1964), and is studied by P. Andrieu-Guitrancourt, *L'archévêque Eudes Rigaud et la vie de l'église au XIIIe siècle* (Paris, 1938). For works on elections see ch. 9.iii. F. Pico discusses the social origins of bishops in 'Non-aristocratic Bishops in the Reign of Louis IX', *Medieval Prosopography* 2 (1981) 41–54.

The evolution of episcopal records is examined by C. R. Cheney, *English Bishops' Chanceries 1100–1250* (Manchester, 1950), and R. Brentano, 'The Bishops' Books of Città di Castello', *Traditio* 16 (1960) 241–54 (which, while it is mainly after 1250, throws light on earlier developments). The earliest surviving episcopal registers are examined by D. Smith, 'The Rolls of Hugh of Wells', *Bulletin of the Institute of Historical Research* 45 (1972) 155–95, and A. D. Frankforter, 'The Origin of Episcopal Registration Procedures in Medieval England', *Manuscripta* 26 (1982) 67–89. C. Morris, 'From Synod to Consistory', *JEH* 22 (1971) 115–23, looks at the changing pattern of tribunals. P. Fournier, *Les officialités au Moyen Âge* (Paris, 1880), has never been superseded, but there are many studies of individual dioceses and for France there is E. Fournier, *Les origines du vicaire général* (Paris, 1922), and *L'origine du vicaire général* (Paris, 1940). On bishops' chaplains see S. Haider, *Das bischöfliche Kapellanat*, vol. 1 *MIOG* Ergänzungsband 25 (1977). There is a general introduction to synodical statutes by O. Pontal, *Les statuts synodaux* (Turnhoult, 1975). The English statutes have been splendidly edited in *C&S*. For France there is O. Pontal, *Les statuts synodaux français du XIIIe siècle*, 2 vols. (Paris, 1971–5), and J. Avril, 'Naissance et évolution des législations synodales', *ZSSRGkA* 103 (1986) 152–249. The process of adapting and publishing such statutes is examined by C. R. Cheney, *English Synodalia of the Thirteenth Century* (Oxford, 1941); R. Foreville, 'La réception des conciles généraux dans l'église . . . de Rouen au XIIIe siècle', *Droit privé et institutions régionales: études historiques à J. Yver* (Paris, 1976), 243–53; and E. Diebold, 'L'application en France du canon 51 du IVe Concile de Latran', *L'année canonique* 2 (1951) 187–95.

ii. Parishes. (See also ch. 12.iii). There is an excellent survey of the development of the parochial ministry in France by G. Devailly, 'L'encadrement paroissial: rigueur et insuffisance', *CF* 11 (1976) 387–417, and valuable information is to be found in O. Dobiache-Rojdestvensky, *La vie paroissiale en France au XIIIe siècle* (Paris, 1911). The case for believing in the relative prosperity of parochial endowments is forcefully stated by B. Tierney, *Medieval Poor Law* (Berkeley, 1959). The significance of incorporation or appropriation is considered in more detail in D. Lindner, *Die Lehre von der Inkorporation in ihrer geschichtlichen Entwicklung* (Munich, 1951). The classic study of the growth of vicarages remains R. A. R. Hartridge, *A History of Vicarages in the Middle Ages* (Cambridge, 1930). D. Kurze, *Pfarrerwahlen im*

Mittelalter (Cologne, 1966), and E. Mason, 'The Role of the English parishioner 1100–1500', *JEH* 27 (1976) 17–29, provide material on the increasing activity of lay parishioners.

iii. Monasteries and cathedrals. (See ch. 3 and 10 above). On the thirteenth-century monasteries there are several older studies which retain their value. These include P. Schmitz, *Histoire de l'ordre de S. Benoît,* iii (Maredsous, 1948), and a series of articles by U. Berlière: 'Innocent III et la réorganisation des monastères bénédictins', *Revue Bénédictine* 32 (1920) 22–42 and 145–59; 'Honorius III et les monastères bénédictins', *Revue Belge de Philologie et d'Histoire* 2 (1923) 237–65 and 461–84; and 'Le nombre des moines dans les anciens monastères', *Revue Bénédictine* 41 (1929) 231–61 and 42 (1930) 19–42. There is useful material in R. H. Snape, *English Monastic Finances in the later Middle Ages* (Cambridge, 1926). The acts of the chapters general in England are much the best source of information for the operation of this system, and are edited by W. A. Pantin, *Chapter of the English Black Monks*, Camden Series, iii.45, 47, 54 (1931–7).

The place to begin for cathedrals and collegiate churches is K. Edwards, *The English Secular Cathedrals in the Middle Ages* (Manchester, 1949), and there is an interesting comparative article by J. Barrow, 'Cathedrals, Provosts and Prebends: a Comparison of Twelfth-century German and English Practice', *JEH* 37 (1986) 536–64. Much recent work has taken the form of the study of individual communities, and among these a book by L. G. Duggan is particularly to be recommended, *Bishop and Chapter: the Governance of the Bishopric of Speyer to 1552* (New Brunswick, 1978). The peculiar developments at Cologne are described by M. Groten, *Priorenkolleg und Domkapitel von Köln im hohen Mittelalter* (Bonn, 1980). Also of importance are J. Oswald, *Das alte Passauer Domkapitel* (Munich, 1933), and an article on Bamberg by K. Guth in *Jb für fränkische Landesforschung* 33 (1973) 13–37. On France, among other studies, there is L. Amiet, *Essai sur l'organisation du chapitre cathédral de Chartres* (Chartres, 1922); M. Legrand, *Le chapitre cathédral de Langres* (Paris, 1931); and L. Walter, 'Le chapitre cathédral de Clermont', *RHEF* 41 (1955) 5–42. The early type of chantry foundation mentioned in the text is studied by A. H. Thompson, 'The Chapel of S. Mary and the Holy Angels', *Yorkshire Archaeological Journal* 36 (1947) 63–77. There is insufficient information to identify the origins and careers of many canons, but some careful prosopographical studies and lists have been provided by W. M. Newman, *Le personnel de la cathédrale d'Amiens 1066–1306* (Paris, 1972), and by F. Pico for Laon in *Catholic Historical Review* 61 (1975) 1–30 and *RHE* 71 (1976) 78–91. See also the English series, *John le Neve: Fasti Ecclesiae Anglicanae 1066–1300*, 3 vols. (London, 1968–71).

Early instances of provisions are assembled in H. Baier, *Päpstliche Provisionen für niedere Pfründen bis zum Jahre 1304* (Münster, 1911), and the basis of the system is given searching analysis by G. Barraclough, *Papal Provisions* (Oxford, 1935). See also G. Mollat, 'Les grâces expectatives du XII^c au XIV^c siècle', *RHE* 42 (1947) 81–102. J. E. Lynch, 'Some Landmarks in the Development of Papal Reservations', *The Jurist* 30 (1970) 145–81, covers the development of papal jurisdiction widely up to 1400. There is a classic study by A. H. Thompson, 'Pluralism in the Medieval Church', *Assoc. Arch. Soc. Reports & Papers*, 33 (1915–6) 35–73 and 34 (1917–8) 1–26, and a good article by K. Pennington, 'The Canonists and Pluralism in the Thirteenth Century', *Speculum* 51 (1976) 35–48. There are not enough studies of the impact of provisions on local churches, for which indeed the evidence itself is usually insufficient, but see C. McCurry, '*Utilia Metensia*: Local Benefices for the Papal Curia 1212–*c*.1370', *Law, Church and Society: Essays in Honor of Stephan Kuttner* (Pennsylvania, 1977) 311–23. Robert Grosseteste of Lincoln is the hero of the anti-provision lobby: accounts of his work have already been mentioned in ch. 20.ii. The materials relating to his protest in 1250 are edited by S. Gieben, 'Robert Grosseteste at the Papal Curia', *Collectanea Franciscana* 41 (1971) 340–93, and an important document in the campaign is assessed by F. A. C. Mantello, 'Letter CXXXI ascribed to Robert Grosseteste', *Franciscan Studies* 39 (1979) 165–79. See also H. Mackenzie, 'The Anti-foreign Movement in England 1231–2', *Haskins Memorial Essays* (New York, 1929), 182–203.

Chapter 22. The Roman Church and the Lay Power in the Thirteenth Century

i. *Papacy, kingdoms and city states.* There are good introductions to the development of the state by E. H. Kantorowicz, *The King's Two Bodies* (Princeton, 1957), and J. R. Strayer, *On the Medieval Origins of the Modern State* (Princeton, 1970). There are also collections of articles by Strayer, *Medieval Statecraft and the Perspectives of History* (Princeton, 1971), and G. Post, *Studies in Medieval Legal Thought* (Princeton, 1964). The canonistic basis is studied in S. Mochi Onory, *Fonti canonistiche dell'idea moderna dello stato* (Milan, 1951). There are also interesting ideas in B. Tierney, *Religion, Law and the Growth of Constitutional Thought 1150–1650* (Cambridge, 1982). For the way in which thirteenth-century changes anticipated later development, see G. de Lagarde, *La naissance de l'esprit laïque au déclin du Moyen Âge*, vol. 1, 3rd edn. (Paris, 1956). The dramatic character of the change in the international situation is indicated in an article by Y. Renouard, '1212–16: comment les traits durables de l'Europe moderne se sont définis', *Études d'histoire médiévale* (Paris, 1968), i. 77–91. The emergence of national cultures is discussed by L. Schmugge, 'Über "nationale" Vorurteile im Mittelalter', *DAEM* 38 (1982) 439–59. The development of representation has been the centre of much scholarly attention, for example by Y. Congar, '*Quod omnes tangit ab omnibus tractari et approbari debet*' in his *Droit ancien et structures ecclésiales* (London, 1982) no. 3; L. Moulin, '*Sanior et maior pars*', *RHDFE* 36 (1958) 368–97 and 491–529; and D. B. Weske, *Convocation of the*

Clergy (London, 1937). For the proposal of Honorius III at Bourges in 1225 we depend on a report which circulated in England, and which has been reconstructed by R. Kay, 'An Eye-witness Account of the 1225 Council of Bourges', *S. Grat.* 12 (1968) 61–80.

The development of the modern state in France (the prime example of the process in the thirteenth century) has naturally been the subject of many studies, among them J. W. Baldwin, *The Government of Philip Augustus* (London, 1986); B. Guenée, 'État et nation en France au Moyen Âge', *Revue Historique* 237 (1967) 17–30; C. T. Wood, '*Regnum Francie*', *Traditio* 23 (1967) 117–47; G. M. Spiegel, ' "Defence of the realm": Evolution of a Capetian Propaganda Slogan', *JMH* 3 (1977) 115–33; R. E. Lerner, 'The Uses of Heterodoxy: the French Monarchy and Unbelief in the Thirteenth Century', *French Historical Studies* 4 (1965) 189–202; and C. T. Wood, 'The Mise of Amiens and S. Louis's theory of kingship', ibid. 6 (1969–70) 300–10. The classic study of Louis's relations with the papacy is E. Berger, *S. Louis et Innocent IV* (Paris, 1893), which is full of valuable information. There are also articles by G. J. Campbell, 'The protest of S. Louis', *Traditio* 15 (1959) 405–18; 'The Attitude of the Monarchy Towards the use of Ecclesiastical Censures in the Reign of S. Louis', *Speculum* 35 (1960) 535–55; and 'Temporal and Spiritual Regalia', *Traditio* 20 (1964) 351–83. On other aspects of Louis's dealing with the Church, see R. Branner, *S. Louis and the Court Style in Gothic Architecture* (London, 1965); O. Pontal, 'Le différend entre Louis IX et les évêques de Beauvais', *Bibliothèque de l'École des Chartes* 123 (1965) 5–34; and E. B. Ham, *Rutebeuf and Louis IX* (Chapel Hill, 1962). The affairs of the English church are discussed in two major books by F. M. Powicke, *King Henry III and the Lord Edward*, 2 vols. (Oxford, 1947), and *The Thirteenth Century* (Oxford, 1953). Aspects of church–state relations are considered by W. R. Jones, 'Bishops, Politics, and the Two Laws: the *Gravamina* of the English Clergy 1237–1399', *Speculum* 41 (1966) 209–45; D. M. Williamson, 'Some Aspects of the Legation of Cardinal Otto in England 1237–41', *EHR* 64 (1949) 145–73; F. Pegues, 'The *clericus* in the Legal Administration of Thirteenth-century England', *EHR* 71 (1956) 529–59; and J. W. Gray, 'The Church and Magna Carta in the Century after Runnymede', *General European Historical Studies* 6 (Dublin, 1968), 23–38

ii. Frederick II. The historiography in the modern period begins with E. H. Kantorowicz, *Kaiser Friedrich II* (Berlin, 1927) (Ergänzungsband Berlin, 1931; English tr. of vol. i, New York, 1957). This was a vivid and imaginative work: if not a historical novel, at least a historical drama. The development of the subject during the next forty years may be followed in the essays edited by G. Wolf, Stupor Mundi: *zur Geschichte Friedrichs II von Hohenstaufen*, Wege der Forschung 101 (1966), and is reviewed by D. Abulafia, 'Kantorowicz and Frederick II', *History* 62 (1977) 193–210. The main modern study in English is F. C. Van Cleve, *The Emperor Frederick II of Hohenstaufen* (London, 1973), and there are penetrating comments by K. Leyser, 'The Emperor Frederick II' in his *Medieval Germany and its Neighbours* (London, 1982) 269–76. See also the discussions in *Probleme um Friedrich II*, VuF 16 (1974) and in *Atti del convegno internazionale di studi federiciani* (Palermo, 1952). The extent of the influence of Greek ideas is considered in a monograph by M. B. Wellas, *Griechisches aus dem Umkreis Kaiser Friedrichs II* (Munich, 1983).

R. Manselli reassessed Frederick's relations with Honorius III in 'Onorio III e Federico II (revisione d'un giudizio?)', *Studi Romani* 11 (1963) 142–59. The basic evaluation of his polemic with the papal curia was by F. Graefe, *Die Publizistik in der letzten Epoche Kaiser Friedrichs II* (Heidelberg, 1909). There have been numerous discussions of particular aspects, including H. M. Schaller, 'Das letzte Rundschreiben Gregors IX gegen Friedrich II', *Festschrift P. E. Schramm* (Wiesbaden, 1964), i.309–21, and 'Die Antwort Gregors IX auf . . . Collegerunt pontifices', *DAEM* 11 (1954–5) 140–65; W. Seegrün, 'Kirche, Papst und Kaiser nach den Anschauungen Kaiser Friedrichs II', *HZ* 207 (1968) 4–41; P. Herde, '*Eger cui lenia*', *DAEM* 23 (1967) 468–538; and H.-E. Hilpert, *Kaiser- und Papstbriefe in den* Chronica majora *des Matthaeus Paris* (Stuttgart, 1981). Frederick's orthodoxy was powerfully defended by A. de Stefano, *Federico II e le correnti spirituali del suo tempo*, 2nd edn. (Parma, n.d.), and J. M. Powell, 'Frederick II and the church: a revisionist view', *Catholic Historic Review* 48 (1963) 487–97. On Frederick's kingship in Sicily, there is H. J. Pybus, 'The Emperor Frederick II and the Sicilian Church', *Cambridge Historical Journal* 3 (1930) 134–63; J. M. Powell, 'Frederick II and the Church in the Kingdom of Sicily', *Church History* 30 (1961) 28–34; and A. Marongiu, 'A Model State in the Middle Ages', *Comparative Studies in Society in Society and History* 6 (1964) 307–24. His legislation has been edited by T. van der Lieck-Buycken, *Die Konstitutionen Friedrichs II von Hohenstaufen für sein Königreich Sizilien* (Vienna, 1973–83); see also J. M. Powell (tr.), *The* Liber Augustalis *or Constitutions of Melfi* (New York, 1971), and (on the prologue) W. Stürner, '*Rerum necessitas* und *divina provisio*', *DAEM* 39 (1983) 467–554. On the council of Lyon 1245 see H. Wolter and H. Holstein, *Lyon I and Lyon II*, Histoire des conciles œcuméniques 7 (Paris, 1966), with references to earlier work.

iii. The papal monarchy in the thirteenth century. The debate over the canonists' conception of papal monarchy took a new departure with the publication of W. Ullmann, *Medieval Papalism* (London, 1949). It is a controversial book, treating the canonists as if they had essentially one opinion, and that wholly in favour of papal absolutism. Its thesis has been widely criticized, for instance by A. M. Stickler, 'Concerning the Political Theories of the Medieval Canonists', *Traditio* 7 (1949–51) 450–63; B. Tierney, 'Some Recent Works on the Political Theories of the Medieval Canonists', *Traditio*

10 (1954) 594–625; and J. Muldoon, '*Extra ecclesiam non est imperium*', S. *Grat.* 9 (1966) 551–80. (On this controversy, see also *under: Papacy* in the *General* section at the beginning of this bibliography). Several major contributions to thirteenth-century papal theory have already been mentioned under Innocent III (ch. 17.iii); to these should be added B. Tierney, *The Foundations of the Conciliar Theory* (Cambridge, 1955), and L. Buisson, Potestas *und* Caritas: *die päpstliche Gewalt im Spätmittelalter.* (Cologne, repr. 1982). On the special problems of the pontificate of Innocent IV there is M. Pacaut, 'L'autorité pontificale selon Innocent IV', *MA* 66 (1960) 85–119.

On the cardinals, in addition to ch. 9.ii, there are A. Paravicini Bagliani, *Cardinali di curia e familiae dal 1227 al 1254* (Padua, 1972) (on which see P. Linehan in *EHR* 89 (1974) 620–2) and H. Singer, '*Quia frequenter*', *ZSSRGkA* 6 (1916) 1–140. C. R. Cheney has written a useful introduction to *The Study of the Medieval Papal Chancery* (Glasgow, 1966), and there is a fine monograph by P. Herde, *Beiträge zum päpstlichen Kanzlei– und Urkundenwesen im 13 Jh.* (Munich, 1961). The writers' college is discussed in B. Schwarz, *Die Organisation kurialer Schreiberkollegien* (Tübingen, 1972), and on two technical points there are R. von Heckel, 'Studien über die Kanzleiordnung Innozenz' III', *HJb* 57 (1937) 258–89, and B. Schwarz, 'Der *corrector litterarum apostolicarum*', *QFIAB* 54 (1974) 122–91. On proctors see R. von Heckel, 'Das Aufkommen der ständigen Prokuratoren an der päpstlichen Kurie im 13 Jh.', *Studi e Testi* 38 (1924) 290–321, and W. Stelzer, 'Beiträge zur Geschichte der Kurienprokuratoren im 13 Jh.', *AHP* 8 (1970) 113–38. One of the most important internal developments is analysed by P. Herde, *Audientia Litterarum Contradictarum* (Tübingen, 1970); G. Barraclough in *Dic. DC* 1 (1935) 1387–99; and J. E. Sayers, 'Canterbury Proctors at the Court of *Audientia litterarum contradictarum*', *Traditio* 22 (1966) 311–45.

There are several books covering the system of legates over a long period. Particularly important is K. Walf, *Die Entwicklung des päpstlichen Gesandtschaftswesen 1159–1815* (Munich, 1966). More recently P. Blet has provided a useful survey in his *Histoire de la représentation du Saint Siège* (Vatican, 1982). On the legal aspects see R. A. Schmutz, 'Medieval papal representatives: legates, nuncios and judges-delegate', *S. Grat.* 15 (1972) 441–63; C. I. Kyer, '*Legatus* and *nuntius* as Used to Denote Papal Envoys 1245–1378', *MS* 40 (1978) 473–7; R. C. Figueira, 'The Classification of Medieval Papal Legates', *AHP* 21 (1983) 211–28; and K. Pennington, 'Johannes Teutonicus and Papal Legates', ibid. 183–94. For judges delegate, start with the works in ch. 9.ii, and see also J. E. Sayers' wider examination of papal activity, *Papal Government and England during the Pontificate of Honorius III* (Cambridge, 1984). There is also an article by J. C. Moore, 'Papal Justice in France around the Time of Pope Innocent III', *Church History* 41 (1972) 295–306. On canon law in the thirteenth century, see G. Fransen, *Les décrétales et les collections de décrétales* (Turnhout, 1972); A. M. Stickler, '*Ordines iudiciarii*', *Dic.DC* 6 (1957) 1132–43; P.-J. Kessler, 'Untersuchungen über die Novellen-Gestetzgebung Papst Innozenz' IV', *ZSSRGkA* 62 (1942) 142–320 and K. Pennington, 'The Making of a Decretal Collection', *ICMCL* 5 (1976) 67–92.

INDEX

Printed in the United States
71414LV00004B/35